1001 BEST BAKING

RECIPES OF ALL TIME

White Lemon

Check out more books by Emma Katie at:
www.amazon.com/author/emmakatie

CONTENTS

Cookies

Muffins and Cupcakes 152

French Desserts

Cheesecakes

Pies and Tarts...............................330

Healthy Desserts.............................348

INTRODUCTION

Baking is a method of cooking that has been used for centuries to dry out various foods, bread being the most common baked goodie. Being looked at as a household activity in its early stages, baking has climbed incredibly high mountains over the last decade, but it still remains the main activity to do and enjoy at home. Women (and men alike) across the globe gather recipes in their notebooks, try them and spoil their families with baked goodies each and every day.

The very first cakes or donuts were simple mixes of flour, water and various seeds, baked on hot rocks. Many of these products back then had religious purposes and were made only on special days. They were dens and only sweetened with honey sometimes. It was only in the XVth century that pastry chefs and bakers began to be more and more popular and baking became a profession as well. And it was then that the French took this profession to a whole new level! Pastries began to be more and more intricate and complex and even the simpler ones started to be more and more comforting. In addition to this, the XVth century marked the moment the Europeans discovered America and with it, the cocoa beans and chocolate and so it began a new era for the world of desserts and baked goodies.

Modern baking however, developed much later. Layered cakes, chocolate cakes, flaky pastries and buttery cookies are a recent addition to the dessert world, but they soon conquered the heart of every baker around the globe. Modern equipment too contributed to this development, especially after it became more and more accessible to the home cooks as well.

But unlike other professions, baking is both a science and an art. And just like a science, it comes with measurements and recipes which often can only be tweaked slightly, but not completely modified. Cups, tablespoons, teaspoons and ounces are perfect to obtain moist cakes, great cookies, amazing muffins or cupcakes, delicious quick breads or fluffy yeasted doughs.

This book aims to become one of the most complete cookbooks referring to desserts on the market. It covers a wide range of desserts and a wide range of flavors, it mixes textures and interesting aromas into excellent recipes waiting to be tried out in your home kitchen. And the great thing about these recipes is that you don't need any special skills to pull it off. As long as you know how to mix, have a bowl and a whisk around, a basic round cake pan and a loaf pan or muffin tin, you're good to go. So keep reading and let's discover together the amazing world of desserts! Put your apron on and let's get start baking, let's discover how fun it is, how much joy it brings and how comforting it makes us feel!

INGREDIENTS

If you're going to take the time to bake a cake or a few muffins, you should have some information about the ingredients you use and their quality. Since homemade desserts don't have stunning decoration, they need to impress with something and their taste is your best bet towards success! And the only thing that matters in the end!

Butter

The natural flavor of butter can't be replaced with just anything so margarine or shortening is rarely a substitute. Softened butter is often used in pound cakes or creams, while cold butter is mostly used when making pie crusts. The recipes in this book call for unsalted butter since it allows you to easier control the saltiness of each baked goodies, but certain desserts, like chocolate cakes, may take advantage of a bit of extra salt, being well known the fact that salt and chocolate are great friends.

But butter has one major quality that most people neglect – it melts in the mouth so desserts made with good quality butter will be soft and simply flood your palate with great flavor and have an amazing texture as well.

Milk

Next to water, milk is the most important liquid used for baking. From cakes to creams, muffins or breads, milk softens up the flour and has the ability to turn any mix of ingredients into delicious desserts. Moreover, milk is the base for other products, from heavy cream, sour cream, buttermilk or cheese.

Flour

There's just a bunch of dessert recipes that don't use flour. Whether it is wheat flour, rye flour, almond flour or coconut flour, this powder seems to be the most used ingredient in baking. Wheat flour can be either white – all-purpose flour – or whole wheat. And while these two categories are pretty straight forward, it gets a bit more complicated when we look into the types of white wheat flour found on the market. The most common is all-purpose flour which is just plain white flour – it's the type I prefer for most recipes because it's easy to find, it's fairly cheap and easy to work with. But apart from this, you'll also find cake flour which has a smoother texture and a lighter color – it's suited for cake sponges and other delicate baked goodies. Pastry flour is similar to cake flour, while self-rising flour is all-purpose flour that has been mixed with baking powder, the proportions being 1 teaspoon of baking powder per each cup of flour.

Flour categories continue with rye flour which doesn't form gluten strands, therefore it's not suited for yeasted dough unless combined with other types of flour. On the other hand, rye flour has a high nutritional profile which recommends it for a healthy diet.

Oat flour is made from oats and it is packed with fibers and proteins. This type of flour is mostly used in healthier baked goodies, such as muffins or quick breads and it doesn't form gluten strands either.

Almond flour is made from raw or blanched almonds, while coconut flour is made from coconuts and has a higher absorption power. Tapioca flour made from tapioca pearls has a high absorption power as well and it's often used as a starch in certain dessert recipes.

Baking powder

I recommend using aluminum free baking powder because it doesn't have a bitter after taste. Any brand of baking powder will do the trick, but keep in mind that baking powder can't be stored for more than 6 months without losing part of its properties.

Baking powder is basically baking soda mixed with an acidic component, usually cream of tartar – and cornstarch. This prevents lumping and brings the leavening power down slightly. Unlike baking soda, baking powder doesn't depend on the addition of an acidic element in order to react, therefore it is more versatile.

Baking soda

Baking soda is usually included in recipes that have an acidic element, such as lemon juice, vinegar or even cocoa powder, molasses, brown sugar, buttermilk, yogurt and chocolate which are acidic. Baking soda can be stored for years without losing its properties and has been proven by scientists to be effective not only in baking, but also for cleaning around the house or certain medical conditions. However, since heat is not needed for the baking soda to react, it is recommend that the batters using it as leavening agent to be baked right away or the soda's power wears off.

Yeast

Found mostly in bread, dinner rolls and similar pastries, yeast is a natural leavening agent which acts by fermenting in the batter or dough, thus raising its volume and incorporating air.

Sugar

Sugars has been blamed for many health problems over the years, starting with obesity, but recent scientific research show that as long as you have a balanced diet and include a variety of foods in your daily eating habits, sugar is the last culprit for your health problems. I too support a balanced diet and having a dessert once in a while shouldn't be looked at as guilty pleasure, but a normal thing to do. That being said, let's see why sugar is so important in baking:

> It adds sweetness to baked goodies.
>
> It adds texture to desserts, making them tenderer and finer.
>
> It turns the curst into a nice golden color.
>
> It retains moisture.
>
> It helps yeasts grow in certain recipes.

Sugar is a very general term to use in baking. Most recipes found in this book are quite specific on which type of sugar to use. The most common type is white granulated sugar which has a mild taste and it's easy to incorporate in most desserts. Powdered sugar or confectioners' sugar is a very fine ground sugar useful mostly in creams or buttercreams because it melts faster and it helps ingredients bind together better. Brown sugar also contains molasses which gives it an intense caramel-like taste. Basically, brown sugar is white sugar that hasn't been completely refined and it is said to be slightly healthier than regular sugar, but not as easy to incorporate in desserts due to its intense taste.

Chocolate

Dark chocolate, milk chocolate and white chocolate are the three main types of chocolate available on the market. I recommend dark chocolate because it has the least amount of sugar added, it has an intense taste and a better texture. A chocolate that has a cocoa content higher than 70% is a proof of quality and can be used in pretty much any recipe found in this book that calls for dark chocolate. In addition to this, chocolate of any kind stores well for up to a few weeks, even more if it's good quality and it well wrapped before storing. A special mention goes to chocolate chips which can easily be replaced with chopped chocolate.

Cocoa powder

Labeled as either natural cocoa powder or Dutch processed cocoa powder, this dark, intense, chocolatey powder is nature's wonder. What would we do without cocoa beans, cocoa powder and chocolate?! The world wouldn't be as cheerful, definitely.

The two types of cocoa powder mentioned above are similar and yet so different. Natural cocoa powder has a lighter color and a higher acidity so it reacts better with baking soda. Dutch cocoa powder has a darker color and a much more intense taste, therefore, unless stated otherwise, it is preferred in the most recipes found in this book.

Eggs

Eggs come in various sizes and qualities, but when it comes to desserts, never make any compromise! Always choose fresh eggs, preferably free ranch and opt for medium size eggs as a general rule, unless stated otherwise in the recipe.

Eggs should be understood by bakers well because they are used in large quantities and are crucial for many baked goodies. First of all, eggs ensure the texture of your cakes or cookies by coagulating and supporting the gluten structure. Moreover, they allow air to be incorporated into the batter in order to obtain a fluffy, airy cake, cupcake or muffin. In addition to this, eggs keep the desserts moist, but also add flavor and nutritional value, as well as color which can be important for yeasted dough for instance.

Gelatin

Gelatin is a water soluble protein extracted from animal tissue. Gelatin is used to stabilize creams or jellies and it requires to be bloomed before use. Also, gelatin shouldn't be boiled as it tends to lose its strength.

Gelatin comes in two variations: powder or granules and leaves. Generally this book calls for powder or granulated gelatin, but leaf gelatin can be used as well.

Nuts

Used is many recipes as the healthy element, nuts are available whole, chopped, halved or ground. They have a high healthy fat content and can easily be incorporated in many recipes. The list of available nuts includes: almonds, coconut, hazelnuts, pecans, peanuts, walnuts, pistachio and macadamia nuts, as well as cashew nuts. The only downside to having them in your pantry all the time is the fact that they change their taste and texture after a few weeks, especially if not kept in a dry and chilled place.

Salt

As the story goes, salt is the most important ingredient found in any recipe across the globe. Salt is the one ingredient that intensifies the flavor of the other ingredients and manages to bring them together into a dessert that tastes amazing. But beyond this, salt also strengthens the gluten structure and interacts with yeast, therefore the quantity of salt in a recipe is not to be looked at as something lacking importance.

Spices

What would the world be without spices?! Spices are to desserts what colors are to the world. They are fun, interesting, tantalizing and fairly cheap, therefore I like to keep a wide selection of spices in my cupboards. The most common spice is definitely vanilla. I recommend using a natural extract which has a far better taste than the industrial kind. As an alternative to this, you can also use fresh vanilla pods – their seeds are the source of the amazing vanilla flavor we all know. But apart from vanilla, I also use cinnamon, ginger (fresh or ground), nutmeg, cardamom, lemon zest, orange zest, lime zest, whole cloves, star anise, lavender buds and the list can go on!

Equipment

While it's nice to have an arsenal of equipment, the truth is that home bakers can easily get by with a few basic pieces of equipment which I decided to list below. It's nothing fancy, just cheap, easy to source things to make your baker life easier.

Baking pans

Whether we're talking about large cookie trays or smaller baking pans, nothing can be done in the kitchen without having a few of these pans.

Round cake pans are suited for cakes or cheesecakes and they come in many sizes. The most common size is 8 or 9 inch diameter and I recommend having two of either size for those cases when you have to bake two sponge cakes at a time.

Bundt cake pans come in various sizes as well and their shape or pattern can be different too. A 10-cup Bundt cake pan will cover any of your needs in terms of size. But when it comes to shape and pattern, it's your choice. However, I recommend avoiding intricate designs as these pans tend to be harder to clean.

Muffin tins usually come in 2 standard sizes – either with 6 cups or 12 cups. Most muffin or cupcake recipes found in this book yield 12 muffins so keep this in mind when buying muffin tins.

Pie and tart pans are similar and one of each is more than enough for your home kitchen.

Mixer

I could easily send you to buy a professional mixer for your home kitchen, but I'm going to say just this – I started baking with a very cheap, weak mixer and I pulled it off. You don't need a powerful, large, fancy mixer to bake any of the recipes found in this book. In fact, a mixer should be the last of your concerns as baking can be done with a whisk as well.

Whisk

I don't know what the pastry world would be without whisks. At least 2 should exist in any kitchen and they should be well made and strong, fitted for your hand size and easy to grab.

Spatulas and wooden spoons

Sometimes a whisk or a mixer can be tricky to use because gluten can form easier under the speed of a mixer. That's when spatulas or wooden spoons step in. They allow bakers to incorporate ingredients at a much slower pace, thus preventing those gluten strands from forming and yielding a better texture for your cake, cookie or bread.

Food processor

Although not compulsory, a food processor comes in handy when grinding certain ingredients or even making pie crust dough. Luckily, they're fairly cheap nowadays so investing in one for your kitchen is never a bad thing.

Measuring spoons and cups

No recipe in this book could be done without these measurements. They come in sets, ranging from ¼ cup to 1 cup and ¼ teaspoon to 1 tablespoon accordingly and you can measure basically anything with them, from flour to sugar and various liquids.

Mixing bowls

Needless to say that mixing bowls are compulsory in any kitchen. I recommend either steel or glass bowls because they don't retain odors or grease.

Baking paper or parchment paper

Before the invention of baking paper, home bakers used to grease their pans and flour them. Sometimes baked goodies would burn or become greasy. It all ended when parchment paper came along. Not only that this kind of paper ease the cleaning after baking, but it also protects the baked products from browning too quickly. It can also be used for chocolate decorations or even storing the baked products. It's cheap and easy to find in most supermarkets.

Cakes

CHOCOLATE FUDGE CAKE

Time: 1 ½ hours

Servings: 12

Ingredients:

Cake:
½ cup dark chocolate chips
1 cup hot water
¼ cup cocoa powder
¾ cup butter, softened
1 cup dark brown sugar
2 eggs
½ cup sour cream
2 tablespoons vegetable oil
1 teaspoon vanilla extract

1 ¾ cups all-purpose flour
1 ½ teaspoons baking powder
½ teaspoon baking soda
¼ teaspoon salt
Frosting:
1 cup butter, softened
2 cups powdered sugar
½ cup cocoa powder
1 pinch salt
2 tablespoons whole milk

Directions:

- To make the cake, mix the chocolate chips, hot water and cocoa powder in a bowl.
- In a different bowl, mix the butter and sugar until creamy and pale. Stir in the eggs, one by one, then add the sour cream, vanilla and oil.
- Sift the flour with baking powder, baking soda and salt then incorporate it in the butter mixture, alternating it with the chocolate mixture. Begin and end with flour.
- Divide the batter between two 9-inch round cake pans lined with parchment paper.
- Bake in the preheated oven at 350F for 25-30 minutes.
- Allow to cool then remove the cakes from the pans and level them. Place aside.
- For the frosting: mix the butter and powdered sugar for at least 5 minutes until creamy and fluffy.
- Add the cocoa powder, salt and milk and give it a good mix for 5 additional minutes.
- Use half of the frosting to fill the cake then decorate it with the remaining half.
- Serve right away or refrigerate until serving.

Nutritional information per serving

Calories: 517
Fat: 34.2g

Protein: 4.8g
Carbohydrates: 52.9g

ANACHE CHOCOLATE CAKE

Time: 1 ¼ hours

Servings: 8

Ingredients:

Cake:
6 eggs, room temperature
2/3 cup white sugar
1 teaspoon vanilla extract
¾ cup all-purpose flour
¼ cup cocoa powder

¼ teaspoon salt
1 teaspoon baking powder
¼ cup butter, melted and cooled
Ganache:
2/3 cup heavy cream
1 cup dark chocolate, chopped

Directions:

- To make the cake, mix the eggs, sugar and vanilla in the bowl of your stand mixer for 5-7 minutes until triple in volume.
- Fold in the flour, cocoa powder, salt and baking powder using a wooden spoon or spatula, being careful not to deflate the eggs.
- Gradually fold in the melted butter.
- Pour the batter in a 10-inch cake pan lined with baking paper and bake in the preheated oven at 350F for 35-40 minutes.

- Allow to cool in the pan then transfer on a platter.
- For the ganache, bring the cream to the boiling point then remove from heat and stir in the chocolate. Mix until melted and smooth then allow to cool completely.
- Spoon the ganache over the cake and serve right away.

Nutritional information per serving
Calories: 358
Fat: 19.4g

Protein: 7.7g
Carbohydrates: 40.5g

*T*ROPICAL CARROT CAKE

Time: 1 ½ hours

Servings: 16

Ingredients:
Cake:
2 cups all-purpose flour
1 teaspoon baking soda
1 teaspoon baking powder
½ teaspoon salt
1 teaspoon cinnamon powder
½ teaspoon ground ginger
½ teaspoon ground cloves
1 cup white sugar
¼ cup dark brown sugar
1 cup vegetable oil

4 eggs
1 teaspoon vanilla extract
4 carrots, grated
1 cup crushed pineapple (with juice)
½ cup chopped walnuts
1 cup shredded coconut
Frosting:
1 cup butter, softened
1 cup cream cheese, softened
2 ½ cups powdered sugar
1 teaspoon vanilla extract

Directions:
- For the cake, mix the flour, baking soda, baking powder, spices and salt in a bowl.
- Combine the sugars, oil, eggs and vanilla in a bowl and mix well until double in volume.
- Stir in the carrots, pineapple, walnuts and coconut then add the dry ingredients.
- Pour the batter in 2 9-inch cake pans and bake in the preheated oven at 350F for 35-40 minutes or until risen and golden brown.
- Allow the cakes to cool in the pans then level them and place aside.
- For the frosting, mix the cream cheese, butter, sugar and vanilla in a bowl for at least 5 minutes until stiff and fluffy.
- Use half of the frosting to fill the cakes and the other half to decorate them.

Nutritional information per serving
Calories: 529
Fat: 35.5g

Protein: 5.5g
Carbohydrates: 50.1g

*R*AINBOW CAKE

Time: 1 hour

Servings: 10

Ingredients:
1 cup butter, softened
1 ½ cups white sugar
2 whole eggs
3 egg whites
1 teaspoon vanilla extract
½ cup sour cream

2 ½ cups all-purpose flour
1 teaspoon baking powder
½ teaspoon baking soda
½ teaspoon salt
Red, green, blue and yellow food coloring

Directions:
- Mix the butter and sugar in a bowl until fluffy and creamy.
- Stir in the eggs, egg whites, vanilla and sour cream and mix well for a few minutes.
- Sift the flour with baking powder, baking soda and salt then fold it in the batter.
- Split the batter into 4 smaller bowls then add a drop of food coloring into each bowl and mix slowly with a spoon in each batch of batter.

- Spoon the colorful batter into a 9-inch cake pan lined with baking paper.
- Using a toothpick, swirl the batter around to mix the colors.
- Bake in the preheated oven at 350F for 35-40 minutes.
- Allow the cake to cool in the pan then slice and serve.

Nutritional information per serving

Calories: 433

Fat: 22.0g

Protein: 6.0g

Carbohydrates: 54.8g

H AZELNUT CHOCOLATE CAKE

Time: 1 hour

Servings: 10

Ingredients:

6 oz. dark chocolate chips

½ cup butter

6 eggs, separated

1 cup Nutella

1 cup ground hazelnuts

½ teaspoon salt

Directions:
- Combine the chocolate chips and butter in a heatproof bowl and place over a hot water bath.
- Melt them together until smooth then remove from heat and fold in the egg yolks, followed by the Nutella and ground hazelnuts.
- Whip the egg whites with a pinch of salt until stiff then fold them in the batter using a spatula.
- Pour the batter in a 9-inch round cake pan lined with baking paper.
- Bake in the preheated oven at 350F for 30 minutes.
- Allow the cake to cool in the pan before slicing and serving.

Nutritional information per serving

Calories: 326

Fat: 25.3g

Protein: 6.5g

Carbohydrates: 22.0g

P OMEGRANATE CAKE

Time: 1 ½ hours

Servings: 10

Ingredients:

White cake:

1 ½ cups all-purpose flour

1 cup white sugar

1 ½ teaspoons baking powder

½ teaspoon salt

1 ¼ cups butter, softened

4 eggs whites

¾ cup whole milk

1 teaspoon vanilla extract

1 teaspoon lemon zest

Pomegranate frosting:

4 egg whites

1 cup white sugar

1 pinch salt

¼ cup pomegranate juice

Directions:
- Mix the flour with sugar, baking powder, salt and butter in a bowl until grainy.
- Combine the egg whites with milk, vanilla and lemon zest in a bowl then pour this mixture over the flour mixture.
- Mix gently then spoon the batter into 2 7-inch round cake pans lined with baking paper.
- Bake in the preheated oven at 350F for 30 minutes.
- Allow the cakes to cool in the pan then level them and cut each cake in half lengthwise.
- For the frosting, mix all the ingredients in a heatproof bowl and place over a hot water bath. Keep over heat, mixing all the time, until the mixture is hot.
- Remove from heat and whip with an electric mixer for at least 7 minutes until stiff and glossy.
- Use half of the frosting to fill the cake and the remaining frosting to frost the cake.
- Serve right away or store in the fridge.

Nutritional information per serving

Calories: 449

Fat: 23.8g

Protein: 5.7g

Carbohydrates: 55.8g

CARAMEL PUMPKIN CAKE

Time: 1 ½ hours

Servings: 12

Ingredients:

Cake:
2 cups all-purpose flour
1 teaspoon baking powder
1 teaspoon baking soda
1 teaspoon cinnamon powder
1 teaspoon ground ginger
½ cup coconut oil, melted
1 cup pumpkin puree
4 eggs

1 cup dark brown sugar
¼ cup white sugar
¼ cup whole milk
1 pinch salt
Caramel frosting:
1 cup butter, softened
2 cups powdered sugar
1 pinch salt
½ cup caramel sauce

Directions:

- For the cake, mix the flour, baking powder, baking soda, spices and salt in a bowl.
- In a different bowl, combine the coconut oil, pumpkin puree, eggs, sugars and milk.
- Pour this mixture over the dry ingredients and mix well.
- Pour the batter in 2 round cake pans lined with baking paper.
- Bake the cakes in the preheated oven at 350F for 35 minutes or until fragrant and well risen.
- Allow the cakes to cool in the pans then level them and place aside.
- For the frosting, mix the butter, sugar and salt in a bowl for 5-7 minutes or until double in volume and stiff.
- Stir in the caramel sauce.
- Use half of the frosting to fill the cake and the remaining half to decorate the cake.
- Serve the cake fresh.

Nutritional information per serving

Calories: 495
Fat: 26.4g

Protein: 4.8g
Carbohydrates: 63.2g

BUTTERSCOTCH SWEET POTATO CAKE

Time: 1 ½ hours

Servings: 10

Ingredients:

Cake:
2 cups all-purpose flour
1 teaspoon baking soda
1 teaspoon baking powder
½ teaspoon salt
1 teaspoon cinnamon powder
½ cup canola oil
½ cup coconut milk
1 cup sweet potato puree

½ cup dark brown sugar
½ cup white sugar
3 eggs
Butterscotch sauce:
¼ cup butter
¼ cup light corn syrup
½ cup dark brown sugar
¼ cup heavy cream
¼ teaspoon salt

Directions:

- To make the cake, mix the dry ingredients in a bowl and the wet ingredients in a different bowl.
- Combine the dry ingredients with the wet ingredients and give it a good mix.
- Pour the batter in a 10-inch round cake pan lined with baking paper and bake in the preheated oven at 350F for 35-40 minutes.
- Allow the cake to cool in the pan then transfer on a platter.
- For the butterscotch sauce, mix all the ingredients in a saucepan and cook for 5-8 minutes until thickened.
- Allow to cool then pour the sauce over each slice of cake in the moment of serving.

Nutritional information per serving

Calories: 426

Fat: 21.1g

Protein: 5.1g

Carbohydrates: 56.2g

LIVE OIL PISTACHIO CAKE

Time: 1 hour

Servings: 10

Ingredients:

1 cup all-purpose flour

½ cup corn meal

½ cup ground pistachios

1 teaspoon baking powder

1 teaspoon baking soda

½ teaspoon salt

½ cup extra virgin olive oil

½ cup white sugar

3 eggs

2 tablespoons orange zest

½ cup whole milk

Directions:

• Mix the dry ingredients in a bowl.

• In a different bowl, combine the oil, sugar, eggs and orange zest and mix well for a few minutes until double in volume.

• Stir in the milk, followed by the dry ingredients.

• Pour the batter in 10-inch round cake pan lined with baking paper.

• Bake the cake in the preheated oven at 350F for 35-40 minutes.

• Serve the cake chilled.

Nutritional information per serving

Calories: 221

Fat: 12.1g

Protein: 4.0g

Carbohydrates: 26.1g

UTTERMILK CHOCOLATE CAKE

Time: 50 minutes

Servings: 8

Ingredients:

1 ½ cups all-purpose flour

1 teaspoon baking powder

½ teaspoon salt

¼ cup cocoa powder

½ cup butter, melted

1 cup sugar

1 cup buttermilk

2 eggs

1 teaspoon vanilla extract

Directions:

• Mix the dry ingredients in a bowl and the wet ingredients in a different bowl.

• Pour the wet ingredients over the dry ones and give it a quick mix.

• Pour the batter in a 9-inch cake pan lined with baking paper.

• Bake in the preheated oven at 350F for 30-35 minutes.

• Allow to cool in the pan before slicing and serving.

Nutritional information per serving

Calories: 323

Fat: 13.8g

Protein: 5.9g

Carbohydrates: 47.8g

PEPPERMINT CHOCOLATE CAKE

Time: 1 ¼ hours

Servings: 10

Ingredients:

Cake:

1 ½ cups all-purpose flour

½ cup cocoa powder

1 teaspoon baking powder

½ teaspoon baking soda
½ teaspoon salt
½ cup canola oil
1 cup buttermilk
½ cup hot coffee
1 teaspoon vanilla extract

Frosting:
½ cup butter, softened
1 ½ cups powdered sugar
1 teaspoon peppermint extract
3 oz. dark chocolate, melted and cooled

Directions:
- To make the cake, mix the dry ingredients in a bowl and the wet ingredients in a different bowl.
- Combine the flour mixture with the wet ingredients and give it a quick mix.
- Pour the batter in a 9-inch cake pan lined with baking paper.
- Bake in the preheated oven at 350F for about 35 minutes.
- Allow the cake to cool in the pan then transfer on a platter.
- For the frosting, mix the butter with the sugar until creamy and fluffy.
- Add the peppermint extract and the melted chocolate and mix well.
- Frost the top of the cake with this chocolate buttercream and serve right away or store in the fridge.

Nutritional information per serving
Calories: 384
Fat: 23.6g

Protein: 4.3g
Carbohydrates: 41.2g

H ONEY FIG CAKE

Time: 1 hour

Servings: 8

Ingredients:
1 ½ cups all-purpose flour
1 teaspoon baking powder
½ teaspoon salt
½ cup butter, softened
½ cup honey

3 egg whites
1 whole egg
1 teaspoon vanilla extract
1 teaspoon orange zest
6 fresh figs, quartered

Directions:
- Mix the butter, honey, egg whites and egg in a bowl until creamy. Add the vanilla and orange zest and mix well.
- Fold in the flour, baking powder and salt then spoon the batter in a 9-inch round cake pan lined with baking paper.
- Top the batter with fig slices and bake in the preheated oven at 350F for 35-40 minutes.
- Allow the cake to cool in the pan before slicing and serving.

Nutritional information per serving
Calories: 304
Fat: 12.4g

Protein: 5.1g
Carbohydrates: 45.0g

F UNFETTI CAKE

Time: 1 hour

Servings: 8

Ingredients:
1 ½ cups all-purpose flour
1 ½ teaspoons baking powder
½ teaspoon salt
½ cup funfetti sprinkles
½ cup whole milk

½ cup canola oil
¼ cup butter, melted
1 cup white sugar
3 eggs
1 teaspoon vanilla extract

Directions:
- Mix the flour, baking powder, salt and sprinkles in a bowl.
- In a different bowl, combine the canola oil, butter and sugar and mix well. Add the eggs and mix well for 5 minutes.
- Stir in the vanilla and milk and mix well then pour this mixture over the dry ingredients and mix gently.
- Spoon the batter in a 9-inch cake pan lined with baking paper and bake in the preheated oven at 350F for 35-40 minu-

tes.
- Allow the cake to cool in the pan before slicing and serving.

Nutritional information per serving

Calories: 392
Fat: 21.8g

Protein: 5.1g
Carbohydrates: 46.0g

$\mathcal{C}$ OCONUT RASPBERRY CAKE

Time: 1 hour

Servings: 8

Ingredients:

1 3/4 cups all-purpose flour
1 cup shredded coconut
½ teaspoon salt
1 teaspoon baking soda
½ cup butter, softened

½ cup coconut oil, melted
1 cup white sugar
4 eggs
¼ cup coconut milk
1 cup fresh raspberries

Directions:

- Mix the flour, shredded coconut, salt and baking soda in a bowl.
- In a different bowl, combine the butter, coconut oil and sugar in a bowl. Mix well until fluffy then add the eggs, one by one, and mix well.
- Stir in the coconut oil then fold in the dry ingredients.
- Spoon the batter in a 9-inch cake pan lined with baking paper.
- Top with fresh raspberries and bake in the preheated oven at 350F for 35-40 minutes or until golden brown and well risen.
- Serve the cake chilled.

Nutritional information per serving

Calories: 505
Fat: 32.8g

Protein: 6.4g
Carbohydrates: 49.8g

$\mathcal{R}$ ASPBERRY LEMON OLIVE OIL CAKE

Time: 1 hour

Servings: 10

Ingredients:

1 ¾ cups all-purpose flour
1 teaspoon baking powder
¼ teaspoon baking soda
½ teaspoon salt
¾ cup extra virgin olive oil
¼ cup butter, softened

¼ cup whole milk
4 eggs
1 cup white sugar
2 tablespoons lemon zest
1 cup fresh raspberries

Directions:

- Mix the flour, baking powder, baking soda and salt in a bowl or platter.
- In a different bowl, combine the oil, butter and sugar and mix well. Stir in the eggs, one by one, then add the milk and lemon zest.
- Fold in the dry ingredients then add the raspberries.
- Spoon the batter in a round cake pan lined with baking paper and bake in the preheated oven at 350F for 35-40 minutes or until the cake passes the toothpick test.
- Serve the cake chilled.

Nutritional information per serving

Calories: 361
Fat: 22.0g
Protein: 4.9g
Carbohydrates: 39.1g

$\mathcal{S}$TRAWBERRY CAKE

Time: 1 ½ hours

Servings: 12

Ingredients:

Cake:
2 cups all-purpose flour
2 teaspoons baking powder
½ teaspoon salt
1 cup white sugar
½ cup canola oil
½ cup coconut milk

1 teaspoon vanilla extract
4 eggs
Strawberry buttercream:
1 cup butter
3 cups powdered sugar
¼ cup strawberry puree

Directions:

- For the cake, mix the flour, baking powder and salt in a bowl.
- In a different bowl, mix the sugar, canola oil and eggs in a bowl until double in volume.
- Stir in the milk and vanilla then fold in the dry ingredients.
- Spoon the batter in 2 9-inch round cake pans and bake in the preheated oven at 350F for 30 minutes.
- Allow the cakes to cool in the pan then level them up.
- For the buttercream, mix the butter and sugar in a bowl until stiff and fluffy.
- Stir in the strawberry puree and mix well.
- Fill the cake with half of the buttercream then use the remaining buttercream to cover the cake.
- Serve right away or store in the fridge.

Nutritional information per serving

Calories: 522
Fat: 28.6g

Protein: 4.4g
Carbohydrates: 64.6g

$\mathcal{B}$ANANA CAKE

Time: 55 minutes

Servings: 8

Ingredients:

1 ½ cups all-purpose flour
1 teaspoon baking soda
¼ teaspoon salt
¼ cup butter, softened
½ cup white sugar

2 tablespoons dark brown sugar
2 eggs
2 ripe bananas, mashed
¼ cup whole milk
½ cup dark chocolate chips

Directions:

- Sift the flour, baking soda and salt in a bowl.
- Combine the butter, sugars and eggs in a bowl and mix well for 5 minutes.
- Add the mashed bananas and milk then fold in the flour, followed by the chocolate chips.
- Spoon the batter in a round cake pan lined with baking paper and bake in the preheated oven at 350F for 30-35 minutes or until golden brown and well risen.
- Allow the cake to cool in the pan before slicing and serving.

Nutritional information per serving

Calories: 273
Fat: 9.4g

Protein: 4.9g
Carbohydrates: 44.8g

$\mathcal{B}$ANANA PEANUT BUTTER CAKE

Time: 1 hour

Servings: 8

Ingredients:

½ cup smooth peanut butter

4 tablespoons butter, softened

2/3 cup white sugar
2 eggs
1 teaspoon vanilla extract
2 ripe bananas, mashed

¼ cup whole milk
1 ½ cups all-purpose flour
1 teaspoon baking soda
½ teaspoon salt

Directions:
- Mix the butter with sugar until creamy and smooth.
- Stir in the eggs one by one, then stir in the vanilla and bananas, as well as milk.
- Fold in the flour, baking soda and salt and mix well.
- Spoon the batter in a 9pinch round cake pan lined with baking paper and bake in the preheated oven at 350F for 30-35 minutes or until golden brown and well risen.
- Allow the cake to cool completely before serving.

Nutritional information per serving

Calories: 342
Fat: 15.6g

Protein: 8.5g
Carbohydrates: 45.0g

*T*AHINI CAKE

Time: 1 ¼ hours

Servings: 10

Ingredients:
½ cup tahini paste
½ cup butter, softened
1 cup white sugar
2 eggs
1 teaspoon vanilla extract

1 cup buttermilk
2 cups all-purpose flour
1 teaspoon baking powder
½ teaspoon baking soda
½ teaspoon salt

Directions:
- Mix the tahini paste, butter and sugar in a bowl and give it a good mix.
- Stir in the eggs, one by one, then add the vanilla and buttermilk.
- Fold in the flour, baking powder, baking soda and salt then spoon the batter in a round cake pan lined with baking paper.
- Bake in the preheated oven at 350F for 30-40 minutes or until the cake is well risen and golden brown.
- Allow the cake to cool in the pan before slicing and serving.

Nutritional information per serving

Calories: 343
Fat: 17.0g

Protein: 6.6g
Carbohydrates: 43.1g

*A*LMOND STRAWBERRY CAKE

Time: 1 ¼ hours

Servings: 8

Ingredients:
½ cup butter, softened
⅓ cup white sugar
2 eggs
½ cup whole milk
1 teaspoon vanilla extract

1 cup all-purpose flour
1 cup ground almonds
1 teaspoon baking soda
½ teaspoon salt
1 cup fresh strawberries, sliced

Directions:
- Mix the butter and sugar in a bowl until creamy. Stir in the eggs, one by one, then add the milk and vanilla.
- Fold in the flour, almonds, baking soda and salt and mix gently.
- Fold in the strawberries then spoon the batter in a round cake pan lined with baking paper.
- Bake the cake in the preheated oven at 350F for 30-35 minutes or until golden brown and well risen.
- Allow the cake to cool in the pan before serving.

Nutritional information per serving

Calories: 306

Fat: 19.2g

Protein: 6.2g

Carbohydrates: 29.2g

$\mathcal{D}$ ARK CHOCOLATE COFFEE CAKE

Time: 1 ¼ hours

Servings: 8

Ingredients:

4 tablespoons butter, softened

3 oz. dark chocolate, melted

4 eggs

½ cup light brown sugar

1 teaspoon vanilla extract

¼ cup sour cream

1 ½ cups all-purpose flour

¼ cup cocoa powder

1 teaspoon baking powder

½ teaspoon salt

Directions:

- Mix the butter and chocolate, then stir in the eggs, sugar, vanilla and sour cream.
- Fold in the flour, cocoa powder, baking powder and salt and mix gently with a spatula.
- Spoon the batter in a 9-inch round cake pan and bake in the preheated oven at 350F for 35-40 minutes or until it passes the toothpicks test.
- Allow the cake to cool in the pan before serving.

Nutritional information per serving

Calories: 282

Fat: 13.2g

Protein: 6.8g

Carbohydrates: 35.4g

$\mathcal{B}$ UTTERY ZUCCHINI CAKE

Time: 1 ½ hours

Servings: 10

Ingredients:

1 cup butter, softened

½ cup dark brown sugar

1/2 cup white sugar

4 eggs

1 cup grated zucchinis

2 cups all-purpose flour

1 teaspoon baking soda

1 teaspoon baking powder

½ teaspoon salt

½ cup dark chocolate chips

Directions:

- Mix the butter, brown sugar and white sugar in a bowl until creamy and stiff.
- Stir in the eggs, one by one, then add the zucchinis.
- Fold in the rest of the ingredients then pour the batter in a round cake pan lined with baking paper.
- Bake the cake in the preheated oven at 350F for 40-45 minutes or until it passes the toothpick test.
- Allow the cake to cool in the pan then slice and serve.

Nutritional information per serving

Calories: 374

Fat: 22.0g

Protein: 5.5g

Carbohydrates: 40.9g

$\mathcal{Y}$ OGURT STRAWBERRY CAKE

Time: 1 hour

Servings: 8

Ingredients:

¾ cup canola oil

¾ cup white sugar

2 eggs

1 teaspoon vanilla extract

1 cup plain yogurt

1 ½ cups all-purpose flour

½ cup cornstarch

1 teaspoon baking powder

½ teaspoon salt

1 cup strawberries, sliced

Directions:
- Mix the canola oil, sugar, eggs and vanilla in a bowl until fluffy.
- Stir in the yogurt and mix well then fold in the flour, cornstarch, baking powder and salt then pour the batter in a 9-inch round cake pan lined with parchment paper.
- Top the cake with fresh strawberries and bake in the preheated oven at 350F for 350-40 minutes or until it passes the toothpick tests.
- Allow the cake to cool in the pan before serving.

Nutritional information per serving

Calories: 412
Fat: 22.2g

Protein: 5.7g
Carbohydrates: 47.9g

*W*ALNUT BANANA CAKE

Time: 1 ¼ hours

Servings: 10

Ingredients:

2 cups all-purpose flour
1 cup ground walnuts
2 teaspoons baking soda
½ teaspoon salt
1 teaspoon cinnamon powder

1 cup butter, softened
1 cup light brown sugar
4 eggs
3 ripe bananas, mashed
¼ cup whole milk

Directions:
- Mix the flour, walnuts, baking soda, salt and cinnamon in a bowl.
- In a different bowl, mix the butter and sugar until creamy, then add the eggs, one by one.
- Add the milk and bananas then fold in the flour mixture.
- Spoon the batter into a 10-inch round cake pan lined with baking paper.
- Bake in the preheated oven at 350F or until the cake passes the toothpick test.
- Allow the cake to cool completely before slicing and serving.

Nutritional information per serving

Calories: 446
Fat: 28.1g

Protein: 8.6g
Carbohydrates: 43.1g

*M*ANGO ICE BOX CAKE

Time: 1 hour

Servings: 8

Ingredients:

15 graham crackers
2 ripe mangos, peeled and cubed
½ cup white sugar

1 tablespoon lemon juice
2 cups heavy cream, whipped
1/3 cup sweetened condensed milk

Directions:
- Mix the mangos, sugar and lemon juice in a saucepan and place over low heat. Cook for 10 minutes until softened. Allow to cool completely.
- To finish the cake, take a loaf pan and line it with plastic wrap.
- Mix the cream and sweetened condensed milk.
- Layer the crackers with the mango mixture and cream in the prepared pan.
- Wrap well and place in the fridge for at least 1 hour.
- Serve the cake chilled.

Nutritional information per serving

Calories: 303
Fat: 14.9g
Protein: 3.5g

Carbohydrates: 40.5g

*B*LUEBERRY CAKE

Time: 1 hour

Servings: 12

Ingredients:
3 ½ cups all-purpose flour
2 teaspoons baking powder
½ teaspoon salt
1 cup butter, softened
1 cup white sugar
1/4 cup light brown sugar

4 eggs
2 tablespoons lemon zest
1 cup buttermilk
2 tablespoons lemon juice
1 cup fresh blueberries

Directions:
- Mix the butter and sugars in a bowl until creamy and fluffy.
- Stir in the eggs, one by one, then add the lemon juice, buttermilk and lemon zest.
- Fold in the flour, baking powder and salt, followed by the fresh blueberries.
- Spoon the batter in a 10-inch round cake pan lined with baking paper.
- Bake in the preheated oven at 350F for 40-45 minutes or until the cake is well risen and golden brown.
- Allow the cake to cool in the pan before slicing and serving.

Nutritional information per serving
Calories: 380
Fat: 17.4g

Protein: 6.6g
Carbohydrates: 50.9g

*T*HE ULTIMATE CHOCOLATE CAKE

Time: 1 ¼ hours

Servings: 14

Ingredients:
Cake:
2 ½ cups all-purpose flour
½ cup cocoa powder
½ teaspoon salt
2 teaspoons baking powder
1 cup butter, softened
1 ½ cups white sugar

2 egg yolks
4 eggs
1 cup buttermilk
¼ cup canola oil
Frosting:
1 cup heavy cream
1 ½ cups dark chocolate chips

Directions:
- Mix the butter and sugar in a bowl until creamy and fluffy.
- Stir in the eggs and egg yolks and mix well.
- Add the buttermilk and oil and mix well then fold in the dry ingredients.
- Pour the batter in a 10-inch round cake pan and bake in the preheated oven at 350F for 45 minutes or until the tooth-pick inserted in the center of the cake comes out clean.
- Allow the cake to cool in the pan then transfer on a platter.
- For the frosting, bring the cream to the boiling point then remove from heat and add the chocolate. Allow the frosting to cool in the fridge for a few hours then whip it with an electric mixer until fluffy.
- Cover the cake with the chocolate frosting and serve it fresh.

Nutritional information per serving
Calories: 442
Fat: 26.3g

Protein: 6.6g
Carbohydrates:50.3g

*F*UDGY CHOCOLATE CAKE

Time: 1 hour
Servings: 10

Ingredients:

4 oz. dark chocolate, melted
½ cup butter, melted
1 cup hot coffee
2 eggs
½ cup sour cream
1 cup white sugar

½ cup cocoa powder
1 3/4 cups all-purpose flour
1 teaspoon baking powder
½ teaspoon baking soda
½ teaspoon salt

Directions:

• Mix the butter and chocolate in a bowl. Stir in the coffee, eggs and sour cream, as well as sugar.
• Mix well then fold in the rest of the ingredients.
• Spoon the batter in a 9-inch round cake pan and bake in the preheated oven at 330F for 45-50 minutes.
• Allow the cake to cool in the pan before serving.

Nutritional information per serving

Calories: 344
Fat: 16.6g

Protein: 5.5g
Carbohydrates: 46.6g

𝓑UTTERY ORANGE CAKE

Time: 1 hour

Servings: 8

Ingredients:

½ cup butter, softened
¼ cup canola oil
1 cup white sugar
Zest of 1 lemon
Juice of 1 lemon

4 eggs
2 cups all-purpose flour
2 teaspoons baking powder
½ teaspoon salt
¾ cup whole milk

Directions:

• Sift the flour with baking powder and salt.
• Mix the butter and eggs in a bowl for 5 minutes until creamy then add the eggs, one by one, as well as lemon juice and zest.
• Fold in the flour mixture, alternating it with milk. Start with flour and end with flour.
• Spoon the batter in a 9-inch round cake pan lined with baking paper.
• Bake in the preheated oven at 350F for 35-40 minutes or until golden brown and well risen.
• Allow the cake to cool in the pan before slicing and serving.

Nutritional information per serving

Calories: 417
Fat: 21.6g

Protein: 6.9g
Carbohydrates: 50.8g

𝓥ANILLA STRAWBERRY CAKE

Time: 1 ½ hours

Servings: 10

Ingredients:

Cake:
1 ½ cups all-purpose flour
1 teaspoon baking powder
½ teaspoon baking soda
½ teaspoon salt
½ cup butter, softened
1 cup white sugar
4 egg whites

½ cup whole milk
¼ cup sour cream
1 teaspoon vanilla extract
Filling:
½ cup butter, softened
2 cups powdered sugar
2 teaspoons vanilla extract
1 cup fresh strawberries, sliced

Directions:

• For the cake, sift the flour with baking powder, baking soda and salt in a bowl.

- Add the sugar and butter and mix until grainy.
- Combine the egg whites, milk and sour cream, as well as vanilla in a bowl. Pour this mixture over the dry ingredients and mix just until combined.
- Spoon the batter in 2 8-inch round cake pans lined with baking paper.
- For the filling, mix the butter with sugar for 5 minutes until fluffy and creamy. Add the vanilla and mix well.
- Fill the cake with the buttercream and strawberry slices.
- Serve it fresh.

Nutritional information per serving

Calories: 435

Fat: 20.3g

Protein: 4.2g

Carbohydrates: 60.6g

*C*HAI SPICED STREUSEL CAKE

Time: 1 hour

Servings: 10

Ingredients:

Streusel:

¼ cup light brown sugar

1 cup pecans, chopped

½ teaspoon cinnamon powder

½ teaspoon cardamom powder

½ teaspoon ground cloves

½ teaspoon star anise

¼ cup all-purpose flour

¼ cup butter, melted

Cake:

6 eggs, room temperature

½ cup white sugar

¼ cup whole milk

1 ¼ cups all-purpose flour

1 teaspoon baking powder

¼ cup butter, melted

1 pinch salt

Directions:

- Mix the eggs, sugar and salt for at least 5 minutes until triple in volume.
- Add the milk then fold in the flour and baking powder.
- Gradually stir in the melted butter then pour the batter in a 9-inch cake pan lined with baking paper.
- For the streusel, combine all the ingredients in a bowl and mix well until grainy.
- Spread the streusel over the cake and bake in the preheated oven at 350F for 40-45 minutes or until golden brown and fragrant.
- Allow to cool in the pan before slicing and serving.

Nutritional information per serving

Calories: 254

Fat: 13.3g

Protein: 5.7g

Carbohydrates: 29.0g

*C*ARDAMOM CARROT CAKE

Time: 1 ¼ hours

Servings: 16

Ingredients:

Cake:

2 cups all-purpose flour

1 teaspoon baking soda

½ teaspoon baking powder

½ teaspoon salt

1 teaspoon ground cardamom

1 cup white sugar

4 eggs

¼ cup dark brown sugar

1 cup vegetable oil

1 teaspoon vanilla extract

2 cups grated carrots

1 cup crushed pineapple

1 cup shredded coconut

1 cup pecans, chopped

Frosting:

1 cup cream cheese

½ cup butter, softened

1 cup powdered sugar

1 teaspoon vanilla extract

Directions:

- For the cake, sift the flour, baking soda, baking powder, salt and cardamom in a bowl.

- In a different bowl, mix the eggs and sugars until creamy and fluffy.
- Add the vanilla, carrots, pineapple, coconut and pecans and mix well.
- Fold in the dry ingredients then pour the batter into a 10-inch round cake pan lined with baking paper.
- Bake the cake in the preheated oven at 350F for 45-50 minutes or until fragrant and well risen.
- For the frosting, mix all the ingredients in a bowl for at least 5 minutes.
- Frost the chilled cake with the cream cheese buttercream and serve fresh or store in the fridge.

Nutritional information per serving

Calories: 416

Fat: 28.0g

Protein: 4.6g

Carbohydrates: 38.4g

Chocolate Pumpkin Cake

Time: 1 hour

Servings: 10

Ingredients:

2 cups all-purpose flour

½ cup cocoa powder

1 teaspoon baking powder

1 teaspoon baking soda

½ teaspoon salt

1 teaspoon ground cinnamon

1 teaspoon ground ginger

½ teaspoon ground star anise

½ cup buttermilk

½ cup sour cream

1 cup pumpkin puree

1 teaspoon vanilla extract

1 cup butter, softened

1 cup light brown sugar

4 eggs

Directions:

- Mix the butter and sugar in a bowl until fluffy and creamy.
- Stir in the eggs, one by one, then add the vanilla, pumpkin puree, sour cream and buttermilk and mix well.
- Fold in the dry ingredients then spoon the batter in a 10-inch round cake pan lined with baking paper.
- Bake the cake in the preheated oven at 350F for 45-50 minutes or until it passes the toothpick test.
- Allow the cake to cool in the pan before slicing and serving.

Nutritional information per serving

Calories: 385

Fat: 23.6g

Protein: 6.9g

Carbohydrates: 39.6g

Chocolate Hazelnut Cake

Time: 1 ¼ hours

Servings: 10

Ingredients:

Cake:

1 cup white sugar

6 eggs

1 cup all-purpose flour

½ cup cocoa powder

½ teaspoon baking powder

½ teaspoon salt

1 cup ground hazelnuts

Glaze:

½ cup heavy cream

1 cup dark chocolate chips

Directions:

- To make the cake, mix the eggs with sugar until fluffy, at least double in volume.
- Fold in the flour, cocoa powder, baking powder, salt and hazelnuts then pour the batter in a 9-inch round cake pan lined with baking paper.
- Bake the cake in the preheated oven at 350F for 40 minutes or until it passes the toothpick test.
- Allow the cake to cool in the pan then transfer on a platter.
- For the glaze, bring the cream to the boiling point then add the chocolate and mix well.
- Pour the warm glaze over the cake. Serve right away or store in the fridge.

CARAMEL BANANA CAKE

Time: 1 hour

Servings: 12

Ingredients:

¾ cup butter, softened

1 cup white sugar

¼ cup dark brown sugar

4 eggs

2 ripe bananas, mashed

2 cups all-purpose flour

1 teaspoon cinnamon powder

½ teaspoon ground cardamom

2 teaspoons baking powder

½ teaspoon salt

1 cup buttermilk

½ cup caramel sauce

Directions:

- Mix the butter with sugars for 5 minutes until creamy. Add the eggs, one by one, then stir in the bananas.
- Fold in the flour, spices, baking powder and salt, alternating it with buttermilk.
- Pour the batter in a 9-inch round cake pan.
- Drizzle the batter with caramel sauce and bake the cake in the preheated oven at 350F for 45 minutes or until it passes the toothpick test.
- Allow the cake to cool in the pan before slicing and serving.

Nutritional information per serving

Calories: 334

Fat: 13.4g

Protein: 5.2g

Carbohydrates: 50.6g

MATCHA CHOCOLATE CAKE

Time: 1 ¼ hours

Servings: 8

Ingredients:

Cake:

4 eggs

1 cup white sugar

¼ cup butter, melted

4 tablespoons hot water

1 ¼ cups all-purpose flour

½ teaspoon salt

1 ½ teaspoons matcha powder

1 teaspoon baking powder

Chocolate glaze:

1 cup dark chocolate chips

¼ cup butter

Directions:

- For the cake, sift the flour with salt, matcha powder and baking powder.
- Mix the eggs and white sugar until double in volume.
- Stir in the melted butter and hot water then fold in the flour mixture.
- Spoon the batter in a 9-inch round cake pan lined with baking paper.
- Bake the cake in the preheated oven at 350F for 35-40 minutes or until it passes the toothpick test.
- For the glaze, combine the chocolate chips and butter in a heatproof bowl and place over a hot water bath. Melt them together until smooth.
- Drizzle the glaze over the cake and serve right away or store in the fridge.

Nutritional information per serving

Calories: 371

Fat: 17.9g

Protein: 5.9g

Carbohydrates: 51.0g

CARAMEL SPICE CAKE

Time: 1 ¼ hours

Servings: 8

Ingredients:

Cake:
½ cup butter, softened
¾ cup light brown sugar
3 eggs
½ cup sour cream
1 1/4 cups all-purpose flour
1 teaspoon baking soda
1 teaspoon cinnamon powder
½ teaspoon ground cardamom
½ teaspoon ground ginger
¼ teaspoon ground nutmeg
Glaze:
1 cup white sugar
½ cup heavy cream
½ teaspoon salt

Directions:

- For the cake, sift the flour, baking soda, spices and salt in a bowl.
- In a different bowl, mix the butter and sugar until creamy. Stir in the eggs and mix well then add the sour cream and mix well.
- Fold in the flour mixture then pour the batter in a 9-inch round cake pan lined with parchment paper.
- Bake in the preheated oven at 350F for 35-40 minutes or until it passes the toothpick test.
- Allow the cake to cool in the pan.
- For the glaze, melt the sugar in a heavy saucepan until it has an amber color.
- Stir in the cream and salt and mix well. Keep over low heat until smooth.
- Allow the caramel glaze to cool down then drizzle it over the cake just before serving.

Nutritional information per serving

Calories: 400
Fat: 19.2g
Protein: 4.9g
Carbohydrates: 54.4g

M ISSISSIPPI MUD CAKE

Time: 1 ¼ hours

Servings: 12

Ingredients:

2 cups white sugar
2 eggs
1 cup hot coffee
½ cup cocoa powder
½ teaspoon salt
2 ½ cups all-purpose flour
1 teaspoon baking soda
1 teaspoon baking powder
1 cup canola oil
2 teaspoons vanilla extract
1 cup buttermilk

Directions:

- Mix the sugar, eggs, coffee, oil, vanilla and buttermilk in a bowl.
- In a different bowl, combine the cocoa powder, salt, flour, baking soda and baking powder then stir in the coffee mixture.
- Pour the batter in a 10-inch round cake pan lined with parchment paper.
- Bake in the preheated oven at 330F for 50-55 minutes.
- Allow the cake to cool in the pan before slicing and serving.

Nutritional information per serving

Calories: 410
Fat: 19.8g
Protein: 5.0g
Carbohydrates: 56.5g

C INNAMON CHOCOLATE CAKE

Time: 1 hour

Servings: 10

Ingredients:

1 cup butter, softened
1 ½ cups white sugar
½ cup cocoa powder
3 eggs
1 teaspoon vanilla extract
2 cups all-purpose flour
2 teaspoons baking powder
½ teaspoon salt

1 teaspoon cinnamon powder
1 cup hot coffee

½ cup buttermilk

Directions:
- Mix the butter, sugar and cocoa powder in a bowl until creamy.
- Stir in the eggs and vanilla and mix well.
- Fold in the flour, baking powder and salt then add the cinnamon, coffee and buttermilk and mix gently.
- Pour the batter in a 9-inch round cake pan lined with baking paper and bake for 35-40 minutes or until well risen and fragrant.
- Allow the cake to cool in the pan before serving.

Nutritional information per serving

Calories: 402
Fat: 20.6g

Protein: 5.7g
Carbohydrates: 52.7g

$\mathcal{M}$OIST APPLE CAKE

Time: 1 ½ hours

Servings: 14

Ingredients:
3 cups all-purpose flour
2 teaspoons baking soda
½ teaspoon salt
1 teaspoon cinnamon powder
1 teaspoon ground ginger
1 teaspoon ground cardamom

1 cup butter, softened
1 ½ cups light brown sugar
¼ cup maple syrup
2 eggs
2 cups applesauce
2 green apples, peeled, cored and diced

Directions:
- Mix the flour, baking soda, salt and spices in a bowl.
- In a different bowl, combine the butter, sugar and maple syrup and mix well for a few minutes.
- Stir in the eggs and applesauce then fold in the flour mixture.
- Add the apples then spoon the batter in a 10-inch round cake pan lined with baking paper.
- Bake in the preheated oven at 350F for 45-50 minutes or until the cake passes the toothpick test.
- Allow the cake to cool in the pan before slicing and serving.

Nutritional information per serving

Calories: 326
Fat: 14.1g

Protein: 3.9g
Carbohydrates: 47.2g

$\mathcal{P}$EAR CINNAMON BUNDT CAKE

Time: 1 ¼ hours

Servings: 10

Ingredients:
2 cups all-purpose flour
1 teaspoon cinnamon powder
½ teaspoon ground ginger
2 teaspoons baking powder
½ teaspoon salt

1 cup butter, melted
1 ½ cups light brown sugar
4 eggs
½ cup buttermilk
2 pears, peeled, cored and diced

Directions:
- Mix the flour, cinnamon, ginger, baking powder and salt in a bowl.
- In a different bowl, combine the butter, sugar, eggs and buttermilk and mix well. Pour this mixture over the dry ingredients then fold in the pears.
- Spoon the batter in a Bundt cake pan greased with butter.
- Bake in the preheated oven at 350F for 35-40 minutes or until golden and well risen.
- Allow the cake to cool in the pan before serving.

Nutritional information per serving

Calories: 392
Fat: 20.6g

Protein: 5.6g
Carbohydrates: 48.0g

ERMAN FRUIT BUNDT CAKE

Time: 1 ¼ hours

Servings: 10

Ingredients:

2 cups all-purpose flour
2 teaspoons baking powder
½ teaspoon salt
1 teaspoon cinnamon powder
1 cup butter, softened
1 cup white sugar

¼ cup dark brown sugar
2 eggs
2 pears, peeled, cored and diced
¼ cup golden raisins
¼ cup dried cranberries

Directions:

• Mix the flour, baking powder, salt and cinnamon in a bowl.
• In a different bowl, combine the butter with the sugars and mix well. Stir in the eggs, one by one and mix well.
• Fold in the flour mixture then add the pears, raisins and cranberries.
• Spoon the batter in a Bundt cake pan greased with butter and bake the cake in the preheated oven at 350F for 35-40 minutes or until golden brown and it passes the toothpick test.
• Allow the cake to cool down before slicing and serving.

Nutritional information per serving

Calories: 393
Fat: 19.6g

Protein: 4.1g
Carbohydrates: 52.7g

SPICED WALNUT CAKE

Time: 1 hour

Servings: 8

Ingredients:

3 eggs
1 cup white sugar
¼ cup canola oil
1 cup ground walnuts
1 teaspoon cinnamon powder

½ teaspoon ground ginger
½ teaspoon ground cardamom
¾ cup all-purpose flour
½ teaspoon salt
1 teaspoon baking soda

Directions:

• Mix the eggs and sugar in a bowl until fluffy and double in volume.
• Stir in the canola oil then fold in the walnuts, cinnamon, ginger, cardamom, flour, salt and baking soda.
• Pour the batter in a 8-inch round cake pan lined with baking paper.
• Bake in the preheated oven at 350F for 35-40 minutes or until fragrant and well risen.
• Allow the cake to cool in the pan before slicing and serving.

Nutritional information per serving

Calories: 318
Fat: 17.8g

Protein: 7.1g
Carbohydrates: 35.8g

EVILS BUNDT CAKE

Time: 1 ¼ hours

Servings: 14

Ingredients:

Cake:
1 cup butter, softened

1 ½ cups white sugar
4 eggs

1 cup cocoa powder
1 cup hot water
1 cup sour cream
2 ½ cups all-purpose flour
2 teaspoons baking powder
¼ teaspoon baking soda

½ teaspoon salt
1 cup white chocolate chips
Glaze:
½ cup heavy cream
¾ cup dark chocolate chips

Directions:
- For the cake, mix the cocoa powder, water and sour cream in a bowl.
- In a different bowl, sift the flour, baking powder, baking soda and salt.
- Mix the butter and sugar in a bowl until fluffy. Add the eggs, one by one and mix well.
- Stir in the cocoa powder mixture then fold in the flour.
- Add the chocolate chips then spoon the batter in a Bundt cake greased with butter.
- Bake the cake in the preheated oven at 350F for 40-45 minutes or until it passes the toothpick test.
- Allow the cake to cool in the pan then transfer on a platter.
- For the glaze, mix the two ingredients in a heatproof bowl and place over low heat. Melt them together then drizzle the glaze over the cake.
- Serve right away or store in the fridge.

Nutritional information per serving
Calories: 456
Fat: 26.1g

Protein: 6.9g
Carbohydrates: 54.6g

CREAM BUNDT CAKE

Time: 1 hour

Servings: 10

Ingredients:
2 cups all-purpose flour
2 teaspoons baking powder
½ teaspoon salt
3 eggs

1 ½ cups heavy cream
1 teaspoon vanilla extract
1 cup white sugar

Directions:
- Sift the flour, baking powder and salt.
- Whip the heavy cream on medium speed until soft peaks form. Continue whipping until stiff.
- Stir in the eggs, one by one, then add the sugar and mix well.
- Fold in the flour then spoon the batter in a Bundt cake pan greased with butter.
- Bake in the preheated oven at 350F for 35-40 minutes or until it passes the toothpick test.
- Allow the cake to cool in the pan for 10 minutes then transfer on a platter.

Nutritional information per serving
Calories: 249
Fat: 8.2g

Protein: 4.6g
Carbohydrates: 40.2g

BLACKBERRY BUNDT CAKE

Time: 1 ¼ hours

Servings: 10

Ingredients:
½ cup butter, softened
1 cup white sugar
2 eggs
1 cup whole milk
1 teaspoon vanilla extract

2 cups all-purpose flour
2 teaspoons baking powder
½ teaspoon salt
½ teaspoon ground cardamom
1 cup fresh blackberries

Directions:
- Mix the butter with sugar until creamy, at least 5 minutes.

- Add the eggs and mix well then stir in the milk and vanilla.
- Fold in the flour, baking powder, salt and cardamom then add the blackberries.
- Spoon the batter in a Bundt cake pan greased with butter.
- Bake in the preheated oven at 350F for 35-40 minutes or until it passes the toothpick test.
- Allow the cake to cool in the pan for 10 minutes then turn it upside down on a platter.

Nutritional information per serving

Calories: 283
Fat: 11.2g

Protein: 4.8g
Carbohydrates: 42.2g

 EACH UPSIDE DOWN CAKE

Time: 1 hour

Servings: 8

Ingredients:

4 peaches, sliced
½ cup light brown sugar
2 tablespoons butter
1 cup all-purpose flour
1 teaspoon baking powder

¼ teaspoon salt
1 egg
½ cup sour cream
¼ cup butter, melted
¼ cup whole milk

Directions:
- Arrange the peaches at the bottom of a 9-inch round cake pan lined with baking paper.
- Sprinkle with brown sugar and top with a few pieces of butter.
- For the batter, mix the flour, baking powder and salt in a bowl. Add the rest of the ingredients and give it a quick mix.
- Spoon the batter over the peaches and bake in the preheated oven at 350F for 30-35 minutes.
- When done, turn the cake upside down on a platter.
- Serve chilled.

Nutritional information per serving

Calories: 231
Fat: 12.7g

Protein: 3.6g
Carbohydrates: 26.8g

APLE SYRUP APPLE CAKE

Time: 1 ¼ hours

Servings: 10

Ingredients:

2 cups all-purpose flour
2 teaspoons baking powder
1 teaspoon cinnamon powder
1 teaspoon ground ginger
½ teaspoon salt
¼ cup butter, softened

1 cup maple syrup
4 eggs
½ cup whole milk
2 red apples, peeled, cored and diced
½ cup walnuts, chopped

Directions:
- Mix the flour, baking powder, cinnamon, ginger and salt in a bowl.
- In a different bowl, mix the butter and maple syrup. Stir in the eggs and the milk then fold in the flour.
- Add the apples and walnuts then spoon the batter in a Bundt cake pan greased with butter.
- Bake in the preheated oven at 350F for 35-40 minutes or until well risen and golden brown.
- Allow the cake to cool in the pan before slicing and serving.

Nutritional information per serving

Calories: 306
Fat: 10.8g
Protein: 6.8g
Carbohydrates: 47.1g

Marble Cake

Time: 1 hour

Servings: 10

Ingredients:

½ cup butter, softened
1 cup white sugar
3 eggs
1 cup whole milk
1 teaspoon vanilla extract
2 ½ cups all-purpose flour

2 teaspoon baking powder
½ teaspoon baking soda
½ teaspoon salt
¼ cup cocoa powder
¼ cup hot water

Directions:

- Mix the cocoa powder with hot water in a small bowl.
- Mix the butter and sugar in a bowl until creamy and stiff. Add the eggs, one by one, then stir in the vanilla and milk.
- Fold in the flour, baking powder, baking soda and salt.
- Split the batter in half. Spoon one half in a loaf pan lined with baking paper.
- Mix the remaining half of batter with the cocoa mixture.
- Spoon the cocoa batter over the white one and swirl it around with a toothpick.
- Bake the loaf cake in the preheated oven at 350F for 35-40 minutes or until it passes the toothpick test.
- Allow the cake to cool in the pan before slicing and serving.

Nutritional information per serving

Calories: 311
Fat: 11.9g

Protein: 6.2g
Carbohydrates: 46.8g

Gingerbread Chocolate Cake

Time: 1 ¼ hours

Servings: 10

Ingredients:

½ cup butter, softened
1 ½ cups white sugar
3 eggs
4 oz. dark chocolate, melted
½ cup sour cream
2 cups all-purpose flour
½ cup cocoa powder

2 teaspoons baking powder
½ teaspoon salt
1 teaspoon cinnamon powder
½ teaspoon ground ginger
½ teaspoon ground star anise
½ teaspoon ground cloves
1 teaspoon orange zest

Directions:

- Mix the butter with sugar until creamy. Add the eggs, one by one, then stir in the melted chocolate and sour cream.
- Fold in the flour, cocoa powder, baking powder, salt and spices.
- Spoon the batter in a 9-icnh round cake pan lined with baking paper.
- Bake in the preheated oven at 350F for 40 minutes or until fragrant and well risen.
- Allow the cake to cool in the pan before slicing and serving.

Nutritional information per serving

Calories: 402
Fat: 17.1g

Protein: 6.4g
Carbohydrates: 59.6g

Ginger Sweet Potato Cake

Time: 1 ½ hours

Servings: 10

Ingredients:

1 cup sweet potato puree
1 tablespoon orange zest

¾ cup canola oil
4 eggs

1 cup light brown sugar
1 teaspoon vanilla extract
1 teaspoon cinnamon powder
½ teaspoon salt

1 3/4 cups all-purpose flour
1 teaspoon baking powder
½ teaspoon baking soda

Directions:
- Mix the sweet potato puree with the orange zest, canola oil, eggs, brown sugar and vanilla in a bowl.
- Fold in the rest of the ingredients then spoon the batter in a 9-inch round cake pan lined with baking paper.
- Bake the cake in the preheated oven at 350F for 35-40 minutes or until a toothpick inserted in the center of the cake comes out clean.
- Allow the cake to cool in the pan before slicing and serving.

Nutritional information per serving

Calories: 332
Fat: 18.4g

Protein: 5.0g
Carbohydrates: 37.4g

$\mathcal{C}$ ANDIED GINGER APPLESAUCE CAKE

Time: 1 ¼ hours

Servings: 10

Ingredients:

2 cups all-purpose flour
2 teaspoons baking powder
¼ teaspoon baking soda
½ teaspoon salt
½ teaspoon cinnamon powder
½ teaspoon ground star anise
½ cup butter, room temperature

1 cup white sugar
2 tablespoons molasses
1 ¼ cups applesauce
1 teaspoon vanilla extract
2 eggs
½ cup golden raisins
¼ cup candied ginger, chopped

Directions:
- Mix the flour, baking powder, baking soda, salt and spices in a bowl.
- In a different bowl, mix the butter, sugar and molasses until creamy and stiff. Add the eggs, one by one, then the applesauce and vanilla and mix well.
- Fold in the flour mixture then add the raisins and ginger.
- Spoon the batter in a 9-inch round cake pan lined with baking paper.
- Bake in the preheated oven at 350F for 40-45 minutes or until golden brown and well risen.
- Allow the cake to cool in the pan before slicing and serving.

Nutritional information per serving

Calories: 310
Fat: 10.4g

Protein: 4.1g
Carbohydrates: 52.1g

$\mathcal{P}$ LUM POLENTA CAKE

Time: 1 hour

Servings: 8

Ingredients:

½ pound plums, pitted and sliced
½ cup butter, softened
½ cup honey
4 eggs
2 cups whole milk

1 tablespoon lemon zest
½ teaspoon salt
1 cup instant polenta flour
1 teaspoon baking soda
½ teaspoon salt

Directions:
- Mix the butter with honey until creamy and stiff. Stir in the eggs, one by one, then add the milk and lemon zest.
- Fold in the polenta flour, baking soda and salt then pour the batter in a 9-inch round cake pan lined with baking paper.
- Top with plum slices and bake in the preheated oven at 350F for 35-40 minutes or until golden brown and well risen.
- Allow the cake to cool in the pan then slice and serve.

Nutritional information per serving

Calories: 298

Fat: 15.7g

Protein: 7.1g

Carbohydrates: 33.7g

$\mathcal{S}$ PICY CHOCOLATE CAKE

Time: 1 hour

Servings: 6

Ingredients:

1 ½ cups all-purpose flour

½ cup cocoa powder

1/2 teaspoon chili powder

¼ teaspoon cinnamon powder

1 teaspoon baking soda

½ teaspoon salt

¼ cup canola oil

1 cup hot coffee

2 oz. dark chocolate, chopped

1 teaspoon vanilla extract

Directions:

- Sift the flour with cocoa powder, chili, cinnamon, baking soda and salt.
- Mix the canola oil with coffee and chocolate and mix until melted.
- Add the vanilla, then fold in the flour mixture.
- Pour the batter in a 9-inch round cake pan lined with parchment paper and bake in the preheated oven at 350F for 35-40 minutes or until a toothpick inserted in the center of the cake comes out clean.
- Serve the cake chilled.

Nutritional information per serving

Calories: 264

Fat: 13.2g

Protein: 5.3g

Carbohydrates: 33.6g

$\mathcal{B}$ LOOD ORANGE OLIVE OIL CAKE

Time: 1 ¼ hours

Servings: 12

Ingredients:

3 blood oranges, sliced

½ cup light brown sugar

¾ cup olive oil

2 eggs

1 ½ cups white sugar

1 ½ cups all-purpose flour

1 teaspoon baking powder

½ cup corn meal

½ teaspoon baking soda

½ teaspoon salt

1 cup buttermilk

Directions:

- Arrange the blood orange slices in a 10-inch baking tray lined with parchment paper and sprinkle them with brown sugar.
- Mix the oil with eggs and sugar in a bowl until double in volume.
- Stir in the flour, baking powder, cornmeal, baking soda and salt then add the buttermilk and give it a quick mix.
- Pour the batter over the orange slices and bake in the preheated oven at 350F for 35-40 minutes or until golden brown and well risen.
- Serve the cake chilled, turned upside down on a platter.

Nutritional information per serving

Calories: 342

Fat: 13.9g

Protein: 4.2g

Carbohydrates: 54.0g

$\mathcal{D}$ ARK RUM PECAN CAKE

Time: 1 ¼ hours

Servings: 10

Ingredients:

Cake:
¾ cup butter, softened
½ cup white sugar
½ cup light brown sugar
3 eggs
¼ cup sour cream
1 ½ cups all-purpose flour

1 cup ground pecans
1 teaspoon baking soda
½ teaspoon baking powder
½ teaspoon salt
Glaze:
1 cup powdered sugar
2 tablespoons dark rum

Directions:

- To make the cake, mix the flour, pecans, baking soda, baking powder and salt in a bowl.
- In a different bowl, mix the butter and sugars until creamy. Add the eggs, one after another, then stir in the sour cream and mix well.
- Fold in the flour mixture then spoon the batter in a 9-inch round cake pan lined with parchment paper.
- Bake in the preheated oven at 350F for 35-40 minutes until golden brown and well risen then transfer the cake on a platter and allow to cool.
- For the glaze, mix the sugar with dark rum. Drizzle the glaze over the chilled cake and serve right away.

Nutritional information per serving

Calories: 350
Fat: 17.5g

Protein: 4.1g
Carbohydrates: 44.0g

PPLE AND PEAR MOLASSES CAKE

Time: 1 ¼ hours

Servings: 10

Ingredients:

½ cup canola oil
¼ cup butter, softened
½ cup light molasses
½ cup white sugar
1 egg
1 teaspoon grated ginger
1 teaspoon cinnamon powder

½ cup whole milk
2 cups all-purpose flour
1 teaspoon baking soda
1 teaspoon baking powder
1 red apple, peeled, cored and diced
1 pear, peeled, cored and diced

Directions:

- Mix the canola oil, butter, molasses and sugar in a bowl until creamy. Add the egg, ginger and cinnamon and mix well then stir in the milk.
- Fold in the rest of the ingredients then spoon the batter in a 9-inch round cake pan lined with parchment paper.
- Bake in the preheated oven at 350F for 40-45 minutes or until a toothpick inserted in the center of the cake comes out clean.
- Allow to cool in the pan then cut and serve.

Nutritional information per serving

Calories: 345
Fat: 16.7g

Protein: 3.7g
Carbohydrates: 46.9g

WALNUT COFFEE CAKE

Time: 2 hours

Servings: 16

Ingredients:

Walnut cake:
2 cups all-purpose flour
2 teaspoons baking powder
1 cup ground walnuts
½ teaspoon salt
1 cup butter, softened

1 cup white sugar
4 eggs
¼ cup whole milk
1 teaspoon vanilla extract
Coffee buttercream:
1 cup butter, softened

2 ½ cups powdered sugar
1 teaspoon vanilla extract

2 teaspoons instant coffee

Directions:
- For the cake, mix the flour, baking powder, walnuts and salt in a bowl.
- In a different bowl, mix the butter and sugar until creamy. Stir in the eggs, one by one, then add the milk and vanilla.
- Fold in the flour and mix gently with a spatula.
- Pour the batter in a round cake pan lined with baking paper and bake in the preheated oven at 350F for 35-40 minutes.
- Allow the cake to cool in the pan then transfer on a platter.
- For the buttercream, mix the butter until creamy and light. Add the sugar, gradually and mix well for a few minutes until stiff.
- Mix the vanilla with the coffee then add it into the buttercream. Mix well.
- Cover the cake with the buttercream and serve it fresh.

Nutritional information per serving
Calories: 449
Fat: 29.0g

Protein: 5.2g
Carbohydrates: 44.5g

ADEIRA CAKE

Time: 1 hour

Servings: 8

Ingredients:
¾ cup butter, softened
¾ cup white sugar
3 eggs
1 ½ cups all-purpose flour

1 teaspoon baking powder
¼ teaspoon salt
¼ cup whole milk
1 teaspoon lemon zest

Directions:
- Mix the butter and sugar in a bowl until creamy and stiff. Add the eggs, one by one, then fold in the flour, baking powder and salt, alternating it with milk.
- Add the lemon zest then spoon the batter in a 9-inch round cake pan lined with baking paper.
- Bake the cake in the preheated oven at 350F for 35-40 minutes or until well risen and golden brown.
- Allow the cake to cool in the pan before slicing and serving.

Nutritional information per serving
Calories: 337
Fat: 19.4g

Protein: 4.9g
Carbohydrates: 37.5g

SOUR CHERRY CHOCOLATE CAKE

Time: 1 ¼ hours

Servings: 10

Ingredients:
1 cup butter, softened
1 cup white sugar
1 teaspoon vanilla extract
4 eggs
1 cup all-purpose flour
½ cup cocoa powder

1 teaspoon baking powder
½ teaspoon salt
¼ cup whole milk
1 cup sour cherries, pitted
1 cup heavy cream, whipped

Directions:
- Sift the flour with cocoa, salt and baking powder.
- Mix the butter with sugar and vanilla until creamy. Add the eggs, one by one, then fold in the flour mixture.
- Add the cherries then spoon the batter in a 9-inch round cake pan lined with baking paper.
- Bake in the preheated oven at 350F for 35-40 minutes or until a toothpick inserted in the center of the cake comes out clean.
- Allow the cake to cool then transfer on a platter and cover it in whipped cream.

- Serve fresh or store in the fridge.

Nutritional information per serving

Calories: 373
Fat: 25.5g

Protein: 5.0g
Carbohydrates: 35.0g

Victoria Sponge Cake with Strawberries

Time: 1 ¼ hours

Servings: 8

Ingredients:

1 cup butter, softened
1 cup white sugar
4 eggs
1 ¼ cups all-purpose flour

¼ teaspoon salt
1 teaspoon baking powder
1 cup heavy cream, whipped
1 cup fresh strawberries, sliced

Directions:

- Mix the butter and sugar in a bowl until light and creamy.
- Stir in the eggs, one by one, then fold in the flour, salt and baking powder.
- Spoon the batter in a 9-inch round cake pan lined with parchment paper and bake in the preheated oven at 350F for 30-35 minutes or until well risen and golden brown.
- Allow the cake to cool down then remove it from the pan and cut it in half lengthwise.
- Fill the cake with whipped cream and strawberries and decorate it with a dust of powdered sugar.

Nutritional information per serving

Calories: 458
Fat: 31.0g

Protein: 5.5g
Carbohydrates: 42.2g

Coconut Carrot Bundt Cake

Time: 1 ¼ hours

Servings: 10

Ingredients:

4 eggs
1 cup light brown sugar
1 cup canola oil
1 teaspoon vanilla extract
1 ¼ cups all-purpose flour
2 teaspoons baking powder
½ teaspoon salt

1 tablespoon orange zest
1 cup shredded coconut
1 cup coconut flakes
2 cups grated carrots
½ cup crushed pineapple
½ cup coconut milk

Directions:

- Mix the eggs and sugar in a bowl until double in volume.
- Stir in the oil and vanilla then add the orange zest, coconut, carrots, pineapple and coconut milk.
- Fold in the flour, baking powder and salt then pour the batter in a 9-inch round cake pan lined with baking paper.
- Bake in the preheated oven at 350F for 40-45 minutes or until it passes the toothpick test.
- Allow the cake to cool in the pan before slicing and serving.

Nutritional information per serving

Calories: 430
Fat: 31.9g

Protein: 4.9g
Carbohydrates: 33.3g

Fruit and Brandy Cake

Time: 1 ½ hours

Servings: 16

Ingredients:

½ cup golden syrup

¼ cup black treacle

¼ cup honey
1 cup dark brown sugar
1 cup heavy cream
1 cup butter, softened
1 teaspoon lemon zest
1 teaspoon orange zest
6 eggs
11 cup dried black currants

1 cup golden raisins
½ cup dried pineapple, chopped
½ cup dried apricots, chopped
¼ cup candied ginger, chopped
1 cup brandy
3 cups all-purpose flour
1 teaspoon baking soda

Directions:
- Mix the dried fruits with brandy in a bowl and allow to soak up for a few hours, preferably overnight.
- Mix the golden syrup, treacle, honey, brown sugar, cream, butter, lemon zest and orange zest in a bowl until creamy.
- Stir in the eggs, one by one, then add the flour. And baking soda.
- Fold in the dried fruits and mix gently with a spatula.
- Spoon the batter in a 10-inch round cake pan and bake in the preheated oven at 330F for 1 hour or until a toothpick inserted in the center of the cake comes out clean. If the toothpick is not clean, continue baking for 10 additional minutes and check again.
- Allow the cake to cool in the pan then transfer on a platter and slice.

Nutritional information per serving
Calories: 450
Fat: 16.3g

Protein: 5.2g
Carbohydrates: 73.3g

G INGER WHOLE ORANGE CAKE

Time: 1 ¼ hours

Servings: 10

Ingredients:
Cake:
1 whole orange
2 cups all-purpose flour
2 teaspoons baking powder
½ teaspoon salt
1 cup butter, softened
1 cup white sugar

2 tablespoons dark brown sugar
4 eggs
1 teaspoon grated ginger
Icing:
1 cup powdered sugar
1 teaspoon orange zest
1 tablespoon orange juice

Directions:
- To make the cake, place the orange in a saucepan and cover it with water. Cook for 30 minutes then drain well and place in a food processor. Pulse until smooth. Add the ginger and mix well. Place aside.
- Mix the butter with the sugars in a bowl until creamy and fluffy. Stir in the eggs, one by one and mix well.
- Fold in the flour, baking powder and salt, alternating it with the orange mixture.
- Spoon the batter in a 9-inch round cake pan lined with baking paper and bake in the preheated oven at 350F for 40-45 minutes or until a toothpick inserted in the center of the cake comes out clean.
- Allow the cake to cool then transfer it on a platter.
- For the icing, mix all the ingredients in a bowl and drizzle it over the chilled cake. Serve right away.

Nutritional information per serving
Calories: 430
Fat: 21.1g

Protein: 5.8g
Carbohydrates: 56.2g

L EMON DRIZZLE CAKE

Time: 1 ¼ hours

Servings: 10

Ingredients:
Cake:
5 eggs
1 cup white sugar

½ cup butter, melted
½ cup sour cream
2 tablespoons lemon zest

2 tablespoons lemon juice
1 ½ cups all-purpose flour
1 teaspoon baking powder
Icing:

1 cup powdered sugar
1 tablespoon lemon juice
1 teaspoon lemon zest

Directions:
- For the cake, mix the eggs and sugar in a bowl until double in volume and fluffy.
- Add the melted butter and mix gently. Stir in the sour cream, lemon zest and lemon juice.
- Fold in the flour, baking powder and salt then pour the batter in a 9-inch round cake pan lined with parchment paper.
- Bake in the preheated oven at 350F for 35-40 minutes or until golden brown and well risen.
- Allow the cake to cool in the pan then transfer on a platter.
- For the icing, mix all the ingredients then drizzle it over the cake.
- Serve right away.

Nutritional information per serving
Calories: 330
Fat: 14.0g

Protein: 5.2g
Carbohydrates: 47.5g

AM STUDDED CAKE

Time: 1 hour

Servings: 8

Ingredients:
5 eggs
¾ cup white sugar
¼ cup canola oil
1 teaspoon vanilla extract
1 teaspoon orange zest

1 cup all-purpose flour
1 teaspoon baking powder
¼ teaspoon salt
1 cup apricot jam

Directions:
- Mix the eggs and sugar in a bowl until triple in volume.
- Stir in the oil, vanilla and orange zest then fold in the flour, baking powder and salt.
- Spoon the batter in 1 9-inch round cake pan lined with baking paper.
- Drop spoonfuls of apricot jam over the batter and bake in the preheated oven at 350F for 35-40 minutes or until golden brown and well risen.
- Allow the cake to cool in the pan before slicing and serving.

Nutritional information per serving
Calories: 326
Fat: 9.8g

Protein: 5.4g
Carbohydrates: 57.1g

R UM PINEAPPLE UPSIDE DOWN CAKE

Time: 1 ¼ hours

Servings: 10

Ingredients:
1 can pineapple rings, drained
4 eggs
1 cup white sugar
¼ cup light rum

¼ cup butter, melted
2 cups all-purpose flour
1 ½ teaspoons baking powder
¼ teaspoon salt

Directions:
- Arrange the pineapple rings at the bottom of a 9-inch round cake pan lined with baking paper.
- Mix the eggs and sugar in a bowl until double in volume.
- Stir in the rum and melted butter then fold in the flour, baking powder and salt.
- Pour the batter over the pineapple and bake in the preheated oven at 350F for 35-40 minutes.
- When done, turn it upside down on a platter and allow to cool before serving.

Nutritional information per serving

Calories: 254

Fat: 6.6g

Protein: 4.9g

Carbohydrates: 41.7g

CHOCOLATE BISCUIT CAKE

Time: 3 hours

Servings: 10

Ingredients:

10 oz. digestive biscuits, chopped

½ cup dark chocolate chips

½ cup milk chocolate chips

½ cup butter

½ cup golden syrup

1 cup heavy cream

1 cup milk

¼ cup cocoa powder

1 cup golden raisins

¼ cup dried cranberries

½ cup pecans, chopped

Directions:

- Melt the chocolate chips and butter in a heatproof bowl over a hot water bath.
- Mix the cream, milk and cocoa powder and place over low heat. Bring to a boil and cook just until slightly thickened. Remove from heat and stir in the chocolate mixture.
- Combine this mixture with the rest of the ingredients in a bowl then transfer in a 8-inch cake pan lined with plastic wrap.
- Place in the fridge to set for 2 hours then slice and serve.

Nutritional information per serving

Calories: 408

Fat: 24.0g

Protein: 4.3g

Carbohydrates: 49.1g

LEMON GINGER CAKE

Time: 1 ¼ hours

Servings: 10

Ingredients:

2 ½ cups all-purpose flour

1 teaspoon baking soda

½ teaspoon baking powder

¼ teaspoon salt

1 cup butter, softened

1 ½ cups white sugar

4 eggs

¼ cup lemon juice

1 tablespoon lemon zest

1 teaspoon grated ginger

1 cup sour cream

Directions:

- Sift the flour, baking soda, baking powder and salt.
- Mix the butter and sugar in a bowl until creamy and fluffy.
- Add the eggs, one by one, then stir in the lemon juice, lemon zest and ginger, as well as the sour cream.
- Fold in the sifted flour then spoon the batter in a 9-inch round cake pan lined with baking paper.
- Bake in the preheated oven at 350F for 35-40 minutes or until a toothpick inserted in the center of the cake comes out clean.
- Allow the cake to cool in the pan before slicing and serving.

Nutritional information per serving

Calories: 466

Fat: 25.4g

Protein: 6.4g

Carbohydrates: 55.5g

MOLASSES PEAR BUNDT CAKE

Time: 1 ¼ hours

Servings: 10

Ingredients:

1 cup butter, softened
½ cup molasses
½ cup light brown sugar
3 eggs
2 cups all-purpose flour
1 teaspoon baking powder
1 teaspoon baking soda

½ teaspoon salt
½ teaspoon ground ginger
1 teaspoon cinnamon powder
1 teaspoon all-spice
½ cup whole milk
½ cup sour cream
2 pears, peeled, cored and diced

Directions:

- Mix the butter, molasses and sugar in a bowl until creamy and pale.
- Stir in the eggs, one at a time, mixing well after each addition.
- Sift the flour with baking powder, baking soda, salt and spices.
- Mix the milk with cream.
- Fold the flour into the butter mixture, alternating it with the milk and sour cream mix.
- Add the pears then spoon the batter in a greased Bundt cake pan.
- Bake in the preheated oven at 350F for 40-45 minutes or until it passes the toothpick test.
- Allow the cake to cool in the pan for 10 minutes then turn upside down on a platter.
- Serve chilled.

Nutritional information per serving

Calories: 405
Fat: 22.9g

Protein: 5.3g
Carbohydrates: 46.3g

P EANUT BUTTER CHOCOLATE BUNDT CAKE

Time: 1 ¼ hours

Servings: 10

Ingredients:

2 cups all-purpose flour
2 teaspoons baking powder
½ teaspoon baking soda
½ teaspoon salt
½ cup cocoa powder
1 cup smooth peanut butter

¼ cup butter, softened
1 cup light brown sugar
3 eggs
1 teaspoon vanilla extract
1 cup buttermilk
½ cup dark chocolate chips

Directions:

- Sift the flour, baking powder, baking soda, salt and cocoa powder.
- Mix the peanut butter, butter and sugar in a bowl until creamy and light.
- Add the eggs and mix well then stir in the vanilla.
- Fold in the flour, alternating it with buttermilk. Start and end with flour.
- Add the chocolate chips then spoon the batter in a Bundt cake pan greased with butter.
- Bake the cake in the preheated oven at 350F for 40-45 minutes or until well risen and golden brown.
- When done, turn the cake upside down on a platter and serve it only when chilled.

Nutritional information per serving

Calories: 407
Fat: 21.6g

Protein: 12.8g
Carbohydrates: 46.5g

S WEET POTATO BUNDT CAKE

Time: 1 hour

Servings: 10

Ingredients:

1 cup sweet potato puree
3/4 cup maple syrup
2 eggs
½ cup sour cream

¼ cup canola oil
1 teaspoon vanilla extract
2 cups all-purpose flour
2 teaspoons baking powder

½ teaspoon salt   ½ cup dark chocolate chips

Directions:
- Mix the potato puree, maple syrup, eggs, sour cream, canola oil and vanilla in a bowl.
- Stir in the rest of the ingredients then spoon the batter in a greased Bundt cake pan.
- Bake in the preheated oven at 350F for 40-45 minutes or until a toothpick inserted in the center of the cake comes out clean.
- Allow the cake to cool in the pan then slice and serve.

Nutritional information per serving

Calories: 294

Fat: 10.7g

Protein: 5.0g

Carbohydrates: 45.9g

H ot Chocolate Bundt Cake

Time: 1 hour

Servings: 12

Ingredients:

Cake:

¾ cup butter, softened

½ cup canola oil

1 cup light brown sugar

3 eggs

1 teaspoon vanilla extract

4 oz. dark chocolate, melted

2 cups all-purpose flour

¾ cup cocoa powder

2 teaspoons baking powder

½ teaspoon salt

1 cup hot water

Glaze:

½ cup heavy cream

1 cup dark chocolate chips

Directions:
- For the cake, mix the butter, oil and sugar in a bowl until creamy and light.
- Stir in the eggs, vanilla and melted chocolate.
- Sift the flour with cocoa powder, baking powder and salt and fold it in the butter mixture.
- Gradually stir in the hot water then spoon the batter in a greased Bundt cake pan.
- Bake in the preheated oven at 350F for 40-45 minutes or until the cake passes the toothpick test.
- When done, remove from the pan on a platter.
- For the glaze, bring the cream to the boiling point then stir in the chocolate. Mix until melted and smooth.
- Drizzle the glaze over the cake and serve chilled.

Nutritional information per serving

Calories: 448

Fat: 29.9g

Protein: 6.1g

Carbohydrates: 43.6g

Y ogurt Bundt Cake

Time: 1 ¼ hours

Servings: 12

Ingredients:

6 eggs, separated

1 ½ cups white sugar

1 cup butter, softened

2 tablespoons lemon zest

2 tablespoons lemon juice

3 cups all-purpose flour

1 teaspoon baking soda

1 teaspoon baking powder

½ teaspoon salt

1 ½ cups plain yogurt

Directions:
- Mix the egg yolks with sugar until pale and fluffy. Stir in the butter and mix well.
- Add the lemon zest and juice then stir in the yogurt.
- Fold in the flour, baking powder, baking soda and salt.
- Spoon the batter in a greased Bundt cake pan and bake in the preheated oven at 350F for 40-45 minutes or until the cake passes the toothpick test.
- Allow the cake to cool in the pan before transferring on a platter.

Nutritional information per serving

Calories: 398
Fat: 18.2g

Protein: 7.9g
Carbohydrates: 51.7g

𝓕LUFFY PEAR BUNDT CAKE

Time: 1 ¼ hours

Servings: 14

Ingredients:

3 cups all-purpose flour
2 teaspoons baking powder
½ teaspoon salt
2 teaspoons pumpkin pie spice
1 cup canola oil

1 ½ cups white sugar
3 eggs
1 teaspoon vanilla extract
½ cup whole milk
3 pears, peeled, cored and diced

Directions:

• Mix the flour, baking powder, salt and pumpkin pie spice in a bowl.
• In a different bowl, mix the canola oil with sugar and eggs until double in volume.
• Add the vanilla extract and milk then fold in the flour, followed by the pears.
• Spoon the batter in a greased Bundt cake pan and bake in the preheated oven at 350F for 45-50 minutes or until a toothpick inserted in the center of the cake comes out clean.
• Allow the cake to cool in the pan then slice and serve it.

Nutritional information per serving

Calories: 363
Fat: 17.1g

Protein: 4.4g
Carbohydrates: 49 7g

𝓑ROWN SUGAR PINEAPPLE BUNDT CAKE

Time: 1 ¼ hours

Servings: 12

Ingredients:

½ cup light brown sugar
4 pineapple slices, cubed
2 cups all-purpose flour
½ cup cornstarch
1 teaspoon baking soda
1 teaspoon baking powder
½ teaspoon salt

¾ cup butter, softened
1 cup white sugar
1 teaspoon vanilla extract
3 eggs
1 tablespoon lemon zest
½ cup buttermilk

Directions:

• Arrange the pineapple slices at the bottom of a greased Bundt cake pan and sprinkle with brown sugar.
• Sift the flour with cornstarch, baking soda, baking powder and salt.
• Mix the butter with sugar in a bowl until light and creamy then stir in the eggs and vanilla, as well as the lemon zest and buttermilk.
• Fold in the flour then pour the batter over the pineapple.
• Bake in the preheated oven at 350F for 40-45 minutes or until well risen and golden brown.
• Allow the cake to cool in the pan for 10 minutes then turn it upside down on a platter.

Nutritional information per serving

Calories: 332
Fat: 13.0g

Protein: 4.3g
Carbohydrates: 51.5g

𝓖RAHAM CRACKER CAKE

Time: 1 ¼ hours
Servings: 10

Ingredients:

1 cup graham cracker crumbs
2 cups all-purpose flour
2 teaspoons baking powder
½ teaspoon baking powder
½ teaspoon salt
½ teaspoon cinnamon powder

¾ cup butter, softened
¼ cup dark brown sugar
1 cup white sugar
3 eggs
½ cup heavy cream

Directions:

- Mix the graham cracker crumbs, flour, baking powder, baking soda, salt and cinnamon in a bowl.
- In another bowl, mix the butter and sugars until creamy and light.
- Stir in the eggs, one after another, and mix well then add the cream.
- Fold in the flour mixture then pour the batter in a 10-inch round cake pan lined with baking paper.
- Bake for 45 minutes in the preheated oven at 350F or until a toothpick inserted in the center of the cake comes out clean.
- Allow the cake to cool in the pan before slicing and serving.

Nutritional information per serving

Calories: 380
Fat: 18.4g

Protein: 5.0g
Carbohydrates: 50.4g

𝒟 UO BUNDT CAKE

Time: 1 ¼ hours

Servings: 14

Ingredients:

½ cup butter, softened
4 oz. dark chocolate, melted
2 cups white sugar
3 eggs
½ cup cream cheese
1 cup buttermilk

3 cups all-purpose flour
2 teaspoons baking powder
½ teaspoon baking soda
½ teaspoon salt
¼ cup cocoa powder
¼ cup hot water

Directions:

- Mix the butter and sugar in a bowl until creamy and fluffy.
- Stir in the chocolate and eggs and mix well, then add the cream cheese.
- Sift the flour, baking powder, baking soda and salt then fold it in the batter.
- Split the batter in half. Mix one half with the cocoa powder and hot water.
- Spoon the white batter in a greased Bundt cake pan.
- Top with the cocoa batter and bake in the preheated oven at 350F for 45-50 minutes or until well risen and it passes the toothpick test.
- Allow the cake to cool in the pan then transfer on a platter.

Nutritional information per serving

Calories: 360
Fat: 13.4g

Protein: 6.1g
Carbohydrates: 56.1g

𝓑 ROWN SUGAR CAKE

Time: 1 ¼ hours

Servings: 10

Ingredients:

2 cups all-purpose flour
2 teaspoons baking powder
½ teaspoon salt
1 cup butter, softened
1 cup light brown sugar
½ cup dark brown sugar

4 eggs
1 teaspoon vanilla extract
½ cup milk

Directions:
- Sift the flour, baking powder and salt in a bowl.
- In another bowl, mix the butter and sugars until creamy and light.
- Stir in the eggs, one by one, then add the vanilla and milk.
- Fold in the flour then spoon the batter in a 9-inch round cake pan lined with parchment paper.
- Bake in the preheated oven at 350F for 40 minutes or until well risen and golden brown.
- Allow the cake to cool in the pan before slicing and serving.

Nutritional information per serving

Calories: 370

Fat: 20.7g

Protein: 5.4g

Carbohydrates: 41.7g

$\mathcal{B}$ oozy Raisin Bundt Cake

Time: 2 hours

Servings: 12

Ingredients:

1 cup butter, softened

1 ½ cups white sugar

1 cup apricot jam

2 eggs

3 cups all-purpose flour

2 teaspoons baking powder

½ teaspoon salt

1 cup golden raisins

½ cup brandy

1 cup buttermilk

½ cup whole milk

Directions:
- Sift the flour, salt and baking powder.
- Mix the butter, sugar and jam in a bowl until creamy and light
- Stir in the eggs, one by one, then begin incorporating the flour mixture, alternating it with the buttermilk and milk.
- Spoon the batter in a greased Bundt cake pan and bake in the preheated oven at 350F for 45-50 minutes or until it passes the toothpick test.
- Allow the cake to cool in the pan before serving.

Nutritional information per serving

Calories: 474

Fat: 17.0g

Protein: 5.9g

Carbohydrates: 77.5g

$\mathcal{R}$ aspberry Chocolate Cake

Time: 1 ¼ hours

Servings: 10

Ingredients:

6 eggs

1 cup white sugar

½ cup butter, melted

3 oz. dark chocolate, melted

1 teaspoon vanilla extract

1 ¼ cups all-purpose flour

½ teaspoon baking powder

½ teaspoon salt

2 cups fresh raspberries

Directions:
- Mix the eggs and sugar in a bowl until triple in volume.
- Stir in the melted butter and chocolate, as well as vanilla.
- Fold in the baking powder and salt then add the raspberries and mix gently.
- Pour the batter in a 9-inch round cake pan and bake in the preheated oven at 350F for 35-40 minutes or until the cake passes the toothpick test.
- Allow to cool in the pan then slice and serve.

Nutritional information per serving

Calories: 311

Fat: 14.7g

Protein: 6.0g

Carbohydrates: 40.3g

ORANGE POUND CAKE

Time: 1 ¼ hours

Servings: 16

Ingredients:

1 ½ cups butter, softened
2 cups white sugar
6 eggs
1 teaspoon vanilla extract
1 orange, zested and juiced

3 cups all-purpose flour
2 teaspoons baking powder
½ teaspoon salt
1 cup sour cream

Directions:
- Sift the flour with salt and baking powder.
- Mix the butter with sugar for 5 minutes until creamy and fluffy.
- Add the vanilla, orange zest and orange juice and mix well.
- Stir in the sour cream then fold in the flour mixture.
- Pour the batter in a large loaf cake pan lined with baking paper.
- Bake in the preheated oven at 330F for 40 minutes then turn the heat on 350F for another 10 minutes.
- Allow the cake to cool in the pan before slicing and serving.

Nutritional information per serving

Calories: 393
Fat: 22.2g

Protein: 5.2g
Carbohydrates: 45.3g

GRAND MARNIER INFUSED LOAF CAKE

Time: 2 hours

Servings: 14

Ingredients:

1 cup dried cranberries
¼ cup grand Marnier
½ cup butter, softened
1 cup cream cheese
1 ½ cups white sugar
4 eggs

1 teaspoon vanilla extract
3 cups all-purpose flour
2 teaspoons baking powder
½ teaspoon salt
½ teaspoon baking soda
½ cup whole milk

Directions:
- Mix the cranberries and Grand Marnier in a jar and allow to soak up for 1 hour.
- Sift the flour with baking powder, baking soda and salt.
- Mix the butter, cream cheese and sugar in a bowl until fluffy.
- Stir in the eggs, one by one, then add the vanilla and milk.
- Fold in the flour mixture and mix just until incorporated.
- Add the cranberries.
- Spoon the batter in a large loaf pan lined with baking paper.
- Bake in the preheated oven at 350F for 50-55 minutes or until it passes the toothpick test.
- Allow the cake to cool in the pan then slice and serve.

Nutritional information per serving

Calories: 336
Fat: 14.1g

Protein: 6.0g
Carbohydrates: 43.9g

CREAM CHEESE PUMPKIN CAKE

Time: 1 ¼ hours

Servings: 14

Ingredients:
Cake:

1 ½ cups pumpkin puree

2 cups white sugar
4 eggs
1 cup canola oil
2 cups all-purpose flour
2 teaspoons baking soda
1 teaspoon cinnamon powder
1 teaspoon ground ginger

½ teaspoon ground cloves
½ teaspoon salt
½ teaspoon ground ginger
Cream cheese frosting:
1 cup cream cheese
½ cup butter, softened
1 cup powdered sugar

Directions:
- For the cake, mix the pumpkin puree, sugar, eggs and canola oil in a bowl.
- Stir in the rest of the ingredients and mix just until incorporated, don't over mix it!
- Pour the batter in a 10-inch round cake pan lined with baking paper.
- Bake in the preheated oven at 350F for 45 minutes or until well risen and golden brown.
- Allow the cake to cool in the pan then transfer on a platter.
- For the frosting, mix all the ingredients in a bowl. Spread the frosting over the cake and serve fresh or store in the fridge.

Nutritional information per serving
Calories: 487
Fat: 29.5g

Protein: 5.0g
Carbohydrates: 53.6g

*G*RAND MARNIER INFUSED LOAF CAKE

Time: 2 hours

Servings: 14

Ingredients:
1 cup dried cranberries
¼ cup grand Marnier
½ cup butter, softened
1 cup cream cheese
1 ½ cups white sugar
4 eggs

1 teaspoon vanilla extract
3 cups all-purpose flour
2 teaspoons baking powder
½ teaspoon salt
½ teaspoon baking soda
½ cup whole milk

Directions:
- Mix the cranberries and Grand Marnier in a jar and allow to soak up for 1 hour.
- Sift the flour with baking powder, baking soda and salt.
- Mix the butter, cream cheese and sugar in a bowl until fluffy.
- Stir in the eggs, one by one, then add the vanilla and milk.
- Fold in the flour mixture and mix just until incorporated.
- Add the cranberries.
- Spoon the batter in a large loaf pan lined with baking paper.
- Bake in the preheated oven at 350F for 50-55 minutes or until it passes the toothpick test.
- Allow the cake to cool in the pan then slice and serve.

Nutritional information per serving
Calories: 336
Fat: 14.1g

Protein: 6.0g
Carbohydrates: 43.9g

*C*REAM CHEESE PUMPKIN CAKE

Time: 1 ¼ hours

Servings: 14

Ingredients:
Cake:
1 ½ cups pumpkin puree
2 cups white sugar
4 eggs
1 cup canola oil

2 cups all-purpose flour
2 teaspoons baking soda
1 teaspoon cinnamon powder
1 teaspoon ground ginger
½ teaspoon ground cloves

½ teaspoon salt
½ teaspoon ground ginger
Cream cheese frosting:

1 cup cream cheese
½ cup butter, softened
1 cup powdered sugar

Directions:

- For the cake, mix the pumpkin puree, sugar, eggs and canola oil in a bowl.
- Stir in the rest of the ingredients and mix just until incorporated, don't over mix it!
- Pour the batter in a 10-inch round cake pan lined with baking paper.
- Bake in the preheated oven at 350F for 45 minutes or until well risen and golden brown.
- Allow the cake to cool in the pan then transfer on a platter.
- For the frosting, mix all the ingredients in a bowl. Spread the frosting over the cake and serve fresh or store in the fridge.

Nutritional information per serving

Calories: 487
Fat: 29.5g

Protein: 5.0g
Carbohydrates: 53.6g

RAHAM CRACKER PUMPKIN CAKE

Time: 1 ¼ hours

Servings: 12

Ingredients:

½ cup butter, softened
1 cup light brown sugar
¼ cup dark brown sugar
4 eggs
1 ¼ cups pumpkin puree

1 ½ cups graham crackers
1 cup all-purpose flour
2 teaspoons baking powder
½ teaspoon salt
½ cup whole milk

Directions:

- Mix the butter with the sugars in a bowl until creamy and fluffy.
- Stir in the eggs, one by one, then add the pumpkin puree and milk.
- Add the rest of the ingredients and mix well with a spatula.
- Pour the batter in a greased Bundt cake pan and bake in the preheated oven at 350F for 40 minutes or until well risen and golden brown.
- Allow the cake to cool in the pan before serving.

Nutritional information per serving

Calories: 244
Fat: 10.7g

Protein: 4.4g
Carbohydrates: 33.9g

ℋOLIDAY POUND CAKE

Time: 1 ¼ hours

Servings: 16

Ingredients:

1 cup butter, softened
1 cup cream cheese
2 cups white sugar
6 eggs
3 cups all-purpose flour
2 teaspoons baking powder

½ teaspoon salt
1 cup buttermilk
1 teaspoon orange zest
1 teaspoon lemon zest
1 teaspoon vanilla extract

Directions:

- Mix the butter and sugar in a bowl until pale and light. Stir in the cream cheese and mix well.
- Add the eggs, one after another, then stir in the flour, baking powder and salt, alternating it with buttermilk.
- Fold in the citrus zest and vanilla extract then spoon the batter in a large loaf cake pan lined with baking paper.
- Bake the cake in the preheated oven at 350F for 50-55 minutes or until the cake passes the toothpick test.
- Allow the cake to cool in the pan before slicing and serving.

$\mathcal{P}$ ECAN BUTTER CAKE

Time: 1 ¼ hours

Servings: 12

Ingredients:

1 cup pecan butter
½ cup butter, softened
1 cup white sugar
4 eggs
1 teaspoon vanilla extract

1 teaspoon lemon zest
2 cups all-purpose flour
1 ½ teaspoons baking powder
½ teaspoon salt
1 ½ cups pecans, chopped

Directions:

- Mix the two types of butter with sugar until creamy and light.
- Stir in the eggs, one by one, then add the vanilla and lemon zest then fold in the dry ingredients.
- Spoon the batter in a 9-inch round cake pan lined with baking paper.
- Bake in the preheated oven at 350F for 40-45 minutes or until well risen and golden brown.
- Allow the cake to cool in the pan then dust it with powdered sugar and serve.

Nutritional information per serving
Calories: 377
Fat: 24.2g

Protein: 6.2g
Carbohydrates: 37.9g

$\mathcal{F}$ RUITY BUNDT CAKE

Time: 1 ¼ hours

Servings: 12

Ingredients:

1 cup cream cheese, room temperature
1 cup butter, softened
1 ½ cups white sugar
4 eggs
1 teaspoon vanilla extract
2 cups all-purpose flour

1 ½ teaspoons baking powder
½ cup chopped pecans
½ cup chopped almonds
½ cup candied cherries, chopped
¼ cup dried apricots, chopped
¼ cup golden raisins

Directions:

- Mix the cream cheese, butter and sugar in a bowl until fluffy and creamy.
- Stir in the eggs, one by one, then add the eggs and vanilla.
- Mix well then fold in the remaining ingredients.
- Spoon the batter in a greased Bundt cake pan and bake in the preheated oven at 350F for 40-45 minutes or until well risen and golden brown.
- Allow the cake to cool in the pan before serving.

Nutritional information per serving
Calories: 447
Fat: 26.6g

Protein: 6.8g
Carbohydrates: 48.0g

$\mathcal{C}$ REAM CHEESE APPLE CAKE

Time: 1 ¼ hours

Servings:10

Ingredients:

1 cup cream cheese
½ cup canola oil

1 ½ cups white sugar
3 eggs

1 teaspoon vanilla extract
2 cups all-purpose flour
2 teaspoons baking powder

½ teaspoon salt
2 red apples, peeled, cored and diced

Directions:
- Mix the cream cheese, canola oil and sugar in a bowl until pale and creamy.
- Add the eggs and mix well then stir in the vanilla, followed by the remaining dry ingredients.
- Mix in the apples then spoon the batter in a 9-inch round cake pan lined with baking paper.
- Bake in the preheated oven at 350F for 45-50 minutes or until well risen and golden brown.
- Allow the cake to cool in the pan before serving.

Nutritional information per serving

Calories: 421
Fat: 20.6g

Protein: 6.1g
Carbohydrates: 55.4g

*C*HOCOLATE CHIP PUMPKIN BUNDT CAKE

Time: 1 ¼ hours

Servings: 12

Ingredients:

1 cup butter, softened
1 ½ cups white sugar
2 tablespoons molasses
1 teaspoon vanilla extract
2 eggs

1 cup pumpkin puree
2 cups all-purpose flour
1 ½ teaspoons baking powder
½ teaspoon salt
1 cup dark chocolate chips

Directions:
- Mix the butter, sugar and molasses in a bowl until creamy and light.
- Stir in the vanilla and eggs, as well as the pumpkin puree.
- Fold in the rest of the ingredients and mix gently.
- Spoon the batter in a greased Bundt cake pan. Bake in the preheated oven at 350F for 45 minutes or until the cake passes the toothpick test.
- Allow the cake to cool in the pan before serving.

Nutritional information per serving

Calories: 381
Fat: 19.0g

Protein: 4.1g
Carbohydrates: 52.1g

*M*OIST PUMPKIN CAKE

Time: 1 ¼ hours

Servings: 12

Ingredients:

2 cups white sugar
1 cup canola oil
4 eggs
1 ½ cups pumpkin puree
3 cups all-purpose flour

2 teaspoons baking powder
½ teaspoon salt
1 teaspoon cinnamon powder
½ teaspoon ground ginger
¼ teaspoon ground nutmeg

Directions:
- Mix the sugar, canola oil and eggs in a bowl until creamy and double in volume.
- Stir in the pumpkin puree, then fold in the rest of the ingredients.
- Pour the batter in a 9-inch round cake pan lined with baking paper.
- Bake in the preheated oven at 350F for 35-40 minutes or until well risen and fragrant.
- Allow the cake to cool in the pan before slicing and serving.

Nutritional information per serving

Calories: 432
Fat: 20.1g

Protein: 5.4g
Carbohydrates: 60.2g

Moist Chocolate Cake

Time: 1 ¼ hours

Servings: 12

Ingredients:

2 cups white sugar
2 eggs
½ cup canola oil
1 teaspoon vanilla extract
2 cups all-purpose flour

½ cup cocoa powder
½ teaspoon salt
1 ½ teaspoon baking powder
1 cup hot coffee
1 cup buttermilk

Directions:
- Mix the sugar, eggs and canola oil in a bowl until creamy.
- Stir in the vanilla, coffee and buttermilk then add the rest of the ingredients.
- Pour the batter in a 9-inch round cake pan lined with baking paper.
- Bake in the preheated oven at 350F for 45 minutes or until a toothpick inserted in the center of the cake comes out clean.
- Allow the cake to cool in the pan before serving.

Nutritional information per serving

Calories: 310
Fat: 10.7g

Protein: 4.4g
Carbohydrates: 52.6g

Lemon Blueberry Bundt Cake

Time: 1 ¼ hours

Servings: 10

Ingredients:

½ cup butter, softened
½ cup cream cheese
1 cup white sugar
2 eggs
2 egg whites
1 tablespoon lemon zest

1 teaspoon vanilla extract
2 cups all-purpose flour
1 ½ teaspoons baking powder
½ teaspoon salt
1 cup plain yogurt
1 cup fresh blueberries

Directions:
- Mix the butter, cream cheese and sugar in a bowl until creamy.
- Stir in the eggs, egg whites, lemon zest and vanilla.
- Fold in the flour, baking powder and salt, alternating it with yogurt.
- Add the blueberries then spoon the batter in a greased Bundt cake pan.
- Bake in the preheated oven at 350F for 40-45 minutes or until it passes the toothpick test.
- Allow the cake to cool in the pan before slicing and serving.

Nutritional information per serving

Calories: 332
Fat: 14.7g

Protein: 6.9g
Carbohydrates: 43.9g

Chocolate Bundt Cake

Time: 1 ¼ hours

Servings: 10

Ingredients:

½ cup butter, softened
2 tablespoons canola oil
1 cup white sugar
3 eggs
1 teaspoon vanilla extract

1 ½ cups all-purpose flour
½ cup cocoa powder
1 teaspoon baking powder
½ teaspoon baking soda
½ teaspoon salt

½ cup dark chocolate chips

Directions:
- Mix the butter, canola oil and sugar in a bowl until light and pale.
- Stir in the eggs and vanilla and mix well.
- Fold in the flour, cocoa powder, baking powder, baking soda and salt.
- Add the chocolate chips then spoon the batter in a greased Bundt cake pan.
- Bake in the preheated oven at 350F for 40-45 minutes or until well risen and it passes the toothpick test.
- Allow the cake to cool in the pan before slicing and serving.

Nutritional information per serving

Calories: 308

Fat: 15.7g

Protein: 4.9g

Carbohydrates: 41.1g

*L*IME POUND CAKE

Time: 1 ¼ hours

Servings: 12

Ingredients:

1 cup butter, softened

¼ cup canola oil

1 ½ cups white sugar

4 eggs

1 lime, zested and juiced

2 cups all-purpose flour

1 teaspoon baking soda

½ teaspoon salt

½ cup sour cream

Directions:
- Mix the butter, oil and sugar in a bowl until pale and creamy.
- Stir in the eggs and mix well then add the lime zest and lime juice. Mix well.
- Fold in the dry ingredients then add the sour cream.
- Turn the mixer on high speed and mix for 1 minute.
- Spoon the batter in a loaf cake pan and bake in the preheated oven at 350F for 40-45 minutes or until well risen and golden brown.
- Allow the cake to cool in the pan before slicing and serving.

Nutritional information per serving

Calories: 389

Fat: 23.6g

Protein: 4.5g

Carbohydrates: 42.0g

*P*ISTACHIO BUNDT CAKE

Time: 1 hour

Servings: 10

Ingredients:

¾ cup butter, softened

1 cup white sugar

4 eggs

1 teaspoon vanilla extract

1 ½ cups all-purpose flour

1 cup ground pistachio

1 ½ teaspoons baking powder

½ teaspoon salt

Directions:
- Mix the butter and sugar until pale and light. Stir in the eggs and vanilla and mix well.
- Fold in the flour, pistachio, baking powder and salt then spoon the batter in a greased Bundt cake pan.
- Bake in the preheated oven at 350F for 40-45 minutes or until well risen and golden brown.
- Allow the cake to cool in the pan before serving.

Nutritional information per serving

Calories: 292

Fat: 15.7g

Protein: 4.3g

Carbohydrates: 34.9g

ANILLA WHITE CHOCOLATE CHIP CAKE

Time: 1 ¼ hours

Servings: 12

Ingredients:

1 cup butter, softened
1 cup white sugar
4 eggs
1 tablespoon vanilla extract
1 cup whole milk

2 cups all-purpose flour
1 ½ teaspoons baking powder
½ teaspoon salt
1 cup white chocolate chips

Directions:

- Mix the butter and sugar in a bowl until fluffy and pale.
- Stir in the eggs, one by one, then add the vanilla and milk.
- Stir in the flour, baking powder and salt then fold in the chocolate chips.
- Spoon the batter in a 9-inch round cake pan lined with baking paper.
- Bake in the preheated oven at 350F for 40-45 minutes.
- Allow the cake to cool in the pan before slicing and serving.

Nutritional information per serving

Calories: 387
Fat: 22.2g

Protein: 5.6g
Carbohydrates: 42.4g

ERRY LEMON CAKE

Time: 1 ¼ hours

Servings: 10

Ingredients:

½ cup butter, softened
1 cup white sugar
3 eggs
1 tablespoon lemon zest
2 tablespoons lemon juice

½ cup plain yogurt
2 cups all-purpose flour
1 ½ teaspoons baking powder
½ teaspoon salt
1 cup mixed berries

Directions:

- Mix the butter and sugar in a bowl until creamy and fluffy.
- Stir in the eggs, one by one, then add the lemon zest and lemon juice, as well as the yogurt.
- Fold in the flour, baking powder and salt then add the berries.
- Pour the batter in a 8-inch round cake pan and bake in the preheated oven at 350F for 35-40 minutes or until well risen and golden brown.
- Allow the cake to cool in the pan before serving.

Nutritional information per serving

Calories: 285
Fat: 11.0g

Protein: 5.2g
Carbohydrates: 42.3g

POPPY SEED LEMON BUNDT CAKE

Time: 1 ¼ hours

Servings: 12

Ingredients:

1 cup butter, softened
1 cup white sugar
4 eggs
1 teaspoon vanilla extract
1 tablespoon lemon zest
2 tablespoons lemon juice

½ cup sour cream
2 cups all-purpose flour
½ cup cornstarch
1 teaspoon baking soda
1 teaspoon baking powder
½ teaspoon salt

2 tablespoons poppy seeds

Directions:
- Sift the flour, cornstarch, baking powder, baking soda and salt then mix it with the poppy seeds.
- Mix the butter and sugar in a bowl until creamy and fluffy.
- Stir in the eggs, lemon zest and lemon juice and mix well.
- Fold in the flour mixture then add the sour cream and mix well.
- Spoon the batter in a greased Bundt cake pan and bake in the preheated oven at 350F for 40-45 minutes or until a toothpick inserted in the center of the cake comes out clean.
- Allow the cake to cool in the pan before serving.

Nutritional information per serving

Calories: 346

Fat: 19.7g

Protein: 4.8g

Carbohydrates: 38.7g

INGERSNAP PUMPKIN BUNDT CAKE

Time: 1 ¼ hours

Servings: 12

Ingredients:

½ cup butter, softened

¼ cup canola oil

1 cup white sugar

2 tablespoons dark brown sugar

3 eggs

1 ½ cups pumpkin puree

1 teaspoon vanilla extract

2 cups all-purpose flour

2 teaspoons baking powder

½ teaspoon salt

6 gingersnaps, crushed

Directions:
- Mix the butter, oil and sugars in a bowl until light and creamy.
- Stir in the eggs, one by one, then add the pumpkin and vanilla and mix well.
- Fold in the flour, baking powder and salt then add the crushed gingersnaps.
- Spoon the batter in a greased Bundt cake pan and bake in the preheated oven at 350F for 45 minutes or until a toothpick inserted in the center of the cake comes out clean.
- Allow to cool in the pan then transfer on a platter.

Nutritional information per serving

Calories: 350

Fat: 16.1g

Protein: 5.0g

Carbohydrates: 48.0g

HOCOLATE CHIP BUNDT CAKE

Time: 1 ¼ hours

Servings: 12

Ingredients:

1 cup butter, softened

1 cup white sugar

1 cup plain yogurt

3 eggs

1 teaspoon vanilla extract

2 cups all-purpose flour

2 teaspoons baking powder

½ teaspoon salt

¾ cup dark chocolate chips

Directions:
- Sift the flour with baking powder and salt.
- Mix the butter with sugar until creamy. Add the eggs, one by one, then stir in the vanilla and mix well.
- Add the yogurt and mix well then fold in the flour, followed by the chocolate chips.
- Spoon the batter in a greased Bundt cake pan.
- Bake in the preheated oven at 350F for 40-45 minutes or until a toothpick inserted in the cake comes out clean.

Nutritional information per serving

Calories: 341

Fat: 18.9g

Protein: 5.3g   Carbohydrates: 39.5g

$\mathcal{M}$ILK CHOCOLATE CHUNK CAKE

Time: 1 1/5 hours   Servings: 12

Ingredients:

8 oz. milk chocolate, chopped
½ cup chocolate syrup
1 cup butter, softened
1 cup white sugar
4 eggs
1 teaspoon vanilla extract

2 cups all-purpose flour
½ cup cocoa powder
1 teaspoon baking powder
½ teaspoon baking soda
½ teaspoon salt
1 cup buttermilk

Directions:

- Sift the flour, cocoa powder, baking powder, baking soda and salt.
- Mix the butter with sugar until creamy and fluffy. Add the chocolate syrup then stir in the eggs and vanilla.
- Fold in the flour, alternating it with buttermilk. Start and end with flour.
- Add the chocolate chunks then spoon the batter in a round cake pan lined with baking paper.
- Bake in the preheated oven at 350F for 40-45 minutes or until a toothpick inserted in the center of the cake comes out clean.

Nutritional information per serving

Calories: 449
Fat: 23.4g
Protein: 7.2g
Carbohydrates: 55.2g

$\mathcal{P}$ECAN RUM CAKE

Time: 1 ¼ hours   Servings: 12

Ingredients:

Cake:
1 cup butter, softened
1 cup white sugar
3 eggs
1 teaspoon vanilla extract
¼ cup dark rum
½ cup whole milk

1 cup ground pecans
1 ¼ cups all-purpose flour
1 teaspoon baking soda
½ teaspoon salt
Glaze:
1 cup powdered sugar
1 tablespoon dark rum

Directions:

- For the cake, mix the flour with baking soda, salt and pecans.
- In a different bowl, mix the butter and sugar until fluffy and creamy.
- Stir in the eggs, one after another, then add the vanilla, rum and milk and mix well.
- Fold in the pecan and flour mixture then spoon the batter in a 8-inch round cake pan lined with baking paper.
- Bake in the preheated oven at 350F for 35-40 minutes or until well risen and fragrant.
- Allow the cake to cool in the pan then transfer on a platter.
- For the glaze, mix the ingredients in a bowl. Drizzle the glaze over the cake and serve fresh.

Nutritional information per serving

Calories: 329
Fat: 17.8g
Protein: 3.3g
Carbohydrates: 37.3g

Orange Pumpkin Bundt Cake

Time: 1 ¼ hours

Servings: 12

Ingredients:

¾ cup butter, softened
1 ¼ cups white sugar
4 eggs
1 teaspoon vanilla extract
1 orange, zested and juiced
1 cup pumpkin puree

2 ½ cups all-purpose flour
1 ½ teaspoons baking soda
½ teaspoon salt
½ teaspoon ground ginger
½ teaspoon cinnamon powder
½ teaspoon ground cardamom

Directions:

- Mix the butter with sugar in a bowl until creamy and fluffy.
- Stir in the eggs and vanilla and mix well then add the orange zest and juice, as well as pumpkin puree.
- Fold in the remaining ingredients then spoon the batter in a loaf cake pan lined with baking paper.
- Bake the cake in the preheated oven at 350F for 40-45 minutes.
- Allow the cake to cool in the pan before serving.

Nutritional information per serving

Calories: 311
Fat: 13.3g

Protein: 5.0g
Carbohydrates: 44.4g

Black Pepper Chocolate Cake

Time: 1 ¼ hours

Servings: 16

Ingredients:

1 cup butter
1 ½ cups white sugar
1 teaspoon ground black pepper
1 teaspoon lemon zest
4 eggs

1 cup sour cream
2 cups all-purpose flour
1 ½ teaspoons baking powder
½ teaspoon salt

Directions:

- Sift the flour with baking powder and salt in a bowl.
- In a different bowl, mix the butter and sugar until fluffy and pale.
- Stir in the black pepper, lemon zest and eggs and mix well.
- Add the sour cream and give it a good mix.
- Fold in the flour, baking powder and salt then spoon the batter in a 9-inch round cake pan lined with baking paper.
- Bake in the preheated oven at 350F for 40-45 minutes or until the cake passes the toothpick test.
- Allow the cake to cool in the pan before serving.

Nutritional information per serving

Calories: 276
Fat: 15.8g

Protein: 3.6g
Carbohydrates: 31.7g

Banana Chocolate Chip Cake

Time: 1 ¼ hours

Servings: 12

Ingredients:

½ cup butter, softened
1 cup white sugar
3 eggs
1 teaspoon vanilla extract
3 ripe bananas, mashed

1 ¾ cups all-purpose flour
1 teaspoon baking soda
¼ teaspoon salt
½ cup walnuts, chopped
½ cup dark chocolate chips

Directions:

- Sift the flour, baking soda and salt on a platter.
- Mix the butter with sugar until creamy and fluffy.
- Stir in the eggs, one by one, then add the vanilla and bananas.
- Mix well then fold in the flour, followed by the walnuts and chocolate chips.
- Spoon the batter in a 9-inch round cake pan lined with parchment paper.
- Bake in the preheated oven at 350F for 40-45 minutes or until the cake passes the toothpick test.
- Allow the cake to cool in the pan before slicing and serving.

Nutritional information per serving

Calories: 295
Fat: 13.4g

Protein: 5.2g
Carbohydrates: 41.3g

$\mathcal{P}$ ECAN CARROT BUNDT CAKE

Time: 1 ½ hours

Servings: 14

Ingredients:

1 cup butter, softened
½ cup dark brown sugar
1 cup white sugar
4 eggs
1 tablespoon orange zest
1 tablespoon lemon zest
2 cups grated carrots
¼ cup orange juice

1 cup crushed pineapple
2 ½ cups all-purpose flour
1 teaspoon baking soda
½ teaspoon baking powder
½ teaspoon salt
1 teaspoon cinnamon powder
½ teaspoon cardamom powder

Directions:

- Sift the flour, baking soda, baking powder, salt and spices in a bowl.
- In a different bowl, mix the butter and sugars until creamy and fluffy.
- Stir in the eggs, one by one, then add the citrus zest, carrots, orange juice and pineapple.
- Fold in the flour and mix gently with a spatula.
- Pour the batter in a greased Bundt cake pan.
- Bake in the preheated oven at 350F for 45-50 minutes or until the cake passes the toothpick test.
- Allow the cake to cool in the pan before serving.

Nutritional information per serving

Calories: 304
Fat: 14.6g

Protein: 4.3g
Carbohydrates: 40.4g

PPLESAUCE CARROT CAKE

Time: 1 ½ hours

Servings: 12

Ingredients:

3 eggs
1 egg white
1 cup white sugar
¼ cup dark brown sugar
1 teaspoon vanilla extract
½ cup canola oil
1 cup applesauce

1 cup grated carrots
½ cup shredded coconut
2 apples, peeled, cored and diced
2 ½ cups all-purpose flour
1 teaspoon baking soda
½ teaspoon baking powder
½ teaspoon salt

Directions:

- Mix the eggs, egg white, sugars and vanilla in a bowl until fluffy and pale.
- Stir in the canola oil and applesauce and mix well then add the carrots, coconut and apples, as well as the flour, baking soda, baking powder and salt.
- Mix gently with a spatula just until incorporated.

- Pour the batter in a 9-inch round cake pan and bake in the preheated oven at 350F for 50-55 minutes or until fragrant and the cake passes the toothpick test.
- Allow the cake to cool in the pan before serving.

Nutritional information per serving

Calories: 307
Fat: 11.6g

Protein: 4.7g
Carbohydrates: 47.6g

LMOND BUTTER BANANA CAKE

Time: 1 ¼ hours

Servings: 12

Ingredients:

1 cup almond butter
1 ½ cups white sugar
3 eggs
1 teaspoon vanilla extract
2 bananas, mashed
¼ cup canola oil

2 cups all-purpose flour
1 teaspoon baking soda
½ teaspoon salt
1 teaspoon cinnamon powder
½ teaspoon ground ginger
½ cup shredded coconut

Directions:

- Sift the flour, baking soda, salt, cinnamon and ginger. Mix it with the shredded coconut.
- Mix the almond butter and sugar in a bowl until creamy.
- Stir in the eggs, one by one, then add the vanilla, bananas and canola oil. Mix well.
- Fold in the flour mixture then pour the batter in a 9-inch round cake pan lined with baking paper.
- Bake in the preheated oven at 350F for 45 minutes or until well risen and golden brown.
- Allow the cake to cool in the pan before serving.

Nutritional information per serving

Calories: 388
Fat: 18.8g

Protein: 8.3g
Carbohydrates: 49.8g

CITRUS POPPY SEED BUNDT CAKE

Time: 1 ¼ hours

Servings: 12

Ingredients:

½ cup canola oil
½ cup butter, softened
1 cup white sugar
2 eggs
1 cup sour cream
1 lime, zested and juiced

1 lemon, zested and juiced
2 cups all-purpose flour
2 teaspoons baking powder
½ teaspoon salt
2 tablespoons poppy seeds

Directions:

- Mix the canola oil, butter and sugar in a bowl until creamy and pale.
- Stir in the eggs and mix well then add the sour cream.
- Mix in the lime zest and juice, as well as the lemon zest and juice.
- Fold in the rest of the ingredients then spoon the batter in a greased Bundt cake pan.
- Bake in the preheated oven at 350F for 40-45 minutes or until well risen and golden brown.
- Allow the cake to cool in the pan before serving.

Nutritional information per serving

Calories: 350
Fat: 22.4g
Protein: 4.1g
Carbohydrates: 35.2g

IRAMISU CAKE

Time: 2 hours

Servings: 12

Ingredients:

2 cups mascarpone cheese
1 cup powdered sugar
1 tablespoon vanilla extract
2 cups heavy cream, whipped

¼ cup Grand Marnier
2 cups brewed coffee
10 oz. ladyfingers

Directions:

- Line a 9-inch round cake pan with plastic wrap.
- Mix the mascarpone cheese with sugar then fold in the whipped cream.
- Mix the coffee and Grand Marnier in a bowl.
- Dip the ladyfingers in the coffee mixture and layer them at the bottom of the pan.
- Top with 1/3 of the cream, followed by another layer of ladyfingers.
- Continue until you run out of ingredients and refrigerate at least 1 hour.
- Serve the cake chilled.

Nutritional information per serving

Calories: 285
Fat: 14.9g

Protein: 7.6g
Carbohydrates: 26.0g

RANGE CHOCOLATE CAKE

Time: 1 ¼ hours

Servings: 12

Ingredients:

1 cup white sugar
4 eggs
8 oz. dark chocolate, melted
2 cups ground almonds

1 teaspoon baking soda
½ teaspoon salt
½ cup candied orange peel, chopped

Directions:

- Mix the eggs with sugar until fluffy and pale.
- Stir in the melted chocolate then add the almonds, baking soda and salt.
- Fold in the candied orange peel then pour the batter in 1 8-inch round cake pan lined with baking paper.
- Bake in the preheated oven at 350F for 30-35 minutes.
- Allow the cake to cool in the pan before serving.

Nutritional information per serving

Calories: 280
Fat: 15.0g

Protein: 6.7g
Carbohydrates: 32.4g

ALMOND WHITE CHOCOLATE CAKE

Time: 1 ½ hours

Servings: 10

Ingredients:

1 cup butter, softened
1 cup light brown sugar
1 tablespoon orange zest
3 eggs
½ cup sour cream
1 cup all-purpose flour

1 cup ground almonds
1 ½ teaspoons baking soda
½ teaspoon salt
½ cup dried cranberries
1 cup white chocolate chips
½ cup sliced almonds

Directions:

- Mix the butter and sugar in a bowl until creamy and fluffy.

- Stir in the eggs, one by one, then add the orange zest and sour cream.
- Fold in the flour, almonds, baking soda and salt then add the cranberries and chocolate chips.
- Spoon the batter in a 9-inch round cake pan and top with sliced almonds.
- Bake in the preheated oven at 350F for 40-45 minutes or until well risen and golden brown.
- Allow the cake to cool in the pan before slicing and serving.

Nutritional information per serving

Calories: 485

Fat: 34.8g

Protein: 7.5g

Carbohydrates: 38.1g

LMOND APPLE CAKE

Time: 1 ¼ hours

Servings: 10

Ingredients:

¾ cup butter, softened

1 cup white sugar

1 teaspoon vanilla extract

3 eggs

1 cup almond flour

¾ cup all-purpose flour

1 teaspoon baking powder

¼ teaspoon salt

½ cup whole milk

2 red apples, cored and diced

Directions:
- Mix the butter with sugar in a bowl until creamy.
- Add the vanilla and eggs and mix well then fold in the almond flour, flour, salt and baking powder.
- Add the milk and mix gently then fold in the apples.
- Spoon the batter in a 8-inch round cake pan lined with baking paper and bake in the preheated oven at 350F for 40 minutes or until well risen and golden.
- Allow the cake to cool in the pan before serving.

Nutritional information per serving

Calories: 294

Fat: 17.1g

Protein: 3.9g

Carbohydrates: 33.7g

 EACH BRANDY CAKE

Time: 1 ½ hours

Servings: 10

Ingredients:

Cake:

2 cups almond flour

1 teaspoon baking powder

½ teaspoon salt

1 teaspoon ground cardamom

1 cup white sugar

5 eggs

½ cup butter, melted

1 cup sweet red win

4 peaches, pitted and sliced

Brandy glaze:

1 cup powdered sugar

1 tablespoon brandy

Directions:
- To make the cake, mix the almond flour, baking powder, salt and cinnamon.
- In a different bowl, mix the sugar and eggs until fluffy and pale. Add the butter and mix well, then stir in the red wine.
- Fold in the almond flour then pour the batter in a 9-inch round cake pan lined with baking paper.
- Top with sliced peaches and bake in the preheated oven at 350F for 45 minutes or until a toothpick inserted in the center of the cake comes out clean.
- Allow the cake to cool in the pan then transfer it on a platter.
- For the glaze, mix the sugar with brandy. Drizzle the glaze over the cake and serve it fresh.

Nutritional information per serving

Calories: 317

Fat: 15.8g

Protein: 8.3g

Carbohydrates: 37.4g

LMOND DATE CAKE

Time: 1 hour

Servings: 8

Ingredients:

2 eggs
4 egg whites
½ lemon , zested and juiced
½ cup white sugar
1 cup dates, pitted

1 ½ cups almond flour
¼ cup rice flour
¼ cup cocoa powder
1 teaspoon baking soda
¼ teaspoon salt

Directions:

- Mix the eggs, egg whites, lemon zest, lemon juice, sugar and dates in a food processor.
- Add the almond flour, rice flour, cocoa powder, baking soda and salt and mix gently with a spatula.
- Pour the batter in a 8-inch round cake pan lined with baking paper.
- Bake in the preheated oven at 350F for 35-40 minutes.
- Allow the cake to cool in the pan before serving.

Nutritional information per serving

Calories: 188
Fat: 4.3g

Protein: 5.6g
Carbohydrates: 35.9g

LMOND FIG CAKE

Time: 1 ¼ hours

Servings: 10

Ingredients:

2 eggs
4 egg whites
1 cup white sugar
½ cup butter, melted
1 cup all-purpose flour

1 teaspoon baking powder
¼ teaspoon salt
1 cup ground almonds
6 figs, sliced

Directions:

- Mix the eggs, egg whites and sugar in a bowl until creamy and double in volume.
- Add the melted butter, gradually, then fold in the flour, baking powder, salt and almonds.
- Pour the batter in a 8-inch round cake pan lined with baking paper.
- Top with figs and bake in the preheated oven at 350F for 35-40 minutes or until well risen and golden brown.
- Allow the cake to cool in the pan before slicing and serving.

Nutritional information per serving

Calories: 305
Fat: 15.1g

Protein: 6.3g
Carbohydrates: 39.3g

EMON RICOTTA CAKE

Time: 1 hour

Servings: 8

Ingredients:

1 cup ricotta cheese
2 eggs
¾ cup white sugar
¼ cup butter, melted
2 tablespoons lemon zest

1 ¼ cups all-purpose flour
½ cup almond flour
1 teaspoon baking powder
¼ teaspoon salt

Directions:

- Mix the cheese, eggs, sugar, butter and lemon zest in a bowl.

- Fold in the flours, baking powder and salt then spoon the batter in a 8-inch round cake pan lined with baking paper.
- Bake in the preheated oven at 350F for 35-40 minutes or until a toothpick inserted in the center of the cake comes out clean.
- Serve the cake chilled.

Nutritional information per serving

Calories: 262

Fat: 10.4g

Protein: 7.4g

Carbohydrates: 36.3g

S UMMER FRUIT CAKE

Time: 1 ¼ hours

Servings: 12

Ingredients:

½ cup butter, softened

½ cup canola oil

1 cup white sugar

1 teaspoon vanilla extract

6 eggs

1 cup ground almonds

1 cup all-purpose flour

1 teaspoon baking powder

1 cup mixed berries

1 cup cherries, pitted

Directions:
- Mix the butter, oil and sugar in a bowl until creamy and fluffy. Add the vanilla and eggs, one by one, and mix well.
- Stir in the almonds, flour and baking powder then pour the batter in a 9-inch round cake pan lined with baking paper.
- Top with berries and cherries and bake in the preheated oven at 350F for 40-45 minutes or until well risen and golden brown.
- Allow the cake to cool in the pan before slicing and serving.

Nutritional information per serving

Calories: 341

Fat: 23.0g

Protein: 5.7g

Carbohydrates: 29.9g

A PRICOT CAKE

Time: 1 hour

Servings: 10

Ingredients:

6 eggs

1 cup white sugar

1 teaspoon vanilla extract

1 tablespoon lemon zest

½ cup canola oil

½ cup sour cream

2 cups all-purpose flour

1 ½ teaspoons baking powder

½ teaspoon salt

6 apricots, halved and sliced

Directions:
- Mix the eggs with sugar, vanilla and lemon zest in a bowl until fluffy and creamy.
- Add the canola oil and sour cream and mix well.
- Fold in the rest of the ingredients then pour the batter in a 9-inch round cake pan lined with baking paper.
- Bake in the preheated oven at 350F for 40-45 minutes or until it passes the toothpick test.
- Allow the cake to cool in the pan before serving.

Nutritional information per serving

Calories: 337

Fat: 16.3g

Protein: 6.5g

Carbohydrates: 42.6g

Y EASTED PLUM CAKE

Time: 2 hours

Servings: 16

Ingredients:

3 cups all-purpose flour
½ teaspoon salt
1 ¼ teaspoons instant yeast
1 cup warm water
½ cup warm milk
¼ cup butter, melted

2 eggs
1 teaspoon vanilla extract
1 tablespoon lemon zest
1 pound plums, pitted and sliced
½ cup light brown sugar

Directions:

- Mix the flour, salt and yeast in a bowl.
- Add the water, milk, butter, eggs, vanilla and lemon zest and knead the dough at least 10 minutes until it looks and feels elastic.
- Allow the dough to rest for 1 hour then roll it into a rectangle and transfer it in a sheet cake pan lined with baking paper.
- Top with plums and sprinkle with brown sugar.
- Bake in the preheated oven at 350F for 40-45 minutes or until well risen and golden brown.
- Allow the cake to cool in the pan before serving.

Nutritional information per serving

Calories: 150
Fat: 3.9g

Protein: 3.7g
Carbohydrates. 25.1g

LMOND STRAWBERRY CAKE

Time: 1 ¼ hours

Servings: 10

Ingredients:

1 cup butter, softened
1 cup white sugar
1 teaspoon vanilla
4 eggs
½ cup plain yogurt

1 cup almond flour
1 cup all-purpose flour
1 teaspoon baking soda
2 cups fresh strawberries

Directions:

- Mix the butter with sugar and vanilla in a bowl until creamy.
- Stir in the eggs, one by one, then add the yogurt and mix well.
- Fold in the almond flour, all-purpose flour, baking soda and a pinch of salt and mix gently with a spatula.
- Pour the batter in a 9-inch round cake pan and top with strawberries.
- Bake in the preheated oven at 350F for 45 minutes or until a toothpick inserted in the center of the cake comes out clean.
- Serve the cake chilled.

Nutritional information per serving

Calories· 344
Fat: 21.9g

Protein: 5.2g
Carbohydrates: 33.4g

EACH MERINGUE CAKE

Time: 1 ½ hours

Servings: 10

Ingredients:

Cake:
½ cup butter, softened
½ cup canola oil
¾ cup white sugar
3 eggs
1 teaspoon vanilla extract
½ cup plain yogurt

2 cups all-purpose flour
1 teaspoon baking soda
½ teaspoon salt
3 peaches, pitted and sliced
Meringue:
3 egg whites
½ cup white sugar

1 teaspoon vanilla extract

Directions:
- For the cake, mix the butter, oil and sugar in a bowl until fluffy and creamy.
- Stir in the egg, vanilla and yogurt and mix well.
- Fold in the flour, baking soda and salt then spoon the batter in a round cake pan lined with baking paper.
- Top with peach slices and bake in the preheated oven at 350F for 40-45 minutes or until well risen and golden brown.
- While the cake bakes, mix the egg whites and sugar in a heatproof bowl. Place over a hot water bath and mix with a whisk until the mixture is hot.
- Remove from heat and continue mixing until stiff and glossy. Add the vanilla and mix well.
- Spoon the meringue over the hot cake and allow to cool.
- Serve right away.

Nutritional information per serving

Calories: 411
Fat: 21.9g

Protein: 6.4g
Carbohydrates: 48.5g

CRANBERRY UPSIDE DOWN CAKE

Time: 1 hour

Servings: 10

Ingredients:

6 eggs
1 cup white sugar
1 teaspoon vanilla extract
½ cup butter, melted and chilled
1 ½ cups all-purpose flour

½ teaspoon baking powder
¼ teaspoon salt
1 cup fresh cranberries
½ cup light brown sugar

Directions:
- Arrange the cranberries at the bottom of a round cake pan. Sprinkle with brown sugar.
- Mix the eggs and sugar in a bowl until fluffy and double in volume.
- Stir in the butter and mix gently.
- Fold in the flour, baking powder and salt.
- Pour the batter over the cranberries and bake in the preheated oven at 350F for 40-45 minutes or until well risen and golden brown.
- When done, turn the cake upside down on a platter and serve chilled.

Nutritional information per serving

Calories: 297
Fat: 12.0g

Protein: 5.4g
Carbohydrates: 42.8g

STRAWBERRY CRUMBLE CAKE

Time: 1 ¼ hours

Servings: 12

Ingredients:

Cake:
6 eggs
1 cup white sugar
1 teaspoon vanilla extract
1 cup plain yogurt
¼ cup canola oil
1 ½ cups all-purpose flour

½ teaspoon baking powder
¼ teaspoon salt
2 cups fresh strawberries, sliced
Crumble:
¼ cup chilled butter
½ cup all-purpose flour
2 tablespoons white sugar

Directions:
- For the cake, mix the eggs, sugar and vanilla in a bowl until fluffy and double in volume at least.
- Stir in the yogurt and oil then fold in the flour, baking powder and salt.
- Pour the batter in a 9-inch round cake pan lined with baking paper.
- Top with strawberries.

- For the streusel, mix all the ingredients in a bowl until grainy.
- Top the cake with streusel and bake in the preheated oven at 350F for 45 minutes or until a toothpick inserted in the center of the cake comes out clean.
- Serve the cake chilled.

Nutritional information per serving

Calories: 275
Fat: 11.1g

Protein: 6.3g
Carbohydrates: 38.2g

HUBARB UPSIDE DOWN CAKE

Time: 1 ¼ hours

Servings: 10

Ingredients:

4 rhubarb stalks, peeled and sliced
½ cup white sugar
¾ cup butter, softened
¾ cup white sugar
3 eggs

½ cup sour cream
1 teaspoon vanilla extract
2 cups all-purpose flour
1 ½ teaspoons baking powder
½ teaspoon salt

Directions:
- Arrange the stalks of rhubarb in a 9-inch round cake pan lined with baking paper.
- Top with ½ cup white sugar.
- Mix the butter with 1 cup sugar until fluffy and pale.
- Add the eggs and sour cream and mix well.
- Stir in the vanilla then fold in the flour, baking powder and salt.
- Pour the batter in the pan and bake in the preheated oven at 350F for 40-45 minutes.
- When done, turn the cake upside down on a platter.

Nutritional information per serving

Calories: 357
Fat: 17.8g

Protein: 4.9g
Carbohydrates: 46.0g

PPLE VANILLA LOAF CAKE

Time: 1 ¼ hours

Servings: 10

Ingredients:

½ cup butter, softened
½ cup canola oil
¾ cup white sugar
3 eggs
½ cup whole milk
1 tablespoon vanilla extract

1 cup all-purpose flour
½ cup cornstarch
1 teaspoon baking powder
¼ teaspoon salt
2 red apples, cored and diced

Directions:
- Mix the butter, oil and sugar in a bowl. Mix well until creamy.
- Add the eggs, one by one, then stir in the milk and vanilla.
- Fold in the flour, cornstarch, baking powder and salt, then incorporate the apples.
- Spoon the batter in a loaf cake pan lined with baking paper.
- Bake in the preheated oven at 350F for 35-40 minutes or until the cake passes the toothpick test.
- Serve the cake chilled.

Nutritional information per serving

Calories: 353
Fat: 22.0g
Protein: 3.6g
Carbohydrates: 36.5g

GRANNY SMITH CAKE

Time: 1 ½ hours

Servings: 12

Ingredients:

1 ½ cups all-purpose flour
2 teaspoons baking powder
¼ teaspoon salt
1 teaspoon cinnamon powder
1 cup canola oil

2 eggs
1 cup white sugar
1 cup whole milk
1 tablespoon lemon zest
3 Granny Smith apples, peeled and diced

Directions:

- Sift the flour, baking powder, salt and cinnamon in a bowl.
- In a different bowl, mix the canola oil, eggs and sugar until fluffy and pale. Add the milk and lemon zest and mix well.
- Fold in the flour then stir in the apples.
- Spoon the batter in a 9-inch round cake pan lined with baking paper.
- Bake in the preheated oven at 350F for 35-40 minutes or until a toothpick inserted in the center of the cake comes out clean.
- Serve chilled.

Nutritional information per serving

Calories: 328
Fat: 19.8g

Protein: 3.3g
Carbohydrates: 36.4g

APRICOT YOGURT LOAF CAKE

Time: 1 ¼ hours

Servings: 10

Ingredients:

½ cup butter, softened
¾ cup white sugar
2 eggs
1 cup plain yogurt
1 teaspoon vanilla extract

1 ¼ cups all-purpose flour
1 teaspoon baking powder
¼ teaspoon salt
4 apricots, pitted and sliced
¼ cup sliced almonds

Directions:

- Mix the butter and sugar in a bowl until fluffy and pale. Stir in the eggs, one by one, then add the yogurt and vanilla and mix well.
- Fold in the flour, baking powder and salt.
- Spoon the batter in a loaf cake pan lined with baking paper.
- Top with apricots and sprinkle with sliced almonds.
- Bake in the preheated oven at 350F for 35-40 minutes or until well risen and golden brown.
- Allow the cake to cool in the pan before serving.

Nutritional information per serving

Calories: 247
Fat: 11.8g

Protein: 4.9g
Carbohydrates: 31.1g

ALMOND HONEY CAKE

Time: 1 ¼ hours

Servings: 10

Ingredients:

¾ cup butter, softened
½ cup honey
¼ cup light brown sugar
3 eggs

1 ½ cups all-purpose flour
½ cup ground almonds
1 teaspoon baking powder
¼ teaspoon salt

¼ teaspoon cinnamon powder

½ cup sliced almonds

Directions:
- Mix the butter, honey and sugar in a bowl until creamy and pale.
- Add the eggs and mix well.
- Fold in the flour, almonds, baking powder, salt and cinnamon powder.
- Spoon the batter in a loaf cake pan lined with baking paper.
- Top with sliced almonds and bake in the preheated oven at 350F for 40 minutes or until the cake passes the toothpick test.
- Serve the cake chilled.

Nutritional information per serving

Calories: 330
Fat: 20.1g

Protein: 5.8g
Carbohydrates: 34.2g

*O*RANGE RICOTTA CAKE

Time: 1 ¼ hours

Servings: 10

Ingredients:

3 cups ricotta cheese
1 teaspoon vanilla extract
1 teaspoon orange zest
¾ cup white sugar
3 eggs

½ cup white chocolate, chopped
½ cup all-purpose flour
1 teaspoon baking powder
1 cup fresh raspberries

Directions:
- Mix the ricotta cheese, vanilla, orange zest, sugar and eggs in a bowl.
- Stir in rest of the ingredients then spoon the batter in a 9-inch round cake pan lined with baking paper.
- Bake in the preheated oven at 350F for 35-40 minutes or until golden brown.
- Serve the cake chilled.

Nutritional information per serving

Calories: 255
Fat: 10.1g

Protein: 11.4g
Carbohydrates: 30.5g

*B*ANANA MARS BAR CAKE

Time: 1 ¼ hours

Servings: 10

Ingredients:

½ cup butter, softened
⅓ cup light brown sugar
2 tablespoons maple syrup
2 eggs
2 bananas, mashed

½ cup whole milk
2 cups all-purpose flour
2 teaspoons baking powder
½ teaspoon salt
2 Mars bars, chopped

Directions:
- Mix the butter, sugar and maple syrup in a bowl until fluffy and pale.
- Add the eggs and mix well then stir in the mashed bananas and milk.
- Fold in the rest of the ingredients then spoon the batter in a loaf cake pan lined with baking paper.
- Bake in the preheated oven at 350F for 40-45 minutes or until golden brown and well risen.
- Serve the cake chilled.

Nutritional information per serving

Calories: 299
Fat: 13.1g
Protein: 5.3g
Carbohydrates: 41.6g

CINNAMON FROSTED BANANA CAKE

Time: 1 ½ hours

Servings: 16

Ingredients:

Cake:
2 cups all-purpose flour
2 teaspoons baking powder
½ teaspoon salt
1 cup canola oil
1 cup light brown sugar
2 eggs

3 bananas, mashed
1 cup sour cream
½ cup dark chocolate chips
Cinnamon cream:
½ cup butter, softened
1 cup cream cheese
1 cup powdered sugar

Directions:

- For the cake, mix the flour, baking powder and salt in a bowl.
- In a different bowl, mix the oil, sugar and eggs until fluffy and pale. Add the bananas and sour cream and mix well then fold in the flour. Add the chocolate chips too.
- Spoon the batter in a 9-inch round cake pan and bake in the preheated oven at 350F for 35-40 minutes.
- Allow the cake to cool in the pan then transfer on a platter.
- For the frosting, mix the butter, cream cheese and sugar in a bowl for 5 minutes.
- Cover the cake in frosting and serve it fresh.

Nutritional information per serving

Calories: 419
Fat: 29.2g

Protein: 4.4g
Carbohydrates: 37.2g

BUTTER CAKE

Time: 1 hour

Servings: 8

Ingredients:

½ cup butter, softened
¾ cup white sugar
1 teaspoon vanilla extract
2 eggs

1 cup all-purpose flour
1 teaspoon baking powder
¼ teaspoon salt
½ cup whole milk

Directions:

- Mix the butter, sugar and vanilla in a bowl until fluffy and pale.
- Stir in the eggs and mix well.
- Fold in the flour, baking powder and salt, alternating it with milk. Start and end with flour.
- Spoon the batter in a 6-inch round cake pan lined with baking paper.
- Bake in the preheated oven at 350F for 30 minutes or until golden brown.
- Allow the cake to cool in the pan before serving.

Nutritional information per serving

Calories: 256
Fat: 13.2g

Protein: 3.6g
Carbohydrates: 31.8g

VANILLA GENOISE CAKE

Time: 1 hour

Servings: 8

Ingredients:

6 eggs
¾ cup white sugar
1 teaspoon vanilla extract
1 cup all-purpose flour

¼ teaspoon salt
¼ teaspoon baking powder

Directions:
- Mix the eggs, sugar and vanilla in a bowl until fluffy and light.
- Fold in the flour, salt and baking powder then spoon the batter in a 8-inch round cake pan lined with baking paper.
- Bake in the preheated oven at 350F for 30-35 minutes or until well risen and golden brown.
- Allow the cake to cool down before serving.

Nutritional information per serving

Calories: 176

Fat: 3.4g

Protein: 5.8g

Carbohydrates: 31.1g

TRAWBERRY LEMON OLIVE OIL CAKE

Time: 1 ¼ hours

Servings: 10

Ingredients:

¾ cup olive oil

4 eggs

¾ cup white sugar

1 lemon, zested and juiced

1 ¼ cups all-purpose flour

1 teaspoon baking powder

¼ teaspoon salt

1 ½ cups strawberries, sliced

Directions:
- Mix the eggs, oil and sugar in a bowl until fluffy and pale.
- Add the lemon zest and juice and mix well.
- Fold in the flour, baking powder and salt then spoon the batter in a 9-inch round cake pan lined with baking paper.
- Top with strawberries and bake in the preheated oven at 350F for 40-45 minutes.
- Allow the cake to cool in the pan before serving.

Nutritional information per serving

Calories: 277

Fat: 17.1g

Protein: 4.0g

Carbohydrates: 29.5g

EETROOT CARROT CAKE

Time: 1 ½ hours

Servings: 10

Ingredients:

1 ½ cups all-purpose flour

½ teaspoon salt

1 teaspoon baking powder

1 teaspoon cinnamon powder

½ teaspoon ground ginger

½ teaspoon ground cardamom

¾ cup vegetable oil

¼ cup maple syrup

½ cup light brown sugar

3 eggs

1 teaspoon vanilla extract

2 cups grated carrots

½ cup grated beetroots

½ cup pecans, chopped

Directions:
- Mix the flour, salt, baking powder, cinnamon, ginger and cardamom in a bowl.
- In a different bowl, mix the oil, maple syrup, sugar, eggs and vanilla until fluffy.
- Stir in the carrots and beetroots, as well as pecans then fold in the flour.
- Spoon the batter in a 9-inch round cake pan lined with baking paper.
- Bake in the preheated oven at 350F for 40-45 minutes or until the cake passes the toothpick test.
- Serve the cake chilled.

Nutritional information per serving

Calories: 305

Fat: 18.9g

Protein: 4.1g

Carbohydrates: 30.4g

ℬEETROOT CHOCOLATE FUDGE CAKE

Time: 1 ¼ hours

Servings: 10

Ingredients:

3 eggs
1 cup light brown sugar
2 tablespoons honey
¼ cup canola oil
1 cup all-purpose flour

½ cup cocoa powder
1 teaspoon baking soda
½ cup almond flour
¼ teaspoon salt
1 ½ cups grated beetroot

Directions:

- Mix the eggs with sugar until fluffy and pale. Add the oil and honey and mix well.
- Fold in the flour, cocoa powder, baking soda, almond flour and salt.
- Add the beetroot and mix gently with a spatula.
- Pour the batter in a 9-inch round cake pan lined with baking paper.
- Bake in the preheated oven at 350F for 30 minutes.
- Allow the cake to cool in the pan before serving.

Nutritional information per serving

Calories: 209
Fat: 8.2g

Protein: 4.5g
Carbohydrates: 32.5g

ℋEALTHIER CARROT CAKE

Time: 1 ½ hours

Servings: 10

Ingredients:

1 cup low-fat yogurt cake
¼ cup orange juice
½ cup coconut oil, melted
1 tablespoon orange zest
1 ½ cups grated carrots
½ cup grated apples
½ cup raisins

½ cup quinoa powder
1 cup whole wheat flour
½ cup rolled oats
2 teaspoons baking powder
½ teaspoon salt
1 teaspoon cinnamon powder
½ teaspoon ground ginger

Directions:

- Mix the yogurt, orange juice, coconut oil, orange zest, carrots, apples and raisins.
- Fold in the rest of the ingredients and mix with a spatula.
- Pour the batter in a 9-inch round cake pan lined with baking paper.
- Bake in the preheated oven at 350F for 45-50 minutes or until the cake passes the toothpick test.
- Serve the cake chilled.

Nutritional information per serving

Calories: 215
Fat: 12.0g

Protein: 2.9g
Carbohydrates: 25.1g

ℳERINGUE BLACK FOREST CAKE

Time: 2 ½ hours

Servings: 8

Ingredients:

4 egg whites
½ teaspoon cream of tartar
1 cup white sugar
2 tablespoons cocoa powder
¼ teaspoon salt

1 cup sour cherries, pitted
1 cup heavy cream
1 ½ cups dark chocolate chips
1 teaspoon vanilla extract

Directions:

- Mix the egg whites, cream of tartar and salt in a bowl for at least 5 minutes or until stiff and fluffy.
- Add the sugar, gradually, whipping until glossy and stiff.
- Fold in the cocoa powder then spoon the meringue on a large baking sheet lined with baking paper, shaping it into 2 8-inch rounds.
- Bake in the preheated oven at 250F for 2 hours.
- Bring the cream to the boiling point in a saucepan. Add the chocolate and mix until melted. Allow this cream to cool down then add the vanilla.
- Layer the baked meringue with chocolate cream and sour cherries.
- Serve the cake fresh.

Nutritional information per serving

Calories: 275
Fat: 11.8g

Protein: 3.9g
Carbohydrates: 44.1g

*W*HITE CHOCOLATE BLACKBERRY CAKE

Time: 2 hours

Servings: 10

Ingredients:

Sponge cake:
5 eggs
½ cup white sugar
¼ teaspoon salt
1 cup all-purpose flour

½ teaspoon baking powder
Filling:
1 ½ cups heavy cream
2 ½ cups white chocolate chips
2 cups fresh blackberries

Directions:

- For the sponge cake, whip the eggs, sugar and salt in a bowl until double in volume.
- Fold in the flour and baking powder then spoon the batter in a 8-inch round cake pan lined with baking paper.
- Bake in the preheated oven at 350F for 35-40 minutes then allow the cake to cool in the pan.
- Slice the cake in half lengthwise.
- For the filling, bring the cream to the boiling point in a saucepan. Remove from heat and add the chocolate. Mix until melted then allow to cool in the fridge.
- Whip the white chocolate cream for 2-3 minutes until fluffy.
- Fill the cake with half of the cream and half of the blackberries. Cover the cake with the remaining cream and decorate with blackberries.
- Serve the cake chilled.

Nutritional information per serving

Calories: 418
Fat: 22.8g

Protein: 7.3g
Carbohydrates: 48.3g

*C*HOCOLATE CHIP BLACKBERRY CAKE

Time: 1 ¼ hours

Servings: 10

Ingredients:

½ cup butter, softened
¼ cup canola oil
1 cup white sugar
½ cup plain yogurt
3 eggs
1 ½ cups all-purpose flour

¼ cup cornstarch
¼ teaspoon salt
1 teaspoon baking powder
½ cup dark chocolate chips
1 cup fresh blackberries

Directions:

- Mix the butter, oil and sugar in a bowl until creamy and fluffy.
- Add the eggs and yogurt and mix well.
- Fold in the flour, cornstarch, baking powder and salt and mix with a spatula.

- Add the chocolate chips and blackberries then spoon the batter in a 9-inch round cake pan lined with baking paper.
- Bake the cake in the preheated oven at 350F for 40-45 minutes or until well risen and golden brown.
- Allow the cake to cool in the pan before serving.

Nutritional information per serving

Calories: 347

Fat: 18.0

Protein: 5.0g

Carbohydrates: 43.8g

LUEBERRY STREUSEL CAKE

Time: 1 ¼ hours

Servings: 10

Ingredients:

Cake:

¾ cup butter, softened

1 cup white sugar

4 eggs

½ cup sour cream

1 tablespoon lemon zest

2 tablespoons lemon juice

2 cups all-purpose flour

1 teaspoon baking soda

½ teaspoon salt

1 ½ cups fresh blueberries

Streusel:

¼ cup butter, chilled

½ cup all-purpose flour

1 pinch salt

2 tablespoons powdered sugar

Directions:
- To make the cake, mix the butter, sugar, eggs and sour cream in a bowl for 5 minutes until creamy.
- Add the lemon zest, lemon juice, flour, baking soda and salt and mix with a spatula.
- Fold in the fruits then spoon the batter in a 9-inch round cake pan.
- For the streusel, mix all the ingredients in a bowl until grainy.
- Spread the streusel over the cake and bake in the preheated oven at 350F for 40-45 minutes or until it passes the toothpick test.
- Allow the cake to cool in the pan before serving.

Nutritional information per serving

Calories: 421

Fat: 23.0g

Protein: 6.2g

Carbohydrates: 49.4g

STRAWBERRY YOGURT CAKE

Time: 1 hour

Servings: 8

Ingredients:

½ cup butter, softened

1 cup white sugar

3 eggs

1/2 cup plain yogurt

1 teaspoon vanilla extract

1 cup all-purpose flour

1 teaspoon baking powder

1 cup strawberries, sliced

Directions:
- Mix the butter and sugar until softened and creamy.
- Add the eggs, one by one, then stir in the yogurt and vanilla.
- Fold in the flour and baking powder with a spatula then add the strawberries.
- Pour the batter in a round cake pan lined with baking paper.
- Bake in the preheated oven at 350F for 40-45 minutes or until the cake passes the toothpick test.
- Allow the cake to cool in the pan before serving.

Nutritional information per serving

Calories: 295

Fat: 13.5g

Protein: 4.8g

Carbohydrates: 39.9g

*B*oozy Chocolate Cake

Time: 1 ¼ hours

Servings: 14

Ingredients:

Cake:
2 cups all-purpose flour
½ cup cocoa powder
1 teaspoon baking soda
1 teaspoon baking powder
½ teaspoon salt
1 cup buttermilk
2 eggs

½ cup canola oil
¼ cup brandy
½ cup hot coffee
Frosting:
1 cup heavy cream
2 cups dark chocolate chips
¼ cup brandy
2 tablespoons butter

Directions:

- For the cake, mix the flour, cocoa powder, baking soda, baking powder and salt in a bowl.
- Add the rest of the ingredients and mix well.
- Pour the batter in a 9-inch round cake pan and bake in the preheated oven at 330F for 50 minutes.
- When done, allow the cake to cool in the pan then transfer on a platter.
- For the frosting, bring the cream to the boiling point in a saucepan. Remove from heat and add the chocolate. Mix well until melted and smooth.
- Allow the frosting to cool down then cover the cake with it.
- Serve fresh or chilled.

Nutritional information per serving

Calories: 281
Fat: 18.5g

Protein: 5.1g
Carbohydrates: 28.0g

*R*ich Vanilla Cake

Time: 1 hour

Servings: 10

Ingredients:

1 cup butter, softened
1 cup white sugar
1 tablespoon vanilla extract
6 egg yolks

2 egg whites
2 cups all-purpose flour
2 teaspoons baking powder
½ teaspoon salt

Directions:

- Mix the butter, sugar and vanilla in a bowl until fluffy and creamy
- Add the egg yolks and whole eggs, one by one, mixing well after each addition.
- Fold in the flour, baking powder and salt then spoon the batter in a 9-inch round cake pan lined with baking paper.
- Bake in the preheated oven at 350F for 35-40 minutes or until the cake passes the toothpick test.
- Allow the cake to cool in the pan before serving.

Nutritional information per serving

Calories: 369
Fat: 21.4g

Protein: 5.1g
Carbohydrates: 40.1g

*P*ear Brownie Cake

Time: 1 ¼ hours

Servings: 10

Ingredients:

½ cup butter, softened
1 cup dark chocolate chips
4 eggs

½ cup white sugar
½ cup all-purpose flour
¼ cup cocoa powder

¼ teaspoon salt

2 pears, peeled, cored and diced

Directions:
- Mix the butter and chocolate in a heatproof bowl over a hot water bath. Melt them together until smooth.
- Add the eggs, one by one, then stir in the sugar.
- Fold in the flour, cocoa powder and salt then spoon the batter in a 8-inch round cake pan lined with baking paper.
- Top with pear dices and bake in the preheated oven at 350F for 25 minutes.
- Allow the cake to cool in the pan before serving.

Nutritional information per serving

Calories: 252

Fat: 14.6g

Protein: 4.3g

Carbohydrates: 30.5g

LL BUTTER CAKE

Time: 1 ½ hours

Servings: 14

Ingredients:

Cake:

1 cup butter, softened

1 cup white sugar

1 teaspoon vanilla extract

4 eggs

½ cup whole milk

2 cups all-purpose flour

2 teaspoons baking powder

¼ teaspoon salt

Frosting:

1 cup butter, softened

2 cups powdered sugar

1 teaspoon vanilla extract

Directions:
- To make the cake, mix the butter, sugar and vanilla in a bowl until fluffy and creamy.
- Add the eggs, one by one then stir in the milk.
- Fold in the flour, baking powder and salt then spoon the batter in a 9-inch round cake pan lined with baking paper.
- Bake in the preheated oven at 350F for 40-45 minutes.
- Allow the cake to cool in the pan then cut it in half lengthwise.
- For the frosting, mix the butter, sugar and vanilla in a bowl until fluffy and pale.
- Use half of the buttercream to fill the cake and the remaining half to frost the cake.
- Serve the cake fresh or chilled.

Nutritional information per serving

Calories: 443

Fat: 28.0g

Protein: 4.0g

Carbohydrates: 45.9g

CARAMEL APPLE CAKE

Time: 1 ½ hours

Servings: 12

Ingredients:

Cake:

1 ¼ cups white sugar

1 cup butter, softened

4 eggs

½ cup applesauce

2 cups all-purpose flour

1 teaspoon baking soda

½ teaspoon salt

½ teaspoon cinnamon powder

½ teaspoon ground ginger

2 red apples, cored and diced

Glaze:

½ cup heavy cream

1 cup white sugar

¼ teaspoon salt

Directions:
- For the cake, mix the sugar, butter and eggs in a bowl until creamy.
- Stir in the applesauce then add the flour, baking soda, salt and cinnamon, as well as ginger and apples.
- Spoon the batter in a 9-inch round cake pan lined with baking paper.

- Bake in the preheated oven at 350F for 45 minutes.
- Allow the cake to cool in the pan then transfer on a platter.
- For the glaze, melt the sugar in a heavy saucepan until it has an amber color.
- Add the cream and salt and mix until melted and smooth.
- Allow the glaze to cool in the pan then drizzle it over the cake.

Nutritional information per serving

Calories: 411
Fat: 18.9g

Protein: 4.4g
Carbohydrates: 59.1g

$\mathcal{B}$ ERRY MERINGUE CAKE

Time: 2 ½ hours

Servings: 8

Ingredients:

4 egg whites
½ teaspoon salt
1 cup white sugar
1 teaspoon vanilla extract

2 tablespoons cornstarch
1 ½ cups fresh berries
1 cup heavy cream, whipped

Directions:

- Mix the egg whites, salt and sugar in a bowl. Place over a hot water bath and keep over heat until the sugar is melted.
- Remove from heat and whip the egg whites until glossy and fluffy.
- Fold in the cornstarch then spoon the meringue on a baking sheet lined with baking paper, shaping it into 2 rounds.
- Bake in the preheated oven at 250F for 2 hours.
- Fill and cover the cake with whipped cream and fresh berries.
- Serve right away.

Nutritional information per serving

Calories: 178
Fat: 5.7g

Protein: 2.3g
Carbohydrates: 30.6g

$\mathcal{W}$ HOLE PEAR SPONGE CAKE

Time: 2 hours

Servings: 14

Ingredients:

4 pears
2 star anise
1 cinnamon stick
¼ cup honey
2 cups white wine
½ cup butter, softened
¼ cup canola oil

2 eggs
½ cup sour cream
1 ½ cups all-purpose flour
½ cup cocoa powder
1 teaspoon baking soda
¼ teaspoon salt

Directions:

- Peel the pears and place them in a saucepan. Add the star anise, cinnamon, honey and wine and cook over low heat for 30 minutes. Allow to cool then arrange the pears in a 9-inch round cake pan lined with baking paper.
- Mix the butter, canola oil and eggs in a bowl until creamy.
- Add the sour cream and mix well then fold in the flour, cocoa powder, baking soda and salt.
- Spoon the batter over the pears.
- Bake the cake in the preheated oven at 350F for 45 minutes or until the cake passes the toothpick test.
- Allow the cake to cool before serving.

Nutritional information per serving

Calories: 257
Fat: 13.5g
Protein: 3.4g

Carbohydrates: 27.6g

CARAMEL PINEAPPLE UPSIDE DOWN CAKE

Time: 1 ½ hours

Servings: 14

Ingredients:

½ cup white sugar
2 tablespoons butter
6 slices pineapple
½ cup butter, softened
½ cup canola oil
½ cup light brown sugar
3 eggs

¼ cup whole milk
1 cup shredded coconut
1 cup all-purpose flour
½ cup cornstarch
1 teaspoon baking soda
¼ teaspoon salt

Directions:

- Melt the white sugar in a saucepan until it has an amber color.
- Drizzle the melted sugar on the bottom of a 9-inch round cake pan lined with baking paper.
- Top the caramelized sugar with butter and place aside.
- For the batter, mix the butter, oil and brown sugar until fluffy and creamy.
- Fold in the eggs and milk then add the rest of the ingredients and mix with a spatula.
- Spoon the batter over the pineapple slices and bake in the preheated oven at 350F for 40-45 minutes or until it passes the toothpick test.
- Allow the cake to cool in the pan for 10 minutes then turn it upside down on a platter.
- Serve chilled.

Nutritional information per serving

Calories: 309
Fat: 19.2g

Protein: 2.9g
Carbohydrates: 33.6g

WALNUT CARROT CAKE

Time: 1 ½ hours

Servings: 16

Ingredients:

Cake:
2 cups all-purpose flour
1 teaspoon all-spice powder
1 teaspoon cinnamon powder
1 teaspoon baking soda
1 teaspoon baking powder
½ teaspoon salt
1 cup white sugar
2 cups grated carrots

1 cup crushed pineapple
1 cup canola oil
3 eggs
1 cup chopped walnuts
½ cup ground walnuts
Frosting:
1 cup cream cheese, softened
¼ cup butter
3 cups powdered sugar

Directions:

- To make the cake, mix the dry ingredients in a bowl and the wet ingredients in another bowl.
- Pour the wet ingredients over the dry ones and mix with a spatula.
- Pour the batter in 9-inch round cake pan lined with baking paper.
- Bake the cakes in the preheated oven at 350F for 40-45 minutes or until they pass the toothpick test.
- Allow the cakes to cool completely.
- For the frosting, mix the cream cheese and butter in a bowl until creamy.
- Add the sugar, gradually, mixing well after each addition.
- Whip the frosting well until fluffy.
- Fill the cake with 1/3 of the frosting and cover it with the remaining cream cheese frosting.
- Serve the cake fresh or store in the fridge.

Nutritional information per serving

Calories: 483
Fat: 29.5g

Protein: 6.8g
Carbohydrates: 51.3g

$\mathcal{B}$UTTERSCOTCH PECAN CAKE

Time: 1 ½ hours

Servings: 10

Ingredients:

½ cup butter, softened
¼ cup canola oil
2 eggs
¼ cup plain yogurt
¼ teaspoon salt

1 ½ cups all-purpose flour
¼ cup cocoa powder
1 teaspoon baking powder
2 cups pecans
½ cup caramel sauce

Directions:

- Mix the butter, canola oil, eggs and yogurt in a bowl until fluffy.
- Add the flour, salt, baking powder and cocoa and mix gently with a spatula.
- Pour the batter in a 9-inch round cake pan and cover with half of the walnuts.
- Mix the remaining pecans with caramel and place aside.
- Bake the cake in the preheated oven at 350F for 35-40 minutes.
- Allow to cool then top with butterscotch pecans and serve fresh.

Nutritional information per serving

Calories: 281
Fat: 18.1g

Protein: 4.4g
Carbohydrates: 27.4g

$\mathcal{A}$MARETTO ALMOND CAKE

Time: 1 hour

Servings: 8

Ingredients:

½ cup butter, softened
½ cup light brown sugar
1 teaspoon orange zest
3 eggs
1 teaspoon lemon zest

1 ½ cups almond flour
¼ cup cocoa powder
¼ teaspoon salt
1 teaspoon baking powder
2 tablespoons Amaretto

Directions:

- Mix the butter, sugar, orange zest and lemon zest in a bowl until fluffy and creamy.
- Add the eggs, one by one, then stir in the almond flour, cocoa, salt and baking powder, preferably using a spatula.
- Spoon the batter in a 8-inch round cake pan and bake in the preheated oven at 350F for 35 minutes or until a toothpick inserted in the center of the cake comes out clean.
- Right after you remove it from the oven, brush it with Amaretto.
- Serve chilled.

Nutritional information per serving

Calories: 208
Fat: 16.1g

Protein: 3.8g
Carbohydrates: 12.0g

$\mathcal{C}$HAI SPICED CAKE

Time: 1 ½ hours

Servings: 10

Ingredients:

Cake:
1 cup butter, softened
1 ½ cups white sugar
1 teaspoon vanilla extract
6 eggs
2 cups all-purpose flour

2 teaspoons baking powder
½ teaspoon salt
1 teaspoon cinnamon powder
½ teaspoon ground ginger
½ teaspoon turmeric
¼ teaspoon ground cloves

Frosting:
1 cup cream cheese
½ cup butter, softened

¼ cup light brown sugar
2 cups powdered sugar
1 teaspoon grated ginger

Directions:
- For the cake, sift the flour with baking powder, salt and spices on a platter.
- Mix the butter and sugar in a bowl until pale and thick.
- Add the eggs, one by one, then stir in the dry ingredients, mixing gently with a spatula.
- Spoon the batter in a 9-inch round cake pan lined with baking paper.
- For the frosting, mix the cream cheese, butter and brown sugar in a bowl for at least 5 minutes.
- Add the rest of the ingredients and mix well. Cover the cake with buttercream and serve fresh.

Nutritional information per serving
Calories: 484
Fat: 27.6g

Protein: 5.7g
Carbohydrates: 55.8g

ARSNIP CARROT CAKE

Time: 1 ½ hours

Servings: 12

Ingredients:
2 cups all-purpose flour
½ teaspoon salt
1 teaspoon baking soda
1 teaspoon baking powder
1 teaspoon cinnamon powder
1 teaspoon ground ginger
4 eggs

1 cup light brown sugar
¼ cup white sugar
1 cup canola oil
1 cup grated carrots
1 cup grated parsnips
1 cup crushed pineapple
½ cup walnuts, chopped

Directions:
- Mix the flour, salt, baking soda, baking powder and spices in a bowl.
- In a different bowl, mix the eggs with the sugars until fluffy and pale.
- Add the oil then stir in the carrots, parsnips, pineapple and walnuts.
- Fold in the dry ingredients you prepared earlier.
- Pour the batter in a 9-inch round cake pan lined with baking paper.
- Bake in the preheated oven at 350F for 40-45 minutes or until it passes the toothpick test.
- Dust with powdered sugar and serve chilled.

Nutritional information per serving
Calories: 371
Fat: 23.0g

Protein: 5.5g
Carbohydrates: 37.6g

CHERRY CHOCOLATE CAKE

Time: 1 ¼ hours

Servings: 10

Ingredients:
3 eggs
1 cup white sugar
½ cup milk
½ cup butter, melted
1 teaspoon vanilla extract

1 ½ cups all-purpose flour
1 teaspoon baking powder
¼ teaspoon salt
½ cup pine nuts, ground
2 cups cherries, pitted

Directions:
- Mix the eggs and sugar in a bowl until double in volume.
- Stir in the milk then gradually pour in the butter, mixing well.
- Add the vanilla then fold in the flour, baking powder and salt.
- Add the ground pine nuts then fold in the cherries.

- Pour the batter in a 9-inch round cake pan lined with baking paper.
- Bake in the preheated oven at 350F for 40-45 minutes or until the cake passes the toothpick test.
- Allow the cake to cool in the pan before serving.

Nutritional information per serving

Calories: 314
Fat: 15.6g

Protein: 5.1g
Carbohydrates: 40.3g

CHERRY BROWNIE CAKE

Time: 1 hour

Servings: 8

Ingredients:

¾ cup butter
1 cup dark chocolate chips
3 eggs
1 teaspoon vanilla extract

¾ cup light brown sugar
1 cup all-purpose flour
¼ teaspoon salt
1 cup cherries, pitted

Directions:

- Mix the butter and chocolate chips in a heatproof bowl. Place over a hot water bath and melt them until smooth.
- Remove from heat and stir in the eggs, vanilla and sugar.
- Fold in the flour and salt then pour the batter in a 8-inch round cake pan lined with baking paper.
- Top with cherries and bake in the preheated oven at 350F for 20 minutes.
- Serve the cake chilled.

Nutritional information per serving

Calories: 367
Fat: 23.1g

Protein: 4.9g
Carbohydrates: 38.1g

SULTANA CAKE

Time: 1 ½ hours

Servings: 10

Ingredients:

½ cup butter, softened
1 cup white sugar
2 tablespoons dark brown sugar
¼ cup orange marmalade
2 eggs

½ cup brandy
1 ½ cups sultanas
1 cup all-purpose flour
¼ teaspoon salt
1 teaspoon baking soda

Directions:

- Mix the sultanas with the brandy and allow to soak up for 30 minutes.
- Mix the butter, sugars and marmalade in a bowl until creamy.
- Add the eggs and mix well.
- Fold in the flour, salt and baking soda then add the sultanas.
- Spoon the batter in a 8-inch round cake pan lined with baking paper.
- Bake in the preheated oven at 350F for 45-50 minutes or until the cake passes the toothpick test.
- Allow the cake to cool down before serving.

Nutritional information per serving

Calories: 262
Fat: 10.2g

Protein: 2.7g
Carbohydrates: 40.7g

RASPBERRY CHOCOLATE MUD CAKE

Time: 1 ½ hours
Servings: 12

Ingredients:

1 cup butter, softened
1 cup dark chocolate chips
1 ½ cups white sugar
1 cup hot water
2 cups all-purpose flour
2 teaspoons baking powder
½ teaspoon salt

½ cup cocoa powder
3 eggs
½ cup buttermilk
½ cup heavy cream
2 tablespoons brandy
1 ½ cups fresh raspberries

Directions:

- Mix the butter and chocolate chips in a heatproof bowl and place over a hot water bath. Melt them together until smooth.
- Stir in the sugar and hot water and mix well.
- Add the buttermilk, cream, eggs and brandy.
- Fold in the dry ingredients and mix well.
- Add the raspberries and pour the batter in a 9-inch round cake pan lined with baking paper.
- Bake in the preheated oven at 350F for 50 minutes.
- Allow the cake to cool in the pan before slicing and serving.

Nutritional information per serving

Calories: 415
Fat: 21.8g

Protein: 5.6g
Carbohydrates: 52.5g

Chocolate Hazelnut Cake

Time: 1 ¼ hours

Servings: 10

Ingredients:

1 cup ground hazelnuts
1 cup all-purpose flour
1 teaspoon baking powder
½ teaspoon baking soda
½ teaspoon salt
½ cup cocoa powder

2 whole eggs
6 egg yolks
½ cup white sugar
¼ cup heavy cream
½ cup cherry jam

Directions:

- Mix the hazelnuts, flour, baking powder, baking soda and salt in a bowl. Add the cocoa powder as well.
- Mix the eggs, egg yolks and sugar in a bowl until thickened and fluffy. Stir in the cream and cherry jam.
- Fold in the flour then spoon the cake in a 8-inch round cake pan lined with baking paper.
- Bake in the preheated oven at 350F for 35-40 minutes or until the cake passes the toothpick test.
- Serve the cake chilled.

Nutritional information per serving

Calories: 240
Fat: 9.9g

Protein: 6.0g
Carbohydrates: 34.9g

Chocolate Dulce de Leche Cake

Time: 1 ¼ hours

Servings: 12

Ingredients:

½ cup butter, softened
½ cup canola oil
1 cup white sugar
3 eggs
½ cup sour cream
1 ¾ cups all-purpose flour
2 teaspoons baking powder

½ teaspoon salt
1 cup dark chocolate chips
½ cup dulce de leche

Directions:
- Mix the butter and oil in a bowl. Add the sugar and give it a good mix until creamy.
- Add the eggs and sour cream and mix well.
- Fold in the flour, baking powder and salt then add the chocolate chips. Pour the batter in a 9-inch round cake pan lined with baking paper.
- Drop spoonfuls of dulce de leche over the batter and bake in the preheated oven at 350F for 40-45 minutes or until the cake passes the toothpick test.
- Serve the cake chilled.

Nutritional information per serving

Calories: 397

Fat: 23.2g

Protein: 5.0g

Carbohydrates: 45.8g

ASPBERRY RICOTTA CAKE

Time: 1 hour

Servings: 10

Ingredients:

1 cup ricotta cheese

½ cup butter, softened

1 cup hot water

¾ cup white sugar

2 cups all-purpose flour

¼ cup cocoa powder

2 teaspoons baking powder

¼ teaspoon salt

1 cup raspberries

Directions:
- Mix the ricotta cheese, butter and sugar in a bowl until creamy.
- Add the water and mix well.
- Fold in the flour, cocoa powder, baking powder and salt.
- Add the raspberries then spoon the batter in a 9-inch round cake pan lined with baking paper.
- Bake in the preheated oven at 350F for 40 minutes or until the cake passes the toothpick test.
- Serve the cake chilled.

Nutritional information per serving

Calories: 275

Fat: 11.8g

Protein: 6.0g

Carbohydrates: 38.5g

HOCOLATE COFFEE CAKE

Time: 1 hour

Servings: 12

Ingredients:

Cake:

1 cup buttermilk

½ cup canola oil

1 cup hot coffee

3 eggs

2 cups all-purpose flour

1 cup white sugar

2 teaspoons baking powder

½ teaspoon salt

2 teaspoons instant coffee

Frosting:

1 cup heavy cream

2 cups dark chocolate chips

2 teaspoons instant coffee

Directions:
- For the cake, mix the buttermilk, canola oil, hot coffee and eggs in a bowl.
- Stir in the dry ingredients and mix well.
- Pour the batter in a 9-inch round cake pan lined with baking paper.
- Bake in the preheated oven at 350F for 45-50 minutes.
- When done, transfer the chilled cake on a platter.
- For the frosting, bring the cream to the boiling point in a saucepan. Add the chocolate and mix until melted. Stir in the coffee.
- Cover the cake with chocolate coffee frosting and serve it fresh.

Calories: 371
Fat: 19.6g

Protein: 5.8g
Carbohydrates: 47.6g

*F*UDGY CHOCOLATE CAKE

Time: 1 hour

Servings: 10

Ingredients:
2 cups dark chocolate chips
1 cup butter
1 cup white sugar
3 eggs

¾ cup all-purpose flour
½ cup cocoa powder
¼ teaspoon salt
1 cup ground walnuts

Directions:
- Mix the chocolate chips and butter in a bowl and place over a hot water bath. Melt it over heat until smooth.
- Add the sugar and mix well then stir in the eggs.
- Fold in the flour, cocoa powder, salt and walnuts then spoon the batter in a 8-inch round cake pan lined with baking paper.
- Bake in the preheated oven at 350F for 35 minutes.
- Allow the cake to cool in the pan before serving.

Nutritional information per serving
Calories: 490
Fat: 34.1g

Protein: 8.2g
Carbohydrates: 46.9g

*C*HESTNUT PUREE CHOCOLATE CAKE

Time: 1 ¼ hours

Servings: 10

Ingredients:
½ cup canola oil
¼ cup butter
1 cup dark chocolate chips
1 cup white sugar
1 cup chestnut puree

½ cup cocoa powder
1 cup all-purpose flour
½ cup ground almonds
¼ teaspoon salt
1 teaspoon baking powder

Directions:
- Mix the canola oil, butter and chocolate chips in a heatproof bowl. Place over heatproof bowl and melt them together.
- Remove from heat and stir in the sugar and chestnut puree.
- Fold in the cocoa powder, flour, almonds, salt and baking powder.
- Spoon the batter in a 9-inch round cake pan lined with baking paper.
- Bake in the preheated oven at 350F for 35-40 minutes or until the cake passes the toothpick test.
- Serve the cake chilled.

Nutritional information per serving
Calories: 354
Fat: 21.8g

Protein: 3.9g
Carbohydrates: 41.6g

*M*ORELLO CHERRY CAKE

Time: 1 ¼ hours

Servings: 12

Ingredients:
1 cup maple syrup
½ cup coconut oil, melted
¼ cup brandy

3 eggs
½ cup white sugar
½ cup cocoa powder

1 cup almond flour
¾ cup all-purpose flour
½ teaspoon salt

½ cup cocoa powder
1 cup Morello cherries

Directions:
- Mix the maple syrup, coconut oil, brandy and eggs in a bowl.
- Stir in the sugar and mix well.
- Fold in the cocoa powder, almond flour, all-purpose flour, salt and cocoa powder.
- Spoon the batter in a 9-inch round cake pan and top with cherries.
- Bake in the preheated oven at 350F for 40 minutes.
- Serve the cake chilled.

Nutritional information per serving
Calories: 270
Fat: 12.4g

Protein: 4.2g
Carbohydrates: 40.9g

*C*HERRY LIQUEUR SOAKED CAKE

Time: 1 ¼ hours

Servings: 8

Ingredients:
1 ½ cups dark chocolate chips
½ cup hot coffee
½ cup white sugar
¼ cup dark brown sugar
½ cup butter, melted
2 eggs

1 cup almond flour
½ cup all-purpose flour
¼ teaspoon salt
½ teaspoon baking powder
¼ cup cherry liqueurs

Directions:
- Mix the coffee and chocolate in a bowl. Mix until melted and smooth.
- Stir in the sugars, butter and eggs then fold in the almond flour, all-purpose flour, salt and baking powder.
- Pour the batter in a 8-inch round cake pan lined with baking paper.
- Bake in the preheated oven at 350F for 35 minutes.
- Allow the cake to cool down then transfer on a platter.
- Brush the cherry liqueur over the cake.
- Serve the cake chilled.

Nutritional information per serving
Calories: 343
Fat: 20.8g

Protein: 4.6g
Carbohydrates: 39.7g

*C*HOCOLATE COCONUT CAKE

Time: 1 ¼ hours

Servings: 10

Ingredients:
½ cup butter
2 tablespoons canola oil
1 cup white sugar
2 eggs
1 ½ cups all-purpose flour

¼ cup cocoa powder
1 cup shredded coconut
1 teaspoon baking powder
¼ teaspoon salt
¾ cup milk

Directions:
- Mix the butter, oil and sugar in a bowl until fluffy and creamy.
- Add the eggs, one by one, then stir in the milk.
- Add the dry ingredients and mix gently with a spatula.
- Spoon the batter in a 8-inch round cake pan lined with baking paper.
- Bake in the preheated oven at 350F for 35-40 minutes or until the cake passes the toothpick test.
- Serve the cake chilled.

Nutritional information per serving

Calories: 305
Fat: 16.4g

Protein: 4.4g
Carbohydrates: 37.9g

ECADENT CHOCOLATE CAKE

Time: 1 hour

Servings: 10

Ingredients:

1 cup butter, softened
3 cups dark chocolate chips
6 eggs, separated
2/3 cup white sugar

½ cup cocoa powder
¼ cup all-purpose flour
½ teaspoon salt

Directions:

- Melt the butter and chocolate chips in a heatproof bowl over a hot water bath.
- Mix the egg yolks and sugar in a bowl until fluffy and pale.
- Stir in the melted chocolate, then add the cocoa powder, flour and salt.
- Whip the egg whites until fluffy and stiff. Fold the meringue into the batter then pour the batter in a 9-inch round cake pan.
- Bake in the preheated oven at 350F for 35-40 minutes or until well risen.
- Serve the cake chilled.

Nutritional information per serving

Calories: 439
Fat: 31.2g

Protein: 7.0g
Carbohydrates: 42.3g

R ASPBERRY GANACHE CAKE

Time: 1 ¼ hours

Servings: 8

Ingredients:

Cake:
½ cup butter, softened
½ cup white sugar
4 eggs
1 cup all-purpose flour
¼ teaspoon salt

1 teaspoon baking powder
1 cup fresh raspberries
Ganache:
½ cup heavy cream
1 cup dark chocolate chips

Directions:

- For the cake, mix the butter and sugar in a bowl until fluffy. Add the eggs, one by one, then stir in the flour, salt and baking powder.
- Spoon the batter in a 8-inch round cake pan lined with baking paper.
- Top with raspberries and bake in the preheated oven at 350F for 35-40 minutes or until well risen and golden brown.
- Allow the cake to cool in the pan then transfer on a platter.
- For the ganache, bring the cream to the boiling point in a saucepan. Remove from heat and stir in the chocolate. Mix until melted.
- Drizzle the ganache over the cake and serve the cake chilled.

Nutritional information per serving

Calories: 341
Fat: 20.7g

Protein: 5.8g
Carbohydrates: 37.0g

B UTTERMILK CHOCOLATE CAKE

Time: 1 ¼ hours
Servings: 10

Ingredients:

2 cups all-purpose flour
2 teaspoons baking powder
½ cup cocoa powder
½ teaspoon salt
1 cup butter, melted

1 cup white sugar
1 teaspoon vanilla extract
2 eggs
1 ¼ cups buttermilk

Directions:

- Combine all the ingredients in a bowl.
- Give it a quick mix just until incorporated.
- Pour the batter in a 9-inch round cake pan lined with baking paper.
- Bake the cake in the preheated oven at 350F for 40-45 minutes or until the cake is well risen and it passes the toothpick test.
- Allow the cake to cool in the pan then serve it chilled.

Nutritional information per serving

Calories: 365
Fat: 20.4g

Protein: 5.7g
Carbohydrates: 43.5g

Chocolate Mousse Cake

Time: 1 ½ hours

Servings: 10

Ingredients:

Cake:
1 cup all-purpose flour
¼ cup cocoa powder
1 teaspoon baking powder
¼ teaspoon salt
1 egg
1 cup buttermilk

¼ cup heavy cream
½ cup dark chocolate chips
Chocolate mousse:
½ cup heavy cream, heated
1 cup dark chocolate chips
1 cup heavy cream, whipped

Directions:

- For the cake, melt the cream and chocolate together in a heatproof bowl.
- Stir in the rest of the ingredients and give it a quick mix.
- Pour the batter in a 9-inch round cake pan lined with baking paper.
- Bake in the preheated oven at 350F for 35-40 minutes or until well risen and fragrant.
- When done, transfer the cake in a cake ring and place it on a platter.
- For the chocolate mousse, mix the cream and chocolate chips in a bowl. Mix until melted and smooth. Allow to cool down.
- Fold in the whipped cream then pour the mousse over the cake.
- Chill the cake before serving.

Nutritional information per serving

Calories: 223
Fat: 13.6g

Protein: 4.7g
Carbohydrates: 24.7g

Blood Orange Cornmeal Cake

Time: 1 ½ hours

Servings: 12

Ingredients:

1 cup butter, softened
1 cup white sugar
2 tablespoons blood orange zest
1 cup fresh blood orange juice
1 cup all-purpose flour
1 cup cornmeal

2 teaspoons baking powder
½ teaspoon salt
2 blood oranges, sliced

Directions:
- Mix the butter, sugar and orange zest in a bowl until creamy and fluffy.
- Mix the flour, cornmeal, baking powder and salt.
- Stir the flour into the butter mixture, alternating it with the orange juice.
- Arrange the orange slices at the bottom of a 9-inch round cake pan lined with baking paper.
- Pour the batter over the orange slices and bake in the preheated oven at 350F for 45 minutes or until the cake passes the toothpick test.
- When done, turn the cake upside down on a platter and serve it chilled.

Nutritional information per serving

Calories: 298

Fat: 15.9g

Protein: 2.5g

Carbohydrates: 38.8g

RANGE CHOCOLATE MUD CAKE

Time: 1 ¼ hours

Servings: 10

Ingredients:

2 cups white sugar

1 cup butter, softened

½ cup brewed coffee

4 eggs

1 teaspoon vanilla extract

1 tablespoon orange zest

¾ cup cocoa powder

1 ½ cups all-purpose flour

2 tablespoons cornstarch

½ teaspoon salt

1 teaspoon baking soda

½ cup candied orange peel, chopped

Directions:
- Mix the sugar and butter in a bowl until fluffy and pale.
- Add the coffee, eggs, vanilla and orange zest.
- Stir in the rest of the ingredients and mix well.
- Pour the batter in a 9-inch round cake pan lined with baking paper.
- Bake the cake in the preheated oven at 350F for 50-55 minutes or until the cake looks set.
- Serve the cake chilled.

Nutritional information per serving

Calories: 433

Fat: 21.2g

Protein: 5.6g

Carbohydrates: 60.9g

CHOCOLATE OLIVE OIL CAKE

Time: 1 ¼ hours

Servings: 10

Ingredients:

2 eggs

1 cup white sugar

1 teaspoon vanilla extract

1 teaspoon orange zest

2/3 cup olive oil

¼ cup whole milk

½ cup cocoa powder

1 cup all-purpose flour

¼ teaspoon salt

1 teaspoon baking powder

Directions:
- Mix the eggs with sugar until fluffy and pale. Stir in the vanilla and orange zest and mix well.
- Add the olive oil and milk then fold in the cocoa powder, flour, salt and baking powder.
- Pour the batter in a 8-inch round cake pan lined with baking paper.
- Bake in the preheated oven at 350F for 40 minutes or until it passes the toothpick test.
- Serve the cake chilled.

Nutritional information per serving

Calories: 263

Fat: 15.2g

Protein: 3.4g

Carbohydrates: 32.6g

Chocolate Peppermint Cake

Time: 1 ½ hours

Servings: 8

Ingredients:

Cake:
1 cup dark chocolate chips
½ cup butter, cubed
½ cup light brown sugar
2 eggs
1 cup all-purpose flour
2 tablespoons cocoa powder

1 teaspoon baking powder
¼ teaspoon salt
Glaze:
¼ cup heavy cream
¼ cup whole milk
3 tablespoons cocoa powder
1 pinch salt

Directions:

- For the cake, mix the chocolate chips and butter in a heatproof bowl and place over a hot water bath. Melt them together until smooth.
- Add the sugar and eggs and mix well.
- Stir in the flour, cocoa powder, baking powder and salt. Pour the batter in a 8-inch round cake pan lined with baking paper.
- Bake in the preheated oven at 350F for 30 minutes.
- For the glaze, mix all the ingredients in a saucepan and place over low heat. Cook until thickened.
- Drizzle the glaze over the cake and serve chilled.

Nutritional information per serving

Calories: 304
Fat: 18.8g

Protein: 5.1g
Carbohydrates: 33.5g

Classic Fruit Cake

Time: 2 hours

Servings: 16

Ingredients:

1 cup sultanas
1 cup golden raisins
½ cup dates, pitted and chopped
½ cup dried apricots, chopped
½ cup dried cranberries
½ cup dried pineapple, chopped
1 cup brandy
1 cup butter, softened
1 cup light brown sugar

2 tablespoons orange zest
½ cup fresh orange juice
4 eggs
2 cups all-purpose flour
½ cup sliced almonds
1 teaspoon baking soda
½ teaspoon baking powder
½ teaspoon salt

Directions:

- Mix the dried fruits and brandy in a bowl. Allow to soak up for at least 1 hour.
- Mix the butter and sugar in a bowl until creamy and pale.
- Add the orange zest and orange juice and mix well then stir in the eggs, one by one.
- Fold in the flour, almonds, baking soda, baking powder and salt.
- Add the fruits and mix gently with a spatula.
- Spoon the batter in a 9-inch round cake pan lined with baking paper.
- Bake in the preheated oven at 350F for 55-60 minutes. The cake is done when a toothpick inserted in the center comes out clean.
- Allow the cake to cool in the pan then slice and serve.

Nutritional information per serving

Calories: 290
Fat: 14.4g
Protein: 4.4g
Carbohydrates: 37.2g

CHIA SEED CHOCOLATE CAKE

Time: 1 ¼ hours

Servings: 10

Ingredients:

½ cup dark chocolate chips
½ cup butter
3 eggs
1 tablespoon orange zest
1 cup white sugar
1 cup canola oil

¼ cup cocoa powder
2 tablespoons chia seeds
1 ½ cups all-purpose flour
1 teaspoon baking powder
¼ teaspoon salt

Directions:

- Melt the chocolate and butter in a bowl until smooth.
- Remove from heat and stir in the eggs, orange zest, sugar and canola oil.
- Fold in the cocoa powder, chia seeds, flour, baking powder and salt then pour the batter in a 9-inch round cake pan lined with baking paper.
- Bake in the preheated oven at 350F for 35-40 minutes or until the cake passes the toothpick test.
- Serve the cake chilled.

Nutritional information per serving

Calories: 470
Fat: 34.4g

Protein: 4.5g
Carbohydrates: 40.0g

CINNAMON MAPLE PUMPKIN CAKE

Time: 1 ¼ hours

Servings: 10

Ingredients:

2 ½ cups all-purpose flour
2 teaspoons baking powder
¼ teaspoon salt
½ teaspoon baking soda
1 tablespoon cinnamon powder
½ cup canola oil

3/4 cup white sugar
½ cup maple syrup
2 eggs
1 ½ cups pumpkin puree
1 teaspoon vanilla extract
½ cup whole milk

Directions:

- Mix the flour, baking powder, salt, baking soda and cinnamon in a bowl.
- Mix the oil and sugar in a bowl for 2 minutes. Add the eggs and mix well.
- Stir in the pumpkin puree, vanilla and milk and mix well.
- Fold in the flour mixture and mix with a spatula. Pour the batter in a 9-inch round cake pan lined with baking paper.
- Bake in the preheated oven at 350F for 45 minutes or until the cake passes the toothpick test.
- Serve the cake chilled.

Nutritional information per serving

Calories: 342
Fat: 12.6g

Protein: 5.1g
Carbohydrates: 53.5g

SNICKERDOODLE BUNDT CAKE

Time: 1 ½ hours

Servings: 12

Ingredients:

Filling:
1 cup white sugar
1 tablespoon cinnamon powder
Cake:

2 ½ cups all-purpose flour
1 teaspoon ground ginger
1 teaspoon baking powder
½ teaspoon baking soda

½ teaspoon salt
1 cup butter, softened
1 cup white sugar

2 tablespoons dark brown sugar
3 eggs
1 cup sour cream

Directions:
- For the filling, mix the sugar with cinnamon in a bowl.
- For the cake, sift the flour, ginger, baking powder, baking soda and salt.
- Mix the butter and sugars in a bowl until fluffy and light.
- Add the eggs, one by one, then stir in the sour cream.
- Fold in the flour then spoon half of the batter in a greased Bundt cake pan. Sprinkle with the cinnamon sugar mixture then top with the remaining batter.
- Bake in the preheated oven at 350F for 45 minutes or until golden brown and the cake passes the toothpick test.
- Serve the cake chilled.

Nutritional information per serving

Calories: 419
Fat: 20.7g

Protein: 4.9g
Carbohydrates: 55.9g

 CHOCOLATE NUTELLA CAKE

Time: 1 ½ hours

Servings: 10

Ingredients:

1 cup ground hazelnuts
2 cups all-purpose flour
2 teaspoons baking powder
½ teaspoon salt
2 eggs
1 cup whole milk

½ cup canola oil
2 tablespoons Kahlua
1 teaspoon vanilla extract
½ cup brewed coffee
1 cup Nutella

Directions:
- Mix the ground hazelnuts, flour, baking powder and salt in a bowl.
- Mix the eggs, milk, canola oil, Kahlua, vanilla and coffee in a different bowl. Stir in the flour mixture then spoon the batter in a 9-inch round cake pan lined with baking paper.
- Drop spoonfuls of Nutella over the batter and bake in the preheated oven at 350F for 40-45 minutes or until the cake passes the toothpick test.
- Serve the cake chilled.

Nutritional information per serving

Calories: 295
Fat: 18.5g

Protein: 5.8g
Carbohydrates: 25.4g

 PISTACHIO CAKE

Time: 1 hour

Servings: 8

Ingredients:

1 cup ground pistachio
½ cup all-purpose flour
¼ teaspoon salt
1 teaspoon baking powder
½ cup butter, softened
½ cup white sugar

2 eggs
¼ cup whole milk
1 teaspoon lemon zest
½ teaspoon ground cardamom
¼ teaspoon cinnamon powder

Directions:
- Mix the pistachio, flour, salt, baking powder, cardamom and cinnamon in a bowl.
- Mix the butter and sugar in a bowl until fluffy and light. Stir in the eggs and milk, as well as lemon zest.
- Fold in the flour and pistachio mixture then spoon the batter in a 8-inch round cake pan lined with baking paper.

- Bake in the preheated oven at 350F for 35-40 minutes.
- Serve the cake chilled, dusted with powdered sugar.

Nutritional information per serving

Calories: 214
Fat: 14.1g

Protein: 3.2g
Carbohydrates: 20.1g

$\mathcal{S}$ PICED PUMPKIN SHEET CAKE

Time: 1 ¼ hours

Servings: 16

Ingredients:

2 cups all-purpose flour
2 teaspoons baking powder
¼ teaspoon baking soda
½ teaspoon salt
1 teaspoon cinnamon powder
1 teaspoon ground ginger
½ teaspoon ground cloves

½ teaspoon ground star anise
1 ½ cups white sugar
1 cup canola oil
4 eggs
1 ½ cups pumpkin puree
½ cup walnuts, chopped

Directions:

- Sift the flour, baking powder, baking soda, salt and spices in a bowl.
- Mix the sugar, canola oil and eggs in a bowl until pale and fluffy.
- Stir in the pumpkin puree then incorporate the flour, ½ cup at a time, mixing gently with a spatula.
- Fold in the walnuts then spoon the batter in a 10x10 inch rectangle pan lined with baking paper.
- Bake in the preheated oven at 350F for 35-40 minutes or until the cake passes the toothpick test.
- Serve the cake chilled, cut into small squares.

Nutritional information per serving

Calories: 297
Fat: 17.3g

Protein: 4.2g
Carbohydrates: 33.5g

$\mathcal{S}$ TRAWBERRY POLENTA CAKE

Time: 1 ¼ hours

Servings: 10

Ingredients:

1 cup polenta flour
2 tablespoons all-purpose flour
¼ teaspoon salt
1 teaspoon baking soda
2 cups whole milk

2 cups water
½ cup white sugar
1 teaspoon vanilla extract
¼ cup butter, melted
2 cups strawberries, sliced

Directions:

- Mix the polenta flour, flour, salt and baking soda in a bowl.
- Stir in the milk, water, sugar, vanilla and melted butter.
- Pour the batter in a 8x8-inch and top with strawberry slices.
- Bake in the preheated oven at 350F for 35-40 minutes or until the cake passes the toothpick test.
- When done, remove from the oven, allow to cool down then cut into small squares.
- Serve right away.

Nutritional information per serving

Calories: 147
Fat: 6.4g
Protein: 2.4g
Carbohydrates: 20.7g

$\mathcal{W}$ALNUT HONEY POUND CAKE

Time: 1 ¼ hours

Servings: 12

Ingredients:

2 cups all-purpose flour
2 teaspoons baking powder
½ teaspoon salt
½ cup butter, softened
1 cup honey

2 eggs
1 teaspoon vanilla extract
1 cup whole milk
1 ½ cups walnuts, chopped

Directions:

- Sift the flour, baking powder and salt in a bowl.
- In a different bowl, mix the butter and honey until fluffy. Stir in the eggs and vanilla and mix well.
- Add the flour mixture, alternating it with the milk.
- Fold in the walnuts then spoon the batter in a 9-inch round cake pan lined with baking paper.
- Bake in the preheated oven at 350F for 40-45 minutes or until well risen and golden brown.
- Allow the cake to cool in the pan before slicing and serving.

Nutritional information per serving

Calories: 351
Fat: 18.5g

Protein: 7.6g
Carbohydrates: 42.1g

$\mathcal{A}$PPLE POUND CAKE

Time: 1 ¼ hours

Servings: 10

Ingredients:

¾ cup butter, softened
½ cup cream cheese, softened
1 cup white sugar
3 eggs
1 teaspoon vanilla extract
1 ½ cups all-purpose flour

1 teaspoon baking powder
½ teaspoon baking soda
¼ teaspoon salt
½ teaspoon cinnamon powder
2 granny Smith apples, peeled, cored and diced

Directions:

- Mix the butter, cream cheese and sugar in a bowl until creamy and fluffy.
- Stir in the eggs and vanilla and mix well.
- Fold in the flour, baking powder, baking soda, salt and cinnamon.
- Add the apple dices then spoon the batter in a loaf cake pan lined with baking paper.
- Bake in the preheated oven at 350F for 40 minutes or until the cake passes the toothpick test.
- Serve the cake chilled.

Nutritional information per serving

Calories: 345
Fat: 19.4g

Protein: 4.7g
Carbohydrates: 40.0g

$\mathcal{P}$EANUT BUTTER JELLY CAKE

Time: 1 ½ hours

Servings: 12

Ingredients:

2 cups all-purpose flour
2 teaspoons baking powder
½ teaspoon salt
½ cup peanut butter
½ cup butter, softened

2 tablespoons canola oil
1 cup white sugar
½ cup light brown sugar
2 eggs
1 teaspoon vanilla extract

½ cup whole milk

½ cup cranberry jelly

Directions:
- Sift the flour, baking powder and salt.
- Mix the peanut butter, butter, canola oil and sugars in a bowl until creamy and fluffy.
- Stir in the eggs and vanilla and mix well.
- Fold in the flour mixture, alternating it with the milk. Start and end with flour.
- Spoon the batter in a round cake pan lined with baking paper.
- Bake in the preheated oven at 350F for 40-45 minutes or until the cake passes the toothpick test.
- When done, brush the cake with cranberry jelly and serve it fresh.

Nutritional information per serving

Calories: 334
Fat: 16.7g

Protein: 6.2g
Carbohydrates: 42.0g

LEMON RASPBERRY POUND CAKE

Time: 1 ¼ hours

Servings: 10

Ingredients:

Cake:
2 ¼ cups all-purpose flour
1 teaspoon baking soda
1 teaspoon baking powder
½ teaspoon salt
1 cup butter, softened
½ cup cream cheese
1 cup white sugar
1 teaspoon vanilla extract

1 teaspoon lemon zest
4 eggs
2 tablespoons lemon juice
1 ½ cups fresh raspberries
Glaze:
½ cup cream cheese
2 tablespoons lemon juice
1 teaspoon lemon zest
2 tablespoons powdered sugar

Directions:
- For the cake, sift the flour, baking soda, baking powder and salt in a bowl.
- In a different bowl, mix the butter, cream cheese, sugar, vanilla and lemon zest until creamy.
- Stir in the eggs, one by one, then add the lemon juice.
- Fold in the flour, mixing with a spatula.
- Add the raspberries then spoon the batter in a loaf cake pan lined with baking paper.
- Bake in the preheated oven at 350F for 40-45 minutes or until the cake passes the toothpick test.
- When the cake is done, transfer it on a platter.
- For the glaze, mix all the ingredients in a bowl.
- Drizzle the glaze over the cake and serve it fresh.

Nutritional information per serving

Calories: 466
Fat: 28.7g

Protein: 7.3g
Carbohydrates: 46.5g

CINNAMON STREUSEL RASPBERRY CAKE

Time: 1 ¼ hours

Servings: 12

Ingredients:

Cake:
2 cups all-purpose flour
2 teaspoons baking powder
½ teaspoon salt
½ cup butter, softened
¼ cup canola oil
2 eggs
¾ cup whole milk

1 teaspoon vanilla extract
1 cup fresh raspberries
Cinnamon streusel:
¼ cup light brown sugar
½ cup butter, chilled
½ cup all-purpose flour
1 teaspoon cinnamon powder
1 pinch salt

Directions:

- To make the cake, sift the flour, baking powder and salt in a bowl.
- In a different bowl, mix the butter, oil and eggs until creamy. Stir in the milk and vanilla then fold in the flour.
- Add the raspberries then spoon the batter in a 8x8-inch cake pan lined with baking paper.
- Make the cinnamon by mixing all the ingredients in a bowl until grainy. Spread the streusel over the cake and bake in the preheated oven at 350F for 40-45 minutes or until fragrant and golden brown.
- Allow the cake to cool in the pan before slicing and serving.

Nutritional information per serving

Calories: 309
Fat: 21.4g

Protein: 4.4g
Carbohydrates: 25.3g

 # ASPBERRY MATCHA CAKE

Time: 1 ¼ hours

Servings: 10

Ingredients:

1 ½ cups all-purpose flour
1 tablespoons matcha powder
2 teaspoons baking powder
½ teaspoon salt
2/3 cup butter, softened

2/3 cup white sugar
4 eggs
1 teaspoon vanilla extract
1 cup fresh raspberries

Directions:

- Sift the flour, matcha powder, baking powder and salt in a bowl.
- Mix the butter and sugar until fluffy and creamy.
- Add the eggs, one by one, and mix well after each addition. Stir in the vanilla then fold in the flour.
- Add the raspberries then spoon the batter in a loaf cake pan lined with baking paper.
- Bake in the preheated oven at 350F for 35-40 minutes or until the cake passes the toothpick test.
- Serve the cake chilled.

Nutritional information per serving

Calories: 262
Fat: 14.3g

Protein: 4.4g
Carbohydrates: 30.3g

 # ANANA BUNDT CAKE WITH PEANUT BUTTER FROSTING

Time: 1 ¼ hours

Servings: 12

Ingredients:

Cake:
1 cup canola oil
1 cup white sugar
2 eggs
1 teaspoon vanilla extract
1 cup buttermilk
2 ripe bananas, mashed

2 cups all-purpose flour
2 teaspoons baking powder
½ teaspoon salt
Frosting:
½ cup peanut butter, softened
½ cup cream cheese
½ cup powdered sugar

Directions:

- To make the cake, mix the oil and sugar in a bowl then stir in the eggs and vanilla. Mix well then add the buttermilk and bananas.
- Fold in the flour, baking powder and salt then spoon the batter in a greased Bundt cake pan.
- Bake in the preheated oven at 350F for 40-45 minutes or until the cake passes the toothpick test.
- Transfer the cake on a platter.
- For the frosting, mix the ingredients in a bowl until creamy.
- Cover the cake with peanut butter frosting and serve fresh.

Nutritional information per serving

Calories: 453

Fat: 28.1g

Protein: 7.4g   Carbohydrates: 45.9g

Chocolate Peanut Butter Bundt Cake

Time: 1 ¼ hours   Servings: 10

Ingredients:

1 cup butter, softened   1 ½ cups all-purpose flour
1 cup light brown sugar   ½ cup cocoa powder
1 teaspoon vanilla extract   1 teaspoon baking powder
3 eggs   1 teaspoon baking soda
1 cup sour cream   ½ teaspoon salt
¼ cup whole milk   2/3 cup smooth peanut butter

Directions:

- Mix the butter, sugar and vanilla in a bowl until fluffy and creamy.
- Add the eggs, one by one, then stir in the sour cream and milk.
- Fold in the flour, cocoa powder, baking powder, baking soda and salt.
- Spoon half of the batter in a greased Bundt cake pan. Top with spoonfuls of peanut butter then cover with the remaining batter.
- Bake in the preheated oven at 350F for 40-45 minutes or until the cake passes the toothpick test.
- Serve the cake chilled.

Nutritional information per serving

Calories: 470   Protein: 9.8g
Fat: 34.1g   Carbohydrates: 35.9g

Vanilla Cardamom Cake

Time: 1 ¼ hours   Servings: 12

Ingredients:

Cake: ½ cup canola oil
1 ½ cups all-purpose flour   Frosting:
1 teaspoon baking powder   ½ cup butter, softened
¼ teaspoon salt   1 cup cream cheese
1 teaspoon cardamom powder   1 ½ cups powdered sugar
6 eggs   1 teaspoon vanilla extract
1 cup white sugar

Directions:

- For the cake, sift the flour with baking powder, salt and cardamom.
- Mix the eggs with sugar until fluffy and pale.
- Add the oil and mix well then fold in the flour.
- Pour the batter in a 9-inch round cake pan lined with baking paper.
- Bake in the preheated oven at 350F for 40-45 minutes.
- When done, allow the cake to cool in the pan then cut it in half lengthwise.
- For the frosting, mix the butter and cream cheese in a bowl until fluffy. Add the vanilla and sugar and continue mixing for at least 5 minutes until pale.
- Use half of the frosting as filling and the other half to cover the cake.
- Serve the cake fresh.

Nutritional information per serving

Calories: 427
Fat: 25.9g
Protein: 5.9g
Carbohydrates: 44.6g

RENCH APPLE CAKE

Time: 1 ¼ hours

Servings: 8

Ingredients:

1 ½ cups all-purpose flour
1 teaspoon baking powder
¼ teaspoon salt
2 eggs
1 cup light brown sugar

¼ cup brandy
½ cup butter, softened
3 red apples, peeled, cored and sliced
½ teaspoon cinnamon powder

Directions:
- Sift the flour, baking powder and salt in a bowl.
- Mix the eggs, sugar, brandy and butter in a bowl until fluffy and pale.
- Fold in the flour then spoon the batter in a 8-inch round cake pan.
- Top with apple slices and bake in the preheated oven at 350F for 35-40 minutes or until golden brown and well risen.
- Serve the cake chilled.

Nutritional information per serving

Calories: 315
Fat: 12.9g

Protein: 4.1g
Carbohydrates: 45.5g

ATURAL RED VELVET CAKE

Time: 1 ¼ hours

Servings: 10

Ingredients:

Cake:
2 beetroots, peeled and pureed
½ cup canola oil
2 eggs
½ cup light brown sugar
¼ cup white sugar
1 ¼ cups all-purpose flour
1 teaspoon baking powder

½ teaspoon salt
2 tablespoons cornstarch
½ teaspoon cinnamon powder
Frosting:
¼ cup butter, softened
1 cup cream cheese
1 cup powdered sugar

Directions:
- For the cake, mix the beetroot puree, canola oil, eggs and sugar in a bowl.
- Stir in the rest of the ingredients and mix well.
- Pour the batter in a 8-inch round cake pan lined with baking paper.
- Bake in the preheated oven at 350F for 40 minutes.
- When done, allow the cake to cool in the pan then transfer the cake on a platter.
- For the frosting, mix all the ingredients in a bowl until fluffy.
- Cover the cake with the frosting and serve it fresh.

Nutritional information per serving

Calories: 395
Fat: 24.7g

Protein: 4.8g
Carbohydrates: 40.1g

ATCHA POUND CAKE

Time: 1 hour

Servings: 10

Ingredients:

1 cup all-purpose flour
¼ teaspoon salt
1 teaspoon baking powder

2 teaspoons matcha powder
4 eggs, separated
½ cup butter, softened

½ cup light brown sugar
1 teaspoon lemon zest

1 tablespoon lemon juice

Directions:
- Sift the flour, salt, baking powder and matcha powder in a bowl.
- Mix the butter with sugar until creamy and pale. Stir in the egg yolks and mix well. Add the lemon zest and lemon juice and give it a good mix.
- Fold in the flour.
- Whip the egg whites until fluffy and stiff. Fold the meringue into the cake batter.
- Pour the batter in a loaf cake pan lined with baking paper.
- Bake in the preheated oven at 350F for 40-45 minutes or until the cake passes the toothpick test.
- Serve the cake chilled.

Nutritional information per serving

Calories: 185
Fat: 11.1g

Protein: 3.6g
Carbohydrates: 18.1g

ROWN BUTTER WALNUT CAKE

Time: 1 ¼ hours

Servings: 12

Ingredients:

1 ½ cups white sugar
1 cup butter
2 eggs
1 cup sour cream
1 teaspoon vanilla extract

1 ½ cups all-purpose flour
1 teaspoon baking powder
½ teaspoon salt
1 cup ground walnuts
1 cup walnuts, chopped

Directions:
- Place the butter in a saucepan and melt it. Keep on heat until slightly browned and caramelized. Allow the butter to cool then transfer it in a bowl.
- Add the sugar and mix well.
- Stir in the eggs and mix well then add the sour cream and vanilla.
- Fold in the flour, baking powder, salt and ground walnuts.
- Spoon the batter in a 9-inch round cake pan and top with chopped walnuts.
- Bake in the preheated oven at 350F for 45 minutes or until the cake passes the toothpick test.
- Serve the cake chilled.

Nutritional information per serving

Calories: 468
Fat: 32.5g

Protein: 8.3g
Carbohydrates: 40.1g

VANILLA FUNFETTI CAKE

Time: 1 ½ hours

Servings: 12

Ingredients:

Cake:
1 cup butter, softened
1 cup white sugar
3 eggs
1 teaspoon vanilla extract
1 cup sour cream
2 cups all-purpose flour

1 ½ teaspoons baking powder
½ teaspoon salt
½ cup sprinkles
Frosting:
½ cup butter, softened
1 ½ cups powdered sugar
1 teaspoon vanilla extract

Directions:
- For the cake, mix the butter and sugar in a bowl until fluffy and creamy.
- Add the eggs and vanilla and mix well for a few minutes.
- Stir in the sour cream then fold in the flour, baking powder and salt, as well as sprinkles.

- Spoon the batter in a 9-inch round cake pan lined with baking paper.
- Bake in the preheated oven at 350F for 40-45 minutes or until well risen and golden brown.
- For the frosting, mix the butter, sugar and vanilla and mix well until fluffy and pale.
- Top the cake with frosting and serve it fresh.

Nutritional information per serving

Calories: 464
Fat: 28.3g
Protein: 4.4g
Carbohydrates: 50.0g

Cookies

Coconut Shortbread Cookies

Time: 2 hours

Servings: 20

Ingredients:

1 cup butter, softened
½ cup powdered sugar
1 teaspoon coconut extract
1 egg

2 cups all-purpose flour
¼ teaspoon salt
1 cup shredded coconut
¼ teaspoon baking powder

Directions:

- Mix the butter, sugar and coconut extract in a bowl.
- Stir in the egg and mix well then add the flour, salt, coconut and baking powder.
- Wrap the dough in a plastic wrap and place in the fridge for 30 minutes.
- Transfer the dough on a working surface and roll it into a thin sheet.
- Cut the dough into small cookies using your favorite cookie cutter.
- Place the cookies in a baking tray lined with baking paper.
- Bake in the preheated oven at 350F for 10-15 minutes or until golden brown on the edges.
- Serve them chilled.

Nutritional information per serving

Calories: 157
Fat: 10.9g

Protein: 1.8g
Carbohydrates: 13.2g

Cardamom Chocolate Chip Cookies

Time: 1 hour

Servings: 20

Ingredients:

1 cup butter, softened
½ cup light brown sugar
½ cup white sugar
2 eggs
2 ½ cups all-purpose flour

1 teaspoon baking powder
½ teaspoon salt
1 teaspoon cardamom powder
1 cup dark chocolate chips

Directions:

- Mix the butter and sugars in a bowl until creamy and fluffy.
- Stir in the eggs, one by one, then add the flour, salt, baking powder and cardamom powder.
- Fold in the chocolate chips then drop spoonfuls of batter on a baking sheet lined with baking paper.
- Bake in the preheated oven at 350F for 10-15 minutes.
- Allow the cookies to cool in the pan before serving.

Nutritional information per serving

Calories: 206
Fat: 11.4g

Protein: 2.7g
Carbohydrates: 24.7g

Peanut Butter Shortbread Cookies

Time: 2 hours

Servings: 25

Ingredients:

½ cup smooth peanut butter
½ cup butter, softened

½ cup powdered sugar
1 teaspoon vanilla extract

1 egg
1 tablespoon cocoa powder
1 ¾ cups all-purpose flour

½ teaspoon salt
½ teaspoon baking powder

Directions:
- Mix the peanut butter, butter, sugar and vanilla in a bowl until creamy and fluffy.
- Stir in the egg and mix well then add the cocoa powder, flour, salt and baking powder.
- Wrap the dough in plastic wrap and place in the fridge for 30 minutes.
- Transfer the dough on a floured working surface and roll it into a thin sheet.
- Cut small cookies with your favorite cookie cutter.
- Place the cookies in a baking sheet lined with baking paper.
- Bake in the preheated oven at 350F for 12-15 minutes until fragrant and golden.
- Serve the cookies chilled.

Nutritional information per serving
Calories: 108
Fat: 6.6g

Protein: 2.5g
Carbohydrates: 10.3g

COFFEE SHORTBREAD COOKIES

Time: 1 hour

Servings: 20

Ingredients:
½ cup butter, softened
½ cup powdered sugar
1 teaspoon vanilla extract
1 egg

2 cups all-purpose flour
½ teaspoon salt
½ teaspoon baking powder
2 teaspoons instant coffee

Directions:
- Mix the butter, sugar and vanilla and mix until smooth and fluffy.
- Add the egg and mix well then fold in the flour, salt, baking powder and coffee.
- Place the dough on a floured working surface and roll it into a thin sheet.
- Cut small cookies with your favorite cookie cutters and arrange the cookies on a baking sheet lined with baking paper.
- Bake the cookies in the preheated oven at 350F for 10-15 minutes or until fragrant and golden brown on the edges.
- Serve the cookies chilled or store them in an airtight container.

Nutritional information per serving
Calories: 102
Fat: 5.0g

Protein: 1.6g
Carbohydrates: 12.6g

BROWN BUTTER CHOCOLATE CHIP COOKIES

Time: 2 hours

Servings: 20

Ingredients:
1 ½ cups all-purpose flour
1 teaspoon baking powder
½ teaspoon baking soda
¼ teaspoon salt
½ cup butter

1 cup light brown sugar
1 egg
1 egg yolk
1 teaspoon vanilla extract
1 cup dark chocolate chips

Directions:
- Mix the flour, baking powder, baking soda and salt in a bowl.
- Melt the butter in a saucepan until it begins to look slightly golden brown and caramelized. Allow to cool then transfer in a bowl.
- Stir in the sugar, egg, egg yolk, vanilla and flour. Mix gently with a spatula.
- Fold in the chocolate chips then drop spoonfuls of dough on a baking sheet lined with baking paper.
- Freeze the cookies for 30 minutes then bake in the preheated oven at 350F for 15 minutes until golden brown.
- Serve chilled.

Nutritional information per serving
Calories: 137
Fat: 6.8g

Protein: 1.8g
Carbohydrates: 18.5g

EANUT BUTTER CHOCOLATE COOKIES

Time: 1 hour

Servings: 20

Ingredients:

¼ cup smooth peanut butter
¼ cup butter, softened
½ cup light brown sugar
1 egg
1 cup all-purpose flour

½ teaspoon baking soda
½ teaspoon baking powder
¼ teaspoon salt
½ cup chocolate chips

Directions:

- Mix the butters and sugar in a bowl until creamy and fluffy.
- Stir in the egg and mix well.
- Fold in the flour, baking soda, baking powder and salt.
- Add the chocolate chips then drop spoonfuls of batter on a baking sheet lined with baking paper.
- Bake the cookies in the preheated oven at 350F for 12-15 minutes or until golden brown.
- Allow the cookies to cool in the pan before serving.

Nutritional information per serving
Calories: 102
Fat: 5.5g

Protein: 2.1g
Carbohydrates: 11.5g

CHOCOLATE HAZELNUT COOKIES

Time: 1 ½ hours

Servings: 30

Ingredients:

1 cup butter, softened
½ cup cream cheese, softened
1 egg yolk
¼ teaspoon salt

1 ½ cups all-purpose flour
¼ cup cocoa powder
½ cup ground hazelnuts

Directions:

- Mix the butter, cream cheese and egg yolk in a bowl until creamy.
- Add the salt, flour, cocoa powder and hazelnuts and mix with a spatula.
- Wrap the plastic wrap and place in the fridge for 30 minutes.
- Transfer the dough on a floured working surface and roll it into a thin sheet.
- Cut small cookies using your favorite cookie cutters.
- Place the cookies in a baking sheet lined with baking paper and bake in the preheated oven at 350F for 10-12 minutes or until golden brown on the edges.
- Serve the cookies chilled.

Nutritional information per serving
Calories: 102
Fat: 8.6g

Protein: 1.4g
Carbohydrates: 5.5g

TOFFEE CHOCOLATE CHIP COOKIES

Time: 1 ¼ hours

Servings: 30

Ingredients:

2 ½ cups all-purpose flour

½ teaspoon salt

1 teaspoon baking powder
1 cup butter, softened
½ cup light brown sugar
¼ cup white sugar

2 eggs
1 cup chopped toffee pieces
½ cup dark chocolate chips

Directions:
- Mix the flour, salt and baking powder in a bowl.
- In a different bowl, combine the butter and sugars and mix well. Add the eggs and give it a good mix.
- Add the flour then fold in the toffee pieces and chocolate chips.
- Drop spoonfuls of batter on a baking sheet lined with baking paper.
- Bake the cookies in the preheated oven at 350F for 10-15 minutes or until golden brown on the edges.
- Serve the cookies chilled.

Nutritional information per serving
Calories: 129
Fat: 7.3g

Protein: 1.7g
Carbohydrates: 14.5g

*C*HOCOLATE **B**UTTERCREAM **C**OOKIES

Time: 1 ½ hours

Servings: 20

Ingredients:
Cookies:
2 cups all-purpose flour
½ cup cocoa powder
½ teaspoon salt
½ teaspoon baking powder
½ cup coconut oil
½ cup butter, softened

½ cup powdered sugar
1 egg
2 tablespoons whole milk
Filling:
½ cup butter, softened
1 cup powdered sugar

Directions:
- For the cookies, mix the flour, cocoa powder, salt and baking powder in a bowl.
- In a different bowl, mix the coconut oil, butter and sugar in a bowl until creamy and fluffy.
- Add the egg and mix well, then stir in the flour and the milk.
- Wrap the dough in plastic wrap and place in the fridge for 30 minutes.
- Transfer the dough on a floured working surface and roll into a thin sheet.
- Cut small round cookies and arrange them on a baking sheet.
- Bake in the preheated oven at 350F for 10-15 minutes.
- Allow the cookies to cool down completely.
- For the filling, mix the butter with sugar until fluffy and creamy.
- Fill the cookies, two by two with the buttercream.
- Serve fresh or store in an airtight container.

Nutritional information per serving
Calories: 218
Fat: 15.4g

Protein: 2.1g
Carbohydrates: 19.8g

O ATMEAL **C**OOKIES

Time: 1 hour

Servings: 30

Ingredients:
1 ½ cups all-purpose flour
1 cup rolled oats
½ teaspoon baking soda
½ teaspoon salt
½ cup dried cranberries
1 cup pecans, chopped

¾ cup butter, softened
½ cup light brown sugar
2 tablespoons dark brown sugar
1 egg
1 teaspoon vanilla extract

Directions:

- Mix the butter and sugars in a bowl until fluffy and creamy.
- Stir in the egg and vanilla and mix well.
- Fold in the rest of the ingredients.
- Drop spoonfuls of batter on a baking sheet lined with baking paper.
- Bake the cookies in the preheated oven at 350F for 15 minutes or until well risen and golden.
- Allow the cookies to cool in the pan before serving.

Nutritional information per serving

Calories: 92

Fat: 5.3g

Protein: 1.3g

Carbohydrates: 9.8g

COFFEE GINGERSNAP COOKIES

Time: 1 ¼ hours

Servings: 20

Ingredients:

½ cup butter, softened

¼ cup coconut oil

1 cup light brown sugar

1 egg

1 teaspoon vanilla extract

2 cups all-purpose flour

1 teaspoon baking soda

¼ teaspoon salt

1 teaspoon cinnamon powder

1 teaspoon ground ginger

½ teaspoon ground cardamom

2 teaspoons instant coffee

Directions:

- Mix the butter, coconut oil and brown sugar in a bowl until fluffy and creamy.
- Add the egg and vanilla and mix well.
- Fold in the rest of the ingredients then drop spoonfuls of batter on a baking sheet lined with baking paper.
- Bake in the preheated oven at 350F for 15 minutes or until fragrant and crisp.
- Serve the cookies chilled.

Nutritional information per serving

Calories: 142

Fat: 7.7g

Protein: 1.7g

Carbohydrates: 16.8g

VANILLA MALTED COOKIES

Time: 1 ¼ hours

Servings: 30

Ingredients:

2 ½ cups all-purpose flour

½ cup malted milk powder

1 teaspoon baking powder

½ teaspoon baking soda

½ teaspoon salt

1 cup butter, softened

½ cup cream cheese

1 cup white sugar

1 teaspoon vanilla extract

1 egg

½ cup white chocolate chips

Directions:

- Sift the flour, milk powder, baking powder, baking soda and salt.
- Mix the butter, cream cheese and sugar in a bowl until creamy and fluffy.
- Add the vanilla and egg and mix well.
- Fold in the flour mixture then add the chocolate chips.
- Drop spoonfuls of batter on a baking sheet lined with baking paper.
- Bake the cookies in the preheated oven at 350F for 10-15 minutes or until golden brown on the edges.
- Serve the cookies chilled.

Nutritional information per serving

Calories: 161

Fat: 8.8g

Protein: 2.1g   Carbohydrates: 19.0g

EANUT BUTTER NUTELLA COOKIES

Time: 1 ¼ hours   Servings: 20

Ingredients:

½ cup peanut butter, softened   1 ½ cups all-purpose flour
¼ cup butter, softened   ½ teaspoon baking soda
½ cup dark brown sugar   ½ teaspoon baking powder
1 egg   ¼ teaspoon salt
1 teaspoon vanilla extract   ½ cup Nutella

Directions:

- Mix the butter, peanut butter and sugar in a bowl until creamy and fluffy.
- Add the egg and vanilla and give it a good mix.
- Fold in the flour, baking soda, baking powder and salt.
- Add the Nutella and swirl it into the batter.
- Drop spoonfuls of batter on a baking sheet lined with baking paper.
- Bake the cookies in the preheated oven at 350F for 15 minutes or until golden brown on the edges.
- Serve the cookies chilled.

Nutritional information per serving

Calories: 120   Protein: 3.0g
Fat: 6.5g   Carbohydrates: 13.2g

HONEY LEMON COOKIES

Time: 1 ¼ hours   Servings: 40

Ingredients:

3 cups all-purpose flour   ¾ cup white sugar
1 teaspoon baking soda   ¼ cup honey
½ teaspoon salt   1 lemon, zested and juiced
1 cup butter, softened   1 egg

Directions:

- Sift the flour, baking soda and salt in a bowl.
- In a different bowl, mix the butter, sugar and honey and mix well.
- Stir in the lemon zest and juice, as well as the egg.
- Fold in the flour mixture then roll the dough into a thin sheet over a floured working surface.
- Cut the cookies with your favorite cookie cutters.
- Place the cookies in the preheated oven at 350F for 10-15 minutes or until golden brown on the edges.
- Serve the cookies chilled.

Nutritional information per serving

Calories: 97   Protein: 1.2g
Fat: 4.8g   Carbohydrates: 12.8g

BUTTER VANILLA COOKIES

Time: 1 hour   Servings: 30

Ingredients:

2 cups all-purpose flour   ½ cup powdered sugar
¼ cup cornstarch   1 cup butter, softened
¼ teaspoon salt   1 egg

1 tablespoon vanilla extract

Directions:
- Mix the butter and sugar in a bowl until fluffy and creamy.
- Add the egg and vanilla and mix well.
- Fold in the flour, cornstarch and salt and mix well.
- Drop spoonfuls of batter on a baking sheet lined with baking paper.
- Bake in the preheated oven at 350F for 10-15 minutes or until golden brown on the edges.
- Serve the cookies chilled.

Nutritional information per serving

Calories: 100

Fat: 6.4g

Protein: 1.1g

Carbohydrates: 9.4g

*F*UDGY CHOCOLATE COOKIES

Time: 1 ¼ hours

Servings: 30

Ingredients:

1 ½ cups dark chocolate chips

½ cup butter

2 eggs

½ cup light brown sugar

2 tablespoons white sugar

1 teaspoon vanilla extract

2/3 cup all-purpose flour

1 teaspoon baking powder

¼ teaspoon salt

Directions:
- Melt the butter and chocolate in a heatproof bowl over a hot water bath.
- Mix the eggs and sugars in a bowl until fluffy and pale.
- Stir in the chocolate and mix with a spatula.
- Fold in the flour, baking powder and salt then drop spoonfuls of batter in a baking sheet lined with baking paper.
- Bake the cookies in the preheated oven at 350F for 12-14 minutes.
- Serve the cookies chilled.

Nutritional information per serving

Calories: 82

Fat: 5.0g

Protein: 1.1g

Carbohydrates: 9.4g

*T*RIPLE CHOCOLATE COOKIES

Time: 1 ¼ hours

Servings: 30

Ingredients:

1 cup butter, softened

1 cup light brown sugar

½ cup dark chocolate chips, melted

2 eggs

1 teaspoon vanilla extract

2 tablespoons whole milk

2 cups all-purpose flour

¼ cup cocoa powder

1 ½ teaspoons baking powder

¼ teaspoon baking soda

¼ teaspoon salt

½ cup dark chocolate chips

Directions:
- Mix the butter and sugar in a bowl until fluffy and pale.
- Add the melted chocolate, eggs and vanilla, as well as the milk.
- Fold in the flour, cocoa powder, baking powder, baking soda and salt then add the chocolate chips.
- Drop spoonfuls of batter on a baking sheet lined with baking paper.
- Bake the cookies in the preheated oven at 350F for 10-15 minutes or until the cookies are golden brown on the edges.
- Serve the cookies chilled.

Nutritional information per serving

Calories: 129

Fat: 7.7g

Protein: 1.7g   Carbohydrates: 14.4g

ASPBERRY JAM COOKIES

Time: 2 hours   Servings: 20

Ingredients:

½ cup butter, softened   1 ¼ cups all-purpose flour
½ cup powdered sugar   ¼ teaspoon salt
1 egg   ½ teaspoon baking powder
2 tablespoons whole milk   ½ cup seedless raspberry jam
1 cup almond flour

Directions:

- Mix the butter and sugar in a bowl until fluffy and creamy.
- Stir in the egg and milk and mix well then fold in the flours, salt and baking powder.
- Transfer the dough on a floured working surface and roll it into a thin sheet.
- Cut 40 small cookies.
- Bake the cookies in the preheated oven at 350F for 12-15 minutes.
- When done, chill the cookies and fill them two by two with raspberry jam.
- Serve right away.

Nutritional information per serving

Calories: 115   Protein: 1.5g
Fat: 5.7g   Carbohydrates: 14.9g

C ORNFLAKE CHOCOLATE CHIP COOKIES

Time: 1 hour   Servings: 20

Ingredients:

½ cup butter, softened   ½ teaspoon baking soda
¾ cup white sugar   2/4 teaspoon salt
1 teaspoon vanilla extract   1 cup cornflakes
1 egg   ½ cup dark chocolate chips
1 ¼ cup all-purpose flour

Directions:

- Mix the butter, sugar and vanilla in a bowl until creamy and pale.
- Add the egg then mix in the flour, baking soda and salt.
- Fold in the cornflakes and chocolate chips.
- Drop spoonfuls of batter on a baking sheet lined with baking paper.
- Bake the cookies in the preheated oven at 350F for 10-15 minutes or until golden brown on the edges.
- Serve the cookies chilled.

Nutritional information per serving

Calories: 120   Protein: 1.4g
Fat: 5.7g   Carbohydrates: 16.7g

INGERBREAD COOKIES

Time: 1 ¼ hours   Servings: 30

Ingredients:

1 cup butter, softened   2 tablespoons dark molasses
½ cup golden syrup   1 egg
½ cup white sugar   2 cups all-purpose flour

1 teaspoon ground ginger
1 teaspoon cinnamon powder
½ teaspoon ground cardamom

1 teaspoon baking soda
¼ teaspoon salt

Directions:
- Mix the butter, golden syrup, sugar and molasses in a bowl until fluffy and pale.
- Add the egg and mix well then fold in the flour, spices, baking soda and salt.
- Form small balls of dough and place them on a baking sheet lined with baking paper.
- Bake in the preheated oven at 350F for 15 minutes or until fragrant and golden.
- Serve the cookies chilled.

Nutritional information per serving
Calories: 119
Fat: 6.4g

Protein: 1.1g
Carbohydrates: 15.0g

 # LMOND COOKIES

Time: 1 ¼ hours

Servings: 20

Ingredients:
½ cup butter, softened
2/3 cup white sugar
1 teaspoon almond extract
2 egg yolks
1 ½ cups all-purpose flour

½ cup almond flour
¼ teaspoon salt
1 teaspoon baking powder
½ cup sliced almonds

Directions:
- Mix the butter, sugar and almond extract in a bowl until fluffy and pale.
- Add the egg yolks and give it a good mix.
- Fold in the flours, salt and baking powder.
- Drop spoonfuls of batter on a baking sheet lined with baking paper.
- Top each cookie with sliced almonds and bake in the preheated oven at 350F for 10-15 minutes until golden brown on the edges.
- Serve the cookies chilled.

Nutritional information per serving
Calories: 124
Fat: 6.7g

Protein: 1.9g
Carbohydrates: 14.7g

 # PRICOT COCONUT COOKIES

Time: 1 ½ hours

Servings: 25

Ingredients:
1 cup all-purpose flour
1 cup shredded coconut
½ cup rolled oats
½ cup dried apricots, chopped
½ teaspoon baking soda
¼ teaspoon salt

½ cup butter, softened
¼ cup light brown sugar
½ cup white sugar
1 teaspoon vanilla extract
2 eggs
½ cup dark chocolate chips

Directions:
- Mix the flour, coconut, oats, apricots, salt and baking soda in a bowl.
- In a different bowl, combine the butter and the sugars and vanilla and mix well.
- Fold in the flour mixture and the chocolate chips.
- Drop spoonful of batter on a baking sheet lined with baking paper.
- Bake in the preheated oven at 350F for 10-15 minutes or until golden brown on the edges.
- Allow the cookies to cool before serving.

Nutritional information per serving

Calories: 107
Fat: 5.9g

Protein: 1.5g
Carbohydrates: 12.8g

D RIED CRANBERRY OATMEAL COOKIES

Time: 1 ¼ hours

Servings: 20

Ingredients:

1 cup rolled oats
1 cup all-purpose flour
1 teaspoon baking soda
½ cup dried cranberries
½ cup butter, softened, melted

4 tablespoons golden syrup
½ cup light brown sugar
½ teaspoon cinnamon powder
½ teaspoon ground ginger
¼ teaspoon salt

Directions:

- Mix the oats, flour, baking soda, spices, salt and cranberries in a bowl.
- Stir in the butter, golden syrup and sugar and mix well.
- Form small balls for dough and place the balls on a baking sheet lined with baking paper.
- Flatten the cookies slightly and bake in the preheated oven at 350F for 15 minutes or until golden brown and fragrant.
- Serve the cookies chilled.

Nutritional information per serving

Calories: 106
Fat: 4.9g

Protein: 1.2g
Carbohydrates: 14.5g

C ANDY CANE CHOCOLATE COOKIES

Time: 1 ¼ hours

Servings: 20

Ingredients:

½ cup butter, softened
2 tablespoons canola oil
2/3 cup light brown sugar
1 teaspoon vanilla extract
1 egg
1 cup all-purpose flour

¼ cup cocoa powder
¼ cup shredded coconut
½ teaspoon baking soda
¼ teaspoon salt
½ cup crushed candy cane cookies

Directions:

- Mix the butter, canola oil, sugar and vanilla in a bowl until fluffy and creamy.
- Stir in the egg then add the flour, cocoa powder, coconut, baking soda and salt.
- Fold in the crushed candy then drop spoonfuls of batter on a baking sheet lined with baking paper.
- Bake the cookies in the preheated oven at 350F for 10-15 minutes or until fragrant and risen.
- Serve the cookies chilled.

Nutritional information per serving

Calories: 108
Fat: 7.0g

Protein: 1.3g
Carbohydrates: 10.8g

M APLE SESAME COOKIES

Time: 1 ½ hours

Servings: 25

Ingredients:

½ cup butter, softened
½ cup maple syrup
1 egg

2 tablespoons dark brown sugar
1 ½ cups all-purpose flour
¼ teaspoon salt

1 teaspoon baking powder ¼ cup sesame seeds

Directions:
- Mix the butter, maple syrup and egg in a bowl until creamy and pale.
- Stir in the sugar and mix well then add the flour, salt, baking powder and sesame seeds.
- Spoon the batter in a plastic wrap and shape it into a log. Place in the freezer for 30 minutes.
- Remove from the freezer and cut into thin slices. Arrange the slices on a baking sheet lined with baking paper with the cut facing up.
- Bake in the preheated oven at 350F for 10-12 minutes or until slightly golden brown on the edges.
- Serve the cookies chilled.

Nutritional information per serving

Calories: 90

Fat: 4.6g

Protein: 1.3g

Carbohydrates: 11.1g

Chocolate Chunk Cookies

Time: 1 ¼ hours

Servings: 20

Ingredients:

½ cup butter, softened

2 tablespoons honey

2/3 cup light brown sugar

1 egg

1 ½ cups all-purpose flour

1 teaspoon baking powder

¼ teaspoon salt

4 oz. dark chocolate, chopped

Directions:
- Mix the butter, honey and sugar in a bowl until fluffy and pale.
- Add the egg and mix well then stir in the flour, baking powder and salt.
- Fold in the chocolate then drop spoonfuls of dough on a baking sheet lined with baking paper.
- Bake the cookies in the preheated oven at 350F for 15 minutes or until golden brown on the edges.
- Serve the cookies chilled.

Nutritional information per serving

Calories: 133

Fat: 6.6g

Protein: 1.8g

Carbohydrates: 17.1g

Chocolate Dipped Sugar Cookies

Time: 1 ¼ hours

Servings: 30

Ingredients:

1 cup butter, softened

1 cup powdered sugar

2 egg yolks

1 teaspoon vanilla extract

3 cups all-purpose flour

1 teaspoon baking powder

¼ teaspoon salt

1 cup dark chocolate, melted

Directions:
- Mix the butter and sugar in a bowl until pale and fluffy.
- Stir in the egg yolks and vanilla and mix well.
- Fold in the flour, baking powder and salt then wrap the dough in plastic wrap and place in the fridge for 30 minutes.
- Transfer the dough on a floured working surface and roll into a thin sheet.
- Cut cookies with your favorite cookie cutters and place them on a baking sheet lined with baking paper.
- Bake in the preheated oven at 350F for 10-14 minutes or until slightly golden brown on the edges.
- When done, allow the cookies to cool then dip them in melted chocolate.
- Serve the cookies chilled.

Nutritional information per serving

Calories: 149

Fat: 8.2g

Protein: 2.0g

Carbohydrates: 17.0g

OFT CHOCOLATE CHIP COOKIES

Time: 1 ¼ hours

Servings: 20

Ingredients:

½ cup butter, softened
1 cup light brown sugar
2 eggs
2 cups all-purpose flour

1 teaspoon baking powder
½ teaspoon salt
1 cup dark chocolate chips

Directions:
- Mix the butter and sugar in a bowl until fluffy and pale.
- Add the eggs, one by one, mixing well after each addition.
- Fold in the rest of the ingredients then drop spoonfuls of batter on a baking sheet lined with baking paper.
- Bake in the preheated oven at 350F for 10-15 minutes or until golden brown on the edges.
- Serve the cookies chilled.

Nutritional information per serving

Calories: 148
Fat: 6.8g

Protein: 2.3g
Carbohydrates: 20.8g

LIVE OIL CHOCOLATE CHIP COOKIES

Time: 1 ¼ hours

Servings: 30

Ingredients:

½ cup olive oil
¼ cup butter, softened
½ cup light brown sugar
¼ cup white sugar
1 teaspoon vanilla extract
1 egg

2 cups all-purpose flour
¼ teaspoon salt
1 teaspoon baking powder
½ cup dark chocolate chips
½ cup white chocolate chips

Directions:
- Mix the oil, butter and sugars in a bowl until creamy and fluffy.
- Add the vanilla and egg and mix well.
- Fold in the flour, salt and baking powder, then add the chocolate chips.
- Drop spoonfuls of batter on a baking sheet lined with baking paper.
- Bake in the preheated oven at 350F for 10-15 minutes or until golden brown on the edges.
- Serve the cookies chilled.

Nutritional information per serving

Calories: 115
Fat: 6.6g

Protein: 1.4g
Carbohydrates: 13.5g

OUBLE CHOCOLATE COOKIES

Time: 1 ½ hours

Servings: 30

Ingredients:

2/3 cup butter, softened
1 cup white sugar
1 egg
1 teaspoon vanilla extract
1 ½ cups all-purpose flour
½ cup cocoa powder
¼ teaspoon salt

½ teaspoon baking powder
½ cup mini chocolate chips

Directions:

- Mix the butter and sugar until fluffy and creamy.
- Add the egg and vanilla and mix well then fold in the rest of the ingredients and mix well.
- Wrap the dough in plastic wrap and place in the fridge for 30 minutes.
- Transfer the dough on a floured working surface and roll it into a thin sheet.
- Cut small cookies with your favorite cookie cutters and arrange them on a baking pan lined with baking paper.
- Bake in the preheated oven at 350F for 10-15 minutes.
- Serve the cookies chilled.

Nutritional information per serving

Calories: 93

Fat: 4.6g

Protein: 1.2g

Carbohydrates: 12.8g

COLORFUL CHOCOLATE COOKIES

Time: 1 ¼ hors

Servings: 30

Ingredients:

1 cup butter, softened

1 cup light brown sugar

1 teaspoon vanilla extract

1 egg

2 cups all-purpose flour

½ cup cocoa powder

1 teaspoon baking powder

½ teaspoon salt

½ cup M&M candies

½ cup crushed candy cane cookies

Directions:

- Mix the butter, sugar and vanilla and mix well until fluffy and pale.
- Stir in the egg and mix well then add the rest of the ingredients.
- Drop spoonfuls of batter on a baking tray lined with baking paper.
- Bake in the preheated oven at 350F for 10-15 minutes.
- Allow the cookies to cool in the pan before serving.

Nutritional information per serving

Calories: 129

Fat: 7.4g

Protein: 1.5g

Carbohydrates: 14.8g

MINTY CHOCOLATE COOKIES

Time: 1 ¼ hours

Servings: 20

Ingredients:

½ cup butter, softened

½ cup white sugar

2 tablespoons honey

1 egg

1 teaspoon vanilla extract

1 teaspoon peppermint extract

1 ¼ cups all-purpose flour

¼ cup cocoa powder

¼ teaspoon salt

1 teaspoon baking powder

Directions:

- Mix the butter, sugar, honey, peppermint and vanilla in a bowl until fluffy and pale.
- Add the egg and mix well then fold in the rest of the ingredients.
- Drop spoonfuls of batter on a baking sheet lined with baking paper.
- Bake the cookies in the preheated oven at 350F for 10-15 minutes or until fragrant and well risen.
- Serve the cookies chilled.

Nutritional information per serving

Calories: 101

Fat: 5.0g

Protein: 1.4g

Carbohydrates: 13.5g

ℛ AINBOW COOKIES

Time: 1 ¼ hours

Servings: 25

Ingredients:

½ cup butter, softened
¼ cup coconut oil, melted
1 cup white sugar
1 egg
1 teaspoon vanilla extract

1 ½ cups all-purpose flour
¼ teaspoon salt
1 teaspoon baking powder
½ cup colorful sprinkles

Directions:

- Mix the butter, coconut oil and sugar in a bowl until fluffy and pale.
- Stir in the egg and vanilla and mix well.
- Fold in the flour, salt and baking powder then add the sprinkles.
- Drop spoonfuls of batter on a baking sheet lined with baking paper.
- Bake in the preheated oven at 350F for 10-15 minutes or until golden brown on the edges.
- Serve the cookies chilled.

Nutritional information per serving

Calories: 118
Fat: 6.3g

Protein: 1.1g
Carbohydrates: 14.8g

𝒞 HOCOLATE SANDWICH COOKIES WITH PASSIONFRUIT GANACHE

Time: 2 hours

Servings: 30

Ingredients:

Cookies:
2 cups all-purpose flour
½ cup cocoa powder
1 teaspoon baking powder
½ teaspoon salt
2/3 cup butter, softened
1 cup white sugar

1 egg
1 teaspoon vanilla extract
Passionfruit ganache:
1 cup white chocolate chips
½ cup heavy cream
¼ cup passionfruit juice
2 tablespoons butter

Directions:

- For the cookies, mix the flour, cocoa powder, baking powder and salt in a bowl.
- In a different bowl, mix the butter and sugar until fluffy and pale.
- Stir in the egg and vanilla and mix well then fold in the flour.
- Transfer the dough on a floured working surface and roll it into a thin sheet.
- Cut 40 small cookies using a round cookie cutter and place them on a baking sheet lined with baking paper.
- For the ganache, bring the cream to the boiling point. Stir in the chocolate and mix until melted. Add the passionfruit juice and butter and mix well. Allow to cool in the fridge.
- Fill the cookies with chilled ganache.

Nutritional information per serving

Calories: 143
Fat: 7.8g

Protein: 1.7g
Carbohydrates: 17.6g

𝒮 PICED CHOCOLATE COOKIES

Time: 1 ¼ hours

Servings: 20

Ingredients:

½ cup butter, softened
½ cup dark brown sugar

2 tablespoons honey
1 egg

1 ¼ cups all-purpose flour
¼ cup cocoa powder
¼ teaspoon salt

½ teaspoon baking powder
1 teaspoon all-spice powder

Directions:
- Mix the butter, brown sugar and honey in a bowl until creamy and fluffy.
- Add the egg and mix well then fold in the flour, cocoa powder, salt, baking powder and all-spice powder.
- Transfer the dough on a floured working surface and roll it into a thin sheet.
- Cut the dough with your favorite cookie cutters and transfer the cookies on a baking sheet lined with baking paper.
- Bake in the preheated oven at 350F for 12 minutes.
- Serve the cookies chilled.

Nutritional information per serving

Calories: 95
Fat: 5.0g

Protein: 1.4g
Carbohydrates: 11.9g

Chocolate Drizzled Lavender Cookies

Time: 1 ½ hours

Servings: 20

Ingredients:
½ cup butter, softened
½ cup powdered sugar
1 egg
1 egg yolk
2 tablespoons whole milk
1 ½ cups all-purpose flour

¼ cup cornstarch
¼ teaspoon baking soda
¼ teaspoon salt
1 teaspoon lavender buds
½ cup white chocolate chips, melted

Directions:
- Mix the butter with sugar in a bowl until fluffy and pale.
- Stir in the egg and egg yolk and mix well.
- Add the milk and mix then fold in the rest of the ingredients. Mix the dough then transfer it on a floured working surface and roll it into a thin sheet.
- Cut small cookies with your favorite cookie cutters.
- Arrange the cookies on a baking sheet lined with baking paper.
- Bake in the preheated oven at 350F for 10-15 minutes or until golden brown on the edges.
- When done, allow to cool in the pan then drizzle the cookies with melted chocolate.
- Serve chilled.

Nutritional information per serving

Calories: 122
Fat: 6.6g

Protein: 1.7g
Carbohydrates: 14.2g

Custard Powder Cookies

Time: 1 ¼ hours

Servings: 20

Ingredients:
½ cup butter, softened
½ cup white sugar
¼ cup whole milk
1 teaspoon vanilla extract

1 ½ cups all-purpose flour
½ cup vanilla custard powder
1 teaspoon baking powder
¼ teaspoon salt

Directions:
- Mix the butter and sugar in a bowl until creamy and fluffy.
- Stir in the milk and vanilla then fold in the rest of the ingredients.
- Drop spoonfuls of batter on a baking sheet lined with baking paper.
- Bake the cookies in the preheated oven at 350F for 10-15 minutes or until golden brown on the edges.
- Serve the cookies chilled.

Nutritional information per serving

Calories: 115
Fat: 4.8g

Protein: 1.1g
Carbohydrates: 17.3g

Confetti Cookies

Time: 1 ¼ hours

Servings: 20

Ingredients:

2/3 cup butter, softened
2/3 cup white sugar
1 teaspoon vanilla extract
1 egg

2 cups all-purpose flour
1 teaspoon baking powder
¼ teaspoon salt
½ cup colorful sprinkles

Directions:
- Mix the butter with sugar and vanilla in a bowl until creamy and fluffy.
- Stir in the egg and mix well then fold in the rest of the ingredients.
- Drop in the sprinkles and mix with a spatula.
- Drop spoonfuls of batter on a baking sheet lined with baking paper.
- Bake in the preheated oven at 350F for 10-15 minutes or until golden brown on the edges.
- Serve the cookies chilled.

Nutritional information per serving

Calories: 136
Fat: 6.7g

Protein: 1.7g
Carbohydrates: 17.5g

Rice Flour Cookies

Time: 1 hour

Servings: 20

Ingredients:

½ cup butter, softened
1/3 cup white sugar
1 teaspoon vanilla extract
1 egg
½ cup all-purpose flour

½ cup rice flour
1 teaspoon baking powder
¼ teaspoon cardamom powder
¼ teaspoon salt

Directions:
- Mix the butter, sugar and vanilla and mix until fluffy.
- Add the egg and mix well then fold in the rest of the ingredients.
- Drop spoonfuls of batter on a baking sheet lined with baking paper.
- Bake the cookies in the preheated oven at 350F for 10-15 minutes or until golden brown on the edges.
- Serve the cookies chilled.

Nutritional information per serving

Calories: 83
Fat: 4.9g

Protein: 0.9g
Carbohydrates: 9.1g

Honey Cornflake Cookies

Time: 1 ¼ hours

Servings: 20

Ingredients:

2/3 cup butter, softened
½ cup honey
½ cup light brown sugar
1 egg

1 teaspoon vanilla extract
1 ¾ cups all-purpose flour
¼ teaspoon salt
1 teaspoon baking powder

1 cup cornflakes

2 tablespoons pine nuts

Directions:
- Mix the butter, honey and sugar in a bowl.
- Stir in the egg and vanilla and mix well then fold in the rest of the ingredients.
- Drop spoonfuls of batter on a baking sheet lined with baking paper.
- Bake in the preheated oven at 350F for 12-15 minutes or until golden brown on the edges.
- Serve the cookies chilled.

Nutritional information per serving

Calories: 148

Fat: 7.1g

Protein: 1.7g

Carbohydrates: 20.4g

M ARSHMALLOW CHOCOLATE CHIP COOKIES

Time: 1 ¼ hours

Servings: 20

Ingredients:

½ cup butter, softened

2 tablespoons coconut oil

¾ cup light brown sugar

1 teaspoon vanilla extract

2 tablespoons whole milk

1 ½ cups all-purpose flour

½ teaspoon baking soda

¼ teaspoon salt

½ cup cornflakes

½ cup dark chocolate chips

1 cup mini marshmallows

Directions:
- Mix the butter, coconut oil, sugar and vanilla in a bowl until pale and fluffy.
- Stir in the milk then add the flour, baking soda and salt then fold in the cornflakes, chocolate chips and marshmallows.
- Drop spoonfuls of batter on a baking sheet lined with baking paper.
- Bake the cookies in the preheated oven at 350F for 10-15 minutes or until golden brown on the edges.
- Serve the cookies chilled.

Nutritional information per serving

Calories: 130

Fat: 6.9g

Protein: 1.3g

Carbohydrates: 16.3g

B ANANA CHOCOLATE COOKIES

Time: 1 ¼ hours

Servings: 20

Ingredients:

¼ cup butter, softened

¼ cup coconut oil, melted

2/3 cup white sugar

2 bananas, mashed

1 ¾ cups all-purpose flour

¼ teaspoon baking soda

½ teaspoon baking powder

¼ teaspoon salt

¼ cup cocoa powder

½ cup walnuts, chopped

Directions:
- Mix the butter, oil and sugar in a bowl until creamy and fluffy.
- Stir in the bananas then fold in the flour, baking soda, baking powder, salt and cocoa powder.
- Add the walnuts then drop spoonfuls of batter on a baking sheet lined with baking paper.
- Bake the cookies in the preheated oven at 350F for 15 minutes or until fragrant.
- Serve the cookies chilled.

Nutritional information per serving

Calories: 141

Fat: 7.2g

Protein: 2.2g

Carbohydrates: 18.7g

ATE PECAN GINGER COOKIES

Time: 1 ½ hours

Servings: 30

Ingredients:

1 cup dates, pitted and chopped
1 cup pecans, chopped
1 cup light brown sugar
½ cup olive oil
1 egg
1 teaspoon vanilla extract

1 teaspoon grated ginger
½ cup whole wheat flour
1 cup all-purpose flour
1 teaspoon baking powder
¼ teaspoon salt

Directions:

• Mix the oil and sugar in a bowl until fluffy and pale.
• Add the vanilla and ginger and mix well then fold in the flours, baking powder and salt.
• Stir in the dates and pecans then drop spoonfuls of batter on a baking sheet lined with baking paper.
• Bake the cookies in the preheated oven at 350F for 15 minutes or until golden brown on the edges.
• Serve the cookies chilled.

Nutritional information per serving

Calories: 93
Fat: 3.9g

Protein: 1.0g
Carbohydrates: 14.2g

GINGER CHOCOLATE OATMEAL COOKIES

Time: 1 ¼ hours

Servings: 30

Ingredients:

2/3 cup butter, softened
1 cup light brown sugar
1 egg
1 teaspoon grated ginger
½ teaspoon cinnamon powder

1 cup all-purpose flour
1 cup rolled oats
2 tablespoons cocoa powder
½ teaspoon baking soda
¼ teaspoon salt

Directions:

• Mix the butter and sugar until fluffy and creamy. Stir in the egg and mix well.
• Add the rest of the ingredients and mix with a spatula.
• Drop spoonfuls of batter on a baking sheet lined with baking paper.
• Bake in the preheated oven at 350F for 15 minutes.
• Serve the cookies chilled.

Nutritional information per serving

Calories: 83
Fat: 4.5g

Protein: 1.1g
Carbohydrates: 10.0g

EGGLESS COOKIES

Time: 1 hour

Servings: 20

Ingredients:

1 ½ cups all-purpose flour
¼ teaspoon salt
½ teaspoon baking soda
½ cup light brown sugar

½ cup butter, melted
¼ cup whole milk
½ cup dried cranberries

Directions:

• Mix the flour, salt, baking soda and sugar in a bowl.

- Stir in the butter and milk and mix with a spatula.
- Fold in the cranberries then drop spoonfuls of batter on a baking sheet lined with baking paper.
- Bake in the preheated oven at 350F for 10-15 minutes or until golden brown on the edges.
- Serve the cookies chilled.

Nutritional information per serving

Calories: 92

Fat: 4.8g

Protein: 1.1g

Carbohydrates: 11.1g

M UESLI COOKIES

Time: 1 ¼ hours

Servings: 20

Ingredients:

½ cup butter, softened

½ cup white sugar

1 egg

1 cup all-purpose flour

1 teaspoon baking powder

¼ teaspoon salt

1 cup muesli

½ cup white chocolate chips

Directions:
- Mix the butter and sugar until fluffy and creamy. Add the egg and mix well.
- Stir in the flour, baking powder and salt then add the muesli and chocolate chips.
- Drop spoonfuls of batter on a baking sheet lined with baking paper.
- Bake the cookies in the preheated oven at 350F for 15 minutes or until golden brown on the edges.
- Serve the cookies chilled.

Nutritional information per serving

Calories: 124

Fat: 6.5g

Protein: 1.6g

Carbohydrates: 15.6g

M OLTEN CHOCOLATE COOKIES

Time: 1 hour

Servings: 20

Ingredients:

2/3 cup butter, melted

1 cup light brown sugar

¼ cup white sugar

1 egg

1 egg yolk

1 ¾ cups all-purpose flour

¼ cup cocoa powder

½ teaspoon baking soda

¼ teaspoon salt

Directions:
- Mix the butter, sugars, egg and egg yolk in bowl until creamy and fluffy.
- Add the rest of the ingredients then drop large spoonfuls of batter on a baking sheet lined with baking paper.
- Bake in the preheated oven at 350F for 12 minutes.
- Serve the cookies chilled.

Nutritional information per serving

Calories: 139

Fat: 6.8g

Protein: 1.8g

Carbohydrates: 18.6g

M ILKY COOKIES

Time: 1 ¼ hours

Servings: 30

Ingredients:

1 cup butter, softened

1 cup white sugar

1 teaspoon vanilla extract

1 teaspoon lemon zest

2 egg yolks
¼ cup whole milk
2 cups all-purpose flour

¼ cup milk powder
1 teaspoon baking powder
¼ teaspoon salt

Directions:
- Mix the butter, sugar, vanilla and lemon zest in a bowl until fluffy and pale.
- Add the egg yolks and milk and mix well then stir in the flour, milk powder, baking powder and salt.
- Drop spoonfuls of batter on a baking tray lined with baking paper.
- Bake in the preheated oven at 350F for 12-15 minutes or until golden brown on the edges.
- Allow the cookies to cool before serving.

Nutritional information per serving

Calories: 119
Fat: 6.6g

Protein: 1.6g
Carbohydrates: 13.8g

ℳ &M Cookies

Time: 1 ¼ hours

Servings: 30

Ingredients:

1 cup butter, softened
2/3 cup light brown sugar
2 eggs
2 cups all-purpose flour

1 teaspoon baking powder
¼ teaspoon salt
1 cup M&M candies

Directions:
- Mix the butter and sugar in a bowl until creamy and fluffy.
- Stir in the eggs, one by one, then add the flour, baking powder and salt.
- Fold in the candies then drop spoonfuls of batter on a baking tray lined with baking paper.
- Bake the cookies in the preheated oven at 350F for 15 minutes or until golden brown on the edges.
- Serve the cookies chilled.

Nutritional information per serving

Calories: 102
Fat: 6.5g

Protein: 1.3g
Carbohydrates: 9.8g

𝒫 ecan Marshmallow Cookies

Time: 1 ½ hours

Servings: 30

Ingredients:

2/3 cup butter
1 cup white sugar
1 teaspoon vanilla extract
1 egg
2 ¼ cups all-purpose flour

1 teaspoon baking powder
¼ teaspoon salt
1 cup pecans, chopped
1 cup mini marshmallows

Directions:
- Mix the butter and sugar in a bowl until fluffy and creamy.
- Stir in the vanilla and egg then add the flour, salt and baking powder.
- Fold in the pecans and marshmallows then drop spoonfuls of batter on a baking sheet lined with baking paper.
- Bake in the preheated oven at 350F for 10-15 minutes or until golden brown on the edges.
- Serve the cookies chilled.

Nutritional information per serving

Calories: 104
Fat: 4.7g
Protein: 1.2g
Carbohydrates: 14.7g

P OLENTA COOKIES

Time: 1 ¼ hours

Servings: 30

Ingredients:

1 ¾ cups all-purpose flour
1 cup polenta flour
½ teaspoon salt
1 teaspoon baking powder
1 cup butter, softened

½ cup light brown sugar
¼ cup dark brown sugar
1 egg
1 egg yolk
1 teaspoon vanilla extract

Directions:

- Mix the flours, salt and baking powder in a bowl.
- In a different bowl, mix the butter and sugars in a bowl until fluffy and pale.
- Add the egg and egg yolk, as well as the vanilla and mix well.
- Stir in the flour then drop spoonfuls of batter on a baking sheet lined with baking paper.
- Bake in the preheated oven at 350F for 10-15 minutes or until golden brown on the edges.
- Serve the cookies chilled or store them in an airtight container.

Nutritional information per serving

Calories: 101
Fat: 6.5g

Protein: 1.2g
Carbohydrates: 9.7g

O UTRAGEOUS CHOCOLATE COOKIES

Time: 1 ¼ hours

Servings: 20

Ingredients:

¼ cup butter, softened
¼ cup coconut oil
2 eggs
4 oz. dark chocolate, melted
¾ cup light brown sugar

1 teaspoon vanilla extract
1 cup all-purpose flour
½ teaspoon salt
1 teaspoon baking powder
½ cup dark chocolate chips

Directions:

- Mix the butter, coconut oil and sugar in a bowl until pale and creamy.
- Mix the eggs, one by one, then stir in the chocolate and vanilla.
- Fold in the flour, salt and baking powder, as well as the chocolate chips.
- Drop spoonfuls of batter on a baking tray lined with baking paper.
- Bake in the preheated oven at 350F for 10-15 minutes or until golden brown and well risen.
- Serve the cookies chilled.

Nutritional information per serving

Calories: 139
Fat: 8.0g

Protein: 1.9g
Carbohydrates: 15.7g

M ACADAMIA COOKIES

Time: 1 ¼ hours

Servings: 20

Ingredients:

1 cup rolled oats
1 cup all-purpose flour
1 teaspoon baking powder
½ teaspoon salt
½ cup shredded coconut
2/3 cup macadamia nuts, chopped

½ cup butter, softened
¼ cup golden syrup
¼ cup light brown sugar

Directions:
- Mix the oats, flour, baking powder, salt, coconut and macadamia nuts in a bowl.
- Mix the butter and syrup and sugar in a bowl until creamy and pale.
- Fold in the rest of the ingredients then drop spoonfuls of batter on a baking sheet lined with baking paper.
- Bake in the preheated oven at 350F for 10-15 minutes or until golden brown on the edges.
- Serve the cookies chilled.

Nutritional information per serving

Calories: 137

Fat: 9.0g

Protein: 1.7g

Carbohydrates: 13.5g

 ATMEAL RAISINS COOKIES

Time: 2 hours

Servings: 20

Ingredients:

2/3 cup butter, softened

½ cup light brown sugar

1 egg

1 teaspoon vanilla extract

1 cup whole wheat flour

¼ teaspoon salt

1 teaspoon baking powder

1 cup rolled oats

½ cup golden raisins

¼ cup brandy

Directions:
- Mix the raisins and brandy in a bowl and let them soak up for 1 hour.
- Mix the butter and sugar in a bowl until fluffy and pale.
- Add the egg and vanilla and mix well.
- Add the flour, salt, baking powder and oats then fold in the raisins.
- Drop spoonfuls of batter on a baking sheet lined with baking paper.
- Bake in the preheated oven at 350F for 15 minutes or until the edges turn golden brown.
- Serve the cookies chilled.

Nutritional information per serving

Calories: 124

Fat: 6.7g

Protein: 1.6g

Carbohydrates: 14.1g

B ANANA OATMEAL COOKIES

Time: 1 hour

Servings: 10

Ingredients:

3 ripe bananas, mashed

2 tablespoons maple syrup

1 cup rolled oats

¼ teaspoon baking soda

1 pinch salt

Directions:
- Mix all the ingredients in a bowl.
- Drop spoonfuls of batter on a baking sheet lined with baking paper.
- Bake the cookies in the preheated oven at 350F for 10 minutes or until golden brown on the edges.
- Serve the cookies chilled.

Nutritional information per serving

Calories: 73

Fat: 0.7g

Protein: 1.5g

Carbohydrates: 16.3g

O RANGE PISTACHIO COOKIES

Time: 1 ¼ hours

Servings: 20

Ingredients:

½ cup almond flour
½ cup ground pistachio
¼ cup powdered sugar
½ cup butter, softened
1 egg

2 tablespoons fresh orange juice
1 teaspoon orange zest
1 cup all-purpose flour
¼ teaspoon salt
½ teaspoon baking soda

Directions:

- Mix the almonds and pistachio in a bowl.
- Mix the butter with sugar until fluffy and pale.
- Stir in the egg, orange juice and orange zest.
- Stir in the flour, salt, baking soda and pistachio mixture.
- Drop spoonfuls of batter on a baking sheet lined with baking paper.
- Bake the cookies in the preheated oven at 350F for 10-15 minutes or until golden brown on the edges.
- Serve the cookies chilled.

Nutritional information per serving

Calories: 88
Fat: 5.7g

Protein: 1.4g
Carbohydrates: 8.0g

RANGE PASSIONFRUIT COOKIES

Time: 1 ¼ hours

Servings: 20

Ingredients:

2/3 cup butter, softened
2/3 cup white sugar
1 teaspoon vanilla extract
1 egg
1 teaspoon orange zest

Juice from 2 passionfruits
2 cups all-purpose flour
¼ teaspoon salt
1 teaspoon baking powder

Directions:

- Mix the butter, sugar and vanilla until creamy and fluffy.
- Add the egg, orange zest and passionfruit juice then stir in the dry ingredients.
- Drop spoonfuls of batter on a baking tray lined with baking paper.
- Bake the cookies in the preheated oven at 350F for 10-15 minutes or until the edges turn golden brown.
- Serve the cookies chilled.

Nutritional information per serving

Calories: 129
Fat: 6.5g

Protein: 1.6g
Carbohydrates: 16.4g

CHUNKY PEANUT BUTTER COOKIES

Time: 1 ¼ hours

Servings: 30

Ingredients:

½ cup butter, softened
1 cup peanut butter, softened
1 cup light brown sugar
1 egg

2 cups all-purpose flour
1 teaspoon baking powder
¼ teaspoon salt
1 cup peanuts, chopped

Directions:

- Mix the butter and peanut butter in a bowl until creamy. Add the sugar and mix for 5 minutes until fluffy.
- Add the egg and mix well then fold in the rest of the ingredients.
- Drop spoonfuls of batter on a baking tray lined with baking paper.
- Bake the cookies in the preheated oven at 350F for 10-15 minutes or until golden brown on the edges.
- Allow the cookies cool down before serving.

Nutritional information per serving

Calories: 156
Fat: 10.0g

Protein: 4.5g
Carbohydrates: 13.7g

INK DOTTED SUGAR COOKIES

Time: 1 ½ hours

Servings: 20

Ingredients:

½ cup butter, softened
½ cup powdered sugar
1 egg
2 cups all-purpose flour

¼ teaspoon salt
1 teaspoon baking powder
½ cup pink sprinkles

Directions:

- Mix the butter and sugar in a bowl until fluffy and creamy.
- Stir in the egg then fold in the flour, salt and baking powder, as well as sprinkles.
- Transfer the dough on a floured working surface and roll it into a thin sheet.
- Cut the cookies with your favorite cookie cutter then place them on a baking sheet lined with baking paper.
- Bake the cookies in the preheated oven at 350F for 10-15 minutes or until golden brown on the edges.
- Serve the cookies chilled.

Nutritional information per serving

Calories: 119
Fat: 5.0g

Protein: 1.6g
Carbohydrates: 17.5g

AMARETTI COOKIES

Time: 1 ¼ hours

Servings: 10

Ingredients:

2 cups almond flour
½ cup light brown sugar
¼ cup all-purpose flour
½ teaspoon baking powder

¼ teaspoon salt
2 egg whites
1 teaspoon vanilla extract

Directions:

- Whip the egg whites with salt and vanilla in a bowl until fluffy.
- Add the sugar and continue mixing until glossy and stiff.
- Drop spoonfuls of batter on a baking tray lined with baking paper.
- Bake in the preheated oven at 350F for 20 minutes or until golden brown and crisp.
- Serve the cookies chilled.

Nutritional information per serving

Calories: 76
Fat: 2.8g

Protein: 2.2g
Carbohydrates: 10.9g

ROCKY ROAD COOKIES

Time: 1 ¼ hours

Servings: 20

Ingredients:

1 cup macadamia nuts, chopped
½ cup glace cherries, halved
½ cup dried cranberries
½ cup walnuts, chopped
½ cup mini marshmallows

2 eggs
1/3 cup butter, softened
¼ cup light brown sugar
1 cup all-purpose flour

Directions:
- Mix the butter and sugar in a bowl until creamy.
- Add the eggs, one by one, then stir in the flour, followed by the rest of the ingredients.
- Drop spoonfuls of batter on a baking tray lined with baking paper.
- Bake the cookies in the preheated oven at 350F for 10-15 minutes or until golden brown on the edges.
- Serve the cookies chilled.

Nutritional information per serving

Calories: 139

Fat: 10.5g

Protein: 2.6g

Carbohydrates: 9.7g

S ALTED CHOCOLATE COOKIES

Time: 1 ½ hours

Servings: 30

Ingredients:

2 cups dark chocolate chips

½ cup butter

2 tablespoons coconut oil

1 cup light brown sugar

2 tablespoons dark brown sugar

2 eggs

1 ½ cups all-purpose flour

¼ cup cocoa powder

1 teaspoon sea salt

1 teaspoon baking powder

Directions:
- Mix the chocolate and butter in a heatproof bowl over a hot water bath and melt them together until smooth.
- Add the coconut oil and mix well then stir in the sugars and eggs. Mix well.
- Fold in the rest of the ingredients then drop spoonfuls of batter on a baking sheet lined with baking paper.
- Bake the cookies in the preheated oven at 350F for 15 minutes.
- Serve the cookies chilled.

Nutritional information per serving

Calories: 122

Fat: 6.5g

Protein: 1.7g

Carbohydrates: 15.9g

M OLASSES COOKIES

Time: 1 ½ hours

Servings: 20

Ingredients:

½ cup butter, softened

4 tablespoons dark molasses

½ cup light brown sugar

1 egg

1 teaspoon vanilla extract

1 ½ cups all-purpose flour

¼ teaspoon salt

1 teaspoon baking powder

Directions:
- Mix the butter, molasses and sugar in a bowl until creamy and fluffy.
- Add the egg and vanilla and mix well.
- Fold in the rest of the ingredients then drop spoonfuls of batter on a baking tray lined with baking paper.
- Bake the cookies in the preheated oven at 350F for 10-15 minutes or until fragrant and crisp.
- Serve the cookies chilled.

Nutritional information per serving

Calories: 104

Fat: 4.9g

Protein: 1.3g

Carbohydrates: 13.9g

G INGER QUINOA COOKIES

Time: 1 ¼ hours

Servings: 30

Ingredients:

½ cup coconut oil, melted
2 tablespoons butter, softened
2 tablespoons molasses
1 egg
½ cup light brown sugar
1 cup all-purpose flour
½ cup almond flour

¼ cup quinoa flour
¼ cup quinoa flakes
½ teaspoon ground ginger
½ teaspoon cinnamon powder
¼ teaspoon salt
½ teaspoon baking soda

Directions:

- Mix the coconut oil and butter, molasses and sugar in a bowl until creamy and fluffy.
- Add the egg and mix well.
- Stir in the rest of the ingredients then drop spoonfuls of batter on a baking sheet lined with baking paper.
- Bake the cookies in the preheated oven at 350F for 10-15 minutes or until golden brown on the edges.
- Serve the cookies chilled.

Nutritional information per serving

Calories: 79
Fat: 5.0g

Protein: 1.2g
Carbohydrates: 7.6g

$\mathcal{P}$ UFFED RICE COOKIES

Time: 1 ¼ hours

Servings: 20

Ingredients:

½ cup butter, softened
½ cup light brown sugar
2 tablespoons golden syrup
1 egg

1 ½ cup all-purpose flour
1 teaspoon baking powder
½ teaspoon salt
2 cups puffed rice cereals

Directions:

- Mix the butter, sugar and golden syrup in a bowl until fluffy and creamy.
- Add the egg and mix well then fold in the rest of the ingredients.
- Drop spoonfuls of batter on a baking sheet lined with baking paper.
- Bake in the preheated oven at 350F for 10-15 minutes or until golden brown on the edges.
- Serve the cookies chilled.

Nutritional information per serving

Calories: 103
Fat: 4.9g

Protein: 1.4g
Carbohydrates: 13.6g

$\mathcal{D}$ OUBLE GINGER COOKIES

Time: 1 ¼ hours

Servings: 20

Ingredients:

2 cups all-purpose flour
1 teaspoon ground ginger
½ teaspoon cinnamon powder
¼ teaspoon salt
½ teaspoon baking soda

1/3 cup butter, softened
2/3 cup light brown sugar
1 teaspoon vanilla extract
2 tablespoons golden syrup
¼ cup candied ginger, chopped

Directions:

- Sift the flour, ginger, cinnamon, salt and baking soda in a bowl.
- Mix the butter, sugar, vanilla and syrup in a bowl until fluffy and pale.
- Fold in the flour then add the candied ginger.
- Drop spoonfuls of batter on a baking sheet lined with baking paper.
- Bake in the preheated oven at 350F for 10-15 minutes or until risen and golden brown.

- Serve the cookies chilled.

Nutritional information per serving

Calories: 98
Fat: 3.2g

Protein: 1.4g
Carbohydrates: 16.1g

*C*ASHEW CRANBERRY COOKIES

Time: 1 ¼ house

Servings: 30

Ingredients:

1 ½ cups ground cashew nuts
½ cup all-purpose flour
¼ teaspoon salt
½ cup baking soda
½ cup coconut oil, melted

2 eggs
1 teaspoon vanilla extract
½ cup light brown sugar
2 tablespoons golden syrup
1 cup dried cranberries

Directions:
- Mix the cashew nuts, flour, salt and baking soda in a bowl.
- In a different bowl, mix the coconut oil, eggs, vanilla, sugar and syrup until creamy.
- Add the flour mixture then fold in the cranberries.
- Drop spoonfuls of batter on a baking sheet lined with baking paper.
- Bake the cookies in the preheated oven at 350F for 10-15 minutes or until golden brown on the edges.
- Serve the cookies chilled.

Nutritional information per serving

Calories: 106
Fat: 7.7g

Protein: 2.0g
Carbohydrates: 7.6g

*C*HILI CHOCOLATE COOKIES

Time: 1 ¼ hours

Servings: 30

Ingredients:

1 cup butter, softened
½ cup white sugar
¼ cup dark brown sugar
1 teaspoon vanilla extract
2 eggs
2 cups all-purpose flour

½ cup cocoa powder
½ teaspoon salt
1 teaspoon chili powder
1 teaspoon baking powder
1 cup dark chocolate chips

Directions:
- Mix the butter and sugars in a bowl until creamy and fluffy.
- Add the vanilla and eggs and mix well.
- Fold in the flour, cocoa powder, salt, chili powder and baking powder then add the chocolate chips.
- Drop spoonfuls of batter on a baking sheet lined with baking paper.
- Bake the cookies in the preheated oven at 350F for 10-15 minutes or until risen and fragrant.
- Serve the cookies chilled.

Nutritional information per serving

Calories: 129
Fat: 7.8g

Protein: 1.8g
Carbohydrates: 14.5g

*F*LOURLESS PEANUT BUTTER COOKIES

Time: 1 hour
Servings: 30

Ingredients:

2 cups smooth peanut butter

1 cup light brown sugar

½ teaspoon salt

2 eggs

Directions:

- Mix all the ingredients in a bowl until smooth.
- Drop spoonfuls of mixture on a baking sheet lined with baking paper.
- Score the top of each cookie with a fork then bake the cookies in the preheated oven at 350F for 10-12 minutes.
- Serve the cookies chilled.

Nutritional information per serving

Calories: 124

Fat: 9.0g

Protein: 4.7g

Carbohydrates: 8.1g

S UGAR COVERED COOKIES

Time: 1 ½ hours

Servings: 30

Ingredients:

1 cup butter, softened

⅓ cup white sugar

1 egg

2 egg yolks

1 teaspoon vanilla extract

½ cup rice flour

2 cups all-purpose flour

¼ teaspoon salt

½ teaspoon baking powder

1 cup powdered sugar

Directions:

- Mix the butter and sugar in a bowl until fluffy and pale.
- Add the egg and egg yolks, as well as the vanilla and mix well.
- Stir in the rice flour, flour, salt and baking powder in a bowl.
- Form small balls and place them on baking trays lined with baking paper.
- Flatten the cookies then bake them in the preheated oven at 350F for 10-15 minutes or until golden brown on the edges.
- Transfer the cookies in a bowl and dust them with powdered sugar.
- Serve the cookies chilled.

Nutritional information per serving

Calories: 128

Fat: 6.7g

Protein: 1.4g

Carbohydrates: 15.9g

C HOCOLATE CHIP PECAN COOKIES

Time: 1 ¼ hours

Servings: 20

Ingredients:

½ cup butter, softened

½ cup powdered sugar

2 tablespoon honey

1 egg

1 cup all-purpose flour

1 cup ground pecans

½ teaspoon baking soda

¼ teaspoon salt

½ cup chocolate chips

Directions:

- Mix the butter, sugar and honey in a bowl until creamy and pale.
- Add the egg and mix well then add the flour, pecans, baking soda and salt.
- Fold in the chocolate chips then drop spoonfuls of batter on a baking sheet lined with baking paper.
- Bake in the preheated oven at 350F for 10-15 minutes or until golden brown and fragrant.
- Serve the cookies chilled.

Nutritional information per serving

Calories: 112

Fat: 6.6g

Protein: 1.4g   Carbohydrates: 12.1g

OOEY CHOCOLATE CHERRY COOKIES

Time: 1 hour   Servings: 20

Ingredients:

½ cup butter, melted   1 ½ cups all-purpose flour
½ cup muscovado sugar   2 tablespoons cocoa powder
¼ cup white sugar   ½ cup dark chocolate chips
1 egg   ½ cup glace cherries, halved

Directions:
- Mix all the ingredients in a bowl with a spatula.
- Drop spoonfuls of batter on a baking tray lined with baking paper.
- Bake in the preheated oven at 350F for 10 minutes.
- Serve the cookies chilled.

Nutritional information per serving

Calories: 128   Protein: 1.7g
Fat: 5.8g   Carbohydrates: 18.2g

INNAMON OATMEAL COOKIES

Time: 1 ¼ hours   Servings: 30

Ingredients:

2/3 cup butter   2 cups rolled oats
2/3 cup light brown sugar   1 teaspoon cinnamon powder
¼ cup golden syrup   ¼ teaspoon salt
1 egg   ½ teaspoon baking soda
2/3 cup all-purpose flour

Directions:
- Mix the butter, sugar and syrup in a bowl until fluffy and creamy.
- Add the egg and mix well then fold in the rest of the ingredients.
- Drop spoonfuls of batter on a baking sheet lined with baking paper.
- Bake the cookies in the preheated oven at 350F for 10-15 minutes or until golden brown on the edges.
- Allow the cookies to cool down before serving.

Nutritional information per serving

Calories: 89   Protein: 1.2g
Fat: 4.6g   Carbohydrates: 11.1g

AMERICAN CHOCOLATE CHUNK COOKIES

Time: 1 ¼ hours   Servings: 20

Ingredients:

½ cup smooth peanut butter   1 cup all-purpose flour
1/3 cup butter, softened   ¼ teaspoon salt
½ cup light brown sugar   ½ teaspoon baking powder
1 egg   ½ cup peanuts, chopped
1 teaspoon vanilla extract   3 oz. dark chocolate, chopped

Directions:
- Mix the peanut butter, butter and sugar in a bowl until fluffy and creamy.
- Add the egg and vanilla and mix well.

- Fold in the flour, salt, baking powder, peanuts and dark chocolate.
- Drop spoonfuls of batter on a baking tray lined with baking paper.
- Bake the cookies in the preheated oven at 350F for 10-15 minutes or until golden brown on the edges.
- Serve the cookies chilled.

Nutritional information per serving

Calories: 149

Fat: 9.7g

Protein: 3.9g

Carbohydrates: 12.8g

*C*HOCOLATE PECAN COOKIES

Time: 1 hour

Servings: 10

Ingredients:

2 egg whites

¼ teaspoon salt

2/3 cup white sugar

1 teaspoon vanilla extract

1 cup ground pecans

½ cup dark chocolate chips

Directions:

- Whip the egg whites and salt in a bowl until fluffy and airy
- Add the sugar, gradually, and mix until glossy.
- Fold in the pecans and chocolate chips then drop spoonfuls of batter on a baking sheet lined with baking paper.
- Bake the cookies in the preheated oven at 350F for 10-15 minutes or until golden brown.
- Serve the cookies chilled.

Nutritional information per serving

Calories: 92

Fat: 2.6g

Protein: 1.3g

Carbohydrates: 17.6g

*I*CING DECORATED COOKIES

Time: 1 ¼ hours

Servings: 20

Ingredients:

Cookies:

½ cup butter, softened

½ cup powdered sugar

1 egg yolk

1 ½ cups all-purpose flour

¼ teaspoon salt

½ teaspoon baking powder

Icing:

1 cup powdered sugar

1 egg white

¼ teaspoon vanilla extract

Directions:

- For the cookies, mix the butter and sugar in a bowl until fluffy and pale.
- Add the egg yolk and mix well then fold in the flour, salt and baking powder.
- Transfer the dough on a floured working surface and roll the dough into thin sheet.
- Cut small cookies with a cookie cutter and place the cookies in a baking tray lined with baking paper.
- Bake the cookies in the preheated oven at 350F for 10-12 minutes or until golden brown on the edges.
- For the icing, mix the sugar, egg white and vanilla in a bowl.
- Spoon the icing in a small piping bag and decorate the chilled cookies with it.

Nutritional information per serving

Calories: 114

Fat: 4.9g

Protein: 1.3g

Carbohydrates: 16.2g

*S*PICED APPLE COOKIES

Time: 1 ¼ hours

Servings: 20

Ingredients:
½ cup coconut oil, melted
½ cup light brown sugar
1 egg
2 tablespoons water
1 ½ cups all-purpose flour

¼ teaspoon salt
1 teaspoon baking powder
½ teaspoon cinnamon powder
2 red apples, cored and diced

Directions:
- Mix the oil, sugar and egg in a bowl until fluffy and light.
- Add the water and mix well then stir in the flour, salt, baking powder and cinnamon.
- Add the apples then drop spoonfuls of batter on a baking tray lined with baking paper.
- Bake the cookies in the preheated oven at 350F for 12-15 minutes or until fragrant and golden brown.
- Serve the cookies chilled.

Nutritional information per serving
Calories: 108
Fat: 5.8g

Protein: 1.3g
Carbohydrates: 13.4g

𝓕 RUITY COOKIES

Time: 1 ½ hours

Servings: 30

Ingredients:
2/3 cup butter, softened
2/3 cup white sugar
2 tablespoons molasses
2 tablespoons golden syrup
1 egg
¼ cup milk
2 cups all-purpose flour

¼ teaspoon salt
1 teaspoon baking soda
½ cup sultanas
½ cup dried cranberries
½ cup raisins
½ cup dried apricots, chopped
¼ cup Grand Marnier

Directions:
- Mix the fruits with Grand Marnier in a bowl and allow to soak up for 30 minutes.
- Mix the butter, sugar, molasses and golden syrup in a bowl until pale.
- Add the egg and milk and mix well.
- Add the dry ingredients then fold in the fruits.
- Drop spoonfuls of batter on a baking sheet lined with baking paper and bake the cookies in the preheated oven at 350F for 15 minutes.
- Allow the cookies to cool down before serving.

Nutritional information per serving
Calories: 111
Fat: 4.4g

Protein: 1.3g
Carbohydrates: 15.7g

𝓞 RANGE PUMPKIN COOKIES

Time: 1 hour

Servings: 20

Ingredients:
½ cup butter, softened
½ cup powdered sugar
1 orange, zested and juiced
½ cup pumpkin puree

1 ½ cups all-purpose flour
½ cup almond flour
¼ teaspoon salt
1 teaspoon baking powder

Directions:
- Mix the butter and sugar in a bowl until pale and creamy.
- Add the orange zest and juice, as well as the pumpkin puree and mix well.
- Fold in the flour, almond flour, salt and baking powder then drop spoonfuls of batter on a baking tray lined with baking

paper.
- Bake the cookies in the preheated oven at 350F for 10-15 minutes or until golden brown or until golden brown and fragrant.
- Serve the cookies chilled.

Nutritional information per serving

Calories: 97
Fat: 5.1g

Protein: 1.3g
Carbohydrates: 12.0g

 NZAC COOKIES

Time: 1 ¼ hours

Servings: 20

Ingredients:

1 cup rolled oats
½ cup shredded coconut
¾ cup all-purpose flour
½ teaspoon baking soda

¼ teaspoon salt
¾ cup butter, melted
4 tablespoons golden syrup
1 teaspoon lemon juice

Directions:
- Mix the oats, coconut, flour, baking soda and salt in a bowl.
- Add the rest of the ingredients and mix well.
- Form small balls of dough and place them in a baking tray lined with baking paper.
- Flatten the cookies slightly then bake in the preheated oven at 350F for 10-15 minutes or until golden brown on the edges.
- Serve the cookies chilled.

Nutritional information per serving

Calories: 112
Fat: 7.9g

Protein: 1.2g
Carbohydrates: 9.8g

RIED PRUNE OATMEAL COOKIES

Time: 1 ¼ hours

Servings: 25

Ingredients:

1 cup dried prunes, chopped
½ cup coconut oil, melted
½ cup maple syrup
1 teaspoon vanilla extract
1 teaspoon lemon juice

2 cups rolled oats
¾ cup all-purpose flour
½ teaspoon baking soda
¼ teaspoon salt

Directions:
- Mix the prunes, oats, flour, baking soda and salt in a bowl.
- Add the rest of the ingredients and mix with a spatula.
- Form small balls of dough and place them on a baking sheet lined with baking paper.
- Bake the cookies in the preheated oven at 350F for 12-15 minutes or until golden brown.
- Serve the cookies chilled.

Nutritional information per serving

Calories: 109
Fat: 4.9g

Protein: 1.4g
Carbohydrates: 15.9g

MANGO CRUNCH COOKIES

Time: 1 ¼ hours
Servings: 20

Ingredients:
½ cup butter, softened
¼ cup white sugar
1 egg
1 teaspoon vanilla extract

1 ½ cups all-purpose flour
¼ teaspoon salt
½ teaspoon baking soda
1 cup dried mango, chopped

Directions:
- Mix the butter, sugar and egg in a bowl until creamy. Add the vanilla and mix well then fold in the flour, salt and baking soda.
- Add the mango and mix with a spatula.
- Drop spoonfuls of batter on a baking tray lined with baking paper.
- Bake in the preheated oven at 350F for 10-15 minutes or until golden brown on the edges.
- Serve the cookies chilled.

Nutritional information per serving
Calories: 95
Fat: 5.0g

Protein: 1.4g
Carbohydrates: 11.5g

EANUT BUTTER PRETZEL COOKIES

Time: 1 ¼ hours

Servings: 30

Ingredients:
¾ cup butter, softened
½ cup smooth peanut butter
1 cup light brown sugar
1 egg
1 teaspoon vanilla extract

2 cups all-purpose flour
¼ teaspoon salt
½ teaspoon baking soda
1 cup crushed pretzels

Directions:
- Mix the butter, peanut butter and sugar in a bowl until creamy and fluffy.
- Add the egg and vanilla and mix well.
- Fold in the flour, salt and baking soda then add the pretzels.
- Drop spoonfuls of batter on a baking tray lined with baking paper.
- Bake in the preheated oven at 350F for 15-20 minutes or until golden brown on the edges.
- Serve the cookies chilled.

Nutritional information per serving
Calories: 121
Fat: 7.0g

Protein: 2.2g
Carbohydrates: 12.7g

CLOVE SUGAR COOKIES

Time: 1 ¼ hours

Servings: 30

Ingredients:
1 cup butter, softened
½ cup powdered sugar
1 teaspoon vanilla extract
1 egg yolk
1 teaspoon ground whole cloves

2 cups all-purpose flour
1 cup ground hazelnuts
¼ teaspoon salt
½ teaspoon baking powder

Directions:
- Mix the butter and sugar in a bowl until pale and fluffy.
- Add the vanilla and egg yolk and mix well.
- Fold in the flour, hazelnuts, cloves, salt and baking powder.
- Transfer the dough on a floured working surface then roll the dough into a thin sheet.
- Cut small cookies with a cookie cutter and place them on a baking tray lined with baking paper.

- Bake the cookies in the preheated oven at 350F for 10-15 minutes or until golden brown and fragrant.
- Serve the cookies chilled.

Nutritional information per serving

Calories: 115

Fat: 7.9g

Protein: 1.5g

Carbohydrates: 9.7g

$\mathcal{B}$ROWN BUTTER AMERICAN COOKIES

Time: 1 ¼ hours

Servings: 20

Ingredients:

1 cup butter

1 cup light brown sugar

1 egg

1 teaspoon vanilla extract

1 ½ cups all-purpose flour

½ teaspoon baking soda

¼ teaspoon salt

½ cup pecans, chopped

Directions:

- Place the butter in a saucepan and melt it then cook it until golden and caramelized. Allow to cool then transfer in a bowl.
- Mix the butter and sugar in a fluffy and pale.
- Add the egg and vanilla and mix well then stir in the flour, baking soda, salt and pecans.
- Drop spoonfuls of batter on a baking tray lined with baking paper.
- Bake in the preheated oven at 350F for 10-15 minutes or until golden brown on the edges.
- Serve the cookies chilled.

Nutritional information per serving

Calories: 152

Fat: 10.0g

Protein: 1.4g

Carbohydrates: 14.4g

$\mathcal{C}$INNAMON SUGAR COOKIES

Time: 1 ½ hours

Servings: 25

Ingredients:

2 eggs

1 cup white sugar

½ cup coconut oil, melted

1 teaspoon vanilla extract

2 cups all-purpose flour

¼ teaspoon salt

1 teaspoon baking powder

½ cup light brown sugar

1 teaspoon cinnamon powder

Directions:

- Mix the brown sugar and cinnamon in a bowl and place aside.
- Combine the eggs and sugar in a different bowl and mix until double in volume.
- Add the coconut oil and vanilla and mix well.
- Add the flour, salt and baking powder and mix with a spatula.
- Form small balls of dough and roll them through cinnamon sugar.
- Bake the cookies in the preheated oven at 350F for 10-15 minutes or until golden brown and fragrant.
- Serve the cookies chilled.

Nutritional information per serving

Calories: 121

Fat: 4.8g

Protein: 1.5g

Carbohydrates: 18.6g

℘ RALINE COOKIES

Time: 1 ¼ hours

Servings: 30

Ingredients:

½ cup butter, softened
½ cup praline paste
½ cup light brown sugar
2 eggs
1 teaspoon vanilla extract

1 tablespoon praline liqueur
2 cups all-purpose flour
¼ teaspoon salt
1 teaspoon baking soda

Directions:
- Mix the butter, praline paste and sugar in a bowl until pale and fluffy.
- Add the egg yolks, vanilla and praline liqueur and mix well.
- Stir in the flour, salt and baking soda then mix with a spatula.
- Transfer the dough on a floured working surface and roll it into a thin sheet.
- Cut small cookies with a cookie cutter and place them all on a baking tray lined with baking paper.
- Bake the cookies in the preheated oven at 350F for 10-15 minutes or until golden brown on the edges.
- Serve the cookies chilled.

Nutritional information per serving

Calories: 91
Fat: 4.6g

Protein: 1.5g
Carbohydrates: 10.9g

℘ ECAN BUTTER COOKIES

Time: 1 ¼ hours

Servings: 20

Ingredients:

½ cup pecan butter, softened
1/3 cup dark brown sugar
1 egg
1 teaspoon vanilla extract
1 cup all-purpose flour

1 cup ground pecans
¼ teaspoon salt
½ teaspoon baking soda
1 cup pecans, chopped

Directions:
- Mix the butter, sugar, egg and vanilla in a bowl.
- Add the flour, salt, baking soda and ground pecans. Fold in the chopped pecans then drop spoonfuls of batter on a baking tray lined with baking paper.
- Bake in the preheated oven at 350F for 10-15 minutes or until fragrant and golden brown on the edges.
- Serve the cookies chilled and store them in an airtight container.

Nutritional information per serving

Calories: 86
Fat: 5.9g

Protein: 1.1g
Carbohydrates: 7.4g

ℭ OCONUT BUTTER COOKIES

Time: 1 ¼ hours

Servings: 20

Ingredients:

½ cup coconut butter, softened
2 tablespoons coconut oil
2/3 cup white sugar
1 egg
1 teaspoon coconut extract
2 cups all-purpose flour

1 cup shredded coconut
1 teaspoon baking powder
¼ teaspoon salt

Directions:
- Mix the coconut butter, coconut oil and sugar in a bowl until pale and creamy.
- Add the egg and coconut extract and mix well.
- Stir in the flour, coconut, baking powder and salt then form small balls of dough.
- Place the balls on baking trays lined with baking paper and bake in the preheated oven at 350F for 10-15 minutes or until golden brown,
- When done, transfer the cookies in a bowl and dust them with powdered sugar.
- Serve the cookies chilled.

Nutritional information per serving

Calories: 100

Fat: 3.0g

Protein: 1.7g

Carbohydrates: 17.0g

UICK BROWN BUTTER COOKIES

Time: 1 hour

Servings: 20

Ingredients:

¾ cup butter

¾ cup white sugar

1 teaspoon vanilla extract

1 egg

1 ½ cups all-purpose flour

¼ teaspoon salt

1 teaspoon baking powder

½ cup sliced almonds

Directions:
- Place the butter in a saucepan and cook it until melted and slightly golden.
- Allow to cool then transfer in a bowl and stir in the rest of the ingredients in the same order they are written in.
- Drop spoonfuls of batter on a baking tray lined with baking paper.
- Bake the cookies in the preheated oven at 350F for 10-15 minutes or until golden brown.
- Serve the cookies chilled.

Nutritional information per serving

Calories: 141

Fat: 8.4g

Protein: 1.8g

Carbohydrates: 15.3g

INGER BUTTER COOKIES

Time: 1 ¼ hours

Servings: 20

Ingredients:

½ cup butter, softened

¾ cup light brown sugar

1 egg

1 teaspoon vanilla extract

1 ½ cups all-purpose flour

1 teaspoon ground ginger

½ teaspoon ground cardamom

½ teaspoon baking soda

¼ teaspoon salt

Directions:
- Mix the butter and sugar until fluffy and pale. Add the egg and vanilla and mix well.
- Stir in the flour, ginger, cardamom, salt and baking soda.
- Drop spoonfuls of batter on baking trays lined with baking paper.
- Bake the cookies in the preheated oven at 350F for 10-15 minutes or until golden brown and crisp on the edges.
- Serve the cookies chilled.

Nutritional information per serving

Calories: 100

Fat: 4.9g

Protein: 1.3g

Carbohydrates: 12.6g

*B*ROWN BUTTER CHOCOLATE OATMEAL COOKIES

Time: 1 ¼ hours

Servings: 30

Ingredients:

1 cup butter
1 cup light brown sugar
1 egg
1 teaspoon vanilla extract
1 1/2 cups rolled oats

1 cup all-purpose flour
1 teaspoon baking soda
¼ teaspoon salt
½ cup dark chocolate chips

Directions:
- Melt the butter in a saucepan until it becomes slightly golden.
- Add the sugar and mix well then stir in the egg and vanilla.
- Add the oats, flour, baking soda and salt then fold in the chocolate chips.
- Drop spoonfuls of batter on a baking tray lined with baking paper.
- Bake the cookies in the preheated oven at 350F for 10-15 minutes or until golden brown on the edges.
- Serve the cookies chilled.

Nutritional information per serving

Calories: 115
Fat: 7.1g

Protein: 1.4g
Carbohydrates: 12.0g

*C*HEWY SUGAR COOKIES

Time: 1 ¼ hours

Servings: 40

Ingredients:

2 ½ cups all-purpose flour
1 teaspoon baking soda
½ teaspoon salt
1 cup butter, softened

2 cups white sugar
2 eggs
1 teaspoon vanilla extract

Directions:
- Mix the butter with sugar until creamy and pale. Add the eggs, one by one, then stir in the vanilla.
- Fold in the flour, baking soda and salt then shape the dough into small balls.
- Place the balls on a baking tray lined with baking paper and flatten them slightly.
- Bake the cookies in the preheated oven at 350F for 10-15 minutes or until slightly golden brown.
- Serve the cookies chilled.

Nutritional information per serving

Calories: 110
Fat: 4.9g

Protein: 1.1g
Carbohydrates: 16.0g

*C*RACKED SUGAR COOKIES

Time: 1 ¼ hours

Servings: 30

Ingredients:

1 cup white sugar
1 cup butter, softened
3 egg yolks
1 teaspoon vanilla extract

2 ½ cups all-purpose flour
1 teaspoon baking soda
½ teaspoon salt
1 cup powdered sugar

Directions:
- Mix the butter and sugar in a bowl until creamy and fluffy.
- Add the egg yolks and mix well then stir in the vanilla.
- Fold in the flour, baking soda and salt then form small balls of dough and roll them through powdered sugar.

- Place the balls on a baking tray lined with baking paper.
- Bake in the preheated oven at 350F for 10-15 minutes or until slightly golden brown.
- Serve the cookies chilled, handling them with care.

Nutritional information per serving

Calories: 139
Fat: 6.7g

Protein: 1.4g
Carbohydrates: 18.7g

C HOCOLATE CRINKLES

Time: 2 hours

Servings: 40

Ingredients:

½ cup coconut oil, melted
4 oz. dark chocolate, melted
2 cups white sugar
4 eggs
1 teaspoon vanilla extract

2 cups all-purpose flour
1 ½ teaspoons baking powder
½ cup cocoa powder
½ teaspoon salt
2 cups powdered sugar

Directions:
- Mix the coconut oil and melted chocolate in a bowl.
- Add the sugar and eggs and mix well then stir in the vanilla.
- Fold in the flour, baking powder, cocoa and salt then cover the dough with plastic wrap.
- Place in the fridge for 1 hour then form small balls of dough and roll them through powdered sugar.
- Place the cookies on a baking tray lined with baking paper and bake in the preheated oven at 350F for 10-12 minutes.
- Serve the cookies chilled.

Nutritional information per serving

Calories: 131
Fat: 4.2g

Protein: 1.6g
Carbohydrates: 23.1g

S OFT GINGER COOKIES

Time: 1 ¼ hours

Servings: 30

Ingredients:

2 cups all-purpose flour
¼ teaspoon salt
1 teaspoon baking soda
1/2 teaspoon cinnamon powder
1 teaspoon ground ginger

¾ cup butter, softened
1 cup white sugar
1 egg
3 tablespoons molasses
1 teaspoon vanilla extract

Directions:
- Mix the flour, salt, baking soda and spices in a bowl.
- In a different bowl, combine the butter and sugar and mix well. Add the egg and molasses and give it a good mix. Stir in the vanilla.
- Fold in the flour mixture then drop spoonfuls of batter on baking trays lined with baking paper.
- Bake the cookies in the preheated oven at 350F for 10-15 minutes or until fragrant and golden brown.
- Serve the cookies chilled.

Nutritional information per serving

Calories: 105
Fat: 4.8g

Protein: 1.1g
Carbohydrates: 14.6g

C HEWY COCONUT COOKIES

Time: 1 hour

Servings: 20

Ingredients:

1 ¼ cups all-purpose flour
¼ cup cornstarch
½ teaspoon baking soda
¼ teaspoon salt
1 cup shredded coconut

1 egg
1 cup white sugar
¼ cup coconut oil, melted
1 teaspoon vanilla extract
½ teaspoon coconut extract

Directions:

- Mix the egg and sugar in a bowl until double in volume. Stir in the coconut oil then add the coconut oil, vanilla and coconut extract.
- Fold in the flour, cornstarch, baking soda, salt and coconut.
- Drop spoonfuls of batter on a baking sheet pan lined with baking paper.
- Bake the cookies in the preheated oven at 350F for 10-15 minutes or until golden brown on the edges.
- Serve the cookies chilled.

Nutritional information per serving

Calories: 114
Fat: 4.4g

Protein: 1.2g
Carbohydrates: 18.1g

C RANBERRY BISCOTTI

Time: 1 ½ hours

Servings: 20

Ingredients:

½ cup butter, softened
½ cup white sugar
1 egg
1 tablespoon lemon zest

2 cups all-purpose flour
½ teaspoon baking soda
¼ teaspoon salt
1 cup dried cranberries

Directions:

- Mix the butter and sugar in a bowl until creamy and fluffy.
- Add the egg and lemon zest and mix well.
- Stir in the flour, baking soda and salt then add the cranberries.
- Place the dough on a baking tray lined with baking paper. Shape the dough into a log and bake it in the preheated oven at 350F for 15 minutes.
- Remove the tray from the oven and allow it to cool down for 10 minutes. Cut the log into 1cm wide slices and place them back on the tray with the cut facing up.
- Continue baking for 15 minutes or until golden brown and crisp.
- Allow to cool before serving or storing.

Nutritional information per serving

Calories: 111
Fat: 5.0g

Protein: 1.6g
Carbohydrates: 15.1g

W HITE CHOCOLATE CRANBERRY COOKIES

Time: 1 ¼ hours

Servings: 30

Ingredients:

½ cup butter, softened
¼ cup coconut oil, melted
½ cup light brown sugar
1 egg
1 tablespoon brandy
1 ½ cups all-purpose flour

¼ teaspoon salt
1 teaspoon baking powder
¼ teaspoon cinnamon powder
½ cup dried cranberries
½ cup white chocolate chips

Directions:

- Mix the butter, coconut oil and sugar in a bowl until fluffy and pale.

- Add the egg and brandy and mix well.
- Fold in the rest of the ingredients and mix with a spatula.
- Drop spoonfuls of batter on a baking tray lined with baking paper.
- Bake the cookies in the preheated oven at 350F for 10-15 minutes or until golden brown on the edges.
- Serve the cookies chilled.

Nutritional information per serving

Calories: 95

Fat: 6.0g

Protein: 1.0g

Carbohydrates: 9.1g

INGERBREAD COOKIES

Time: 1 ¼ hours

Servings: 20

Ingredients:

½ cup butter, softened

¼ cup molasses

½ cup light brown sugar

1 egg

2 cups all-purpose flour

½ cup ground almonds

¼ teaspoon salt

½ teaspoon baking soda

½ teaspoon cinnamon powder

½ teaspoon ground ginger

½ teaspoon ground cloves

Directions:

- Mix the butter, molasses and sugar in a bowl until pale and creamy.
- Add the egg and mix well then stir in the rest of the ingredients.
- Form small balls of dough and place them on a baking tray lined with baking paper.
- Bake the cookies in the preheated oven at 350F for 12-14 minutes or until fragrant, risen and golden.
- Serve the cookies chilled.

Nutritional information per serving

Calories: 129

Fat: 6.2g

Protein: 2.1g

Carbohydrates: 16.8g

EANUT BUTTER OATMEAL COOKIES

Time: 1 ½ hours

Servings: 30

Ingredients:

½ cup smooth peanut butter

¼ cup butter, softened

½ cup light brown sugar

½ cup white sugar

1 egg

1 teaspoon vanilla extract

¼ cup heavy cream

1 cup all-purpose flour

2 cups rolled oats

½ teaspoon baking soda

¼ teaspoon salt

Directions:

- Mix the peanut butter, butter and sugars in a bowl until pale and creamy.
- Add the egg and vanilla and mix well.
- Add the cream as well then fold in the flour, oats, baking soda and salt.
- Drop spoonfuls of batter on a baking tray lined with baking paper.
- Bake the cookies in the preheated oven at 350F for 10-15 minutes or until the cookies turn golden brown on the edges.
- Serve the cookies chilled.

Nutritional information per serving

Calories: 102

Fat: 4.6g

Protein: 2.5g

Carbohydrates: 13.5g

Coconut Macaroons

Time: 1 ½ hours

Servings: 20

Ingredients:

4 cups shredded coconut
¼ teaspoon salt
½ cup all-purpose flour

1 can sweetened condensed milk
1 teaspoon vanilla extract

Directions:

- Mix the coconut, salt and flour in a bowl.
- Add the milk and vanilla and mix well.
- Drop spoonfuls of mixture on baking trays lined with baking paper.
- Bake the cookies in the preheated oven at 350F for 15 minutes or until crisp and golden brown.
- Serve the cookies chilled.

Nutritional information per serving

Calories: 118
Fat: 6.7g

Protein: 2.1g
Carbohydrates: 13.2g

Russian Tea Cookies

Time: 1 hour

Servings: 30

Ingredients:

1 cup butter, softened
½ cup powdered sugar
1 egg
1 teaspoon vanilla extract
2 cups all-purpose flour

1 cup ground walnuts
¼ teaspoon salt
1 teaspoon baking powder
1 cup powdered sugar

Directions:

- Mix the butter and sugar in a bowl until creamy and pale.
- Add the egg and vanilla and mix well then stir in the flour, walnuts, salt and baking powder.
- Form small balls of dough and place them on a baking tray lined with baking paper.
- Transfer the baked cookies in a bowl and dust them with plenty of powdered sugar.
- Serve the cookies chilled.

Nutritional information per serving

Calories: 136
Fat: 8.8g

Protein: 2.1g
Carbohydrates: 12.9g

Healthy Banana Cookies

Time: 1 hour

Servings: 25

Ingredients:

4 ripe bananas, mashed
¼ cup coconut oil, melted
2 cups rolled oats
1 cup dates, pitted and chopped

¼ cup dried cranberries
¼ cup coconut flakes
¼ cup dried mango, chopped

Directions:

- Mix the bananas and oil then stir in the rest of the ingredients.
- Drop spoonfuls of batter on baking trays lined with baking paper.
- Bake in the preheated oven at 350F for 10-15 minutes or until golden brown.
- Serve the cookies chilled.

Calories: 114
Fat: 3.0g

Protein: 1.3g
Carbohydrates: 21.8g

*M*INTY CHOCOLATE COOKIES

Time: 1 ¼ hours

Servings: 20

Ingredients:
¾ cup butter, softened
1 cup light brown sugar
1 teaspoon vanilla extract
2 tablespoons milk
1 teaspoon peppermint extract
1 egg

1 1/4 cups all-purpose flour
¼ cup cocoa powder
¼ teaspoon salt
1 teaspoon baking powder
½ cup dark chocolate chips

Directions:
- Mix the butter, sugar and vanilla in a bowl until creamy and pale.
- Add the milk, peppermint extract and egg and mix well then fold in the rest of the ingredients.
- Drop spoonfuls of batter on baking trays lined with baking paper.
- Bake the cookies in the preheated oven at 350F for 12-14 minutes or until fragrant.
- Serve the cookies chilled.

Nutritional information per serving
Calories: 139
Fat: 8.2g

Protein: 1.6g
Carbohydrates: 15.9g

*G*INGERSNAP COOKIES

Time: 1 hour

Servings: 20

Ingredients:
¾ cup canola oil
¼ cup molasses
¾ cup light brown sugar
1 egg
2 cups all-purpose flour

1 teaspoon baking soda
½ teaspoon baking powder
¼ teaspoon salt
1 teaspoon ground ginger
½ teaspoon cinnamon powder

Directions:
- Mix the oil, molasses and sugar in a bowl.
- Add the egg and mix until creamy and pale.
- Fold in the rest of the ingredients then form small balls and place them on baking trays lined with baking paper.
- Bake the cookies in the preheated oven at 350F for 12-15 minutes or until crisp and fragrant.
- Serve the cookies chilled.

Nutritional information per serving
Calories: 154
Fat: 8.5g

Protein: 1.6g
Carbohydrates: 18.1g

*F*OUR INGREDIENT PEANUT BUTTER COOKIES

Time: 1 hour

Servings: 20

Ingredients:
1 cup smooth peanut butter
1 egg
2/3 cup light brown sugar

1 cup rolled oats

Directions:
- Mix the peanut butter, egg and sugar in a bowl until creamy then add the oats.
- Drop spoonfuls of batter on a baking tray lined with baking paper.
- Bake the cookies in the preheated oven at 350F for 10-15 minutes or until golden brown on the edges.
- Serve the cookies chilled.

Nutritional information per serving

Calories: 113

Fat: 7.0g

Protein: 4.1g

Carbohydrates: 10.1g

Candied Ginger Oatmeal Cookies

Time: 1 hour

Servings: 30

Ingredients:

2 cups all-purpose flour

1 teaspoon baking soda

½ teaspoon salt

2 cups rolled oats

½ cup canola oil

¼ cup butter, softened

1 cup light brown sugar

2 eggs

1 teaspoon vanilla extract

½ cup candied ginger, chopped

Directions:
- Mix the butter and sugar in a bowl until creamy and pale.
- Add the eggs and mix well then stir in the vanilla.
- Fold in the dry ingredients and ginger then drop spoonfuls of batter on a baking sheet lined with baking paper.
- Bake the cookies in the preheated oven at 350F for 10-15 minutes or until fragrant and golden brown on the edges.
- Serve the cookies chilled.

Nutritional information per serving

Calories: 121

Fat: 5.9g

Protein: 2.0g

Carbohydrates: 15.0g

Nutty Cookies

Time: 1 hour

Servings: 20

Ingredients:

½ cup almond butter

½ cup light brown sugar

¼ cup white sugar

1 egg

1 teaspoon vanilla extract

1 ¼ cups all-purpose flour

½ cup ground walnuts

½ cup ground cashew nuts

½ teaspoon baking soda

¼ teaspoon salt

Directions:
- Mix the almond butter and sugars in a bowl until pale and light. Add the egg and vanilla and mix well.
- Stir in the rest of the ingredients then drop spoonfuls of batter on a baking tray lined with baking paper.
- Bake the cookies in the preheated oven at 350F for 12-15 minutes or until crisp and golden brown.
- Serve the cookies chilled or store them in an airtight container.

Nutritional information per serving

Calories: 138

Fat: 7.6g

Protein: 3.9g

Carbohydrates: 14.6g

Peanut Butter Cups Cookies

Time: 1 ¼ hours

Servings: 25

Ingredients:

½ cup butter, softened
¼ cup smooth peanut butter
¾ cup light brown sugar
2 tablespoons golden syrup
1 egg

1 teaspoon vanilla extract
1 ½ cups all-purpose flour
½ teaspoon baking soda
¼ teaspoon salt
1 cup peanut butter, chopped

Directions:

- Mix the butter and smooth peanut butter in a bowl until smooth and creamy.
- Add the sugar and golden syrup then stir in the egg and vanilla extract.
- Add the flour, baking soda and salt then fold in the peanut butter cups.
- Drop spoonfuls of batter on a baking tray lined with parchment paper.
- Bake the cookies in the preheated oven at 350F for 10-15 minutes or until golden brown on the edges.
- Serve the cookies chilled.

Nutritional information per serving

Calories: 160
Fat: 10.4g

Protein: 4.3g
Carbohydrates: 13.8g

$\mathcal{B}$ ANANA CHOCOLATE CHIP COOKIES

Time: 1 ¼ hours

Servings: 20

Ingredients:

1 ½ cups all-purpose flour
1 teaspoon baking powder
¼ teaspoon salt
½ cup white sugar
½ cup butter, melted

1 egg
1 teaspoon vanilla extract
2 bananas, mashed
½ cup dark chocolate chips

Directions:

- Mix all the dry ingredients in a bowl.
- Add the rest of the ingredients and mix well with a spatula.
- Drop spoonfuls of batter on a baking tray lined with parchment paper.
- Bake the cookies in the preheated oven at 350F for 10-15 minutes or until golden brown on the edges.
- Serve the cookies chilled.

Nutritional information per serving

Calories: 122
Fat: 5.8g

Protein: 1.6g
Carbohydrates: 17.0g

MARETTI COOKIES

Time: 1 hour

Servings: 10

Ingredients:

2 cups almond flour
2/3 cup light brown sugar
1 teaspoon vanilla extract

½ teaspoon almond extract
2 egg whites

Directions:

- Mix the egg whites until fluffy.
- Add the vanilla and sugar and continue whipping until glossy and stiff.
- Fold in the almond flour then drop spoonfuls of batter on a baking tray lined with baking paper.
- Bake the cookies in the preheated oven at 350F for 10-15 minutes or until golden brown on the edges.
- Serve the cookies chilled.

Nutritional information per serving

Calories: 74

Fat: 2.8g

Walnut Crescent Cookies

Time: 1 ¼ hours   Servings: 20

Ingredients:

2/3 cup butter, softened
2/3 cup white sugar
1 teaspoon vanilla extract
½ teaspoon almond extract
1 egg

1 cup all-purpose flour
1 ½ cups ground walnuts
½ teaspoon salt
½ teaspoon baking powder

Directions:
- Mix the butter, sugar, vanilla and almond extract in a bowl until fluffy and creamy.
- Add the egg and mix well then fold in the flour, walnuts, salt and baking powder.
- Take small pieces of dough and shape them into small logs.
- Place them on a baking tray lined with baking paper and bake in the preheated oven at 350F for 10-15 minutes or until golden brown on the edges.
- Serve the cookies chilled.

Nutritional information per serving

Calories: 164
Fat: 11.9g

Protein: 3.2g
Carbohydrates: 12.5g

Chocolate Nutella Cookies

Time: 1 ¼ hours   Servings: 30

Ingredients:

1 cup butter, softened
¾ cup light brown sugar
¼ cup white sugar
1 cup Nutella
1 teaspoon vanilla extract
2 eggs

2 cups all-purpose flour
¼ cup cocoa powder
½ teaspoon salt
½ teaspoon baking soda
1 cup dark chocolate chips

Directions:
- Mix the butter and sugars in a bowl until creamy and fluffy.
- Add the Nutella, vanilla and eggs and mix well.
- Fold in the rest of the ingredients then drop spoonfuls of batter on a baking tray lined with parchment paper.
- Bake the cookies in the preheated oven at 350F for 10-15 minutes or until golden brown.
- Serve the cookie chilled.

Nutritional information per serving

Calories: 136
Fat: 8.0g

Protein: 1.8g
Carbohydrates: 15.5g

Chocolate Orange Shortbread Cookies

Time: 1 hour   Servings: 20

Ingredients:

½ cup butter, softened
¼ cup cocoa powder
½ cup white sugar
1 egg

1 teaspoon vanilla extract
1 tablespoon orange zest
1 ½ cups all-purpose flour
½ cup almond flour

¼ teaspoon salt

½ teaspoon baking soda

Directions:
- Mix the butter, cocoa powder and sugar in a bowl until fluffy and pale.
- Add the egg, vanilla and orange zest and mix well.
- Fold in the flour, almond flour, salt and baking soda then transfer the dough on a floured working surface.
- Roll the dough into a thin sheet then cut small cookies with your favorite cookie cutter.
- Bake the cookies in the preheated oven at 350F for 10-15 minutes or until golden brown and fragrant.
- Serve the cookies chilled.

Nutritional information per serving

Calories: 104
Fat: 5.4g

Protein: 1.6g
Carbohydrates: 13.0g

*C*INNAMON SNAP COOKIES

Time: 1 ¼ hours

Servings: 30

Ingredients:

2 cups all purpose flour
¼ cup cocoa powder
1 teaspoon baking soda
½ teaspoon salt
½ teaspoon ground ginger
1 teaspoon cinnamon powder

½ teaspoon ground cloves
1 cup butter, softened
2/3 cup white sugar
1 teaspoon vanilla extract
2 tablespoons golden syrup
1 egg

Directions:
- Mix the butter, sugar, vanilla and golden syrup in a bowl until pale and creamy.
- Add the egg and mix well then add the flour mixture.
- Form small balls of dough and place the cookies on a baking sheet lined with baking paper.
- Bake the cookies in the preheated oven at 350F for 10-15 minutes until fragrant and golden brown.
- Serve the cookies chilled.

Nutritional information per serving

Calories: 109
Fat: 6.5g

Protein: 1.2g
Carbohydrates: 12.3g

*T*HIN COCONUT COOKIES

Time: 1 hour

Servings: 20

Ingredients:

½ cup butter, softened
½ cup white sugar
2 egg whites

¼ cup all-purpose flour
1 ¾ cups shredded coconut
¼ teaspoon salt

Directions:
- Mix all the ingredients in a bowl until creamy. Place the dough in the fridge until firm.
- Form small balls of dough and place them on baking trays lined with baking paper.
- Flatten the cookies and bake them in the preheated oven at 350F for 10-15 minutes or until golden brown and crisp on the edges.
- Serve the cookies chilled.

Nutritional information per serving

Calories: 92
Fat: 7.0g
Protein: 0.8g
Carbohydrates: 7.3g

*L*EMON POPPY SEED COOKIES

Time: 1 hour

Servings: 20

Ingredients:

¼ cup butter, softened
¼ cup coconut oil
2/3 cup white sugar
1 egg
1 tablespoon lemon zest
2 tablespoons lemon juice

1 cup all-purpose flour
¼ cup cornstarch
¼ teaspoon salt
½ teaspoon baking soda
2 tablespoons poppy seeds

Directions:

- Mix the butter, coconut oil and sugar in a bowl until fluffy and pale.
- Add the egg, lemon zest and lemon juice and mix well.
- Fold in the rest of the ingredients and mix with a spatula.
- Drop spoonfuls of batter on baking trays lined with baking paper.
- Bake the cookies in the preheated oven at 350F for 10-15 minutes or until golden brown or until golden brown on the edges.
- Serve the cookies chilled.

Nutritional information per serving

Calories: 106
Fat: 5.7g

Protein: 1.1g
Carbohydrates: 13.2g

*G*INGER ALMOND BISCOTTI

Time: 1 ¼ hours

Servings: 20

Ingredients:

¾ cup white sugar
2 tablespoons dark brown sugar
2 tablespoons molasses
2 eggs
½ cup butter, softened
1 teaspoon vanilla extract

2 cups all-purpose flour
½ teaspoon salt
1 teaspoon baking powder
¼ teaspoon baking soda
1 teaspoon ground ginger
½ cup blanched almonds

Directions:

- Mix the sugars, molasses, eggs and butter in a bowl until creamy.
- Add the vanilla then fold in the rest of the ingredients.
- Transfer the dough on a baking tray lined with parchment paper and shape it into a log.
- Bake the log in the preheated oven at 350F for 15 minutes or until golden brown on the edges.
- When done, allow to cool down slightly then cut the log into thin slices and place them back on the baking tray with the cut facing up.
- Bake the cookies in the preheated oven at 350F for 10-15 additional minutes.
- Serve the biscotti chilled.

Nutritional information per serving

Calories: 145
Fat: 6.4g

Protein: 2.4g
Carbohydrates: 20.2g

*P*ECAN CREAM CHEESE COOKIES

Time: 2 hours

Servings: 40

Ingredients:

1 cup cream cheese

2/3 cup butter, softened

1 cup white sugar
1 teaspoon vanilla extract
1 egg
3 cups all-purpose flour

1 ½ cups ground pecans
¼ teaspoon salt
1 teaspoon baking powder

Directions:
- Mix the cream cheese, butter, sugar and vanilla and mix well. Add the egg and mix well.
- Fold in the rest of the ingredients then transfer the dough on plastic wrap and roll it into a log. Wrap tightly and place in the freezer for 1 hour.
- Remove the dough from the freezer and cut into thin cookies.
- Place them on a baking tray lined with baking paper and bake in the preheated oven at 350F for 10-15 minutes or until slightly golden brown on the edges.
- Serve the cookies chilled.

Nutritional information per serving

Calories: 105
Fat: 5.5g

Protein: 1.6g
Carbohydrates: 12.4g

RANGE POPPY SEED COOKIES

Time: 1 ¼ hours

Servings: 20

Ingredients:
½ cup butter, softened
½ cup white sugar
1 egg
1 tablespoon orange zest

1 ½ cups all-purpose flour
¼ teaspoon salt
½ teaspoon baking powder
1 tablespoon poppy seeds

Directions:
- Mix the butter and sugar in a bowl until fluffy and creamy.
- Add the egg and orange zest and mix well then fold in the flour, salt, baking powder and poppy seeds.
- Drop spoonfuls of batter on a baking tray lined with baking paper.
- Bake the cookies in the preheated oven at 350F for 10-15 minutes or until golden brown on the edges.
- Serve the cookies chilled.

Nutritional information per serving

Calories: 100
Fat: 5.1g

Protein: 1.4g
Carbohydrates: 12.4g

ONSTER COOKIE RECIPES

Time: 1 ¼ hours

Servings: 30

Ingredients:
½ cup butter, softened
½ cup smooth peanut butter
¾ cup light brown sugar
¼ cup white sugar
1 teaspoon vanilla extract
2 eggs
2 ¼ cups all-purpose flour

½ teaspoon salt
1 teaspoon baking soda
½ cup walnuts, chopped
½ cup pecans, chopped
½ cup M&M candies
½ cup mini marshmallows

Directions:
- Mix the butter, peanut butter and sugars in a bowl. Add the vanilla and eggs and mix well.
- Fold in the flour, salt and baking soda then add the rest of the ingredients.
- Drop spoonfuls of batter on a baking tray lined with parchment paper.
- Bake the cookies in the preheated oven at 350F for 10-15 minutes or until golden brown on the edges.
- Serve the cookies chilled.

Nutritional information per serving

Calories: 149

Fat: 7.2g

Protein: 3.2g

Carbohydrates: 18.9g

M APLE FLAVORED COOKIES

Time: 1 ¼ hours

Servings: 30

Ingredients:

½ cup butter, softened

1/2 cup light brown sugar

1 teaspoon vanilla extract

1 egg

½ cup maple syrup

2 cups all-purpose flour

¼ teaspoon salt

1 teaspoon baking powder

1 cup walnuts, chopped

Directions:

- Mix the butter, sugar and maple syrup in a bowl until fluffy and creamy.
- Add the vanilla and eggs and mix well then stir in the rest of the ingredients.
- Drop spoonfuls of batter on baking trays lined with baking paper.
- Bake the cookies in the preheated oven at 350F for 10-15 minutes or until golden brown on the edges.
- Serve the cookies chilled.

Nutritional information per serving

Calories: 109

Fat: 5.8g

Protein: 2.1g

Carbohydrates: 12.8g

W HITE CHOCOLATE PISTACHIO COOKIES

Time: 1 ¼ hours

Servings: 40

Ingredients:

1 cup butter, softened

1 cup white sugar

½ cup light brown sugar

2 eggs

¼ cup whole milk

1 teaspoon vanilla extract

2 ½ cups all-purpose flour

½ teaspoon salt

1 teaspoon baking soda

½ teaspoon baking powder

1 cup pistachio, chopped

½ cup white chocolate chips

Directions:

- Mix the butter and sugars in a bowl until fluffy and pale.
- Add the eggs and mix well then stir in the vanilla.
- Add the rest of the ingredients and mix with a spatula.
- Drop spoonfuls of batter on baking trays lined with baking paper.
- Bake the cookies in the preheated oven at 350F for 10-15 minutes or until golden brown on the edges.
- Serve the cookies chilled.

Nutritional information per serving

Calories: 119

Fat: 6.3g

Protein: 1.6g

Carbohydrates: 14.5g

P INE NUT COOKIES

Time: 1 hour

Servings: 20

Ingredients:

1 ½ cups almond paste

½ cup sugar

1 egg

2 egg whites

¼ teaspoon salt   ½ cup pine nuts

Directions:
- Mix the almond paste, sugar and egg and mix well until creamy.
- Whip the egg whites and salt until fluffy then fold the meringue into the almond paste.
- Drop spoonfuls of mixture on baking trays lined with baking paper.
- Top with pine nuts and bake in the preheated oven at 350F for 10-15 minutes or until golden brown and crisp.
- Serve the cookies chilled.

Nutritional information per serving

Calories: 125   Protein: 2.6g
Fat: 7.3g   Carbohydrates: 13.6g

*L*EMON RICOTTA COOKIES

Time: 2 hours   Servings: 40

Ingredients:

1 cup ricotta cheese   2 tablespoons lemon juice
1 cup white sugar   2 ½ cups all-purpose flour
2 eggs   ½ teaspoon salt
¼ cup butter, softened   1 teaspoon baking powder
1 tablespoon lemon zest

Directions:
- Mix the cheese, sugar, eggs and butter in a bowl until creamy.
- Add the lemon zest and lemon juice then fold in the flour, salt and baking powder.
- Drop spoonfuls of baking batter on a baking tray lined with parchment paper.
- Bake the cookies in the preheated oven at 350F for 10-15 minutes or until golden brown on the edges.
- Serve the cookies chilled.

Nutritional information per serving

Calories: 69   Protein: 1.8g
Fat: 1.9g   Carbohydrates: 11.4g

*C*OCONUT LIME BUTTER COOKIES

Time: 1 ¼ hours   Servings: 30

Ingredients:

1 cup butter, softened   2 cups all-purpose flour
1 cup white sugar   ½ teaspoon salt
2 egg yolks   1 cup shredded coconut
1 lime, zested and juiced   ½ teaspoon baking powder
1 teaspoon coconut extract

Directions:
- Mix the butter and sugar in a bowl until creamy and pale.
- Add the egg yolks, lime zest and lime juice, as well as the coconut extract.
- Stir in the flour, salt, coconut and baking powder then transfer the dough on a floured working surface.
- Roll the dough into a thin sheet then cut small cookies with your favorite cookie cutter.
- Place the cookies on a baking tray lined with parchment paper.
- Bake the cookies in the preheated oven at 350F for 10-15 minutes or until golden brown on the edges.
- Serve the cookies chilled.

Nutritional information per serving

Calories: 124   Carbohydrates: 13.8g
Fat: 7.4g
Protein: 1.2g

E ARL GREY COOKIES

Time: 1 ¼ hours

Servings: 20

Ingredients:

2 cups all-purpose flour
½ teaspoon salt
1 teaspoon baking powder
1 tablespoon loose Earl grey leaves

1 cup butter, softened
½ cup powdered sugar
1 egg
1 teaspoon vanilla extract

Directions:
- Mix the butter and sugar in a bowl until fluffy and pale.
- Add the egg and vanilla and mix well.
- Stir in the rest of the ingredients and mix with a spatula.
- Transfer the dough on a floured working surface and roll it into a thin sheet.
- Cut small cookies with your cookie cutters and place them on a baking tray lined with baking paper.
- Bake in the preheated oven at 350F for 10-12 minutes or until golden brown on the edges.
- Serve the cookies chilled.

Nutritional information per serving

Calories: 143
Fat: 9.6g

Protein: 1.7g
Carbohydrates: 12.7g

H AZELNUT CHOCOLATE CHIP COOKIES

Time: 1 ¼ hours

Servings: 30

Ingredients:

½ cup rolled oats, ground
2 cups all-purpose flour
1 cup ground hazelnuts
1 teaspoon baking powder
½ teaspoon salt
1 cup butter, softened

1 cup light brown sugar
1 egg
¼ cup sour cream
1 teaspoon vanilla extract
½ cup mini chocolate chip cookies

Directions:
- Mix the butter and sugar in a bowl until creamy and fluffy.
- Add the egg and vanilla and sour cream and mix well the stir in the dry ingredients and chocolate chips.
- Transfer the dough on a floured working surface and roll it into a thin sheet.
- Cut small cookies with your cookie cutters and place the cookies on baking trays lined with baking paper.
- Bake the cookies in the preheated oven at 350F for 10-15 minutes or until golden brown on the edges.
- Serve the cookies chilled.

Nutritional information per serving

Calories: 135
Fat: 8.6g

Protein: 1.8g
Carbohydrates: 13.1g

D OUBLE CHOCOLATE ESPRESSO COOKIES

Time: 1 hour

Servings: 20

Ingredients:

2 eggs
2/3 cup white sugar
1 teaspoon vanilla extract
¼ cup coconut oil, melted
1 teaspoon instant coffee

6 oz. dark chocolate
¼ cup butter
2 tablespoons all-purpose flour
¼ teaspoon salt

Directions:

- Mix the chocolate and butter in a heatproof bowl and place over a hot water bath. Melt them together until smooth and melted.
- Mix the eggs and sugar in a bowl until fluffy and pale. Add the vanilla and oil and mix gently. Stir in the coffee.
- Add the melted chocolate and mix gently then fold in the flour and salt.
- Drop spoonfuls of batter on a baking tray lined with baking paper.
- Bake in the preheated oven at 350F for 10-12 minutes or until set.
- Serve the cookies chilled.

Nutritional information per serving

Calories: 124
Fat: 8.0g

Protein: 1.3g
Carbohydrates: 12.4g

WHITE **C**HOCOLATE **C**HUNK **C**OOKIES

Time: 1 ¼ hours

Servings: 30

Ingredients:

½ cup butter, softened
1 cup light brown sugar
¼ cup white sugar
1 teaspoon vanilla extract
2 eggs

2 cups all-purpose flour
½ cup cocoa powder
½ teaspoon salt
1 teaspoon baking soda
4 oz. white chocolate, chopped

Directions:

- Mix the butter and sugars in a bowl until fluffy and pale.
- Add the vanilla and eggs and mix well.
- Fold in the flour, cocoa powder, salt and baking soda.
- Add the white chocolate chips then drop spoonfuls of batter on baking trays lined with baking paper.
- Bake the cookies in the preheated oven at 350F for 10-15 minutes or until risen.
- Serve the cookies chilled.

Nutritional information per serving

Calories: 110
Fat: 4.8g

Protein: 1.8g
Carbohydrates: 15.8g

GERMAN **C**HOCOLATE **C**OOKIES

Time: 1 ¼ hours

Servings: 30

Ingredients:

1 cup butter, softened
1 cup light brown sugar
½ cup white sugar
2 eggs
2 ¼ cups all-purpose flour
¼ cup cocoa powder

1 teaspoon baking soda
½ teaspoon salt
½ cup dark chocolate chips
½ cup coconut flakes
1 cup pecans, chopped

Directions:

- Mix the butter and sugars in a bowl until pale and creamy.
- Add the eggs and mix well then fold in the flour, cocoa powder, baking soda and salt.
- Fold in the chocolate chips, coconut flakes and pecans.
- Drop spoonfuls of batter on baking trays lined with baking paper.
- Bake the cookies in the preheated oven at 350F for 10-15 minutes or until risen.
- Serve the cookies chilled.

Nutritional information per serving

Calories: 142
Fat: 7.9g

Protein: 1.8g
Carbohydrates: 17.2g

Chocolate Star Anise Cookies

Time: 1 ¼ hours

Servings: 20

Ingredients:
½ cup butter, softened
2 tablespoons coconut oil
1 egg
¾ cup white sugar
1 ½ cups all-purpose flour

½ cup cocoa powder
½ teaspoon salt
½ teaspoon baking soda
1 teaspoon ground star anise
½ cup pecans, chopped

Directions:
- Mix the butter and coconut oil in a bowl. Add the sugar and mix until fluffy.
- Stir in the egg and give it a good mix.
- Fold in the rest of the ingredients and mix with a spatula.
- Drop spoonfuls of batter on baking trays lined with parchment paper.
- Bake in the preheated oven at 350F for 10-15 minutes or until risen and fragrant.
- Serve the cookies chilled.

Nutritional information per serving
Calories: 129
Fat: 7.1g

Protein: 1.8g
Carbohydrates: 16.1g

Lemony Lavender Cookies

Time: 1 ¼ hours

Servings: 25

Ingredients:
½ cup butter, softened
2 tablespoons honey
1 egg
1 tablespoon lemon zest
½ cup white sugar

1 teaspoon lavender buds
1 cup all-purpose flour
1 cup almond flour
½ teaspoon salt
½ teaspoon baking soda

Directions:
- Mix the butter, honey, egg, lemon zest, sugar and lavender in a bowl until pale and light.
- Add the rest of the ingredients and mix with a spatula.
- Drop spoonfuls of batter on a baking tray lined with baking paper.
- Bake the cookies in the preheated oven at 350F for 10-15 minutes or until golden brown on the edges.
- Serve the cookies chilled.

Nutritional information per serving
Calories: 82
Fat: 4.5g

Protein: 1.1g
Carbohydrates: 9.9g

Fig and Almond Cookies

Time: 1 ¼ hours

Servings: 20

Ingredients:
½ cup butter, softened
1 cup powdered sugar
1 teaspoon vanilla extract
1 egg
1 ¾ cups all-purpose flour
½ cup ground almonds
½ teaspoon baking soda

½ teaspoon salt
1 ½ cups dried figs, chopped

Directions:
- Mix the butter, sugar and vanilla in a bowl until fluffy and pale.
- Add the egg and mix well then fold in the rest of the ingredients.
- Drop spoonfuls of batter on a baking tray lined with baking paper.
- Bake in the preheated oven at 350F for 10-15 minutes or until golden brown on the edges and slightly crisp.
- Serve the cookies chilled.

Nutritional information per serving

Calories: 159

Fat: 6.3g

Protein: 2.5g

Carbohydrates: 24.4g

EVERYTHING-BUT-THE-KITCHEN-SINK COOKIES

Time: 1 ¼ hours

Servings: 20

Ingredients:

¼ cup coconut oil, melted

2 tablespoons butter, softened

1 teaspoon vanilla extract

1 egg

¼ cup applesauce

1 cup whole wheat flour

1 cup rolled oats

¼ teaspoon cinnamon powder

½ teaspoon ground ginger

½ teaspoon salt

½ cup walnuts, chopped

¼ cup dried apricots, chopped

¼ cup dried cranberries

¼ cup dark chocolate chips

¼ cup shredded coconut

Directions:
- Mix the coconut oil, butter, vanilla, egg and applesauce in a bowl.
- Add the flour, oats, spices and salt then fold in the walnuts, apricots, cranberries, apricots, chocolate chips and coconut.
- Drop spoonfuls of batter on baking trays lined with baking paper.
- Bake the cookies in the preheated oven at 350F for 12-15 minutes or until golden brown and crisp on the edges.
- Serve the cookies chilled.

Nutritional information per serving

Calories: 109

Fat: 7.0g

Protein: 2.4g

Carbohydrates: 9.8g

DRIED FRUIT WHOLESOME COOKIES

Time: 1 ¼ hours

Servings: 20

Ingredients:

¼ cup coconut oil, melted

¼ cup applesauce

1 egg

1 teaspoon vanilla extract

1 ¼ cups whole wheat flour

¼ teaspoon salt

½ teaspoon baking soda

½ teaspoon cinnamon powder

¼ cup rolled oats

¼ cup golden raisins

¼ cup dried cranberries

¼ cup dried apricots, chopped

Directions:
- Mix the coconut oil, applesauce, egg and vanilla and mix well.
- Stir in the flour, salt, baking soda and cinnamon then add the oats and dried fruits.
- Drop spoonfuls of batter on a baking tray lined with baking paper.
- Bake the cookies in the preheated oven at 350F for 10-12 minutes or until golden brown and crisp on the edges.
- Serve the cookies chilled.

Nutritional information per serving

Calories: 68

Fat: 3.1g

Protein: 1.3g   Carbohydrates: 8.8g

F RESH **B**LUEBERRY **C**OOKIES

Time: 1 ½ hours   Servings: 30

Ingredients:

1 cup butter, softened   1 tablespoon lemon zest
1 teaspoon vanilla extract   2 cups all-purpose flour
1 cup powdered sugar   ½ teaspoon salt
1 egg   ½ teaspoon baking soda
¼ cup whole milk   1 cup fresh blueberries

Directions:

- Mix the butter, vanilla and sugar in a bowl until fluffy and light.
- Add the egg, milk and lemon zest and mix well.
- Stir in the flour, salt and baking soda and mix with a spatula then fold in the blueberries.
- Drop spoonfuls of batter on a baking tray lined with parchment paper.
- Bake in the preheated oven at 350F for 10-14 minutes or until golden brown on the edges.
- Serve the cookies chilled.

Nutritional information per serving

Calories: 107   Protein: 1.2g
Fat: 6.5g   Carbohydrates: 11.2g

A LMOND **B**LUEBERRY **C**OOKIES

Time: 1 ¼ hours   Servings: 20

Ingredients:

½ cup butter, softened   1 ¼ cups all-purpose flour
2/3 cup white sugar   1 cup ground almonds
1 teaspoon lemon zest   ¼ teaspoon salt
1 egg   ½ teaspoon baking soda
¼ cup whole milk   ½ cup dried blueberries
1 teaspoon almond extract   ¼ cup sliced almonds

Directions:

- Mix the butter, sugar and lemon zest in a bowl until fluffy and pale.
- Add the egg and milk and mix well then fold in the flour, ground almonds, baking soda, salt and blueberries.
- Drop spoonfuls of batter on a baking tray lined with parchment paper and top each cookie with almond slices.
- Bake the cookies in the preheated oven at 350F for 10-15 minutes or until golden brown and fragrant.
- Serve the cookies chilled or store them in an airtight container for up to 1 week.

Nutritional information per serving

Calories: 136   Protein: 2.5g
Fat: 8.0g   Carbohydrates: 14.6g

L ENTIL **C**OOKIES

Time: 1 ¼ hours   Servings: 30

Ingredients:

4 oz. lentil, cooked and pureed   ¾ cup light brown sugar
½ cup butter, melted   1 ½ cups all-purpose flour
1 egg   ¼ teaspoon salt
1 teaspoon vanilla extract   ½ teaspoon baking powder

½ teaspoon cinnamon powder
½ teaspoon ground ginger

½ cup walnuts, chopped

Directions:
- Mix the lentil puree, butter, egg, vanilla and sugar in a bowl until creamy and light.
- Add the rest of the ingredients and mix well.
- Form small balls of mixture and place them on a baking tray lined with baking paper.
- Bake the cookies in the preheated oven at 350F for 10-15 minutes or until golden brown and fragrant.
- Serve the cookies chilled.

Nutritional information per serving

Calories: 93
Fat: 4.5g

Protein: 2.3g
Carbohydrates: 10.9g

Coconut Florentine Cookies

Time: 1 ¼ hours

Servings: 25

Ingredients:

1 cup butter, softened
½ cup light brown sugar
¼ cup honey
1 cup shredded coconut

1 ½ cups sliced almonds
¼ teaspoon salt
4 tablespoons all-purpose flour

Directions:
- Mix the butter, sugar and honey in a heatproof bowl over a hot water bath until smooth and melted.
- Remove from heat and add the coconut, almonds, salt and flour.
- Drop spoonfuls of batter on a baking tray lined with baking paper.
- Spread the mixture slightly then bake the cookies in the preheated oven at 350F for 10-15 minutes or until golden brown and crisp.
- Allow the cookies to cool down before serving.

Nutritional information per serving

Calories: 135
Fat: 11.3g

Protein: 1.5g
Carbohydrates: 8.3g

Vanilla Sugared Cookies

Time: 2 hours

Servings: 20

Ingredients:

½ cup butter, softened
½ cup powdered sugar
1 tablespoon vanilla extract
1 egg

2 cups all-purpose flour
¼ teaspoon salt
¼ teaspoon baking powder
Powdered sugar for coating the cookies

Directions:
- Mix the butter and sugar in a bowl until pale and light.
- Add the vanilla and egg and mix well.
- Stir in the flour, salt and baking powder then transfer the dough on a plastic wrap and roll it into a log.
- Wrap the dough and place it in the freezer for 30 minutes.
- When done, cut the log of dough into thin slices.
- Place the cookies in a baking tray lined with parchment paper and bake in the preheated oven at 350F for 10-12 minutes or until golden brown on the edges.
- Serve the cookies chilled.

Nutritional information per serving

Calories: 103
Fat: 5.0g

Protein: 1.6g
Carbohydrates: 12.7g

TOFFEE APPLE COOKIES

Time: 1 ¼ hours

Servings: 20

Ingredients:

½ cup butter, softened
1 cup light brown sugar
2 egg yolks
½ cup almond flour
1 ½ cups all-purpose flour

½ teaspoon baking soda
¼ teaspoon salt
2 apples, peeled and cored
½ cup toffee bits

Directions:

- Mix the butter and sugar in a bowl until fluffy and pale.
- Add the egg yolks and mix well then stir in the almond flour, flour, baking soda and salt in the bowl.
- Add the eggs and toffee bits then drop spoonfuls of batter on a baking tray lined with baking paper.
- Bake the cookies in the preheated oven at 350F for 10-15 minutes or until golden brown on the edges.
- Serve the cookies chilled.

Nutritional information per serving

Calories: 129
Fat: 5.8g

Protein: 2.1g
Carbohydrates: 17.8g

SOFT BAKED CHOCOLATE COOKIES

Time: 1 ½ hours

Servings: 30

Ingredients:

½ cup butter, softened
1 cup dark brown sugar
¼ cup light corn syrup
2 eggs
1 teaspoon vanilla extract

2 ½ cups all-purpose flour
½ teaspoon salt
½ teaspoon baking soda
1 ¼ cups chocolate chips

Directions:

- Mix the butter and sugar in a bowl until pale and creamy.
- Add the corn syrup, eggs and vanilla and mix well.
- Fold in the flour, salt and baking soda then add the chocolate chips and mix well.
- Drop spoonfuls of batter on baking trays lined with baking paper and bake the cookies in the preheated oven at 350F for 10-15 minutes or until golden brown and crisp on the edges.
- Serve the cookies chilled.

Nutritional information per serving

Calories: 133
Fat: 5.5g

Protein: 2.0g
Carbohydrates: 18.9g

BROWN SUGAR CHOCOLATE CHIP COOKIES

Time: 1 ½ hours

Servings: 40

Ingredients:

1 ½ cups butter, softened
1 cup light brown sugar
1 cup dark brown sugar
½ cup white sugar
2 eggs
1 teaspoon vanilla extract
3 cups all-purpose flour

½ teaspoon salt
1 teaspoon baking soda
1 ½ cups dark chocolate chips

Directions:
- Mix the butter and sugars in a bowl until creamy and fluffy.
- Add the eggs and vanilla and mix well then fold in the rest of the ingredients.
- Drop spoonfuls of batter on a baking tray lined with baking paper.
- Bake the cookies in the preheated oven at 350F for 10-15 minutes or until golden brown on the edges and crisp.
- Serve the cookies chilled.

Nutritional information per serving

Calories: 157
Fat: 8.4g

Protein: 1.6g
Carbohydrates: 19.8g

$\mathcal{P}$ ECAN STUDDED COOKIES

Time: 1 hour

Servings: 20

Ingredients:

½ cup butter
2/3 cup light brown sugar
1 teaspoon lemon juice
1 egg
1 ½ cups all-purpose flour

¼ cup cocoa powder
¼ teaspoon salt
½ teaspoon baking soda
½ cup dark chocolate chips

Directions:
- Melt the butter in a saucepan until it becomes slightly golden brown.
- Remove from heat and stir in the lemon juice and egg, as well as sugar.
- Add the rest of the ingredients and mix with a spatula.
- Drop spoonfuls of batter on a baking tray lined with baking paper.
- Bake the cookies in the preheated oven at 350F for 10-15 minutes or until slightly golden brown and crisp on the edges.
- Serve the cookies chilled.

Nutritional information per serving

Calories: 113
Fat: 5.9g

Protein: 1.7g
Carbohydrates: 14.5g

$\mathcal{L}$ AYERED CHOCOLATE CHIP COOKIES

Time: 1 ¼ hours

Servings: 30

Ingredients:

1 cup butter, softened
¾ cup light brown sugar
¼ cup dark brown sugar
1 teaspoon vanilla extract
2 eggs

2 ¼ cups all-purpose flour
½ teaspoon salt
1 teaspoon baking soda
1 cup dark chocolate chips

Directions:
- Mix the butter and sugars in a bowl until fluffy and pale.
- Add the eggs and mix well then fold in the rest of the ingredients.
- Drop spoonfuls of batter on baking trays lined with parchment paper.
- Bake the cookies in the preheated oven at 350F for 12-14 minutes or until golden brown.
- Serve the cookies chilled.

Nutritional information per serving

Calories: 130
Fat: 7.6g
Protein: 1.7g
Carbohydrates: 14.6g

Walnut Banana Cookies

Time: 1 hour

Servings: 20

Ingredients:

1 cup whole wheat flour
½ cup all-purpose flour
½ teaspoon salt
½ teaspoon baking powder
½ cup butter, softened
½ cup white sugar

¼ cup dark brown sugar
1 egg
1 teaspoon vanilla extract
1 banana, mashed
½ cup dark chocolate chips
½ cup walnuts, chopped

Directions:

- Mix the butter and sugars in a bowl until fluffy and pale.
- Add the egg, vanilla and banana and mix well.
- Stir in the flours, salt and baking powder then fold in the chocolate chips and walnuts.
- Drop spoonfuls of batter on a baking tray lined with parchment paper and bake in the preheated oven at 350F for 10-14 minutes or until golden brown and crisp on the edges.
- The cookies are best served chilled.

Nutritional information per serving

Calories: 143
Fat: 7.6g

Protein: 2.3g
Carbohydrates: 17.7g

Peanut Butter Cinnamon Cookies

Time: 1 hour

Servings: 20

Ingredients:

1 ½ cups smooth peanut butter
2 eggs
½ cup white sugar
¼ cup almond milk

1 cup all-purpose flour
½ teaspoon salt
1 teaspoon cinnamon powder
½ teaspoon baking soda

Directions:

- Mix the peanut butter, eggs and sugar in a bowl until creamy.
- Add the flour, salt, cinnamon and baking soda and give it a quick mix.
- Drop spoonfuls of batter on baking trays lined with parchment paper and bake the cookies in the preheated oven at 350F for 10-15 minutes or until fragrant and crisp on the edges.
- Serve the cookies chilled

Nutritional information per serving

Calories: 168
Fat: 11.0g

Protein: 6.1g
Carbohydrates: 13.7g

Cakey Chocolate Chip Cookies

Time: 1 hour

Servings: 20

Ingredients:

1 egg
½ cup white sugar
¼ cup coconut oil, melted
¼ cup whole milk

1 ½ cups all-purpose flour
¼ teaspoon salt
½ teaspoon baking powder
½ cup dark chocolate chips

Directions:

- Mix the egg and sugar in a bowl until double in volume.
- Add the coconut oil and milk and mix well.

- Stir in the rest of the ingredients then drop spoonfuls of batter on a baking tray lined with baking paper.
- Bake the cookies in the preheated oven at 350F for 10-12 minutes or until risen and golden.
- Allow to cool in the pan before serving.

Nutritional information per serving
Calories: 96
Fat: 3.9g
Protein: 1.6g
Carbohydrates: 14.4g

Muffins and Cupcakes

Coconut Cupcakes

Time: 1 ½ hours

Servings: 12

Ingredients:

Cupcakes:
½ cup butter, softened
¾ cup white sugar
1 teaspoon vanilla extract
3 eggs
1 ¾ cup all-purpose flour
1 ½ teaspoons baking powder
½ teaspoon salt

½ cup shredded coconut
¾ cup coconut milk
Frosting:
½ cup butter, softened
½ cup cream cheese, softened
2 cups powdered sugar
1 teaspoon vanilla extract

Directions:
- For the cupcakes, mix the butter, sugar and vanilla in a bowl until fluffy and pale.
- Add the eggs, one by one, then fold in the flour, baking powder, salt and coconut, alternating it with milk. Start with flour and end with flour.
- Spoon the batter in 12 muffin cups lined with muffin papers.
- Bake in the preheated oven at 350F for 15-20 minutes or until well risen and golden brown.
- Allow the cupcakes to cool in the pan.
- For the frosting, mix the butter, cream cheese and sugar in a bowl for 5 minutes or until fluffy and pale.
- Stir in the vanilla and mix well then spoon the frosting in a pastry bag and pipe it over the cupcakes.

Nutritional information per serving

Calories: 425
Fat: 24.7g

Protein: 4.6g
Carbohydrates: 48.4g

Banana Buttermilk Muffins

Time: 1 hour

Servings: 12

Ingredients:

1 ¾ cups all-purpose flour
½ cup white sugar
1 teaspoon baking powder
1 teaspoon baking soda
½ teaspoon salt

½ cup rolled oats
¼ cup butter, melted
1 egg
1 cup buttermilk
2 ripe bananas, mashed

Directions:
- Mix the dry ingredients in a bowl and the wet ingredients in a different bowl.
- Pour the wet ingredients over the dry ones and mix quickly.
- Spoon the batter in a muffin pan lined with muffin papers.
- Bake the muffins in the preheated oven at 350F for 20 minutes or until golden brown or until slightly golden brown and well risen.
- Serve the muffins chilled.

Nutritional information per serving

Calories: 176
Fat: 4.8g
Protein: 3.7g
Carbohydrates: 30.2g

INTY CHOCOLATE CUPCAKES

Time: 1 ½ hours

Servings: 12

Ingredients:

Cupcakes:
1 ½ cups all-purpose flour
½ cup cocoa powder
1 cup white sugar
1 teaspoon baking soda
½ teaspoon baking powder
½ teaspoon salt
1 cup buttermilk

2 eggs
¼ cup canola oil
1 teaspoon vanilla extract
Frosting:
2/3 cup heavy cream
1 ½ cups dark chocolate chips
2 tablespoons butter
1 teaspoon peppermint extract

Directions:

- For the cupcakes, mix the flour, cocoa powder, sugar, baking soda, baking powder and salt in a bowl.
- Add the buttermilk, eggs, canola oil and vanilla and mix quickly.
- Spoon the batter in a muffin cup lined with muffin papers.
- Bake the cupcakes in the preheated oven at 350F for 20 25 minutes or until well risen.
- Allow to cool in the pan.
- For the frosting, bring the cream to the boiling in a saucepan. Remove from heat and stir in the chocolate chips. Mix until melted and smooth then add the peppermint extract and butter and mix well.
- Allow the frosting to cool then top each cupcake with the frosting.
- Serve chilled.

Nutritional information per serving

Calories: 298
Fat: 14.5g

Protein: 5.0g
Carbohydrates: 42.0g

P EACHY MUFFINS

Time: 1 hour

Servings: 12

Ingredients:

1 cup all-purpose flour
½ cup whole wheat flour
½ teaspoon salt
1 teaspoon baking soda
2 tablespoons chia seeds

½ cup canola oil
¾ cup white sugar
2 eggs
½ cup plain yogurt
2 peaches, pitted and diced

Directions:

- Mix the flours, salt, chia seeds and baking soda in a bowl.
- Mix the oil, sugar and eggs in another bowl and whip until double in volume.
- Add the yogurt then stir in the flour. Fold in the peaches.
- Spoon the batter in a muffin tin lined with muffin papers.
- Bake the muffins in the preheated oven at 350F for 20-25 minutes or until well risen and golden brown.
- Serve the muffins chilled.

Nutritional information per serving

Calories: 219
Fat: 10.9g

Protein: 3.8g
Carbohydrates: 26.9g

M OCHA CUPCAKES

Time: 1 ½ hours
Servings: 14

Ingredients:

Cupcakes:

2 cups all-purpose flour

2 teaspoons baking powder

½ teaspoon salt

½ cup canola oil

1 cup light brown sugar

2 eggs

1 teaspoon vanilla extract

½ cup sour cream

½ cup espresso

Frosting:

1 cup cream cheese

½ cup butter, softened

2 cups powdered sugar

1 teaspoon instant coffee

½ cup dark chocolate chips, melted

Directions:

- For the cupcakes, mix the oil and sugar in a bowl for 2 minutes then add the eggs and mix well.
- Stir in the vanilla, sour cream and espresso then add the flour, baking powder and salt.
- Pour the batter in a muffin tin lined with muffin papers.
- Bake the cupcakes in the preheated oven at 350F for 20-25 minutes.
- Allow to cool in the pan.
- For the frosting, mix the cream cheese and butter in a bowl until pale. Add the sugar and continue whipping until fluffy.
- Stir in the coffee and melted chocolate.
- Spoon the frosting in a pastry bag and pipe it on top of each cupcake.
- Serve the cupcakes fresh.

Nutritional information per serving

Calories: 404

Fat: 23.8g

Protein: 4.5g

Carbohydrates: 44.9g

TRAWBERRY MUFFINS

Time: 1 hour

Servings: 12

Ingredients:

1 cup all-purpose flour

¾ cup whole wheat flour

1 teaspoon baking soda

½ teaspoon salt

½ cup canola oil

¾ cup white sugar

2 eggs

½ cup milk

1 ½ cups strawberries, sliced

Directions:

- Mix the flours, baking soda and salt in a bowl.
- Add the canola oil, sugar, eggs and mix and give it a quick mix.
- Fold in the strawberries then spoon the batter in12 muffin cups lined with muffin papers.
- Bake the muffins in the preheated oven at 350F for 20-25 minutes or until golden brown and well risen.
- Allow to cool down before serving.

Nutritional information per serving

Calories: 215

Fat: 10.3g

Protein: 3.3g

Carbohydrates: 28.3g

STRAWBERRY AND CREAM CUPCAKES

Time: 1 ½ hours

Servings: 12

Ingredients:

½ cup butter, softened

2/3 cup white sugar

3 eggs

1 teaspoon vanilla extract

1 ½ cups all-purpose flour

½ teaspoon salt

1 ½ teaspoons baking powder

1 cup fresh strawberries, sliced

1 ½ cups heavy cream, whipped

Directions:
- Mix the butter and sugar in a bowl until fluffy and pale.
- Add the eggs, one by one, then stir in the vanilla.
- Fold in the flour, salt and baking powder then add the strawberries.
- Spoon the batter into 12 muffin cups lined with muffin papers and bake in the preheated oven at 350F for 20-25 minutes or until golden brown and well risen.
- Allow to cool down then top each cupcake with whipped cream.
- Serve the cupcakes chilled.

Nutritional information per serving
Calories: 239

Fat: 14.5g

Protein: 3.5g

Carbohydrates: 24.8g

OUBLE CHOCOLATE CUPCAKES

Time: 1 ½ hours

Servings: 12

Ingredients:
Cupcakes:

2 eggs

1 cup brewed coffee

¾ cup white sugar

1 teaspoon lemon juice

1 teaspoon vanilla extract

½ cup canola oil

½ cup cocoa powder

1 ½ cups all purpose flour

½ teaspoon salt

1 teaspoon baking soda

Frosting:

1 cup heavy cream

2 cups dark chocolate chips

1 teaspoon vanilla extract

Directions:
- For the cupcakes, mix all the ingredients in a bowl and give it a quick mix.
- Pour the batter into 12 muffin cups lined with muffin papers.
- Bake the cupcakes in the preheated oven at 350F for 20-25 minutes or until well risen and set.
- Allow to cool in the pan.
- For the frosting, bring the cream to the boiling point in a saucepan.
- Add the chocolate chips and mix well until melted. Stir in the vanilla and mix well.
- Allow the frosting to cool down.
- Top each cupcake with the chilled frosting.

Nutritional information per serving
Calories: 333

Fat: 19.5g

Protein: 4.7g

Carbohydrates: 40.1g

ANANA PEANUT BUTTER MUFFINS

Time: 1 hour

Servings: 12

Ingredients:
¼ cup smooth peanut butter

2 ripe bananas, mashed

2 eggs

½ cup buttermilk

¼ cup canola oil

1 teaspoon vanilla extract

½ cup light brown sugar

1 ½ cups all-purpose flour

½ teaspoon salt

1 teaspoon baking soda

Directions:
- Mix the peanut butter, bananas, oil, eggs and buttermilk in a bowl.
- Add the vanilla and mix well then fold in the rest of the ingredients.
- Spoon the batter in 12 muffin cups lined with muffin papers.
- Bake the muffins in the preheated oven at 350F for 20-25 minutes or until well risen and fragrant.
- Serve the muffins chilled.

Nutritional information per serving

Calories: 185
Fat: 8.3g

Protein: 4.4g
Carbohydrates: 24.0g

ED VELVET CUPCAKES

Time: 1 ½ hours

Servings: 12

Ingredients:

Cupcakes:
1 ½ cups all-purpose flour
1 tablespoon cocoa powder
½ teaspoon baking soda
1 teaspoon baking powder
½ teaspoon salt
¾ cup canola oil
1 egg
¾ cup white sugar

½ cup buttermilk
1 teaspoon red food coloring
½ teaspoon white wine vinegar
1 teaspoon vanilla extract
Frosting:
1 cup cream cheese, softened
½ cup butter, softened
3 cups powdered sugar
1 teaspoon vanilla extract

Directions:
- For the cupcakes, sift the flour, baking soda, baking powder and cocoa powder in a bowl.
- In a different bowl, mix the oil, egg and sugar until creamy and pale.
- Stir in the buttermilk, red food coloring, vinegar and vanilla extract.
- Spoon the batter in a muffin tin lined with muffin papers.
- Bake the cupcakes in the preheated oven at 350F for 20-25 minutes or until well risen.
- Allow the cupcakes to cool in the pan.
- For the frosting, mix the cream cheese and butter in a bowl. Add the vanilla and mix well then stir in the sugar and continue mixing for 5 minutes until fluffy and airy.
- Spoon the frosting in a pastry bag and pipe it over the cupcakes.
- Serve the cupcakes fresh.

Nutritional information per serving

Calories: 489
Fat: 28.7g

Protein: 4.0g
Carbohydrates: 55.9g

ANILLA CUPCAKES WITH MAPLE FROSTING

Time: 1 ½ hours

Servings: 10

Ingredients:

Cupcakes:
½ cup butter, softened
¾ cup white sugar
1 teaspoon vanilla extract
3 eggs
1 ½ cups all-purpose flour
½ teaspoon salt

1 teaspoon baking powder
½ cup whole milk
Frosting:
1 cup butter, softened
2 cups powdered sugar
1 teaspoon vanilla extract

Directions:
- For the cupcakes, mix the butter and sugar until fluffy and pale.
- Add the vanilla then stir in the eggs and mix well.
- Fold in the flour, salt and baking powder, alternating it with the milk.
- Spoon the batter in a muffin tin lined with muffin papers.
- Bake in the preheated oven at 350F for 20-25 minutes or until they pass the toothpick test.
- For the frosting, mix the butter in a bowl until fluffy. Add the sugar and continue mixing until airy and pale.
- Add the vanilla then spoon the frosting in a pastry bag and pipe it over the chilled cupcakes.

S WEET POTATO CUPCAKES

Time: 1 ½ hours

Servings: 16

Ingredients:

Cupcakes:

2 cups all-purpose flour

2 teaspoons baking powder

½ teaspoon salt

1 teaspoon cinnamon powder

½ teaspoon ground ginger

1 cup butter, softened

1 cup white sugar

3 eggs

1 ½ cups sweet potato puree

1 teaspoon vanilla extract

½ cup mini marshmallows

Frosting:

1 cup cream cheese

½ cup butter, softened

2 cups powdered sugar

Directions:

- For the cupcakes, sift the flour, baking powder, salt, cinnamon and ginger in a bowl.
- In a different bowl, mix the butter and sugar until fluffy and pale.
- Add the eggs and mix well then stir in the pumpkin puree and vanilla.
- Fold in the flour then spoon the batter in 12 muffin cups lined with baking muffin papers.
- Bake the cupcakes in the preheated oven at 350F for 20-25 minutes or until well risen and fragrant.
- For the frosting, mix all the ingredients in a bowl until pale and fluffy.
- Spoon the frosting in a pastry bag and pipe it over the cupcakes.

Nutritional information per serving

Calories: 408

Fat: 23.4g

Protein: 4.5g

Carbohydrates: 47.1g

C HOCOLATE GRAHAM CUPCAKES

Time: 1 ½ hours

Servings: 12

Ingredients:

Cupcakes:

1 cup whole wheat flour

½ cup all-purpose flour

½ cup crushed graham crackers

½ teaspoon salt

1 teaspoon baking soda

1/2 teaspoon cinnamon powder

1 cup butter, softened

1 cup light brown sugar

1 teaspoon vanilla extract

4 eggs

¼ cup whole milk

Frosting:

1 cup heavy cream

2 cups dark chocolate chips

½ cup crushed graham crackers

Directions:

- For the cupcakes, mix the butter and sugar in a bowl until pale and creamy.
- Add the vanilla and eggs, one by one and mix well.
- Fold in the flours, graham crackers, salt, baking soda and cinnamon powder, alternating it with the milk.
- Spoon the batter in a muffin tin lined with baking muffin papers.
- Bake in the preheated oven at 350F for 20-25 minutes or until the cupcakes pass the toothpick test.
- Allow to cool in the pan.
- For the frosting, bring the cream to a boil in a saucepan. Remove from heat and add the chocolate. Mix until melted and smooth then allow to cool down.
- Top each cupcake with frosting and sprinkle with crushed graham crackers.

Nutritional information per serving

Calories: 421

Fat: 26.9g

Protein: 5.8g   Carbohydrates: 43.2g

*M*ATCHA STRAWBERRY CUPCAKES

Time: 1 ½ hours   Servings: 14

Ingredients:

Cupcakes: 3 eggs
1 ½ cups all-purpose flour   1 teaspoon vanilla extract
¼ cup cornstarch   2/3 cup whole milk
½ teaspoon salt   Frosting:
1 teaspoon baking powder   1 cup butter, softened
1 tablespoon matcha   2 cups powdered sugar
½ cup butter, softened   1 cup fresh strawberries, sliced
1 cup white sugar

Directions:

- For the cupcakes, mix the butter and sugar in a bowl until fluffy and pale.
- Add the eggs and vanilla and mix well.
- Fold in the dry ingredients, alternating them with milk.
- Spoon the batter in a muffin tin lined with muffin papers.
- Bake the cupcakes in the preheated oven at 350F for 20-25 minutes or until well risen.
- Allow the cupcakes to cool down.
- For the frosting, mix the butter and sugar in a bowl until airy and fluffy.
- Spoon the frosting into a pastry bag and pipe it over the cupcakes. Arrange one strawberry on top of each cupcake and serve fresh.

Nutritional information per serving

Calories: 377   Protein: 3.2g
Fat: 21.2g   Carbohydrates: 45.3g

*B*LACKBERRY MUFFINS

Time: 1 hour   Servings: 10

Ingredients:

1 ½ cups all-purpose flour   2 eggs
½ cup rolled oats   1 cup buttermilk
1 teaspoon baking soda   1 teaspoon vanilla extract
½ teaspoon salt   1 cup fresh blackberries
2/3 cup white sugar

Directions:

- Mix the flour, oats, baking soda, salt and sugar in a bowl.
- Add the eggs, buttermilk and vanilla and mix quickly.
- Fold in the blackberries then scoop the batter in a muffin tin lined with muffin papers.
- Bake the muffins in the preheated oven at 350F for 20-25 minutes or until well risen and golden.
- Serve the muffins chilled.

Nutritional information per serving

Calories: 164   Protein: 4.6g
Fat: 1.6g   Carbohydrates: 33.1g

*B*LUEBERRY FROSTED CUPCAKES

Time: 1 ½ hours
Servings: 12

Ingredients:

Cupcakes:
½ cup butter, softened
2/3 cup white sugar
2 tablespoons dark brown sugar
3 eggs
1 teaspoon vanilla extract
1 ¾ cups all-purpose flour
1 teaspoon baking powder
½ teaspoon salt
1 cup buttermilk
1 cup fresh blueberries
Frosting:
1 cup butter, softened
2 ½ cups powdered sugar
¼ cup blueberry puree

Directions:

- For the cupcakes, mix the butter and sugars in a bowl until fluffy and pale.
- Add the eggs and vanilla and mix well then fold in the flour, baking powder and salt.
- Stir in the buttermilk then fold in the blueberries.
- Spoon the batter in 12 muffin cups lined with muffin papers.
- Bake the cupcakes in the preheated oven at 350F for 20-25 minutes or until well risen and golden brown.
- Allow the cupcakes to cool down in the pan.
- For the frosting, mix the butter and sugar in a bowl until fluffy and pale, at least 5 minutes.
- Add the blueberry puree and mix well.
- Spoon the frosting into a pastry bag and pipe it on cupcakes.

Nutritional information per serving

Calories: 463
Fat: 24.5g
Protein: 4.3g
Carbohydrates: 58.8g

*B*LACK SESAME CUPCAKES WITH CREAM CHEESE FROSTING

Time: 1 ½ hours

Servings: 14

Ingredients:

Cupcakes:
2/3 cup butter, softened
1 cup white sugar
2 eggs
¾ cup milk
1 teaspoon vanilla extract
1 ½ cups all-purpose flour
¼ cup black sesame powder
½ teaspoon salt
1 teaspoon baking powder
Frosting:
2/3 cup butter, softened
1 cup cream cheese
3 cups powdered sugar

Directions:

- For the cupcakes, mix the butter and sugar in a bowl until fluffy and airy. Add the eggs, one by one, then stir in the milk and vanilla.
- Fold in the dry ingredients and mix with a spatula.
- Spoon the batter into 12 muffin cups lined with muffin papers.
- Bake the cupcakes in the preheated oven at 350F for 20-25 minutes or until the cupcakes pass the toothpick test.
- Allow to cool in the pan.
- For the frosting, mix the butter and cream cheese in a bowl until creamy.
- Add the sugar and continue mixing well until fluffy and pale.
- Spoon the frosting in a pastry bag and pipe it over each cupcake.

Nutritional information per serving

Calories: 445
Fat: 25.0g
Protein: 4.0g
Carbohydrates: 53.3g

*C*HOCOLATE PEANUT BUTTER CUPCAKES

Time: 1 ½ hours
Servings: 12

Ingredients:

Cupcakes:
½ cup butter, softened
¼ cup smooth peanut butter
2 eggs
½ cup sour cream
1 teaspoon vanilla extract
1 cup all-purpose flour

1 cup almond flour
¼ teaspoon salt
1 teaspoon baking powder
Frosting:
1 cup heavy cream
2 cups dark chocolate chips
1 teaspoon vanilla extract

Directions:

- For the cupcakes, mix the butter and peanut butter in a bowl until creamy.
- Add the eggs and sour cream and mix well. Stir in the vanilla too.
- Add the flours, salt and baking powder and mix them with a spatula.
- Spoon the batter in 12 muffin cups lined with muffin papers.
- Bake the cupcakes in the preheated oven at 350F for 20-25 minutes or until well risen and golden.
- Allow them to cool in the pan.
- For the frosting, bring the cream to the boiling point in a saucepan.
- Remove from heat and add the chocolate chips. Mix until melted and smooth then allow to cool.
- Top each cupcake with a dollop of frosting.

Nutritional information per serving

Calories: 312
Fat: 23.4g

Protein: 5.8g
Carbohydrates: 23.9g

EMON BLUEBERRY MUFFINS

Time: 1 hour

Servings: 12

Ingredients:

2 cups all-purpose flour
2 teaspoons baking powder
½ teaspoon salt
2 tablespoons chia seeds
½ cup white sugar

2 eggs
1 cup buttermilk
1 teaspoon vanilla extract
1 tablespoon lemon zest
1 cup fresh blueberries

Directions:

- Mix the flour, baking powder, salt, chia seeds and sugar in a bowl.
- Add the rest of the ingredients and mix with a spatula.
- Spoon the batter into 12 muffin cups lined with muffin papers.
- Bake the muffins in the preheated oven at 350F for 20-25 minutes or until well risen and golden brown.
- Serve the muffins chilled.

Nutritional information per serving

Calories: 146
Fat: 1.9g

Protein: 4.4g
Carbohydrates: 27.7g

RAISIN BRAN MUFFINS

Time: 1 hour

Servings: 10

Ingredients:

1 cup all-purpose flour
1 cup wheat bran
2 teaspoons baking powder
½ teaspoon salt
½ teaspoon cinnamon powder
¼ teaspoon ground ginger
½ cup white sugar

½ cup canola oil
2 eggs
½ cup whole milk
½ cup golden raisins

Directions:
- Mix the flour, wheat bran, baking powder, salt, cinnamon, ginger and raisins in a bowl.
- Add the sugar, canola oil and eggs, as well as milk and mix with a spatula.
- Spoon the batter in a muffin tin lined with muffin papers.
- Bake the muffins in the preheated oven at 350F for 20 minutes or until well risen and golden brown.
- Serve the muffins cooled.

Nutritional information per serving

Calories: 235

Fat: 12.6g

Protein: 3.9g

Carbohydrates: 30.1g

*W*HOLESOME BLUEBERRY MUFFINS

Time: 1 hour

Servings: 12

Ingredients:

1 cup whole wheat flour

1 cup all-purpose flour

¼ cup wheat bran

2 teaspoons baking powder

½ teaspoon salt

½ cup butter, melted

2 eggs

½ cup milk

2 tablespoons orange marmalade

1 cup fresh blueberries

Directions:
- Mix the flours, bran, baking powder and salt in a bowl.
- Add the butter, eggs, milk and marmalade then fold in blueberries.
- Spoon the batter in a muffin tin lined with muffin papers and bake in the preheated oven at 350F for 20 minutes or until well risen and golden brown.
- Serve the muffins chilled.

Nutritional information per serving

Calories: 213

Fat: 10.7g

Protein: 4.5g

Carbohydrates: 25.9g

*R*ASPBERRY MUFFINS

Time: 1 hour

Servings: 10

Ingredients:

2 cups all-purpose flour

½ cup white sugar

½ teaspoon salt

1 ½ teaspoons baking powder

3 eggs

½ cup milk

1 teaspoon vanilla extract

1 cup fresh raspberries

Directions:
- Mix the flour, sugar, salt and baking powder in a bowl.
- Add the rest of the ingredients and mix with a spatula.
- Spoon the batter in a muffin tin lined with muffin papers.
- Bake the muffins in the preheated oven at 350F for 20 minutes or until the muffins pass the toothpick test.
- Serve the muffins chilled.

Nutritional information per serving

Calories: 162

Fat: 1.9g

Protein: 4.8g

Carbohydrates: 31.7g

*I*NTENSE CHOCOLATE CUPCAKES

Time: 1 ½ hours

Servings: 12

Ingredients:

Cupcakes:

1 cup brewed coffee

3 oz. dark chocolate

1 teaspoon vanilla extract

1 egg

½ cup buttermilk

¼ cup canola oil

1 ½ cups all-purpose flour

1 teaspoon baking soda

½ teaspoon baking powder

½ teaspoon salt

¼ cup cocoa powder

Frosting:

1 cup butter, softened

2 cups powdered sugar

2 tablespoons cocoa powder

2 tablespoons heavy cream

Directions:

- For the cupcakes, mix the wet ingredients in a bowl. Add the dry ingredients and mix quickly.
- Pour the cupcakes in 12 muffin cups lined with muffin papers.
- Bake the cupcakes in the preheated oven at 350F for 20 minutes.
- For the frosting, mix the butter and sugar in a bowl until fluffy and pale.
- Add the rest of the ingredients and mix well.
- Spoon the frosting in a pastry bag and pipe it over each cupcake.

Nutritional information per serving

Calories: 374

Fat: 23.9g

Protein: 3.7g

Carbohydrates: 38.3g

CHOCOLATE CHIP MUFFINS

Time: 1 hour

Servings: 12

Ingredients:

1 cup all-purpose flour

1 cup whole wheat flour

1 ½ teaspoons baking powder

½ teaspoon salt

½ cup white sugar

1 egg

2/3 cup milk

½ cup canola oil

1 teaspoon vanilla extract

½ cup chocolate chips

Directions:

- Mix the flours, baking powder and salt in a bowl.
- Add the sugar, egg, milk, oil and vanilla and mix with a spatula.
- Fold in the chocolate chips then spoon the batter in a muffin tin lined with muffin papers.
- Bake the muffins in the preheated oven at 350F for 20-25 minutes or until golden brown and well risen.
- Serve the muffins chilled.

Nutritional information per serving

Calories: 238

Fat: 12.0g

Protein: 3.6g

Carbohydrates: 29.4g

CINNAMON BLUEBERRY MUFFINS

Time: 1 hour

Servings: 12

Ingredients:

2 cups all-purpose flour

½ cup light brown sugar

½ teaspoon salt

1 teaspoon baking soda

½ teaspoon cinnamon powder

½ cup milk

2 eggs

½ cup butter, melted

1 cup blueberries

Directions:

- Mix the flour, sugar, salt, baking soda and cinnamon in a bowl.

- Add the milk, eggs and melted butter and fold in the blueberries then spoon the batter in a muffin tin lined with muffin papers.
- Bake the muffins in the preheated oven at 350F for 20 minutes or until well risen and golden brown.
- Serve the muffins chilled.

Nutritional information per serving

Calories: 189

Fat: 8.8g

Protein: 3.6g

Carbohydrates: 24.1g

*C*OCONUT MUFFINS

Time: 1 hour

Servings: 12

Ingredients:

1 ½ cups all-purpose flour

½ cup quinoa flour

1 teaspoon baking soda

½ teaspoon salt

½ cup shredded coconut

½ cup light brown sugar

1 egg

2/3 cup milk

½ cup canola oil

1 teaspoon vanilla extract

½ cup raspberry jam

Directions:

- Mix the flours, baking soda, salt, coconut and sugar.
- Stir in the egg, milk, oil and vanilla and give it a quick mix with a spatula.
- Spoon the batter in a muffin tin lined with muffin papers.
- Drop a dollop of raspberry jam on top of each muffin and bake in the preheated oven at 350F for 20 minutes or until well risen and golden brown.
- Serve the muffins chilled.

Nutritional information per serving

Calories: 237

Fat: 11.5g

Protein: 4.4g

Carbohydrates: 28.9g

*P*INK COCONUT CUPCAKES

Time: 1 ½ hours

Servings: 12

Ingredients:

Cupcakes:

½ cup butter, softened

½ cup white sugar

1 teaspoon vanilla extract

2 eggs

1 ½ cups all-purpose flour

½ teaspoon salt

1 teaspoon baking powder

½ cup shredded coconut

2/3 cup whole milk

Frosting:

1 cup butter, softened

2 cups powdered sugar

2 tablespoons heavy cream

½ teaspoon pink food coloring

Directions:

- For the cupcakes, mix the butter, sugar and vanilla in a bowl until fluffy and pale.
- Add the eggs and mix well then fold in the flour, salt, baking powder and coconut, alternating it with milk.
- Spoon the batter in a muffin tin lined with muffin papers and bake in the preheated oven at 350F for 20 minutes or until golden brown and well risen.
- Allow the cupcakes to cool down.
- For the frosting, mix the butter and sugar in a bowl until fluffy and pale.
- Add the cream and food coloring and continue mixing a few additional minutes until airy.
- Top each cupcake with a dollop of frosting before serving.

Nutritional information per serving

Calories: 410
Fat:26.4g

Protein: 3.4g
Carbohydrates: 41.7g

D OUBLE CHOCOLATE MUFFINS

Time: 1 hour

Servings: 12

Ingredients:

1 ½ cups all-purpose flour
½ cup cocoa powder
½ teaspoon salt
1 teaspoon baking powder
2 eggs

½ cup canola oil
½ cup whole milk
1 teaspoon vanilla extract
½ cup dark chocolate chips

Directions:

- Mix the flour, cocoa powder, salt and baking powder in a bowl.
- Add the rest of the ingredients and give it a quick mix with a whisk.
- Spoon the batter into 12 muffin cups lined with muffin papers and bake in the preheated oven at 350F for 15-20 minutes.
- Serve the muffins chilled.

Nutritional information per serving

Calories: 186
Fat: 12.1g

Protein: 3.8g
Carbohydrates: 18.0g

G INGERBREAD MUFFINS

Time: 1 hour

Servings: 12

Ingredients:

1 ½ cups all-purpose flour
½ cup wheat bran
1 teaspoon cinnamon powder
½ teaspoon ground ginger
½ teaspoon ground star anise
½ teaspoon salt

2 tablespoons dark molasses
½ cup white sugar
1 egg
1 teaspoon vanilla extract
1 cup buttermilk
½ cup raisins

Directions:

- Mix the dry ingredients in a bowl.
- Add the wet ingredients and give it a quick mix.
- Spoon the batter in a muffin tin lined with muffin papers.
- Bake the muffins in the preheated oven at 350F for 15-20 minutes or until fragrant and golden.
- Serve them chilled.

Nutritional information per serving

Calories: 137
Fat: 0.8g

Protein: 3.4g
Carbohydrates: 30.3g

L EMON CURD CUPCAKES

Time: 1 ½ hours

Servings: 12

Ingredients:

1 ½ cups all-purpose flour
½ cup almond flour
2 teaspoons baking powder

½ teaspoon salt
¾ cup butter, softened
¾ cup white sugar

3 eggs
1 tablespoon lemon zest
2 tablespoons lemon juice

1 teaspoon vanilla extract
1 cup lemon curd

Directions:
- Mix the butter and sugar in a bowl until pale and fluffy.
- Add the eggs, one by one, and mix well then stir in the lemon zest and juice, as well as vanilla.
- Fold in the flours, salt and baking powder then spoon the batter in 12 muffin cups lined with muffin papers.
- Bake the cupcakes in the preheated oven at 350F for 20 minutes or until well risen and golden brown.
- When done, allow to cool and top each cupcake with a dollop of lemon curd.

Nutritional information per serving

Calories: 311
Fat: 21.4g

Protein: 4.7g
Carbohydrates: 30.7g

*L*EMON POPPY SEED MUFFINS

Time: 1 hour

Servings: 12

Ingredients:

1 ¾ cups all-purpose flour
½ teaspoon salt
1 ½ teaspoons baking powder
2 tablespoons poppy seeds
2 eggs

½ cup white sugar
½ cup canola oil
½ cup milk
1 tablespoon lemon zest
2 tablespoons lemon juice

Directions:
- Mix the flour, salt, baking powder and poppy seeds in a bowl.
- In a different bowl, mix the eggs and sugar until fluffy and pale. Add the oil and milk and mix well then stir in the lemon zest and juice.
- Fold in the flour mixture then spoon the batter in 12 muffin cups lined with muffin papers.
- Bake the muffins in the preheated oven at 350F for 20 minutes or until golden brown and well risen.
- Serve the muffins chilled.

Nutritional information per serving

Calories: 203
Fat: 10.9g

Protein: 3.4g
Carbohydrates: 23.6g

*C*ITRUS COCONUT MUFFINS

Time: 1 hour

Servings: 12

Ingredients:

2 cups all-purpose flour
2 teaspoons baking powder
½ teaspoon salt
2 eggs
½ cup white sugar
½ cup butter, melted

1 teaspoon orange zest
1 teaspoon lemon zest
1 teaspoon lime zest
¼ cup milk
1 cup coconut flakes

Directions:
- Mix the eggs and sugar in a bowl until pale and light. Add the melted butter and citrus zest and mix well.
- Fold in the dry ingredients, as well as the coconut flakes then spoon the batter in 12 muffin cups lined with muffin papers.
- Bake the muffins in the preheated oven at 350F for 20 minutes or until golden brown and well risen.
- Allow to cool in the pan before serving.

Nutritional information per serving

Calories: 213

Fat: 10.9g

$\mathcal{P}$ URE VANILLA MUFFINS

Time: 1 hour   Servings: 10

Ingredients:

1 ½ cups all-purpose flour
½ teaspoon salt
1 teaspoon baking powder
2 eggs

½ cup white sugar
½ cup canola oil
1 teaspoon vanilla extract
¼ cup sour cream

Directions:

- Mix the eggs and sugar in a bowl until pale and light.
- Add the canola oil, vanilla and sour cream and mix well.
- Fold in the flour, salt and baking powder then spoon the batter in a muffin tin lined with muffin papers.
- Bake in the preheated oven at 350F for 15-20 minutes or until well risen and golden.
- Serve the muffins chilled.

Nutritional information per serving

Calories: 229
Fat: 13.2g

Protein: 3.2g
Carbohydrates: 24.9g

$\mathcal{P}$ INK VELVET CUPCAKES

Time: 1 ½ hours   Servings: 12

Ingredients:

Cupcakes:
1 2/3 cups all-purpose flour
½ teaspoon salt
1 ½ teaspoon baking powder
1 egg
½ cup white sugar
1 teaspoon vanilla extract

½ cup sour cream
¼ teaspoon red food coloring
Frosting:
1 cup butter, softened
2 cups powdered sugar
1 teaspoon vanilla extract

Directions:

- For the cupcakes, mix the egg and sugar until pale. Add the vanilla and mix well then stir in the sour cream and food coloring.
- Stir in the rest of the ingredients and give it a quick mix.
- Spoon the batter in 12 muffin cups lined with muffin papers.
- Bake the cupcakes in the preheated oven at 350F for 20 minutes or until the cupcake pass the toothpick test.
- Allow the cupcakes to cool down.
- For the frosting, mix the butter until pale. Add the sugar and give it a good mix.
- Stir in the vanilla and mix well then spoon the buttercream in a pastry bag and pipe on each cupcake.

Nutritional information per serving

Calories: 336
Fat: 17.9g

Protein: 2.7g
Carbohydrates: 42.3g

$\mathcal{L}$ OADED MUFFINS

Time: 1 ¼ hours   Servings: 10

Ingredients:

1 ½ cups all-purpose flour
¼ cup cocoa powder

½ teaspoon salt
1 ½ teaspoons baking powder

2 tablespoons candied orange peel, chopped
¼ cup dried apricots, chopped
¼ cup dried cranberries

2 eggs
½ cup milk
¼ cup canola oil

Directions:
- Mix the dry ingredients in a bowl.
- Add the rest of the ingredients and give it a quick mix.
- Spoon the batter in a muffin tin lined with muffin papers.
- Bake the muffins in the preheated oven at 350F for 20 minutes or until golden brown and well risen.
- Serve the muffins chilled.

Nutritional information per serving
Calories: 145
Fat: 7.1g

Protein: 3.9g
Carbohydrates: 17.5g

*C*HOCOLATE CHUNK CUPCAKES

Time: 1 ½ hours

Servings: 12

Ingredients:
Cupcakes:
2 cups all-purpose flour
2 teaspoons baking powder
½ teaspoon salt
½ cup butter, melted
½ cup white sugar

2 eggs
½ cup sour cream
4 oz. dark chocolate, chopped
Frosting:
1 ½ cups heavy cream, whipped
2 oz. dark chocolate, chopped

Directions:
- For the cupcakes, mix the butter, sugar and eggs in a bowl until pale.
- Add the sour cream and mix well.
- Fold in the flour, baking powder and salt then fold in the dark chocolate.
- Spoon the batter in a muffin tin lined with muffin papers.
- Bake the cupcakes in the preheated oven at 350F for 20 minutes or until golden brown and well risen.
- Allow the cupcakes to cool then top each of them with a dollop of whipped cream.
- Sprinkle each cream with chopped chocolate and serve.

Nutritional information per serving
Calories: 334
Fat: 20.4g

Protein: 4.8g
Carbohydrates: 33.9g

*W*HOLEMEAL MUFFINS

Time: 1 hour

Servings: 12

Ingredients:
1 ½ cups all-purpose flour
½ cup whole wheat flour
2 teaspoons baking powder
½ teaspoon salt
2 tablespoons chia seeds

2 tablespoons hemp seeds
½ cup white sugar
1 egg
1 cup milk
¼ cup canola oil

Directions:
- Mix the flour, wheat flour, baking powder, salt, chia seeds and hemp seeds.
- Add the sugar, egg, milk and canola oil and give it a quick mix.
- Spoon the batter into a muffin tin lined with muffin papers and bake in the preheated oven at 350F for 20 minutes or until golden brown and well risen.
- Serve the muffins chilled.

Nutritional information per serving

Calories: 182

Fat: 6.9g

Protein: 4.2g

Carbohydrates: 25.9g

LMOND VANILLA CUPCAKES

Time: 1 ½ hours

Servings: 12

Ingredients:

Cupcakes:

½ cup butter, softened

½ cup white sugar

1 teaspoon vanilla extract

2 eggs

1 teaspoon lemon zest

1 cup all-purpose flour

1 cup ground almonds

½ teaspoon salt

1 teaspoon baking powder

¼ cup milk

Glaze:

1 tablespoon butter, melted

1 teaspoon lemon zest

1 cup powdered sugar

Directions:

- For the cupcakes, mix the butter, sugar and vanilla in a bowl until fluffy and pale.
- Add the eggs, one by one, then stir in the lemon zest and add the flour, almonds, salt and baking powder.
- Stir in the milk and mix for 1 minute on high speed.
- Spoon the batter in a muffin tin lined with muffin papers and bake in the preheated oven at 350F for 20 minutes or until golden brown and well risen.
- Allow the cupcakes to cool in the pan.
- For the glaze, mix all the ingredients in a bowl. Drizzle the glaze over each cupcake and serve fresh.

Nutritional information per serving

Calories: 245

Fat: 13.5g

Protein: 3.9g

Carbohydrates: 28.6g

UTTY DOUBLE CHOCOLATE MUFFINS

Time: 1 hour

Servings: 12

Ingredients:

1 1/2 cup all-purpose flour

½ cup ground hazelnuts

¼ cup cocoa powder

½ teaspoon salt

1 teaspoon baking powder

1 cup white sugar

1 egg

¼ cup canola oil

1 cup milk

1 teaspoon vanilla extract

1 cup dark chocolate chips

Directions:

- Mix the flour, cocoa powder, ground hazelnuts, salt, baking powder and sugar in a bowl.
- Add the egg, canola oil, milk and vanilla and give it a quick mix.
- Fold in the chocolate chips then spoon the batter in a muffin tin lined with muffin papers.
- Bake the muffins in the preheated oven at 350F for 20 minutes or until they pass the toothpick test.
- Serve the muffins chilled.

Nutritional information per serving

Calories: 247

Fat: 10.3g

Protein: 4.2g

Carbohydrates: 38.0g

FUDGY CHOCOLATE MUFFINS

Time: 1 hour

Servings: 12

Ingredients:

1 ¾ cups all-purpose flour
2 tablespoons cocoa powder
2 teaspoons baking powder
½ teaspoon salt
1 egg

1 cup milk
3 oz. dark chocolate
½ cup canola oil
1 teaspoon vanilla extract
1 cup dark chocolate chips

Directions:

- Mix the dark chocolate and canola oil in a heatproof bowl and place over a hot water bath. Melt them together until smooth then remove from heat and add the egg, milk, sugar and vanilla.
- Fold in the flour, cocoa powder, baking powder and salt then add the chocolate chips.
- Spoon the batter in a muffin tin lined with muffin papers.
- Bake the muffins in the preheated oven at 350F for 20 minutes or until well risen and the muffins pass the toothpick test.
- Serve the muffins chilled.

Nutritional information per serving

Calories: 250
Fat: 14.9g

Protein: 4.4g
Carbohydrates: 26.7g

Ɛxtra Chocolate Muffins

Time: 1 hour

Servings: 12

Ingredients:

1 ¾ cups all-purpose flour
¼ cup cocoa powder
½ cup light brown sugar
½ teaspoon baking soda
½ teaspoon baking powder
½ teaspoon salt

2 eggs
1 cup milk
1/3 cup canola oil
½ cup dark chocolate chips
½ cup white chocolate chips

Directions:

- Mix the dry ingredients in a bowl then add the wet ingredients.
- Fold in the chocolate chips then spoon the batter in a muffin cups lined with muffin papers.
- Bake the muffins in the preheated oven at 350F for 20 minutes or until well risen.
- Serve the muffins chilled.

Nutritional information per serving

Calories: 229
Fat: 11.2g

Protein: 4.5g
Carbohydrates: 29.5g

Rhubarb Strawberry Muffins

Time: 1 hour

Servings: 12

Ingredients:

1 cup all-purpose flour
½ cup whole wheat flour
½ teaspoon salt
1 teaspoon baking soda
3 eggs

½ cup light brown sugar
1 teaspoon vanilla extract
½ cup milk
1 rhubarb stalk, sliced
1 cup strawberries, sliced

Directions:

- Mix the flours, salt and baking soda in a bowl.
- Whip the eggs and sugar in a bowl until pale and light.
- Add the milk and vanilla and mix well.
- Fold in the flour mixture then add the rhubarb and strawberries.

- Spoon the batter in a muffin tin lined with muffin papers.
- Bake the muffins in the preheated oven at 350F for 20 minutes or until golden brown and fluffy.
- Serve the muffins chilled.

Nutritional information per serving

Calories: 106

Fat: 1.5g

Protein: 3.5g

Carbohydrates: 19.6g

ORANGE ALMOND MUFFINS

Time: 1 ½ hours

Servings: 12

Ingredients:

2 small oranges

6 eggs

1 cup white sugar

1 teaspoon vanilla extract

2 cups almond flour

1 teaspoon baking powder

½ teaspoon salt

Directions:
- Place the oranges in a saucepan and cover them with water. Boil the oranges for 30 minutes until softened. Drain the oranges well and place them in a blender. Pulse until smooth.
- Mix the eggs and sugar in a bowl until fluffy and pale.
- Stir in the oranges then fold in the almond flour, baking powder and salt.
- Spoon the batter in a muffin tin lined with muffin papers.
- Bake the muffins in the preheated oven at 350F for 20-25 minutes or until well risen and golden brown.
- Allow the muffins to cool down before serving.

Nutritional information per serving

Calories: 130

Fat: 4.5g

Protein: 3.9g

Carbohydrates: 20.0g

APPLE MUFFINS

Time: 1 hour

Servings: 12

Ingredients:

1 cup all-purpose flour

½ cup whole wheat flour

½ cup ground walnuts

½ teaspoon salt

1 teaspoon baking soda

½ teaspoon cinnamon powder

2 eggs

½ cup white sugar

1 teaspoon vanilla extract

¼ cup canola oil

½ cup plain yogurt

2 apples, peeled, cored and diced

Directions:
- Mix the eggs and sugar until fluffy and pale.
- Add the vanilla, oil and yogurt and give it a good mix.
- Fold in the flour mixture then add the apples.
- Spoon the batter in a muffin tin lined with muffin papers and bake in the preheated oven at 350F for 20-25 minutes or until golden brown and well risen.
- Serve the muffins chilled.

Nutritional information per serving

Calories: 195

Fat: 8.7g Protein: 4.5g

Carbohydrates: 25.8g

*B*LACK BOTTOM MUFFINS

Time: 1 hour

Servings: 12

Ingredients:

1 cup cream cheese
¼ cup white sugar
1 egg
½ cup butter, melted
2 eggs

½ cup light brown sugar
1/3 cup all-purpose flour
1 ½ cups almond flour
1 teaspoon baking powder
½ teaspoon salt

Directions:

- Mix the cream cheese, 1 egg and ¼ cup sugar in a bowl.
- Spoon the mixture into 12 muffin cups lined with muffin papers.
- Mix 2 eggs with butter and sugar until pale.
- Add the flour, almond flour, baking powder and salt.
- Spoon the batter over the cream cheese mixture.
- Bake the muffins in the preheated oven at 350F for 20 minutes or until well risen.
- Serve the muffins chilled.

Nutritional information per serving

Calories: 223
Fat: 17.3g

Protein: 4.0g
Carbohydrates: 14.3g

*B*LUEBERRY WHITE CHOCOLATE MUFFINS

Time: 1 hour

Servings: 12

Ingredients:

1 1/2 cups all-purpose flour
2 teaspoons baking powder
½ teaspoon salt
½ cup shredded coconut
½ cup white chocolate chips

1 cup milk
2 eggs
¼ cup canola oil
1 teaspoon vanilla extract

Directions:

- Mix the flour, baking powder, salt, coconut and chocolate chips in a bowl.
- Add the rest of the ingredients and mix well.
- Spoon the batter in a muffin tin lined with special muffin papers.
- Bake the muffins in the preheated oven at 350F for 20 minutes or until golden brown and well risen.
- Serve the muffins chilled.

Nutritional information per serving

Calories: 169
Fat: 9.2g

Protein: 3.7g
Carbohydrates: 18.1g

*M*ILK CHOCOLATE CUPCAKES

Time: 1 ½ hours

Servings: 12

Ingredients:

Cupcakes:
½ cup butter, softened
¾ cup white sugar
2 eggs
1 teaspoon vanilla extract
1 cup milk

2 cups all-purpose flour
2 teaspoons baking powder
½ teaspoon salt
Frosting:
1 cup butter, softened
2 cups powdered sugar

½ cup milk chocolate chips, melted and chilled

Directions:
- For the cupcakes, mix the butter and sugar until fluffy and pale.
- Add the eggs, one by one, then stir in the vanilla and milk.
- Add the flour, baking powder and salt and mix with a spatula.
- Spoon the batter into 12 muffin cups lined with muffin papers.
- Bake the cupcakes in the preheated oven at 350F for 20 minutes or until golden brown and well risen.
- Allow to cool down.
- For the frosting, mix the butter in a bowl until fluffy and pale.
- Add the sugar and mix well for 5 minutes.
- Stir in the chocolate and mix well.
- Spoon the frosting in a pastry bag and pipe it over each cupcake.
- Serve the cupcakes fresh.

Nutritional information per serving

Calories: 438
Fat: 25.0g

Protein: 4.0g
Carbohydrates: 51.3g

*T*URKISH DELIGHT MUFFINS

Time: 1 hour

Servings: 12

Ingredients:

4 eggs
½ cup white sugar
1 teaspoon vanilla extract
½ cup canola oil
½ cup sour cream

2 cups all-purpose flour
¼ teaspoon salt
1 teaspoon baking powder
1 cup Turkish delight, diced

Directions:
- Mix the eggs and sugar in a bowl until fluffy and light.
- Add the vanilla, oil and sour cream and mix well.
- Fold in the flour, salt and baking powder then stir in the Turkish delight.
- Spoon the batter in a muffin tin lined with muffin papers.
- Bake in the preheated oven at 350F for 20 minutes or until golden brown and well risen.
- Serve the muffins chilled.

Nutritional information per serving

Calories: 239
Fat: 13.0g

Protein: 4.3g
Carbohydrates: 27.0g

*C*ARROT WHITE CHOCOLATE MUFFINS

Time: 1 hour

Servings: 12

Ingredients:

1 cup all-purpose flour
½ cup whole wheat flour
½ teaspoon salt
1 teaspoon baking powder
¼ teaspoon baking soda
½ teaspoon salt
1 egg

½ cup white sugar
¼ cup canola oil
½ cup plain yogurt
1 cup crushed pineapple
1 cup grated carrots
½ cup white chocolate chips

Directions:
- Mix the egg and sugar in a bowl until pale and light.
- Add the oil and yogurt and mix well.
- Fold in the flours, salt, baking powder, baking soda and salt.

- Add the crushed pineapple, carrots and chocolate chips.
- Spoon the batter in a muffin tin lined with muffin papers and bake in the preheated oven at 350F for 20 minutes or until the muffins pass the toothpick test.
- Serve the muffins chilled.

Nutritional information per serving

Calories: 190
Fat: 7.5g

Protein: 3.2g
Carbohydrates: 28.1g

*C*HERRY MUFFINS

Time: 1 hour

Servings: 10

Ingredients:

4 eggs
½ cup white sugar
1 teaspoon vanilla extract
½ cup butter, melted

1 cup all-purpose flour
¼ teaspoon salt
1 teaspoon baking powder
1 cup cherries, pitted

Directions:

- Mix the eggs, sugar and vanilla in a bowl until triple in volume.
- Stir in the butter and mix well.
- Fold in the flour, salt and baking powder.
- Add the cherries then spoon the batter in a muffin tin lined with muffin papers.
- Bake the muffins in the preheated oven at 350F for 20 minutes or until golden brown and well risen.
- Serve the muffins chilled.

Nutritional information per serving

Calories: 200
Fat: 11.1g

Protein: 3.6g
Carbohydrates: 22.0g

B LACK FOREST CUPCAKES

Time: 1 ½ hours

Servings: 12

Ingredients:

Cupcakes:
1 cup brewed coffee
½ cup canola oil
1 egg
1 teaspoon vanilla extract
1 ¼ cups all-purpose flour

¼ cup cocoa powder
½ teaspoon salt
1 teaspoon baking soda
Frosting:
2 cups heavy cream, whipped
1 cup sour cherries, pitted

Directions:

- For the cupcakes, mix the coffee, oil, egg and vanilla in a bowl.
- Stir in the flour, cocoa powder, salt and baking soda and give it a quick mix.
- Pour the batter in a muffin tin lined with muffin papers.
- Bake in the preheated oven at 350F for 20 minutes or until well risen and fragrant.
- Allow the muffins to cool down.
- Top each muffin with whipped cream and garnish with sour cherries.

Nutritional information per serving

Calories: 264
Fat: 17.2g
Protein: 2.7g
Carbohydrates: 25.4g

CHOCOLATE CHIP CINNAMON MUFFINS

Time: 1 hour

Servings: 12

Ingredients:

4 eggs
½ cup white sugar
2 tablespoons dark brown sugar
1 teaspoon vanilla extract
1 teaspoon orange zest
½ cup butter, melted

1 cup all-purpose flour
1 teaspoon cinnamon powder
½ teaspoon salt
1 teaspoon baking powder
¼ cup milk
½ cup dark chocolate chips

Directions:
- Mix the eggs and sugars in a bowl until fluffy and pale.
- Add the vanilla, orange zest and melted butter.
- Fold in the flour, cinnamon, salt and baking powder then add the milk and chocolate chips.
- Spoon the batter in a muffin tin lined with muffin papers.
- Bake in the preheated oven at 350F for 20 minutes or until golden brown and well risen.
- Serve the muffins chilled.

Nutritional information per serving

Calories: 191
Fat: 10.7g

Protein: 3.5g
Carbohydrates: 21.7g

RICOTTA LEMON MUFFINS

Time: 1 hour

Servings: 12

Ingredients:

1 cup ricotta cheese
¼ cup butter, melted
2 eggs
1 teaspoon vanilla extract
½ cup white sugar

1 tablespoon lemon zest
1 ½ cups all-purpose flour
½ teaspoon salt
1 teaspoon baking powder

Directions:
- Mix the cheese, butter, eggs, vanilla and sugar in a bowl.
- Add the flour, salt and baking powder and mix with a spatula.
- Spoon the batter in a muffin tin lined with muffin papers.
- Bake the muffins in the preheated oven at 350F for 20 minutes or until golden brown and well risen.
- Serve the muffins chilled.

Nutritional information per serving

Calories: 163
Fat: 6.3g

Protein: 4.9g
Carbohydrates: 21.7g

FUDGY CHOCOLATE DATE MUFFINS

Time: 1 hour

Servings: 12

Ingredients:

1 cup dates, pitted
½ cup fresh orange juice
1 teaspoon orange zest
2 eggs
1 teaspoon vanilla extract
¼ cup milk

1 cup all-purpose flour
½ cup cocoa powder
¼ cup cornstarch
1 teaspoon baking soda
½ teaspoon salt

Directions:
- Mix the dates, orange juice, orange zest, eggs and vanilla in a blender and pulse until smooth. Add the milk and mix well.
- Fold in the rest of the ingredients and mix well.
- Pour the batter in a muffin tin lined with muffin papers.
- Bake the muffins in the preheated oven at 350F for 15-20 minutes or until the muffins pass the toothpick test.
- Serve the muffins chilled.

Nutritional information per serving
Calories: 117
Fat: 1.5g

Protein: 3.3g
Carbohydrates: 24.9g

*C*HOCOLATE PEAR MUFFINS

Time: 1 hour

Servings: 12

Ingredients:
2 eggs
½ cup milk
½ cup light brown sugar
½ cup buttermilk
1 1/3 cups all-purpose flour

1/3 cup cocoa powder
¼ teaspoon salt
1 teaspoon baking powder
2 pears, peeled and diced

Directions:
- Mix the eggs, milk, sugar and buttermilk in a bowl.
- Stir in the dry ingredients and give it a quick mix.
- Fold in the pears then spoon the batter in a muffin tin lined with muffin papers.
- Bake the muffins in the preheated oven at 350F for 15-20 minutes or until well risen.
- Serve the muffins chilled.

Nutritional information per serving
Calories: 119
Fat: 1.5g

Protein: 3.6g
Carbohydrates: 24.4g

*B*ANANA CHOCOLATE CHIP MUFFINS

Time: 1 hour

Servings: 12

Ingredients:
3 bananas, mashed
½ cup white sugar
1 egg
1/3 cup butter, melted
¼ cup milk

1 ½ cups all-purpose flour
1 teaspoon baking soda
½ teaspoon salt
½ cup dark chocolate chips

Directions:
- Mix the bananas, sugar, egg, butter and milk in a bowl until creamy.
- Add the rest of the ingredients and fold them in with a spatula.
- Spoon the batter into 12 muffin cups lined with muffin papers.
- Bake in the preheated oven at 350F for 20 minutes.
- Serve the muffins chilled.

Nutritional information per serving
Calories: 191
Fat: 7.2g
Protein: 2.9g
Carbohydrates: 30.6g

ℬ ANANA YOGURT MUFFINS

Time: 1 hour

Servings: 12

Ingredients:

1 bananas, mashed
1 cup plain yogurt
1 egg
½ cup light brown sugar
½ cup canola oil

2 cups all-purpose flour
1 teaspoon baking powder
½ teaspoon baking soda
½ teaspoon salt

Directions:

- Mix the bananas, yogurt, egg, sugar and oil in a bowl until creamy.
- Add the rest of the ingredients and give it a quick mix.
- Spoon the batter in a muffin tin lined with muffin papers.
- Bake the muffins in the preheated oven at 350F for 20 minutes or until golden brown and well risen.
- Serve the muffins chilled.

Nutritional information per serving

Calories: 208
Fat: 9.9g

Protein: 3.9g
Carbohydrates: 25.7g

ℬ LUEBERRY POPPY SEED MUFFINS

Time: 1 hour

Servings: 12

Ingredients:

2 eggs
1 cup plain yogurt
1 tablespoon lemon zest
1 tablespoon lemon juice
½ cup canola oil
½ cup white sugar

1 1/2 cups all-purpose flour
2 teaspoons baking powder
½ teaspoon salt
2 tablespoons poppy seeds
1 cup fresh blueberries

Directions:

- Mix the eggs, yogurt, lemon zest, lemon juice and oil in a bowl.
- Add the sugar and mix well then fold in the rest of the ingredients.
- Spoon the batter in a muffin tin lined with muffin papers and bake in the preheated oven at 350F for 20 minutes or until they pass the toothpick test.
- Serve them chilled.

Nutritional information per serving

Calories: 210
Fat: 10.9g

Protein: 4.1g
Carbohydrates: 24.4g

ℬ ANANA CHIA MUFFINS

Time: 1 hour

Servings: 12

Ingredients:

2 cups all-purpose flour
3 tablespoons chia seeds
½ teaspoon salt
2 teaspoons baking powder
½ cup white sugar
2 eggs
½ cup canola oil

1 cup buttermilk
¼ cup whole milk
2 bananas, mashed

Directions:
- Mix the flour, chia seeds, sugar, salt and baking powder in a bowl.
- Add the rest of the ingredients and give it a quick mix.
- Spoon the batter in a muffin tin lined with muffin papers and bake in the preheated oven at 350F for 20-25 minutes or until the muffins pass the toothpick test.
- Allow them to cool in the pan before serving.

Nutritional information per serving

Calories: 266

Fat: 12.8g

Protein: 5.7g

Carbohydrates: 33.0g

 ALMOND VANILLA CUPCAKES

Time: 1 ½ hours

Servings: 12

Ingredients:

Cupcakes:

1 ½ cups almond flour

⅓ cup all-purpose flour

½ teaspoon salt

1 teaspoon baking soda

½ cup butter, softened

½ cup white sugar

2 eggs

1 teaspoon vanilla extract

½ cup buttermilk

½ teaspoon almond extract

Frosting:

1 cup butter, softened

2 cups powdered sugar

1 tablespoon vanilla extract

Directions:
- For the cupcakes, mix the flours, salt and baking soda in a bowl.
- In a different bowl, mix the butter, sugar and vanilla until fluffy and creamy.
- Add the eggs, one by one, then stir in the buttermilk and almond extract.
- Fold in the flour mixture then spoon the batter in a muffin tin lined with muffin papers.
- Bake in the preheated oven at 350F for 20-25 minutes or until golden brown.
- Allow them to cool in the pan.
- For the frosting, mix the butter and sugar for 5 minutes until pale and fluffy.
- Add the vanilla and mix well.
- Spoon the frosting in a pastry bag and pipe it over the cupcakes.

Nutritional information per serving

Calories: 371

Fat: 25.7g

Protein: 2.8g

Carbohydrates: 33.8g

HONEY CARDAMOM CUPCAKES

Time: 1 ½ hours

Servings: 12

Ingredients:

Cupcakes:

½ cup butter, softened

½ cup honey

2 tablespoons dark brown sugar

1 teaspoon vanilla extract

2 eggs

1 ½ cups all-purpose flour

½ teaspoon salt

1 ½ teaspoons baking powder

1 teaspoon ground cardamom

1/3 cup milk

Frosting:

1 cup butter, softened

2 cups powdered sugar

1 teaspoon vanilla extract

¼ cup honey

Directions:
- For the cupcakes, mix the butter, honey and sugar in a bowl until fluffy and pale. Add the vanilla and eggs and mix well.
- Fold in the flour, salt, baking powder and cardamom, alternating them with milk.

- Spoon the batter in a muffin tin lined with muffin papers.
- Bake in the preheated oven at 350F for 20-25 minutes or until golden brown.
- Allow them to cool in the pan.
- For the frosting, mix the butter and sugar in a bowl for 5-7 minutes until fluffy and pale. Stir in the vanilla and mix well.
- Spoon the frosting into a pastry and pipe it over each cupcake.
- Drizzle the frosted cupcakes with honey.

Nutritional information per serving

Calories: 425
Fat: 24.1g

Protein: 3.1g
Carbohydrates: 51.7g

ANANA HONEY MUFFINS

Time: 1 hour

Servings: 12

Ingredients:

2 ripe bananas, mashed
½ cup honey
½ cup buttermilk
1 egg
1 teaspoon vanilla extract

1 ½ cups all-purpose flour
½ cup rolled oats
½ teaspoon salt
1 teaspoon baking soda

Directions:
- Mix the bananas, honey, buttermilk, egg and vanilla in a bowl.
- Add the rest of the ingredients and mix with a spatula.
- Spoon the batter in a muffin tin lined with muffin papers and bake in the preheated oven at 350F for 20-25 minutes or until well risen and golden brown.
- Serve the muffins chilled.

Nutritional information per serving

Calories: 141
Fat: 0.9g

Protein: 3.1g
Carbohydrates: 30.9g

ONEY NUTMEG PEACH MUFFINS

Time: 1 hour

Servings: 12

Ingredients:

1 ½ cups all-purpose flour
½ cup ground walnuts
½ cup white sugar
½ teaspoon ground nutmeg
¼ teaspoon salt
1 teaspoon baking soda

2 eggs
¼ cup honey
1 banana, mashed
½ cup buttermilk
2 peaches, pitted and diced

Directions:
- Mix the dry ingredients in a bowl.
- Stir in the eggs, honey, banana and buttermilk and give it a quick mix.
- Fold in the peaches and spoon the batter in a muffin tin lined with muffin papers.
- Bake in the preheated oven at 350F for 20 minutes or until well risen and golden brown.
- Allow the muffins to cool in the pan before serving.

Nutritional information per serving

Calories: 172
Fat: 4.1g
Protein: 4.4g
Carbohydrates: 31.0g

CHOCOLATE RASPBERRY CUPCAKES

Time: 1 ½ hours

Servings: 12

Ingredients:

Cupcakes:
2/3 cup butter, softened
2/3 cup white sugar
2 eggs
1 teaspoon vanilla extract
¼ cup milk
1 ½ cups all-purpose flour
½ teaspoon salt

1 ½ teaspoons baking powder
¼ cup cocoa powder
Frosting:
1 cup cream cheese
1 cup butter, softened
2 cups powdered sugar
½ cup dark chocolate chips, melted and chilled

Directions:

- For the cupcakes, mix the butter and sugar in a bowl until fluffy and airy.
- Add the eggs and vanilla and mix well. Stir in the milk.
- Fold in the flour, salt, baking powder and cocoa and mix with a spatula.
- Spoon the batter in a muffin tin lined with muffin papers and bake in the preheated oven at 350F for 20 minutes or until well risen.
- Allow them to cool in the pan.
- For frosting, mix the cream cheese and butter in a bowl until pale.
- Add the sugar, gradually, and mix for 5 minutes on high speed.
- Stir in the melted chocolate then spoon a dollop of frosting over each cupcake and serve fresh.

Nutritional information per serving

Calories: 512
Fat: 34.9g

Protein: 5.1g
Carbohydrates: 48.5g

THE ULTIMATE BLUEBERRY MUFFINS

Time: 1 hour

Servings: 12

Ingredients:

2 eggs
2/3 cup white sugar
½ cup canola oil
1 teaspoon lemon zest
1 teaspoon vanilla extract

2 cups all-purpose flour
½ teaspoon salt
2 teaspoons baking powder
1 cup sour cream
1 cup fresh blueberries

Directions:

- Mix the eggs and sugar in a bowl until fluffy and pale.
- Add the oil and vanilla and mix well.
- Fold in the flour, salt and baking powder then add the sour cream and mix for 1 minute on high speed.
- Fold in the blueberries then spoon the batter in a muffin tin lined with muffin papers.
- Bake the muffins in the preheated oven at 350F for 20-25 minutes or until well risen and golden.
- Allow them to cool before serving or storing.

Nutritional information per serving

Calories: 258
Fat: 14.1g

Protein: 3.8g
Carbohydrates: 30.1g

RASPBERRY WHITE CHOCOLATE MUFFINS

Time: 1 hour
Servings: 12

Ingredients:
2 eggs
½ cup white sugar
1 teaspoon vanilla extract
½ cup sour cream
1 ½ cups all-purpose flour

½ teaspoon salt
1 teaspoon baking powder
1 cup fresh raspberries
½ cup white chocolate chips

Directions:
- Mix the eggs, sugar and vanilla in a bowl until fluffy and creamy.
- Add the sour cream and mix well then fold in the dry ingredients.
- Stir in using a spatula the raspberries and white chocolate.
- Spoon the batter in a muffin tin lined with muffin papers and bake in the preheated oven at 350F for 20 minutes or until golden brown and well risen.
- Allow the muffins to cool down before serving.

Nutritional information per serving
Calories: 164
Fat: 5.2g

Protein: 3.4g
Carbohydrates: 26.4g

LACKBERRY BRAN MUFFINS

Time: 1 hour

Servings: 12

Ingredients:
1 cup all-purpose flour
½ cup wheat bran
1 teaspoon baking soda
½ teaspoon salt
2 eggs

¾ cup milk
¼ cup honey
¼ cup light brown sugar
¼ cup rice bran oil
1 cup fresh blackberries

Directions:
- Mix the flour, wheat bran, baking soda and salt in a bowl.
- Stir in the eggs, milk, honey, sugar and oil and give it a quick mix.
- Fold in the blackberries then spoon the batter in a muffin tin lined with muffin papers.
- Bake in the preheated oven at 350F for 20 minutes or until well risen and golden.
- Serve the muffins chilled.

Nutritional information per serving
Calories: 140
Fat: 5.8g

Protein: 3.1g
Carbohydrates: 20.2g

ASPBERRY VANILLA CUPCAKES

Time: 1 ½ hours

Servings: 12

Ingredients:
Cupcakes:
½ cup butter, softened
2/3 cup white sugar
2 eggs
1 tablespoon vanilla extract
2/3 cup buttermilk
1 ½ cups all-purpose flour

¼ teaspoon salt
1 ½ teaspoons baking powder
Frosting:
2 cups heavy cream
2 tablespoons powdered sugar
1 teaspoon vanilla extract
1 cup fresh raspberries

Directions:
- For the cupcakes, mix the butter and sugar until pale and light.
- Add the eggs, one by one, then stir in the vanilla and buttermilk.
- Fold in the flour, salt and baking powder then spoon the batter in a muffin tin lined with muffin papers.

- Bake the cupcakes in the preheated oven at 350F for 20-25 minutes until they pass the toothpick test then allow them to cool down.
- For the frosting, whip the cream in a bowl until airy and puffed up. Add the sugar and vanilla and mix well.
- Drop a dollop of cream over each cupcake and decorate with a few raspberries.

Nutritional information per serving

Calories: 267

Fat: 16.1g

Protein: 3.6g

Carbohydrates: 27.3g

RANGE ICED CUPCAKES

Time: 1 ¼ hours

Servings: 12

Ingredients:

½ cup butter, softened

¾ cup white sugar

3 eggs

1 teaspoon vanilla extract

½ cup buttermilk

1 ¾ cups all-purpose flour

1 ½ teaspoons baking powder

½ teaspoon salt

¼ cup candied orange peel, diced

Frosting:

1 tablespoon butter, melted

1 tablespoon orange juice

1 teaspoon orange zest

1 ½ cups powdered sugar

Directions:

- For the cupcakes, mix the butter and sugar in a bowl until fluffy and pale.
- Add the eggs and mix well then stir in the vanilla and buttermilk.
- Fold in the flour, baking powder, salt and orange peel then spoon the batter in a muffin tin lined with muffin papers.
- Bake in the preheated oven at 350F for 20 minutes or until they pass the toothpick test. Allow them to cool in the pan.
- For the glaze, mix all the ingredients in a bowl and mix well.
- Drizzle each cupcake with frosting.

Nutritional information per serving

Calories: 272

Fat: 10.0g

Protein: 3.7g

Carbohydrates: 42.9g

ITRUS ICED COCONUT CUPCAKES

Time: 1 ¼ hours

Servings: 12

Ingredients:

Cupcakes:

½ cup coconut butter

½ cup white sugar

2 eggs

½ cup coconut milk

1 ½ cups all-purpose flour

½ cup coconut flakes

¼ teaspoon salt

1 ½ teaspoons baking powder

Icing:

1 teaspoon lime zest

1 teaspoon lemon zest

1 tablespoon lime juice

1 ½ cups powdered sugar

Directions:

- For the cupcakes, mix the coconut butter and sugar until creamy.
- Add the eggs, one by one, then stir in the coconut milk.
- Fold in the flour, coconut flakes, salt and baking powder then spoon the batter in a muffin tin lined with muffin papers.
- Bake the muffins in the preheated oven at 350F for 20 minutes or until golden brown and well risen. Allow them to cool in the pan.
- For the icing, mix all the ingredients in a bowl.
- Drizzle the icing over each cupcake and serve them fresh.

Nutritional information per serving

Calories: 212
Fat: 6.2g

Protein: 3.1g
Carbohydrates: 37.7g

𝒫 LUM WHOLE WHEAT MUFFINS

Time: 1 hour

Servings: 12

Ingredients:

1 ½ cups whole wheat flour
¼ cup all-purpose flour
2 teaspoons baking powder
½ teaspoon salt
1 tablespoon chia seeds

2 eggs
½ cup buttermilk
¼ cup canola oil
1 teaspoon vanilla extract
4 plums, pitted and diced

Directions:

- Mix the flours, baking powder, salt and chia seeds in a bowl.
- Add the rest of the ingredients and give it a quick mix with a spatula.
- Spoon the batter in a muffin tin lined with muffin papers.
- Bake the muffins in the preheated oven at 350F for 20 minutes or until well risen and golden.
- Serve the muffins chilled.

Nutritional information per serving

Calories: 142
Fat: 6.4g

Protein: 3.8g
Carbohydrates: 17.4g

𝒲 HITE CHOCOLATE LIME CUPCAKES

Time: 1 ½ hours

Servings: 12

Ingredients:

Cupcakes:
2/3 cup butter, softened
2/3 cup light brown sugar
3 eggs
1 teaspoon vanilla extract
1 tablespoon lime zest
1 tablespoon lime juice
½ cup buttermilk
1 ½ cups all-purpose flour

¼ cup cornstarch
½ teaspoon salt
1 teaspoon baking soda
½ cup white chocolate chips
Frosting:
1 cup cream cheese, softened
½ cup butter, softened
2 cups powdered sugar
1 tablespoon lime zest

Directions:

- For the cupcakes, mix the butter and sugar in a bowl until pale and fluffy.
- Add the eggs, one by one, then stir in the vanilla, lime zest and juice and buttermilk.
- Fold in the flour, cornstarch, salt and baking soda then add the chocolate chips.
- Spoon the batter in a muffin tin lined with muffin papers and bake in the preheated oven at 350F for 20 minutes until well risen and golden brown.
- Allow them to cool in the pan.
- For the frosting, mix the cream cheese and butter in a bowl until pale.
- Add the sugar and mix well until airy and light.
- Stir in the lime zest then spoon the frosting over each cupcake.
- Serve the cupcakes fresh.

Nutritional information per serving

Calories: 462
Fat: 28.3g
Protein: 5.5g
Carbohydrates: 48.0g

ALMOND WHITE CHOCOLATE CUPCAKES

Time: 1 ½ hours

Servings: 12

Ingredients:

Cupcakes:
1 cup almond flour
½ cup all-purpose flour
½ teaspoon salt
1 ½ teaspoons baking powder
½ cup butter, softened
¾ cup white sugar

1 teaspoon vanilla extract
½ teaspoon almond extract
3 eggs
½ cup plain yogurt
Frosting:
1 cup heavy cream
2 cups white chocolate chips

Directions:

- For the cupcakes, mix the butter and sugar in a bowl until fluffy and pale.
- Add the vanilla, almond extract and eggs and mix well.
- Stir in the yogurt and give it a good mix.
- Fold in the flours, salt, baking powder and mix with a spatula.
- Spoon the batter in a muffin tin lined with muffin papers and bake in the preheated oven at 350F for 20 minutes or until well risen and golden.
- Allow them to cool in the pan.
- For the frosting, bring the cream to the boiling point then remove from the heat and add the chocolate. Mix until melted and smooth then allow to cool in the fridge for a few hours.
- When chilled, whip the frosting until airy and fluffy. Spoon the frosting in a pastry bag and pipe it on top of each cupcake.
- Serve them right away.

Nutritional information per serving

Calories: 359
Fat: 22.9g

Protein: 5.0g
Carbohydrates: 35.2g

PEAR AND GINGER MUFFINS

Time: 1 hour

Servings: 12

Ingredients:

2 eggs
½ cup light brown sugar
½ cup canola oil
¼ cup buttermilk
1 teaspoon vanilla extract
1 teaspoon grated ginger

1 ½ cups all-purpose flour
¼ teaspoon salt
1 teaspoon baking soda
2 pears, cored and diced
½ cup dark chocolate chips

Directions:

- Mix the eggs and sugar in a bowl until fluffy and pale. Stir in the oil and mix well then add the buttermilk and mix well.
- Stir in the vanilla and ginger then fold in the flour, salt and baking powder.
- Add the pears and dark chocolate and mix gently with a spatula.
- Spoon the batter in a muffin tin lined with muffin papers and bake in the preheated oven at 350F for 20 minutes or until well risen and golden brown.
- Serve the muffins chilled.

Nutritional information per serving

Calories: 220
Fat: 11.4g
Protein: 3.4g
Carbohydrates: 27.2g

CINNAMON APPLE CUPCAKES

Time: 1 ½ hours

Servings: 12

Ingredients:

Cupcakes:
½ cup butter, softened
½ cup light brown sugar
3 eggs
1 teaspoon vanilla extract
1 teaspoon grated ginger
1 ½ cups all-purpose flour
½ teaspoon salt

1 teaspoon baking powder
¼ cup milk
2 red apples, cored and diced
Frosting:
1 cup butter, softened
2 cups powdered sugar
1 teaspoon cinnamon powder
1 teaspoon vanilla extract

Directions:

- For the cupcakes, mix the butter and sugar in a bowl until fluffy and creamy.
- Add the eggs, one by one, and mix well then stir in the vanilla and ginger.
- Fold in the flour, salt and baking powder, alternating it with milk. Fold in the apples.
- Spoon the batter in a muffin tin lined with muffin papers.
- Bake the cupcakes in the preheated oven at 350F for 20 minutes. Allow the cupcakes to cool in the pan.
- For the frosting, mix the butter in a bowl until fluffy. Add the sugar and mix well then stir in the cinnamon and vanilla. Whip on high speed for 5 minutes.
- Spoon the frosting on top of each cupcake and serve them fresh.

Nutritional information per serving

Calories: 398
Fat: 24.4g

Protein: 3.5g
Carbohydrates: 42.7g

APRICOT ORANGE MUFFINS

Time: 1 hour

Servings: 12

Ingredients:

1 ½ cups all-purpose flour
¼ cup wheat bran
½ teaspoon salt
1 ½ teaspoons baking powder
2 eggs
½ cup light brown sugar

½ cup canola oil
½ cup buttermilk
1 tablespoon orange zest
¼ teaspoon orange juice
6 apricots, halved

Directions:

- Mix the flour, wheat bran, salt and baking powder in a bowl.
- Add the eggs, sugar, buttermilk, orange zest and orange juice and give it a quick mix.
- Spoon the batter in a muffin tin lined with muffin papers.
- Top each muffin with one apricot half and bake in the preheated oven at 350F for 20-25 minutes or until golden brown and well risen.
- Serve the muffins chilled.

Nutritional information per serving

Calories: 187
Fat: 10.2g

Protein: 3.3g
Carbohydrates: 21.5g

BANANA OLIVE OIL MUFFINS

Time: 1 hour
Servings: 12

Ingredients:

2 eggs
½ cup light brown sugar
¼ cup extra virgin olive oil
1 teaspoon lemon zest
1 tablespoon lemon juice

2 bananas, mashed
½ cup buttermilk
1 ½ cups all-purpose flour
½ teaspoon salt
1 ½ teaspoons baking powder

Directions:

- Mix the eggs and sugar in a bowl until creamy. Add the olive oil and lemon zest and mix well. Stir in the lemon juice and bananas, as well as the buttermilk.
- Fold in the flour, salt and baking powder then spoon the batter in a muffin tin lined with muffin papers.
- Bake in the preheated oven at 350F for 20-25 minutes or until well risen and golden.
- Serve the muffins chilled.

Nutritional information per serving

Calories: 149
Fat: 5.2g

Protein: 3.1g
Carbohydrates: 23.3g

S IMPLE LAVENDER CUPCAKES

Time: 1 ½ hours

Servings: 12

Ingredients:

Cupcakes:
½ cup butter, softened
2/3 cup white sugar
2 eggs
1 teaspoon vanilla extract
1 teaspoon lavender buds
½ cup heavy cream

1 ½ cups all-purpose flour
½ teaspoon salt
1 teaspoon baking powder
Frosting:
1 cup cream cheese
¾ cup butter, softened
2 ½ cups powdered sugar

Directions:

- For the cupcakes, mix the butter and sugar in a bowl until creamy and pale.
- Add the eggs and vanilla and mix well. Stir in the lavender buds and cream and mix well.
- Fold in the flour, salt and baking powder then spoon the batter in a muffin tin lined with baking muffin papers.
- Bake in the preheated oven at 350F for 20 minutes or until well risen and golden brown.
- Allow them to cool in the pan.
- For the frosting, mix the cream cheese and butter in a bowl until fluffy.
- Add the sugar and mix well for 5 minutes on high speed.
- Spoon the frosting over each cupcake and serve them fresh.

Nutritional information per serving

Calories: 466
Fat: 28.8g

Protein: 4.4g
Carbohydrates: 49.8g

C HERRY COCONUT MUFFINS

Time: 1 hour

Servings: 12

Ingredients:

2 eggs
½ cup white sugar
¼ cup canola oil
¾ cup coconut milk
1 cup shredded coconut

1 cup all-purpose flour
½ teaspoon salt
1 teaspoon baking soda
1 cup cherries, pitted

Directions:

- Mix the eggs and sugar in a bowl until fluffy and pale. Add the oil and milk and mix well.

- Fold in the coconut, flour, salt, baking soda and cherries.
- Spoon the batter in a muffin tin lined with muffin papers.
- Bake the muffins in the preheated oven at 350F for 20 minutes or until they pass the toothpick test.
- Serve the muffins chilled.

Nutritional information per serving

Calories: 185
Fat: 11.2g

Protein: 2.6g
Carbohydrates: 19.9g

H UMMINGBIRD MUFFINS

Time: 1 ½ hours

Servings: 12

Ingredients:

1 ½ cups all-purpose flour
½ teaspoon salt
1 ½ teaspoons baking powder
½ cup shredded coconut
¼ teaspoon cinnamon powder
½ cup walnuts, chopped
2 eggs

½ cup white sugar
2 bananas, mashed
½ cup canola oil
1 teaspoon vanilla extract
½ cup crushed pineapple
1 teaspoon orange zest
½ cup grated carrots

Directions:
- Mix the eggs and sugar in a bowl until fluffy and pale.
- Add the bananas and oil, as well as vanilla and mix well.
- Fold in the flour, salt, baking powder and cinnamon then add the coconut, walnuts, pineapple, carrots and orange zest.
- Pour the batter in a muffin tin lined with muffin papers.
- Bake the muffins in the preheated oven at 350F for 20-25 minutes or until golden brown and well risen.
- Serve the muffins chilled.

Nutritional information per serving

Calories: 247
Fat: 14.2g

Protein: 4.2g
Carbohydrates: 27.6g

C OCONUT FLAKES CUPCAKES

Time: 1 ½ hours

Servings: 12

Ingredients:

Cupcakes:
½ cup butter, softened
½ cup white sugar
1 teaspoon coconut extract
3 eggs
1 cup all-purpose flour
¼ teaspoon salt

1 teaspoon baking powder
1 cup shredded coconut
Frosting:
1 cup butter, softened
2 cups powdered sugar
1 cup coconut flakes

Directions:
- For the cupcakes, mix the butter and sugar in a bowl until pale and light.
- Add the coconut extract and eggs and mix well.
- Fold in the flour, salt, baking powder and shredded coconut.
- Spoon the batter in a muffin tin lined with muffin papers.
- Bake the cupcakes in the preheated oven at 350F for 20 minutes or until well risen and golden. Allow the cupcakes to cool down.
- For the frosting, mix the butter until pale. Add the sugar and mix well for 5 minutes.
- Spoon the frosting in a pastry bag and pipe it over each cupcake.
- Decorate the frosted cupcakes with coconut flakes.
- Serve the cupcakes fresh.

Nutritional information per serving

Calories: 415
Fat: 28.7g

Protein: 3.2g
Carbohydrates: 38.6g

H ONEY PEAR MUFFINS

Time: 1 hour

Servings: 12

Ingredients:

1 ½ cups all-purpose flour
½ teaspoon salt
½ teaspoon cinnamon powder
1 ½ teaspoons baking powder
¼ teaspoon ground nutmeg
½ cup light brown sugar

2 eggs
¼ cup butter, melted
1 teaspoon vanilla extract
½ cup buttermilk
2 pears, cored and diced

Directions:

• Mix the dry ingredients in a bowl and the wet ingredients in a different bowl.
• Combine the two mixtures together and mix quickly with a whisk or spatula.
• Fold in the pears then spoon the batter in a muffin tin lined with muffin papers.
• Bake the muffins in the preheated oven at 350F for 20 minutes or until golden brown and well risen.
• Serve the muffins chilled.

Nutritional information per serving

Calories: 150
Fat: 4.9g

Protein: 3.0g
Carbohydrates: 24.1g

P ASSIONFRUIT CUPCAKES

Time: 1 ½ hours

Servings: 12

Ingredients:

Cupcakes:
½ cup butter, softened
½ cup white sugar
2 eggs
1 teaspoon vanilla extract
¼ cup passionfruit juice
½ cup milk

1 13/4 cups all-purpose flour
½ teaspoon salt
1 ½ teaspoons baking powder
Frosting:
1 cup butter, softened
2 cups powdered sugar
2 tablespoons passionfruit juice

Directions:

• For the cupcakes, mix the butter and sugar in a bowl until pale and light.
• Add the eggs and mix well then stir in the vanilla, passionfruit juice and milk.
• Fold in the flour, salt and baking powder then spoon the batter in a muffin tin lined with muffin papers.
• Bake in the preheated oven at 350F for 20 minutes or until golden brown.
• Allow the cupcakes to cool down.
• For the frosting, mix the butter and sugar in a bowl for 5 minutes until pale.
• Stir in the passionfruit juice and mix well.
• Spoon the frosting over each cupcake and serve fresh.

Nutritional information per serving

Calories: 494
Fat: 24.4g

Protein: 6.1g
Carbohydrates: 63.8g

C OCONUT CARAMEL CUPCAKES

Time: 1 ½ hours

Servings: 14

Ingredients:

Cupcakes:

1 cup white sugar

½ cup butter, softened

3 eggs

½ cup coconut cream

½ cup coconut milk

1 teaspoon vanilla extract

1 ½ cups all-purpose flour

2/3 cup shredded coconut

½ teaspoon salt

2 teaspoons baking powder

Frosting:

1 cup butter, softened

2 cups powdered sugar

1 teaspoon vanilla extract

1 cup coconut flakes

½ cup caramel sauce

Directions:

- For the cupcakes, mix the butter and sugar in a bowl until fluffy and pale.
- Add the eggs and mix well then stir in the coconut cream, milk and vanilla.
- Fold in the flour, coconut, salt and baking powder.
- Spoon the batter in a muffin tin lined with muffin papers and bake in the preheated oven at 350F for 20 minutes or until golden brown and well risen.
- Allow the cupcakes to cool down.
- For the frosting, mix the butter and sugar in a bowl for 5-7 minutes or until fluffy and pale.
- Add the vanilla and mix well. Spoon the frosting over each cupcake then decorate with coconut flakes.
- Just before serving, drizzle the cupcakes with caramel sauce.

Nutritional information per serving

Calories: 462

Fat: 28.1g

Protein: 3.7g

Carbohydrates: 52.2g

Chocolate Sprinkle Cupcakes

Time: 1 ½ hours

Servings: 12

Ingredients:

Cupcakes:

1 ½ cups all-purpose flour

½ teaspoon salt

1 ½ teaspoons baking powder

¼ cup cocoa powder

2 eggs

1 teaspoon vanilla extract

1 cup buttermilk

¼ cup brewed coffee

¼ cup canola oil

Frosting:

1 cup butter, softened

2 cups powdered sugar

1 tablespoon cocoa powder

1 tablespoon dark rum

Directions:

- For the cupcakes, mix the flour, salt, baking powder and cocoa powder in a bowl.
- Add the eggs, vanilla, buttermilk, coffee and canola oil and give it a quick mix.
- Pour the batter in 12 muffin cups lined with muffin papers and bake in the preheated oven at 350F for 20-25 minutes or until they pass the toothpick test.
- Allow to cool down.
- For the frosting, mix the butter until fluffy. Add the sugar and mix for 5-7 minutes or until pale and light.
- Stir in the rum and mix well.
- Cover each cupcake with frosting and serve them fresh.

Nutritional information per serving

Calories: 338

Fat: 21.3g

Protein: 3.8g

Carbohydrates: 34.5g

Hazelnut Fig Muffins

Time: 1 hour

Servings: 12

Ingredients:

1 cup ground hazelnuts
½ cup all-purpose flour
½ teaspoon salt
1 teaspoon baking powder

4 eggs
½ cup light brown sugar
¼ cup canola oil
12 fresh figs

Directions:
- Mix the hazelnuts, flour, salt and baking powder in a bowl.
- Mix the eggs and sugar in a bowl until pale and light. Add the oil and mix well.
- Fold in the flour and hazelnut mixture then pour the batter in a muffin tin lined with muffin papers.
- Top each muffin with a fig and bake in the preheated oven at 350F for 20 minutes or until well risen and golden.
- Serve the muffins chilled.

Nutritional information per serving

Calories: 190
Fat: 10.0g

Protein: 4.0g
Carbohydrates: 23.4g

M APLE SYRUP PECAN CUPCAKES

Time: 1 ½ hours

Servings: 12

Ingredients:

Cupcakes:
¼ cup butter, softened
¼ cup heavy cream
½ cup white sugar
¼ cup maple syrup
2 eggs
1 teaspoon vanilla extract
1 cup ground pecans

1 cup all-purpose flour
½ teaspoon salt
1 teaspoon baking powder
1 cup dates, pitted and chopped
Frosting:
1 cup butter, softened
¼ cup maple syrup

Directions:
- For the syrup, mix the butter, cream, sugar and maple syrup in a bowl until pale and creamy.
- Add the eggs and vanilla and mix well.
- Fold in the pecans, flour, salt and baking powder then add the dates.
- Spoon the batter in a muffin tin lined with muffin papers.
- Bake in the preheated oven at 350F for 20 minutes or until golden brown and well risen.
- Allow them to cool in the pan.
- For the frosting, mix the butter and cream in a bowl.
- Drizzle the frosting over each cupcake and serve fresh.

Nutritional information per serving

Calories: 343
Fat: 21.9g

Protein: 2.7g
Carbohydrates: 36.8g

C HOCOLATE CANDIED ORANGE MUFFINS

Time: 1 hour

Servings: 12

Ingredients:

½ cup white sugar
½ cup fresh orange juice
2 eggs
½ cup canola oil
½ cup plain yogurt
1 teaspoon orange zest
1 ½ cups all-purpose flour
½ teaspoon salt

1 ½ teaspoons baking powder
½ cup dark chocolate chips
¼ cup candied orange peel, chopped

Directions:
- Mix the sugar, orange juice, eggs, oil, yogurt and orange zest in a bowl.
- Stir in the flour, salt, baking powder, chocolate chips and orange peel and mix with a spatula.
- Pour the batter in a muffin tin lined with muffin papers and bake in the preheated oven at 350F for 20 minutes or until they pass the toothpick test.
- Serve the muffins chilled.

Nutritional information per serving

Calories: 217
Fat:11.4g

Protein: 3.5g
Carbohydrates: 26.3g

S PICED STRAWBERRY CUPCAKES

Time: 1 ½ hours
Servings: 12
Ingredients
Cupcakes:
1 cup all-purpose flour
1 cup white sugar
1 teaspoon baking soda
½ teaspoon baking powder
½ teaspoon salt
½ teaspoon cinnamon powder

½ teaspoon ground ginger
¼ teaspoon ground nutmeg
½ cup canola oil
1 cup milk
1 teaspoon apple cider vinegar
1 egg
Frosting:
1 cup butter, softened
2 ½ cups powdered sugar
½ cup strawberry puree

Directions:
- For the cupcakes, mix all the ingredients in a bowl and give it a quick mix.
- Pour the batter in a muffin tin lined with baking muffin papers.
- Bake in the preheated oven at 350F for 20 minutes or until well risen and fragrant.
- Allow to cool in the pan.
- For the frosting, mix the butter in a bowl until fluffy. Add the sugar and mix well then stir in the strawberry puree.
- Spoon the frosting over each cupcake and serve them fresh.

Nutritional information per serving

Calories: 435
Fat: 25.4g

Protein: 2.4g
Carbohydrates: 51.8g

C HOCOLATE SPICE CUPCAKES

Time: 1 ½ hours

Servings: 12

Ingredients:
Cupcakes:
1/2 cup butter, softened
½ cup white sugar
1 teaspoon vanilla extract
2 eggs
¾ cup milk
1 ¼ cups all-purpose flour
¼ cup cocoa powder

½ teaspoon salt
1 ½ teaspoons baking powder
½ teaspoon cinnamon powder
½ teaspoon ground ginger
½ teaspoon ground star anise
Frosting:
½ cup heavy cream
1 cup dark chocolate chips

Directions:
- For the cupcakes, mix the butter, sugar and vanilla in a bowl until fluffy and pale.
- Add the eggs and mix well then stir in the milk.
- Fold in the flour, cocoa powder, salt, baking powder, cinnamon, ginger and star anise.
- Spoon the batter in a muffin tin lined with muffin papers.
- Bake the cupcakes in the preheated oven at 350F for 20 minutes or until fragrant and well risen.
- Allow the cupcakes to cool down.

- For the frosting, bring the cream to the boiling point in a saucepan. Remove from heat and stir in the chocolate chips. Mix until melted then spoon the frosting over each cupcake.
- Serve the cupcakes fresh or store them in an airtight container.

Nutritional information per serving

Calories: 235
Fat: 13.6g

Protein: 4.0g
Carbohydrates: 27.4g

OIST CHOCOLATE COFFEE CUPCAKES

Time: 1 ½ hours

Servings: 12

Ingredients:

Cupcakes:
½ cup cocoa powder
1 ½ cups all-purpose flour
½ teaspoon salt
1 teaspoon baking soda
1 egg
1 cup brewed coffee
1 teaspoon instant coffee

½ cup buttermilk
¼ cup canola oil
1 teaspoon vanilla extract
Frosting:
2 cups dark chocolate chips
1 cup heavy cream
1 teaspoon vanilla extract

Directions:
- For the cupcakes, mix the cocoa powder, flour, salt and baking soda in a bowl.
- Stir in the egg, coffee, instant coffee, buttermilk, oil and vanilla and mix well.
- Pour the batter in a muffin tin lined with muffin papers.
- Bake the cupcakes in the preheated oven at 350F for 20 minutes or until well risen. Allow them to cool in the pan.
- For the frosting, bring the cream to the boiling point. Remove from heat and add the chocolate. Mix until melted and smooth then allow to cool completely.
- Stir in the vanilla then whip the cream with an electric mixer just until pale and stiff.
- Decorate each cupcake with whipped frosting and serve them fresh.

Nutritional information per serving

Calories: 244
Fat: 14.6g

Protein: 4.6g
Carbohydrates: 28.1g

OUBLE BERRY CUPCAKES

Time: 1 ½ hours

Servings: 12

Ingredients:

Cupcakes:
½ cup butter, softened
½ cup white sugar
1 teaspoon vanilla extract
2 eggs
2/3 cup buttermilk
1 ¼ cups all-purpose flour

½ cup almond flour
½ teaspoon salt
1 ½ teaspoons baking powder
1 cup fresh strawberries, sliced
Frosting:
2 cups heavy cream
1 cup fresh raspberries

Directions:
- For the cupcakes, mix the butter and sugar in a bowl until creamy and pale. Add the eggs and vanilla and mix well.
- Stir in the buttermilk then fold in the flours, salt and baking powder.
- Add the strawberries and mix gently.
- Spoon the batter in a muffin tin lined with baking muffin papers and bake in the preheated oven at 350F for 20 minutes or until golden brown and well risen.
- Allow them to cool in the pan.
- Top each cupcake with whipped cream and decorate with raspberries.

Nutritional information per serving

Calories: 249
Fat: 16.7g

Protein: 3.7g
Carbohydrates: 22.3g

$\mathcal{E}$ SPRESSO SOUR CREAM CUPCAKES

Time: 1 ½ hours

Servings: 12

Ingredients:

Cupcakes:
2/3 cup butter, softened
2/3 cup white sugar
1 teaspoon vanilla extract
2 eggs
½ cup sour cream
¼ cup brewed espresso
1 ½ cups all-purpose flour

½ teaspoon salt
1 ½ teaspoons baking powder
¼ cup cornstarch
Frosting:
1 cup butter, softened
2 cups powdered sugar
2 teaspoons instant coffee
1 teaspoon vanilla extract

Directions:

- For the cupcakes, mix the butter and sugar in a bowl until pale and creamy.
- Add the vanilla and eggs and mix well. Stir in the espresso and sour cream.
- Add the rest of the ingredients and mix with a spatula.
- Spoon the batter in a muffin tin lined with muffin papers.
- Bake in the preheated oven at 350F for 20 minutes or until well risen and golden brown.
- Allow the cupcakes to cool in the pan.
- For the frosting, mix the butter and sugar in a bowl for at least 5 minutes or until pale and creamy.
- Add the coffee and vanilla and mix well.
- Spoon the frosting in a pastry bag and pipe it over the cupcakes.
- Serve them fresh.

Nutritional information per serving

Calories: 447
Fat: 28.5g

Protein: 3.1g
Carbohydrates: 46.4g

$\mathcal{T}$ HE ULTIMATE VANILLA CUPCAKES

Time: 1 ½ hours

Servings: 12

Ingredients:

Cupcakes:
2 cups all-purpose flour
½ teaspoon salt
2 teaspoons baking powder
2/3 cup white sugar
2/3 cup butter, softened
2 eggs
1 cup buttermilk

1 tablespoon vanilla extract
Frosting:
4 egg whites
1 cup white sugar
½ teaspoon salt
1 cup butter, softened
1 teaspoon vanilla extract

Directions:

- For the cupcakes, mix the flour, salt, baking powder and sugar in a bowl.
- Add the butter and mix until grainy.
- In a bowl, combine the eggs, buttermilk and vanilla and mix well. Pour over the flour and mix for 1 minute on high speed.
- Spoon the batter in a muffin tin lined with baking muffins papers.
- Bake in the preheated oven at 350F for 20 minutes or until well risen and golden brown.
- Allow to cool in the pan.
- For the frosting, mix the egg whites and sugar in a bowl and place over hot water bath. Keep on heat and mix until

heated and the sugar has melted.
- Remove from heat and mix for 5-7 minutes until fluffy and thickened, glossy and stiff.
- Add the butter, all at once, and mix well for 2 minutes. It will curdle up at first then it will come back together.
- Add the vanilla and mix well.
- Spoon the frosting in a pastry bag and pipe it over the cupcakes.
- Serve them fresh.

Nutritional information per serving

Calories: 435

Fat: 26.7g

Protein: 5.2g

Carbohydrates: 45.4g

H ONEY SPICED MUFFINS

Time: 1 hour

Servings: 12

Ingredients:

½ cup butter, melted

2 eggs

½ cup honey

2 tablespoons dark brown sugar

1 teaspoon vanilla extract

1 cup ground almonds

1 cup all-purpose flour

½ teaspoon cinnamon powder

½ teaspoon ground ginger

½ teaspoon ground star anise

½ teaspoon ground cardamom

½ teaspoon salt

1 teaspoon baking soda

Directions:
- Mix the butter, eggs, honey and sugar in a bowl.
- Stir in the rest of the ingredients and mix with a spatula just until incorporated.
- Pour the batter in a muffin tin lined with muffin papers.
- Bake in the preheated oven at 350F for 20 minutes or until fragrant and well risen.
- Serve the muffins chilled.

Nutritional information per serving

Calories: 213

Fat: 12.5g

Protein: 3.9g

Carbohydrates: 23.1g

G LUTEN FREE CHOCOLATE MUFFINS

Time: 1 hour

Servings: 10

Ingredients:

3 eggs

½ cup white sugar

1 teaspoon vanilla extract

½ cup canola oil

½ cup white rice flour

½ cup tapioca flour

½ cup shredded coconut

¼ cup cocoa powder

1 teaspoon baking powder

½ teaspoon salt

½ cup dark chocolate chips

Directions:
- Mix the eggs, sugar and vanilla in a bowl until fluffy and pale.
- Add the oil then stir in the rest of the ingredients.
- Spoon the batter in a muffin tin lined with muffin papers and bake in the preheated oven at 350F for 15-20 minutes or until well risen and fragrant.
- Serve the muffins chilled.

Nutritional information per serving

Calories: 251

Fat: 15.4g

Protein: 2.9g

Carbohydrates: 28.7g

ℛ ASPBERRY JAM MUFFINS

Time: 1 hour

Servings: 12

Ingredients:

2 eggs
2/3 cup white sugar
1 teaspoon vanilla extract
½ cup canola oil
¾ cup sour cream

1 ¾ cups all-purpose flour
½ teaspoon salt
1 ½ teaspoons baking powder
1 cup raspberry jam

Directions:

- Mix the eggs and sugar in a bowl until fluffy and pale, at least double in volume.
- Stir in the vanilla, sour cream and oil and mix well.
- Fold in the flour, salt and baking powder then spoon the batter in a muffin tin lined with baking muffin papers.
- Spoon the jam over each muffin and bake in the preheated oven at 350F for 20 minutes or until golden brown and well risen.
- Allow to cool down before serving.

Nutritional information per serving

Calories: 298
Fat: 13.0g

Protein: 3.4g
Carbohydrates: 43.4g

𝒮 PRINKLES CHOCOLATE CUPCAKES

Time: 1 ½ hours

Servings: 12

Ingredients:

Cupcakes:
½ cup butter, softened
1 cup white sugar
2 eggs
1 teaspoon vanilla extract
1 ½ cups all-purpose flour
¼ cup cocoa powder

½ teaspoon salt
1 ½ teaspoons baking powder
1 cup whole milk
Frosting:
1 cup butter, softened
2 cups powdered sugar
½ cup dark chocolate chips, melted

Directions:

- For the cupcakes, mix the butter and sugar in a bowl until creamy and pale.
- Add the eggs and vanilla and mix well then stir in the flour, cocoa powder, salt and baking powder, alternating them with milk.
- Spoon the batter in a muffin tin lined with baking muffin papers.
- Bake the cupcakes in the preheated oven at 350F for 20 minutes or until they pass the toothpick test.
- For the frosting, mix the butter and sugar in a bowl until fluffy and pale. Add the melted and cooled chocolate.
- Decorate the cupcakes with frosting and serve them fresh.

Nutritional information per serving

Calories: 452
Fat: 26.1g

Protein: 4.1g
Carbohydrates: 54.2g

ℒ EMON FIG MUFFINS

Time: 1 hour

Servings: 12

Ingredients:

1/3 cup butter, melted
½ cup white sugar
3 eggs

½ cup buttermilk
1 lemon, zested and juiced
1 cup ground almonds

1 cup all-purpose flour
½ teaspoon salt

1 teaspoon baking soda
4 fresh figs, chopped

Directions:
- Mix the butter, sugar, eggs, buttermilk, lemon zest and lemon juice in a bowl until creamy.
- Add the flour, salt and baking soda and mix with a spatula.
- Fold in the figs then spoon the batter in a muffin tin lined with muffin papers.
- Bake in the preheated oven at 350F for 20 minutes or until they pass the toothpick test.
- Serve them chilled.

Nutritional information per serving

Calories: 197
Fat: 10.4g

Protein: 4.8g
Carbohydrates: 23.0g

*L*EMON RICOTTA MUFFINS

Time: 1 hour

Servings: 12

Ingredients:

⅓ cup butter, melted
1 teaspoon vanilla extract
2 eggs
½ cup ricotta cheese
¼ cup milk

1 tablespoon lemon zest
1 cup almond flour
1 cup all-purpose flour
½ teaspoon salt
1 ½ teaspoons baking powder

Directions:
- Mix the butter, vanilla, eggs, ricotta, milk and lemon zest in a bowl.
- Add the flours, salt and baking powder and mix with a spatula.
- Spoon the batter in 12 muffin cups lined with baking muffin papers of your desire.
- Bake in the preheated oven at 350F for 20 minutes or until well risen and golden brown.
- Serve the muffins chilled.

Nutritional information per serving

Calories: 148
Fat: 10.6g

Protein: 3.9g
Carbohydrates: 9.7g

*C*OCONUT MANGO MUFFINS

Time: 1 hour

Servings: 12

Ingredients:

½ cup canola oil
2 eggs
½ cup white sugar
1 teaspoon vanilla extract
½ cup coconut milk

1 cup shredded coconut
1 cup all-purpose flour
½ teaspoon salt
1 ½ teaspoons baking powder
1 mango, peeled and diced

Directions:
- Mix the oil, eggs, sugar, vanilla and coconut milk in a bowl.
- Add the coconut, flour, salt and baking powder then fold in the mango.
- Spoon the batter in a muffin tin lined with muffin papers or greased and bake in the preheated oven at 350F for 20 minutes or until well risen and golden brown.
- Serve the muffins chilled.

Nutritional information per serving

Calories: 220
Fat: 14.6g
Protein: 2.5g
Carbohydrates: 21.2g

B ANANA PEANUT BUTTER CUPS MUFFINS

Time: 1 hour

Servings: 12

Ingredients:

2 bananas, mashed
2 eggs
1 cup buttermilk
1 teaspoon vanilla extract
½ cup light brown sugar

1 ½ cups all-purpose flour
½ teaspoon salt
1 teaspoon baking soda
½ peanut butter cups, chopped

Directions:

- Mix the bananas, eggs, buttermilk and vanilla in a bowl.
- Add the sugar, flour, salt and baking soda and mix with a spatula.
- Fold in the peanut butter cups then spoon the batter in a muffin tin lined with muffin papers.
- Bake the muffins in the preheated oven at 350F for 15-20 minutes or until golden brown and well risen.
- Serve the muffins chilled.

Nutritional information per serving

Calories: 180
Fat: 6.5g

Protein: 6.1g
Carbohydrates: 25.5g

F UNFETTI CREAM CHEESE CUPCAKES

Time: 1 ½ hours

Servings: 12

Ingredients:

Cupcakes:
1 ¾ cups all-purpose flour
½ teaspoon salt
1 teaspoon baking powder
½ teaspoon baking soda
½ cup butter, softened
2/3 cup white sugar
2 eggs
½ cup sour cream

½ cup milk
1 teaspoon vanilla extract
½ cup colorful sprinkles
Frosting:
1 cup cream cheese
½ cup butter, softened
2 cups powdered sugar
Sprinkles to decorate

Directions:

- For the cupcakes, mix the butter and sugar in a bowl until creamy and pale.
- Add the eggs and mix well then stir in the sour cream, milk and vanilla.
- Fold in the sprinkles then spoon the batter in a muffin tin lined with baking muffin papers.
- Bake in the preheated oven at 350F for 20 minutes or until well risen and golden brown.
- Allow the cupcakes to cool down.
- For the frosting, mix the cream cheese and butter in a bowl until pale.
- Add the sugar and mix well for 5-7 minutes or until fluffy and light.
- Decorate the cupcakes with cream cheese frosting.
- Top with colorful sprinkles.

Nutritional information per serving

Calories: 438
Fat: 25.7g

Protein: 5.2g
Carbohydrates: 48.6g

B LUEBERRY LEMON CUPCAKES

Time: 1 ½ hours
Servings: 12

Ingredients:

Cupcakes:
½ cup butter, softened
1 cup white sugar
3 eggs
1 tablespoon lemon zest
2 tablespoons lemon juice
1 teaspoon vanilla extract
1 ¾ cups all-purpose flour

½ teaspoon salt
1 ½ teaspoons baking powder
1 cup fresh blueberries
Frosting:
4 egg yolks
3 lemons, zested and juiced
½ cup butter
1 cup white sugar

Directions:

- For the cupcakes, mix the butter and sugar in a bowl until fluffy and creamy.
- Add the eggs and mix well then stir in the lemon zest, lemon juice and vanilla.
- Fold in the flour, salt, baking powder and blueberries.
- Spoon the batter in a muffin tin lined with muffin papers.
- Bake in the preheated oven at 350F for 20 minutes or until they pass the toothpick test.
- Allow them to cool in the pan.
- For the frosting, mix all the ingredients in a heatproof bowl and place over a hot water bath.
- Cook the mixture for 15-20 minutes, stirring all the time with a whisk until it thickens and it looks smooth and shiny.
- Allow to cool then top each cupcake with the lemon cream.

Nutritional information per serving

Calories: 374
Fat: 18.2g

Protein: 4.6g
Carbohydrates: 51.1g

G RAPEFRUIT CREAM CHEESE CUPCAKES

Time: 1 ½ hours

Servings: 12

Ingredients:

Cupcakes:
½ cup butter, softened
¾ cup white sugar
1 teaspoon grapefruit zest
2 eggs
¾ cup buttermilk
1 ¾ cups all-purpose flour

½ teaspoon salt
1 ½ teaspoons baking powder
Frosting:
1 cup cream cheese
½ cup butter
2 cups powder sugar
1 tablespoon grapefruit zest

Directions:

- For the cupcakes, mix the butter and sugar in a bowl until fluffy and creamy.
- Add the zest and eggs and mix well.
- Stir in the flour, salt and baking powder then add the milk and mix well.
- Spoon the batter in a muffin tin lined with muffin papers and bake in the preheated oven at 350F for 20-25 minutes.
- Allow the cupcakes to cool in the pan.
- For the frosting, mix the cream cheese and butter in a bowl until fluffy.
- Add the eggs and mix well for 4-5 minutes then stir in the zest.
- Decorate each cupcake with frosting and serve them fresh.

Nutritional information per serving

Calories: 412
Fat: 23.1g

Protein: 4.9g
Carbohydrates: 48.1g

O RANGE POPPY SEED MUFFINS

Time: 1 ½ hours

Servings: 12

Ingredients:

1 orange, washed

½ cup coconut oil

3 eggs
1 teaspoon vanilla extract
1 cup all-purpose flour
½ cup whole wheat flour

1 ½ teaspoon baking powder
½ teaspoon salt
2 tablespoons poppy seed

Directions:
- Place the orange in a saucepan and cover it with water. Cook until softened then drain and place the orange in a blender.
- Add the coconut oil, eggs and vanilla and blend until smooth.
- Stir in the flours, salt, baking powder and poppy seed and mix with a spatula.
- Spoon the batter in a muffin tin lined with muffin papers and bake in the preheated oven at 350F for 20-25 minutes or until well risen and golden.
- Serve the muffins chilled.

Nutritional information per serving
Calories: 168
Fat: 11.0g

Protein: 3.4g
Carbohydrates: 14.5g

$\mathcal{B}$ANANA MASCARPONE CUPCAKES

Time: 1 ½ hours

Servings: 12

Ingredients:
Cupcakes:
2 bananas, mashed
2 eggs
1 teaspoon vanilla extract
¼ cup canola oil
1 cup buttermilk
1 ½ cups all-purpose flour

½ cup oat flour
½ teaspoon salt
2 teaspoons baking powder
Frosting:
1 ½ cups mascarpone cheese
1 cup powdered sugar
1 teaspoon vanilla extract

Directions:
- For the cupcakes, mix the bananas, eggs, vanilla, oil and buttermilk in a bowl.
- Add the rest of the ingredients and mix well.
- Spoon the batter in a muffin tin lined with muffin papers.
- Bake in the preheated oven at 350F for 20-25 minutes or until golden brown and well risen.
- Allow them to cool in the pan.
- For the frosting, mix the mascarpone cheese and sugar in a bowl until pale and fluffy.
- Add the vanilla and mix well.
- Top the cupcakes with frosting and serve them fresh.

Nutritional information per serving
Calories: 244
Fat: 9.9g

Protein: 7.4g
Carbohydrates: 31.5g

$\mathcal{C}$HOCOLATE RASPBERRY CRUMBLE MUFFINS

Time: 1 ¼ hours

Servings: 12

Ingredients:
Muffins:
3 eggs
½ cup white sugar
½ cup butter, melted
1 teaspoon vanilla extract
½ cup milk
1 ½ cups all-purpose flour
¼ cup cocoa powder

½ teaspoon salt
2 teaspoons baking powder
1 cup fresh raspberries
Crumble topping:
¼ cup butter, chilled
½ cup all-purpose flour
¼ teaspoon salt

Directions:

- For the muffins, mix the eggs, sugar and vanilla in a bowl until creamy.
- Stir in the milk and butter and mix well.
- Fold in the flour, cocoa powder, salt and baking powder then spoon the batter in a muffin pan lined with muffin papers.
- For the topping, mix the ingredients in a bowl until grainy.
- Top the muffins with the crumble topping and bake in the preheated oven at 350F for 20 minutes or until well risen.
- Serve the muffins chilled.

Nutritional information per serving

Calories: 241

Fat: 13.3g

Protein: 4.4g

Carbohydrates: 27.5g

UTTERNUT ALMOND MUFFINS

Time: 1 hour

Servings: 12

Ingredients:

1 cup butternut squash puree

½ cup golden syrup

2 eggs

1 teaspoon vanilla extract

¼ cup canola oil

1 cup almond flour

1 cup all purpose flour

½ teaspoon salt

1 ½ teaspoons baking powder

1 teaspoon pumpkin pie spices

¼ cup sliced almonds

Directions:

- Mix the butternut squash puree, golden syrup, eggs, vanilla and canola oil in a bowl.
- Add the flours, salt, baking powder and spices and mix gently.
- Spoon the batter in a muffin tin lined with muffin papers and top with sliced almonds.
- Bake in the preheated oven at 350F for 20-25 minutes or until golden brown and well risen.
- Serve the muffins chilled.

Nutritional information per serving

Calories: 158

Fat: 7.6g

Protein: 3.0g

Carbohydrates: 20.9g

PPLE PUREE MUFFINS

Time: 1 hour

Servings: 12

Ingredients:

1 ½ cups all-purpose flour

2/3 cup light brown sugar

1 teaspoon cinnamon powder

½ teaspoon ground ginger

1 teaspoon baking soda

2 eggs

½ cup apple puree

¼ cup peanut oil

1 teaspoon vanilla extract

2 apples, cored and diced

½ cup golden raisins

Directions:

- Mix the flour, sugar, cinnamon, ginger and baking soda in a bowl.
- Add the rest of the ingredients and give it a quick mix.
- Pour the batter in a muffin tin lined with baking muffin papers.
- Bake the muffins in the preheated oven at 350F for 20-25 minutes or until fragrant and golden brown.
- Serve the muffins chilled.

Nutritional information per serving

Calories: 179

Fat: 5.5g

Protein: 2.8g

Carbohydrates: 30.4g

GINGER PINEAPPLE MUFFINS

Time: 1 hour

Servings: 12

Ingredients:

½ cup canola oil
¾ cup light brown sugar
1 egg
½ cup milk
1 ½ cups all-purpose flour
½ cup shredded coconut

½ teaspoon salt
1 ½ teaspoons baking powder
1 teaspoon ground ginger
½ teaspoon cinnamon powder
1 cup crushed pineapple

Directions:

- Mix the oil and sugar until creamy. Add the egg and mix well then stir in the milk and mix very well.
- Fold in the flour, coconut, salt, baking powder, ginger and cinnamon and mix well.
- Fold in the pineapple then spoon the batter in a muffin tin lined with muffin papers.
- Bake in the preheated oven at 350F for 15-20 minutes or until well risen and golden brown.
- Serve the muffins chilled.

Nutritional information per serving

Calories: 202
Fat: 10.9g

Protein: 2.6g
Carbohydrates: 24.1g

DUO CHOCOLATE CHIP MUFFINS

Time: 1 hour

Servings: 12

Ingredients:

½ cup canola oil
1 cup white sugar
2 eggs
1 cup milk
2 cups all-purpose flour

½ teaspoon salt
1 ½ teaspoons baking powder
½ cup dark chocolate chips
½ cup white chocolate chips

Directions:

- Mix the oil and sugar in a bowl. Add the eggs and mix well then stir in the milk.
- Fold in the flour, salt and baking powder then add the chocolate chips.
- Spoon the batter in a muffin tin lined with muffin papers and bake in the preheated oven at 350F for 20 minutes or until golden brown.
- Serve the muffins chilled.

Nutritional information per serving

Calories: 301
Fat: 14.0g

Protein: 4.5g
Carbohydrates: 41.4g

MILKY BANANA MUFFINS

Time: 1 hour

Servings: 12

Ingredients:

1 ½ cups all-purpose flour
½ teaspoon salt
1 teaspoon baking soda
2 bananas, mashed

2 eggs
½ cup heavy cream
¼ cup canola oil
1 teaspoon vanilla extract

Directions:

- Mix the bananas, eggs, cream, oil and vanilla in a bowl.

- Add the flour, salt and baking soda then spoon the batter in a muffin tin lined with muffin papers.
- Bake the muffins in the preheated oven at 350F for 15-20 minutes or until well risen and fragrant.
- Serve the muffins chilled.

Nutritional information per serving

Calories: 143
Fat: 7.3g

Protein: 2.8g
Carbohydrates: 16.7g

OCHA CHOCOLATE CHIP BANANA MUFFINS

Time: 1 hour

Servings: 12

Ingredients:

2 bananas, mashed
2 eggs
2 teaspoons instant coffee
1 teaspoon vanilla extract
½ cup milk
½ cup light brown sugar

1 ½ cups all-purpose flour
1 teaspoon baking powder
½ teaspoon baking soda
¼ teaspoon salt
½ cup dark chocolate chips

Directions:

- Mix the bananas, eggs, instant coffee, vanilla, milk and sugar in a bowl.
- Stir in the rest of the ingredients and mix well.
- Fold in the chocolate chips then spoon the batter in 12 muffin cups lined with muffin papers.
- Bake in the preheated oven at 350F for 15-20 minutes or until golden brown and well risen.
- Serve the muffins chilled.

Nutritional information per serving

Calories: 138
Fat: 2.5g

Protein: 3.4g
Carbohydrates: 26.5g

LUEBERRY OATMEAL MUFFINS

Time: 1 hour

Servings: 12

Ingredients:

1 cup all-purpose flour
1 cup oat flour
1 teaspoon baking powder
½ teaspoon baking soda
¼ teaspoon salt

¾ cup light brown sugar
2 eggs
1 cup buttermilk
½ cup canola oil
1 cup fresh blueberries

Directions:

- Mix the flours, baking powder, baking soda, salt and sugar in a bowl.
- Add the eggs, buttermilk and canola oil and mix well.
- Fold in the blueberries then spoon the batter in a muffin tin lined with muffin papers of your desire.
- Bake in the preheated oven at 350F for 20 minutes or until well risen and golden brown.
- Allow to cool in the pan before serving.

Nutritional information per serving

Calories: 209
Fat: 10.6g

Protein: 3.8g
Carbohydrates: 25.1g

RICH CHOCOLATE MUFFINS

Time: 1 hour
Servings: 12

Ingredients:

1 ¾ cups all-purpose flour
½ cup cocoa powder
½ teaspoon salt
1 teaspoon baking powder
¼ teaspoon baking soda

1 cup white sugar
½ cup canola oil
¾ cup milk
2 eggs
1 teaspoon vanilla extract

Directions:

- Mix the flour, cocoa powder, salt, baking powder, baking soda and salt in a bowl.
- Add the rest of the ingredients and mix well.
- Pour the batter in a muffin tin lined with muffin papers.
- Bake the muffins in the preheated oven at 350F for 15-20 minutes.
- Allow them to cool in the pan before serving or storing.

Nutritional information per serving

Calories: 237
Fat: 10.8g

Protein: 3.9g
Carbohydrates: 33.6g

C INNAMON PLUM MUFFINS

Time: 1 hour

Servings: 12

Ingredients:

1 ½ cups all-purpose flour
½ cup light brown sugar
1 teaspoon baking soda
1 teaspoon cinnamon powder
½ teaspoon ground ginger
½ cup ground walnuts

1 cup buttermilk
¼ cup canola oil
1 egg
1 teaspoon vanilla extract
6 plums, pitted and diced

Directions:

- Mix the flour, sugar, baking soda, cinnamon, ginger and walnuts in a bowl.
- Add the rest of the ingredients and mix well. Add the plums as well.
- Spoon the batter in a muffin tin lined with your favorite muffin papers.
- Bake in the preheated oven at 350F for 20-25 minutes or until well risen and golden brown.
- Serve the muffins chilled.

Nutritional information per serving

Calories: 177
Fat: 8.4g

Protein: 4.2g
Carbohydrates: 22.0g

C ARROT CAKE PECAN MUFFINS

Time: 1 hour

Servings: 12

Ingredients:

1 ½ cups all-purpose flour
¼ teaspoon salt
1 teaspoon baking soda
1 teaspoon cinnamon powder
½ teaspoon ground ginger
½ cup milk

1 egg
½ cup canola oil
½ cup light brown sugar
1 cup grated carrot
½ cup crushed pineapple
½ cup walnuts, chopped

Directions:

- Mix the flour, salt, baking soda, cinnamon and ginger.
- Add the milk, egg, oil, sugar, carrot, pineapple and walnuts and mix well.
- Spoon the batter in a muffin tin lined with muffin papers.
- Bake in the preheated oven at 350F for 20 minutes or until well risen and fragrant.

- Serve the muffins chilled or store them in an airtight container for up to 4 days.

Nutritional information per serving

Calories: 210
Fat: 12.9g

Protein: 3.8g
Carbohydrates: 20.8g

*M*IXED BERRY BUTTERMILK MUFFINS

Time: 1 hour

Servings: 12

Ingredients:

2 cups all-purpose flour
½ teaspoon salt
1 teaspoon baking powder
½ teaspoon baking soda
1 egg

¼ cup olive oil
1 ¼ cups buttermilk
1 teaspoon vanilla extract
½ cup white sugar
1 cup mixed berries

Directions:

- Mix the flour, salt, baking powder and baking soda in a bowl.
- Add the egg, olive oil, buttermilk and vanilla and mix well then stir in the sugar.
- Fold in the berries then spoon the batter in a muffin tin lined with your favorite muffin papers.
- Bake the muffins in the preheated oven at 350F for 15-20 minutes or until they pass the toothpick test.
- Serve the muffins chilled.

Nutritional information per serving

Calories: 167
Fat: 5.0g

Protein: 3.5g
Carbohydrates: 27.1g

*P*EANUT BUTTER BANANA CUPCAKES

Time: 1 ½ hours

Servings: 12

Ingredients:

Cupcakes:
2 bananas, mashed
½ cup canola oil
½ cup milk
1 egg
1 teaspoon vanilla extract
1 ¾ cups all-purpose flour

¼ teaspoon salt
1 teaspoon baking soda
Frosting:
½ cup smooth peanut butter
1 cup cream cheese
1 cup powdered sugar

Directions:

- For the cupcakes, mix the bananas, canola oil, milk, egg and vanilla.
- Stir in the flour, salt and baking soda then spoon the batter in a muffin tin lined with muffin papers.
- Bake in the preheated oven at 350F for 15-20 minutes or until well risen and golden brown.
- For the frosting, mix all the ingredients in a bowl until creamy and fluffy.
- Top each chilled cupcake with frosting and serve them fresh.

Nutritional information per serving

Calories: 345
Fat: 22.1g

Protein: 7.0g
Carbohydrates: 31.5g

*S*TRAWBERRY CHIA SEED MUFFINS

Time: 1 hour

Servings: 12

Ingredients:

1 ¾ cups all-purpose flour

2 tablespoons chia seeds

½ teaspoon salt
2 teaspoons baking powder
1/3 cup canola oil
1 cup plain yogurt

2 eggs
4 tablespoons milk
1 cup strawberries, sliced

Directions:
- Mix the dry ingredients in a bowl.
- Add the oil, yogurt, eggs and milk and give it a quick mix.
- Fold in the strawberries then spoon the batter in 12 muffin cups lined with muffin papers.
- Bake the muffins in the preheated oven at 350F for 2- minutes or until well risen and golden brown.
- Allow the muffins to cool down before serving.

Nutritional information per serving
Calories: 178
Fat: 9.0g

Protein: 5.3g
Carbohydrates: 18.7g

S PICY PINEAPPLE MUFFINS

Time: 1 hour

Servings: 12

Ingredients:
1 ½ cups all-purpose flour
½ teaspoon salt
1 teaspoon baking soda
½ cup sultanas
¼ teaspoon cayenne pepper

½ teaspoon ground ginger
2 eggs
½ cup light brown sugar
1/3 cup canola oil
2 cups crushed pineapple

Directions:
- Mix the flour, salt, baking soda and sultanas in a bowl.
- Add the cayenne pepper and ginger then stir in the rest of the ingredients and give it a quick mix.
- Spoon the batter in a muffin tin lined with muffin papers.
- Bake in the preheated oven at 350F for 15-20 minutes or until well risen and golden brown.
- Serve the muffins chilled or store them in an airtight container.

Nutritional information per serving
Calories: 162
Fat: 7.0g

Protein: 2.7g
Carbohydrates: 22.7g

O RANGE YOGURT MUFFINS

Time: 1 hour

Servings: 12

Ingredients:
2 cups all-purpose flour
2 teaspoons baking powder
½ teaspoon salt
1 cup plain yogurt

1 orange, zested and juice
½ cup canola oil
1 egg
¼ cup candied orange peel, chopped

Directions:
- Mix the flour, baking powder and salt in a bowl.
- Add the yogurt, orange zest, orange juice, oil and egg and mix well.
- Fold in the orange peel then spoon the batter in a muffin tin lined with your favorite muffin papers.
- Bake in the preheated oven at 350F for 15-20 minutes or until well risen and golden brown.
- Serve the muffins chilled.

Nutritional information per serving
Calories: 186
Fat: 9.9g
Protein: 3.9g

Carbohydrates: 20.1g

*M*UESLI APPLE MUFFINS

Time: 1 hour

Servings: 16

Ingredients:

2 ½ cups all-purpose flour
½ teaspoon salt
2 teaspoons baking powder
½ teaspoon cinnamon powder
1 cup muesli

2 eggs
½ cup canola oil
1 ½ cups milk
2 red apples, cored and diced

Directions:

- Mix the flour, salt, baking powder, cinnamon and muesli in a bowl.
- Add the eggs, canola oil and milk and mix well with a spatula.
- Fold in the apples then spoon the batter in a muffin tin lined with your favorite muffin papers.
- Bake in the preheated oven at 350F for 20-25 minutes or until well risen and golden brown.
- Serve the muffins chilled or store them in an airtight container.

Nutritional information per serving

Calories: 182
Fat: 8.4g

Protein: 4.0g
Carbohydrates: 23.5g

*A*PPLE CRANBERRY MUFFINS

Time: 1 hour

Servings: 12

Ingredients:

1 ¾ cups all-purpose flour
½ cup light brown sugar
1 teaspoon baking soda
¼ teaspoon salt
½ teaspoon cinnamon powder
½ cup butter, melted

½ cup milk
1 egg
1 teaspoon vanilla extract
1 red apple, cored and diced
½ cup dried cranberries

Directions:

- Mix the flour, sugar, baking soda, salt and cinnamon in a bowl.
- Stir in the butter, milk, egg and vanilla and give it a quick mix.
- Fold in the apple and cranberries and spoon the batter in a muffin tin lined with your favorite muffin papers.
- Bake the muffins in the preheated oven at 350F for 15-20 minutes or until well risen and golden.
- Serve the muffins chilled.

Nutritional information per serving

Calories: 179
Fat: 8.4g

Protein: 2.8g
Carbohydrates: 22.9g

*A*PRICOT ROSEMARY MUFFINS

Time: 1 hour

Servings: 12

Ingredients:

1 ½ cups all-purpose flour
¼ teaspoon salt
1 teaspoon baking powder
½ cup rolled oats
½ cup ground almonds
1 teaspoon dried rosemary
½ cup honey

½ cup plain yogurt
¼ cup milk
1 egg
½ cup dried apricots, chopped

Directions:
- Mix the flour, salt, baking powder, oats, almonds and rosemary in a bowl.
- Stir in the honey, yogurt, milk and egg and mix well then fold in the apricots.
- Spoon the batter in a muffin pan lined with your favorite muffin papers and bake in the preheated oven at 350F for 20-25 minutes or until well risen and golden brown.
- Serve the muffins chilled.

Nutritional information per serving

Calories: 155

Fat: 3.0g

Protein: 4.2g

Carbohydrates: 28.7g

B ASIC MUFFINS

Time: 1 hour

Servings: 12

Ingredients:

2 ¼ cups all-purpose flour

½ teaspoon baking soda

½ teaspoon baking powder

¼ teaspoon salt

¾ cup white sugar

1 egg

½ cup canola oil

1 cup whole milk

1 teaspoon vanilla extract

Directions:
- Mix the flour, sugar, salt, baking powder and baking soda in a bowl.
- Stir in the egg, oil, milk and vanilla and give it a quick mix.
- Spoon the batter in a muffin tin lined with muffin papers and bake in the preheated oven at 350F for 15-20 minutes or until well risen and golden.
- Serve the muffins chilled.

Nutritional information per serving

Calories: 231

Fat: 10.3g

Protein: 3.5g

Carbohydrates: 31.5g

B EETROOT RASPBERRY MUFFINS

Time: 1 ½ hours

Servings: 12

Ingredients:

1 cup beetroot puree

1 egg

½ cup buttermilk

½ cup canola oil

½ cup white sugar

1 teaspoon vanilla extract

2 cups all-purpose flour

½ teaspoon salt

1 ½ teaspoons baking powder

1 cup fresh raspberries

Directions:
- Mix the beetroot puree, egg, buttermilk and oil in a bowl.
- Add the sugar and vanilla and mix well then fold in the flour, salt and baking powder.
- Fold in the raspberries then spoon the batter in a muffin tin lined with baking muffin papers.
- Bake in the preheated oven at 350F for 20 minutes or until well risen and golden brown.
- Serve the muffins chilled.

Nutritional information per serving

Calories: 206

Fat: 9.8g

Protein: 3.2g

Carbohydrates: 26.8g

Cinnamon Autumn Muffins

Time: 1 hour

Servings: 12

Ingredients:

2 cups all-purpose flour
½ teaspoon salt
2 teaspoons baking powder
1 teaspoon cinnamon powder
2/3 cup light brown sugar
½ cup butter, melted

2 eggs
½ cup milk
1 teaspoon vanilla extract
1 apple, cored and diced
1 pear, cored and diced
½ cup butternut squash cubes

Directions:

- Mix the flour, salt, baking powder, cinnamon and sugar in a bowl.
- Add the butter, eggs, milk and vanilla and mix well.
- Fold in the apple, pear and butternut squash cubes.
- Spoon the batter in a muffin tin lined with baking muffin papers.
- Bake in the preheated oven at 350F for 15-20 minutes or until well risen and golden.
- Serve the muffins chilled.

Nutritional information per serving

Calories: 208
Fat: 8.9g

Protein: 3.6g
Carbohydrates: 29.1g

Sultana Bran Muffins

Time: 1 hour

Servings: 12

Ingredients:

¾ cup wheat bran
1 ¼ cups all-purpose flour
2 teaspoons baking powder
¼ cup shredded coconut
½ teaspoon cinnamon powder
½ teaspoon salt

2 bananas, mashed
1 egg
¾ cup plain yogurt
¼ cup olive oil
1 teaspoon vanilla extract
½ cup sultanas

Directions:

- Mix the wheat bran, flour, baking powder, coconut, cinnamon and salt in a bowl.
- Stir in the bananas, egg, yogurt, olive oil and vanilla.
- Fold in the sultanas then spoon the batter in a muffin tin lined with muffin papers.
- Bake in the preheated oven at 350F for 20-25 minutes or until well risen and golden brown.
- Serve the muffins chilled.

Nutritional information per serving

Calories: 137
Fat: 5.7g

Protein: 3.5g
Carbohydrates: 19.7g

Blueberry Banana Muffins

Time: 1 hour

Servings: 12

Ingredients:

1 cup all-purpose flour
1 cup wheat flour
½ teaspoon cinnamon powder
½ teaspoon salt
2 teaspoons baking powder

2 bananas, mashed
2 eggs
1 cup plain yogurt
½ cup canola oil
1 cup fresh blueberries

Directions:
- Mix the flours, cinnamon, salt and baking powder in a bowl.
- Add the rest of the ingredients and give it a quick mix.
- Fold in the blueberries then spoon the batter in a muffin tin lined.
- Bake in the preheated oven at 350F for 20 minutes or until well risen and golden brown.
- Serve the muffins chilled.

Nutritional information per serving

Calories: 206

Fat: 10.4g

Protein: 4.5g

Carbohydrates: 24.0g

$\mathcal{W}$ALNUT BANANA MUFFINS

Time: 1 hour

Servings: 12

Ingredients:

3 bananas, mashed

½ cup light brown sugar

2 eggs

½ cup plain yogurt

¼ cup butter, melted

1 cup all-purpose flour

1 cup ground walnuts

½ teaspoon salt

1 ½ teaspoons baking powder

½ cup walnuts, chopped

Directions:
- Mix the bananas, sugar, eggs, yogurt and butter and mix well.
- Fold in the flour, walnuts, salt and baking powder.
- Fold in the walnuts then spoon the batter in a muffin tin lined with muffin papers and bake in the preheated oven at 350F for 20 minutes or until well risen and golden.
- Serve the muffins chilled.

Nutritional information per serving

Calories: 236

Fat: 14.1g

Protein: 6.7g

Carbohydrates: 23.2g

$\mathcal{B}$LACK FOREST MUFFINS

Time: 1 hour

Servings: 12

Ingredients:

2 eggs

1 cup buttermilk

½ cup brewed coffee

¼ cup canola oil

1 teaspoon vanilla extract

1 ½ cups all-purpose flour

¼ cup cocoa powder

½ teaspoon baking soda

1 teaspoon baking powder

¼ teaspoon salt

1 cup cherries, pitted

Directions:
- Mix the eggs, buttermilk, coffee, oil and vanilla and mix well.
- Fold in the flour, cocoa powder, baking soda, baking powder and salt then add the cherries and mix them in gently.
- Spoon the batter in a muffin tin lined with baking muffin papers and bake in the preheated oven at 350F for 20 minutes or until well risen.
- Serve the muffins chilled.

Nutritional information per serving

Calories: 128

Fat: 5.8g

Protein: 3.6g

Carbohydrates: 15.9g

MANGO BUTTERMILK MUFFINS

Time: 1 hour

Servings: 12

Ingredients:

2 cups all-purpose flour
½ cup white sugar
¼ teaspoon salt
1 teaspoon baking soda
2 eggs

1 ½ cups buttermilk
¼ cup canola oil
1 teaspoon vanilla extract
1 mango, peeled and diced

Directions:

- Mix the flour, sugar, salt and baking soda in a bowl.
- Add the eggs, buttermilk, oil and vanilla and give it a quick mix.
- Fold in the mango then spoon the batter in a muffin tin lined with muffin papers.
- Bake the muffins in the preheated oven at 350F for 20 minutes or until well risen and golden brown.
- Serve the muffins chilled.

Nutritional information per serving

Calories: 171
Fat: 5.7g

Protein: 4.1g
Carbohydrates: 25.8g

RASPBERRY RICOTTA MUFFINS

Time: 1 hour

Servings: 12

Ingredients:

1/3 cup butter, softened
¾ cup ricotta cheese
1/3 cup white sugar
2 eggs
½ cup milk

1 teaspoon vanilla extract
1 ¾ cups all-purpose flour
¼ teaspoon salt
1 ½ teaspoons baking powder
1 cup raspberries

Directions:

- Mix the butter, cheese, sugar, eggs, milk and vanilla in a bowl.
- Add the flour, salt and baking powder then spoon the batter in a muffin tin lined with muffin papers.
- Top each muffin with fresh raspberries and bake in the preheated oven at 350F for 20 minutes or until well risen and golden brown.
- Serve the muffins chilled.

Nutritional information per serving

Calories: 176
Fat: 7.5g

Protein: 5.1g
Carbohydrates: 22.4g

BLACKBERRY WHITE CHOCOLATE MUFFINS

Time: 1 hour

Servings: 12

Ingredients:

2 cups all-purpose flour
2 teaspoons baking powder
½ teaspoon salt
½ cup white sugar
¼ cup shredded coconut
½ cup white chocolate chips
1 cup milk
2 eggs

½ cup canola oil
1 teaspoon vanilla extract
1 cup blueberries

Directions:
- Mix the flour, baking powder, salt, sugar, coconut and chocolate chips in a bowl.
- Stir in the milk, eggs, canola oil and vanilla and mix with a spatula.
- Fold in the blueberries then spoon the batter in a muffin tin lined with baking muffin papers.
- Bake the muffins in the preheated oven at 350F for 15-20 minutes or until well risen and golden brown.
- Serve the muffins chilled.

Nutritional information per serving

Calories: 261

Fat: 13.3g

Protein: 4.3g

Carbohydrates: 31.9g

C ARAMEL VANILLA CUPCAKES

Time: 1 ½ hours

Servings: 12

Ingredients:

Cupcakes:

1 ¾ cups all-purpose flour

¼ teaspoon salt

1 ½ teaspoons baking powder

2 eggs

1/3 cup butter, melted

1 cup milk

1 egg

1 teaspoon vanilla extract

Frosting:

1 cup butter, softened

2 cups powdered sugar

1 teaspoon vanilla extract

½ cup caramel sauce

Directions:
- For the cupcakes, mix the flour, salt and baking powder in a bowl.
- Combine the eggs, butter, milk, egg and vanilla then pour this mixture over the flour. Give it a quick mix then spoon the batter in a muffin tin lined with muffin papers.
- Bake in the preheated oven at 350F for 20 minutes or until well risen and golden brown. Allow them to cool down.
- For the frosting, mix the butter in a bowl until fluffy. Add the sugar and vanilla and keep mixing for 5 minutes.
- Pipe the frosting over the cupcakes and drizzle them with caramel sauce.
- Serve the cupcakes fresh.

Nutritional information per serving

Calories: 388

Fat: 22.2g

Protein: 4.3g

Carbohydrates: 44.3g

M ORNING GLORY MUFFINS

Time: 1 hour

Servings: 12

Ingredients:

1 ¾ cups all-purpose flour

1 teaspoon baking soda

½ teaspoon baking powder

½ teaspoon salt

3 eggs

½ cup canola oil

½ cup applesauce

1 cup grated carrots

½ cup raisins

½ cup shredded coconut

½ cup walnuts, chopped

2 tablespoons chia seeds

Directions:
- Mix the flour, baking soda, baking powder and salt in a bowl.
- Add the eggs, canola oil and applesauce and give it a quick mix.
- Fold in the carrots, raisins, walnuts, coconut and chia seeds then spoon the batter in a muffin tin lined with muffin papers.
- Bake in the preheated oven at 350F for 20 minutes or until well risen and golden brown.
- Serve the muffins chilled.

Nutritional information per serving

Calories: 259
Fat: 16.2g

Protein: 6.0g
Carbohydrates: 23.7g

UMPKIN APPLE MUFFINS

Time: 1 ¼ hours

Servings: 12

Ingredients:

1 ½ cups whole wheat flour
½ cup all-purpose flour
1 teaspoon baking soda
½ teaspoon baking powder
½ teaspoon salt
1 teaspoon pumpkin pie spices

2 eggs
1 cup pumpkin puree
¼ cup milk
½ cup canola oil
½ cup light brown sugar
2 red apples, cored and diced

Directions:

- Mix the flours, baking soda, baking powder, salt and spices in a bowl.
- Add the eggs, pumpkin puree, milk, oil and sugar and give it a quick mix.
- Fold in the apples then spoon the batter in a muffin tin lined with muffin papers.
- Bake in the preheated oven at 350F for 20 minutes or until well risen and golden brown.
- Serve the muffins chilled.

Nutritional information per serving

Calories: 215
Fat: 10.2g

Protein: 3.6g
Carbohydrates. 28.2g

ATMEAL CARROT MUFFINS

Time: 1 hour

Servings: 12

Ingredients:

1 cup rolled oats
1 cup all-purpose flour
½ teaspoon baking soda
1 teaspoon baking powder
¼ teaspoon salt
½ teaspoon cinnamon powder
½ teaspoon ground ginger

½ cup light brown sugar
2 eggs
½ cup canola oil
1 cup buttermilk
2 cups grated carrots
½ cup crushed pineapple

Directions:

- Mix the oats, flour, baking soda, baking powder, salt, cinnamon, ginger and sugar in a bowl.
- Stir in the eggs, oil and buttermilk and give it a quick mix.
- Fold in the carrots and pineapple then spoon the batter in a muffin tin lined with muffin papers.
- Bake the muffins in the preheated oven at 350F for 20 minutes or until well risen and golden brown.
- Serve the muffins chilled.

Nutritional information per serving

Calories: 197
Fat: 10.5g

Protein: 3.8g
Carbohydrates: 22.5g

STREUSEL BANANA MUFFINS

Time: 1 ¼ hours

Servings: 12

Ingredients:
Muffins:

2 bananas, mashed

2 eggs
½ cup buttermilk
1 teaspoon vanilla extract
1 ¾ cups all-purpose flour
2 tablespoons wheat bran
1 teaspoon baking soda
¼ teaspoon salt

½ teaspoon cinnamon powder
Streusel:
½ cup butter, chilled
1 cup all-purpose flour
2 tablespoons dark brown sugar
¼ teaspoon salt

Directions:
- For the muffins, mix the bananas, eggs and buttermilk in a bowl.
- Stir in the flour, wheat bran, baking soda, salt and cinnamon and give it a quick mix.
- Spoon the batter in a muffin tin lined with muffin papers.
- For the streusel, mix all the ingredients in a bowl until grainy.
- Top each muffin with the streusel and bake in the preheated oven at 350F for 20 minutes or until golden brown and well risen.
- Serve the muffins chilled.

Nutritional information per serving

Calories: 212
Fat: 8.9g

Protein: 4.6g
Carbohydrates: 28.8g

UMPKIN CHOCOLATE CHIP MUFFINS

Time: 1 hour

Servings: 12

Ingredients:

1 cup pumpkin puree
¼ cup canola oil
2 eggs
1 teaspoon vanilla extract
1 ½ cups all-purpose flour
½ cup oat flour

¼ teaspoon salt
1 teaspoon baking soda
½ teaspoon cinnamon powder
½ teaspoon ground ginger
½ teaspoon ground star anise
½ cup dark chocolate chips

Directions:
- Mix the pumpkin puree, oil, eggs and vanilla in a bowl and mix well.
- Fold in the flours, salt, baking soda and spices.
- Spoon the batter in a muffin tin lined with muffin papers.
- Bake the muffins in the preheated oven at 350F for 15-20 minutes or until well risen and golden brown.
- Serve the muffins chilled.

Nutritional information per serving

Calories: 155
Fat: 7.1g

Protein: 3.6g
Carbohydrates: 19.8g

RAN FLAX BLUEBERRY MUFFINS

Time: 1 hour

Servings: 12

Ingredients:

1 ½ cups all-purpose flour
½ cup ground flax seeds
½ cup oat bran
2 teaspoons baking powder
½ teaspoon salt
1 cup milk
2 eggs
½ cup canola oil
1 teaspoon vanilla extract

1 cup grated carrots
1 red apple, peeled and grated
½ cup raisins
1 cup blueberries

Directions:
- Mix the flour, flax seeds, oat bran, baking powder and salt in a bowl.
- Add the milk, eggs, canola oil and vanilla and give it a quick mix.
- Fold in the carrots, apple, raisins and blueberries then spoon the batter in a muffin tin lined with muffin papers.
- Bake the muffins in the preheated oven at 350F for 20 minutes or until the muffins pass the toothpick test.
- Serve the muffins chilled.

Nutritional information per serving

Calories: 227

Fat: 12.1g

Protein: 4.9g

Carbohydrates: 25.9g

*W*HOLE **W**HEAT **S**TRAWBERRY **M**UFFINS

Time: 1 hour

Servings: 12

Ingredients:

2 eggs

½ cup applesauce

½ cup canola oil

2 bananas, mashed

½ cup light brown sugar

1 teaspoon vanilla extract

2 cups whole wheat flour

1 teaspoon baking soda

1 teaspoon baking powder

1 cup strawberries, sliced

Directions:
- Mix the eggs, applesauce, canola oil, bananas, sugar and vanilla in a bowl.
- Add the flour, baking soda and baking powder and mix quickly.
- Fold in the strawberries then spoon the batter in a muffin tin lined with baking muffin papers.
- Bake the muffins in the preheated oven at 350F for 20-25 minutes or until they pass the toothpick test.
- Serve the muffins chilled.

Nutritional information per serving

Calories: 217

Fat: 10.1g

Protein: 3.4g

Carbohydrates: 28.7g

*H*ONEY **P**UMPKIN **M**UFFINS

Time: 1 hour

Servings: 12

Ingredients:

1 cup pumpkin puree

½ cup honey

1 teaspoon vanilla extract

2 eggs

1 cup all-purpose flour

1 cup oat flour

2 teaspoons baking powder

¼ teaspoon salt

2 tablespoons pumpkin seeds

Directions:
- Mix the honey, pumpkin puree, vanilla and eggs in a bowl.
- Add the rest of the ingredients then pour the batter in a muffin tin lined with muffin papers of your desire.
- Bake in the preheated oven at 350F for 20 minutes or until well risen and golden brown.
- Serve the muffins chilled.

Nutritional information per serving

Calories: 138

Fat: 2.1g

Protein: 3.6g

Carbohydrates: 27.2g

*N*UTTY **C**HOCOLATE **C**HIP **M**UFFINS

Time: 1 hour

Servings: 12

Ingredients:

1 ½ cups all-purpose flour
½ cup cocoa powder
1 cup white sugar
½ teaspoon baking soda
1 teaspoon baking powder
¼ teaspoon salt

2 eggs
¼ cup canola oil
1 teaspoon vanilla extract
1 cup buttermilk
1 cup walnuts, chopped
½ cup dark chocolate chips

Directions:

- Mix the flour, cocoa powder, sugar, baking soda, baking powder and salt in a bowl.
- Add the eggs, oil, vanilla and buttermilk and give it a quick mix.
- Fold in the walnuts and chocolate chips then pour the batter in a muffin tin lined with your favorite muffin papers.
- Bake in the preheated oven at 350F for 20 minutes or until they pass the toothpick test.
- Serve the muffins chilled.

Nutritional information per serving

Calories: 275
Fat: 13.6g

Protein: 6.7g
Carbohydrates: 36.2g

HUBARB STREUSEL MUFFINS

Time: 1 ¼ hours

Servings: 12

Ingredients:

Muffins:
2 cups all-purpose flour
½ teaspoon baking soda
1 teaspoon baking powder
¼ teaspoon salt
½ cup light brown sugar
¼ cup white sugar
2 eggs

1 cup buttermilk
¼ cup canola oil
2 rhubarb stalks, sliced
Streusel:
½ cup butter, melted
1 cup all-purpose flour
2 tablespoons white sugar
1 pinch salt

Directions:

- For the muffins, mix the flour, baking soda, baking powder, salt and sugars in a bowl.
- Add the eggs, buttermilk and oil and mix with a spatula.
- Fold in the rhubarb then spoon the batter in a muffin tin lined with baking muffin papers.
- For the streusel, mix the ingredients in a bowl until grainy. Spread the streusel over each muffin.
- Bake in the preheated oven at 350F for 20 minutes or until golden brown and well risen.
- Serve the muffins chilled.

Nutritional information per serving

Calories: 289
Fat: 13.4g

Protein: 5.0g
Carbohydrates: 37.6g

ZUCCHINI CHOCOLATE MUFFINS

Time: 1 hour

Servings: 12

Ingredients:

1 ½ cups all-purpose flour
½ cup cocoa powder
¾ cup white sugar
1 teaspoon baking soda
½ teaspoon cinnamon powder
½ teaspoon salt
1 egg
½ cup canola oil

¼ cup buttermilk
1 cup grated zucchinis
½ cup walnuts, chopped

Directions:
- Mix the flour, cocoa powder, sugar, baking soda, cinnamon and salt in a bowl.
- Stir in the egg, canola oil, buttermilk and zucchinis then fold in the walnuts.
- Pour the batter in a muffin tin lined with your favorite muffin papers and bake in the preheated oven at 350F for 20 minutes or until well risen and fragrant.
- Allow the muffins to cool in the pan before serving.

Nutritional information per serving

Calories: 233
Fat: 13.2g

Protein: 4.2g
Carbohydrates: 27.5g

OIST BANANA MUFFINS

Time: 1 hour

Servings: 12

Ingredients:

2 cups all-purpose flour
1 teaspoon baking soda
1 teaspoon baking powder
1 cup white sugar
3 bananas, mashed

2 eggs
½ cup canola oil
1 teaspoon vanilla extract
½ cup dark chocolate chips

Directions:
- Mix the flour, baking soda, baking powder and sugar in a bowl.
- Add the rest of the ingredients and give it a quick mix.
- Fold in the chocolate chips then spoon the batter in a muffin tin lined with muffin papers.
- Bake in the preheated oven at 350F for 20 minutes or until well risen and fragrant.
- Serve the muffins chilled or store them in an airtight container.

Nutritional information per serving

Calories: 280
Fat: 11.4g

Protein: 3.7g
Carbohydrates: 42.9g

UINOA PEACH MUFFINS

Time: 1 hour

Servings: 12

Ingredients:

1 cup cooked quinoa
¼ cup canola oil
1 egg
1 cup buttermilk
1 teaspoon vanilla extract

¾ cups light brown sugar
2 cups all-purpose flour
¼ teaspoon salt
1 teaspoon baking powder
½ teaspoon baking soda

Directions:
- Mix the quinoa, canola oil, egg, buttermilk and vanilla in a bowl.
- Stir in the sugar and mix well then add the flour, salt, baking powder and baking soda.
- Spoon the batter in a muffin tin lined with muffin papers.
- Bake in the preheated oven at 350F for 20 minutes or until well risen.
- Allow to cool down before serving.

Nutritional information per serving

Calories: 217
Fat: 6.1g
Protein: 5.3g
Carbohydrates: 35.1g

*S*UGARLESS MUFFINS

Time: 1 hour

Servings: 12

Ingredients:

2 eggs

3 bananas, mashed

½ cup applesauce

1 ½ cups all-purpose flour

¼ teaspoon salt

1 teaspoon baking soda

½ cup walnuts, chopped

Directions:

- Mix the eggs, bananas and applesauce in a bowl.
- Add the flour, salt and baking soda then stir in the walnuts.
- Spoon the batter in a muffin tin lined with your favorite muffin papers and bake in the preheated oven at 350F for 20 minutes.
- Serve the muffins chilled.

Nutritional information per serving

Calories: 130

Fat: 4.1g

Protein: 4.1g

Carbohydrates: 20.4g

*S*UGARY PUMPKIN MUFFINS

Time: 1 hour

Servings: 12

Ingredients:

¾ cup butter, softened

¾ cup light brown sugar

2 eggs

¼ cup buttermilk

½ cup pumpkin puree

2 cups all-purpose flour

½ teaspoon salt

2 teaspoons baking powder

1 teaspoon ground ginger

½ cup white sugar

1 teaspoon cinnamon powder

Directions:

- Mix the butter and brown sugar in a bowl until pale and light.
- Add the eggs, buttermilk and pumpkin puree and mix well.
- Fold in the flour, salt, baking powder and ginger then spoon the batter in a muffin tin lined with your favorite muffin papers.
- Mix the sugar and cinnamon in a bowl. Top each muffin with the cinnamon sugar and bake in the preheated oven at 350F for 20 minutes or until well risen and golden brown.
- Serve the muffins chilled.

Nutritional information per serving

Calories: 261

Fat: 12.5g

Protein: 3.5g

Carbohydrates: 34.8g

*B*LACKBERRY OAT BRAN MUFFINS

Time: 1 hour

Servings: 12

Ingredients:

1 ½ cups all-purpose flour

½ cup oat bran

1 ½ teaspoons baking powder

¼ teaspoon salt

½ teaspoon cinnamon powder

½ cup butter, melted

½ cup white sugar

2 eggs

1 cup buttermilk

1 teaspoon vanilla extract

1 cup blackberries

Directions:

- Mix the flour, oat bran, baking powder, salt and cinnamon in a bowl.
- In a different bowl, combine the butter, sugar, eggs, buttermilk and vanilla. Pour this mixture over the dry ingredients and give them a quick whisk.
- Fold in the blackberries then spoon the batter in a muffin tin lined with your favorite muffin papers.
- Bake in the preheated oven at 350F for 20 minutes or until well risen and golden.
- Serve the muffins chilled.

Nutritional information per serving

Calories: 188
Fat: 9.0g

Protein: 3.9g
Carbohydrates: 24.5g

 ## REAKFAST MUFFINS

Time: 1 hour

Servings: 16

Ingredients:

1 cup rolled oats
1 ½ cups all purpose flour
2 teaspoons baking powder
½ teaspoon salt
½ teaspoon ground nutmeg
½ teaspoon cinnamon powder
½ teaspoon ground ginger

1 cup golden raisins
½ cup olive oil
2 eggs
1 cup milk
1 cup grated carrots
1 banana, mashed
½ cup shredded coconut

Directions:

- Mix the oats, flour, baking powder, salt and spices in a bowl. Stir in the raisins and coconut.
- Add the olive oil, eggs, milk, carrots and banana and mix with a spatula.
- Spoon the batter in a muffin tin lined with your favorite muffin papers.
- Bake in the preheated oven at 350F for 20-25 minutes or until well risen and the muffins pass the toothpick test.
- Serve the muffins chilled.

Nutritional information per serving

Calories: 178
Fat: 8.5g

Protein: 3.6g
Carbohydrates: 23.5g

 ## ASIC CHOCOLATE MUFFINS

Time: 1 hour

Servings: 12

Ingredients:

2 cups all-purpose flour
2 tablespoons cocoa powder
¼ teaspoon salt
1 ½ teaspoons baking powder
½ cup canola oil

¾ cup light brown sugar
½ cup milk
2 eggs
1 teaspoon vanilla extract

Directions:

- Mix the flour, cocoa powder, salt and baking powder.
- Mix the sugar and oil in a bowl for 2 minutes. Add the eggs, vanilla and milk and mix well.
- Fold in the flour then spoon the batter in a muffin tin lined with muffin papers of your desire.
- Bake in the preheated oven at 350F for 15-20 minutes or until they pass the toothpick test.
- Serve the muffins chilled.

Nutritional information per serving

Calories: 210
Fat: 10.3g
Protein: 3.6g

Carbohydrates: 26.2g

$\mathcal{P}$ ECAN PIE MUFFINS

Time: 1 hour

Servings: 10

Ingredients:

2 eggs
1 cup light brown sugar
1 teaspoon vanilla extract
1 cup butter, melted

½ cup all-purpose flour
1 ½ cups pecans, chopped
¼ teaspoon salt

Directions:
- Mix the eggs and sugar in a bowl until fluffy and double in volume.
- Add the vanilla and melted butter and mix well.
- Fold in the flour, pecans and salt then spoon the batter in a muffin tin lined with muffin papers.
- Bake in the preheated oven at 350F for 15-20 minutes or until golden brown.
- Serve the muffins chilled.

Nutritional information per serving

Calories: 264
Fat: 20.3g

Protein: 2.1g
Carbohydrates: 19.3g

$\mathcal{S}$ TRAWBERRY MATCHA MUFFINS

Time: 1 hour

Servings: 12

Ingredients:

2 cups all-purpose flour
1 tablespoon matcha powder
1 teaspoon baking powder
½ teaspoon baking soda
¼ teaspoon salt

½ cup butter, melted
2 eggs
1 cup milk
1 cup white sugar
1 cup strawberries, sliced

Directions:
- Mix the flour, matcha powder, baking powder, baking soda and salt in a bowl.
- Stir in the butter, eggs, milk and sugar and give it a quick whisk.
- Fold in the strawberries then spoon the batter in a muffin tin lined with your favorite muffin papers.
- Bake in the preheated oven at 350F for 15-20 minutes or until they pass the toothpick test.
- Serve the muffins chilled or store them in an airtight container.

Nutritional information per serving

Calories: 233
Fat: 9.1g

Protein: 3.9g
Carbohydrates: 35.2g

$\mathcal{H}$ ARVEST MUFFINS

Time: 1 hour

Servings: 12

Ingredients:

2 cups all-purpose flour
1 teaspoon baking powder
½ teaspoon baking soda
¼ teaspoon salt
½ teaspoon cinnamon powder
½ teaspoon ground ginger
½ cup light brown sugar
2 eggs
1 cup milk

½ cup butter, melted
1 apple, cored and diced
1 pear, cored and diced
½ cup dried cranberries

Directions:
- Mix the flour, baking powder, baking soda, salt, cinnamon, ginger and sugar in a bowl.
- Add the eggs, milk and butter and give it a quick mix.
- Fold in the apple, pear and cranberries then spoon the batter in a muffin pan lined with muffin papers.
- Bake in the preheated oven at 350F for 20 minutes or until well risen and fragrant.
- Allow the muffins to cool down before serving.

Nutritional information per serving

Calories: 205

Fat: 9.1g

Protein: 3.9g

Carbohydrates: 27.4g

 ANANA CRUNCH MUFFINS

Time: 1 hour

Servings: 12

Ingredients:

2 bananas, mashed

½ cup light brown sugar

2 eggs

½ cup milk

1 teaspoon vanilla extract

½ cup canola oil

2 cups all-purpose flour

¼ teaspoon salt

1 ½ teaspoons baking powder

½ cup shredded coconut

1 cup rolled oats

Directions:
- Mix the bananas, sugar, eggs, milk, vanilla and oil in a bowl.
- Stir in the flour, salt, baking powder and coconut and mix with a spatula.
- Spoon the batter in a muffin tin lined with muffin papers and top each muffin with rolled oats.
- Bake in the preheated oven at 350F for 20-25 minutes or until well risen and golden brown.
- Serve the muffins chilled.

Nutritional information per serving

Calories: 251

Fat: 11.8g

Protein: 4.6g

Carbohydrates: 32.3g

 HUNKY BANANA MUFFINS

Time: 1 hour

Servings: 12

Ingredients:

2 eggs

½ cup light brown sugar

2 tablespoons molasses

1 teaspoon vanilla extract

¼ cup butter, melted

1 cup buttermilk

1 ½ cups all-purpose flour

½ cup cocoa powder

¼ teaspoon salt

2 teaspoons baking powder

2 bananas, sliced

Directions:
- Mix the eggs and sugar in a bowl until pale and light. Add the molasses and vanilla and mix well.
- Stir in the butter and buttermilk then add the flour, cocoa powder, salt and baking powder.
- Fold in the banana slices and spoon the batter in a muffin tin lined with your favorite muffin papers.
- Bake in the preheated oven at 350F for 15-20 minutes. When done, allow them to cool in the pan before serving.

Nutritional information per serving

Calories: 169

Fat: 5.4g

Protein: 4.1g

Carbohydrates: 28.3g

ORNING MUFFINS

Time: 1 ¼ hours

Servings: 12

Ingredients:

2 eggs
½ cup light brown sugar
1 teaspoon vanilla extract
1 cup buttermilk
1 ½ cups all-purpose flour
½ cup oat flour

¼ teaspoon salt
1 teaspoon baking soda
1 cup grated carrots
½ cup dried cranberries
1 apple, cored and diced

Directions:

- Mix the eggs and sugar in a bowl until pale and airy.
- Add the vanilla and buttermilk and mix well.
- Fold in the flours, salt and baking soda then add the carrots, cranberries and apple.
- Spoon the batter in a muffin tin lined with your favorite muffin papers.
- Bake in the preheated oven at 350F for 20 minutes or until they pass the toothpick test.
- Serve the muffins chilled.

Nutritional information per serving

Calories: 129
Fat: 1.3g

Protein: 3.8g
Carbohydrates: 25.0g

EXICAN CHOCOLATE MUFFINS

Time: 1 hour

Servings: 12

Ingredients:

1 ½ cups all-purpose flour
¼ cup cocoa powder
¾ cup white sugar
¼ teaspoon salt
1 teaspoon baking powder
¼ teaspoon baking soda

½ teaspoon chili powder
3 bananas, mashed
1 egg
½ cup butter, melted
¼ cup milk
1 cup dark chocolate chips

Directions:

- Mix the flour, cocoa powder, sugar, salt, baking powder, baking soda and chili powder.
- Add the bananas, egg, butter and milk and give it a quick mix.
- Fold in the chocolate chips then spoon the batter in a muffin tin lined with muffin papers.
- Bake the muffins in the preheated oven at 350F for 15-20 minutes or until well risen and fragrant.
- Serve the muffins chilled.

Nutritional information per serving

Calories: 257
Fat: 11.3g

Protein: 3.6g
Carbohydrates: 39.4g

O RANGE OLIVE OIL MUFFINS

Time: 1 hour

Servings: 12

Ingredients:

4 eggs
1 cup white sugar
½ cup fresh orange juice
¼ cup olive oil
1 teaspoon vanilla extract

1 tablespoon orange zest
1 cup almond flour
1 cup all-purpose flour
¼ teaspoon salt
1 teaspoon baking powder

½ cup sliced almonds

Directions:
- Mix the eggs and sugar in a bowl until fluffy and pale.
- Add the orange juice, oil, vanilla and orange zest and mix well.
- Fold in the flours, salt and baking powder then spoon the batter in a muffin tin lined with baking muffin papers.
- Top each muffin with sliced almonds and bake in the preheated oven at 350F for 15-20 minutes or until well risen and golden brown.
- Serve the muffins chilled.

Nutritional information per serving

Calories: 200

Fat: 8.9g

Protein: 4.4g

Carbohydrates: 27.5g

 ZUCCHINI CARROT MUFFINS

Time: 1 hour

Servings: 12

Ingredients:

1 cup almond flour

½ cup brown rice flour

¼ teaspoon salt

1 ½ teaspoons baking powder

½ teaspoon cinnamon powder

½ cup canola oil

¼ cup maple syrup

1 egg

1 cup grated carrots

1 cup grated zucchinis

½ cup golden raisins

Directions:
- Mix the flours, salt, baking powder and cinnamon in a bowl.
- Stir in the canola oil, maple syrup and egg and give it a quick mix.
- Fold in the carrots, zucchinis and raisins then spoon the batter in a muffin tin lined with muffin papers.
- Bake in the preheated oven at 350F for 20 minutes or until they pass the toothpick test.
- Serve the muffins chilled.

Nutritional information per serving

Calories: 164

Fat: 10.8g

Protein: 1.8g

Carbohydrates: 16.3g

P ERSIMMON MUFFINS

Time: 1 hour

Servings: 12

Ingredients:

1 ½ cups all-purpose flour

½ cup whole wheat flour

½ teaspoon salt

2 teaspoons baking powder

½ teaspoon ground ginger

½ teaspoon cinnamon powder

2 eggs

½ cup butter, melted

¾ cup buttermilk

1 teaspoon vanilla extract

2 persimmon fruits, diced

Directions:
- Mix the flours, salt, baking powder, ginger and cinnamon in a bowl.
- Stir in the eggs, butter, buttermilk and vanilla and give it a quick mix.
- Fold in the persimmon then spoon the batter in a muffin tin lined with muffin papers.
- Bake in the preheated oven at 350F for 15-20 minutes or until well risen and golden brown.
- Serve the muffins chilled or store them in an airtight container for up to 4 days.

Nutritional information per serving

Calories: 182

Fat: 8.7g

Protein: 3.8g

Carbohydrates: 22.4g

Sour Cream Muffins

Time: 1 hour   Servings: 12

Ingredients:

2 cups all-purpose flour   1 cup butter, softened
¼ teaspoon salt   1 ½ cups sour cream
2 teaspoons baking powder   1 teaspoon vanilla extract

Directions:

- Mix the butter, vanilla and sour cream in a bowl until creamy.
- Add the flour, salt and baking powder then spoon the batter in a muffin tin lined with baking muffin papers.
- Bake in the preheated oven at 350F for 15-20 minutes or until well risen and golden brown.
- Serve the muffins chilled.

Nutritional information per serving

Calories: 275   Protein: 3.2g
Fat: 21.6g   Carbohydrates: 17.6g

Multigrain Muffins

Time: 1 hour   Servings: 12

Ingredients:

1 cup whole wheat flour   1 ½ cups buttermilk
½ cup wheat bran   ¼ cup canola oil
½ cup all-purpose flour   ½ cup light brown sugar
2 teaspoons baking powder   ½ cup walnuts
¼ teaspoon salt   2 tablespoons pumpkin seeds
2 eggs   2 tablespoons sunflower seeds

Directions:

- Mix the flours, bran, baking powder and salt in a bowl.
- Add the eggs, buttermilk, oil, sugar, walnuts and seeds and mix with a spatula.
- Spoon the batter in a muffin tin lined with muffin papers and bake in the preheated oven at 350F for 15-20 minutes or until well risen and golden brown.
- Serve the muffins chilled.

Nutritional information per serving

Calories: 192   Protein: 5.6g
Fat: 9.8g   Carbohydrates: 22.2g

Caribbean Muffins

Time: 1 hour   Servings: 12

Ingredients:

1 ½ cups all-purpose flour   ½ cup shredded coconut
¼ cup wheat bran   1 egg
¼ teaspoon salt   1 cup buttermilk
1 ½ teaspoons baking powder   1 cup crushed pineapple
2 tablespoons chia seeds   1 mango, peeled and diced

Directions:

- Mix the flour, wheat bran, salt, baking powder, chia seeds and coconut in a bowl.
- Add the egg, buttermilk and pineapple and mix well.
- Fold in the mango then spoon the batter in a muffin tin lined with muffin papers.
- Bake the muffins in the preheated oven at 350F for 20 minutes or until well risen and golden brown.

- Serve the muffins chilled.

Nutritional information per serving

Calories: 130
Fat: 3.5g

Protein: 4.3g
Carbohydrates: 21.0g

W HITE CHOCOLATE PUMPKIN CUPCAKES

Time: 1 ½ hours

Servings: 14

Ingredients:

Cupcakes:
2 cups all-purpose flour
1 teaspoon baking powder
½ teaspoon baking soda
½ teaspoon cinnamon powder
½ teaspoon ground ginger
½ teaspoon ground cardamom
½ teaspoon salt
2 eggs
½ cup light brown sugar

½ cup milk
1 cup pumpkin puree
¼ cup canola oil
1 teaspoon vanilla extract
½ cup dark chocolate chips
Frosting:
1 cup heavy cream
2 cups white chocolate chips
1 teaspoon vanilla extract
2 tablespoons butter

Directions:

- For the cupcakes, mix the flour, baking powder, baking soda, spices and salt in a bowl.
- Mix the eggs and sugar in a bowl until fluffy and pale.
- Add the milk, pumpkin puree, canola oil and vanilla and mix well.
- Fold in the flour mixture then spoon the batter in a muffin tin lined with muffin papers.
- Bake in the preheated oven at 350F for 20 minutes or until the cupcakes pass the toothpick test.
- Allow them to cool in the pan.
- For the frosting, bring the cream to the boiling point. Remove from heat and stir in the chocolate. Mix until melted and smooth.
- Add the vanilla and butter and mix well.
- Allow to cool completely then whip the cream until fluffy and pale.
- Top the cupcakes with the frosting and decorate with a dusting of cinnamon powder.

Nutritional information per serving

Calories: 336
Fat: 18.7g

Protein: 5.1g
Carbohydrates: 38.4g

D ECADENT BROWNIE MUFFINS

Time: 1 hour

Servings: 12

Ingredients:

¾ cup butter
1 ½ cups dark chocolate chips
4 eggs
1 cup light brown sugar

1 teaspoon vanilla extract
1 cup all-purpose flour
½ teaspoon baking soda
¼ teaspoon salt

Directions:

- Melt the butter and chocolate in a heatproof bowl over a hot water bath. Allow to cool down slightly.
- Mix the eggs and sugar in a bowl until fluffy and pale. Add the vanilla then stir in the chocolate mixture.
- Fold in the flour, baking soda and salt then spoon the batter in a muffin tin lined with muffin papers.
- Bake in the preheated oven at 350F for 10-15 minutes or until set.
- Allow to cool in the pan then serve.

Nutritional information per serving

Calories: 278

Fat: 17.1g

Protein: 4.1g   Carbohydrates: 30.0g

*L*EMON CHIA SEED MUFFINS

Time: 1 hour   Servings: 12

Ingredients:

2 tablespoons chia seeds   1 cup plain yogurt
2 cups all-purpose flour   ½ cup coconut oil, melted
1 ½ teaspoons baking powder   1 teaspoon vanilla extract
½ teaspoon baking soda   1 cup white sugar
¼ teaspoon salt   2 eggs

Directions:

- Mix the chia seeds, flour, baking powder, baking soda and salt in a bowl.
- Add the yogurt, coconut oil, vanilla, sugar and eggs and give it a quick mix.
- Spoon the batter in a muffin tin lined with muffin papers.
- Bake in the preheated oven at 350F for 20 minutes or until they pass the toothpick test.
- Serve the muffins chilled.

Nutritional information per serving

Calories: 269   Protein: 5.3g
Fat: 11.9g   Carbohydrates: 36.2g

*S*WEET RASPBERRY CORN MUFFINS

Time: 1 hour   Servings: 12

Ingredients:

1 ½ cups all-purpose flour   ½ cup apricot jam
1 cup yellow cornmeal   ¼ cup canola oil
½ cup white sugar   1 tablespoon orange zest
2 teaspoons baking powder   2 eggs
¼ teaspoon salt   1 cup raspberries
1 cup buttermilk

Directions:

- Mix the flour, cornmeal, sugar, baking powder and salt in a bowl.
- Stir in the buttermilk, apricot jam, oil, orange zest and eggs and mix well.
- Fold in the raspberries then spoon the batter in a muffin tin lined with baking muffin papers.
- Bake the muffins in the preheated oven at 350F for 20 minutes or until well risen and golden brown.
- Allow the muffins to cool in the pan before serving.

Nutritional information per serving

Calories: 223   Protein: 4.3g
Fat: 6.1g   Carbohydrates: 39.4g

*P*EACH AND CREAM MUFFINS

Time: 1 hour   Servings: 12

Ingredients:

2 cups all-purpose flour   ½ cup white sugar
2 teaspoons baking powder   1 teaspoon vanilla extract
¼ teaspoon salt   2 peaches, pitted and diced
1 cup butter, melted
1 cup sour cream

Directions:
- Mix the butter, sour cream, sugar and vanilla in a bowl until creamy.
- Add the flour, baking powder and salt then fold in the peaches.
- Spoon the batter in a muffin tin lined with muffin papers and bake in the preheated oven at 350F for 20 minutes or until golden brown and well risen.
- Serve the muffins chilled.

Nutritional information per serving

Calories: 292

Fat: 19.6g

Protein: 3.1g

Carbohydrates: 27.1g

RESH GINGER MUFFINS

Time: 1 hour

Servings: 12

Ingredients:

½ cup butter, softened

2 eggs

1 cup buttermilk

1 ½ teaspoons grated ginger

1 teaspoon vanilla extract

½ cup light brown sugar

2 cups all-purpose flour

½ teaspoon salt

2 teaspoons baking powder

Directions:
- Mix the butter, eggs, buttermilk, ginger and vanilla in a bowl.
- Stir in the sugar and mix well.
- Fold in the flour, salt and baking powder then spoon the batter in a muffin tin lined with muffin papers.
- Bake in the preheated oven at 350F for 20 minutes or until well risen and golden brown.
- Serve the muffins chilled.

Nutritional information per serving

Calories: 188

Fat: 8.8g

Protein: 3.9g

Carbohydrates: 23.5g

GERMAN CHOCOLATE CUPCAKES

Time: 1 ½ hours

Servings: 18

Ingredients:

Cupcakes:

1 cup butter, softened

2/3 cup white sugar

¼ cup light brown sugar

2 eggs

1 teaspoon vanilla extract

1 cup buttermilk

½ cup sour cream

1 3/4 cups all-purpose flour

1 cup cocoa powder

¼ teaspoon salt

1 ½ teaspoons baking powder

½ teaspoon baking soda

Frosting:

1 cup butter, softened

1 cup evaporated milk

1 cup light brown sugar

2 cups shredded coconut

1 cup sliced almonds

½ cup pecans, chopped

Directions:
- For the cupcakes, mix the butter, sugars and vanilla in a bowl until fluffy and pale.
- Add the eggs, one by one, and mix well then stir in the buttermilk and sour cream.
- Fold in the flour, cocoa powder, salt, baking powder and baking soda.
- Spoon the batter in a muffin tin lined with muffin papers.
- Bake in the preheated oven at 350F for 20 minutes.
- For the frosting, mix the butter, sugar and evaporated milk in a bowl until creamy and fluffy.
- Add the coconut, almonds and pecans and mix well.
- Spoon the frosting over each cupcake and serve them fresh.

Nutritional information per serving

Calories: 415
Fat: 30.4g

Protein: 6.1g
Carbohydrates: 34.4g

*C*HOCOLATE CUPCAKES WITH PEANUT BUTTER FROSTING

Time: 1 ½ hours

Servings: 16

Ingredients:

Cupcakes:
½ cup butter, softened
1 cup white sugar
3 eggs
1 teaspoon vanilla extract
½ cup sour cream
1 cup buttermilk
1 ½ cups all-purpose flour
½ cup cocoa powder

¼ teaspoon salt
1 ½ teaspoons baking powder
Frosting:
1 cup smooth peanut butter
1 cup powdered sugar
½ cup butter, softened
1 teaspoon vanilla extract
2 tablespoons heavy cream

Directions:
- For the cupcakes, mix the butter and sugar in a bowl until creamy and pale.
- Add the eggs and mix well then stir in the vanilla, sour cream and buttermilk.
- Fold in the flour, cocoa powder, salt and baking powder then spoon the batter in a muffin tin lined with muffin papers.
- Bake the muffins in the preheated oven at 350F for 20 minutes.
- Allow the cupcakes to cool down.
- For the frosting, mix the peanut butter, butter and sugar in a bowl until fluffy and pale.
- Add the vanilla and cream and continue whipping for 5 minutes until fluffy and airy.
- Decorate the cupcakes with the peanut butter frosting.
- Serve the cupcakes fresh.

Nutritional information per serving

Calories: 363
Fat: 23.3g

Protein: 7.7g
Carbohydrates: 35.0g

*O*RANGE GLAZED CUPCAKES

Time: 1 ½ hours

Servings: 12

Ingredients:

Cupcakes:
½ cup butter, softened
¼ cup molasses
1 cup light brown sugar
1 cup sour cream
1 tablespoon orange zest
1 teaspoon grated ginger
2 eggs
2 cups all-purpose flour
¼ teaspoon salt

1 teaspoon baking soda
½ teaspoon baking powder
1 teaspoon cinnamon powder
½ teaspoon ground ginger
½ teaspoon ground cloves
¼ cup candied ginger, chopped
Glaze:
1 teaspoon vanilla extract
1 tablespoon orange juice
1 cup powdered sugar

Directions:
- For the cupcakes, mix the butter, molasses and sugar in a bowl until creamy and pale.
- Add the sour cream, orange zest, ginger and eggs and mix well.
- Fold in the flour, salt, baking soda, baking powder, cinnamon, ginger and cloves.
- Fold in the ginger and mix with a spatula.
- Spoon the batter in a muffin tin lined with baking muffin papers.
- Bake in the preheated oven at 350F for 20 minutes or until well risen and fragrant.

- Allow them to cool down in the pan.
- For the glaze, mix all the ingredients in a bowl.
- Drizzle the glaze over the cupcakes and serve them fresh.

Nutritional information per serving

Calories: 304
Fat: 12.7g

Protein: 3.8g
Carbohydrates: 44.6g

ROWN BUTTER BANANA MUFFINS

Time: 1 hour

Servings: 12

Ingredients:

½ cup butter
¾ cup light brown sugar
4 bananas, mashed
1/2 cup milk
2 eggs
1 cup ground walnuts

1 cup all-purpose flour
½ teaspoon baking soda
¼ teaspoon salt
½ teaspoon baking powder

Directions:
- Place the butter in a saucepan and place over medium flame. Cook the butter until it begins to turn golden brown, slightly caramelized.
- Mix the butter, sugar, milk and eggs in a bowl.
- Stir in the walnuts, flour, baking soda, salt and baking powder.
- Spoon the batter in a muffin tin lined with special muffin papers and bake in the preheated oven at 350F for 20 minutes or until well risen and golden brown.
- Serve the muffins chilled.

Nutritional information per serving

Calories: 255
Fat: 15.0g

Protein: 5.4g
Carbohydrates: 27.5g

RANBERRY EGGNOG MUFFINS

Time: 1 hour

Servings: 12

Ingredients:

1 cup dried cranberries
½ cup eggnog
2 cups all-purpose flour
2 teaspoons baking powder
¼ teaspoon salt

¾ cup light brown sugar
½ cup butter, softened
1 cup eggnog
2 eggs
1 teaspoon vanilla extract

Directions:
- Mix the cranberries and eggnog in a bowl and place aside to soak up.
- Mix the butter, sugar, eggnog, eggs and vanilla in a bowl until creamy.
- Fold in the flour and mix well then add the cranberries.
- Spoon the batter in a muffin tin lined with muffin papers.
- Bake in the preheated oven at 350F for 20 minutes or until well risen and golden brown.
- Serve the muffins chilled.

Nutritional information per serving

Calories: 238
Fat: 11.0g
Protein: 4.4g
Carbohydrates: 30.4g

EGAN BLUEBERRIES MUFFINS

Time: 1 hour   Servings: 12

Ingredients:

2 cups all-purpose flour   ½ cup canola oil
2 teaspoons baking powder   1 cup almond milk
¼ teaspoon salt   ½ cup soy yogurt
¾ cup light brown sugar   1 teaspoon vanilla extract
2 tablespoons ground flaxseeds   1 cup blueberries

Directions:
• Mix the flour, baking powder, salt and sugar in a bowl.
• Stir in the flaxseeds then add the canola oil, almond milk, soy yogurt and vanilla.
• Fold in the blueberries then spoon the batter in a muffin tin lined with muffin papers.
• Bake in the preheated oven at 350F for 20 minutes or until they pass the toothpick test.
• Serve the muffins chilled.

Nutritional information per serving

Calories: 259   Protein: 3.3g
Fat: 14.7g   Carbohydrates: 29.4g

UINOA CRANBERRY MUFFINS

Time: 1 hour   Servings: 12

Ingredients:

1 cup whole wheat flour   1 cup plain yogurt
½ cup quinoa flour   ¼ cup butter, melted
¼ cup all-purpose flour   2 eggs
¼ teaspoon salt   ¼ cup white sugar
2 teaspoons baking powder   1 cup cranberries
2 tablespoons sunflower seeds

Directions:
• Mix the flours, salt, baking powder, sunflower seeds in a bowl.
• Add the yogurt, eggs, sugar and butter and give it a quick mix.
• Fold in the cranberries then spoon the batter in a muffin tin lined with baking muffin papers.
• Bake in the preheated oven at 350F for 15-20 minutes or until well risen and golden.
• Allow to cool down before serving.

Nutritional information per serving

Calories: 149   Protein: 5.2g
Fat: 5.7g   Carbohydrates: 18.1g

O RANGE PECAN MUFFINS

Time: 1 ¼ hours   Servings: 12

Ingredients:

1 ¾ cups all-purpose flour   ½ cup milk
¼ teaspoon salt   ¼ cup fresh orange juice
1 ½ teaspoons baking powder   1 tablespoon orange zest
½ cup white sugar   1 cup pecans, chopped
¼ teaspoon cinnamon   ½ cup dried cranberries
2 eggs
6 tablespoons butter, melted

Directions:

- Mix the flour, salt, baking powder, sugar and cinnamon in a bowl.
- Add the eggs, butter, milk, orange juice and orange zest and give it a quick mix.
- Fold in the pecans and cranberries then spoon the batter in a muffin tin lined with baking muffin papers.
- Bake the muffins in the preheated oven at 350F for 20 minutes or until well risen and golden.
- Allow to cool down before serving.

Nutritional information per serving

Calories: 178

Fat: 7.7g

Protein: 3.4g

Carbohydrates: 24.4g

*F*RAGRANT DATE BANANA MUFFINS

Time: 1 ¼ hours

Servings: 12

Ingredients:

½ cup butter, melted

2 eggs

4 bananas, mashed

½ cup light brown sugar

1 ½ cups all-purpose flour

2 teaspoons baking powder

¼ teaspoon salt

1 cup dates, pitted and chopped

Directions:

- Mix the butter, eggs, bananas and sugar in a bowl.
- Add the flour, baking powder and salt and mix quickly.
- Fold in the dates then spoon the batter in a muffin tin lined with muffin papers.
- Bake in the preheated oven at 350F for 20 minutes or until well risen and golden brown.
- Allow to cool down before serving.

Nutritional information per serving

Calories: 236

Fat: 8.7g

Protein: 3.4g

Carbohydrates: 38.4g

*M*OIST BANANA MUFFINS

Time: 1 hour

Servings: 12

Ingredients:

3 bananas, mashed

2/3 cup white sugar

1 teaspoon vanilla extract

2 eggs

½ cup sour cream

½ cup coconut oil, melted

2 cups all-purpose flour

¼ teaspoon salt

2 teaspoons baking powder

Directions:

- Mix the bananas, sugar, vanilla, eggs, sour cream and coconut oil in a bowl.
- Add the flour, salt and baking powder and mix quickly.
- Spoon the batter in a muffin tin lined with muffin papers.
- Bake in the preheated oven at 350F for 20 minutes or until the muffins pass the toothpick test.
- Serve the muffins chilled.

Nutritional information per serving

Calories: 255

Fat: 12.1g

Protein: 3.7g

Carbohydrates: 34.6g

*C*AKEY BLUEBERRY MUFFINS

Time: 1 hour

Servings: 12

Ingredients:

2 eggs
¾ cup white sugar
1 teaspoon vanilla extract
½ cup canola oil
2/3 cup sour cream

1 ½ cups all-purpose flour
¼ cup cornstarch
¼ teaspoon salt
1 ½ teaspoons baking powder
1 cup blueberries

Directions:

- Mix the eggs and sugar in a bowl until double in volume. Stir in the vanilla and oil and mix well then add the sour cream and give it a good mix.
- Fold in the flour, cornstarch, salt and baking powder then fold in the blueberries.
- Spoon the batter in a muffin tin lined with muffin papers.
- Bake in the preheated oven at 350F for 20 minutes or until they pass the toothpick test.
- Serve the muffins chilled.

Nutritional information per serving

Calories: 241
Fat: 12.7g

Protein: 3.0g
Carbohydrates: 29.6g

S PELT ZUCCHINI MUFFINS

Time: 1 ¼ hours

Servings: 12

Ingredients:

1 cup spelt flour
1 cup whole wheat flour
¼ teaspoon salt
1 teaspoon baking soda
1 egg
½ cup plain yogurt

¼ cup maple syrup
¼ cup coconut oil, melted
1 teaspoon vanilla extract
1 cup grated zucchinis
2 tablespoons chia seeds

Directions:

- Mix the spelt flour, wheat flour, salt and baking soda in a bowl.
- Add the rest of the ingredients and give it a quick mix.
- Spoon the batter in a muffin tin lined with muffin papers and bake in the preheated oven at 350F for 20-25 minutes or until a toothpick inserted in the center comes out clean.
- Allow to cool down before serving.

Nutritional information per serving

Calories: 169
Fat: 6.9g

Protein: 4.7g
Carbohydrates: 22.5g

L EMON GLAZED APPLE CIDER MUFFINS

Time: 1 hour

Servings: 12

Ingredients:

½ cup coconut oil
½ cup light brown sugar
1 teaspoon vanilla extract
2 eggs
½ cup apple cider
2 cups all-purpose flour
1 teaspoon baking powder

½ teaspoon baking soda
¼ teaspoon salt
½ teaspoon cinnamon powder
2 red apples, cored and diced
1 cup powdered sugar
1 tablespoon lemon juice

Directions:

- Mix the coconut oil and sugar in a bowl for 2 minutes. Add the eggs and vanilla and mix well.
- Stir in the apple cider then fold in the flour, baking powder, baking soda, salt and cinnamon and mix with a spatula.

- Fold in the apples then spoon the batter in a muffin tin lined with muffin papers.
- Bake in the preheated oven at 350F for 20-25 minutes or until set and golden brown.
- For the glaze, mix the lemon juice and sugar in a bowl.
- Drizzle the mixture over the muffins and serve chilled.

Nutritional information per serving

Calories: 249
Fat: 10.1g

Protein: 3.2g
Carbohydrates: 37.5g

S PICED ZUCCHINI MUFFINS

Time: 1 ¼ hours

Servings: 12

Ingredients:

1 cup grated zucchinis
1 apple, cored and grated
½ cup almond butter, softened
¼ cup honey
2 eggs
1 teaspoon vanilla extract

1 ½ cups all-purpose flour
½ teaspoon cinnamon
½ teaspoon ground ginger
½ teaspoon ground cardamom
¼ teaspoon salt
1 ½ teaspoons baking powder

Directions:

- Mix the zucchinis, apples, almond butter, honey, eggs and vanilla in a bowl.
- Stir in the flour, cinnamon, ginger, cardamom, salt and baking powder.
- Spoon the batter in a muffin tin lined with muffin papers and bake in the preheated oven at 350F for 15-20 minutes or until they pass the toothpick test.
- Allow to cool down before serving.

Nutritional information per serving

Calories: 167
Fat: 6.8g

Protein: 4.9g
Carbohydrates: 22.6g

O ATMEAL CRANBERRY MUFFINS

Time: 1 hour

Servings: 12

Ingredients:

2 bananas, mashed
2 eggs
¼ cup milk
¼ cup olive oil
¼ cup light brown sugar
1 teaspoon vanilla extract
1 cup all-purpose flour

2 tablespoons ground flaxseeds
1 cup rolled oats
2 teaspoons baking powder
¼ teaspoon salt
1 cup fresh cranberries
¼ cup candied orange peel, diced

Directions:

- Mix the bananas, eggs, milk, olive oil, sugar and vanilla in a bowl.
- Fold in the flour, flaxseeds, oats, baking powder and salt then add the cranberries and orange peel.
- Spoon the batter in a muffin tin lined with muffin papers.
- Bake in the preheated oven at 350F for 20 minutes or until fragrant and well risen.
- Allow to cool in the pan before serving.

Nutritional information per serving

Calories: 157
Fat: 6.0g
Protein: 3.5g
Carbohydrates: 22.4g

*P*UMPKIN APPLE STREUSEL MUFFINS

Time: 1 ¼ hours

Servings: 14

Ingredients:

Muffins:
2 cups all-purpose flour
½ cup oat flour
1 cup white sugar
1 teaspoon baking soda
1 teaspoon baking powder
¼ teaspoon salt
1 teaspoon pumpkin pie spices
1 ¼ cups pumpkin puree

2 eggs
¼ cup canola oil
2 apples, peeled and diced
Streusel:
½ cup all-purpose flour
1 pinch salt
2 tablespoons dark brown sugar
¼ cup rolled oats
¼ cup butter

Directions:
- For the muffins, mix the flours, sugar, baking soda, baking powder, salt and spices in a bowl.
- Add the pumpkin puree, eggs, canola oil and apples and give it a quick mix.
- Spoon the batter in a muffin tin lined with muffin papers.
- Bake in the preheated oven at 350F for 20 minutes or until fragrant and well risen.
- Allow to cool down before serving.

Nutritional information per serving

Calories: 252
Fat: 8.5g

Protein: 4.1g
Carbohydrates: 41.5g

*G*RAIN FREE APPLE CINNAMON

Time: 1 ¼ hours

Servings: 12

Ingredients:

1 ½ cups almond flour
½ cup tapioca flour
1 teaspoon cinnamon powder
½ teaspoon baking soda
½ teaspoon baking powder
¼ teaspoon salt
3 eggs

½ cup coconut milk
¼ cup coconut oil, melted
¼ cup honey
1 teaspoon lemon juice
1 teaspoon vanilla extract
2 red apples, cored and diced

Directions:
- Mix the flours, cinnamon, baking soda, baking powder and salt in a bowl.
- Add the eggs and the rest of the ingredients and mix well.
- Spoon the batter in a muffin tin lined with baking muffin papers then bake in the preheated oven at 350F for 20 minutes or until golden brown and well risen.
- Serve the muffins chilled.

Nutritional information per serving

Calories: 163
Fat: 9.8g

Protein: 2.5g
Carbohydrates: 18.5g

*B*ROWN BUTTER CHOCOLATE CHIP MUFFINS

Time: 1 ¼ hours

Servings: 14

Ingredients:

½ cup brown butter
2 eggs

¾ cup milk
¾ cup white sugar

1 ½ cups all-purpose flour
1 ½ teaspoons baking powder

¼ teaspoon salt
½ cup dark chocolate chips

Directions:

- Mix the brown butter and sugar in a bowl until creamy. Add the eggs and milk and mix well then stir in the flour, baking powder and salt.
- Spoon the batter in a muffin tin lined with muffin papers.
- Top with chocolate chips and bake in the preheated oven at 350F for 20 minutes or until well risen and golden brown.
- When done, allow to cool in the pan before serving.

Nutritional information per serving

Calories: 267
Fat: 10.6g

Protein: 7.4g
Carbohydrates: 36.4g

UMPKIN NUTELLA MUFFINS

Time: 1 hour

Servings: 12

Ingredients:

2 cups all-purpose flour
1 cup white sugar
1 teaspoon baking powder
1 teaspoon baking soda
¼ teaspoon salt
1 teaspoon cinnamon powder
½ teaspoon ground nutmeg

½ teaspoon ground ginger
2 eggs
1 teaspoon vanilla extract
1 ½ cups pumpkin puree
½ cup coconut oil, melted
½ cup Nutella

Directions:

- Mix the flour, sugar, baking powder, baking soda, salt, cinnamon, nutmeg and ginger.
- Add the eggs, vanilla, pumpkin puree and coconut oil and give it a quick mix.
- Spoon the batter in a muffin tin lined with muffin papers.
- Drop a spoonful of Nutella on top of each muffin then swirl it with a toothpick.
- Bake in the preheated oven at 350F for 15-20 minutes or until well risen and golden brown.
- Serve the muffins chilled.

Nutritional information per serving

Calories: 256
Fat: 11.1g

Protein: 3.6g
Carbohydrates: 37.2g

TREUSEL CRANBERRY MUFFINS

Time: 1 hour

Servings: 12

Ingredients:

Muffins:
½ cup butter, melted
2 eggs
½ cup milk
1 cup white sugar
1 teaspoon vanilla extract
1 ½ cups all-purpose flour
¼ teaspoon salt

1 cup ground pecans
1 ½ teaspoons baking powder
1 cup fresh cranberries
Streusel:
½ cup whole wheat flour
¼ cup butter, chilled
2 tablespoons brown sugar

Directions:

- For the muffins, mix the butter, eggs, milk, sugar and vanilla in a bowl.
- Stir in the flour, salt, pecans and baking powder then fold in the cranberries.
- Spoon the batter in a muffin tin lined with muffin papers.
- For the streusel, mix all the ingredients in a bowl until grainy.

- Top each muffin with streusel and bake in the preheated oven at 350F for 20 minutes or until golden brown and well risen.
- Serve the muffins chilled.

Nutritional information per serving

Calories: 276

Fat: 13.5g

Protein: 3.7g

Carbohydrates: 36.0g

ROWN BUTTER BANANA CUPCAKES

Time: 1 ½ hours

Servings: 20

Ingredients:

Cupcakes:

1 cup all-purpose flour

¾ cup whole wheat flour

¼ teaspoon salt

½ teaspoon baking soda

1 teaspoon baking powder

½ cup brown butter

¼ cup coconut oil, melted

¾ cup light brown sugar

2 eggs

½ cup buttermilk

2 bananas, mashed

Frosting:

1 cup butter, softened

2 cups powdered sugar

½ teaspoon cinnamon powder

Directions:
- For the cupcakes, mix the flours, salt, baking soda and baking powder in a bowl.
- In a different bowl, mix the butter, coconut oil and sugar in a bowl until fluffy and creamy.
- Add the eggs and mix well then stir in the buttermilk and bananas.
- Fold in the flour then spoon the batter in a muffin tin lined with muffin papers.
- Bake in the preheated oven at 350F for 20 minutes or until fragrant and golden.
- Allow to cool in the pan.
- For the frosting, mix all the ingredients in a bowl for 5-7 minutes until pale and fluffy.
- Top each cupcake with the butter frosting.
- Serve chilled.

Nutritional information per serving

Calories: 331

Fat: 18.5g

Protein: 5.3g

Carbohydrates: 37.0g

MAPLE SPICE MUFFINS

Time: 1 hour

Servings: 12

Ingredients:

2 ¼ cups all-purpose flour

¼ teaspoon salt

2 teaspoons baking powder

½ teaspoon cinnamon powder

½ teaspoon all-spice powder

½ teaspoon ground ginger

¾ cup maple syrup

½ cup canola oil

½ cup milk

1 egg

1 teaspoon vanilla extract

½ cup walnuts, chopped

½ cup dark chocolate chips

Directions:
- Mix the flour, salt, baking powder and spices in a bowl.
- Add the rest of the ingredients and give it a good mix.
- Fold in the walnuts and chocolate chips then spoon the batter in a muffin tin lined with muffin papers.
- Bake in the preheated oven at 350F for 15-20 minutes or until they pass the toothpick test.
- Serve the muffins chilled.

Nutritional information per serving
Calories: 285
Fat: 14.3g

Protein: 4.8g
Carbohydrates: 36.0g

*C*HOCOLATE PRETZEL MUFFINS

Time: 1 ½ hours

Servings: 12

Ingredients:
Cupcakes:
1 ¼ cups all-purpose flour
¼ cup cocoa powder
¼ teaspoon salt
1 ½ teaspoons baking powder
1 cup buttermilk
2 eggs
½ cup brewed coffee

¼ cup canola oil
1 teaspoon vanilla extract
Frosting:
1 cup butter, softened
2 cups powdered sugar
½ cup dark chocolate chips, melted and chilled
1 cup pretzels, crushed

Directions:
- For the cupcakes, mix the flour, cocoa powder, salt and baking powder in a bowl.
- Add the rest of the ingredients and give it a quick mix.
- Pour the batter in a muffin tin lined with muffin papers.
- Bake in the preheated oven at 350F for 20 minutes or until the muffins pass the toothpick test.
- Allow to cool down.
- For the frosting, mix the butter and sugar in a bowl until fluffy and pale.
- Stir in the chocolate and mix well.
- Top each cupcake with the frosting and sprinkle with pretzels.
- Serve the cupcakes fresh.

Nutritional information per serving
Calories: 368
Fat: 22.6g

Protein: 4.3g
Carbohydrates: 39.5g

*B*OURBON GLAZED PUMPKIN MUFFINS

Time: 1 hour

Servings: 12

Ingredients:
Muffins:
1 ½ cups whole wheat flour
½ cup white sugar
2 teaspoons baking powder
½ teaspoon salt
1 teaspoon cinnamon powder
½ teaspoon ground ginger

1 cup pumpkin puree
½ cup buttermilk
1 egg
¼ cup coconut oil
Glaze:
2 tablespoons bourbon
1 ½ cups powdered sugar

Directions:
- For the muffins, mix the dry ingredients in a bowl.
- Add the wet ingredients and give it a quick mix.
- Spoon the batter in a muffin tin lined with muffin papers.
- Bake in the preheated oven at 350F for 20 minutes.
- When done, allow to cool in the pan.
- For the glaze, mix the ingredients in a bowl.
- Drizzle the glaze over each muffin and serve the muffins chilled.

Nutritional information per serving
Calories: 208
Fat: 5.2g

Protein: 2.6g
Carbohydrates: 37.8g

ROWN BUTTER STREUSEL PUMPKIN MUFFINS

Time: 1 hour

Servings: 12

Ingredients:

Muffins:
1 cup pumpkin puree
2 eggs
½ cup buttermilk
¼ cup canola oil
1 teaspoon vanilla extract
½ cup light brown sugar
1 ½ cups all-purpose flour
½ teaspoon baking powder

½ teaspoon baking soda
1 pinch salt
1 teaspoon pumpkin pie spices
Streusel:
¼ cup brown sugar
½ cup all-purpose flour
2 tablespoons light brown sugar
1 pinch salt
2 tablespoons pumpkin seeds

Directions:

- For the muffins, mix the wet ingredients in a bowl.
- Add the dry ingredients and give it a quick mix.
- Spoon the batter in a muffin tin lined with muffin papers.
- For the streusel, combine all the ingredients in a bowl and mix until grainy.
- Spread the streusel over the muffins and bake in the preheated oven at 350F for 15-20 minutes or until they're fragrant and well risen.
- Allow to cool in the pan before serving.

Nutritional information per serving

Calories: 187
Fat: 6.3g

Protein: 4.0g
Carbohydrates: 29.0g

B ANANA PEAR MUFFINS

Time: 1 hour

Servings: 12

Ingredients:

2 bananas, mashed
1 egg
¼ cup canola oil
¼ cup buttermilk
½ cup white sugar
1 cup all-purpose flour

½ cup whole wheat flour
¼ teaspoon salt
1 teaspoon cinnamon powder
½ teaspoon ground ginger
1 teaspoon baking soda
2 pears, cored and diced

Directions:

- Mix the bananas, egg, oil, buttermilk and sugar in a bowl.
- Add the flours, salt, spices and baking soda and give it a quick mix just until incorporated.
- Fold in the pears then spoon the batter in a muffin tin lined with muffin papers.
- Bake in the preheated oven at 350F for 15-20 minutes or until golden brown and fragrant.
- Serve the muffins chilled.

Nutritional information per serving

Calories: 173
Fat: 5.2g

Protein: 2.6g
Carbohydrates: 30.4g

F LAXSEED PUMPKIN MUFFINS

Time: 1 hour

Servings: 12

Ingredients:

1 ¼ cups all-purpose flour

¼ cup ground flaxseeds

1 teaspoon pumpkin pie spices
1 teaspoon baking powder
¼ teaspoon baking soda
¼ teaspoon salt
1 cup pumpkin puree

½ cup buttermilk
1 egg
¼ cup canola oil
1 teaspoon vanilla extract

Directions:
- Mix the flour, flaxseeds, spices, baking powder, baking soda and salt in a bowl.
- Add the rest of the ingredients and mix well.
- Spoon the batter in a muffin tin lined with special muffin papers.
- Bake the muffins in the preheated oven at 350F for 15-20minutes or until they pass the toothpick test.
- Allow to cool in the pan before serving.

Nutritional information per serving

Calories: 118
Fat: 5.9g

Protein: 2.8g
Carbohydrates: 13.1g

ℰ GGLESS PUMPKIN MUFFINS

Time: 1 hour

Servings: 12

Ingredients:

3/4 cup almond milk
1 teaspoon lemon juice
½ cup maple syrup
½ cup coconut oil, melted
1 teaspoon vanilla extract

1 cup pumpkin puree
2 cups all-purpose flour
2 teaspoons baking powder
¼ teaspoon salt
1 teaspoon pumpkin pie spices

Directions:
- Mix the wet ingredients in a bowl.
- Add the rest of the ingredients and give it a quick mix.
- Spoon the batter in a muffin tin lined with muffin papers and bake in the preheated oven at 350F for 15-20 minutes or until they pass the toothpick test.
- Serve the muffins chilled.

Nutritional information per serving

Calories: 232
Fat: 13.0g

Protein: 2.7g
Carbohydrates: 27.7g

LUTEN FREE MAPLE MUFFINS

Time: 1 hour

Servings: 12

Ingredients:

½ cup butter, melted
2 eggs
½ cup maple syrup
2 tablespoons dark brown sugar
1 teaspoon vanilla extract
½ cup coconut flour

½ cup sorghum flour
¼ cup tapioca flour
¼ teaspoon salt
1 ½ teaspoons baking powder
¾ cup milk

Directions:
- Mix the eggs, butter, maple syrup, sugar and vanilla in a bowl until creamy.
- Add the rest of the ingredients and mix well.
- Pour the batter in a muffin tin lined with muffin papers.
- Bake in the preheated oven at 350F for 20 minutes or until the muffins pass the toothpick test.
- Allow the muffins to cool down before serving.

Calories: 203
Fat: 9.7g

Protein: 3.1g
Carbohydrates: 27.3g

S UGARY BLUEBERRY MUFFINS

Time: 1 hour

Servings: 12

Ingredients:

½ cup butter, melted
½ cup white sugar
2 eggs
1 teaspoon vanilla extract
¼ cup milk

2 cups all-purpose flour
2 teaspoons baking powder
¼ teaspoon salt
1 ½ cups blueberries
½ cup Demerara sugar

Directions:

- Mix the butter and sugar in a bowl. Add the eggs and mix well then stir in the milk and vanilla.
- Fold in the flour, baking powder and salt then add the blueberries.
- Spoon the batter in a muffin tin lined with muffin papers.
- Top each muffin with Demerara sugar and bake in the preheated oven at 350F for 20 minutes or until well risen and golden brown.
- Allow to cool down before serving.

Nutritional information per serving

Calories: 223
Fat: 8.8g

Protein: 3.5g
Carbohydrates: 33.5g

B LUEBERRY CHEESE MUFFINS

Time: 1 hour

Servings: 12

Ingredients:

¾ cup butter, melted
1 cup white sugar
2 eggs
1 cup milk
½ cup coconut flour
½ cup sorghum flour

½ cup tapioca flour
¼ cup white rice flour
1 ½ teaspoons baking powder
¼ teaspoon salt
1 cup fresh blueberries
½ cup cream cheese

Directions:

- Mix the butter, sugar and eggs in a bowl until creamy.
- Add the milk and mix well then stir in the flours, salt and baking powder.
- Add the blueberries then spoon the batter in a muffin tin lined with baking muffin papers.
- Top each muffin with a dollop of cream cheese and bake in the preheated oven at 350F for 20 minutes or until golden brown and well risen.
- Allow the muffins to cool down before serving.

Nutritional information per serving

Calories: 314
Fat: 17.1g

Protein: 4.3g
Carbohydrates: 38.6g

R ED BERRIES CREAM CHEESE MUFFINS

Time: 1 hour

Servings: 12

Ingredients:

1 cup cream cheese

½ cup butter, softened

2 eggs
¾ cup white sugar
½ cup heavy cream
1 teaspoon vanilla extract
1 ½ cups all-purpose flour

¼ teaspoon salt
2 teaspoons baking powder
1 cup mixed berries
½ cup sliced almonds

Directions:

- Mix the cream cheese and butter in a bowl.
- Add the sugar and eggs and mix well. Stir in the cream and vanilla and give it a good mix.
- Fold in the flour, salt and baking powder then add the berries.
- Spoon the batter in a muffin tin lined with muffin papers.
- Top the muffins with sliced almonds and bake in the preheated oven at 350F for 15-20 minutes or until well risen and golden brown.
- Allow to cool down before serving.

Nutritional information per serving

Calories: 298
Fat: 19.2g

Protein: 5.1g
Carbohydrates: 27.9g

NICKERDOODLE MUFFINS

Time: 1 hour

Servings: 12

Ingredients:

Muffins:
½ cup butter, softened
½ cup light brown sugar
1 teaspoon vanilla extract
2 eggs
2/3 cup buttermilk
2 ¼ cups all-purpose flour

½ teaspoon salt
2 teaspoons baking powder
½ teaspoon ground ginger
Topping:
2/3 cup white sugar
1 teaspoon cinnamon powder

Directions:

- For the muffins, mix the butter and sugar in a bowl.
- Add the vanilla and eggs and mix well then stir in the buttermilk.
- Fold in the flour, salt, baking powder and ginger then spoon the batter in a muffin tin lined with muffin papers.
- Bake in the preheated oven at 350F for 20 minutes or until golden brown and well risen.
- For the topping, mix the ingredients in a bowl.
- While the muffins are still hot, dip them in cinnamon sugar.
- Serve the muffins chilled.

Nutritional information per serving

Calories: 236
Fat: 8.8g

Protein: 3.9g
Carbohydrates: 36.1g

FIG WALNUT MUFFINS

Time: 1 hour

Servings: 12

Ingredients:

1 ½ cups whole wheat flour
1 teaspoon baking powder
¼ teaspoon baking soda
¼ teaspoon salt
1 pinch cinnamon powder
½ cup white sugar
½ cup shredded coconut
1 cup ground walnuts

1/3 cup olive oil
1 cup coconut milk
1 egg
1 teaspoon vanilla extract
6 fresh figs, quartered

Directions:

- Mix the flour, baking powder, baking soda, salt, cinnamon, sugar, coconut and walnuts in a bowl.
- Add the rest of the ingredients and mix well.
- Pour the batter in a muffin tin lined with muffin papers and top with figs.
- Bake in the preheated oven at 350F for 20 minutes or until they pass the toothpick test.
- Allow the muffins to cool in the pan before serving.

Nutritional information per serving

Calories: 289   Protein: 5.5g
Fat: 18.2g   Carbohydrates: 29.3g

 VEGAN CHOCOLATE MUFFINS

Time: 1 hour   Servings: 12

Ingredients:

1 ½ cups all-purpose flour   1/3 cup coconut oil, melted
½ cup almond flour   1 cup coconut milk
¼ cup cocoa powder   1 teaspoon vanilla extract
1 ½ teaspoons baking powder   ½ cup dark chocolate chips
1 cup coconut sugar

Directions:

- Mix the flours, cocoa powder, baking powder and sugar in a bowl.
- Add the rest of the ingredient and give it a quick mix.
- Fold in the chocolate chips then spoon the batter in a muffin tin lined with baking muffin papers.
- Bake in the preheated oven at 350F for 20 minutes or until the muffins pass the toothpick test.
- Serve the muffins chilled.

Nutritional information per serving

Calories: 251   Protein: 3.0g
Fat: 13.1g   Carbohydrates: 33.9g

ALMOND POPPY SEED MUFFINS

Time: 1 hour   Servings: 12

Ingredients:

1 ½ cups almond flour   2 eggs
1 teaspoon baking powder   ½ cup sour cream
¼ teaspoon salt   1 teaspoon vanilla extract
2 tablespoons poppy seeds   1 teaspoon lemon zest
½ cup white sugar   1 pinch salt
½ cup butter, melted

Directions:

- Mix the almond flour, baking powder, salt and poppy seeds in a bowl.
- In another bowl, mix the sugar, butter, eggs, sour cream, lemon zest and salt. Pour this mixture over the dry ingredients and mix well.
- Spoon the batter in a muffin tin lined with muffin papers.
- Bake in the preheated oven at 350F for 15-20 minutes or until golden brown and well risen.
- Allow the muffins to cool in the pan before serving.

Nutritional information per serving

Calories: 159
Fat: 12.8g
Protein: 2.3g
Carbohydrates: 10.2g

Coconut Lemon Chia Seed Muffins

Time: 1 hour

Servings: 10

Ingredients:

2 tablespoons chia seeds
1 ½ cups almond flour
¼ teaspoon salt
1 teaspoon baking powder
½ cup milk
½ cup honey

4 eggs
¼ cup coconut oil, melted
1 teaspoon vanilla extract
1 teaspoon lemon zest
1 teaspoon lemon juice

Directions:

- Mix the chia seeds, almond flour, salt and baking powder in a bowl.
- Add the rest of the ingredients and give it a quick mix.
- Pour the batter in a muffin tin lined with muffin papers.
- Bake in the preheated oven at 350F for 20 minutes or until well risen and golden.
- Allow the muffins to cool in the pan before serving.

Nutritional information per serving

Calories: 187
Fat: 11.5g

Protein: 4.8g
Carbohydrates: 18.0g

Spiced Cupcakes with Cream Cheese Cupcakes

Time: 1 ½ hours

Servings: 16

Ingredients:

Cupcakes:
½ cup butter, softened
1 cup white sugar
2 eggs
¾ cup plain yogurt
1 teaspoon vanilla extract
2 cups all-purpose flour
1 teaspoon cinnamon powder

½ teaspoon grated ginger
½ teaspoon ground cardamom
¼ teaspoon salt
1 ½ teaspoons baking powder
Frosting:
1 cup cream cheese
½ cup butter, softened
3 cups powdered sugar

Directions:

- For the cupcakes, mix the butter and sugar in a bowl until fluffy and pale.
- Add the eggs and mix well then stir in the yogurt and vanilla.
- Fold in the flour, spices, salt and baking powder then spoon the batter in a muffin tin lined with muffin papers.
- Bake the cupcakes in the preheated oven at 350F for 20 minutes.
- For the frosting, mix the cream cheese and butter in a bowl until creamy.
- Add the sugar, gradually, and mix well for a few minutes until fluffy.
- Pipe the frosting over each cupcake and serve the cupcakes fresh.

Nutritional information per serving

Calories: 361
Fat: 17.4g

Protein: 4.2g
Carbohydrates: 48.4g

Sweet Potato Cinnamon Cupcakes

Time: 1 ½ hours

Servings: 16

Ingredients:

Cupcakes:
2 cups all-purpose flour

1 teaspoon cinnamon powder
½ teaspoon ground ginger

½ teaspoon baking soda
½ teaspoon baking powder
¼ teaspoon salt
1 cup butter, softened
1 cup light brown sugar
2 cups sweet potato puree

½ cup crushed pineapple
Frosting:
1 cup butter, softened
2 cups powdered sugar, sifted
1 teaspoon cinnamon powder

Directions:
- For the cupcakes, sift the flour, spices, baking soda, baking powder and salt in a bowl.
- Mix the butter and sugar in a different bowl until fluffy and creamy. Add the sweet potato puree and pineapple then fold in the flour.
- Spoon the batter in a muffin tin lined with paper liners.
- Bake in the preheated oven at 350F for 20 minutes or until they pass the toothpick test.
- Allow the cupcakes to cool down.
- For the frosting, mix the butter in a bowl until creamy.
- Add the sugar, ½ cup at a time, and mix well until fluffy and pale.
- Pipe the frosting on top of each cupcake and sprinkle with cinnamon powder.
- Serve the cupcakes fresh.

Nutritional information per serving
Calories: 388
Fat: 23.3g

Protein: 2.5g
Carbohydrates: 44.0g

PPLE PIE CARAMEL CUPCAKES

Time: 1 ½ hours

Servings: 14

Ingredients:
2/3 cup butter, softened
2/3 cup light brown sugar
2 eggs
1 teaspoon vanilla extract
2/3 cup buttermilk
1 ½ cups all-purpose flour
½ teaspoon ground ginger
1 teaspoon baking powder
½ teaspoon baking soda

1 pinch salt
Frosting:
1 cup butter, softened
2 cups powdered sugar
½ teaspoon cinnamon powder
Topping:
2 apples, peeled, cored and diced
¼ cup light brown sugar
1 tablespoon lemon juice

Directions:
- For the cupcakes, mix the butter and sugar in a bowl until creamy and fluffy.
- Add the eggs and vanilla and mix well then stir in the buttermilk.
- Add the flour, spices, baking powder, baking soda and salt then pour the batter in a muffin tin lined with muffin papers.
- Bake in the preheated oven at 350F for 20 minutes or until they pass the toothpick test.
- For the frosting, mix the butter and sugar in a bowl for 5 minutes until pale and airy. Add the cinnamon and mix well.
- Top each cupcake with the frosting.
- For the topping, combine the ingredients in a saucepan and cook over low heat just until the apples are tender. Allow to cool down then top each cupcake with a spoonfuls of apple mixture.
- Serve the cupcakes fresh.

Nutritional information per serving
Calories: 374
Fat: 22.9g

Protein: 2.9g
Carbohydrates: 41.1g

CHOCOLATE AVOCADO CUPCAKES

Time: 1 ½ hours

Servings: 12

Ingredients:

Cupcakes:
1 large avocado, mashed
2/3 cup coconut sugar
1 cup coconut milk
1 teaspoon vanilla extract
1 egg
2 egg whites
1 cup whole wheat flour
1 cup all-purpose flour

¼ teaspoon salt
2 teaspoons baking powder
½ cup cocoa powder
Frosting:
1 large avocado, mashed
2 tablespoons coconut oil
¼ cup cocoa powder
2 tablespoons coconut sugar
½ teaspoon vanilla extract

Directions:

- For the cupcakes, mix the avocado, coconut sugar, coconut milk, vanilla, egg and egg whites in a bowl until creamy.
- Add the rest of the ingredients and mix quickly.
- Spoon the batter in a muffin tin lined with muffin papers.
- Bake in the preheated oven at 350F for 20 minutes or until a toothpick inserted in the muffins comes out clean.
- Allow to cool in the pan.
- For the frosting, mix all the ingredients in a blender or food processor and pulse until well mixed.
- Pipe the frosting over each cupcake and serve fresh.

Nutritional information per serving

Calories: 280
Fat: 14.8g

Protein: 5.3g
Carbohydrates: 36.0g

'MORES CHOCOLATE CUPCAKES

Time: 1 ½ hours

Servings: 12

Ingredients:

Cupcakes:
1 ½ cups all-purpose flour
¼ cup cocoa powder
½ teaspoon baking soda
1 teaspoon baking powder
¼ teaspoon salt
½ cup white sugar
2 tablespoons dark brown sugar
½ cup butter, softened

2 eggs
½ cup buttermilk
1 teaspoon vanilla extract
Frosting:
2 egg whites
½ cup white sugar
1 teaspoon vanilla extract
½ cup dark chocolate chips
½ cup crushed graham crackers

Directions:

- For the cupcakes, mix the flour, cocoa powder, baking soda, baking powder and salt in a bowl.
- Mix the butter and sugars in a different bowl until creamy and pale.
- Add the eggs, buttermilk and vanilla and mix well.
- Fold in the flour mixture then spoon the batter in a muffin tin lined with baking muffin papers.
- Bake in the preheated oven at 350F for 20 minutes or until fragrant and golden brown.
- Allow to cool in the pan.
- For the frosting, mix the egg whites, sugar and vanilla in a bowl and place over a hot water bath. Keep on heat until the sugar is melted.
- Remove from heat and whip with an electric mixer until fluffy, stiff and glossy.
- Top each cupcake with frosting and sprinkle with chocolate chips and graham crackers.
- Serve the cupcakes fresh.

Nutritional information per serving

Calories: 255
Fat: 10.6g
Protein: 4.4g
Carbohydrates: 37.9g

RED WINE FIG CUPCAKES

Time: 1 ½ hours

Servings: 16

Ingredients:

Cupcakes:
2/3 cup butter, softened
2/3 cup white sugar
½ cup red wine
1 teaspoon vanilla extract
2 eggs
1 ½ cups all-purpose flour
¼ cup cocoa powder
¼ teaspoon salt
1 ½ teaspoons baking powder

Frosting:
1 cup cream cheese
½ cup butter, softened
2 cups powdered sugar
Fig compote:
6 figs, halved
½ cup red wine
¼ cup light brown sugar
1 cinnamon stick

Directions:
- For the cupcakes, mix the butter and sugar in a bowl until creamy. Add the wine, vanilla and eggs and mix well.
- Fold in the flour, cocoa powder, salt and baking powder and mix with a spatula.
- Spoon the batter in a muffin tin lined with muffin papers.
- Bake in the preheated oven at 350F for 20 minutes or until well risen and golden.
- Allow the muffins to cool down in the pan.
- For the frosting, mix the butter and cream cheese in a bowl until fluffy and pale.
- Add the sugar, ½ cup at a time and mix well for 4-5 minutes until airy.
- Pipe the frosting over each cupcake.
- For the compote, combine the ingredients in a saucepan and cook for 5-6 minutes just until softened.
- Spoon the compote over each cupcake and serve fresh.

Nutritional information per serving

Calories: 353
Fat: 19.4g

Protein: 3.6g
Carbohydrates: 40.9g

GLUTEN FREE CHOCOLATE CUPCAKES WITH PUMPKIN FROSTING

Time: 1 ½ hours

Servings: 12

Ingredients:

Cupcakes:
½ cup buckwheat flour
1 cup shredded coconut
½ cup coconut flour
½ cup cocoa powder
1 teaspoon baking soda
¼ teaspoon salt
½ cup maple syrup
1 cup sparkling water
¼ cup coconut oil, melted

1 teaspoon vanilla extract
Frosting:
1 cup dates, pitted
½ cup walnuts
2 tablespoons maple syrup
2 tablespoons coconut oil
½ cup pumpkin puree
¼ teaspoon cinnamon powder
¼ teaspoon ground ginger

Directions:
- For the cupcakes, mix the flours, shredded coconut, cocoa powder, baking soda and salt in a bowl.
- In a different bowl, combine the maple syrup, sparkling water, coconut oil and vanilla and mix well. Add the dry ingredients and give it a quick mix.
- Pour the batter in a muffin tin lined with muffin papers and bake in the preheated oven at 350F for 20 minutes or until they pass the toothpick test.
- Allow the cupcakes to cool down.
- For the frosting, place the dates and the remaining ingredients in a food processor or blender and pulse until well mixed.

- Top each cupcake with the frosting and serve fresh.

Nutritional information per serving

Calories: 249

Fat: 13.5g

Protein: 3.9g

Carbohydrates: 32.8g

ROOKLYN BLACKOUT CUPCAKES

Time: 1 ½ hours

Servings: 12

Ingredients:

Cupcakes:

½ cup butter, softened

1 cup white sugar

2 eggs

2 teaspoons instant coffee

½ cup buttermilk

1 teaspoon vanilla extract

1 cup all-purpose flour

½ cup cocoa powder

½ teaspoon baking soda

1 teaspoon baking powder

¼ teaspoon salt

Frosting:

1 cup milk

¼ cup white sugar

1 pinch salt

1 teaspoon instant coffee

2 tablespoons cornstarch

2 tablespoons cocoa powder

2 tablespoons butter

Directions:

- For the cupcakes, mix the butter and sugar in a bowl until creamy.
- Add the eggs, one by one, and mix well then stir in the coffee powder, buttermilk and vanilla.
- Add the flour, cocoa powder, baking soda, baking powder and salt and mix with a spatula or whisk.
- Pour the batter in a muffin tin lined with muffin papers and bake in the preheated oven at 350F for 20 minutes or until they pass the toothpick test.
- Allow to cool down in the pan.
- For the frosting, bring the milk to the boiling point in a saucepan.
- In a bowl, combine the rest of the ingredients.
- Pour in the milk and mix well then return on low heat and cook until thickened.
- Allow the frosting to cool down then spoon it over each cupcake.
- Serve the cupcakes chilled.

Nutritional information per serving

Calories: 242

Fat: 11.5g

Protein: 3.9g

Carbohydrates: 34.2g

OGURT BLACKBERRY MUFFINS

Time: 1 hour

Servings: 12

Ingredients:

2 cups all-purpose flour

2 teaspoons baking powder

¼ teaspoon salt

2 eggs

2 egg whites

1 teaspoon vanilla extract

1 cup white sugar

½ cup butter, melted

½ cup heavy cream

1 cup blackberries

Directions:

- Mix the flour, baking powder and salt in a bowl.
- Whip the eggs, egg whites, vanilla and sugar until fluffy and pale.
- Add the butter and mix well then stir in the cream.
- Fold in the flour then add the blackberries.
- Spoon the batter in a muffin tin lined with muffin papers.
- Bake in the preheated oven at 350F for 20 minutes or until well risen and golden brown.
- Allow the muffins to cool down before serving.

Nutritional information per serving

Calories: 244

Fat: 10.5g

Protein: 4.0g

Carbohydrates: 34.4g

N UTELLA PEANUT BUTTER CUPCAKES

Time: 1 ½ hours

Servings: 12

Ingredients:

Cupcakes:

½ cup smooth peanut butter

¼ cup butter, softened

¾ cup light brown sugar

1 teaspoon vanilla extract

2 eggs

½ cup buttermilk

1 ½ cups all-purpose flour

¼ teaspoon salt

1 ½ teaspoons baking powder

Frosting:

1 cup Nutella

Directions:

- For the cupcakes, mix the peanut butter, butter, sugar and vanilla in a bowl until creamy.
- Add the eggs and buttermilk and mix well.
- Fold in the rest of the ingredients then spoon the batter in a muffin tin lined with muffin papers.
- Bake in the preheated oven at 350F for 20 minutes or until well risen and golden brown.
- When chilled, top with Nutella and serve fresh.

Nutritional information per serving

Calories: 221

Fat: 11.2g

Protein: 5.8g

Carbohydrates: 25.7g

B ROWN SUGAR BOURBON CUPCAKES

Time: 1 hour

Servings: 12

Ingredients:

Cupcakes:

1 cup light brown sugar

½ cup butter, softened

½ cup heavy cream

1 teaspoon vanilla extract

2 tablespoons bourbon

3 eggs

1 ¾ cups all-purpose flour

¼ teaspoon salt

1 ½ teaspoons baking powder

Frosting:

1 cup butter, softened

½ cup dark brown sugar

1 cup powdered sugar

Directions:

- For the cupcakes, mix the sugar and butter in a bowl until creamy.
- Add the cream, vanilla and bourbon and mix well.
- Stir in the eggs and give it a good mix.
- Fold in the flour, salt and baking powder then spoon the batter in a muffin tin lined with muffin papers.
- Bake in the preheated oven at 350F for 20 minutes or until they pass the toothpick test.
- Allow to cool in the pan.
- For the frosting, mix all the ingredients in a bowl for 5-7 minutes or until fluffy and pale.
- Top the cupcakes with the frosting and serve them fresh.

Nutritional information per serving

Calories: 418

Fat: 26.2g

Protein: 3.6g

Carbohydrates: 42.2g

C HAI VANILLA FROSTED CUPCAKES

Time: 1 ½ hours

Servings: 12

Ingredients:

Cupcakes:
½ cup butter, softened
2/3 cup white sugar
2 eggs
1 teaspoon vanilla extract
2/3 cup buttermilk
1 ½ cups all-purpose flour
1 teaspoon baking powder
½ teaspoon baking soda
¼ teaspoon cinnamon powder
¼ teaspoon ground ginger
¼ teaspoon ground star anise
¼ teaspoon ground cardamom
Frosting:
1 cup butter, softened
2 cups powdered sugar
1 teaspoon vanilla extract

Directions:

- For the cupcakes, mix the butter and sugar in a bowl until creamy and stiff.
- Add the eggs and vanilla, then stir in the buttermilk.
- Add the flour, baking powder, baking soda, cinnamon powder, ginger, star anise and cardamom, as well as a pinch of salt.
- Pour the batter in a muffin tin lined with muffin papers and bake in the preheated oven at 350F for 20 minutes or until golden brown.
- Allow to cool down in the pan.
- For the frosting, mix the butter in a bowl until creamy and light.
- Add the sugar, ½ cup at a time, and mix well for at least 5 minutes.
- Add the vanilla and mix well.
- Top each cupcake with the frosting and serve fresh.

Nutritional information per serving

Calories: 399
Fat: 24.0g
Protein: 3.2g
Carbohydrates: 44.1g

LACK MAGIC CUPCAKES

Time: 1 ½ hours

Servings: 14

Ingredients:

Cupcakes:
1 ½ cups all-purpose flour
¼ teaspoon salt
1 ½ teaspoons baking powder
¾ cup cocoa powder
1 teaspoon instant coffee
½ cup buttermilk
2 eggs
½ cup canola oil
¼ cup butter, softened
1 teaspoon vanilla extract
1 cup white sugar
Frosting:
1 cup butter, softened
2 cups powdered sugar
1 teaspoon instant coffee
¼ cup cocoa powder
2 tablespoons milk

Directions:

- For the cupcakes, mix the butter, oil and sugar in a bowl until creamy and pale.
- Add the eggs and mix well. Stir in the vanilla and buttermilk then add the rest of the ingredients and mix with a spatula.
- Spoon the batter in a muffin tin lined with muffin papers.
- Bake the muffins in the preheated oven at 350F for 20 minutes or until they pass the toothpick test.
- Allow to cool in the pan.
- For the frosting, mix the butter in a bowl until creamy and pale.
- Add the sugar, gradually, then whip until fluffy.
- Stir in the coffee, cocoa powder and milk and mix for a few additional minutes.
- Spoon the frosting in a pastry bag and pipe it over each cupcake.
- Serve the cupcakes chilled.

Nutritional information per serving

Calories: 412
Fat: 25.9g

Protein: 3.8g   Carbohydrates: 45.8g

LMOND ROSE CUPCAKES

Time: 1 ½ hours   Servings: 12

Ingredients:

Cupcakes: ¼ teaspoon salt
½ cup butter, softened   1 ½ teaspoons baking powder
½ cup white sugar   Frosting:
1 teaspoon rose water   1 cup butter, softened
1 /2 teaspoon almond extract   2 cups powdered sugar
2 eggs   1 teaspoon rose water
1 ¼ cups almond flour   Rose petals to decorate
¼ cup all-purpose flour

Directions:

- For the cupcakes, mix the butter and sugar in a bowl until creamy and fluffy. Add the rose water and almond extract, as well as the eggs and mix well.
- Fold in the flours, salt and baking powder and mix with a spatula.
- Spoon the batter in a muffin tin lined with muffin papers and bake in the preheated oven at 350F for 20 minutes or until well risen and golden brown.
- Allow to cool in the pan.
- For the frosting, mix the butter and sugar in a bowl until creamy and fluffy and pale.
- Add the rose water and mix well.
- Pipe the frosting on top of each cupcake and decorate with rose petals.

Nutritional information per serving

Calories: 350   Protein: 2.1g
Fat: 25.3g   Carbohydrates: 31.3g

ONEY LEMON MUFFINS

Time: 1 hour   Servings: 12

Ingredients:

1 ½ cups all-purpose flour   ¼ cup honey
¼ teaspoon salt   1 tablespoon lemon zest
1 ½ teaspoons baking powder   2 tablespoons lemon juice
2 eggs   ¼ cup canola oil
½ cup milk   ½ cup white chocolate chips

Directions:

- Mix the flour, salt and baking powder in a bowl.
- Add the rest of the ingredients and mix well.
- Spoon the batter in a muffin tin lined with baking muffin papers and bake in the preheated oven at 350F for 20 minutes or until well risen and golden brown.
- Allow to cool down before serving.

Nutritional information per serving

Calories: 174   Protein: 3.3g
Fat: 7.9g   Carbohydrates: 23.0g

CHOCOLATE MALT CUPCAKES

Time: 1 hour
Servings: 18

Ingredients:
Cupcakes:
2 ¼ cups all-purpose flour
¾ cups cocoa powder
½ teaspoon salt
½ teaspoon baking soda
1 teaspoon baking powder
1 cup milk
1 cup malted milk powder
4 eggs

1 cup sour cream
1 teaspoon vanilla extract
¼ cup canola oil
Frosting:
1 ½ cups butter, softened
½ cup malted milk powder
2 cups powdered sugar
1 teaspoon vanilla extract

Directions:
- For the cupcakes, mix the milk, milk powder, eggs, sour cream, vanilla and oil in a bowl.
- Add the flour, cocoa powder, salt, baking soda and baking powder and mix with a spatula.
- Spoon the batter in a muffin tin lined with muffin papers.
- Bake in the preheated oven at 350F for 20-25 minutes or until they pass the toothpick test.
- Allow to cool down before serving.
- For the frosting, mix the butter in a bowl until airy.
- Add the milk powder and mix 2 minutes on high speed, then stir in the sugar and vanilla and continue mixing for 5 minutes on high speed.
- Pipe the frosting on top of the cupcakes and serve them fresh.

Nutritional information per serving
Calories: 389
Fat: 23.6g

Protein: 5.8g
Carbohydrates: 41.3g

S NICKERS CUPCAKES

Time: 1 ½ hours

Servings: 16

Ingredients:
Cupcakes:
1 ½ cups all-purpose flour
½ cup cocoa powder
¼ teaspoon salt
1 ½ teaspoons baking powder
4 eggs
1 cup light brown sugar
½ cup canola oil
1 cup buttermilk
1 teaspoon lemon juice

1 teaspoon vanilla extract
Frosting:
½ cup smooth peanut butter
½ cup butter, softened
½ cup cocoa powder
2 cups powdered sugar
1 teaspoon vanilla extract
Topping:
6 snickers, chopped

Directions:
- For the cupcakes, mix the eggs and sugar in a bowl until fluffy and pale. Add the oil and mix well then stir in the buttermilk, lemon juice and vanilla.
- Fold in the flour, cocoa powder, salt and baking powder then spoon the batter in a muffin tin lined with muffin papers.
- Bake the cupcakes in the preheated oven at 350F for 20 minutes or until they pass the toothpick test.
- Allow to cool down in the pan.
- For the frosting, mix the butter and peanut butter in a bowl until fluffy.
- Stir in the sugar, cocoa powder and vanilla and mix well for a few additional minutes until fluffy and well mixed.
- Pipe the frosting over each cupcake and serve them fresh.

Nutritional information per serving
Calories: 399
Fat: 22.4g
Protein: 7.4g
Carbohydrates: 45.8g

S WEET POTATO MAPLE MUFFINS

Time: 1 hour

Servings: 12

Ingredients:

2 cups all-purpose flour
¼ teaspoon salt
1 ½ teaspoons baking powder
½ teaspoon cinnamon powder
½ teaspoon ground ginger
½ teaspoon all-spice powder

3 eggs
1 cup light brown sugar
2/3 cup canola oil
1 cup sweet potato puree
1 cup milk
1 teaspoon vanilla extract

Directions:
- Mix the flour, salt, baking powder, cinnamon, ginger and all-spice powder in a bowl.
- Add the rest of the ingredients and mix well then pour the batter in a muffin tin lined with muffin papers.
- Bake the muffins in the preheated oven at 350F for 20 minutes or until golden brown and fragrant.
- Allow to cool down before serving.

Nutritional information per serving

Calories: 278
Fat: 13.9g

Protein: 4.6g
Carbohydrates: 34.2g

D EEP CHOCOLATE PUMPKIN MUFFINS

Time: 1 hour

Servings: 12

Ingredients:

1 ½ cups all-purpose flour
¼ cup cocoa powder
1 teaspoon baking soda
½ teaspoon baking powder
¼ teaspoon cinnamon powder
1 pinch nutmeg
1 cup pumpkin puree

½ cup buttermilk
1 teaspoon vanilla extract
½ cup canola oil
3 eggs
2/3 cup light brown sugar
½ cup dark chocolate chips

Directions:
- Mix the eggs and sugar in a bowl until fluffy and pale.
- Add the canola oil and vanilla, as well as buttermilk and pumpkin puree.
- Fold in the dry ingredients then add the chocolate chips.
- Spoon the batter in a muffin tin lined with muffin papers.
- Bake the muffins in the preheated oven at 350F for 20 minutes or until they pass the toothpick test.
- Allow to cool in the pan before serving.

Nutritional information per serving

Calories: 223
Fat: 12.0g

Protein: 4.2g
Carbohydrates: 26.5g

W HITE CHOCOLATE PUMPKIN CUPCAKES

Time: 1 ½ hours

Servings: 12

Ingredients:

Cupcakes:
½ cup butter, softened
2 tablespoons canola oil
2/3 cup light brown sugar
2 eggs

1 cup pumpkin puree
½ cup buttermilk
1 ½ cups all-purpose flour
¼ teaspoon salt
1 teaspoon cinnamon powder

½ teaspoon ground ginger
¼ teaspoon ground cardamom
Frosting:

1 cup heavy cream
2 cups white chocolate chips

Directions:
- For the cupcakes, mix the butter, oil and sugar in a bowl until fluffy and pale.
- Add the eggs and mix well then stir in the pumpkin puree and buttermilk.
- Fold in the rest of the ingredients then spoon the batter in a muffin tin lined with muffin papers.
- Bake in the preheated oven at 350F for 20-25 minutes or until well risen and fragrant.
- Allow to cool in the pan completely.
- For the frosting, bring the cream to the boiling point in a saucepan. Remove from heat and add the chocolate. Mix until melted then allow to cool down.
- Pipe the frosting over each cupcake and serve them fresh.

Nutritional information per serving

Calories: 385
Fat: 23.8g

Protein: 5.1g
Carbohydrates: 39.2g

UICK COFFEE MUFFINS

Time: 1 hour

Servings: 12

Ingredients:

1 ½ cups white sugar
1 ¾ cups all-purpose flour
¾ cup cocoa powder
½ teaspoon baking soda
1 teaspoon baking powder
¼ teaspoon salt

2 eggs
1 cup buttermilk
½ cup canola oil
1 teaspoon vanilla extract
¼ cup brewed espresso
½ cup hot water

Directions:
- Mix the dry ingredients in a bowl.
- Add the rest of the ingredients and give it a quick mix.
- Pour the batter in a muffin tin lined with muffin papers and bake in the preheated oven at 350F for 20-25 minutes or until they pass the toothpick test.
- Allow to cool down before serving.

Nutritional information per serving

Calories: 277
Fat: 10.9g

Protein: 4.6g
Carbohydrates: 44.1g

Z ESTY PISTACHIO MUFFINS

Time: 1 hour

Servings: 12

Ingredients:

3 eggs
1 cup white sugar
¼ cup canola oil
1 teaspoon vanilla extract
¼ cup plain yogurt

1 cup ground pistachio
1 cup all-purpose flour
¼ teaspoon salt
1 teaspoon baking powder
1 cup fresh raspberries

Directions:
- Mix the eggs and sugar in a bowl until double in volume.
- Add the oil, vanilla and yogurt and mix well.
- Fold in the rest of the ingredients then spoon the batter in a muffin tin lined with muffin papers.
- Bake the muffins in the preheated oven at 350F for 20 minutes or until well risen and golden brown.
- Allow to cool in the pan before serving.

Nutritional information per serving

Calories: 184

Fat: 6.7g

Protein: 3.3g

Carbohydrates: 28.8g

*F*UNFETTI BANANA MUFFINS

Time: 1 hour

Servings: 12

Ingredients:

1 ½ cups all-purpose flour

½ cup almond flour

¼ teaspoon salt

1 teaspoon baking powder

2 eggs

½ cup white sugar

½ cup canola oil

1 teaspoon vanilla extract

½ cup milk

¼ cup colorful sprinkles

Directions:

- Mix the eggs and sugar in a bowl until fluffy and pale.
- Add the oil, vanilla and milk and mix well.
- Fold in the flours, salt and baking powder then add the sprinkles.
- Spoon the batter in a muffin tin lined with muffin papers and bake in the preheated oven at 350F for 20 minutes or until golden brown and well risen.
- Allow to cool down before serving.

Nutritional information per serving

Calories: 204

Fat: 11.2g

Protein: 3.3g

Carbohydrates: 23.3g

*V*ANILLA CUPCAKES WITH CHOCOLATE BUTTERCREAM

Time: 1 ½ hours

Servings: 14

Ingredients:

Cupcakes:

2 cups all-purpose flour

2/3 cup white sugar

¼ teaspoon salt

2 teaspoons baking powder

1 cup butter, softened

2 eggs

1 cup milk

1 tablespoon vanilla extract

Frosting:

2 egg whites

½ cup white sugar

1 teaspoon vanilla extract

1 cup butter, softened

1 cup dark chocolate chips, melted

Directions:

- For the cupcakes, mix the flour, sugar, salt and baking powder in a bowl. Add the butter and mix until grainy.
- Stir in the eggs, milk and vanilla and give it a quick mix.
- Spoon the batter in a muffin tin lined with muffin papers and bake in the preheated oven at 350F for 20 minutes or until they pass the toothpick test.
- Allow the cupcakes to cool in the pan.
- For the frosting, mix the egg whites and sugar in a bowl. Place over a hot water bath and keep over heat until the sugar has melted.
- Remove from heat and whip for 5-7 minutes until glossy and fluffy.
- Add the butter and mix for 2-3 minutes until fluffy and creamy.
- Stir in the chocolate and mix briefly then pipe the buttercream over each cupcake.
- Serve the cupcakes fresh.

Nutritional information per serving

Calories: 424

Fat: 29.8g

Protein: 4.6g

Carbohydrates: 37.5g

$\mathcal{O}$ RANGE SODA CUPCAKES

Time: 1 ½ cups

Servings: 12

Ingredients:

Cupcakes:
1 ½ cups all-purpose flour
¼ teaspoon salt
1 ½ teaspoons baking powder
½ cup white sugar
3 egg whites
¼ cup vegetable oil
1 ¼ cups orange soda

1 teaspoon orange zest
Frosting:
½ cup butter, softened
1 cup cream cheese
2 cups powdered sugar
2 tablespoons heavy cream
1 teaspoon vanilla extract

Directions:
- For the cupcakes, mix the egg whites, oil, orange soda and orange zest in a bowl.
- Add the rest of the ingredients then spoon the batter in a muffin tin lined with muffin papers.
- Bake in the preheated oven at 350F for 20 minutes or until they pass the toothpick test.
- Allow to cool in the pan.
- For the frosting, mix the butter and cream cheese in a bowl until fluffy.
- Add the sugar and mix for 5 minutes on high speed.
- Stir in the cream and vanilla and mix for 1 additional minute.
- Pipe the frosting over each cupcake and serve them fresh.

Nutritional information per serving

Calories: 368
Fat: 20.1g

Protein: 4.1g
Carbohydrates: 44.4g

$\mathcal{P}$ INK LEMONADE CUPCAKES

Time: 1 ½ hours

Servings: 12

Ingredients:

Cupcakes:
2 ½ cups all-purpose flour
¼ teaspoon salt
2 teaspoons baking powder
1 cup white sugar
¾ cup butter, softened
2 eggs
1 egg white
1 teaspoon vanilla extract

2 tablespoons lemon juice
1 tablespoon lemon zest
½ cup milk
1 drop red food coloring
Frosting:
1 cup butter
2 cups powdered sugar
1 drop red food coloring

Directions:
- For the cupcakes, mix the butter and sugar in a bowl until fluffy and pale.
- Add the eggs and egg white and mix well.
- Stir in the vanilla, lemon juice, lemon zest, milk and food coloring and mix well.
- Add the dry ingredients and fold them in with a spatula.
- Spoon the batter in a muffin tin lined with muffin papers.
- Bake in the preheated oven at 350F for 20 minutes or until golden brown and well risen.
- Allow to cool in the pan.
- For the frosting, mix the butter in a bowl until fluffy. Add the sugar and continue mixing for a few minutes on high speed.
- Add the food coloring then pipe the frosting over each cupcake.
- Serve the cupcakes chilled.

Nutritional information per serving

Calories: 442

Fat: 24.1g

Protein: 3.9g   Carbohydrates: 54.6g

REO CREAM CUPCAKES

Time: 1 ½ hours   Servings: 12

Ingredients:

Cupcakes: 1 cup buttermilk
2 cups all-purpose flour   1 tablespoon vanilla extract
¼ teaspoon salt   6 Oreo cookies, crushed
2 teaspoons baking powder   Topping:
1 cup white sugar   2 cups heavy cream, whipped
1 cup butter, softened   6 Oreo cookies, chopped
2 eggs

Directions:
- For the cupcakes, mix the flour, salt, baking powder and sugar in a bowl.
- Add the butter and mix until grainy.
- In a small bowl, combine the eggs, buttermilk and vanilla. Pour this mixture gradually over the flour and mix for 1 minute on high speed.
- Spoon the batter in a muffin tin lined with muffin papers.
- Bake in the preheated oven at 350F for 20 minutes or until well risen and golden brown.
- Allow to cool down before serving.

Nutritional information per serving

Calories: 412   Protein: 4.9g
Fat: 25.8g   Carbohydrates: 41.9g

$\mathcal{V}$ODKA CUPCAKES

Time: 1 ½ hours   Servings: 12

Ingredients:

Cupcakes: Frosting:
1 cup heavy cream   1 cup butter, softened
2 eggs   2 ½ cups powdered sugar
¼ cup vodka   1 tablespoon heavy cream
½ cup white sugar   Topping:
1 teaspoon vanilla extract   ½ cup dark chocolate chips
2 cups all-purpose flour   ¼ cup heavy cream
2 teaspoons baking powder   2 tablespoons vodka
¼ teaspoon salt

Directions:
- For the cupcakes, mix the cream, eggs, vodka, sugar and vanilla in a bowl.
- Stir in the flour, baking powder and salt and mix quickly.
- Spoon the batter in a muffin tin lined with muffin papers and bake in the preheated oven at 350F for 20 minutes or until well risen and golden brown.
- Allow to cool down in the pan.
- For the frosting, mix the butter in a bowl until pale. Add the sugar and mix on high speed until fluffy and light.
- Stir in the cream and mix for a few more minutes.
- Pipe the frosting over each cupcake.
- For the topping, melt the chocolate and cream together in a heatproof bowl over a hot water bath.
- Remove from heat and add the vodka. Allow to cool down then drizzle it over the frosted cupcakes.
- Serve the cupcakes fresh.

Nutritional information per serving

Calories: 439   Fat: 22.7g

Protein: 3.9g   Carbohydrates: 53.3g

OCHA MADNESS CUPCAKES

Time: 1 ½ hours   Servings: 12

Ingredients:

Cupcakes: 1 teaspoon baking soda
2 eggs   ¼ teaspoon salt
1 cup white sugar   Frosting:
2 teaspoon vanilla extract   2 egg whites
1 teaspoon apple cider vinegar   ½ cup white sugar
½ cup water   1 pinch salt
1 teaspoon instant coffee   1 cup butter, softened
½ cup canola oil   1 cup dark chocolate chips, melted and cooled
1 ½ cups all-purpose flour   1 teaspoon instant coffee
½ cup cocoa powder

Directions:

- For the cupcakes, mix the eggs and sugar in a bowl until fluffy and pale.
- Add the vanilla, vinegar, water, coffee and oil and mix well.
- Stir in the dry ingredients then pour the batter in a muffin tin lined with muffin papers.
- Bake the cupcakes in the preheated oven at 350F for 20 minutes or until they pass the toothpick test.
- Allow to cool in the pan.
- For the frosting, mix the egg whites, sugar and salt in a bowl and place over a hot water bath. Keep on heat until the sugar has melted then remove and start whipping until stiff and glossy and chilled.
- Add the butter, all at once, and mix a few minutes until it comes together into a silky cream.
- Stir in the chocolate and coffee and mix well.
- Pipe the frosting over each cupcake and serve them fresh.

Nutritional information per serving

Calories: 437   Protein: 4.6g
Fat: 28.5g   Carbohydrates: 45.8g

UTELLA STUFFED STRAWBERRY MUFFINS

Time: 1 hour   Servings: 12

Ingredients:

2 eggs   2 cups all purpose flour
1 cup white sugar   ¼ teaspoon salt
1 teaspoon vanilla extract   2 teaspoons baking powder
½ cup canola oil   1 cup strawberries, sliced
¾ cup milk   ½ cup Nutella

Directions:

- Mix the eggs and sugar in a bowl until fluffy and pale.
- Add the vanilla and oil and mix well.
- Stir in the milk then add the flour, salt and baking powder and mix with a spatula.
- Spoon half of the batter evenly in a muffin tin lined with muffin papers.
- Top with a dollop of Nutella then spoon the remaining batter over the Nutella.
- Bake in the preheated oven at 350F for 20 minutes or until fluffy and golden brown.
- Allow to cool in the pan before serving.

Nutritional information per serving

Calories: 259   Carbohydrates: 36.5g
Fat: 11.4g
Protein: 3.8g

$\mathcal{M}$ILLET FLOUR PLUM MUFFINS

Time: 1 hour

Servings: 12

Ingredients:

1 cup millet flour
1 cup whole wheat flour
½ cup light brown sugar
¼ teaspoon salt
1 teaspoon baking soda

2 eggs
1 cup almond milk
¼ cup coconut oil, melted
6 plums, pitted and sliced

Directions:
- Mix the flours, salt, sugar and baking soda in a bowl.
- Add the rest of the ingredients and mix well.
- Fold in the plums then spoon the batter in a muffin tin lined with special muffin papers.
- Bake the muffins in the preheated oven at 350F for 20 minutes or until golden brown and well risen.
- Allow to cool down before serving.

Nutritional information per serving

Calories: 210
Fat: 10.7g

Protein: 4.0g
Carbohydrates: 26.2g

$\mathcal{Y}$OGURT VANILLA BERRY MUFFINS

Time: 1 hour

Servings: 12

Ingredients:

2 eggs
¼ cup canola oil
1 cup Greek yogurt
1 tablespoon vanilla extract
1 ¾ cups all-purpose flour

¼ teaspoon salt
1 teaspoon baking powder
½ teaspoon baking soda
1 cup mixed berries

Directions:
- Mix the eggs, oil, yogurt and vanilla in a bowl.
- Add the flour, salt, baking powder and baking soda and give it a quick mix just until incorporated.
- Fold in the berries then spoon the batter in a muffin tin lined with muffin papers.
- Bake in the preheated oven at 350F for 20 minutes or until they pass the toothpick test.
- Allow to cool in the pan before serving.

Nutritional information per serving

Calories: 140
Fat: 5.8g

Protein: 4.6g
Carbohydrates: 16.4g

$\mathcal{P}$UMPKIN PECAN CRUNCH MUFFINS

Time: 1 ¼ hours

Servings: 12

Ingredients:

Muffins:
1 ½ cups all-purpose flour
½ cup ground pecans
¼ teaspoon salt
1 teaspoon baking soda
1 teaspoon pumpkin pie spices
½ cup light brown sugar
1 cup pumpkin puree

½ cup coconut oil, melted
2 eggs
½ cup coconut milk
Pecan crunch:
½ cup pecans, chopped
½ cup all-purpose flour
¼ cup butter, chilled
2 tablespoons light brown sugar

Directions:
- For the muffins, mix the dry ingredients in a bowl.
- Add the rest of the ingredients, all at once, and give it a quick mix just until incorporated.
- Spoon the batter in a muffin tin lined with baking muffin papers.
- For the pecan crunch, mix the ingredients in a bowl until sandy.
- Spread the crunch over the muffins and bake in the preheated oven at 350F for 20 minutes or until the top is crunchy and golden brown.
- Allow to cool in the pan before serving.

Nutritional information per serving

Calories: 274
Fat: 18.0g

Protein: 3.8g
Carbohydrates: 26.0g

*H*EALTHY CHOCOLATE MUFFINS

Time: 1 hour

Servings: 12

Ingredients:

1 ½ cups whole wheat flour
1 ½ teaspoons baking powder
¼ teaspoon salt
½ cup cocoa powder
1 cup plain yogurt

1 egg
⅓ cup maple syrup
½ cup low fat milk
1 teaspoon vanilla extract

Directions:
- Mix the flour, baking powder, salt and cocoa powder in a bowl.
- Add the rest of the ingredients and give it a quick mix.
- Spoon the batter in a muffin tin lined with muffin papers and bake in the preheated oven at 350F for 20 minutes or until they pass the toothpick test.
- Allow to cool in the pan before serving.

Nutritional information per serving

Calories: 125
Fat: 1.4g

Protein: 4.2g
Carbohydrates: 25.0g

*W*HOLE WHEAT BANANA MUFFINS

Time: 1 hour

Servings: 12

Ingredients:

2 cups whole wheat flour
2 teaspoons baking powder
¼ teaspoon salt
¼ teaspoon cinnamon powder
½ cup light brown sugar

2 eggs
2 bananas, mashed
¼ cup canola oil
1 cup buttermilk

Directions:
- Mix the dry ingredients in a bowl.
- Add the rest of the ingredients, all at once, and give it a quick mix with a whisk.
- Pour the batter in a muffin tin lined with baking muffin papers and bake in the preheated oven at 350F for 20 minutes or until they pass the toothpick test.
- Allow to cool down before serving.

Nutritional information per serving

Calories: 176
Fat: 5.7g
Protein: 4.0g
Carbohydrates: 27.7g

*C*HOCOLATE TAHINI MUFFINS

Time: 1 hour

Servings: 12

Ingredients:

4 eggs
¼ cup tahini paste
¼ cup maple syrup
¼ cup light brown sugar
1 teaspoon vanilla extract

¼ cup milk
1 ½ cups all-purpose flour
¼ cup cocoa powder
¼ teaspoon salt
1 teaspoon baking powder

Directions:
- Mix the eggs, tahini paste, maple syrup, sugar, vanilla and milk in a bowl.
- Add the flour, cocoa powder, salt and baking powder and give it a quick mix.
- Spoon the batter in a muffin tin lined with baking muffin papers.
- Bake in the preheated oven at 350F for 20 minutes or until a toothpick inserted in the center of the muffins comes out clean.
- Allow the muffins to cool down completely in the pan.

Nutritional information per serving

Calories: 144
Fat: 4.6g

Protein: 4.8g
Carbohydrates: 21.9g

*D*OUBLE CHOCOLATE NUTELLA MUFFINS

Time: 1 hour

Servings: 12

Ingredients:

½ cup Nutella
3 eggs
1 teaspoon vanilla extract
½ cup canola oil
½ cup milk
2 cups all-purpose flour
¼ cup cocoa powder

¼ cup white sugar
¼ teaspoon salt
1 teaspoon baking powder
½ teaspoon baking soda
½ cup dark chocolate chips
½ cup chopped hazelnuts

Directions:
- Mix the Nutella, eggs, vanilla, oil and milk in a bowl.
- Add the flour, cocoa powder, sugar, salt, baking powder and baking soda and give it a quick mix.
- Fold in the chocolate chips then spoon the batter in a muffin tin lined with your favorite muffin papers.
- Top with chopped hazelnuts and bake in the preheated oven at 350F for 20 minutes or until they pass the toothpick test.
- Allow to cool in the pan before serving or storing away.

Nutritional information per serving

Calories: 258
Fat: 15.0g

Protein: 5.1g
Carbohydrates: 27.5g

*S*WEET POTATO ZUCCHINI MUFFINS

Time: 1 hour

Servings: 12

Ingredients:

1 cup sweet potato puree
1 cup grated zucchinis
¼ cup light brown sugar
¼ cup heavy cream

2 eggs
¼ cup canola oil
1 teaspoon orange zest
2 cups all-purpose flour

1 teaspoon baking powder
½ teaspoon baking soda

¼ teaspoon salt

Directions:
- Mix the sweet potato puree, zucchinis, sugar, cream, eggs, oil and orange zest in a bowl.
- Add the dry ingredients and give it a quick mix with a spatula.
- Spoon the batter in a muffin tin lined with your favorite muffin papers.
- Bake in the preheated oven at 350F for 20 minutes or until well risen and the muffins pass the toothpick test.
- Allow to cool in the pan before serving.

Nutritional information per serving
Calories: 170
Fat: 6.5g
Protein: 3.6g
Carbohydrates: 24.5g

French Desserts

CLASSIC FRENCH TOAST WITH HONEY

Time: 20 minutes

Servings: 4

Ingredients:

4 slices brioche bread
2 eggs, beaten
1 cup milk

1 teaspoon vanilla extract
2 tablespoons butter
¼ cup honey for serving

Directions:
- Mix the eggs, milk and vanilla in a bowl.
- Heat the butter in a skillet.
- Dip the bread slices in the egg and milk mixture then drop them in the hot butter.
- Fry on each side until golden brown and crusty.
- Serve the French toast warm, drizzled with honey.

Nutritional information per serving

Calories: 302
Fat: 12.3g

Protein: 7.7g
Carbohydrates: 41.1g

FRENCH APPLE TART

Time: 1 ½ hours

Servings: 10

Ingredients:

Crust:
3/4 cup butter, chilled and cubed
1 ¼ cups all-purpose flour
¼ teaspoon salt
2 tablespoons powdered sugar
4-6 tablespoons cold water
Filling:

4 egg yolks
2/3 cup white sugar
¼ cup cornstarch
2 cups milk
1 teaspoon vanilla extract
1 pinch salt
4 apples, peeled and finely sliced

Directions:
- For the crust, mix the flour, salt and sugar in a bowl. Add the butter and mix until grainy.
- Stir in the water, spoon by spoon, and mix until the dough comes together.
- Wrap the dough in plastic wrap and place in the fridge for 30 minutes.
- In the meantime, bring the milk to the boiling point in a saucepan.
- Mix the eggs, sugar and cornstarch in a bowl until fluffy and pale.
- Add the hot milk and place back on heat. Cook until thickened then remove from heat and allow to cool. Stir in the vanilla extract.
- Place the dough on a floured working surface and roll it into a thin sheet. Transfer the dough in a 9-inch tart pan and press it well on the bottom and sides of the pan. Trim the edges if needed.
- Bake the crust in the preheated oven at 350F for 10 minutes.
- Remove from the oven and fill the crust with the vanilla pastry cream.
- Top with apple slices and continue baking for 15-20 additional minutes.
- Serve the tart chilled.

Nutritional information per serving

Calories: 332
Fat: 16.9g
Protein: 4.6g
Carbohydrates: 42.5g

CHOCOLATE ÉCLAIRS

Time: 1 ½ hours

Servings: 20

Ingredients:

Éclairs:
½ cup water
½ cup milk
¾ cup butter
1 teaspoon sugar
½ teaspoon salt
1 cup all-purpose flour
5 eggs, beaten

Chocolate filling:
1 ½ cups heavy cream
1 ½ cups dark chocolate chips
1 teaspoon vanilla extract
Glaze:
1 ½ cups dark chocolate chips
1 tablespoon canola oil

Directions:

- For the éclairs, mix the water, milk, butter, sugar and salt in a saucepan.
- Place over medium flame and bring to a boil.
- Add the flour, all at once, and mix well with a spatula until thickened and the dough comes together into a ball.
- Allow the dough to cool down for 10 minutes then stir in the eggs and mix well.
- Spoon the batter in a pastry bag and pipe it on a baking tray lined with parchment paper.
- Bake in the preheated oven at 350F for 15-20 minutes or until well risen, golden and crisp.
- Allow to cool in the pan.
- For the filling, bring the cream to the boiling point. Remove from heat and add the chocolate. Mix until melted and smooth then allow to cool down and stir in the vanilla.
- Fill the éclairs with the chocolate cream.
- For the glaze, melt the chocolate with the oil in a heatproof bowl over a hot water bath.
- Dip the éclairs in the glaze and place on a wire rack.
- Serve them chilled and set.

Nutritional information per serving

Calories: 225
Fat: 17.0g

Protein: 3.7g
Carbohydrates: 17.6g

CHERRY CLAFOUTIS

Time: 1 hour

Servings: 8

Ingredients:

1 ½ cups milk
1 teaspoon vanilla extract
½ cup white sugar
2 tablespoons brandy

6 eggs
¼ cup all-purpose flour
¼ teaspoon salt
3 cups cherries, pitted or unpitted

Directions:

- Mix the milk, vanilla, sugar, brandy and eggs in a bowl.
- Stir in the flour and salt and mix well.
- Place the cherries in a deep dish baking tray greased with butter.
- Pour the batter over the cherries and bake in the preheated oven at 350F for 25 minutes or until set.
- Serve the clafoutis chilled.

Nutritional information per serving

Calories: 203
Fat: 4.4g

Protein: 7.3g
Carbohydrates: 31.0g

TART TATIN

Time: 1 hour

Servings: 8

Ingredients:

½ cup butter, chilled and cubed
1 ¼ cups all-purpose flour
¼ teaspoon salt
4-6 tablespoons cold water

4 apples, peeled, cored and quartered
1 cup white sugar
1 teaspoon cinnamon powder

Directions:

- Melt the sugar in a heavy saucepan until it has an amber color.
- Drizzle the sugar on the bottom of a round cake pan.
- Arrange the apple slices over the dark color.
- For the dough, mix the butter, flour and salt in a bowl until grainy.
- Add the water, spoon after spoon, until the dough comes together.
- Place the dough on a floured working surface and roll it into a thin sheet, as large as your pan.
- Place the dough over the apples.
- Bake in the preheated oven at 350F for 25 minutes or until golden brown.
- When the tart is done, turn it upside down on a platter and serve it chilled.

Nutritional information per serving

Calories: 314
Fat: 11.9g

Protein: 2.4g
Carbohydrates: 52.5g

C RÈME BRULEE

Time: 1 hour

Servings: 6

Ingredients:

2 cups milk
1 cup heavy cream
6 egg yolks

1 teaspoon vanilla extract
1 cup white sugar

Directions:

- Mix the milk, cream, egg yolks and vanilla in a bowl.
- Pour the mixture in 4 ramekins and arrange them in a deep dish baking pan.
- Pour hot water in the pan, around the ramekins and bake in the preheated oven at 300F for 40 minutes.
- When done, top the ramekins with sugar and place under the broiler for 2 minutes until caramelized and golden.
- Serve the crème brulee chilled.

Nutritional information per serving

Calories: 291
Fat: 13.6g

Protein: 5.8g
Carbohydrates: 38.6g

F AR BRETON

Time: 1 hour

Servings: 10

Ingredients:

4 eggs
3 cups milk
½ cup heavy cream
1 teaspoon vanilla extract

1 ½ cups all-purpose flour
¼ teaspoon salt
1 ½ cups dried prunes, pitted

Directions:

- Mix the eggs, milk, cream and vanilla in a bowl.
- Add the flour and salt and mix well.
- Fold in the prunes then pour the mixture in a greased deep dish baking pan.
- Bake in the preheated oven at 350F for 25 minutes or until set.
- Serve the dessert chilled.

Nutritional information per serving

Calories: 213
Fat: 5.8g

Protein: 7.2g
Carbohydrates: 34.6g

F RENCH LEMON TART

Time: 1 ½ hour

Servings: 10

Ingredients:

Tart:
½ cup butter, softened
½ cup powdered sugar
1 egg
2 cups all-purpose flour
½ teaspoon baking powder
¼ teaspoon salt

Filling:
½ cup butter
1 cup white sugar
1 pinch salt
½ cup lemon juice
2 tablespoons lemon zest

Directions:

- For the tart crust, mix the butter with sugar until creamy and fluffy
- Add the egg and mix well then stir in the flour, baking powder and salt.
- Place the dough on a floured working surface and roll it into a thin sheet.
- Place the dough on a tart pan and press it on the bottom and sides. Trim off the edges.
- Bake the crust in the preheated oven at 350F for 20 minutes or until golden brown on the edges.
- Allow the crust to cool down.
- For the filling, mix all the ingredients in a heatproof bowl. Place over a hot water bath and cook until thickened.
- Pour the filling into the crust and allow to cool down and set before serving.

Nutritional information per serving

Calories: 362
Fat: 19.2g

Protein: 3.5g
Carbohydrates: 45.7g

F RENCH CANNELES

Time: 1 ½ hours

Servings: 20

Ingredients:

2 cups milk
2 tablespoons butter
1 teaspoon vanilla extract
1 pinch salt

½ cup white sugar
3 eggs
2 tablespoons dark rum

Directions:

- Mix all the ingredients in a bowl until creamy.
- Pour the canneles in a caneles pan. Place the pan in another pan, slightly deeper and pour hot water in the pan.
- Bake in the preheated oven at 350F until they turn golden brown.
- Allow them to cool down slightly then remove them from the pan and serve them chilled.

Nutritional information per serving

Calories: 54
Fat: 2.3g

Protein: 1.6g
Carbohydrates: 6.3g

F RENCH BEIGNETS

Time: 1 hour

Servings: 20

Ingredients:

2 cups all-purpose flour

¼ teaspoon salt

¼ cup sugar

2 eggs

¼ cup butter, melted

1 teaspoon orange blossom water

1 teaspoon vanilla extract

Oil for frying

Directions:
- Mix the sugar, eggs, butter, orange water and vanilla in a bowl until pale and creamy.
- Add the flour and salt and knead the dough for a few minutes until elastic.
- Allow the dough to rest for 10 minutes then place it on a floured working surface and roll it into a thin sheet.
- Cut strips of dough with a sharp knife.
- Heat enough oil in a deep frying pan.
- Drop the strips of dough in the hot pan and fry them on each side until golden brown.
- Remove the beignets on paper towels and serve them with powdered sugar.

Nutritional information per serving

Calories: 82

Fat: 2.9g

Protein: 1.9g

Carbohydrates: 12.1g

*T*ARTE *T*ROPEZIENNE

Time: 2 hours

Servings: 10

Ingredients:

Brioche dough:

2 cups all-purpose flour

¼ teaspoon salt

¼ teaspoon instant yeast

2 tablespoons milk

¼ cup white sugar

3 eggs

1 teaspoon vanilla extract

1/4 cup butter, melted

Filling:

2 cups milk

4 egg yolks

½ cup white sugar

¼ cup cornstarch

¼ teaspoon salt

1 tablespoon vanilla extract

1 cup butter, softened

Directions:
- For the brioche dough, mix the warm milk with the yeast in a bowl until melted.
- Add the eggs, sugar, vanilla and butter then stir in the flour and salt.
- Knead the dough for a few minutes until elastic.
- Allow the dough to rest and rise for 1 hour.
- Place the dough on a floured working surface and roll it into a disc.
- Bake the brioche in the preheated oven at 350F for 25-30 minutes or until well risen and golden brown.
- Allow to cool down.
- For the filling, mix the egg yolks, sugar and cornstarch in a bowl.
- Heat the milk and pour it over the egg yolks. Place back over heat and cook until thickened.
- Allow the cream to cool down then stir in the vanilla.
- Whip the butter in a bowl until fluffy. Add the pastry cream, spoon by spoon, and mix well.
- Cut the brioche disc in half lengthwise and fill it with the pastry cream.
- Serve it fresh.

Nutritional information per serving

Calories: 435

Fat: 27.4g

Protein: 7.3g

Carbohydrates: 40.1g

*F*IG *G*ALETTE

Time: 1 hour

Servings: 10

Ingredients:

½ cup butter, chilled and cubed

1 ½ cups all-purpose flour

2 tablespoons powdered sugar

¼ teaspoon salt

¼ cup sour cream
½ cup butter, softened
1 egg

½ cup light brown sugar
1 cup ground almonds
1 pound fresh figs, quartered

Directions:

- For the dough, mix the chilled butter, flour, sugar and salt in a bowl until grainy.
- Add the sour cream and mix until the dough comes together.
- Place the dough on a floured working surface and roll it into a thin sheet.
- Mix the softened butter, light brown sugar and egg in a bowl until creamy and pale.
- Add the almonds and mix gently. Spoon the mixture over the center of the dough.
- Top with fresh figs then pull the edges of the dough over the filling, leaving the center exposed.
- Bake in the preheated oven at 350F for 25-30 minutes or until crisp and golden on the edges.
- Serve the galette chilled.

Nutritional information per serving

Calories: 451
Fat: 25.4g

Protein: 6.4g
Carbohydrates: 54.3g

B UTTERY MADELEINES

Time: 1 hour

Servings: 12

Ingredients:

¾ cup all-purpose flour
1 pinch salt
½ teaspoon baking powder
2 eggs

½ cup white sugar
1 teaspoon vanilla extract
½ cup butter, melted and cooled

Directions:

- Sift the flour, salt and baking powder in a bowl.
- Mix the eggs and sugar in a bowl until fluffy and light. Add the vanilla and mix well.
- Fold in the flour then add the butter, mixing it gently with a spatula.
- Spoon the batter in a madeleine pan and bake in the preheated oven at 350F for 10-12 minutes or until golden brown and well risen.
- Serve the madeleines chilled.

Nutritional information per serving

Calories: 139
Fat: 8.5g

Protein: 1.8g
Carbohydrates: 14.5g

ERINGUES

Time: 2 hours

Servings: 20

Ingredients:

4 egg whites
1 cup white sugar

¼ teaspoon salt
1 tablespoon vanilla extract

Directions:

- Mix the egg whites, sugar and salt in a heatproof bowl. Place the bowl over a hot water bath and mix until the sugar is melted.
- Remove from heat and whip the egg whites for 7-9 minutes or until fluffy, stiff and glossy.
- Add the vanilla extract then spoon the meringue in a pastry bag and pipe small dollops of mixture on a baking tray lined with baking paper.
- Bake in the preheated oven at 250F for 1 ½ hours.
- Serve the meringues chilled.

Nutritional information per serving

Calories: 43

Fat: 0.0g

Protein: 0.7g

Carbohydrates: 10.1g

OUSSE AU CHOCOLAT

Time: 1 hour

Servings: 4

Ingredients:

4 egg yolks
¼ cup white sugar
1 cup heavy cream

¼ teaspoon salt
6 oz. dark chocolate chips
1 cup heavy cream, whipped

Directions:

- Bring 1 cup of cream to the boiling point.
- Mix the egg yolks and sugar in a bowl until creamy. Add the cream and mix well then place back on heat and cook until thickened.
- Remove from heat and stir in the salt and chocolate. Mix until smooth.
- Allow to cool down then fold in the whipped cream.
- Spoon the mousse into small glasses and serve it chilled.

Nutritional information per serving

Calories: 506
Fat: 38.0g

Protein: 6.8g
Carbohydrates: 43.1g

1 LES FLOTTANTES

Time: 1 ½ hours

Servings: 4

Ingredients:

Crème anglaise:
4 egg yolks
½ cup white sugar
1 teaspoon vanilla extract
2 cups milk
1 pinch nutmeg

Iles flottantes:
2 egg whites
½ cup white sugar
½ teaspoon lemon zest
1 pinch salt
2 cups milk

Directions:

- To make the crème anglaise, bring the milk to the boiling point. Mix the egg yolks and sugar in a bowl until creamy. Add the hot milk and mix well then place the mixture back on heat and cook until thickened. Remove from heat and add the vanilla and nutmeg. Allow to cool down.
- For the iles flottante, mix the egg whites, lemon zest and salt in a bowl until fluffy.
- Add the sugar and continue whipping until glossy and stiff.
- Bring the milk to a boil in a saucepan. Drop spoonfuls of whipped egg whites in the hot milk and cook for 1-2 minutes. Carefully remove on serving platters.
- Top with crème anglaise and serve.

Nutritional information per serving

Calories: 376
Fat: 9.6g

Protein: 12.5g
Carbohydrates: 62.9g

B UTTER COOKIES

Time: 1 ½ hours

Servings: 20

Ingredients:

½ cup butter, softened
½ cup powdered sugar
1 teaspoon vanilla extract

1 egg
½ cup ground almonds
2 cups all-purpose flour

¼ teaspoon salt

Directions:
- Mix the butter and sugar in a bowl until fluffy and pale.
- Add the vanilla and egg and mix well then stir in the almonds, flour and salt.
- Shape the dough into a ball and wrap it in foil. Place in the fridge for 30 minutes.
- Transfer the dough on a floured working surface and roll it into a thin sheet.
- Cut small cookies with your favorite cookie cutters and place them on a baking sheet lined with baking papers.
- Bake in the preheated oven at 350F for 10-12 minutes or until the edges turn slightly golden brown.
- Allow the cookies to cool down before serving.

Nutritional information per serving
Calories: 115
Fat: 6.1g

Protein: 2.1g
Carbohydrates: 13.1g

USTIC PEAR GALETTE

Time: 1 hour

Servings: 8

Ingredients:
½ cup butter, chilled
3 tablespoons powdered sugar
1 cup all-purpose flour
¼ cup whole wheat flour
¼ teaspoon salt

½ teaspoon baking powder
¼ cup milk
4 pears, cored and sliced
2 tablespoons dark brown sugar

Directions:
- Mix the flours, sugar, salt and baking powder in a bowl. Add the butter and mix until grainy.
- Stir in the milk and mix until the dough comes together.
- Place the dough on a floured working surface and roll it into a thin sheet.
- Place the pear slices in the center of the dough and wrap the edges over the pears, leaving the center exposed.
- Sprinkle the pears with brown sugar and bake the galette in the preheated oven at 350F for 25-30 minutes or until golden brown and crisp.
- Serve the galette chilled.

Nutritional information per serving
Calories: 258
Fat: 12.0g

Protein: 2.8g
Carbohydrates: 36.6g

REPES SUZZETTE

Time: 1 hour

Servings: 4

Ingredients:
1 ½ cups milk
2 eggs
1 teaspoon vanilla extract
2 tablespoons canola oil
¾ cup all-purpose flour

1 pinch salt
3 tablespoons butter
4 oranges, cut into segments
¼ cup brandy

Directions:
- Mix the milk, eggs, vanilla, oil, flour and salt in a bowl until creamy.
- Heat a non-stick pan over medium to high heat then pour a few tablespoons of batter in the hot pan and swirl it around to evenly cover the bottom of the pan.
- Cook on each side until golden and stack the crepes on a platter.
- Melt the butter in a saucepan.
- Add the oranges and brandy and cook for 1-2 minutes.
- Place the wrapped crepes in the mixture and cook for another minute.
- Serve the crepe suzette warm, topped with powdered sugar to taste.

Nutritional information per serving

Calories: 404

Fat: 20.1g

Protein: 10.0g

Carbohydrates: 44.3g

G ATEAU BASQUE

Time: 1 hour

Servings: 8

Ingredients:

2 sheets puff pastry dough

2 ½ cups milk

½ cup cornstarch

½ cup white sugar

4 egg yolks

1 tablespoon vanilla extract

2 tablespoons brandy

1 cup glace cherries

1 egg for brushing the dough

Directions:

- Bring the milk to a boil in a saucepan.
- Mix the egg yolks, cornstarch and sugar in a bowl. Pour in the hot milk then place back on heat and cook until thickened.
- Remove from heat and stir in the vanilla and brandy. Allow to cool completely.
- Place on sheet of puff pastry dough on a floured working surface.
- Spoon the vanilla cream in the center of the dough. Top with cherries and cover with the remaining sheet of dough.
- Trim the edges around the filling and brush the top with egg.
- Bake in the preheated oven at 350F for 35 minutes or until well risen and golden brown.
- Serve the gateau chilled.

Nutritional information per serving

Calories: 243

Fat: 8.9g

Protein: 5.6g

Carbohydrates: 31.9g

L EMON CHEESE SOUFFLÉ

Time: 1 hour

Servings: 4

Ingredients:

6 tablespoons butter, softened

1/2 cup white sugar

¾ cup water

¼ teaspoon salt

¾ cup all-purpose flour

5 egg yolks

1 lemon, zested and juiced

1 cup ricotta cheese

5 egg whites

Directions:

- Mix the butter, sugar, water and salt in a saucepan. Place over medium flame and bring to a boil.
- Add the flour, all at once, and mix well until a dough forms.
- Remove from heat and allow to cool down then stir in the egg yolks, lemon zest and lemon juice.
- Stir in the cheese.
- Whip the egg whites in a bowl until fluffy and stiff.
- Fold the meringue into the batter then spoon the mixture into 4 ramekins greased with butter.
- Bake in the preheated oven at 350F for 20 minutes until well risen and golden brown.
- Serve the soufflés warm and fresh out of the oven.

Nutritional information per serving

Calories: 510

Fat: 28.2g

Protein: 17.7g

Carbohydrates: 48.5g

C HOCOLATE TART

Time: 1 ½ hour

Servings: 10

Ingredients:
Crust:
½ cup butter, softened
½ cup powdered sugar
1 teaspoon vanilla extract
1 egg
1 ¾ cups all-purpose flour
¼ cup cocoa powder

¼ teaspoon salt
Filling:
1 ½ cups heavy cream
2 cups dark chocolate chips
1 tablespoon vanilla extract
1 pinch salt

Directions:
- For the crust, mix the butter, sugar and vanilla and mix well.
- Stir in the egg and fold in the flour, cocoa powder and salt and mix until the dough comes together.
- Place the dough on a floured working surface and roll it into a thin sheet.
- Transfer the sheet of dough in a tart pan and press it well on the bottom and sides of the pan.
- Bake the crust in the preheated oven at 350F for 20 minutes or until set.
- For the filling, bring the cream to the boiling point in a saucepan.
- Remove from heat and add the chocolate chips and mix until melted and smooth.
- Add the vanilla and salt and mix well.
- Pour the filling in the chilled crust and allow to cool in the pan.
- Serve the chocolate tart chilled.

Nutritional information per serving
Calories: 374
Fat: 23.2g

Protein: 5.3g
Carbohydrates: 40.6g

R HUBARB TART

Time: 1 hour

Servings: 10

Ingredients:
Crust:
1 ½ cups all-purpose flour
2 tablespoons powdered sugar
1 pinch salt
4 oz. butter, chilled and cubed
1 egg
2 tablespoons cold water
Filling:

2 pounds rhubarb stalks, sliced
1 cup white sugar
1 cup heavy cream
2 egg yolks
2 eggs
1 pinch salt
1 teaspoon vanilla extract

Directions:
- For the crust, mix the flour, sugar, salt and butter in a bowl until grainy.
- Add the egg and water and mix well until the dough comes together.
- Place the dough on a floured working surface and roll it into a thin sheet.
- Place the dough in a tart baking pan and press it well on the bottom and sides of the pan. Trim the edges.
- Arrange the rhubarb slices in the crust.
- Mix the sugar, cream, egg yolks, eggs, salt and vanilla in a bowl. Pour this mixture over the rhubarb. Bake in the preheated oven at 350F for 35 minutes.
- Allow to cool down before serving.

Nutritional information per serving
Calories: 322
Fat: 16.2g
Protein: 5.3g
Carbohydrates: 40.6g

P istachio Financiers

Time: 1 hour

Servings: 16

Ingredients:

1 cup ground almonds
½ cup white sugar
2 eggs

½ cup butter, melted
¼ cup all-purpose flour
½ cup pistachio, chopped

Directions:
- Mix the almonds and sugar in a bowl. Stir in the eggs and mix well then add the butter and give it a good mix.
- Fold in the flour and pistachio, as well as a pinch of salt.
- Spoon the batter in small financier pans and bake in the preheated oven at 350F for 10-15 minutes or until well risen and golden on the edges.
- Serve the financiers chilled.

Nutritional information per serving

Calories: 134
Fat: 10.2g

Protein: 2.6g
Carbohydrates: 9.5g

P ure Chocolate Buche de Noel

Time: 1 ½ hours

Servings: 10

Ingredients:

Cake:
6 eggs
¾ cup white sugar
1 teaspoon vanilla extract
1 cup all-purpose flour
¼ teaspoon salt
½ teaspoon baking powder
¼ cup cocoa powder

2 tablespoons butter, melted
Filling:
1 cup heavy cream
2 cups dark chocolate chips
1 tablespoon vanilla extract
Glaze:
1 ½ cups dark chocolate chips
¾ cup heavy cream

Directions:
- For the cake, mix the eggs, sugar and vanilla in a bowl until fluffy and pale and double in volume.
- Fold in the flour, salt, baking powder and cocoa powder then add the butter and mix with a spatula.
- Spread the batter in a large baking pan lined with baking paper and bake in the preheated oven at 350F for 15 minutes or until set.
- Allow the cake to cool in the pan.
- For the filling, melt the cream and chocolate together in a heatproof bowl. Add the vanilla then allow the filling to cool completely in the fridge for a few hours.
- Whip the filling until airy and pale.
- Spread the filling over the cake and roll it tightly. Place it on a platter.
- For the glaze, bring the cream to the boiling point. Add the chocolate and mix until melted. Allow to cool completely and set then spread it over the cake.
- Using a fork, score the top of the cake roulade to resemble a tree.
- Serve fresh and chilled.

Nutritional information per serving

Calories: 438
Fat: 24.3g
Protein: 8.2g
Carbohydrates: 54.8g

OCHA POTS DE CRÈME

Time: 1 ½ hours

Servings: 6

Ingredients:

2 cups heavy cream
1 cup milk
1 ½ cups dark chocolate chips
2 teaspoons instant coffee

6 egg yolks
1 pinch salt
1 teaspoon vanilla extract

Directions:

- Bring the milk to the boiling point in a saucepan. Remove from heat and stir in the chocolate. Mix until melted then allow to cool down slightly.
- Stir in the rest of the ingredients and mix well.
- Pour the mixture in 4 ramekins and place them in a deep baking pan. Pour hot water in the deep pan, around the ramekins. Bake in the preheated oven at 300F for 30 minutes until set.
- Allow to cool in the pan before serving.

Nutritional information per serving

Calories: 354
Fat: 28.1g

Protein: 6.9g
Carbohydrates: 23.8g

 ED WINE CHOCOLATE CAKE:

Time: 1 ¼ hours

Servings: 10

Ingredients:

2 cups all-purpose flour
¾ cup cocoa powder
½ teaspoon salt
1 teaspoon baking soda
1 teaspoon baking powder
1 cup red wine

1 cup buttermilk
½ cup canola oil
1 teaspoon vanilla extract
2 eggs
1 cup dark chocolate chips

Directions:

- Mix the dry ingredients in a bowl.
- Stir in the red wine, buttermilk, oil, vanilla and eggs and give it a quick mix.
- Fold in the chocolate chips then pour the batter in a 9-inch round cake pan lined with baking paper.
- Bake in the preheated oven at 350F for 40 minutes or until the cake passes the toothpick test.
- Serve the cake chilled.

Nutritional information per serving

Calories: 301
Fat: 16.3g

Protein: 6.5g
Carbohydrates: 32.8g

G ASCON FLAN

Time: 1 ¼ hours

Servings: 10

Ingredients:

1 ½ cups all-purpose flour
½ cup white sugar
¼ teaspoon salt

4 cups milk
1 teaspoon vanilla extract
4 eggs

Directions:

- Mix all the ingredients in a blender and pulse until smooth.
- Pour the batter in a deep dish baking pan greased with butter and bake in the preheated oven at 350F for 35-40 minutes or until golden brown.

- Serve the flan chilled.

Nutritional information per serving

Calories: 181

Fat: 3.9g

Protein: 7.4g

Carbohydrates: 29.3g

EEP CHOCOLATE SOUFFLÉ

Time: 1 hour

Servings: 4

Ingredients:

1 cup milk

¼ cup white sugar

¼ cup cocoa powder

2 tablespoons all-purpose flour

4 oz. dark chocolate, chopped

4 egg yolks

6 egg whites

¼ teaspoon salt

Directions:

- Mix the milk and sugar in a saucepan and place over low heat. Bring to a boil then add the flour and cocoa and cook until thickened.
- Remove from heat and stir in the chocolate. Mix until melted and smooth.
- Allow to cool down then add the egg yolks.
- Whip the whites with the salt until fluffy and stiff.
- Fold the meringue into the chocolate mixture then pour the mixture into 4 ramekins.
- Bake in the preheated oven at 350F for 25 minutes.
- Serve the soufflés freshly made.

Nutritional information per serving

Calories: 335

Fat: 15.0g

Protein: 13.6g

Carbohydrates: 39.2g

CHEWY ALMOND MACAROONS

Time: 1 hour

Servings: 20

Ingredients:

16 oz. almond paste

½ cup white sugar

¼ teaspoon salt

¼ cup Amaretto liqueur

1 cup powdered sugar

Directions:

- Mix the almond paste, sugar and salt in a bowl until creamy.
- Add the liqueur and mix well.
- Place the sugar on a platter.
- Form small balls of mixture and roll them through the powdered sugar. Arrange the macaroons on a baking tray lined with parchment paper. Allow to rest for 20 minutes then bake in the preheated oven at 350F for 15 minutes or until golden.
- Serve them chilled.

Nutritional information per serving

Calories: 155

Fat: 6.3g

Protein: 2.0g

Carbohydrates: 21.8g

BOOZY CHOCOLATE TRUFFLES

Time: 2 hours

Servings: 30

Ingredients:

1 pound dark chocolate chips

¼ teaspoon salt

½ cup butter
½ cup heavy cream

¼ cup Amaretto liqueur

Directions:
- Combine the chocolate, salt, butter and heavy cream in a bowl over a hot water bath.
- When melted and smooth, remove from heat and stir in the Amaretto liqueur.
- Cover the mixture with plastic wrap and place in the fridge for at least 1 hour.
- Form small balls of mixture and roll them through cocoa powder.
- Serve the truffles chilled and store them in an airtight container.

Nutritional information per serving
Calories: 111
Fat: 7.8g

Protein: 1.1g
Carbohydrates: 10.1g

IADONE – FRENCH CHEESECAKE

Time: 1 ¼ hours

Servings: 10

Ingredients:
2 pounds ricotta cheese
1 lemon, zested
1 tablespoon vanilla extract

8 eggs
1 cup white sugar
Butter to grease the pan

Directions:
- Mix all the ingredients in a bowl.
- Grease a 9-inch round cake pan with butter then pour the mixture in the pan.
- Bake in the preheated oven at 350F for 40-45 minutes or until golden brown on the edges.
- Allow the cheesecake to cool down before serving.

Nutritional information per serving
Calories: 256
Fat: 10.7g

Protein: 14.8g
Carbohydrates: 25.6g

$\mathcal{P}$ EPIN'S APPLE TART

Time: 1 ¼ hours

Servings: 10

Ingredients:
½ cup butter, softened
½ cup powdered sugar
¼ cup milk
2 eggs
1 teaspoon vanilla extract

1 ¼ cups all-purpose flour
¼ teaspoon salt
1 teaspoon baking powder
4 apples, cored and sliced
½ teaspoon cinnamon powder

Directions:
- Mix the butter and sugar in a bowl until creamy and pale.
- Add the eggs, milk and vanilla and mix well.
- Fold in the flour, salt and baking powder then spoon the batter in a 9-inch tart pan.
- Top with apple slices and sprinkle with cinnamon.
- Bake the tart in the preheated oven at 350F for 35-40 minutes until well risen and golden brown.
- Serve the tart chilled.

Nutritional information per serving
Calories: 217
Fat: 10.5g
Protein: 3.2g
Carbohydrates: 28.6g

*P*ORT WINE POACHED PEARS

Time: 1 hour

Servings: 4

Ingredients:

4 pears, ripe but firm
2 cups Port wine
1 cup fresh orange juice
½ lemon, sliced

1 star anise
2 whole cloves
1 cinnamon stick
2 cardamom pods, crushed

Directions:

- Mix the wine, Port wine, orange juice, lemon slices, star anise, cloves, cinnamon and cardamom in a saucepan.
- Bring to a boil.
- In the meantime, peel the pears and carefully remove their core.
- Drop them in the hot liquid then turn the heat on low and cover with a lid.
- Cook for 30 minutes or until tender.
- Allow the pears to cool in the liquid before serving.

Nutritional information per serving

Calories: 256
Fat: 0.8g

Protein: 1.5g
Carbohydrates: 43.4g

*D*RIED CRANBERRY PEAR CLAFOUTIS

Time: 1 hour

Servings: 8

Ingredients:

Butter to grease the pan
4 eggs
1 cup heavy cream
¼ cup milk
1/3 cup white sugar

2/3 cup all-purpose flour
¼ teaspoon salt
1 teaspoon vanilla extract
4 pears, ripe but firm
½ cup dried cranberries

Directions:

- Grease a 9-inch deep dish baking pan with butter.
- Place the pears and cranberries on the bottom of the pan.
- Mix the cream, milk, sugar, flour, salt and vanilla in bowl.
- Pour this mixture over the pears and bake in the preheated oven at 350F for 35 minutes or until golden brown on the edges.
- Serve the clafoutis chilled.

Nutritional information per serving

Calories: 222
Fat: 8.2g

Protein: 4.8g
Carbohydrates: 33.9g

*H*ONEY FIG AND GOAT CHEESE TART

Time: 1 hour

Servings: 10

Ingredients:

1 sheet puff pastry
1 cup cream cheese
½ cup goat cheese
2 eggs

¼ cup honey
1 pound fresh figs, quartered
½ cup walnuts, chopped
Extra honey for serving

Directions:

- Mix the cream cheese, goat cheese, eggs and honey in a bowl.
- Arrange the puff pastry dough in a baking tray lined with baking paper.

- Spread the goat cheese mixture over the dough and top with fresh figs.
- Sprinkle with walnuts and bake in the preheated oven at 350F for 30-35 minutes.
- Serve the tart chilled, drizzled with extra honey.

Nutritional information per serving

Calories: 304
Fat: 15.5g

Protein: 6.9g
Carbohydrates: 39.3g

RANGE APPLE TERRINE

Time: 2 hours

Servings: 8

Ingredients:

2 pounds Granny Smith apples
2 oranges

½ cup light brown sugar

Directions:
- Peel the apples and carefully core them. Cut them into small slices.
- Cut the oranges into segments as well.
- Begin layering the apple slices and orange segments in a loaf cake pan lined with baking paper. Sprinkle with brown sugar between layers.
- Bake in the preheated oven at 300F for 1 ½ hours.
- When done, remove from the oven and place a weight on top of your terrine. Allow it to cool down completely then turn it upside down on a platter.
- Serve the terrine chilled.

Nutritional information per serving

Calories: 115
Fat: 0.3g

Protein: 0.8g
Carbohydrates: 30.0g

CRÈME CARAMEL

Time: 1 hour

Servings: 6

Ingredients:

6 eggs
3 cups milk
1 tablespoon vanilla extract

¼ cup light brown sugar
1 pinch salt
1 ¼ cups white sugar

Directions:
- Melt the sugar in a heavy saucepan until it has an amber color.
- Pour the hot sugar in a 8-inch deep dish baking pan and swirl it around to cover the bottom and sides. Be careful as it's hot.
- Mix the eggs, milk, vanilla, brown sugar and salt in a bowl.
- Pour this mixture in the pan and bake in the preheated oven at 300F for 35-40 minutes.
- Allow to cool down for 1 hour then turn the crème upside down on a platter.
- Serve chilled.

Nutritional information per serving

Calories: 309
Fat: 6.9g

Protein: 9.5g
Carbohydrates: 54.2g

ORANGE MARMALADE SOUFFLÉS

Time: 1 hour

Servings: 6

Ingredients:

Butter to grease the ramekins

1 cup orange marmalade

¼ cup heavy cream
2 tablespoons lemon juice
1 tablespoon Cointreau

4 egg whites
¼ teaspoon salt

Directions:
- Grease 6 ramekins with butter.
- Mix the marmalade with the cream, lemon juice and Cointreau in a bowl.
- Whip the egg whites and salt in a bowl until fluffy and stiff.
- Add the egg whites into the marmalade, folding it slowly with a spatula.
- Spoon the batter in the greased ramekins and bake in the preheated oven at 350F for 15-20 minutes.
- Serve the soufflés right away.

Nutritional information per serving

Calories: 174
Fat: 1.9g

Protein: 2.7g
Carbohydrates: 35.8g

LMOND SABLES

Time: 2 hours

Servings: 20

Ingredients:
½ cup butter, softened
½ cup powdered sugar
1 egg
1 teaspoon vanilla extract
½ cup ground almonds

2 cups all-purpose flour
¼ teaspoon salt
1 egg white, beaten
1 cup almonds, chopped
¼ cup light brown sugar

Directions:
- Mix the butter and sugar in a bowl until fluffy and pale.
- Add the egg and vanilla and mix well then fold in the almonds, flour and salt and knead just until the dough comes together.
- Shape the dough into an even log.
- Mix the almonds and sugar on a platter.
- Brush the log with egg white then roll it through the almond mixture. Wrap in plastic wrap and place in the freezer for 1 hour.
- After 1 hour, cut the log into ¼-inch thin slices and place them with the cut facing up on a baking tray lined with parchment paper.
- Bake in the preheated oven at 350F for 10-15 minutes or until golden on the edges.
- Serve the sables chilled.

Nutritional information per serving

Calories: 151
Fat: 8.5g
Protein: 3.3g
Carbohydrates: 15.9g

Cheesecakes

ALMOND VANILLA CHEESECAKE

Time: 1 ¼ hours

Servings: 10

Ingredients:

Crust:
1 cup graham crackers, crushed
¼ cup ground almonds
2 tablespoons light brown sugar
2 tablespoons cocoa powder
½ cup butter, melted
Filling:

3 cups cream cheese
1 cup sour cream
3 eggs
2/3 cup white sugar
1 teaspoon vanilla extract
½ teaspoon almond extract
¼ teaspoon salt

Directions:

- For the crust, mix the ingredients in a food processor and pulse until mixed.
- Transfer the mixture in a 9-inch round cake pan lined with baking paper and press it well on the bottom of the pan.
- For the filling, mix all the ingredients in a bowl. Pour the filling over the crust and bake in the preheated oven at 330F for 45 minutes.
- Allow to cool down before serving.

Nutritional information per serving

Calories: 503
Fat: 41.8g

Protein: 9.0g
Carbohydrates: 25.7g

STRAWBERRY LEMON CHEESECAKE

Time: 1 ¼ hours

Servings: 10

Ingredients:

Crust:
1 ¼ cups graham crackers, crushed
½ cup butter, melted
1 teaspoon lemon zest
Filling:
3 cups cream cheese
½ cup plain yogurt

2 eggs
1 lemon, zested and juiced
¾ cup white sugar
1 teaspoon vanilla extract
1 tablespoon cornstarch
Topping:
2 cups fresh strawberries

Directions:

- For the crust, mix all the ingredients in a bowl then transfer in a 9-inch round cake pan. Press it well on the bottom of the pan.
- For the filling, mix all the ingredients in a bowl. Pour the filling over the crust and bake in the preheated oven at 350F for 40-45 minutes until set in the center.
- When done, remove from the oven and allow to chill.
- Top with fresh strawberries and serve chilled.

Nutritional information per serving

Calories: 462
Fat: 35.7g

Protein: 8.1g
Carbohydrates: 29.4g

CLASSIC VANILLA CHEESECAKE

Time: 1 ¼ hours
Servings: 10

Ingredients:

Crust:
1 ½ cups graham crackers
½ cup butter, melted
1 pinch salt
2 tablespoons light brown sugar
Filling:

26 oz. cream cheese
1 tablespoon vanilla extract
3 eggs
2/3 cup white sugar
1 tablespoon cornstarch

Directions:
- For the crust, mix all the ingredients in a food processor and pulse until well mixed.
- Press well on the bottom of the pan.
- For the filling, mix all the ingredients in a bowl. Spoon the filling over the crust and bake in the preheated oven at 330F for 40-45 minutes.
- Allow to cool down before serving.

Nutritional information per serving

Calories: 474
Fat: 37.5g

Protein: 8.2g
Carbohydrates: 27.7g

INGERSNAP CHEESECAKE

Time: 1 ¼ hours

Servings: 14

Ingredients:

Crust:
16 gingersnaps
½ cup butter, melted
Filling:
28 oz. cream cheese

2 eggs
1 cup light brown sugar
1 teaspoon ground ginger
½ cup sour cream
1 teaspoon vanilla extract

Directions:
- For the crust, combine the gingersnaps and butter in a food processor and pulse until well mixed.
- Transfer the mixture in a 9-inch pan and press it well on the bottom of the pan.
- For the filling, mix all the ingredients in a bowl. Pour the mixture over the crust and bake the cheesecake in the pre-heated oven at 330F for 35-40 minutes.
- When done, allow the cheesecake to cool in the pan then slice and serve.

Nutritional information per serving

Calories: 483
Fat: 34.4g

Protein: 7.7g
Carbohydrates: 37.4g

PICED HONEY CHEESECAKE

Time: 1 ¼ hours

Servings: 14

Ingredients:

Crust:
10 gingersnaps
10 graham crackers
½ cup butter, melted
¼ teaspoon cinnamon powder
Filling:
3 cups cream cheese
1 cup sour cream
3 eggs

½ cup light brown sugar
1/4 cup honey
1 tablespoon cornstarch
1 teaspoon vanilla extract
¼ teaspoon ground nutmeg
½ teaspoon ground cardamom
½ teaspoon ground ginger
½ teaspoon cinnamon powder
1 pinch salt

Directions:
- For the crust, mix all the ingredients in a food processor and pulse until well mixed. Transfer the mixture in a 9-inch

round cake pan and press it well on the bottom of the pan.
- For the filling, mix all the ingredients in a bowl. Pour the bowl over the crust and bake the cheesecake in the preheated oven at 330F for 35-40 minutes or until golden brown.
- Allow the cheesecake to cool down in the pan before slicing and serving.

Nutritional information per serving
Calories: 464

Fat: 32.9g

Protein: 7.7g

Carbohydrates: 36.2g

$\mathcal{W}$ALNUT CHEESECAKE

Time: 1 ¼ hours

Servings: 10

Ingredients:
Crust:

10 graham crackers

1 cup walnuts

¼ cup butter, melted

Filling:

2 cups cream cheese

1 cup sour cream

2/3 cup white sugar

1 teaspoon vanilla extract

2 oz. dark chocolate, melted

2 tablespoons dark rum

3 eggs

1 tablespoon cornstarch

Directions:
- For the crust, mix the ingredients in a food processor and pulse until well mixed. Transfer in a 9-inch round cake pan and press it well on the bottom of the pan.
- For the filling, combine the ingredients in a blender and pulse until well mixed. Pour the mixture into the crust and bake in the preheated oven at 330F for 40-45 minutes until set.
- Allow the cheesecake to cool down before slicing and serving.

Nutritional information per serving
Calories: 498

Fat: 37.4g

Protein: 10.3g

Carbohydrates: 31.8g

$\mathcal{A}$MARETTI CHEESECAKE

Time: 1 ¼ hours

Servings: 10

Ingredients:
Crust:

6 oz. Amaretti cookies, crushed

¼ cup butter, melted

Filling:

3 cups cream cheese

3 eggs

½ cup white sugar

1 teaspoon vanilla extract

4 oz. Amaretti cookies, crushed

Directions:
- For the crust, mix the ingredients in a bowl. Transfer in a 8-inch round cake pan and press it well on the bottom of the pan.
- For the filling, mix the cream cheese, eggs, sugar and vanilla in a bowl. Fold in the cookies then pour the batter in the pan.
- Bake in the preheated oven at 330F for 40-45 minutes or until golden brown on the edges.
- Allow to cool down before serving.

Nutritional information per serving
Calories: 476

Fat: 35.7g

Protein: 8.0g

Carbohydrates: 32.4g

MARETTO CHEESECAKE

Time: 1 ¼ hours

Servings: 12

Ingredients:

Crust:
1 ½ cups graham crackers, crushed
½ cup butter, melted
1 tablespoon Amaretto liqueur
Filling:
3 oz. dark chocolate, melted
3 cups cream cheese

2 tablespoons butter, melted
½ cup light brown sugar
1 teaspoon vanilla extract
3 eggs
1 pinch salt
¼ cup Amaretto liqueur
1 tablespoon cornstarch

Directions:

- For the crust, mix the ingredients in a food processor and pulse until well mixed. Transfer in a 9-inch round cake pan and press it well on the bottom of the pan.
- For the filling, mix the cream cheese with melted chocolate until creamy. Add the rest of the ingredients and mix well.
- Pour the mixture over the crust and bake in the preheated oven at 330F for 45 minutes.
- Allow the cheesecake to cool down before slicing and serving.

Nutritional information per serving

Calories: 431
Fat: 34.1g

Protein: 7.1g
Carbohydrates: 20.5g

APPLE CINNAMON CHEESECAKE

Time: 1 ¼ hours

Servings: 12

Ingredients:

Crust:
2 cups graham crackers, crushed
½ cup butter, melted
Filling:
3 cups cream cheese
½ cup sour cream

2/3 cup white sugar
1 teaspoon vanilla extract
3 eggs
2 tablespoons cornstarch
2 Granny Smith apples, peeled, cored and diced
1 teaspoon cinnamon powder

Directions:

- For the crust, mix the ingredients in a bowl then transfer in a 9-inch round cake pan and press it well on the bottom of the pan.
- Top the crust with apple dices and sprinkle with cinnamon powder.
- For the filling, mix the ingredients in a bowl. Pour the filling over the apples and bake in the preheated oven at 330F for 45 minutes until the center of the cheesecake looks set.
- Allow the cheesecake to cool down before slicing and serving.

Nutritional information per serving

Calories: 429
Fat: 32.4g

Protein: 7.2g
Carbohydrates: 29.3g

VANILLA CRUMBLE CHEESECAKE

Time: 1 ¼ hours

Servings: 12

Ingredients:

Crust:
1 ½ cups vanilla biscuits
¼ cup butter, melted
Filling:

3 cups cream cheese
½ cup heavy cream
3 eggs
1 tablespoon cornstarch

1 tablespoon vanilla extract
2/3 cup white sugar
1 pinch salt
Topping:

½ cup butter, chilled
¾ cup all-purpose flour
1 pinch salt

Directions:
- For the crust, mix the two ingredients in a bowl then transfer the mixture in a 9-inch round cake pan lined with baking paper.
- For the filling, mix all the ingredients in a bowl. Pour the mixture over the crust.
- For the topping, mix the butter, flour and salt in a bowl until crumbly, grainy.
- Spread the crumble over the filling then place the cheesecake in the preheated oven at 330F.
- Bake for 45-50 minutes or until golden brown and crusty.
- Allow to cool down before serving.

Nutritional information per serving
Calories: 449
Fat: 35.6g

Protein: 7.4g
Carbohydrates: 25.9g

S PICED PUMPKIN CHEESECAKE

Time: 1 ½ hours

Servings: 10

Ingredients:
Crust:
4 oz. gingersnaps, crushed
½ cup butter, melted
Filling:
1 cup pumpkin puree
2 eggs
3 cups cream cheese

1 teaspoon vanilla extract
1 pinch salt
1 tablespoon cornstarch
½ teaspoon cinnamon powder
½ teaspoon ground ginger
½ teaspoon ground star anise
½ teaspoon ground whole cloves

Directions:
- For the crust, mix the gingersnap and butter in a bowl. Transfer the mixture in a 9-inch round cake pan lined with baking paper.
- For the filling, mix the ingredients in a bowl until creamy. Pour the filling over the crust.
- Bake the cheesecake in the preheated oven at 330F for 45-50 minutes or until fragrant.
- Allow the cheesecake to cool down before slicing and serving.

Nutritional information per serving
Calories: 404
Fat: 36.3g

Protein: 7.5g
Carbohydrates: 13.2g

B ANANA CARAMEL CHEESECAKE

Time: 1 ½ hours

Servings: 12

Ingredients:
Crust:
2 cups graham crackers, crushed
½ cup butter, melted
Filling:
2 bananas, mashed
1 tablespoon lemon juice

½ cup caramel sauce
3 cups cream cheese
1 pinch salt
½ cup sour cream
3 eggs
1 teaspoon vanilla extract

Directions:
- For the crust, mix the crackers and butter and mix well. Transfer the mixture in a 9-inch round cake pan and press it well on the bottom of the pan.
- For the filling, combine all the ingredients in a bowl and mix well. Pour the mixture over the crust.

- Bake the cheesecake in the preheated oven at 330F for 45-50 minutes.
- Allow the cheesecake to cool down completely before slicing and serving.

Nutritional information per serving

Calories: 419

Fat: 32.5g

Protein: 7.5g

Carbohydrates: 26.4g

C ARAMEL DRIZZLED CHEESECAKE

Time: 1 ¼ hours

Servings: 12

Ingredients:

Crust:

1 ½ cups graham crackers, crushed

½ cup butter, melted

1 pinch salt

Filling:

3 cups cream cheese

½ cup sour cream

2 eggs

½ cup caramel sauce

1 tablespoon cornstarch

1 teaspoon vanilla extract

Topping:

1 cup caramel sauce

Directions:

- For the crust, mix the crackers and butter in a bowl. Transfer the mixture in a 9-inch round cake pan lined with baking paper. Press well on the bottom of the pan.
- For the filling, combine the cream cheese and the rest of the ingredients in a bowl. Mix well then pour the mixture over the crust and bake in the preheated oven at 330F for 45-50 minutes or until set.
- Allow the cheesecake to cool down completely then drizzle it with caramel sauce and serve it.

Nutritional information per serving

Calories: 453

Fat: 31.7g

Protein: 7.0g

Carbohydrates: 37.8g

C RUSTLESS ORANGE CHEESECAKE

Time: 1 ½ hours

Servings: 10

Ingredients:

3 cups cream cheese

½ cup sour cream

3 eggs

2 tablespoons cornstarch

2/3 cup white sugar

1 teaspoon vanilla extract

1 tablespoon orange zest

Directions:

- Mix all the ingredients in a bowl.
- Grease a 8-inch baking pan with butter then pour the cheesecake mix in the pan.
- Bake in the preheated oven at 330F for 45-50 minutes or until set.
- Allow the cheesecake to cool down before slicing and serving.

Nutritional information per serving

Calories: 344

Fat: 28.0g

Protein: 7.3g

Carbohydrates: 17.4g

C HUNKY BANANA CHEESECAKE

Time: 1 ½ hours

Servings: 12

Ingredients:

Crust:

2 cups graham crackers

1 tablespoon dark brown sugar

½ cup butter, melted

Filling:
2 bananas, sliced
3 cups cream cheese
2 eggs
½ cup white sugar

1 teaspoon vanilla extract
½ cup plain yogurt
1 pinch salt
1 tablespoon cornstarch

Directions:
- For the crust, mix all the ingredients in a bowl. Transfer the mixture in a deep dish baking pan lined with baking paper and press it well on the bottom and sides of the pan.
- Arrange the banana slices over the crust.
- For the filling, mix all the ingredients in a bowl until creamy pour the filling into the crust and bake in the preheated oven at 330F for 40-45 minutes or until the center of the cheesecake looks slightly set.
- Allow the cheesecake to cool down in the pan then slice and serve. Store it I the fridge for not more than 4 days.

Nutritional information per serving
Calories: 402
Fat: 30.2g

Protein: 7.1g
Carbohydrates: 27.3g

ASSIONFRUIT CHEESECAKE

Time: 1 ¼ hours

Servings: 10

Ingredients:
Crust:
1 ½ cups vanilla biscuits, crushed
½ cup butter, melted
1 teaspoon orange zest
Filling:
24 oz. cream cheese
½ cup sour cream

¾ cup white sugar
3 eggs
¼ cup passionfruit juice
1 teaspoon orange zest
1 teaspoon vanilla extract
1 tablespoon cornstarch

Directions:
- For the crust, mix the biscuits with melted butter and orange zest. Transfer in a 9-inch baking pan and press it well on the bottom of the pan.
- For the filling, mix all the ingredients in a bowl until creamy.
- Pour the filling over the crust then bake the cheesecake in the preheated oven at 330F for 45-50 minutes.
- Allow the cheesecake to cool down before slicing and serving.

Nutritional information per serving
Calories: 439
Fat: 37.2g

Protein: 7.5g
Carbohydrates: 20.6g

HUBARB STRAWBERRY CHEESECAKE

Time: 1 ½ hours

Servings: 12

Ingredients:
Crust:
1 ½ cups graham crackers, crushed
½ cup butter, melted
Filling:
24 oz. cream cheese
1 cup heavy cream
3 eggs

1 tablespoon cornstarch
2/3 cup white sugar
1 teaspoon vanilla extract
Topping:
2 rhubarb stalks, sliced
½ pound strawberries, halved
¼ cup light brown sugar

Directions:
- For the crust, mix the crackers and butter well then transfer in a 9-inch cake pan lined with baking paper. Press the mixture well on the bottom of the pan.

- For the filling, mix the cream cheese, cream, eggs, cornstarch, sugar and vanilla in a bowl. Pour the filling over the crust and bake in the preheated oven at 330F for 45 minutes or until the center looks set.
- Allow the cheesecake to cool down in the pan.
- For the topping, mix the ingredients in a deep dish baking pan and cook in the preheated oven at 350F for 10-15 minutes until softened. Allow to cool down.
- Top the cheesecake with the rhubarb strawberry mixture and serve it fresh.

Nutritional information per serving

Calories: 425
Fat: 33.4g

Protein: 6.9g
Carbohydrates: 26.5g

H AZELNUT CHOCOLATE CHEESECAKE

Time: 1 ¼ hours

Servings: 12

Ingredients:

Crust:
1 cup ground hazelnuts
1 cup graham crackers
¼ cup butter, melted
Filling:
3 oz. dark chocolate, melted

3 cups cream cheese
3 eggs
¾ cup white sugar
1 teaspoon vanilla extract
1 tablespoon cornstarch
2 tablespoons hazelnut liqueur

Directions:

- For the crust, mix the hazelnuts, crackers and butter in a bowl. Transfer the mixture in a 9-inch round cake pan and press it well on the bottom of the pan.
- For the filling, mix the cream cheese and the melted chocolate in a bowl. Stir in the rest of the ingredients. Pour the mixture over the crust then bake the cheesecake in the preheated oven at 330F for 45-50 minutes or until set in the center.
- Allow the cheesecake to cool down before serving.

Nutritional information per serving

Calories: 418
Fat: 32.2g

Protein: 7.8g
Carbohydrates: 25.9g

C HERRY CHOCOLATE CHEESECAKE

Time: 1 ¼ hours

Servings: 12

Ingredients:

Crust:
1 ½ cups chocolate biscuits, crushed
½ cup butter, melted
Filling:
3 cups cream cheese
4 oz. dark chocolate, melted
1 teaspoon vanilla extract

½ cup sour cream
2/3 cup white sugar
3 eggs
1 tablespoon cornstarch
2 cups cherries, pitted
2 tablespoons all-purpose flour

Directions:

- For the crust, mix the chocolate biscuits and butter in a bowl. Transfer the mixture in a 9-inch round cake pan and press it well on the bottom of the pan.
- For the filling, mix the cream cheese with the melted chocolate. Add the sugar, eggs, cornstarch and sour cream, as well as vanilla and mix well.
- Pour the filling over the crust.
- Mix the cherries with the flour. Top the cheesecake with the cherries.
- Bake in the preheated oven at 330F for 45-50 minutes.
- Allow the cheesecake cool down before serving.

Nutritional information per serving

Calories: 432
Fat: 34.3g

Protein: 7.2g
Carbohydrates: 25.3g

CRUSTLESS VANILLA CHEESECAKE

Time: 1 hour

Servings: 10

Ingredients:

24 oz. cream cheese
1 cup sour cream
¾ cup white sugar
1 tablespoon vanilla extract

4 eggs
2 tablespoons all-purpose flour
1 pinch salt
Butter to grease the pan

Directions:

- Combine all the ingredients in a bowl.
- Grease a 9-inch round cake pan with butter. Pour the filling in the pan and bake in the preheated oven at 330F for 40-45 minutes or until set.
- Allow the cake cool in the oven before serving.

Nutritional information per serving

Calories: 378
Fat: 30.3g

Protein: 8.2g
Carbohydrates: 19.3g

TIRAMISU CHEESECAKE

Time: 1 ½ hours

Servings: 10

Ingredients:

Crust:
1 ½ cups chocolate biscuits
1 teaspoon instant coffee
½ cup butter, melted
Filling:
3 cups cream cheese
¾ cup white sugar

3 eggs
¼ cup espresso
1 teaspoon vanilla extract
1 tablespoon cornstarch
Topping:
¼ cup cocoa powder

Directions:

- For the crust, place the biscuits in a food processor and pulse until ground. Add the butter and mix well then transfer the mixture in a 9-inch round cake pan and press it well on the bottom of the pan.
- For the filling, mix all the ingredients in a bowl. Pour the mixture over the crust and bake the cheesecake in the preheated oven at 330F for 45-50 minutes.
- Allow the cheesecake to cool in the pan then top it with a dusting of cocoa powder.
- Serve the cheesecake fresh and chilled.

Nutritional information per serving

Calories: 446
Fat: 37.3g

Protein: 7.9g
Carbohydrates: 22.9g

DULCE DE LECHE CHEESECAKE

Time: 1 ¼ hours

Servings: 10

Ingredients:

Crust:
1 ½ cups graham crackers, crushed
½ cup butter, melted

Filling:
4 cream cheese
4 eggs

¾ cup white sugar
1 tablespoon vanilla extract
1 tablespoon cornstarch

Topping:
1 cup dulce de leche

Directions:
- For the crust, mix the crackers with the butter in a bowl. Transfer the mixture in a 9-inch round cake pan lined with baking paper. Press the mixture well on the bottom of the pan.
- For the filling, mix the cream cheese, eggs, sugar, vanilla and cornstarch in a bowl until creamy.
- Spoon the filling over the crust and bake in the preheated oven at 330F for 40-45 minutes.
- When done, allow the cheesecake to cool down in the pan.
- Top the chilled cheesecake with dulce de leche and serve it right away.

Nutritional information per serving
Calories: 325
Fat: 14.8g

Protein: 5.1g
Carbohydrates: 44.2g

H ONEY RICOTTA CHEESECAKE

Time: 1 hour

Servings: 8

Ingredients:
1 ½ pounds ricotta cheese
3 eggs
¼ cup honey
¼ cup light brown sugar

1 teaspoon vanilla extract
1 teaspoon cornstarch
½ cup golden raisins
Butter to grease the pan

Directions:
- Mix all the ingredients in a bowl.
- Grease a 8-inch round cake pan with butter then pour the cheesecake mixture in the pan.
- Bake in the preheated oven at 330F for 40-45 minutes or until the edges turn slightly golden brown.
- Allow the cheesecake to cool down before serving.

Nutritional information per serving
Calories: 220
Fat: 8.4g

Protein: 12.1g
Carbohydrates: 25.2g

L EMON COCONUT CHEESECAKE

Time: 1 ½ hours

Servings: 10

Ingredients:
Crust:
½ cup shredded coconut
1 cup vanilla biscuits, crushed
¼ cup coconut oil, melted
Filling:
1 ½ pounds cream cheese
2 egg yolks

2 eggs
½ cup white sugar
1 tablespoon lemon zest
2 tablespoons lemon juice
1 teaspoon vanilla extract
1 tablespoon cornstarch

Directions:
- For the crust, mix all the ingredients in a food processor and pulse until mixed. Transfer the mixture in a 9-inch round cake pan lined with baking paper and press it well on the bottom of the pan.
- For the filling, mix all the ingredients in a bowl then pour the filling over the crust.
- Bake the cheesecake in the preheated oven at 330F for 45-50 minutes or until the center looks set.
- Allow the cheesecake to cool down before slicing and serving.

Nutritional information per serving
Calories: 408
Fat: 33.3g

Protein: 7.7g
Carbohydrates: 21.2g

CREAMY LEMON CHEESECAKES

Time: 1 ½ hours

Servings: 10

Ingredients:
Crust:
1 ½ cups vanilla biscuits
1 teaspoon lemon zest
½ cup butter, melted
Filling:
3 cups cream cheese

1 lemon, zested and juiced
¾ cup white sugar
1 teaspoon vanilla extract
3 eggs
1 tablespoon cornstarch

Directions:
- For the crust, mix all the ingredients in a bowl. Transfer the mixture in a 9-inch round cake pan lined with baking paper and press it well on the bottom of the pan.
- For the filling, mix the cream cheese and the rest of the ingredients in a bowl and give it a quick mix.
- Pour the filling over the crust and bake in the preheated oven at 330F for 45 minutes or until slightly golden brown on the edges and set in the center.
- Serve the cheesecake chilled.

Nutritional information per serving
Calories: 448
Fat: 35.8g

Protein: 7.8g
Carbohydrates: 25.9g

NO CRUST CITRUS CHEESECAKE

Time: 1 hour

Servings: 10

Ingredients:
1 ½ pounds cream cheese
¼ cup butter, melted
¾ cup white sugar
1 teaspoon lemon zest
1 teaspoon lime zest
1 teaspoon orange zest

1 pinch salt
1 teaspoon vanilla extract
3 eggs
1 pinch salt
1 tablespoon cornstarch
Butter to grease the pan

Directions:
- Combine all the ingredients in a bowl and give it a quick mix.
- Grease a 8-inch round cake pan with butter then pour the cheesecake mixture in the pan.
- Bake in the preheated oven at 330F for 40-45 minutes or until the center looks set.
- Allow the cheesecake to cool down before slicing and serving.

Nutritional information per serving
Calories: 358
Fat: 29.6g

Protein: 6.8g
Carbohydrates: 17.8g

MANGO RIPPLE CHEESECAKE

Time: 1 ½ hours

Servings: 12

Ingredients:
Crust:
1 ½ cups graham crackers
½ cup butter, melted
Filling:
4 cups cream cheese
4 eggs

¾ cup white sugar
1 teaspoon vanilla extract
¼ cup plain yogurt
1 mango, peeled and cubed
¼ cup light brown sugar
1 lime, zested and juiced

Directions:

- For the crust, mix the crackers and butter in a bowl. Transfer the mixture in a deep dish baking pan lined with baking paper.
- Press the mixture well on the bottom of the pan.
- For the filling, mixing the cream cheese, eggs, sugar, vanilla and yogurt and mix well. Pour the mixture over the crust.
- For the mango ripple, mix the mango flesh, lime zest and juice and sugar in a blender and pulse until smooth.
- Drizzle the mixture over the cheesecake and swirl it around with a fork.
- Serve the cheesecake chilled.

Nutritional information per serving

Calories: 480

Fat: 37.3g

Protein: 8.9g

Carbohydrates: 29.6g

 # AISIN MARSALA CHEESECAKE

Time: 1 ¼ hours

Servings: 10

Ingredients:

Crust:

1 ½ cups graham crackers

½ cup butter, melted

1 tablespoon dark brown sugar

1 tablespoon Marsala

Filling:

3 cups cream cheese

¼ cup Marsala

1 teaspoon vanilla extract

1 pinch salt

3 eggs

1 tablespoon cornstarch

½ cup white sugar

1 cup golden raisins

Directions:

- For the crust, mix the crackers in a food processor until ground. Add the sugar and butter and mix well then transfer the mixture in a round cake pan lined with baking paper. Press it well on the bottom of the pan.
- For the filling, mix all the ingredients in a bowl until creamy.
- Pour the mixture over the crust and bake the cheesecake in the preheated oven at 330F for 45-50 minutes.
- Allow the cheesecake to cool down in the pan before slicing and serving.

Nutritional information per serving

Calories: 491

Fat: 36.1g

Protein: 8.3g

Carbohydrates: 35.0g

 # ICOTTA CHEESECAKE WITH BALSAMIC STRAWBERRIES

Time: 1 ½ hours

Servings: 10

Ingredients:

Crust:

1 1/2cups graham crackers, ground

½ cup olive oil

2 tablespoons dark brown sugar

Filling:

3 cups ricotta cheese

4 eggs

1 teaspoon vanilla extract

1 teaspoon lemon zest

2/3 cup white sugar

1 tablespoon cornstarch

Topping:

2 cups strawberries, halved

1 tablespoon olive oil

1 tablespoon balsamic vinegar

Directions:

- For the crust, mix the ingredients in a bowl. Transfer the mixture in a 9-inch round cake pan lined with baking paper and press it well on the bottom of the pan.
- For the filling, mix the ricotta cheese, eggs, vanilla, lemon zest, sugar and cornstarch in a bowl.
- Pour the mixture over the crust and bake the cheesecake in the preheated oven at 350F for 45 minutes or until it looks set in the center.
- Allow the cheesecake to cool down before slicing and serving.

Calories: 327
Fat: 20.0g

Protein: 11.5g
Carbohydrates: 27.1g

ARSALA INFUSED CHEESECAKE

Time: 1 ½ hours

Servings: 10

Ingredients:

Crust:
1 ½ cups vanilla cookies, crushed
¼ cup butter, melted
2 tablespoons Marsala wine
Filling:
1 cup sultanas
½ cup Marsala wine

3 cups cream cheese
½ cup sour cream
3 eggs
1 tablespoon cornstarch
2/3 cup white sugar
1 teaspoon vanilla extract

Directions:

- For the crust, mix the cookies, butter and wine in a bowl. Transfer the mixture in a 9-inch round cake pan and press it well on the bottom of the pan.
- For the filling, mix the sultanas and wine in a bowl and allow to soak up for 30 minutes.
- Mix the cream cheese, sour cream, eggs, cornstarch and vanilla in a bowl.
- Add the sultanas and wine and mix well. Pour the mixture over the crust and bake in the preheated oven at 350F for 45-50 minutes or until the center looks set.
- Allow the cheesecake to cool down before serving.

Nutritional information per serving

Calories: 409
Fat: 32.8g

Protein: 7.5g
Carbohydrates: 20.4g

PRICOT COMPOTE RICOTTA CHEESECAKE

Time: 1 ½ hours

Servings: 10

Ingredients:

Crust:
1 ½ cups graham crackers, crushed
½ cup butter, melted
Filling:
2 cups ricotta cheese
1 cup cream cheese
½ cup sour cream
4 eggs

1 tablespoon lemon zest
2/3 cup white sugar
1 tablespoon cornstarch
Apricot compote:
1 pound apricots, pitted and sliced
½ cup fresh orange juice
1 teaspoon orange zest

Directions:

- For the crust, mix the ingredients in a bowl. Transfer the mixture in a 9-inch round cake pan and press it well on the bottom of the pan.
- For the filling, mix the ricotta cheese, cream cheese, sour cream, eggs, lemon zest, cornstarch and sugar. Spoon the mixture over the crust and bake in the preheated oven at 350F for 40-45 minutes.
- Allow the cheesecake to cool in the pan.
- For the compote, mix the ingredients in a saucepan and cook for 5 minutes over medium flame.
- Serve the cheesecake with warm or chilled apricot compote.

Nutritional information per serving

Calories: 415
Fat: 27.0g
Protein: 11.6g
Carbohydrates: 34.0g

*H*ONEY FIG RICOTTA CHEESECAKE

Time: 1 ¼ hours

Servings: 10

Ingredients:

Crust:
1 ½ cups graham crackers, crushed
½ cup butter, melted
Filling:
1 ½ pounds ricotta cheese
4 eggs
1 teaspoon vanilla extract

¼ cup honey
¼ cup white sugar
1 tablespoon cornstarch
Topping:
1 pound fresh figs, quartered
¼ cup honey

Directions:
- For the crust, mix the crackers with melted butter in a bowl then transfer the mixture in a 9-inch round cake pan lined with baking paper. Press it well on the bottom of the pan.
- For the filling, mix the cheese, eggs, vanilla, honey, sugar and cornstarch in a bowl.
- Pour the mixture over the crust and bake in the preheated oven at 350F for 45 minutes or until set in the center.
- When done, allow to cool then top with fresh figs.
- Drizzle with honey just before serving.

Nutritional information per serving

Calories: 441
Fat: 18.0g

Protein: 12.5g
Carbohydrates: 62.1g

*S*NICKERS CHEESECAKE

Time: 1 ¼ hours

Servings: 10

Ingredients:

Crust:
1 cup graham crackers
2 tablespoons cocoa powder
¼ cup butter
1 tablespoon Dark rum
Filling:

24 oz. cream cheese, softened
2/3 cup white sugar
3 eggs
1 teaspoon vanilla extract
1 tablespoon cornstarch
4 Snickers bars, chopped

Directions:
- For the crust, mix the ingredients in a food processor and pulse until well mixed. Transfer the mixture in a 8-inch round cake pan and press it well on the bottom of the pan.
- For the filling, mix the cream cheese, sugar, eggs, vanilla and cornstarch in a bowl. Fold in the chopped Snickers then pour the mixture in the prepared pan, over the crust.
- Bake in the preheated oven at 330F for 45-50 minutes or until the center looks set.
- Allow the cheesecake to cool down before slicing and serving.

Nutritional information per serving

Calories: 456
Fat: 33.8g

Protein: 8.8g
Carbohydrates: 31.5g

*S*OUR CREAM MANGO CHEESECAKE

Time: 1 ¼ hours

Servings: 10

Ingredients:

Crust:
1 ½ cups graham cracker, crushed
½ cup butter, melted

Filling:
2 cups sour cream
2 cups cream cheese

1 teaspoon vanilla extract
3 eggs
¾ cup white sugar
1 tablespoon cornstarch

Topping:
1 mango, peeled and cubed
¼ cup light brown sugar
¼ cup fresh orange juice

Directions:
- For the crust, mix the ingredients in a bowl. Transfer the mixture in a 9-inch round cake pan lined with baking paper.
- For the filling, mix all the ingredients in a bowl. Pour the mixture over the crust and bake in the preheated oven at 330F for 45 minutes or until set in the center.
- Allow to cool down in the pan.
- For the topping, mix all the ingredients in a saucepan and cook until softened.
- Allow to cool then top the cheesecake with the mango compote.
- Serve the cheesecake fresh.

Nutritional information per serving
Calories: 491
Fat: 37.6g

Protein: 7.6g
Carbohydrates: 33.0g

N UTMEG RICOTTA CHEESECAKE

Time: 1 ¼ hours

Servings: 10

Ingredients:
Crust:
1 ½ cups graham crackers, crushed
½ cup butter, melted
Filling:
24 oz. ricotta cheese
½ cup heavy cream
2 eggs

¼ cup butter, melted
2/3 cup white sugar
1 teaspoon vanilla extract
¼ teaspoon ground nutmeg
1 tablespoon cornstarch
1 pinch salt

Directions:
- For the crust, mix the ingredients in a bowl. Transfer the mixture in a 9-inch round cake pan and press it well on the bottom of the pan.
- For the filling, mix all the ingredients in a bowl until creamy.
- Pour the mixture over the crust and bake in the preheated oven at 330F for 40-45 minutes or until set in the center.
- Serve the cheesecake chilled.

Nutritional information per serving
Calories: 357
Fat: 23.6g

Protein: 10.0g
Carbohydrates: 27.6g

S HORTCRUST PASTRY CHEESECAKE

Time: 1 ½ hours

Servings: 12

Ingredients:
Crust:
½ cup butter, softened
¼ cup powdered sugar
1 egg yolk
1 ¾ cups all-purpose flour
1 pinch salt
Filling:
3 cups cream cheese

1 cup sour cream
1 teaspoon vanilla extract
3 eggs
½ cup white sugar
1 pinch salt
2 tablespoons butter, melted
1 tablespoon cornstarch

Directions:
- For the crust, mix the butter and sugar in a bowl until creamy. Add the egg yolk and mix well then stir in the rest of the

ingredients.

- Transfer the dough on a floured working surface and roll the dough into a thin sheet.
- Transfer the dough in a 9-inch round cake pan and press it well on the bottom and sides of the pan.
- Bake the crust in the preheated oven at 350F for 12 minutes then allow to cool down.
- For the filling, mix all the ingredients in a bowl. Pour the mixture into the crust and bake in the preheated oven at 300F for 45 minutes or until set in the center.
- Serve the cheesecake chilled.

Nutritional information per serving

Calories: 459

Fat: 35.5g

Protein: 8.6g

Carbohydrates: 27.9g

$\mathcal{W}$ALNUT CRUMBLE CHEESECAKE

Time: 1 ½ hours

Servings: 12

Ingredients:

Crust:

1 cup graham crackers, crushed

1 cup ground walnuts

2 tablespoons butter, melted

Filling:

24 oz. cream cheese

2 eggs

1 teaspoon vanilla extract

2/3 cup white sugar

2 tablespoons dark rum

1 pinch salt

1 tablespoon cornstarch

Topping:

1 cup walnuts, chopped

¼ cup all-purpose flour

1 pinch salt

2 tablespoons butter, chilled

Directions:

- For the crust, mix the ingredients in a food processor and pulse until ground and well mixed.
- Transfer in a 9-inch round cake pan lined with baking paper and press it well on the bottom of the pan.
- For the filling, mix all the ingredients in a bowl. Pour the mixture over the crust.
- For the topping, mix all the ingredients in a bowl until grainy.
- Top the cheesecake with this mixture and bake in the preheated oven at 350F for 45 minutes or until set in the center.
- Allow to cool down before slicing and serving.

Nutritional information per serving

Calories: 461

Fat: 37.4g

Protein: 11.0g

Carbohydrates: 22.8g

$\mathcal{B}$AKLAVA CHEESECAKE

Time: 1 ½ hours

Servings: 12

Ingredients:

Crust:

4 phyllo dough sheets, crumbled

¼ cup butter, melted

Filling:

4 cups cream cheese

2/3 cup white sugar

3 eggs

1 tablespoon vanilla extract

1 tablespoon cornstarch

1 pinch salt

Topping:

1 cup walnuts, chopped

¼ cup honey

Directions:

- For the crust, mix the phyllo dough and butter in a 9-inch baking pan lined with baking paper.
- Press slightly to arrange the dough in an even layer.
- For the filling, mix all the ingredients in a bowl until creamy. Pour the mixture over the phyllo dough and bake in the preheated oven at 330F for 45 minutes or until the center looks set.
- Allow the cheesecake to cool down then top with walnuts and honey.

- Serve chilled.

Nutritional information per serving

Calories: 472
Fat: 38.4g

Protein: 10.2g
Carbohydrates: 24.2g

*L*IME **P**INEAPPLE **C**HEESECAKE

Time: 1 ¼ hours

Servings: 10

Ingredients:

Crust:
1 ½ cups graham crackers, crushed
½ cup butter, melted
Filling:
1 cup crushed pineapple, drained
3 cups cream cheese

1 cup sour cream
3 eggs
1 tablespoon cornstarch
½ cup white sugar
1 lime, zested and juiced
1 pinch salt

Directions:

- For the crust, mix the two ingredients in a bowl. Transfer in a 9-inch round cake pan and press it well on the bottom of the pan.
- Top the crust with pineapple.
- For the filling, mix the cream cheese, sour cream, eggs, cornstarch, sugar, lime zest, lime juice and salt in a bowl. Pour the mixture over the pineapple.
- Bake in the preheated oven at 350F for 45 minutes or until the center looks set.
- Allow the cheesecake to cool in the pan before slicing and serving.

Nutritional information per serving

Calories: 496
Fat: 40.9g

Protein: 8.8g
Carbohydrates: 26.2g

*B*ANOFFEE **P**IE **C**HEESECAKE

Time: 1 ½ hours

Servings: 12

Ingredients:

Crust:
2 cups graham crackers, crushed
½ cup butter, melted
Filling:
2 bananas, sliced
1 cup dulce de leche
3 cups cream cheese

2 eggs
¼ cup heavy cream
1 teaspoon vanilla extract
¼ cup light brown sugar
1 pinch salt
1 tablespoon cornstarch

Directions:

- For the crust, mix the crackers and butter in a bowl. Transfer the mixture in a 9-inch round cake pan and press it on the bottom and sides of the pan.
- Top the crust with banana slices and dulce de leche.
- Mix the cream cheese, eggs, cream, vanilla, sugar, salt and cornstarch in a bowl.
- Spoon the filling over the dulce de leche and bake the cheesecake in the preheated oven at 330F for 40-45 minutes or until set in the center.
- Serve the cheesecake chilled.

Nutritional information per serving

Calories: 454
Fat: 32.0g
Protein: 7.9g
Carbohydrates: 35.9g

$\mathcal{B}$ ASQUE BURNT CHEESECAKE

Time: 1 hour

Servings: 10

Ingredients:

3 cups cream cheese
4 eggs
1 ½ cups white sugar
1 cup heavy cream

1 tablespoon all-purpose flour
1 pinch salt
Butter to grease the pan

Directions:

- Grease a 9-inch round cake pan with butter.
- Mix the cream cheese until fluffy and pale. Add the eggs, one by one, then stir in the rest of the ingredients and mix well.
- Pour the batter in the prepared pan and bake in the preheated oven at 400F for 40-45 minutes or until the cheesecake has a dark brown color.
- Allow to cool in the pan before slicing and serving.

Nutritional information per serving

Calories: 425
Fat: 30.5g

Protein: 7.8g
Carbohydrates: 32.9g

$\mathcal{M}$ IXED BERRY CHEESECAKE

Time: 1 ¼ hours

Servings: 12

Ingredients:

Crust:
1 ½ cups graham crackers, crushed
½ cup butter, melted
1 teaspoon vanilla extract
Filling:
4 cups cream cheese

4 eggs
¾ cup white sugar
1 tablespoon vanilla extract
1 tablespoon cornstarch
Topping:
2 cups mixed berries

Directions:

- For the crust, mix the crackers, butter and vanilla in a bowl. Transfer the mixture in a 9-inch round cake pan and press it well on the bottom of the pan.
- For the filling, mix the cream cheese, sugar, vanilla, eggs and cornstarch in a bowl pour the mixture over the crust and bake in the preheated oven at 330F for 45-50 minutes or until set in the center.
- Allow the cheesecake to cool down in the pan then top with mixed berries.

Nutritional information per serving

Calories: 470
Fat: 37.2g

Protein: 8.7g
Carbohydrates: 26.4g

$\mathcal{M}$ INI RASPBERRY CHEESECAKES

Time: 1 ½ hours

Servings: 14

Ingredients:

Crust:
2 cups graham crackers, crushed
½ cup butter, melted
1 teaspoon vanilla extract
Filling:
4 cups cream cheese
4 eggs

2/3 cup white sugar
1 teaspoon vanilla extract
1 tablespoon cornstarch
1 cup raspberry puree

Directions:

- For the crust, mix the crackers, butter and vanilla in a bowl. Transfer the mixture into 12 muffin cups lined with muffin papers and press it well on the bottom of each cup.
- For the filling, mix the cream cheese, eggs, sugar, vanilla and cornstarch in a bowl.
- Evenly pour the mixture into the muffin cups.
- Top the cheesecakes with a spoonful of raspberry puree. Swirl the puree into the cheesecake with a fork.
- Bake in the preheated oven at 330F for 25 minutes or until set.
- Serve the cheesecakes chilled.

Nutritional information per serving

Calories: 455
Fat: 32.2g

Protein: 7.6g
Carbohydrates: 36.1g

ERRY MASCARPONE CHEESECAKE

Time: 1 ¼ hours

Servings: 10

Ingredients:

Crust:
1 ½ cups Oreo cookies
¼ cup butter, melted
Filling:
1 ½ cups mascarpone cheese
2 cups cream cheese
3 eggs

1 teaspoon vanilla extract
1 tablespoon lemon zest
1 pinch salt
¾ cup white sugar
Topping:
2 cups mixed berries

Directions:

- For the crust, place the cookies in a food processor and pulse until ground. Add the butter and mix well. Transfer the mixture in a 9-inch round cake pan and press it well on the bottom of the pan.
- For the filling, mix the cheese, eggs, vanilla, lemon zest, salt and sugar in a bowl. Pour the mixture over the crust and bake in the preheated oven at 330F for 45 minutes or until set.
- Allow to cool in the pan then top with fresh berries and serve.

Nutritional information per serving

Calories: 361
Fat: 27.1g

Protein: 9.6g
Carbohydrates: 21.2g

ASSIONFRUIT BLUEBERRY CHEESECAKE

Time: 1 ¼ hours

Servings: 10

Ingredients:

Crust:
1 ½ cups vanilla biscuits, crushed
½ cup butter, melted
Filling:
4 cups cream cheese
2/3 cup white sugar

1 tablespoon vanilla extract
3 eggs
1 tablespoon cornstarch
¼ cup passionfruit juice
1 cup fresh blueberries

Directions:

- For the crust, mix the ingredients in a bowl. Transfer the mixture in a 9-inch round cake pan and press it well on the bottom of the pan.
- For the filling, mix the cream cheese, sugar, vanilla, eggs, cornstarch and passionfruit juice in a bowl. Pour the filling over the crust.
- Top with blueberries then bake in the preheated oven at 330F for 45 minutes or until the set looks set.
- Allow the cheesecake to cool down in the pan before slicing and serving.

Nutritional information per serving

Calories: 447

Fat: 36.6g

Protein: 8.0g

Carbohydrates: 22.8g

*T*HE ULTIMATE NO CRUST CHEESECAKE

Time: 1 hour

Servings: 12

Ingredients:

2 cups ricotta cheese

1 cup cream cheese

½ cup sour cream

1 cup sweetened condensed milk

1 teaspoon vanilla extract

3 eggs

2 tablespoons butter, melted

1 pinch salt

1 tablespoon cornstarch

Butter to grease the pan

Directions:

- Grease 1 9-inch round cake pan with butter.
- Mix the ricotta cheese and the rest of the ingredients in a bowl until creamy.
- Pour the mixture in the greased pan and bake in the preheated oven at 350F for 40 minutes or until slightly golden brown on the edges and set in the center.
- Allow the cheesecake to cool down in the pan before slicing and serving.

Nutritional information per serving

Calories: 263

Fat: 17.2g

Protein: 9.9g

Carbohydrates: 17.6g

*D*UO CHEESECAKE

Time: 1 ½ hours

Servings: 12

Ingredients:

Crust:

2 cups graham crackers, crushed

½ cup butter, melted

1 teaspoon vanilla extract

White layer;

1 ½ cups cream cheese

¼ cup sour cream

2 eggs

1 tablespoon cornstarch

¼ cup white sugar

1 teaspoon vanilla extract

Dark layer:

2 cups cream cheese

2 oz. dark chocolate, melted and chilled

2 eggs

1 teaspoon vanilla extract

¼ cup light brown sugar

Directions:

- For the crust, mix the ingredients in a bowl. Transfer the mixture in a 9-inch round cake pan and press it well.
- For the white layer, mix all the ingredients in a bowl until creamy.
- Pour the mixture over the crust.
- For the dark layer, mix the cream cheese with the melted chocolate. Add the rest of the ingredients then pour the mixture over the white one.
- Swirl it around with a fork and bake in the preheated oven at 330F for 45-50 minutes or until the center looks set.
- Serve the cheesecake chilled.

Nutritional information per serving

Calories: 452

Fat: 36.5g

Protein: 8.5g

Carbohydrates: 23.5g

*D*ARK CHERRY CHEESECAKE

Time: 1 ¼ hours

Servings: 12

Ingredients:

Crust:
1 ½ cups Oreo cookies
½ cup butter, melted
Filling:
4 cups cream cheese
4 oz. dark chocolate, melted
3 eggs

¼ cup heavy cream
¾ cup white sugar
2 tablespoons cocoa powder
1 tablespoon dark rum
1 pinch salt
1 tablespoon cornstarch
2 cups dark cherries, pitted

Directions:

- For the crust, place the cookies in a food processor and pulse until ground.
- Add the melted butter and mix well then transfer in a 9-inch round cake pan and press it well on the bottom of the pan.
- Top with the pitted cherries.
- For the filling, mix the cream cheese and chocolate in a bowl.
- Add the rest of the ingredients and mix well.
- Spoon the filling over the cherries and bake the cheesecake in the preheated oven at 330F for 50-55 minutes or until set in the center.
- Allow the cheesecake to cool in the pan before slicing and serving.

Nutritional information per serving

Calories: 480
Fat: 39.6g

Protein: 8.5g
Carbohydrates: 24.7g

ECADENT CHOCOLATE CHEESECAKE

Time: 1 ½ hours

Servings: 14

Ingredients:

Crust:
1 ½ cups chocolate cookies, crushed
½ cup butter, melted
Filling:
3 cups cream cheese
1 cup heavy cream
1 cup dark chocolate chips, melted

¾ cup white sugar
3 eggs
1 teaspoon vanilla extract
1 tablespoon cornstarch
Topping:
1 cup heavy cream
1 ¼ cups dark chocolate chips

Directions:

- For the crust, mix the ingredients in a bowl. Transfer the mixture in a 9-inch round cake pan lined with baking paper and press it well on the bottom of the pan.
- For the filling, mix the ingredients in a bowl until creamy. Pour the mixture over the crust and bake in the preheated oven at 330F for 50 minutes.
- Allow to cool down in the pan.
- For the topping, bring the cream to the boiling point.
- Remove from heat and add the chocolate. Mix until melted then allow to cool
- Top the cheesecake with the chilled topping chocolate cream.
- Serve the cheesecake chilled.

Nutritional information per serving

Calories: 489
Fat: 38.0g

Protein: 7.4g
Carbohydrates: 34.7g

WHITE CHOCOLATE CHEESECAKE

Time: 1 ¼ hours

Servings: 10

Ingredients:

Crust:

1 ½ cups graham crackers, crushed

½ cup butter, melted
Filling:
3 cups cream cheese
4 oz. white chocolate, melted
3 eggs

1 teaspoon vanilla extract
1/3 cups white sugar
1 pinch salt
1 teaspoon cornstarch

Directions:
- For the filling, mix the ingredients in a bowl. Transfer in a 9-inch round cake pan and press it well on the bottom of the pan.
- For the filling, mix the cream cheese, white chocolate, eggs, vanilla, sugar, salt and cornstarch.
- Pour the mixture over the crust and bake in the preheated oven at 330F for 45-50 minutes or until the center looks set if you shake the pan slightly.
- Allow the cheesecake to cool in the pan before slicing and serving.

Nutritional information per serving
Calories: 485
Fat: 39.7g

Protein: 8.5g
Carbohydrates: 25.3g

*B*LACKBERRY GINGER CHEESECAKE

Time: 1 ½ hours

Servings: 16

Ingredients:
Crust:
20 gingersnap cookies, crushed
1/3 cup butter, melted
Filling:
1 ½ cups fresh blackberries
2 tablespoons all-purpose flour
3 cups cream cheese

½ cup sour cream
2/3 cup white sugar
1 tablespoon lemon zest
1 teaspoon orange zest
3 eggs
1 pinch salt

Directions:
- For the crust, mix the ingredients well then transfer in a 9-inch round cake pan lined with baking paper. Press the mixture well on the bottom of the pan.
- Sprinkle the blackberries with flour then place them over the crust.
- For the filling, mix the cream cheese, sour cream, sugar, lemon zest, orange zest, eggs and salt in a bowl.
- Pour this mixture over the blackberries and bake in the preheated oven at 330F for 45-50 minutes or until the center looks set.
- Allow the cheesecake to cool down before slicing and serving.

Nutritional information per serving
Calories: 455
Fat: 29.6g

Protein: 6.4g
Carbohydrates: 42.6g

*A*LMOND COCONUT CHEESECAKE

Time: 1 ½ hours

Servings: 12

Ingredients:
Crust:
1 ½ cups graham crackers, crushed
¼ cup butter
¼ cup coconut cream
Filling:
3 cups cream cheese
½ cup coconut milk
½ cup sweetened condensed milk
1 cup shredded coconut

½ cup sliced almonds
3 eggs
1 teaspoon vanilla extract
1 pinch salt

Directions:

- For the crust, mix the ingredients in a bowl. Transfer in a 9-inch round cake pan lined with parchment paper and press it well on the bottom of the pan.
- For the filling, mix the ingredients in a bowl until creamy.
- Pour the mixture over the crust and bake in the preheated oven at 330F for 45-50 minutes or until the cheesecake looks slightly in the center when you shake the pan lightly.
- When done, remove from the oven and allow to cool down completely before serving.

Nutritional information per serving

Calories: 419
Fat: 35.1g

Protein: 8.9g
Carbohydrates: 19.4g

LEMONY STRAWBERRY CHEESECAKE

Time: 1 ¼ hours

Servings: 10

Ingredients:

Crust:
1 ½ cups vanilla biscuits, crushed
½ cup butter, melted
Filling:
3 cups cream cheese
1 lemon, zested and juiced

2/3 cup white sugar
1 pinch salt
3 eggs
1 tablespoon cornstarch
2 cups fresh strawberries

Directions:

- For the crust, mix the biscuits and butter in a bowl. Transfer in a 9-inch round cake pan lined with baking paper and press It well on the bottom of the pan.
- For the filling, mix the cream cheese, lemon zest, lemon juice, sugar, salt, eggs and cornstarch in a bowl.
- Pour the mixture over the crust and bake in the preheated oven at 350F for 45-50 minutes.
- When done, allow to cool down then top with fresh strawberries.
- Serve the cheesecake chilled.

Nutritional information per serving

Calories: 450
Fat: 35.9g

Protein: 8.0g
Carbohydrates: 26.4g

VERY VANILLA CHEESECAKE

Time: 1 ¼ hours

Servings: 10

Ingredients:

Crust:
1 ½ cups graham crackers, crushed
½ cup butter, melted
1 teaspoon vanilla extract
Filling:
3 cups cream cheese

1 cup sour cream
1 vanilla bean, split lengthwise, seeds removed
3 eggs
1 pinch salt
1 tablespoon cornstarch

Directions:

- For the crust, mix the ingredients in a bowl. Transfer the mixture in a 9-inch round cake pan and press it well on the bottom of the pan.
- For the filling, mix the cream cheese, sour cream, vanilla bean seeds, eggs, salt and cornstarch in a bowl.
- Pour the mixture over the crust and bake the cheesecake in the preheated oven at 330F for 40-45 minutes. Place a pan filled with water under the cheesecake while baking. This ensures a humid atmosphere in the oven and the cheesecake has less chances to crack on top.
- Allow the cheesecake to cool down completely before slicing and serving.

Nutritional information per serving

Calories: 460

Fat: 41.2g

Protein: 8.9g   Carbohydrates: 14.9g

COLORFUL BLUEBERRY CHEESECAKE

Time: 1 ¼ hours   Servings: 10

Ingredients:

Crust: 2/3 cup white sugar
1 ½ cups graham crackers, crushed   2 eggs
½ cup butter, melted   2 tablespoons cornstarch
Filling: 1 pinch salt
1 cup fresh blueberries   1 teaspoon lemon zest
3 cups cream cheese   1 tablespoon lemon juice

Directions:

- For the crust, mix the crackers and butter in a bowl. Transfer the mixture in a 9-inch round cake pan and press it well on the bottom of the pan.
- For the filling, combine all the ingredients in a blender and pulse until smooth.
- Pour the mixture over the filling.
- Bake the cheesecake in the preheated oven at 350F for 45-50 minutes or until the cheesecake looks set in the center if you shake the pan lightly.
- When done, remove from the oven and allow to cool down before serving.

Nutritional information per serving

Calories: 455   Protein: 7.5g
Fat: 35.7g   Carbohydrates: 28.6g

BROWNIE CHEESECAKE

Time: 1 ½ hours   Servings: 12

Ingredients:

Brownie layer: 3 cups cream cheese
3 oz. dark chocolate, melted   ½ cup sour cream
¼ cup butter, melted   2 eggs
2 eggs   1 teaspoon orange zest
¼ cup white sugar   1 teaspoon vanilla extract
½ cup all-purpose flour   ½ cup white sugar
1 pinch salt   1 pinch salt
Filling: 1 tablespoon cornstarch

Directions:

- For the brownie layer, mix the chocolate and butter in a bowl. Add the eggs and sugar and mix well.
- Fold in the flour then pour the batter in a 9-inch round cake pan lined with parchment paper.
- Bake in the preheated oven at 350F for 10 minutes.
- For the filling, mix all the ingredients in a bowl.
- Pour the filling over the brownie layer and continue baking at 330F for 40 additional minutes or until the cheesecake looks set when shaking the pan.
- When done, remove from the oven and allow to cool down in the pan before serving.

Nutritional information per serving

Calories: 385   Protein: 7.6g
Fat: 29.7g   Carbohydrates: 23.4g

CRÈME BRULEE CHEESECAKE

Time: 1 ¼ hours   Servings: 12

Ingredients:

Crust:
1 ½ cups Oreo cookies, crushed
½ cup butter, melted
Filling:
4 cups cream cheese
3 eggs
2/3 cup white sugar
1 teaspoon vanilla extract
1 teaspoon orange zest
1 pinch salt
Topping:
1/2 cup white sugar

Directions:

- For the crust, mix the cookies and butter in a bowl. Transfer the mixture in a 9-inch round cake pan and press it well on the bottom of the pan.
- For the filling, mix the ingredients in a bowl until creamy. Spoon the filling over the crust and bake in the preheated oven at 330F for 45 minutes or until set.
- When done, remove from the oven and allow to cool down slightly.
- Top with sugar and place under the broiler for 2-3 minutes until caramelized.
- Allow to cool down before serving.

Nutritional information per serving

Calories: 429
Fat: 35.8g

Protein: 7.3g
Carbohydrates: 21.8g

B URNT ORANGE CHEESECAKE

Time: 1 hour

Servings: 12

Ingredients:

Crust:
1 1/2 cups graham crackers, crushed
½ cup ground hazelnuts
¼ cup butter, melted
Filling:
3 cups cream cheese
1 cup white sugar
3 eggs
1 pinch salt
1 teaspoon vanilla extract
½ cup heavy cream
Topping:
2 blood oranges, sliced
½ cup light brown sugar

Directions:

- For the crust, mix the crackers, hazelnuts and butter in a bowl. Transfer the mixture in a 9-inch round cake pan lined with parchment paper and press it well on the bottom of the pan.
- For the filling, mix the cream cheese, sugar, eggs, salt, vanilla and cream in a bowl. Pour the filling over the crust and bake in the preheated oven at 330F for 45-50 minutes.
- When done, remove from the oven and allow to cool down.
- Top the cheesecake with orange slices and sprinkle with brown sugar.
- Using a blowtorch, caramelize the sugar on top.
- Serve the cheesecake chilled.

Nutritional information per serving

Calories: 434
Fat: 30.0g

Protein: 7.4g
Carbohydrates: 36.6g

M OCHA CHOCOLATE CHEESECAKE

Time: 1 ¼ hours

Servings: 12

Ingredients:

Crust:
1 ½ cups Oreo cookies, crushed
½ cup butter, melted
Filling:
4 cups cream cheese
4 oz. dark chocolate, melted
2 teaspoons instant coffee
3 eggs
2/3 cup white sugar
1 pinch salt

1 tablespoon dark rum

Directions:
- For the crust, mix the cookies and butter in a bowl. Transfer the mixture in a 9-inch round cake pan lined with parchment paper and press it well on the bottom of the pan.
- For the filling, mix all the ingredients in a bowl until creamy.
- Pour the mixture over the crust and bake in the preheated oven at 330F for 40-45 minutes or until the center looks slightly set.
- When done, allow the cheesecake to cool down before slicing and serving.
- Top it with whipped cream if you want.

Nutritional information per serving

Calories: 449

Fat: 38.6g

Protein: 8.0g

Carbohydrates: 19.0g

$\mathcal{P}$ EPPERMINT CHOCOLATE CHEESECAKE

Time: 1 ¼ hours

Servings: 12

Ingredients:

Crust:

1 ½ cups chocolate biscuits, crushed

½ cup butter, melted

Filling:

3 cups cream cheese

4 oz. dark chocolate, melted

3 eggs

2/3 cup white sugar

1 pinch salt

1 teaspoon vanilla extract

Topping:

1 cup heavy cream

1 cup dark chocolate chips

1 teaspoon peppermint extract

Crushed candy canes to decorate

Directions:
- For the crust, mix the ingredients in a bowl then transfer in a 9-inch round cake pan lined with parchment paper.
- Press the mixture well on the bottom of the pan.
- For the filling, mix the cream cheese and chocolate in a bowl until creamy.
- Add the rest of the ingredients and give it a good mix.
- Allow the cheesecake to cool down.
- For the topping, bring the cream to the boiling point in a saucepan. Remove from heat and add the chocolate. Mix well then stir in the peppermint extract.
- Top the cheesecake with the chocolate glaze.
- Serve the cheesecake chilled.

Nutritional information per serving

Calories: 476

Fat: 39.0g

Protein: 7.6g

Carbohydrates: 27.2g

$\mathcal{C}$ APPUCCINO CHEESECAKE

Time: 1 ¼ hours

Servings: 10

Ingredients:

Crust:

1 ½ cups graham crackers

½ cup butter, melted

1 teaspoon vanilla extract

Filling:

3 cups cream cheese

¼ cup milk powder

2 tablespoons cocoa powder

1 teaspoon instant coffee

1 teaspoon vanilla extract

3 eggs

2/3 cup white sugar

1 pinch salt

1 tablespoon cornstarch

1 tablespoon Amaretto liqueur

Directions:
- Make the crust by mixing the crackers and butter in a bowl. Transfer the mixture in a 9-inch round cake pan and press it well on the bottom of the pan.
- For the filling, combine all the ingredients in a bowl and give them a good mix.
- Pour the filling over the crust and bake the cheesecake in the preheated oven at 330F for 45-50 minutes or until the center of the cheesecake looks set if you shake it slightly.
- Allow the cheesecake to cool down before serving.

Nutritional information per serving

Calories: 471

Fat: 36.2g

Protein: 9.3g

Carbohydrates: 28.1g

CARAMEL PECAN CHEESECAKE

Time: 1 ½ hours

Servings: 14

Ingredients:

Crust:

2 cups graham crackers, crushed

½ cup butter, melted

Filling:

4 cups cream cheese

½ cup heavy cream

3 eggs

1 teaspoon vanilla extract

1 pinch salt

2 tablespoons dark rum

½ cup white sugar

¼ cup light brown sugar

1 tablespoon cornstarch

Topping:

1 cup white sugar

½ cup heavy cream

1 cup pecans

Directions:
- For the crust, mix the ingredients in a bowl. Transfer the mixture in a 10-inch round cake pan and press it well on the bottom of the pan.
- For the filling, mix all the ingredients in a bowl until creamy. Pour the filling over the crust and bake the cheesecake in the preheated oven at 330F for 45-50 minutes or until set in the center.
- Allow to cool down completely once baked.
- For the topping, melt the sugar in a heavy saucepan until it has an amber color.
- Add the cream and mix well until melted.
- Stir in the pecans and remove from heat. Allow to cool down.
- Top the cheesecake with the caramel and pecans just before serving.

Nutritional information per serving

Calories: 481

Fat: 35.0g

Protein: 7.3g

Carbohydrates: 35.8g

CARAMEL SWIRL CHEESECAKE

Time: 1 hour

Servings: 10

Ingredients:

Crust:

1 ½ cups graham crackers, crushed

1/3 butter, melted

Filling:

3 cups cream cheese

½ cup sour cream

3 eggs

½ cup white sugar

1 teaspoon vanilla extract

1 pinch salt

1 tablespoon cornstarch

1 cup caramel sauce

Directions:
- For the crust, mix the crackers and butter in a bowl. Transfer the mixture in a 9-inch round cake pan lined with parchment paper.
- Press it well on the bottom of the pan.

- For the filling, mix the cream cheese, sour cream, eggs, sugar, vanilla, salt and cornstarch in a bowl.
- Spoon the filling over the crust then drizzle the filling with caramel sauce.
- Using a fork, swirl the caramel sauce into the cheesecake.
- Bake in the preheated oven at 330F for 45 minutes or until the center looks set.
- Allow to cool down in the pan before slicing and serving.

Nutritional information per serving

Calories: 464

Fat: 29.3g

Protein: 8.6g

Carbohydrates: 44.5g

C HAI CHEESECAKE

Time: 1 ¼ hours

Servings: 10

Ingredients:

Crust:

1 ½ cups graham crackers, crushed

¼ cup ground almonds

½ teaspoon ground ginger

¼ teaspoon cinnamon powder

½ cup butter, melted

Filling:

3 cups cream cheese

½ cup sour cream

½ cup white sugar

3 eggs

½ teaspoon cinnamon powder

½ teaspoon ground ginger

½ teaspoon ground cardamom

1 pinch nutmeg

1 pinch salt

Directions:

- For the crust, mix all the ingredients in a bowl. Transfer the mixture in a 9-inch round cake pan lined with parchment paper and press it well on the bottom of the pan.
- For the filling, mix the cream cheese and the rest of the ingredients in a bowl until creamy.
- Pour the filling over the crust and bake in the preheated oven at 330F for 40-45 minutes or until the center of the cheesecake looks set.
- Remove from the oven when done and allow it to cool down before serving.

Nutritional information per serving

Calories: 473

Fat: 39.7g

Protein: 8.8g

Carbohydrates: 22.8g

EFRESHING KIWI CHEESECAKE

Time: 1 ½ hours

Servings: 10

Ingredients:

Crust:

1 ½ cups vanilla biscuits, crushed

1/3 cup butter, melted

Filling:

3 cups cream cheese

2 tablespoons butter, melted

¼ cup heavy cream

3 eggs

2/3 cup white sugar

1 teaspoon vanilla extract

1 tablespoon cornstarch

1 pinch salt

Topping:

1 pound kiwi fruits

Directions:

- For the crust, mix the biscuits and butter in a bowl. Transfer the mixture in a 9-inch round cake pan and press it well on the bottom of the pan.
- For the filling, combine all the ingredients in a bowl. Pour the mixture over the crust and bake in the preheated oven at 330F for 45-50 minutes or until the center of the cheesecake looks set.
- When done, remove from the oven and allow to cool down.
- Top the freshly baked cheesecake with kiwi fruit slices and serve it fresh.

Nutritional information per serving

Calories: 472
Fat: 36.4g

Protein: 8.3g
Carbohydrates: 30.4g

CHOCOLATE CHIP CHEESECAKE

Time: 1 ½ hours

Servings: 12

Ingredients:

Crust:
1 ½ cups graham crackers, crushed
1/2 cup butter, melted
2 tablespoons cocoa powder
Filling:
4 cups cream cheese
4 eggs

½ cup white sugar
1 pinch salt
1 teaspoon vanilla extract
2 tablespoons milk
1 tablespoon cornstarch
1 cup dark chocolate chips

Directions:

- For the crust, mix the ingredients in a bowl until well combined. Transfer in a 9-inch round cake pan and press the mixture well on the bottom of the pan.
- For the filling, mix the cream cheese, eggs, sugar, salt, vanilla, milk and cornstarch in a bowl.
- Fold in the chocolate chips then spoon the filling over the crust.
- Bake the cheesecake in the preheated oven at 330F for 45-50 minutes or until set in the center.
- Allow the cheesecake to cool down before slicing and serving.

Nutritional information per serving

Calories: 488
Fat: 40.0g

Protein: 9.4g
Carbohydrates: 26.5g

FRANGELICO CHEESECAKE

Time: 1 ¼ hours

Servings: 10

Ingredients:

Crust:
1 ½ cups graham crackers, crushed
½ cup butter, melted
Filling:
3 cups cream cheese
3 eggs
½ cup white sugar

¼ cup Frangelico liqueur
1 pinch salt
1 teaspoon vanilla extract
1 tablespoon cornstarch
Topping:
2 cups strawberries, sliced

Directions:

- For the crust, mix the ingredients in a bowl. Transfer the mixture in a 9-inch round cake pan and press it well on the bottom of the pan.
- For the filling, mix the ingredients in a bowl until creamy and airy.
- Spoon the filling over the crust and bake in the preheated oven at 330F for 45 minutes or until the center of the cheesecake looks set if you shake the pan.
- When done, remove from the oven and allow to cool down.
- Top the cheesecake with fresh strawberries.
- Serve the cheesecake chilled.

Nutritional information per serving

Calories: 465
Fat: 36.2g
Protein: 8.1g
Carbohydrates: 24.6g

ISTACHIO PASTE CHEESECAKE

Time: 1 ¼ hours

Servings: 10

Ingredients:

Crust:
1 ½ cups Oreo cookies, crushed
1/3 cup butter, melted
Filling:
3 cups cream cheese
½ cup pistachio paste

3 eggs
1 teaspoon vanilla extract
1 pinch salt
½ cup white sugar
1 tablespoon cornstarch

Directions:

- For the crust, mix the ingredients in a bowl. Transfer the mixture in a 9-inch round cake pan lined with parchment paper. Press the mixture well on the bottom of the pan.
- For the filling, mix the cream cheese, pistachio paste, eggs, vanilla, salt, sugar and cornstarch in a bowl until creamy.
- Pour the mixture over the crust and bake the cheesecake in the preheated oven at 330F for 45-50 minutes or until set in the center.
- Allow the cheesecake to cool down before slicing and serving.
- Store the cheesecake in the fridge.

Nutritional information per serving

Calories: 427
Fat: 37.0g

Protein: 8.6g
Carbohydrates: 17.7g

LMOND PRALINE CHEESECAKE

Time: 1 ½ hours

Servings: 12

Ingredients:

Crust:
1 ½ cups graham crackers, crushed
1/3 cup butter, melted
1 tablespoon dark rum
Filling:
3 cups cream cheese
½ cup sour cream
2 eggs

1 pinch salt
1 teaspoon vanilla extract
½ cup white sugar
½ cup almond flour
½ teaspoon almond extract
Topping:
½ cup white sugar
1 cup blanched almonds

Directions:

- For the crust, mix the ingredients in a bowl. Transfer the mixture in a 9-inch round cake pan lined with parchment paper and press it well on the bottom of the pan.
- For the filling, mix all the ingredients in a bowl until creamy. Pour the filling over the crust and bake in the preheated oven at 330F for 40-45 minutes or until the center of the cake looks slightly set is you shake the pan.
- Allow the cheesecake to cool in the pan when done.
- For the topping, melt the sugar in a heavy saucepan until it has an amber color.
- Remove from heat and stir in the almonds. Mix until coated then spoon on a baking tray lined with baking paper. Allow to cool down and set.
- When chilled, crack into smaller pieces. Top the cheesecake with the almond praline and serve the cheesecake fresh.

Nutritional information per serving

Calories: 442
Fat: 33.7g

Protein: 8.3g
Carbohydrates: 28.7g

N O BAKE MASCARPONE CHEESECAKE

Time: 2 hours

Servings: 10

Ingredients:

Crust:
1 ½ cups graham crackers, crushed
1/3 cup butter, melted
Filling:
1 ½ cups mascarpone cheese
¾ cup powdered sugar
1 cup cream cheese

1 tablespoon vanilla extract
1 pinch salt
1 teaspoon gelatin
2 tablespoons cold water
1 cup heavy cream, whipped
2 cups cherries, pitted

Directions:

- For the crust, mix the ingredients in a bowl. Transfer the mixture in a 9-inch round cake pan lined with parchment paper and press it well on the bottom of the pan.
- For the filling, mix the mascarpone cheese, sugar and cream cheese in a bowl for 5 minutes until airy and light.
- Bloom the gelatin in cold water for 10 minutes.
- Mix the cheese mixture with vanilla. Melt the gelatin and stir in the melted gelatin.
- Fold in the whipped cream then add the cherries.
- Spoon the mixture over the crust and place in the fridge to set for at least 1 hour.

Nutritional information per serving

Calories: 353
Fat: 24.8g

Protein: 7.8g
Carbohydrates: 25.0g

N o Bake Passionfruit Cheesecake

Time: 2 hours

Servings: 10

Ingredients:

Crust:
1 ½ cups vanilla biscuits, crushed
¼ cup butter, melted
1 teaspoon vanilla extract
Filling:
2 cups cream cheese

1 cup powdered sugar
1 teaspoon vanilla extract
¼ cup passionfruit juice
1 teaspoon gelatin
2 tablespoons cold water
1 cup heavy cream, whipped

Directions:

- For the crust, mix the biscuits, butter and vanilla in a bowl. Transfer the mixture in a 9-inch round cake pan lined with parchment paper and press it well on the bottom of the pan.
- Bloom the gelatin in cold water for 10 minutes.
- For the filling, mix the cream cheese, sugar and vanilla in a bowl until fluffy.
- Melt the gelatin and stir it in the cream cheese mixture.
- Add the passionfruit juice then fold in the whipped cream. Spoon the mixture over the crust and place in the fridge to set for at least 1 hour.
- Serve the cheesecake chilled.

Nutritional information per serving

Calories: 341
Fat: 26.2g

Protein: 5.1g
Carbohydrates: 21.9g

C hocolate Banana Cheesecake

Time: 1 ½ hours

Servings: 12

Ingredients:

Crust:
2 cups chocolate biscuits, crushed
½ cup butter, melted
2 tablespoons dark rum
Filling:

1 cup mascarpone cheese
4 oz. dark chocolate, melted and chilled
3 cups cream cheese
2 tablespoons dark rum
1 pinch salt

4 eggs
1 tablespoon cornstarch

2/3 cup white sugar
2 bananas, sliced

Directions:

Crust:

- Mix the ingredients in a bowl. Transfer the mixture in a 9-inch round cake pan and press it well on the bottom of the pan.
- Arrange the banana slices over the crust.
- For the filling, mix the mascarpone cheese and chocolate. Stir in the cream cheese, rum, salt, eggs, cornstarch and sugar and mix well.
- Spoon the mixture over the banana slices and bake in the preheated oven at 330F for 45-50 minutes or until set.
- Allow the cheesecake to cool down before slicing and serving.

Nutritional information per serving

Calories: 461
Fat: 35.3g

Protein: 9.8g
Carbohydrates: 25.7g

*C*HOCOLATE **S**TRAWBERRY **C**HEESECAKE

Time: 1 ½ hours

Servings: 10

Ingredients:

Crust:
1 ½ cups Oreo cookies, crushed
1/3 cup butter, melted
Filling:
3 cups cream cheese
3 eggs
1 pinch salt

1 teaspoon vanilla extract
2/3 cup white sugar
1 tablespoon cornstarch
½ cup dark chocolate chips
Topping:
2 cups strawberries, sliced

Directions:

- For the crust, mxi the cookies and butter in a bowl. Transfer in a 9-inch round cake pan lined with parchment paper and press it well on the bottom of the pan.
- For the filling, combine the cream cheese and the rest of the ingredients in a bowl and mix until creamy.
- Fold in the chocolate chips then pour the mixture over the crust.
- Bake the cheesecake in the preheated oven at 330F for 45-50 minutes or until the center looks set.
- Allow to cool down completely in the pan.
- When chilled, top the cheesecake with strawberry slices.
- Serve the cheesecake chilled.

Nutritional information per serving

Calories: 409
Fat: 33.5g

Protein: 7.6g
Carbohydrates: 22.4g

*C*OFFEE **G**LAZED **C**HEESECAKE

Time: 1 ½ hours

Servings: 12

Ingredients:

Crust:
1 ½ cups chocolate biscuits, crushed
½ cup butter, melted
1 teaspoon vanilla extract
Filling:
3 cups cream cheese
½ cup sour cream
3 eggs
1 pinch salt

2/3 cup white sugar
2 teaspoons instant coffee
1 tablespoon cornstarch
Topping:
¾ cup heavy cream
1 cup white chocolate chips
½ cup dark chocolate chips
2 teaspoons instant coffee

Directions:
- For the crust, mix the ingredients in a bowl. Transfer the mixture in a 9-inch round cake pan and press it well on the bottom of the pan.
- For the filling, mix all the ingredients in a bowl until creamy. Pour the mixture over the crust and bake in the preheated oven at 330F for 45-50 minutes.
- When done, allow to cool in the pan completely.
- For the topping, heat the cream in a saucepan just to the boiling point.
- Remove from heat and stir in the chocolate chips and coffee. Mix well then allow to cool down.
- Pour the glaze over the baked cheesecake and serve the dessert fresh.

Nutritional information per serving

Calories: 483

Fat: 39.9g

Protein: 7.5g

Carbohydrates: 26.5g

UTELLA CHEESECAKE

Time: 1 ¼ hours

Servings: 10

Ingredients:

Crust:

1 ½ cups graham crackers, crushed

1/3 cup butter, melted

Filling:

3 cups cream cheese

1 cup Nutella

2 tablespoons cocoa powder

3 eggs

1 teaspoon vanilla extract

1 pinch salt

¼ cup milk

1 tablespoon cornstarch

Directions:
- For the crust, mix the ingredients in a bowl until well combined. Transfer the mixture in a baking tray lined with parchment paper and press it well on the bottom of the pan.
- For the filling, combine all the ingredients in a bowl until creamy.
- Pour the filling over the crust and bake in the preheated oven at 330F for 45-50 minutes or until the center of the cake looks set in the center.
- Allow the cheesecake to cool down in the pan before slicing and serving.

Nutritional information per serving

Calories: 399

Fat: 34.4g

Protein: 8.4g

Carbohydrates: 15.6g

R ASPBERRY CHOCOLATE CHEESECAKE

Time: 1 ½ hours

Servings: 10

Ingredients:

Crust:

1 ½ cups Oreo cookies, crushed

1/3 cup butter, melted

Filling:

3 cups cream cheese

6 oz. dark chocolate, melted and chilled

3 eggs

1 pinch salt

½ cup white sugar

1 teaspoon vanilla extract

Topping:

2 cups fresh raspberries

Directions:
- For the crust, mix the cookies and butter in a bowl. Transfer the mixture in a baking tray lined with parchment paper and press it well on the bottom of the pan.
- For the filling, mix the cream cheese, chocolate, eggs, salt, sugar and vanilla in a bowl. Pour the filling over the crust and bake in the preheated oven at 330F for 45-50 minutes or until the center looks set.
- Allow the cheesecake to cool down in the pan then transfer on a platter. Top with fresh raspberries just before serving.

Nutritional information per serving

Calories: 460

Fat: 37.0g

Protein: 8.6g   Carbohydrates: 25.2g

CHOCOLATE FUDGE CHEESECAKE

Time: 1 ½ hours   Servings: 14

Ingredients:

Crust: ½ cup heavy cream
8 oz. chocolate biscuits, crushed   ¾ cup sweetened condensed milk
½ cup butter, melted   6 oz. dark chocolate, melted
Filling: 1 pinch salt
3 cups cream cheese   1 teaspoon vanilla extract

Directions:
- For the crust, mix all the ingredients in a bowl. Transfer the mixture in a 9-inch round cake pan lined with parchment paper and press it well on the bottom of the pan.
- For the filling, mix the ingredients in a bowl. Pour the filling over the crust and bake in the preheated oven at 330F for 45 minutes or until the center looks set.
- Allow the cheesecake to cool down before slicing and serving.

Nutritional information per serving

Calories: 441   Protein: 7.5g
Fat: 33.4g   Carbohydrates: 28.4g

CHOCOLATE PEANUT BUTTER CHEESECAKE

Time: 1 ¼ hours   Servings: 10

Ingredients:

Crust: 2 cups cream cheese
1 ½ cups graham crackers, crushed   1 cup sour cream
¼ cup butter   3 eggs
¼ cup smooth peanut butter   ½ cup white sugar
1 tablespoon dark brown sugar   ¼ cup light brown sugar
Filling: 1 pinch salt
½ cup smooth peanut butter   1 teaspoon vanilla extract

Directions:
- For the crust, mix the ingredients well then transfer the mixture in a 9-inch round cake pan lined with baking paper.
- Press the mixture well on the bottom of the pan and place aside.
- For the filling, mix all the ingredients in a bowl until smooth and creamy.
- Pour the filling over the crust then bake the cheesecake in the preheated oven at 330F for 45-50 minutes or until the center of the cheesecake looks set.
- Allow the cheesecake to cool down before slicing and serving.

Nutritional information per serving

Calories: 494   Protein: 11.7g
Fat: 37.9g   Carbohydrates: 30.3g

DRIED FRUIT CHEESECAKE

Time: 1 ½ hours   Servings: 12

Ingredients:

Crust: 2 tablespoons brandy
2 cups graham crackers, crushed   Filling:
½ cup butter, melted   3 cups cream cheese

1 cup ricotta cheese
1 cup mixed dried fruits, chopped
¼ cup brandy
½ cup white sugar

1 tablespoon vanilla extract
4 eggs
1 pinch salt
2 tablespoons cornstarch

Directions:
- For the crust, mix the ingredients well in a bowl then transfer the mixture in a 9-inch round cake pan lined with parchment paper.
- Press well on the bottom of the pan and place aside.
- For the filling, first of all mix the fruits with brandy in a bowl and allow to soak up for 30 minutes.
- Mix the cream cheese, ricotta, sugar, vanilla, eggs, salt and cornstarch in a bowl.
- Fold in the dried fruits then pour the filling over the crust.
- Bake in the preheated oven at 330F for 45 minutes or until the center of the cake is set if you shake the pan.
- Allow the cheesecake to cool down completely before slicing and serving.

Nutritional information per serving
Calories: 492
Fat: 32.5g

Protein: 10.2g
Carbohydrates: 38.8g

RÈME FRAICHE CHEESECAKE

Time: 1 ¼ hours

Servings: 10

Ingredients:
Crust:
1 ½ cups vanilla cookies, crushed
1/3 cup butter, melted
1 teaspoon vanilla extract
Filling:
2 cups crème fraiche

1 cup cream cheese
3 eggs
1 teaspoon vanilla extract
1 pinch salt
1 tablespoon cornstarch

Directions:
- For the crust, mix the ingredients in a bowl until well combined. Transfer in a 9-inch round cake pan and press it well on the bottom of the pan.
- For the filling, mix all the ingredients in a bowl until creamy.
- Pour the filling over the crust and bake the cheesecake in the preheated oven at 330F for 45-50 minutes or until the center of the cheesecake looks slightly set if you shake the pan.
- Serve the cheesecake chilled.

Nutritional information per serving
Calories: 285
Fat: 27.0g
Protein: 5.7g
Carbohydrates: 7.0g

INI GINGER CHEESECAKES

Time: 1 ¼ hours

Servings: 12

Ingredients:
Crust:
2 cups graham crackers, crushed
½ cup butter, melted
½ teaspoon ground ginger
Filling:
3 cups cream cheese

3 eggs
½ cup light brown sugar
1 teaspoon grated ginger
¼ teaspoon cinnamon powder
1 tablespoon cornstarch
1 pinch salt

Directions:

- For the crust, mix the ingredients in a bowl. Spoon the mixture in a muffin tin lined with muffin papers. Press it well on the bottom of the tin.
- For the filling, combine all the ingredients in a bowl. Pour the filling over the crust and bake in the preheated oven at 350F for 20 minutes or until set in the center.
- Allow to cool down before serving.

Nutritional information per serving

Calories: 372

Fat: 30.4g

Protein: 6.8g

Carbohydrates: 19.1g

I NDIVIDUAL PUMPKIN CHEESECAKES

Time: 1 ¼ hours

Servings: 12

Ingredients:

Crust:

2 cups gingersnaps, crushed

½ cup butter, melted

Filling:

1 cup pumpkin puree

3 cups cream cheese

2 eggs

½ cup light brown sugar

¼ teaspoon cinnamon powder

½ teaspoon ground ginger

¼ teaspoon salt

½ teaspoon vanilla extract

Directions:

- For the crust, mix the ingredients in a bowl. Spoon the mixture in a muffin tin lined with muffin papers and press it well on the bottom of the pan.
- For the filling, combine all the ingredients in a bowl and mix until creamy.
- Pour the filling over the crust and bake in the preheated oven at 330F for 20 minutes or until the center looks set.
- Allow to cool in the pan before serving.

Nutritional information per serving

Calories: 335

Fat: 29.5g

Protein: 5.9g

Carbohydrates: 12.9g

*N*EW YORK CHEESECAKES

Time: 1 ¼ hours

Servings: 12

Ingredients:

Crust:

1 ½ cups Oreo cookies, crushed

¼ cup butter, melted

Filling:

24 oz. cream cheese

2/3 cup white sugar

3 eggs

1 teaspoon vanilla extract

Topping:

2 cups sour cream

½ cup white sugar

1 teaspoon vanilla extract

Directions:

- For the crust, mix all the ingredients in a bowl. Transfer in a 9-inch round cake pan and press it well on the bottom of the pan.
- For the filling, mix all the ingredients in a bowl. Pour the filling over the crust.
- Wrap the pan in aluminum foil and place it in a deep baking pan.
- Pour hot water in the bigger pan, surrounding the cheesecake.
- Bake in the preheated oven at 330F for 45 minutes or until the center looks set.
- Remove from the oven.
- Mix the ingredients for the topping in a bowl.
- Top the cheesecake with the sour cream mixture and place back in the oven for 10 additional minutes.
- Allow to cool down before serving.

JAPANESE CHEESECAKE

Time: 1 ¼ hours

Servings: 10

Ingredients:

6 oz. white chocolate chips, melted
6 oz. cream cheese
1 teaspoon vanilla extract

6 eggs, separated
1 pinch salt
¼ cup white sugar

Directions:

- Mix the white chocolate, cream cheese and vanilla in a bowl.
- Add the egg yolks and mix well.
- Whip the egg whites with a pinch of salt until fluffy. Add the sugar and continue mixing until glossy and firm.
- Fold the whipped whites into the cream cheese mixture.
- Pour the mixture in a small round cake pan lined with baking paper.
- Bake in the preheated oven at 330F for 25-30 minutes.
- Allow to cool in the pan then slice and serve.

CHOCOLATE CHIP BANANA CHEESECAKE

Time: 1 ½ hours

Servings: 12

Ingredients:

Crust:
2 cups graham crackers, crushed
½ cup butter, melted
Filling:
3 cups cream cheese
2 bananas, mashed
1 teaspoon lemon juice

1 teaspoon vanilla extract
½ cup heavy cream
3 eggs
½ cup white sugar
1 tablespoon cornstarch
1 pinch salt
½ cup dark chocolate chips

Directions:

- For the crust, mix the crackers and butter in a bowl until well combined. Transfer the mixture in a round cake pan lined with baking paper and press it well on the bottom of the pan.
- For the filling, mix the bananas with lemon juice in a bowl.
- Add the rest of the ingredients and mix well.
- Fold in the chocolate chips then pour the mixture over the crust.
- Bake in the preheated oven at 330F for 45 minutes or until the center looks set.
- Allow to cool down before slicing and serving.

LEMON CURD CHEESECAKE

Time: 1 ¼ hours
Servings: 14

Ingredients:

Cheesecake:
3 cups cream cheese
3 eggs
½ cup white sugar
1 tablespoon lemon zest
1 teaspoon vanilla extract
¼ cup butter, melted
2 tablespoons cornstarch

Butter to grease the pan
Lemon curd:
4 egg yolks
½ cup butter
1 cup white sugar
1 pinch salt
1/3 cup lemon juice
2 tablespoons lemon zest

Directions:

- For the cheesecake, combine all the ingredients in a bowl and mix well.
- Grease a 8-inch round cake pan with baking paper then pour the filling in the pan.
- Bake in the preheated oven at 330F for 45-50 minutes or until the center looks set.
- Allow to cool in the pan then transfer on a platter.
- For the lemon curd, combine all the ingredients in a heatproof bowl. Place the bowl over a hot water bath and cook for 20 minutes, stirring all the time with a spatula or whisk, until thickened and creamy.
- Allow to cool down then spread it over the cheesecake.
- Serve chilled.

Nutritional information per serving

Calories: 377
Fat: 29.5g

Protein: 5.9g
Carbohydrates: 24.5g

𝓘 NDIVIDUAL MOCHA CHEESECAKES

Time: 1 ¼ hours

Servings: 12

Ingredients:

Crust:
2 cups Oreo cookies, crushed
½ cup butter, melted
Filling:
3 cups cream cheese
1 cup sour cream

¼ cup cocoa powder
3 teaspoons instant coffee
½ cup white sugar
1 pinch salt
3 eggs

Directions:

- For the crust, mix the cookies and butter in a bowl. Transfer in a muffin tin lined with muffin papers and press it well on the bottom of the muffin cups.
- For the filling, mix all the ingredients in a bowl until creamy. Pour the mixture over the crust and bake in the preheated oven at 330F for 20 minutes or until the center looks set if you shake the pan slightly.
- Allow to cool in the pan before serving.

Nutritional information per serving

Calories: 370
Fat: 33.6g

Protein: 6.9g
Carbohydrates: 13.0g

𝓚 AHLUA CHOCOLATE CHEESECAKE

Time: 1 ¼ hours

Servings: 10

Ingredients:

Crust:
1 ½ cups Oreo cookies, crushed
¼ cup butter, melted
1 tablespoon Kahlua
Filling:
3 cups cream cheese

1 cup dark chocolate chips, melted
2 tablespoons Kahlua
1 pinch salt
3 eggs
1 teaspoon vanilla extract
½ cup light brown sugar

1 tablespoon cornstarch

Directions:
- For the crust, mix the cookies, butter and Kahlua in a bowl until well combined. Transfer in a 9-inch round cake pan and press it well on the bottom of the pan.
- For the filling, mix all the ingredients in a bowl. Pour the mixture over the crust and bake in the preheated oven at 330F for 45-50 minutes or until the center looks set if you shake the pan.
- Allow to cool down before slicing and serving.

Nutritional information per serving

Calories: 411
Fat: 33.6g

Protein: 7.8g
Carbohydrates: 20.2g

ULCE DE LECHE CHEESECAKE

Time: 1 ¼ hours

Servings: 12

Ingredients:

Crust:
1 ½ cups graham crackers, crushed
1/3 cup butter, melted
Filling:
3 cups cream cheese

1 cup dulce de leche
1 teaspoon vanilla extract
3 eggs
1 pinch salt
1 tablespoon cornstarch

Directions:
- For the crust, mix the two ingredients in a bowl. Transfer the mixture in a 9-inch round cake pan and press it well on the bottom of the pan.
- For the filling, mix all the ingredients in a bowl until creamy.
- Pour the filling over the crust and bake the cheesecake in the preheated oven at 330F for 40-45 minutes or until the center looks set.
- Allow to cool in the pan before slicing and serving.

Nutritional information per serving

Calories: 385
Fat: 28.5g

Protein: 7.9g
Carbohydrates: 25.7g

MERINGUE CHEESECAKE

Time: 1 ½ hours

Servings: 12

Ingredients:

Crust:
1 ½ cups graham crackers, crushed
1/3 cup butter, melted
Filling:
24 oz. cream cheese
1 lemon, zested and juiced
2/3 cup white sugar

2 eggs
1 teaspoon vanilla extract
1 tablespoon cornstarch
Topping:
2 egg whites
½ cup sugar

Directions:
- For the crust, mix the ingredients in a bowl. Transfer the mixture in a 8-inch round cake pan and press it well on the bottom of the pan.
- For the filling, mix all the ingredients in a bowl until creamy. Pour the filling over the crust and bake the cheesecake in the preheated oven at 330F for 45 minutes or until the center looks set.
- Allow the cheesecake to cool in the pan.
- For the topping, combine the egg whites and sugar in a bowl and place over a hot water bath. Cook, stirring all the time, just until the sugar has dissolved.
- Remove from heat and whip with an electric mixer for 5-7 minutes until stiff and glossy.
- Top the cheesecake with the whipped whites and place under the broiler for 2 minutes just to brown slightly.

- Serve the cheesecake chilled.

Nutritional information per serving

Calories: 379

Fat: 26.7g

Protein: 6.6g

Carbohydrates: 30.2g

I RISH CREAM CHEESECAKE

Time: 1 ¼ hours

Servings: 12

Ingredients:

Crust:

1 ½ cups Oreo cookies, crushed

1/3 cup butter, melted

Filling:

24 oz. cream cheese

2/3 cup white sugar

2 tablespoons cocoa powder

¼ cup Irish cream liqueur

1 pinch salt

3 eggs

½ cup sour cream

Directions:

- For the crust, mix the ingredients in a bowl until well combined. Transfer in a 9-inch round cake pan and press it well on the bottom of the pan.
- For the filling, mix all the ingredients in a bowl. Pour the filling over the crust and bake the cheesecake in the preheated oven at 350F for 45-50 minutes or until the center looks set if you shake the pan lightly.
- Allow the cheesecake to cool in the pan before slicing and serving.

Nutritional information per serving

Calories: 381

Fat: 30.4g

Protein: 6.7g

Carbohydrates: 18.4g

S 'MORES CHEESECAKE

Time: 1 ½ hours

Servings: 14

Ingredients:

Crust:

2 cups graham crackers, crushed

½ cup butter, melted

Filling:

26 oz. cream cheese

4 oz. dark chocolate, melted

¼ cup cocoa powder

¼ teaspoon salt

1 cup white sugar

3 eggs

2 tablespoons chocolate liqueur

1 teaspoon vanilla extract

1 tablespoon cornstarch

Topping:

2 egg whites

½ cup white sugar

1 teaspoon vanilla extract

Directions:

- For the crust, mix the ingredients in a bowl until well combined.
- Transfer the mixture in a 9-inch round cake pan lined with baking paper and press it well on the bottom of the pan.
- For the filling, mix the cream cheese and melted chocolate in a bowl.
- Add the rest of the ingredients and mix well.
- Pour the filling over the crust.
- Bake in the preheated oven at 330F for 50 minutes or until the center of the cheesecake looks set.
- For the topping, whip the egg whites in a bowl until fluffy. Add the sugar, gradually and mix until fluffy and glossy.
- Stir in the vanilla then spread the meringue over the cheesecake.
- Place under the broiler for 2-3 minutes just until slightly browned on top.
- Allow to cool down before serving.

Nutritional information per serving

Calories: 462

Fat: 30.8g

Protein: 7.6g   Carbohydrates: 41.1g

PURE COCONUT VANILLA CHEESECAKE

Time: 1 ¼ hours   Servings: 12

Ingredients:

Crust: ½ cup shredded coconut
1 cup graham crackers, crushed   3 eggs
1 cup shredded coconut   1 tablespoon coconut flour
¼ cup coconut oil, melted   ½ cup coconut sugar
Filling: 1 tablespoon vanilla extract
1 cup coconut cream   1 pinch salt
3 cups cream cheese

Directions:

- For the crust, mix the ingredients in a bowl until well mixed. Transfer in a 9-inch round cake pan and press it well on the bottom of the pan.
- For the filling, combine all the ingredients in a bowl and mix well. Pour the filling over the crust.
- Bake in the preheated oven at 330F for 50-55 minutes or until the center of the cheesecake looks set if you shake the pan.
- Allow the cheesecake to cool in the pan before slicing and serving.

Nutritional information per serving

Calories: 404   Protein: 7.1g
Fat: 34.8g   Carbohydrates: 18.1g

BLUEBERRY LIME CHEESECAKE

Time: 1 ¼ hours   Servings: 12

Ingredients:

Crust: 1 teaspoon vanilla extract
1 1/2 cups graham crackers, crushed   1 lime, zested and juiced
½ cup butter, melted   2 eggs
Filling: 1 tablespoon cornstarch
3 cups cream cheese   ½ cup white sugar
½ cup sour cream   1 cup fresh blueberries

Directions:

- For the crust, mix the ingredients in a bowl until well combined. Transfer in a 8-inch round cake pan and press it well on the bottom of the pan.
- For the filling, mix the cream cheese, sour cream, vanilla, lime zest and lime juice, eggs, cornstarch and sugar until creamy.
- Pour the filling over the crust then top with blueberries.
- Bake in the preheated oven at 330F for 45-50 minutes or until the cheesecake looks set in the center.
- Allow to cool in the pan before serving.

Nutritional information per serving

Calories: 389   Protein: 6.5g
Fat: 31.7g   Carbohydrates: 21.4g

APPLE PIE CHEESECAKE

Time: 1 ½ hours
Servings: 14

Ingredients:

Crust:
1 ½ cups graham crackers, crushed
¼ teaspoon cinnamon powder
¼ teaspoon ground ginger
2 tablespoons dark brown sugar
1/3 cup butter, melted
Filling:
2 Granny Smith apples, peeled and diced
¼ cup light brown sugar

1 tablespoon lemon juice
1 cinnamon stick
3 cups cream cheese
½ cup heavy cream
2 eggs
1 tablespoon cornstarch
½ cup white sugar
1 teaspoon vanilla extract

Directions:
- For the crust, mix the ingredients in a bowl until well combined and fragrant. Transfer in a 9-inch round cake pan and press it well on the bottom of the pan.
- For the filling, start by mixing the apples, brown sugar, lemon juice and cinnamon stick in a saucepan. Add to the boiling point and cook until tender, about 5-7 minutes on low heat.
- Allow to cool then place it over the crust.
- For the filling, mix the cream cheese, heavy cream, eggs, cornstarch, sugar and vanilla in a bowl.
- Pour over the apples and bake in the preheated oven at 330F for 45-50 minutes or until set in the center.
- Allow to cool in the pan before serving.

Nutritional information per serving

Calories: 333
Fat: 24.9g

Protein: 5.4g
Carbohydrates: 23.6g

S TRAWBERRY JAM CHEESECAKE

Time: 1 ¼ hours

Servings: 14

Ingredients:

Crust:
1 ½ cups graham crackers, crushed
1/3 cup butter, melted
Filling:
4 cups cream cheese

3 eggs
½ cup white sugar
1 teaspoon vanilla extract
1 tablespoon cornstarch
1 cup strawberry jam

Directions:
- For the crust, mix all the ingredients in a bowl until well combined. Transfer in a 9-inch round cake pan and press it well on the bottom of the pan.
- For the filling, mix the cream cheese, eggs, sugar, vanilla and cornstarch in a bowl. Pour the mixture over the crust.
- Top the cheesecake with dollops of strawberry jam.
- Bake in the preheated oven at 330F for 45-50 minutes or until the center of the cake looks set.
- Allow to cool in the pan then slice and serve.

Nutritional information per serving

Calories: 438
Fat: 29.4g

Protein: 6.9g
Carbohydrates: 37.7g

M INTY CHEESECAKE

Time: 1 ¼ hours

Servings: 14

Ingredients:

Crust:
1 ½ cups graham crackers, crushed
1/3 cup butter, melted
Filling:
3 cups cream cheese

4 oz. dark chocolate, melted
3 eggs
1 teaspoon vanilla extract
1 teaspoon peppermint extract
1 pinch salt

½ cup white sugar

1 cup white chocolate chips

Directions:
- For the crust, mix the crackers and butter in a bowl. Transfer in a 9-inch round cake pan and press it well on the bottom of the pan.
- For the filling, combine the cream cheese, chocolate, eggs, vanilla, peppermint extract, salt and sugar in a bowl and mix until creamy.
- Fold in the chocolate chips.
- Pour the mixture over the crust and bake in the preheated oven at 330 for 45-50 minutes or until the center looks set.
- Allow to cool down before slicing and serving.

Nutritional information per serving

Calories: 401

Protein: 6.9g

Fat: 29.9g

Carbohydrates: 27.5g

$\mathcal{T}$WIX CHEESECAKE

Time: 1 ¼ hours

Servings: 14

Ingredients:

Crust:

4 eggs

2 cups Oreo cookies, crushed

2 tablespoons cornstarch

½ cup butter, melted

1 teaspoon vanilla extract

Filling:

½ cup white sugar

3 cups cream cheese

1 pinch salt

1 cup sour cream

4 Twix bars, chopped

Directions:
- For the crust, mix the ingredients in a bowl until combined. Transfer in a 9-inch round cake pan and press it well on the bottom of the pan.
- For the filling, mix the cream cheese, sour cream, eggs, cornstarch, vanilla, sugar and salt in a bowl. Fold in the bars and pour the mixture over the crust.
- Bake in the preheated oven at 330F for 45-50 minutes or until the center of the cheesecake looks set, but still slightly jiggly.
- Allow to cool in the pan before slicing and serving.

Nutritional information per serving

Calories: 406

Protein: 6.7g

Fat: 32.9g

Carbohydrates: 22.0g

$\mathcal{B}$ROWN SUGAR AMARETTO CHEESECAKE

Time: 1 ¼ hours

Servings: 10

Ingredients:

Crust:

¼ cup Amaretto liqueur

1 cup Amaretti biscuits, crushed

½ cup light brown sugar

½ cup graham crackers, crushed

2 eggs

¼ cup butter, melted

2 egg yolks

Filling:

1 pinch salt

1 ½ pounds cream cheese

1 teaspoon vanilla extract

Directions:
- For the crust, mix the biscuits, crackers and butter in a bowl until well combined. Transfer in a 9-inch round cake pan and press it well on the bottom of the pan.
- For the filling, combine all the ingredients in a bowl and mix well.
- Pour the filling over the crust and bake in the preheated oven at 330F for 45 minutes or until set.
- Allow to cool in the pan before slicing and serving.

Nutritional information per serving

Calories: 369
Fat: 30.6g

Protein: 7.2g
Carbohydrates: 12.8g

ED VELVET CHEESECAKE

Time: 1 ¼ hours

Servings: 10

Ingredients:

Crust:
1 ½ cups Oreo cookies, crushed
1/3 cup butter, melted
Filling:
3 cups cream cheese
1 cup sour cream

1 teaspoon red food coloring
1 pinch salt
1 teaspoon vanilla extract
1 teaspoon lemon juice
½ cup white sugar
1 tablespoon cornstarch

Directions:

- For the crust, mix the cookies and butter in a bowl until combined. Transfer the mixture in a 9-inch round cake pan and press it well on the bottom of the pan.
- For the filling, combine all the ingredients in a bowl and mix until creamy.
- Pour the filling over the crust then bake in the preheated oven at 330F for 45 minutes or until set in the center.
- Allow to cool down before slicing and serving.

Nutritional information per serving

Calories: 389
Fat: 35.3g

Protein: 6.1g
Carbohydrates: 13.8g

TIRAMISU INSPIRED CHEESECAKE

Time: 1 ¼ hours

Servings: 10

Ingredients:

Crust:
1 ½ cups Oreo cookies, crushed
1/3 cup butter, melted
1 tablespoon cocoa powder
Filling:
1 cup mascarpone cheese
3 cups cream cheese

1 teaspoon vanilla extract
½ cup white sugar
1 tablespoon instant coffee
1 pinch salt
3 eggs
Cocoa powder for dusting

Directions:

- For the crust, mix all the ingredients in a bowl. Transfer the mixture in a 9-inch round cake pan and press it well on the bottom of the pan.
- For the filling, mix all the ingredients in a bowl until creamy and thick. Pour the filling over the crust and bake in the preheated oven at 330F for 45 minutes or until set in the center.
- Allow to cool down then dust with cocoa powder.
- Serve the cheesecake chilled.

Nutritional information per serving

Calories: 404
Fat: 35.2g

Protein: 9.9g
Carbohydrates: 13.8g

SALTED CHOCOLATE CHEESECAKE

Time: 1 ¼ hours
Servings: 10

Ingredients:

Crust:
1 ½ cups graham crackers, crushed
2 tablespoons cocoa powder
1/3 cup butter, melted
Filling:
24 oz. cream cheese
8 oz. dark chocolate chips, melted

1 teaspoon salt
½ cup white sugar
1 teaspoon vanilla extract
3 eggs
1 tablespoon cornstarch
2 tablespoons cocoa powder

Directions:

- For the crust, mix the crackers, cocoa powder and butter in a bowl. Transfer the mixture in a 9-inch round cake pan and press it well on the bottom of the pan.
- For the filling, mix the cream cheese and chocolate in a bowl until creamy.
- Add the rest of the ingredients and mix well.
- Pour the filling over the crust and bake in the preheated oven at 330F for 45-50 minutes or until set in the center.
- Allow to cool in the pan before slicing and serving.

Nutritional information per serving

Calories: 430
Fat: 32.3g

Protein: 8.0g
Carbohydrates: 32.2g

ATMEAL CRUST CHEESECAKE

Time: 1 ¼ hours

Servings: 12

Ingredients:

Crust:
1 cup rolled oats
½ cup smooth peanut butter
½ cup graham crackers, crushed
Filling:
24 oz. cream cheese

¼ cup smooth peanut butter
½ cup light brown sugar
1 teaspoon vanilla extract
1 pinch salt
3 eggs
½ cup plain yogurt

Directions:

- For the crust, mix the ingredients in a bowl until well combined. Transfer the mixture in a 9-inch round cake pan lined with parchment paper.
- For the filling, mix the cream cheese, peanut butter, sugar, vanilla, salt, eggs and yogurt in a bowl. Pour the mixture over the crust.
- Bake in the preheated oven at 330F for 45-50 minutes or until the center looks set.
- Allow to cool down before serving.

Nutritional information per serving

Calories: 380
Fat: 29.9g

Protein: 11.4g
Carbohydrates: 18.7g

BROWNIE MANGO CHEESECAKE

Time: 1 ½ hours

Servings: 12

Ingredients:

Crust:
¼ cup butter
1 cup dark chocolate chips
2 eggs
¼ cup light brown sugar
¼ cup all-purpose flour
1 pinch salt
Filling:

1 mango, peeled and cubed
2 cups ricotta cheese
1 cup sour cream
2 eggs
1 teaspoon lemon juice
1 teaspoon lemon zest
1 teaspoon vanilla extract
1 tablespoon cornstarch

½ cup white sugar

Directions:
- For the crust, melt the butter and chocolate chips in a heatproof bowl. Add the rest of the ingredients and mix well.
- Pour the mixture in a 9-inch round cake pan lined with baking paper.
- Bake in the preheated oven at 330F for 10 minutes.
- Place aside when baked.
- For the filling, mix all the ingredients in a blender and pulse until smooth.
- Pour the mixture over the brownie crust and bake in the preheated oven at 330F for 45-50 minutes or until set in the center.
- Allow to cool down before serving.

Nutritional information per serving

Calories: 268

Fat: 15.3g

Protein: 8.2g

Carbohydrates: 26.6g

WHITE CHOCOLATE CARAMEL CHEESECAKE

Time: 1 ¼ hours

Servings: 12

Ingredients:

Crust:

1 ½ cups graham crackers, crushed

1/3 cup butter, melted

Filling:

24 oz. cream cheese

6 oz. white chocolate chips, melted

1 tablespoon vanilla extract

1 pinch salt

3 eggs

¼ cup caramel sauce

1 tablespoon cornstarch

Directions:
- For the crust, mix the ingredients in a bowl. Transfer in a 9-inch round cake pan and press it well on the bottom of the pan.
- For the filling, mix the cream cheese and chocolate in a bowl.
- Add the rest of the ingredients and mix well.
- Pour the mixture over the crust and bake in the preheated oven at 330F for 45-50 minutes or until the center looks set.
- Allow to cool down in the pan before slicing and serving.

Nutritional information per serving

Calories: 403

Fat: 31.6g

Protein: 7.4g

Carbohydrates: 23.3g

CRANBERRY EGGNOG CHEESECAKE

Time: 1 ¼ hours

Servings: 12

Ingredients:

Crust:

1 ½ cups graham crackers, crushed

1/3 cup butter, melted

Filling:

1 cup cranberries

3 cups cream cheese

½ cup sour cream

1 teaspoon vanilla extract

2 eggs

½ cup white sugar

1 pinch salt

1 tablespoon cornstarch

¼ cup eggnog

Directions:
- For the crust, mix the ingredients in a bowl then transfer the mixture in a 9-inch round cake pan and press it well on the bottom of the pan.
- Top the crust with cranberries.
- For the filling, mix all the ingredients in a bowl and mix well.

- Pour the mixture over the cranberries and bake in the preheated oven at 330F for 45-50 minutes or until well set in the center.
- Allow to cool in the pan before serving.

Nutritional information per serving

Calories: 370
Fat: 29.5g

Protein: 6.6g
Carbohydrates: 20.6g

*M*APLE CINNAMON CHEESECAKE

Time: 1 ¼ hours

Servings: 12

Ingredients:

Crust:
1 ½ cups gingersnaps, crushed
½ cup ground walnuts
1/3 cup butter, melted
Filling:
3 cups cream cheese

1 cup ricotta cheese
½ cup maple syrup
1 teaspoon vanilla extract
¼ teaspoon cinnamon powder
3 eggs
2 tablespoons butter, melted

Directions:

- For the crust, mix the ingredients in a bowl. Transfer the mixture in a 9-inch round cake pan lined with baking paper.
- Press it well on the bottom of the pan.
- For the filling, mix all the ingredients in a bowl until creamy. Pour the mixture over the crust.
- Bake in the preheated oven at 330F for 45-50 minutes or until set in the center if you shake the pan.
- Allow to cool in the pan before serving.

Nutritional information per serving

Calories: 388
Fat: 33.5g

Protein: 9.6g
Carbohydrates: 13.9g

*G*INGER EGGNOG CHEESECAKE

Time: 1 ¼ hours

Servings: 12

Ingredients:

Crust:
1 ½ cups gingersnaps, crushed
1/3 cup butter, melted
Filling:
3 cups cream cheese
½ cup eggnog
3 eggs

1 teaspoon vanilla extract
1 pinch nutmeg
¼ cup light brown sugar
1 tablespoon cornstarch
Topping:
2 cups heavy cream, whipped

Directions:

- For the crust, mix the gingersnaps and butter in a bowl. Transfer the mixture in a 9-inch round cake batter and press it well on the bottom of the pan.
- For the filling, mix all the ingredients in a bowl until creamy.
- Pour the mixture over the crust and bake in the preheated oven at 330F for 45-50 minutes or until set in the center.
- Allow to cool in the pan before serving.

Nutritional information per serving

Calories: 373
Fat: 35.0g
Protein: 6.8g
Carbohydrates: 9.1g

Chocolate Pumpkin Cheesecake

Time: 1 ¼ hours

Servings: 12

Ingredients:

Crust:
1 ½ cups Oreo cookies, crushed
1/3 cup butter, melted
Filling:
1 cup pumpkin puree
3 cups cream cheese
1 teaspoon vanilla extract
1 pinch salt

½ cup light brown sugar
3 eggs
1 tablespoon cornstarch
½ cup dark chocolate chips
Topping:
1 ½ cups heavy cream, whipped
Cocoa powder

Directions:
- For the crust, mix the cookies and butter in a bowl. Transfer the mixture in a 9-inch round cake pan and press it well on the bottom of the pan.
- For the filling, mix the ingredients in a bowl.
- Pour the mixture over the crust and bake in the preheated oven at 330F for 45-50 minutes or until set in the center.
- Allow to cool in the pan.
- Top the cheesecake with whipped cream and decorate with a dusting of cocoa powder.
- Serve the cheesecake fresh.

Nutritional information per serving

Calories: 376
Fat: 33.5g

Protein: 6.7g
Carbohydrates: 14.2g

Citrus Cheesecake

Time: 1 ¼ hours

Servings: 14

Ingredients:

Crust:
1 ½ cups graham crackers, crushed
1/3 cup butter, melted
Filling:
4 cups cream cheese
3 eggs
½ cup white sugar

1 lime, zested
1 lemon, zested
1 orange, zested
1 pinch salt
1 teaspoon vanilla extract
Fresh raspberries to decorate

Directions:
- For the crust, mix the crackers and butter in a bowl. Transfer the mixture in a 9-inch round cake lined with baking paper. Press it well on the bottom of the pan.
- For the filling, mix all the ingredients in a bowl until creamy. Pour the mixture over the crust and bake in the preheated oven at 330F for 45-50 minutes or until set in the center.
- Allow to cool in the pan before slicing and serving.

Nutritional information per serving

Calories: 358
Fat: 29.4g

Protein: 7.1g
Carbohydrates: 18.3g

Nutella Mocha Cheesecake

Time: 1 ¼ hours

Servings: 12

Ingredients:

Crust:

1 ½ cups chocolate cookies, crushed

1/3 cup butter, melted
Filling:
24 oz. cream cheese
½ cup white sugar
3 eggs
1 teaspoon vanilla extract

2 teaspoons instant coffee
½ cup Nutella
1 pinch salt
Topping:
1 ½ cups heavy cream, whipped
1 teaspoon instant coffee

Directions:
- For the crust, mix the ingredients in a bowl until well combined. Transfer the mixture in a 9-inch round cake pan and press it well on the bottom of the pan.
- For the filling, mix all the ingredients in a different bowl until creamy. Pour the mixture over the crust and bake in the preheated oven at 330F for 45-50 minutes or until the center of the cheesecake looks set if you shake the cheesecake.
- Allow to cool in the pan before slicing and serving.

Nutritional information per serving
Calories: 420
Fat: 34.5g

Protein: 7.1g
Carbohydrates: 22.3g

HAI LATTE CHEESECAKE

Time: 1 ¼ hours

Servings: 10

Ingredients:
Crust:
1 ½ cups gingersnaps, crushed
1/3 cup butter, melted
Filling:
24 oz. cream cheese
¼ cup milk powder
½ teaspoon cinnamon powder

½ teaspoon ground ginger
1 teaspoon vanilla extract
½ cup white sugar
½ cup sour cream
1 pinch salt
2 eggs

Directions:
- For the crust, mix the gingersnaps and butter in a bowl until well combined. Transfer the mixture in a 9-inch round cake pan and press it well on the bottom of the pan with your fingertips.
- For the filling, mix the cream cheese and the rest of the ingredients in a bowl until creamy.
- Pour the filling over the crust and bake in the preheated oven at 330F for 45-50 minutes or until set in the center if you shake the pan.
- Allow to cool in the pan before slicing and serving.

Nutritional information per serving
Calories: 394
Fat: 33.7g

Protein: 8.1g
Carbohydrates: 16.4g

NUTMEG SWEET POTATO CHEESECAKE

Time: 1 ¼ hours

Servings: 12

Ingredients:
Crust:
2 cups gingersnaps, crushed
½ cup butter, melted
Filling:
1 cup sweet potato puree
3 eggs

3 cups cream cheese
½ cup light brown sugar
1 pinch salt
¼ cup heavy cream
1 tablespoon cornstarch
¼ teaspoon nutmeg

Directions:
- For the crust, mix the gingersnaps and butter in a bowl until well combined. Transfer the mixture in a 9-inch round cake pan and press it well on the bottom of the pan.

- For the filling, mix the ingredients in a bowl until creamy and smooth.
- Spoon the filling over the crust and bake in the preheated oven at 330F for 45-50 minutes or until the cheesecake looks set in the center.
- Allow to cool in the pan before slicing and serving.

Nutritional information per serving

Calories: 365

Fat: 30.8g

Protein: 6.6g

Carbohydrates: 16.8g

Condensed Milk Cheesecake

Time: 1 ¼ hours

Servings: 10

Ingredients:

Crust:

1 ½ cups Oreo cookies, crushed

1/3 cup butter, melted

Filling:

2/3 cup sweetened condensed milk

16 oz. cream cheese

1 teaspoon vanilla extract

2 eggs

1 pinch salt

½ cup dark chocolate chips

Directions:

- For the crust, mix the cookies and butter in a bowl until well combined. Transfer the mixture in a 9-inch round cake pan and press it well on the bottom of the pan.
- For the filling, mix the milk, cream cheese, vanilla, eggs and salt in a bowl. Fold in the chocolate chips.
- Pour the filling over the crust and bake in the preheated oven at 330F for 45-50 minutes or until the center looks set.
- Allow to cool down before slicing and serving.

Nutritional information per serving

Calories: 325

Fat: 26.4g

Protein: 6.6g

Carbohydrates: 17.2g

Cranberry Sauce Cheesecake

Time: 1 ½ hours

Servings: 10

Ingredients:

Crust:

1 ½ cups graham crackers, crushed

1/3 cup butter, melted

1 teaspoon vanilla extract

Filling:

24 oz. cream cheese

3 eggs

½ cup white sugar

1 teaspoon vanilla extract

1 tablespoon cornstarch

Cranberry sauce:

1 cup cranberries

¼ cup white sugar

1 tablespoon lemon juice

Directions:

- For the crust, mix the crackers, butter and vanilla in a bowl until well combined. Transfer the mixture in a 9-inch round cake pan and press it well on the bottom of the pan.
- For the filling, mix all the ingredients in a bowl until creamy and smooth.
- Pour the filling over the crust and bake in the preheated oven at 330F for 45 minutes or until set.
- Allow to cool in the pan.
- For the sauce, mix the ingredients in a saucepan and place over low heat. Cook until the cranberries are softened.
- Slice the cheesecake and top it with the sauce just before serving.

Nutritional information per serving

Calories: 432

Fat: 32.5g

Protein: 7.7g

Carbohydrates: 28.5g

Lavender Lemon Cheesecake

Time: 1 ¼ hours

Servings: 12

Ingredients:
Crust:
1 cup graham crackers, crushed
½ cup gingersnaps, crushed
1/3 cup butter, melted
Filling:
24 oz. cream cheese
¼ cup butter, melted
½ cup white sugar
1 teaspoon vanilla extract

1 tablespoon lemon zest
2 tablespoons lemon juice
3 eggs
1 teaspoon lavender buds
1 pinch salt
1 tablespoon cornstarch
Topping:
2 cups heavy cream, whipped

Directions:
- For the crust, mix all the ingredients in a bowl until well combined.
- Transfer in a 9-inch round cake pan and press it well on the bottom of the pan.
- For the filling, mix all the ingredients in a bowl until creamy and smooth. Pour the mixture over the crust then bake in the preheated oven at 330F for 45-50 minutes or until set in the center.
- Allow to cool in the pan then top with whipped cream.
- Serve the cheesecake fresh and chilled.

Nutritional information per serving
Calories: 443
Fat: 38.4g

Protein: 6.9g
Carbohydrates: 19.4g

Chocolate Chip Mint Cheesecake

Time: 1 ¼ hours

Servings: 12

Ingredients:
Crust:
2 cups Oreo cookies, crushed
½ cup butter, melted
Filling:
24 oz. cream cheese
¼ cup butter, melted
½ cup white sugar

1 teaspoon peppermint extract
1 pinch salt
3 eggs
1 tablespoon cornstarch
½ cup dark chocolate chips
Topping:
1 ½ cups heavy cream, whipped

Directions:
- For the crust, mix the cookies and butter in a bowl until well combined. Transfer in a 9-inch round cake pan and press it well on the bottom of the pan.
- For the filling, mix all the ingredients in a bowl. Pour the mixture over the crust and bake in the preheated oven at 330F for 45-50 minutes or until set in the center.
- Allow to cool in the pan then top with whipped cream.
- Serve the cheesecake chilled.

Nutritional information per serving
Calories: 433
Fat: 39.6g

Protein: 6.5g
Carbohydrates: 15.5g

Cherry Vanilla Cheesecake

Time: 1 ¼ hours
Servings: 10

Ingredients:

Crust:
1 cup pecans, ground
1/2 cup graham crackers, crushed
¼ cup butter, melted
Filling:
1 cup cherries, pitted

24 oz. cream cheese
½ cup white sugar
1 tablespoon vanilla extract
1 pinch salt
3 eggs
1 tablespoon cornstarch

Directions:
- For the crust, mix the ingredients in a food processor and pulse until well mixed. Transfer in a 9-inch round cake pan and press it well on the bottom of the pan.
- Top the crust with cherries.
- For the filling, mix the cream cheese, sugar, vanilla, salt, eggs and cornstarch in a bowl. Pour the filling over the cherries and bake the cheesecake in the preheated oven at 330F for 45-50 minutes or until the center looks set.
- Allow to cool down in the pan before slicing and serving.

Nutritional information per serving

Calories: 377
Fat: 31.1g

Protein: 7.3g
Carbohydrates: 18.3g

*C*HOCOLATE SAUCE CHEESECAKE

Time: 1 ¼ hours

Servings: 10

Ingredients:

Crust:
1 ½ cups Oreo cookies, crushed
1/3 cup butter, melted
Filling:
3 cups cream cheese
3 eggs
2/3 cup white sugar

1 teaspoon vanilla extract
1 pinch salt
1 tablespoon cornstarch
Chocolate sauce:
1 cup heavy cream
1 cup dark chocolate chips

Directions:
- For the crust, mix the cookies and butter in a bowl until well combined. Transfer the mixture in a 8-inch round cake pan and press it well on the bottom of the pan.
- For the filling, mix the cream cheeses, eggs, sugar, vanilla, salt and cornstarch in a bowl. Pour the filling over the crust.
- Bake the cheesecake in the preheated oven at 330F for 45 minutes or until the center looks set.
- Allow to cool in the pan.
- For the sauce, bring the cream to the boiling point in a saucepan. Remove from heat and stir in the chocolate. Mix until melted and smooth.
- Serve the cheesecake with chocolate sauce.

Nutritional information per serving

Calories: 472
Fat: 39.6g

Protein: 8.1g
Carbohydrates: 25.1g

*F*UNFETTI CHOCOLATE CHEESECAKE

Time: 1 ½ hours

Servings: 10

Ingredients:

Crust:
1 ½ cups Oreo cookies, crushed
1/3 cup butter, melted
Filling:
20 oz. cream cheese
½ cup sour cream

6 oz. dark chocolate, melted
1 teaspoon vanilla extract
2 eggs
1 pinch salt
½ cup white sugar
1 tablespoon cornstarch

½ cup colorful sprinkles

Directions:
- For the crust, mix the cookies and butter in a bowl until well combined. Transfer the mixture in a 9-icnh round cake pan and press it well on the bottom of the pan.
- For the filling, mix the cream cheese, sour cream, chocolate and vanilla in a bowl. Add the rest of the ingredients and mix well.
- Fold in the sprinkles then pour the filling over the crust.
- Bake in the preheated oven at 330F for 45-50 minutes or until set in the center.
- Allow to cool in the pan before slicing and serving.

Nutritional information per serving
Calories: 441
Fat: 34.9g
Protein: 7.4g
Carbohydrates: 26.0g

Pies and Tarts

*P*EANUT BUTTER CREAM CHEESE TART

Time: 1 ¼ hours

Servings: 12

Ingredients:

Crust:
½ cup butter, softened
½ cup powdered sugar
1 egg
2 cups all-purpose flour
¼ teaspoon salt

Filling:
¾ cup smooth peanut butter
2 cups cream cheese
1 teaspoon vanilla extract
¼ cup maple syrup
1 cup heavy cream, whipped

Directions:
- For the crust, mix the butter and sugar in a bowl. Add the egg and vanilla and mix well. Stir in the flour and salt then transfer the dough on a floured working surface.
- Roll the dough into a thin sheet then transfer it in a tart pan. Press it well on the bottom and sides of the pan then trim the edges.
- Bake the crust in the preheated oven at 350F for 15-20 minutes until golden brown.
- Allow to cool in the pan.
- For the filling, mix the peanut butter and cream cheese in a bowl. Add the vanilla and maple syrup then fold in the whipped cream.
- Pour the cream into the crust and serve the tart chilled.

Nutritional information per serving

Calories: 451
Fat: 33.6g

Protein: 9.9g
Carbohydrates: 29.8g

*B*LUEBERRY PISTACHIO GALETTE

Time: 1 ¼ hours

Servings: 8

Ingredients:

1 ½ cups all-purpose flour
1 pinch salt
½ cup butter, chilled and cubed
¼ cup cold water

2 cups blueberries
¼ cup white sugar
1 teaspoon lemon zest
½ cup pistachios, chopped

Directions:
- Mix the flour, salt and butter in a bowl until grainy. Add the cold water and mix until the dough gets together.
- Transfer the dough on a floured working surface and roll it into a thin sheet, shaped as a round.
- Mix the blueberries, sugar, lemon zest and pistachio in a bowl. Spoon the mixture in the center of the dough and wrap the edges over the filling.
- Bake the galette in the preheated oven at 350F for 30 minutes or until golden brown on the edges.
- Allow to cool in the pan before serving.

Nutritional information per serving

Calories: 251
Fat: 13.6g

Protein: 3.6g
Carbohydrates: 30.5g

*W*HOLE WHEAT STRAWBERRY GALETTE

Time: 1 ¼ hours
Servings: 10

Ingredients:

1 cup whole wheat flour

½ cup all-purpose flour

1 pinch salt

½ cup butter

2-4 tablespoons cold water

2 cups strawberries, halved

1 tablespoon cornstarch

¼ cup white sugar

Directions:

- Mix the flours, salt and butter in a bowl then rub it with your fingertips until grainy.
- Add the water and mix until a dough forms. Transfer the dough on a floured working surface and roll it into a thin sheet, shaping it into a round.
- Mix the strawberries with cornstarch and sugar in a bowl. Place the filling in the center of the dough.
- Wrap the edges of the dough over the fruits, leaving the center exposed.
- Bake the galette in the preheated oven at 350F for 30 minutes or until fragrant and golden brown.
- Allow to cool down before serving.

Nutritional information per serving

Calories: 181

Fat: 9.5g

Protein: 2.2g

Carbohydrates: 22.3g

P UMPKIN CREAM PIE

Time: 1 ¼ hours

Servings: 10

Ingredients:

Crust:

2 cups graham crackers, crushed

1/2 cup butter, melted

Filling:

2 cups pumpkin puree

1 cup heavy cream

2 eggs

1 egg yolk

½ cup light brown sugar

1 tablespoon cornstarch

1 pinch salt

Directions:

- For the crust, mix the crackers and butter in a bowl. Transfer the mixture in a pie pan and press it well on the bottom and sides of the pan.
- For the filling, mix all the ingredients in a bowl until creamy.
- Pour the mixture into the crust and bake in the preheated oven at 330F for 40 minutes.
- Allow to cool in the pan before slicing and serving.

Nutritional information per serving

Calories: 259

Fat: 16.8g

Protein: 3.4g

Carbohydrates: 25.2g

M APLE PECAN PIE

Time: 1 ¼ hours

Servings: 10

Ingredients:

Crust:

1 ½ cups all-purpose flour

1 pinch salt

½ teaspoon cinnamon powder

½ cup butter, chilled and cubed

¼ cup maple syrup

2 tablespoons cold water

Filling:

1 cup pumpkin puree

2 eggs

¼ cup maple syrup

¼ cup heavy cream

1 pinch salt

¼ teaspoon cinnamon powder

2 cups pecan halves

¼ cup light brown sugar

Directions:

- For the crust, mix the flour, salt, cinnamon and butter in a bowl until grainy.

- Add the rest of the ingredients and mix well.
- When a dough has formed, transfer it on a floured working surface and roll it into a thin sheet.
- Transfer the dough on a pie pan and press it well on the bottom and sides of the pan.
- Bake the crust in the preheated oven at 350F for 10-15 minutes or until golden brown.
- Place aside.
- For the filling, mix all the ingredients in a bowl then pour the mixture into the crust.
- Place back in the oven at 330F for 40 minutes.
- Allow to cool down before slicing and serving.

Nutritional information per serving

Calories: 255
Fat: 13.5g

Protein: 3.8g
Carbohydrates: 31.0g

*D*ARK CHOCOLATE PUMPKIN PIE

Time: 1 ¼ hours

Servings: 12

Ingredients:

Crust:
½ cup butter, softened
½ cup powdered sugar
1 egg
2 cups all-purpose flour
1 pinch salt
Filling:
2 cups pumpkin puree

1 cup heavy cream
½ cup light brown sugar
½ teaspoon cinnamon powder
½ teaspoon ground ginger
¼ teaspoon ground cardamom
Topping:
1 cup heavy cream
1 cup dark chocolate chips

Directions:
- For the crust, mix the butter and sugar in a bowl until creamy. Add the egg and mix well then add the flour and salt and mix well.
- Transfer the dough on a floured working surface and roll into a thin sheet.
- Place the dough on a pie pan and press it well on the bottom and sides of the pan.
- Bake the crust in the preheated oven at 350F for 10 minutes. Allow to cool aside.
- For the filling, mix all the ingredients in a bowl. Pour the mixture into the crust then bake at 330F for 40 minutes.
- Allow to cool completely.
- For the topping, melt the cream and chocolate chips in a heatproof bowl over a hot water bath until creamy.
- Pour the chocolate mixture over the pie and allow to set.
- Serve the pie fresh.

Nutritional information per serving

Calories: 321
Fat: 18.4g

Protein: 4.2g
Carbohydrates: 37.5g

*T*ARTE AU CITRON

Time: 1 ¼ hours

Servings: 10

Ingredients:

Crust:
½ cup butter, softened
½ cup powdered sugar
1 egg
2 cups all-purpose flour
1 pinch salt
Filling:

4 eggs
1 egg yolk
¾ cup white sugar
½ cup heavy cream
½ cup fresh lemon juice
2 tablespoons lemon zest
1 pinch salt

Directions:
- For the crust, mix the butter and sugar in a bowl until creamy.

- Add the rest of the ingredients and mix well. Transfer the dough on a floured working surface and roll it into a thin sheet.
- Place the dough on a tart pan and press it well on the bottom and sides of the pan. Trim the edges if needed then bake the crust in the preheated oven at 350F for 15 minutes.
- Allow to cool aside.
- For the filling, mix all the ingredients in a bowl until creamy
- Pour the mixture into the crust then bake in the preheated oven at 330F for 30 minutes.
- Allow to cool in the pan before serving.

Nutritional information per serving

Calories: 313

Fat: 14.4g

Protein: 6.0g

Carbohydrates: 41.0g

PPLE FRANGIPANE TART

Time: 1 ¼ hours

Servings: 12

Ingredients:

Crust:

½ cup butter, softened

½ cup powdered sugar

1 egg

2 cups all-purpose flour

1 pinch salt

Filling:

½ cup butter, softened

½ cup light brown sugar

1 teaspoon vanilla extract

2 eggs

1 egg yolk

1 ½ cups ground almonds

2 Granny Smith apples, peeled, cored and sliced

Directions:

- For the crust, mix the butter and sugar in a bowl until creamy. Add the egg and mix well.
- Stir in the flour and salt then transfer the dough on a floured working surface and roll it into a sheet.
- Place the dough in a tart pan and press it on the bottom and sides of the pan. Trim the edges if needed.
- For the filling, mix the butter and sugar in a bowl until creamy.
- Add the vanilla, eggs, egg yolk and almonds and mix well.
- Spoon the filling into the crust and top with apple slices.
- Bake in the preheated oven at 350F for 45 minutes or until golden brown.
- Allow to cool in the pan before slicing and serving.

Nutritional information per serving

Calories: 360

Fat: 23.0g

Protein: 6.5g

Carbohydrates: 33.7g

LASSIC APPLE PIE

Time: 1 ¼ hours

Servings: 12

Ingredients:

Crust:

2 ½ cups all-purpose flour

½ cup butter, chilled and cubed

¼ cup coconut oil

¼ cup cold water

1 pinch salt

2 tablespoons powdered sugar

Filling:

2 pounds apples, peeled, cored and sliced

2 tablespoons cornstarch

¼ cup light brown sugar

¼ cup golden raisins

1 teaspoon cinnamon powder

1 pinch salt

Directions:

- For the crust, mix the flour, salt and sugar in a bowl.
- Add the butter and coconut oil and mix until grainy.
- Add the water and mix to form a dough.
- Transfer the dough on a floured working surface and cut it in half.

- Roll one half into a thin sheet then place it in a pie pan and press it on the bottom and sides. Trim the edges if needed.
- Mix the apples and the rest of the ingredients in a bowl. Transfer into the crust.
- Take the remaining dough and roll it into a thin sheet.
- Place over the apples and seal the edges, trimming them if needed.
- Make a few holes in the top layer of dough to allow the steams to escape then bake in the preheated oven at 350F for 50 minutes or until golden brown and crusty.
- Allow to cool in the pan then slice and serve.

Nutritional information per serving

Calories: 272

Fat: 12.6g

Protein: 3.1g

Carbohydrates: 38.2g

Ricotta Cheese Pie

Time: 1 ¼ hours

Servings: 10

Ingredients:

Crust:

2 cups graham crackers, crushed

½ cup butter, melted

Filling:

2 cups ricotta cheese

½ cup heavy cream

3 egg yolks

1 pinch salt

¼ cup white sugar

1 tablespoon lemon zest

1 teaspoon vanilla extract

Directions:
- For the crust, mix the ingredients in a bowl. Transfer the mixture in a pie pan and press it well on the bottom and sides of the pan.
- For the filling, mix all the ingredients in a bowl until creamy. Pour the mixture into the crust and bake the pie in the preheated oven at 350F for 35-40 minutes.
- Allow to cool in the pan before slicing and serving.

Nutritional information per serving

Calories: 278

Fat: 18.4g

Protein: 7.8g

Carbohydrates: 21.0g

Easy Banoffee Pie

Time: 1 hour

Servings: 10

Ingredients:

Crust:

2 cups graham crackers, crushed

½ cup butter, melted

Filling:

3 ripe bananas, sliced

1 cup dulce de leche

2 cups heavy cream, whipped

Chocolate curls to decorate

Directions:
- For the crust, mix the crackers and butter in a bowl. Transfer the mixture in a pie pan and press it well on the bottom and sides of the pan.
- Bake the crust in the preheated oven at 350F for 15-20 minutes or until golden brown.
- Allow the crust to cool down then fill it with banana slices.
- Top the bananas with dulce de leche.
- Cover the dulce de leche with whipped cream and decorate with chocolate curls.
- Serve the pie fresh and chilled.

Nutritional information per serving

Calories: 355

Fat: 21.1g

Protein: 3.7g

Carbohydrates: 40.1g

CRUMBLE GINGER PEAR PIE

Time: 1 ½ hours

Servings: 12

Ingredients:

Crust:
½ cup butter, chilled and cubed
1 ½ cups all-purpose flour
1 pinch salt
2 tablespoons powdered sugar
2-4 tablespoons cold water
Filling:
2 pounds pears, peeled, cored and cubed
¼ cup light brown sugar

2 tablespoons cornstarch
1 teaspoon ground ginger
1 pinch salt
Crumble topping:
½ cup butter, cubed
¾ cup all-purpose flour
½ teaspoon cinnamon powder
1 pinch salt
2 tablespoons dark brown sugar

Directions:
- For the crust, mix the flour, salt, sugar and butter in a bowl until grainy.
- Add the water and mix well.
- Transfer the dough on a floured working surface and roll it into a thin sheet.
- Place the dough on a pie pan and press it well on the bottom and sides of the pan.
- For the filling, mix the pears, sugar, cornstarch, ginger and salt in a bowl. Transfer the mixture into the crust.
- For the topping, combine all the ingredients in a food processor and pulse until grainy.
- Spread the topping over the pears and bake in the preheated oven at 350F for 45 minutes.
- Allow to cool in the pan before slicing and serving.

Nutritional information per serving

Calories: 293
Fat: 15.7g

Protein: 2.9g
Carbohydrates: 36.5g

CHOCOLATE RED VELVET PIE

Time: 1 ¼ hours

Servings: 10

Ingredients:

Crust:
½ cup butter, softened
½ cup powdered sugar
1 egg
1 ½ cups all-purpose flour
½ cup cocoa powder
1 pinch salt
Filling:
2 cups cream cheese

½ cup white chocolate chips, melted
¼ cup honey
1 teaspoon red food coloring
1 teaspoon vanilla extract
1 teaspoon lemon zest
2 eggs
1 tablespoon cornstarch
Topping:
1 cup heavy cream, whipped

Directions:
- For the crust, mix the butter, sugar and egg in a bowl until creamy.
- Add the flour, cocoa powder and salt and mix well.
- Transfer the dough on a floured working surface and roll it into a thin sheet.
- Place the dough in a pie pan and press it well on the bottom and sides of the pan. Trim the edges as needed.
- For the filling, mix the ingredients in a bowl until creamy.
- Spoon the filling into the crust and bake the pie in the preheated oven at 350F for 35-40 minutes.
- Allow to cool down then top with whipped cream.
- Serve the pie chilled.

Nutritional information per serving

Calories: 481
Fat: 34.6g

Protein: 8.8g
Carbohydrates: 37.2g

GREEK YOGURT PIE

Time: 1 hour   Servings: 8

Ingredients:

8 phyllo dough sheets, shredded   1 pinch salt
3 cups Greek yogurt   ½ cup white sugar
4 eggs   1 tablespoon cornstarch
1 teaspoon vanilla extract

Directions:

- Mix the yogurt, eggs, vanilla, salt, sugar and cornstarch in a bowl.
- Add the phyllo sheets and mix well.
- Pour the mixture in a greased pie pan and bake in the preheated oven at 350F for 35-40 minutes or until golden brown.
- Allow to cool in the pan then serve.

Nutritional information per serving

Calories: 197   Protein: 11.7g
Fat: 4.8g   Carbohydrates: 26.7g

JUICY PEACH PIE

Time: 1 ¼ hours   Servings: 10

Ingredients:

Crust: 2 pounds peaches, pitted and sliced
2 ½ cups all-purpose flour   2 tablespoons cornstarch
2 tablespoons powdered sugar   1/3 cup light brown sugar
2/3 cup butter, chilled and cubed   ¼ teaspoon cinnamon powder
¼ cup cold water   1 teaspoon lemon zest
Filling: 1 tablespoon lemon juice

Directions:

- For the crust, mix the flour, sugar and a pinch of salt in a bowl. Add the butter and mix until grainy.
- Stir in the water and knead slightly.
- Transfer the dough on a floured working surface and cut it into 2 equal pieces. Roll one half of dough into a thin sheet.
- Place the dough on a pie pan and press it well on the bottom and sides of the pan.
- For the filling, mix the peaches and the rest of the ingredients in a bowl. Transfer the filling into the crust.
- Take the remaining dough and roll it into a thin sheet. Place over the pie and seal the edges.
- Bake in the preheated oven at 330F for 45-50 minutes.
- Allow to cool in the pan before slicing and serving.

Nutritional information per serving

Calories: 289   Protein: 4.2g
Fat: 12.8g   Carbohydrates: 40.4g

LEMON MERINGUE PIE

Time: 1 ½ hours   Servings: 10

Ingredients:

Crust: 1 egg
1 ½ cups all-purpose flour   Filling:
1 pinch salt   1 ½ cups sweetened condensed milk
½ cup butter, softened   ½ cup heavy cream
¼ cup powdered sugar   4 egg yolks

1 egg
1 teaspoon vanilla extract
2 tablespoons lemon zest
½ cup lemon juice

Topping:
2 egg whites
1 pinch salt
½ cup white sugar

Directions:
- For the crust, mix the butter and sugar in a bowl until creamy. Add the egg and mix well then stir in the flour and salt.
- Transfer the dough on a floured working surface and roll it into a thin sheet.
- Place the dough in a pie pan and press it well on the bottom and sides of the pan.
- Trim the edges then bake the crust in the preheated oven at 350F for 10 minutes. Place aside when done.
- For the filling, mix all the ingredients in a bowl. Pour the mixture into the crust and bake for 20 additional minutes.
- Allow to cool in the pan.
- For the topping, mix the egg whites and salt in a bowl until fluffy.
- Add the sugar and mix well until glossy and firm. Pipe the meringue over the pie and place it under the broiler for 2 minutes just until it browns slightly.
- Allow to cool down before serving.

Nutritional information per serving
Calories: 409
Fat: 18.4g

Protein: 8.8g
Carbohydrates: 53.4g

REO BANOFFEE PIE

Time: 1 ¼ hours

Servings: 10

Ingredients:
Crust:
1 ½ cups Oreo cookies, crushed
¼ cup butter, melted
¼ cup chocolate, melted
Filling:
4 bananas, sliced

1 cup dulce de leche
Topping:
1 cup heavy cream
1 cup dark chocolate chips
1 cup heavy cream, whipped

Directions:
- For the crust, mix the ingredients in a bowl. Transfer in a pie pan and press it well on the bottom and sides of the pan.
- Bake the crust in the preheated oven at 350F for 10 minutes. Allow to cool down.
- Fill the crust with banana slices and dulce de leche and place in the fridge.
- For the topping, melt the chocolate and 1 cup heavy cream in a bowl over a hot water bath until smooth.
- Pour this mixture over the banana and dulce de leche and allow to set.
- Top the pie with whipped cream and serve it fresh and chilled.

Nutritional information per serving
Calories: 337
Fat: 19.5g

Protein: 3.8g
Carbohydrates: 41.0g

 HYLLO FIG PIE

Time: 1 hour

Servings: 12

Ingredients:
8 phyllo dough sheets
¼ cup butter, melted
1 ½ pounds figs, quartered

¼ teaspoon cinnamon powder
¼ cup light brown sugar

Directions:
- Take 4 phyllo dough sheets and shred them in a pie pan.
- Drizzle with half of the melted butter and top with figs, cinnamon and sugar.
- Cover the figs with the remaining phyllo dough sheet and drizzle with the remaining butter.
- Bake the pie in the preheated oven at 350F for 35-40 minutes or until golden brown.

- Allow to cool in the pan before serving.

Nutritional information per serving

Calories: 287

Fat: 5.4g

Protein: 5.2g

Carbohydrates: 59.2g

S 'MORES PIE

Time: 1 ¼ hours

Servings: 10

Ingredients:

Crust:

1 ½ cups graham crackers, crushed

1/3 cup butter, melted

Filling:

½ cup butter

1 cup dark chocolate chips

2 eggs

½ cup white sugar

½ cup all-purpose flour

1 pinch salt

Topping:

2 egg whites

½ cup white sugar

Directions:

- For the crust, mix the crackers and butter in a bowl. Transfer in a pie pan and press it well on the bottom and sides of the pan.
- For the filling, mx the butter and chocolate chips in a heatproof bowl and place over a hot water bath until melted and smooth.
- Stir in the rest of the ingredients then pour the mixture into the crust.
- Bake in the preheated oven at 350F for 25 minutes.
- In the meantime, whip the egg whites until stiff. Add the sugar and mix until glossy and firm.
- Top the pie with the meringue and place under the broiler for 2 minutes.
- Allow to cool down before slicing and serving.

Nutritional information per serving

Calories: 359

Fat: 20.8g

Protein: 4.3g

Carbohydrates: 42.6g

HUBARB STRAWBERRY GALETTE

Time: 1 ¼ hours

Servings: 10

Ingredients:

Crust:

½ cup butter, chilled and cubed

1 ½ cups all-purpose flour

2 tablespoons wheat bran

1 pinch salt

2 tablespoons dark brown sugar

4 tablespoons cold water

Filling:

1 pound strawberries

2 rhubarb stalks, sliced

2 tablespoons cornstarch

¼ cup white sugar

Directions:

- For the crust, mix the butter and the rest of the ingredients in a food processor. Pulse until well combined.
- Transfer the dough on a floured working surface and roll it into a thin sheet, shaping it into a round.
- For the filling, mix the strawberries, rhubarb, cornstarch and sugar in a bowl.
- Spoon the filling in the center of the dough and wrap the edges of the crust over the filling, leaving the center exposed.
- Bake the galette in the preheated oven at 350F for 30 minutes.
- Serve the dessert chilled.

Nutritional information per serving

Calories: 200

Fat: 9.6g

Protein: 2.5g

Carbohydrates: 27.0g

$\mathcal{P}$URE BLUEBERRY PIE

Time: 1 ¼ hours

Servings: 10

Ingredients:

Crust:
1 ½ cups all-purpose flour
2 tablespoons powdered sugar
1 pinch salt
¼ teaspoon baking powder
½ cup butter, chilled and cubed
4 tablespoons cold water

Filling:
3 cups blueberries
2 tablespoons cornstarch
¼ cup white sugar
1 tablespoon lemon zest
1 tablespoon lemon juice

Directions:

- For the crust, mix the ingredients in a food processor and pulse until well combined.
- Transfer the dough on a floured working surface and roll it into a thin sheet.
- Transfer the dough on a pie pan and trim the edges as needed.
- Mix the blueberries, cornstarch, sugar, lemon zest and lemon juice in a bowl.
- Transfer the filling into the crust and bake the pie in the preheated oven at 350F for 35-40 minutes.
- Allow to cool in the pan before serving.

Nutritional information per serving

Calories: 206
Fat: 9.6g

Protein: 2.4g
Carbohydrates: 28.9g

$\mathcal{M}$IXED BERRY PIE

Time: 1 ¼ hours

Servings: 10

Ingredients:

1 ½ cups all-purpose flour
2 tablespoons white sugar
1 pinch salt
½ cup butter, chilled and cubed
1 egg yolk
Filling:
3 cups mixed berries

2 tablespoons cornstarch
1 teaspoon lemon zest
1 teaspoon vanilla extract
¼ cup white sugar
Topping:
2 cups heavy cream, whipped

Directions:

- For the crust, mix the flour, sugar, salt and butter in a food processor. Pulse until well mixed and sandy.
- Add the egg yolk and mix well.
- Transfer the dough on a floured working surface and roll it into a thin sheet. Place the dough into a pie pan and press it well on the bottom and sides of the pan.
- For the filling, mix all the ingredients in a bowl. Transfer the mixture into the crust and bake the pie in the preheated oven at 350F for 35-40 minutes.
- Allow the pie to cool down then top it with whipped cream.
- Serve the pie chilled.

Nutritional information per serving

Calories: 297
Fat: 18.9g

Protein: 3.1g
Carbohydrates: 29.1g

$\mathcal{L}$IMONCELLO LIME TART

Time: 1 ¼ hours
Servings: 10

Ingredients:

Crust:
½ cup butter, softened
½ cup powdered sugar
1 egg
2 cups all-purpose flour
1 pinch salt
Filling:

1 ½ cups sweetened condensed milk
4 egg yolks
¼ cup Limoncello
2 limes, zested and juiced
¼ cup lemon juice
1 tablespoon lemon zest

Directions:

- For the crust, mix the butter and sugar in a bowl until creamy.
- Add the egg and mix well then stir in the flour and salt.
- Transfer the dough on a floured working surface and roll it into a thin sheet. Transfer the dough on a tart pan and press it well on the bottom and sides of the pan. Trim the edges.
- Bake the crust in the preheated oven at 350F for 10-15 minutes or until golden brown.
- For the filling, mix all ingredients in a bowl. Pour the filling into the crust and bake the tart for 20 additional minutes.
- Serve the tart chilled.

Nutritional information per serving

Calories: 387
Fat: 15.8g

Protein: 8.1g
Carbohydrates: 53.1g

S PICED PUMPKIN PIE

Time: 1 ¼ hours

Servings: 10

Ingredients:

Crust:
½ cup butter, softened
½ cup powdered sugar
1 egg
2 cups all-purpose flour
½ teaspoon ground ginger
½ teaspoon cinnamon powder
½ teaspoon ground cardamom

1 pinch salt
Filling:
2 cups pumpkin puree
1 cup heavy cream
4 egg yolks
½ cup light brown sugar
½ teaspoon cinnamon powder

Directions:

- For the crust, mix the butter and sugar in a bowl until creamy.
- Add the egg and mix well then stir in the flour, salt and spices.
- Transfer the dough on a floured working surface and roll it into a thin sheet. Place the dough in a pie pan and press it on the bottom and sides of the pan, trimming the edges as needed.
- For the filling, mix all the ingredients in a bowl. Pour the mixture into the crust and bake in the preheated oven at 350F for 35-40 minutes or until fragrant and golden.
- Allow to cool in the pan before serving.

Nutritional information per serving

Calories: 310
Fat: 16.3g

Protein: 5.1g
Carbohydrates: 36.9g

B LACK FOREST TART

Time: 1 ¼ hours

Servings: 10

Ingredients:

Crust:
½ cup butter, softened
½ cup powdered sugar
1 egg

1 ½ cups all-purpose flour
½ cup cocoa powder
¼ teaspoon salt
Filling:

2 cups sour cherries, pitted
½ cup white sugar
¼ cup red wine

1 ¼ cups heavy cream
1 ½ cups dark chocolate

Directions:
- For the crust, mix the butter and sugar in a bowl until creamy.
- Add the egg and mix well then stir in the flour, cocoa powder and salt.
- Transfer the dough on a floured working surface and roll it into a thin sheet.
- Place the dough on a tart baking pan and press it well on the bottom and sides of the pan. Trim the edges as needed.
- For the filling, mix the cherries, sugar and red wine in a saucepan. Cook until softened and thick.
- Spoon the sour cherry mixture into the crust.
- For the chocolate filling, bring the cream to the boiling point in a saucepan.
- Remove from heat and add the dark chocolate. Mix until melted and smooth.
- Pour the chocolate mixture over the sour cherries.
- Place in the fridge to set then slice and serve.

Nutritional information per serving
Calories: 435
Fat: 23.4g

Protein: 5.7g
Carbohydrates: 52.4g

*T*HYME PEAR PIE

Time: 1 ¼ hours

Servings: 10

Ingredients:
Crust:
½ cup white wine
½ cup canola oil
2 tablespoons maple syrup
½ teaspoon vanilla extract
1 ¾ cups all-purpose flour
1 pinch salt

Filling:
2 pounds pears, peeled, cored and sliced
1 teaspoon dried thyme
½ cup light brown sugar
1 tablespoon cornstarch
1 teaspoon lemon zest

Directions:
- For the crust, mix all the ingredients in a bowl and knead to form a dough. Place the dough on a floured working surface and roll it into a thin sheet.
- Place the sheet of dough in a pie pan and press it well on the bottom and sides of the pan. Trim the edges as needed.
- For the filling, mix all the ingredients in a bowl. Transfer the filling into the crust.
- Bake the pie in the preheated oven at 350F for 40-45 minutes or until golden brown on the edges.
- Allow to cool down before slicing and serving.

Nutritional information per serving
Calories: 280
Fat: 11.3g

Protein: 2.6g
Carbohydrates: 41.5g

B LUEBERRY ALMOND PIE

Time: 1 ¼ hours

Servings: 12

Ingredients:
Crust:
½ cup brown butter
2 tablespoons maple syrup
2 tablespoons water
1 ½ cups all-purpose flour
¼ teaspoon salt
Filling:
½ cup butter, softened

½ cup powdered sugar
2 eggs
2 egg yolks
1 ½ cups ground almonds
2 cups blueberries

Directions:
- For the crust, mix the butter, maple syrup and water in a bowl.
- Add the rest of the ingredients and mix well. Knead the dough slightly then transfer it on a floured working surface.
- Roll the dough into a thin sheet then place it in a pie pan and press it well on the bottom and sides of the pan. Trim the edges as needed.
- For the filling, mix the butter and sugar in a bowl until creamy.
- Add the eggs, egg yolks and almonds and mix well.
- Spoon the mixture into the crust then top with fresh blueberries.
- Bake in the preheated oven at 350F for 35-40 minutes or until golden brown on the edges.
- Allow to cool in the pan before serving.

Nutritional information per serving
Calories: 421

Fat: 25.2g

Protein: 11.0g

Carbohydrates: 39.0g

ℬ LACKBERRY LEMON CURD TART

Time: 1 ¼ hours

Servings: 10

Ingredients:
Crust:

½ cup butter, softened

½ cup powdered sugar

1 egg

½ cup ground almonds

1 ¾ cups all-purpose flour

¼ teaspoon salt

Filling:

½ cup butter, cubed

½ cup lemon juice

1 cup white sugar

2 tablespoons lemon zest

1 pinch salt

2 cups fresh blackberries

Directions:
- For the crust, mix the butter and sugar in a bowl until creamy.
- Add the egg and mix well then stir in the almonds, flour and salt.
- Transfer the dough on a floured working surface and roll it into a thin sheet.
- Place the dough in a tart pan and press it well on the bottom and sides of the pan.
- Bake the crust in the preheated oven at 350F for 15 minutes or until golden brown and crisp.
- Allow to cool in the pan.
- For the filling, mix the butter, lemon juice, sugar, lemon zest and a pinch of salt in a heatproof bowl. Place over a hot water bath and cook for 20 minutes, stirring all the time, until thickened.
- When done, remove from heat and pour the curd in the baked crust.
- Allow to cool down then top with blackberries.
- Serve the crust fresh.

Nutritional information per serving
Calories: 391

Fat: 21.7g

Protein: 4.5g

Carbohydrates: 47.0g

ℬ LUEBERRY PEACH CROSTATA

Time: 1 ¼ hours

Servings: 8

Ingredients:
Crust:

½ cup butter, chilled and cubed

1 tablespoon white sugar

1 ½ cups all-purpose flour

1 pinch salt

1 egg

2 tablespoons cold water

Filling:

¼ cup orange marmalade

1 1/2 pounds peaches, pitted and sliced

¼ cup light brown sugar

Directions:
- For the crust, combine all the ingredients in a food processor and pulse until well mixed.
- Transfer the dough on a floured working surface and roll it into a thin sheet, shaping it into a round.
- Spread the dough with orange marmalade. Top with peach slices and sprinkle with sugar.
- Wrap the edges of the dough over the filling and bake in the preheated oven at 350F for 35 minutes or until golden brown and crisp.
- Allow to cool down before serving.

Nutritional information per serving
Calories: 276

Fat: 12.5g

Protein: 4.0g

Carbohydrates: 38.6g

OURBON PEACH GALETTE

Time: 1 hour

Servings: 8

Ingredients:
Crust:

1 ½ cups all purpose flour

1 pinch salt

½ cup butter, chilled and cubed

¼ cup bourbon

Filling:

1 ½ pounds peaches, pitted and sliced

2 tablespoons bourbon

2 tablespoons cornstarch

¼ cup light brown sugar

1 pinch cinnamon powder

Directions:
- For the crust, mix the flour and butter in a food processor and pulse until grainy. Add the rest of the ingredients and pulse until well combined.
- Transfer the dough on a floured working surface and roll it into a thin sheet, shaping it into a round.
- Mix the peaches, bourbon, cornstarch, sugar and cinnamon in a bowl.
- Transfer the filling onto the dough, mainly the center.
- Wrap the edges of the dough over the filling, leaving the center exposed.
- Bake in the preheated oven at 350F for 30-35 minutes or until golden brown and crisp.
- Allow to cool in the pan before serving.

Nutritional information per serving
Calories: 269

Fat: 12.0g

Protein: 3.3g

Carbohydrates: 32.3g

UFF PASTRY BERRY TARTLETS

Time: 1 hour

Servings: 8

Ingredients:
1 puff pastry dough sheet

2 cups mixed berries

1 tablespoon cornstarch

3 tablespoons white sugar

1 teaspoon lemon zest

Directions:
- Cut the puff pastry dough into small squares.
- Mix the berries, cornstarch, sugar and lemon zest in a bowl.
- Top each square of puff pastry dough with the berry mixture.
- Bake in the preheated oven at 350F for 15-20 minutes.
- Allow to cool in the pan before serving.

Nutritional information per serving
Calories: 72

Fat: 2.4g

Protein: 0.6g

Carbohydrates: 12.2g

KEY LIME TARTLETS

Time: 1 ¼ hours   Servings: 12

Ingredients:

Crust: 1 ½ cups sweetened condensed milk
2 cups graham crackers, crushed   3 key limes, zested and juiced
½ cup butter, melted   4 egg yolks
2 tablespoons dark brown sugar   ¼ cup butter, melted
Filling: 1 pinch salt

Directions:

- For the crust, mix the ingredients in a food processor until well combined.
- Transfer the mixture in 12 small tartlet pans and press it well on the bottom and sides of the pan.
- For the filling, mix all the ingredients in a bowl.
- Pour the mixture into each crust and bake in the preheated oven at 350F for 15-20 minutes.
- Allow to cool in the pan before serving.

Nutritional information per serving

Calories: 312   Protein: 5.1g
Fat: 17.8g   Carbohydrates: 35.0g

MIXED FRUIT GALETTE

Time: 1 hour   Servings: 8

Ingredients:

1 sheet puff pastry dough   2 plums, pitted and sliced
¼ cup breadcrumbs   1 tablespoon cornstarch
1 cup blueberries   ¼ cup light brown sugar
1 cup strawberries   1 tablespoon lemon juice
1 peach, pitted and sliced

Directions:

- Spread the breadcrumbs over the puff pastry dough.
- Mix the fruits, cornstarch, sugar and lemon juice in a bowl.
- Top the dough with the fruit mixture then carefully wrap the dough over the fruit filling, leaving the center exposed.
- Bake in the preheated oven at 350F for 30 minutes.
- Allow to cool in the pan before slicing and serving.

Nutritional information per serving

Calories: 92   Protein: 1.3g
Fat: 2.6g   Carbohydrates: 16.8g

PLUM STREUSEL PIE

Time: 1 ¼ hours   Servings: 10

Ingredients:

Crust: ¼ cup light brown sugar
½ cup butter, chilled and cubed   Streusel:
1 ½ cups all-purpose flour   ¼ cup butter, chilled and cubed
1 pinch salt   ½ cup all-purpose flour
4 tablespoons cold water   1 cup ground walnuts
Filling: 2 tablespoons dark brown sugar
2 pounds plums, pitted and sliced
1 tablespoon cornstarch

Directions:

- For the crust, mix all the ingredients in a food processor and pulse until well mixed.
- Transfer the dough on a floured working surface and roll it into a thin sheet. Place it in a pie pan and press it well on the bottom and sides of the pan. Trim the edges as needed.
- For the filling, mix all the ingredients in a bowl. Transfer the mixture into the crust.
- For the streusel, combine all the ingredients in a bowl until grainy. Spread the streusel over the plums and bake the pie in the preheated oven at 350F for 40-45 minutes or until golden brown and fragrant.
- Allow to cool in the pan before slicing and serving.

Nutritional information per serving

Calories: 341   Protein: 6.2g
Fat: 21.6g   Carbohydrates: 33.2g

UTELLA BANANA TART

Time: 1 ¼ hours   Servings: 10

Ingredients:

Crust: 2 tablespoon water
1 ½ cups all-purpose flour   Filling:
2 tablespoons white sugar   2 bananas, sliced
1 pinch salt   2 cups heavy cream, whipped
½ cup butter, chilled and cubed 1 cup Nutella
1 egg yolk   1 teaspoon vanilla extract

Directions:

- For the crust, combine all the ingredients in a food processor. Pulse until well mixed then transfer the dough in a tart pan and press it well on the bottom and sides of the pan.
- Bake the crust in the preheated oven at 350F for 15-20 minutes or until golden brown and crusty.
- Allow to cool down.
- Fill the crust with banana slices.
- Mix the whipped cream with Nutella and vanilla extract. Spoon the cream over the banana slices.
- Serve the tart fresh and chilled.

Nutritional information per serving

Calories: 289   Protein: 3.3g
Fat: 19.9g   Carbohydrates: 25.2g

RAPEFRUIT FLAVORED APPLE PIE

Time: 1 ¼ hours   Servings: 10

Ingredients:

Crust: 2 pounds apples, peeled and cubed
½ cup butter, chilled and cubed 4 tablespoons grapefruit juice
1 ½ cups all-purpose flour   1 tablespoon grapefruit zest
1 pinch salt   2 tablespoons cornstarch
1 egg yolks   ½ teaspoon vanilla extract
2 tablespoons cold water   ¼ teaspoon cinnamon powder
Filling: 1 pinch salt

Directions:

- For the crust, combine all the ingredients in a food processor. Pulse until well mixed then transfer the dough on a floured working surface.
- Roll the dough into a thin sheet then place it in a pie pan. Press it well on the bottom and sides of the pan.
- For the filling, mix all the ingredients in a bowl. Transfer the mixture into the crust.
- Bake the pie in the preheated oven at 350F for 35-40 minutes.
- Allow to cool in the pan before slicing and serving.

Nutritional information per serving
Calories: 211
Fat: 10.0g

Protein: 2.6g
Carbohydrates: 29.0g

PRICOT FRANGIPANE TARTLETS

Time: 1 ¼ hours

Servings: 12

Ingredients:
Crust:
½ cup butter, softened
½ cup powdered sugar
1 egg
½ cup ground almonds
1 ¾ cups all-purpose flour
1 pinch salt
Filling:

1 cup butter, softened
½ cup powdered sugar
2 eggs
2 egg yolks
1 teaspoon vanilla extract
1 ¾ cups ground almonds
1 pinch salt
1 pound apricots, pitted and halved

Directions:
- For the crust, mix the butter and sugar in a bowl until creamy.
- Add the egg and mix well then stir in the rest of the ingredients.
- Transfer the dough on a floured working surface and roll it into a thin sheet.
- Transfer pieces of the dough into 10 small tartlet pans and press it well on the bottom and sides of the pan.
- For the filling, mix the butter and sugar in a bowl until creamy.
- Add the eggs, egg yolks, vanilla, almonds and salt and mix well.
- Spoon the filling into the tartlets and top with apricot halves.
- Bake in the preheated oven at 350F for 20 minutes.
- Allow to cool in the pan before serving.

Nutritional information per serving
Calories: 456
Fat: 34.2g

Protein: 8.2g
Carbohydrates: 32.1g

WALNUT BROWNIE TART

Time: 1 ¼ hours

Servings: 10

Ingredients:
Crust:
1 ½ cups Oreo cookies, crushed
1/3 cup butter, melted
Filling:
½ cup butter
1 ½ cups dark chocolate chips

3 eggs
½ cup white sugar
½ teaspoon vanilla extract
½ cup all-purpose flour
¼ teaspoon salt
1 cup walnuts, chopped

Directions:
- For the crust, mix the ingredients in a bowl. Transfer the mixture in a small tart pan and press it well on the bottom and sides of the pan.
- For the filling, mix the butter and chocolate in a bowl and place over a hot water bath until melted and smooth.
- Remove from heat and stir in the rest of the ingredients.
- Pour the filling into the crust and bake in the preheated oven at 350F for 20-25 minutes.
- Allow to cool in the pan before slicing and serving.

Nutritional information per serving
Calories: 381
Fat: 29.1g
Protein: 6.7g
Carbohydrates: 28.9g

*D*OUBLE CRUST BLUEBERRY PIE

Time: 1 ½ hours

Servings: 10

Ingredients:

Crust:
¾ cup butter, chilled and cubed
2 ½ cups all-purpose flour
1 pinch salt
¼ teaspoon baking powder
1 egg
¼ cup cold water

Filling:
3 cups fresh blueberries
1 tablespoon lemon zest
2 tablespoons cornstarch
½ cup white sugar
1 tablespoon lemon juice
1 pinch salt

Directions:

• For the crust, combine all the ingredients in a food processor. Pulse until well mixed then transfer the dough on a floured working surface and cut it into 2 equal portions.
• Roll one part of the dough into a thin sheet and place it in a baking pie pan. Press it well on the bottom and sides of the pan.
• Mix the blueberries, lemon zest, lemon juice, cornstarch, sugar and salt in a bowl.
• Spoon the filling into the crust.
• Take the remaining half of dough on a floured working surface and roll it into a thin sheet. Place over the blueberries and seal the edges.
• Bake in the preheated oven at 350F for 40-45 minutes or until golden brown.
• Allow to cool in the pan before slicing and serving.

Nutritional information per serving

Calories: 312
Fat: 14.7g

Protein: 4.3g
Carbohydrates: 41.9g

*R*USTIC APPLE TART

Time: 1 hour

Servings: 8

Ingredients:

Crust:
1 ¼ cups all-purpose flour
¼ teaspoon salt
¼ teaspoon baking powder
¼ cup butter, chilled and cubed
½ cup sour cream

Filling:
1 ½ pounds apples, peeled, cored and sliced
¼ cup light brown sugar
1 tablespoon cornstarch
½ teaspoon cinnamon powder
1 tablespoon lemon juice

Directions:

• For the crust, mix the flour, salt and baking powder in a food processor.
• Add the butter and mix until grainy.
• Stir in the sour cream and pulse until well combined.
• Transfer the dough on a floured working surface and roll it into a thin sheet, shaping it into a round.
• Mix the ingredients of the filling in a bowl.
• Top the dough with the apple filling then wrap the edges of the dough over the filling, leaving the center unexposed.
• Bake in the preheated oven at 350F for 30-35 minutes or until golden brown and crusty.
• Allow to cool in the pan before serving.

Nutritional information per serving

Calories: 219
Fat: 9.1g
Protein: 2.8g
Carbohydrates: 32.7g

Healthy Desserts

Thick Berry Smoothie Bowl

Time: 15 minutes   Servings: 4

Ingredients:

1 cup plain yogurt   ½ cup mixed berries for topping
1 banana   ¼ cup rolled oats
1 cup mixed berries   ¼ cup almond slices
2 tablespoons honey   ½ teaspoon cinnamon powder
½ cup almond milk

Directions:

• Mix the yogurt, banana, berries, honey and almond milk in a blender. Pulse until smooth.
• Pour the smoothie in 2 bowls.
• Top each bowl with mixed berries, oats, almond slices and a sprinkle of cinnamon.
• Serve the dessert fresh.

Nutritional information per serving

Calories: 265   Protein: 7.1g
Fat: 12.3g   Carbohydrates: 32.7g

Vegan Sweet Potato Donuts

Time: 1 hour   Servings: 12

Ingredients:

Donuts: 2 tablespoons coconut oil, melted
1 cup sweet potato puree   ¼ teaspoon cinnamon powder
1 cup whole wheat flour   Glaze:
1 cup coconut milk   2 tablespoons smooth peanut butter
¼ cup coconut sugar   ¼ cup maple syrup
1 teaspoon baking powder   2 tablespoons coconut oil, melted

Directions:

• For the donuts, mix all the ingredients in a food processor and pulse until well mixed.
• Pour the batter in a greased donut pan and bake in the preheated oven at 350F for 15-20 minutes.
• Allow to cool in the pan then transfer on a wire rack.
• For the glaze, mix all the ingredients in a bowl.
• Drizzle the donuts with the glaze and serve them fresh.

Nutritional information per serving

Calories: 193   Protein: 2.6g
Fat: 10.8g   Carbohydrates: 23.1g

Vegan Crustless Pumpkin Pie

Time: 1 hour   Servings: 8

Ingredients:

2 cups pumpkin puree   2 tablespoons cornstarch
8 oz. silken tofu, drained   ½ teaspoon cinnamon powder
2 bananas, mashed   ½ cup coconut milk
1 teaspoon lemon juice   ½ cup coconut sugar

Coconut oil to grease the pan

Directions:
- Grease a 8-inch round cake pan with coconut oil.
- For the pie, mix all the ingredients in a bowl until creamy.
- Pour the mixture into the prepared pan and bake in the preheated oven at 330F for 35-40 minutes or until set in the center.
- Allow to cool in the pan before serving.

Nutritional information per serving

Calories: 152

Fat: 4.6g

Protein: 3.3g

Carbohydrates: 27.0g

LIVE OIL BLUEBERRY MUFFINS

Time: 1 hour

Servings: 10

Ingredients:

4 eggs

½ cup coconut sugar

½ cup extra virgin olive oil

¼ cup almond milk

1 teaspoon vanilla extract

1 ½ cups whole wheat flour

1 teaspoon baking powder

¼ teaspoon salt

1 cup blueberries

Directions:
- Mix the eggs and sugar in a bowl until fluffy and double in volume.
- Add the almond milk and oil, as well as vanilla and mix well.
- Stir in the flour, baking powder and salt then fold in the blueberries.
- Spoon the batter in a muffin tin lined with muffin papers.
- Bake in the preheated oven at 350F for 15-20 minutes or until well risen and golden brown.
- Allow to cool in the pan before serving.

Nutritional information per serving

Calories: 240

Fat: 13.5g

Protein: 4.4g

Carbohydrates: 26.8g

𝒫 ECAN ENERGY BALLS

Time: 30 minutes

Servings: 8

Ingredients:

1 cup dates, pitted

2 tablespoons hot water

1 ½ cups pecans, ground

1 cup almond flour

¼ cup maple syrup

1 teaspoon vanilla extract

1 pinch salt

Directions:
- Mix the dates and water in a food processor and pulse until smooth.
- Add the rest of the ingredients and pulse until well mixed.
- Form small balls of mixture and serve them fresh.

Nutritional information per serving

Calories: 122

Fat: 3.1g

Protein: 1.5g

Carbohydrates: 24.4g

𝒞 OCONUT OIL BANANA ALMOND BREAD

Time: 1 hour

Servings: 10

Ingredients:

1/3 cup coconut oil, melted
½ cup maple syrup
2 eggs
2 bananas, mashed
½ cup coconut milk

1 ½ cups whole wheat flour
¼ teaspoon salt
1 ½ teaspoons baking powder
¼ cup sliced almonds

Directions:

- Mix the coconut oil, maple syrup, eggs, bananas and milk in a bowl.
- Stir in the rest of the ingredients then pour the batter in a small loaf pan lined with baking paper.
- Bake in the preheated oven at 350F for 35 minutes or until golden brown.
- Allow to cool in the pan before serving.

Nutritional information per serving

Calories: 248
Fat: 12.5g

Protein: 4.1g
Carbohydrates: 31.9g

WHOLESOME APPLE PIE

Time: 1 ½ hours

Servings: 10

Ingredients:

Crust:
2 cups whole wheat flour
1 pinch salt
½ teaspoon baking powder
½ cup applesauce
¼ cup maple syrup
¼ cup coconut oil, melted

2 tablespoons water
Filling:
1 ½ pounds apples, peeled, cored and sliced
1 tablespoon cornstarch
1 teaspoon cinnamon powder
¼ cup maple syrup
½ cup applesauce

Directions:

- For the crust, mix all the ingredients in a food processor and pulse until well mixed.
- Transfer the dough on a floured working surface and roll it into a thin sheet.
- Place the dough on a pie pan and press it on the bottom and sides of the pan.
- For the filling, mix all the ingredients in a bowl. Pour the mixture into the crust.
- Bake the pie in the preheated oven at 350F for 40 minutes or until golden brown on the edges.
- Allow to cool in the pan before serving.

Nutritional information per serving

Calories: 228
Fat: 5.9g

Protein: 2.8g
Carbohydrates: 42.7g

GRANOLA PUMPKIN PIE

Time: 1 ¼ hours

Servings: 10

Ingredients:

Crust:
1 cup all-purpose flour
1 cup granola
½ cup coconut oil, melted
4 tablespoons maple syrup
Filling:

2 cups pumpkin puree
1 teaspoon pumpkin pie spice
2 eggs
½ cup maple syrup
1 cup plain yogurt
1 pinch salt

Directions:

- For the crust, place the granola in a food processor and pulse until well mixed.
- Add the rest of the ingredients and mix well.
- Transfer the dough on a floured working surface and roll it into a thin sheet.

- Place the dough on a pie pan and press it well on the bottom and sides of the pan.
- For the filling, mix all the ingredients in a bowl until creamy.
- Pour the filling into the crust and bake in the preheated oven at 350F for 35-40 minutes.
- Allow to cool in the pan before serving.

Nutritional information per serving

Calories: 277

Fat: 18.3g

Protein: 8.0g

Carbohydrates: 44.3g

C ARAMELIZED PINEAPPLE ICE CREAM

Time: 2 hours

Servings: 6

Ingredients:

4 slices pineapple

2 tablespoons honey

2 cups plain yogurt

1 teaspoon vanilla extract

¼ cup honey

1 pinch salt

Directions:

- Brush the pineapple with 2 tablespoons honey. Place the pineapple on a hot grill pan and cook on each side until browned. Allow to cool down then chop into small pieces.
- Mix all the ingredients in a bowl.
- Pour the mixture in an ice cream machine and churn according to the machine's instructions.
- Serve the ice cream fresh or store in the freezer for up to 1 month.

Nutritional information per serving

Calories: 179

Fat: 1.1g

Protein: 5.3g

Carbohydrates: 37.7g

W HOLESOME VEGAN WAFFLES

Time: 40 minutes

Servings: 6

Ingredients:

1 cup whole wheat flour

½ cup oat flour

1 teaspoon baking powder

¼ cup coconut sugar

¼ cup coconut oil, melted

3/4 cup coconut milk

1 teaspoon lemon zest

1 pinch salt

Directions:

- Mix all the ingredients in a blender and pulse until well mixed.
- Heat your waffle machine and pour a few tablespoons of batter in the hot machine.
- Bake according to your machine's instructions.
- Serve the waffles fresh.

Nutritional information per serving

Calories: 284

Fat: 16.9g

Protein: 3.8g

Carbohydrates: 31.3g

M OLASSES PUMPKIN LOAF CAKE

Time: 1 hour

Servings: 10

Ingredients:

1 ½ cups pumpkin puree

2 eggs

½ cup coconut oil, melted

2 tablespoons dark molasses

1 cup whole wheat flour

½ cup oat flour

1 pinch salt

1 teaspoon baking soda

½ teaspoon ground ginger
½ teaspoon cinnamon powder

½ teaspoon ground cloves
¼ cup pumpkin seeds

Directions:
- Mix all the ingredients in a bowl.
- Pour the mixture in a loaf cake pan lined with parchment paper.
- Bake in the preheated oven at 350F for 30-35 minutes or until it passes the toothpick test.
- Allow to cool down before slicing and serving.

Nutritional information per serving
Calories: 213
Fat: 13.9g

Protein: 4.3g
Carbohydrates: 19.5g

RAIN FREE PUMPKIN PORRIDGE

Time: 30 minutes

Servings: 6

Ingredients:
1 cup pumpkin puree
1 cup almond milk
2 tablespoons almond butter
1 cup shredded coconut

½ teaspoon cinnamon powder
1/3 cup agave syrup
2 tablespoons almond slices

Directions:
- Mix the pumpkin puree, almond milk, almond butter, agave syrup, coconut and cinnamon in a saucepan.
- Cook over low heat until thickened then pour into 2 bowls.
- Top with almond slices and serve warm or chilled.

Nutritional information per serving
Calories: 303
Fat: 22.1g

Protein: 5.0g
Carbohydrates: 25.2g

PUMPKIN CHIA PUDDING

Time: 1 hour

Servings: 6

Ingredients:
4 tablespoons chia seeds
1 ½ cups almond milk
½ cup pumpkin puree
¼ cup maple syrup

½ teaspoon vanilla extract
½ teaspoon cinnamon powder
1 pinch salt

Directions:
- Mix all the ingredients in a bowl.
- Pour the mixture into 2 small bowls and place in the fridge for at least 30 minutes.
- Serve the pudding chilled.

Nutritional information per serving
Calories: 284
Fat: 20.8g

Protein: 5.8g
Carbohydrates: 20.8g

PLUM AND NECTARINE COMPOTE

Time: 30 minutes

Servings: 4

Ingredients:
1 pound plums, pitted
2 nectarines, pitted and sliced

2 cups water
¼ cup maple syrup

1 cinnamon stick   2 cardamom pods, crushed

Directions:
- Mix all the ingredients in a saucepan.
- Cook for 10 minutes and serve the compote chilled.

Nutritional information per serving

Calories: 121   Protein: 1.4g
Fat: 0.6g   Carbohydrates: 30.3g

ATMEAL YOGURT MUFFINS

Time: 1 hour   Servings: 10

Ingredients:
1 cup plain yogurt   ½ cup coconut sugar
1 cup pumpkin puree   1 ½ teaspoons baking powder
2 eggs   ¼ teaspoon salt
2 cups rolled oats   ½ teaspoon cinnamon powder
¼ cup whole wheat flour   ½ cup raisins

Directions:
- Mix the yogurt, pumpkin puree and eggs in a bowl.
- Add the rest of the ingredients then pour the batter in a muffin tin lined with muffin papers.
- Bake the muffins in the preheated oven at 350F for 15-20 minutes or until they pass the toothpick test.
- Allow to cool in the pan then serve or store in an airtight container.

Nutritional information per serving

Calories: 170   Protein: 5.5g
Fat: 2.4g   Carbohydrates: 32.9g

C HOCOLATE HAZELNUT TRUFFLES

Time: 40 minutes   Servings: 18

Ingredients:
1 cup dates, pitted   1 cup ground hazelnuts
¼ cup hot water   ¼ cup ground flaxseeds
2 tablespoons maple syrup   1 pinch salt
¼ cup coconut oil, melted   1 teaspoon vanilla extract
½ cup cocoa powder   Cocoa powder for coating

Directions:
- Mix the dates and hot water in a blender and pulse until smooth.
- Add the rest of the ingredients and mix well.
- Form small balls and roll them through cocoa powder.
- Serve the truffles fresh or store them in an airtight container.

Nutritional information per serving

Calories: 100   Protein: 1.6g
Fat: 6.4g   Carbohydrates: 11.4g

REEN SMOOTHIE BOWL

Time: 30 minutes   Servings: 4

Ingredients:
1 cup fresh spinach   2 kiwi fruits, peeled

1 banana
1 ½ cups coconut milk
1 cup blueberries
2 tablespoons chia seeds

¼ cup almond slices
2 tablespoons rolled oats
2 tablespoons raisins

Directions:
- Mix the spinach, kiwi fruits, banana and coconut milk in a blender and pulse until smooth.
- Pour the mixture into 2 serving bowls.
- Top the smoothie with blueberries, chia seeds, almond slices, oats and raisins.
- Serve the smoothie bowls as fresh as possible.

Nutritional information per serving

Calories: 425
Fat: 30.7g

Protein: 8.4g
Carbohydrates: 34.9g

LMOND PANCAKES

Time: 1 hour

Servings: 4

Ingredients:

1 cup whole wheat flour
2 tablespoons all-purpose flour
¼ teaspoon salt
1 teaspoon baking powder
1 cup almond milk

1 egg
¼ cup coconut oil, melted
½ teaspoon vanilla extract
¼ cup almond slices
Maple syrup to serve

Directions:
- Mix the flours, salt and baking powder in a bowl.
- Add the egg, almond milk, coconut oil, vanilla and almond slices and give it a quick mix.
- Heat a non-stick pan over medium flame then drop spoonfuls of mixture on the hot pan.
- Fry the pancakes on each side until golden brown.
- Serve the pancakes warm, drizzled with maple syrup.

Nutritional information per serving

Calories: 447
Fat: 33.1g

Protein: 7.9g
Carbohydrates: 32.4g

VEGAN CHAI DONUTS

Time: 1 hour

Servings: 10

Ingredients:

1 cup almond milk
1 teaspoon chai tea powder
1 teaspoon baking powder
1 cup whole wheat flour
¼ teaspoon salt

¼ cup coconut sugar
½ teaspoon cinnamon powder
2 tablespoons ground flaxseeds
4 tablespoons coconut oil, melted

Directions:
- Mix all the ingredients in a bowl until creamy.
- Pour the batter in a donut tin greased with oil and bake in the preheated oven at 350F for 15 minutes.
- Allow to cool in the pan before serving.

Nutritional information per serving

Calories: 173
Fat: 11.7g
Protein: 2.1g
Carbohydrates: 16.3g

S WEET POTATO COCONUT BREAD

Time: 1 hour

Servings: 10

Ingredients:

1 ½ cups sweet potato puree
½ cup plain yogurt
¼ cup coconut oil, melted
1 egg
¼ cup agave syrup
1 cup whole wheat flour
1 cup shredded coconut

2 tablespoons coconut flour
¼ teaspoon salt
1 teaspoon baking powder
½ teaspoon baking soda
½ teaspoon cinnamon powder
½ teaspoon ground ginger

Directions:

- Mix the sweet potato puree, yogurt, coconut oil, egg and agave syrup in a bowl.
- Add the rest of the ingredients and give it a quick mix.
- Pour the batter in a loaf pan lined with baking paper and bake in the preheated oven at 350F for 35-40 minutes or until well risen and golden brown.
- Allow to cool in the pan before serving.

Nutritional information per serving

Calories: 206
Fat: 9.1g

Protein: 3.8g
Carbohydrates: 28.2g

G LUTEN FREE PUMPKIN BREAD

Time: 1 hour

Servings: 10

Ingredients:

2 eggs
1 cup pumpkin puree
1 teaspoon vanilla extract
½ cup coconut cream
¼ cup maple syrup

½ cup brown rice flour
½ cup tapioca flour
¼ teaspoon salt
1 teaspoon baking soda

Directions:

- Mix the eggs, pumpkin puree, vanilla, coconut cream and maple syrup in a bowl.
- Stir in the rest of the ingredients and mix well.
- Pour the batter in a muffin tin lined with parchment paper.
- Bake in the preheated oven at 350F for 30 minutes.
- Allow to cool in the pan before serving.

Nutritional information per serving

Calories: 131
Fat: 4.0g

Protein: 2.2g
Carbohydrates: 22.4g

G INGERBREAD SMOOTHIE

Time: 15 minutes

Servings: 2

Ingredients:

2 bananas
1 cup coconut milk
2 tablespoons coconut cream
½ cup water
½ teaspoon vanilla extract
¼ teaspoon cinnamon

½ teaspoon grated ginger
1 pinch nutmeg
2 tablespoons maple syrup

Directions:
- Mix all the ingredients in a blender and pulse until smooth.
- Pour the smoothie into serving glasses and serve right away.

Nutritional information per serving

Calories: 474

Fat: 32.7g

Protein: 4.4g

Carbohydrates: 48.6g

*H*EALTHY **PUMPKIN BROWNIES**

Time: 45 minutes

Servings: 8

Ingredients:

1 cup pumpkin puree

4 eggs

¼ cup honey

½ cup cocoa powder

¼ teaspoon cinnamon powder

¼ teaspoon salt

Directions:
- Mix all the ingredients in a bowl.
- Pour the mixture in a small square pan lined with baking paper.
- Bake in the preheated oven at 350F for 20 minutes.
- Allow to cool in the pan then cut into small squares.
- Serve fresh or store in an airtight container.

Nutritional information per serving

Calories: 86

Fat: 3.0g

Protein: 4.1g

Carbohydrates: 14.3g

*A*PPLESAUCE **GINGERBREAD LOAF**

Time: 1 hour

Servings: 10

Ingredients:

1 cup oat flour

1 cup whole wheat flour

1 teaspoon ground ginger

½ teaspoon cinnamon powder

½ teaspoon ground cloves

½ teaspoon ground cardamom

1 teaspoon baking powder

½ teaspoon baking soda

½ cup coconut sugar

1 cup applesauce

¼ cup coconut oil, melted

½ cup almond milk

Directions:
- Mix the dry ingredients in a bowl.
- Add the wet ingredients and give it a quick mix.
- Pour the batter in a loaf pan lined with baking paper.
- Bake in the preheated oven at 350F for 30 minutes.
- Allow to cool in the pan then cut and serve.

Nutritional information per serving

Calories: 204

Fat: 9.1g

Protein: 2.8g

Carbohydrates: 29.3g

*S*WEET **COCONUT CORNBREAD**

Time: 1 hour

Servings: 10

Ingredients:

1 cup yellow cornmeal

½ cup coconut flour

1 teaspoon baking powder

½ teaspoon baking soda

¼ teaspoon salt
¼ teaspoon ground ginger
2 cups coconut milk

½ cup date syrup
1 teaspoon vanilla extract
½ cup coconut flakes

Directions:
- Mix all the ingredients in a bowl until creamy.
- Pour the batter in a loaf pan lined with parchment paper and bake in the preheated oven at 350F for 30 minutes or until it passes the toothpick test.
- Allow to cool in the pan then slice and serve.

Nutritional information per serving

Calories: 239
Fat: 14.0g

Protein: 4.6g
Carbohydrates: 29.0g

S EED ENERGY BARS

Time: 40 minutes

Servings: 20

Ingredients:
1 cup oat flour
½ cup sunflower seeds
½ cup pumpkin seeds
½ cup cooked quinoa

¼ cup coconut oil, melted
1 cup pecans, chopped
¼ cup maple syrup
1 cup dates, pitted

Directions:
- Mix the dates, maple syrup and coconut oil in a food processor. Pulse until smooth.
- Add the rest of the ingredients and mix with a spatula.
- Spoon the mixture in a small square pan lined with plastic wrap. Refrigerate until set then cut into small squares.
- Serve the bars fresh or store them in an airtight container.

Nutritional information per serving

Calories: 123
Fat: 6.0g

Protein: 2.6g
Carbohydrates: 16.1g

G LUTEN FREE DEVIL'S FOOD CAKE

Time: 1 hour

Servings: 10

Ingredients:
1 ¼ cups coconut flour
½ cup cocoa powder
½ cup coconut sugar
1 teaspoon baking powder
½ teaspoon baking soda

¼ teaspoon salt
6 eggs
1 cup applesauce
1 cup coconut milk
1 teaspoon vanilla extract

Directions:
- Mix the coconut flour, cocoa powder, coconut sugar, baking powder, baking soda and salt in a bowl.
- Add the rest of the ingredients and give it a quick mix.
- Pour the batter in a 9-inch round cake pan lined with baking paper.
- Bake the cake in the preheated oven at 350F for 40 minutes or until the cake passes the toothpick test.
- Allow to cool in the pan before serving.

Nutritional information per serving

Calories: 211
Fat: 10.9g
Protein: 6.7g
Carbohydrates: 24.5g

*W*HOLE **W**HEAT **A**PPLESAUCE **M**UFFINS

Time: 1 hour

Servings: 12

Ingredients:

½ cup coconut oil, melted
½ cup light brown sugar
2 eggs
1 cup applesauce
1 ½ cups whole wheat flour
½ teaspoon baking soda

1 teaspoon baking powder
½ teaspoon cinnamon powder
½ teaspoon ground ginger
½ teaspoon ground cardamom
2 apples, peeled, cored and diced

Directions:

- Mix the coconut oil, sugar, eggs and applesauce in a bowl.
- Add the rest of the ingredients and give it a quick mix.
- Fold in the apples then spoon the batter in a muffin tin lined with muffin papers.
- Bake the muffins in the preheated oven at 350F for 15-20 minutes or until golden brown and fragrant.
- Allow to cool down before serving.

Nutritional information per serving

Calories: 194
Fat: 10.0g

Protein: 2.7g
Carbohydrates: 24.7g

*C*OCOA **B**ANANA **L**OAF **C**AKE

Time: 1 hour

Servings: 10

Ingredients:

4 bananas, mashed
2 eggs
¼ cup coconut oil, melted
1 ½ cups whole wheat flour

¼ cup cocoa powder
¼ teaspoon salt
1 teaspoon baking soda

Directions:

- Mix the bananas, eggs and coconut oil in a bowl.
- Add the rest of the ingredients and give it a quick mix.
- Pour the batter in a loaf cake pan lined with baking paper.
- Bake in the preheated oven at 350F for 35-40 minutes or until well risen and golden.
- Allow to cool in the pan before slicing and serving.

Nutritional information per serving

Calories: 175
Fat: 6.9g

Protein: 4.0g
Carbohydrates: 26.3g

*M*ANGO **T**URMERIC **S**MOOTHIE

Time: 15 minutes

Servings: 2

Ingredients:

1 cup fresh orange juice
1 mango, peeled and cubed
¼ teaspoon grated ginger

1 teaspoon turmeric powder
2 tablespoons agave syrup
1 cup coconut milk

Directions:

- Combine all the ingredients in a blender.
- Pulse until smooth and creamy.
- Pour the smoothie into serving glasses and drink it as fresh as possible.

Nutritional information per serving

Calories: 473

Fat: 29.3g

Protein: 4.2g

Carbohydrates: 54.8g

*M*IXED FRUIT BOWLS WITH YOGURT DRESSING

Time: 20 minutes

Servings: 2

Ingredients:

1 cup strawberries, halved

1 small mango, peeled and cubed

1 cup fresh blueberries

½ cup grapes, halved

½ cup golden raisins

1 cup plain yogurt

1 lime, zested and juiced

Directions:

- Mix the strawberries, mango, blueberries, grapes and golden raisins in a bowl.
- Spoon the mixture into 2 serving bowls.
- Top the fruits with plain yogurt and drizzle with lime juice.
- Top with lime zest and serve the dessert right away.

Nutritional information per serving

Calories: 358

Fat: 2.6g

Protein: 10.0g

Carbohydrates: 78.4g

*P*OPPY SEED LEMON PANCAKES

Time: 45 minutes

Servings: 4

Ingredients:

2 tablespoons poppy seeds

2 tablespoons ground flaxseeds

1 cup almond flour

¼ teaspoon salt

1 teaspoon baking powder

1 cup coconut milk

½ cup water

2 egg whites

¼ cup maple syrup

1 tablespoon lemon zest

Directions:

- Mix the poppy seeds, flaxseeds, flour, salt and baking powder in a bowl.
- Add the rest of the ingredients in the bowl and give it a quick mix.
- Heat a non-stick pan over medium flame then drop spoonfuls of batter on the hot pan.
- Fry on each side until golden brown.
- Serve the pancakes fresh.

Nutritional information per serving

Calories: 282

Fat: 21.0g

Protein: 6.2g

Carbohydrates: 21.1g

*C*HOCOLATE BROWNIE BALLS

Time: 45 minutes

Servings: 20

Ingredients:

1 cup dates, pitted

2 tablespoons coconut sugar

2 tablespoons coconut oil, melted

2 tablespoons water

1 cup almond flour

¼ cup shredded coconut

2 tablespoons cocoa powder

1 pinch salt

½ cup rolled oats

Directions:
- Mix all the ingredients in a food processor and pulse until well mixed.
- Form small balls and place them on a platter.
- Serve the balls fresh or store them in an airtight container.

Nutritional information per serving

Calories: 62

Fat: 2.6g

Protein: 0.9g

Carbohydrates: 10.0g

S KINNY BANANA MUFFINS

Time: 1 hour

Servings: 12

Ingredients:

4 bananas, mashed

¼ cup honey

1 cup applesauce

1 egg

2 cups whole wheat flour

1 teaspoon baking powder

¼ teaspoon salt

½ teaspoon cinnamon powder

½ teaspoon ground ginger

¼ teaspoon ground cloves

Directions:
- Mix the bananas, honey, applesauce and egg in a bowl.
- Add the rest of the ingredients and mix well.
- Pour the batter in a muffin tin lined with muffin papers and bake in the preheated oven at 350F for 15-20 minutes or until well risen and golden brown.
- Allow to cool in the pan before serving.

Nutritional information per serving

Calories: 147

Fat: 0.7g

Protein: 3.1g

Carbohydrates: 33.3g

O ATMEAL BANANA BREAD

Time: 1 hour

Servings: 10

Ingredients:

2 cups rolled oats

4 bananas, mashed

4 tablespoons coconut oil, melted

¼ cup coconut sugar

½ teaspoon cinnamon powder

¼ teaspoon salt

1 teaspoon baking soda

Directions:
- Mix the bananas, coconut oil and sugar in a bowl.
- Add the rest of the ingredients and mix well.
- Spoon the batter in a loaf cake pan lined with parchment paper.
- Bake in the preheated oven at 350F for 35-40 minutes or until golden brown and sell risen.
- Allow to cool down before serving.

Nutritional information per serving

Calories: 169

Fat: 6.7g

Protein: 2.7g

Carbohydrates: 26.7g

C ARROT CAKE PORRIDGE

Time: 45 minutes

Servings: 4

Ingredients:

1 cup rolled oats

2 cups coconut milk

2 tablespoons ground flaxseeds
¼ teaspoon cinnamon powder
¼ teaspoon ground ginger
½ carrot, grated

½ cup crushed pineapple
¼ cup golden raisins
¼ cup maple syrup

Directions:
- Combine all the ingredients in a saucepan.
- Place over low heat and cook for 10 minutes until thickened.
- Pour the porridge into bowls and serve.

Nutritional information per serving
Calories: 464
Fat: 31.1g

Protein: 6.5g
Carbohydrates: 45.4g

$\mathcal{H}$ONEY HAZELNUT MACAROONS

Time: 1 ¼ hours

Servings: 30

Ingredients:
3 cups ground hazelnuts
¼ cup cocoa powder
¼ teaspoon cinnamon powder

2 eggs
¼ cup honey
1 pinch salt

Directions:
- Mix all the ingredients in a bowl.
- Drop spoonfuls of batter on a baking tray lined with parchment paper.
- Bake in the preheated oven at 250F for 1 hour.
- Serve the macaroons chilled.

Nutritional information per serving
Calories: 61
Fat: 4.9g

Protein: 1.6g
Carbohydrates: 4.0g

$\mathcal{W}$HOLE GRAIN PUMPKIN MUFFINS

Time: 1 hour

Servings: 12

Ingredients:
1 cup pumpkin puree
1 egg
¼ cup coconut oil, melted
¼ cup coconut milk
¼ cup maple syrup

1 cup whole wheat flour
1 cup whole grain flour
1 teaspoon baking powder
½ teaspoon baking soda
¼ teaspoon salt

Directions:
- Mix the pumpkin puree, egg, coconut oil, milk and maple syrup in a bowl.
- Add the rest of the ingredients and mix quickly.
- Pour the mixture in a loaf cake pan lined with baking paper.
- Bake in the preheated oven at 350F for 35-40 minutes or until well risen and golden brown.
- Allow to cool down before slicing and serving.

Nutritional information per serving
Calories: 152
Fat: 6.5g

Protein: 3.2g
Carbohydrates: 21.8g

$\mathcal{H}$EALTHY CARROT MUFFINS

Time: 1 hour

Servings: 12

Ingredients:

1 ½ cups whole wheat flour
¼ cup all-purpose flour
1 teaspoon baking soda
½ teaspoon baking powder
1 teaspoon cinnamon powder
¼ teaspoon salt
½ cup coconut oil, melted

½ cup coconut sugar
1 egg
¼ cup buttermilk
1 apple, peeled, cored and diced
1 pear, peeled, cored and diced
1 carrot, grated

Directions:

- Mix the flours, baking soda, baking powder, cinnamon, coconut sugar and salt in a bowl.
- Add the rest of the ingredients and give it a quick mix.
- Pour the mixture in a loaf cake pan lined with baking paper.
- Bake in the preheated oven at 350F for 35-40 minutes or until the cake passes the toothpick test.
- Allow to cool down before serving.

Nutritional information per serving

Calories: 199
Fat: 9.7g

Protein: 2.6g
Carbohydrates: 26.6g

RIED FRUIT OVERNIGHT OATMEAL

Time: 12 hours

Servings: 4

Ingredients:

1 ½ cups rolled oats
2 cups coconut milk
¼ cup raisins

¼ cup dried cranberries
2 tablespoons chia seeds
¼ cup dried pineapple, chopped

Directions:

- Mix all the ingredients in a bowl.
- Cover with plastic wrap and place in the fridge overnight.
- Serve the oatmeal fresh.

Nutritional information per serving

Calories: 337
Fat: 23.6g

Protein: 6.9g
Carbohydrates: 27.9g

HOMEMADE GRANOLA

Time: 35 minutes

Servings: 10

Ingredients:

4 cups rolled oats
1 cup almond slices
1 cup pecans, chopped
½ cup sunflower seeds
½ cup pumpkin seeds

½ cup raisins
½ cup dried cranberries
¼ cup maple syrup
½ cup coconut oil

Directions:

- Mix the oats, almond slices, pecans, sunflower seeds, pumpkin seeds, cranberries, raisins.
- Mix the maple syrup and oil in a saucepan and melt them together over low heat.
- Pour over the oat mixture and mix well.
- Spread the granola in a baking tray lined with baking paper and bake in the preheated oven at 350F for 20-25 minutes or until golden brown and fragrant.
- Allow to cool in the pan before serving or storing in an airtight container.

Nutritional information per serving

Calories: 342

Fat: 19.9g

Protein: 7.4g   Carbohydrates: 36.2g

B AKED **BROWN SUGAR APPLE CHIPS**

Time: 1 ¼ hours   Servings: 4

Ingredients:

4 apples   ½ cup light brown sugar

Directions:
- Wash the apples and core them.
- Slice the apples finely and arrange them on a baking tray lined with baking paper.
- Sprinkle with brown sugar and bake in the preheated oven at 200F for 1 hour.
- Serve the chips chilled.

Nutritional information per serving

Calories: 164   Protein: 0.5g
Fat: 0.3g   Carbohydrates: 42.9g

L OW **FAT PUMPKIN ROULADE**

Time: 1 ½ hours   Servings: 10

Ingredients:

Cake: 1/2 cup pumpkin puree
4 eggs   1 ½ cups cream cheese
½ cup light brown sugar   ¼ cup light brown sugar
1 cup whole wheat flour   ½ teaspoon cinnamon powder
¼ teaspoon salt   ¼ teaspoon ground ginger
1 teaspoon baking powder   1 cup heavy cream, whipped
Filling:

Directions:
- For the cake, mix the eggs and sugar in a bowl until double in volume.
- Add the flour, salt and baking powder and mix with a spatula.
- Pour the batter in a rectangle baking pan lined with baking paper.
- Bake in the preheated oven at 350F for 25-30 minutes.
- Allow to cool in the pan.
- For the filling, mix the pumpkin puree, cream cheese, sugar, cinnamon and ginger in a bowl.
- Fold in the whipped cream then spread the mixture over the baked cake.
- Carefully roll the cake into a roulade.
- Serve the roulade fresh.

Nutritional information per serving

Calories: 280   Protein: 6.5g
Fat: 18.5g   Carbohydrates: 22.9g

C OCONUT **COOKIES**

Time: 1 hour   Servings: 20

Ingredients:

1 cup coconut flour   2 eggs
1 cup shredded coconut   1 cup coconut oil, melted
¼ teaspoon salt   ½ teaspoon coconut extract
1 teaspoon baking powder
1/2 cup coconut milk

Directions:
- Mix the dry ingredients in a bowl.
- Add the rest of the ingredients and mix well.
- Form small balls of mixture and place them on a baking tray lined with baking paper.
- Bake in the preheated oven at 350F for 12-15 minutes or until golden brown on the edges.
- Allow to cool down before serving.

Nutritional information per serving

Calories: 153

Fat: 14.9g

Protein: 1.6g

Carbohydrates: 4.3g

AIRY FREE PUMPKIN PIE

Time: 1 ¼ hours

Servings: 10

Ingredients:

Crust:

1 ½ cups whole wheat flour

¼ teaspoon salt

½ teaspoon baking powder

½ cup coconut oil, melted

4 tablespoons cold water

Filling:

2 cups pumpkin puree

1 cup coconut milk

½ cup maple syrup

1 pinch salt

2 eggs

¼ teaspoon ground ginger

½ teaspoon cinnamon powder

½ teaspoon ground cardamom

Directions:
- For the crust, mix the flour, salt and baking powder in a bowl.
- Add the coconut oil and water and mix well.
- Transfer the dough on a floured working surface and roll it into a thin sheet.
- Place the dough on a pie pan and press it well on the bottom and sides of the pan.
- For the filling, mix all the ingredients in a bowl.
- Pour the filling into the crust and bake in the preheated oven at 330F for 45 minutes or until golden brown on the edges.
- Serve the pie chilled.

Nutritional information per serving

Calories: 288

Fat: 17.9g

Protein: 4.2g

Carbohydrates: 30.5g

FLOURLESS ORANGE CAKE

Time: 1 ½ hours

Servings: 10

Ingredients:

2 oranges, washed

¼ cup coconut oil, melted

4 eggs

½ cup light brown sugar

1 ½ cups almond flour

1 pinch salt

Directions:
- Place the oranges in a saucepan and cover it with water. Cook for 30 minutes on low heat then drain and place in a blender.
- Add the coconut oil and eggs and blend until smooth.
- Stir in the rest of the ingredients then pour the batter in a 8-inch round cake pan lined with baking paper.
- Bake in the preheated oven at 350F for 30 minutes.
- Allow to cool in the pan before slicing and serving.

Nutritional information per serving

Calories: 141

Fat: 9.3g

Protein: 3.5g

Carbohydrates: 12.5g

S PICED ALMOND CAKE

Time: 1 hour

Servings: 10

Ingredients:

2 cups almond flour
½ cup coconut sugar
¼ cup coconut flour
¼ teaspoon salt
1 teaspoon baking powder
½ teaspoon cinnamon powder

½ teaspoon ground ginger
½ teaspoon ground cardamom
3 eggs
2 egg whites
½ cup pumpkin puree
1 cup coconut milk

Directions:

- Mix the dry ingredients in a bowl.
- Add the rest of the ingredients and give it a quick mix.
- Pour the batter in a 9-inch round cake pan and bake in the preheated oven at 350F for 35-40 minutes or until golden brown.
- Allow to cool in the pan before serving.

Nutritional information per serving

Calories: 163
Fat: 10.3g

Protein: 4.7g
Carbohydrates: 15.2g

A LMOND FLOUR CRANBERRY CAKE

Time: 1 ¼ hours

Servings: 10

Ingredients:

2 cups almond flour
¼ teaspoon salt
1 ½ teaspoons baking powder
3 eggs

½ cup coconut sugar
¼ cup coconut oil, melted
¾ cup coconut milk
1 cup fresh cranberries

Directions:

- Mix the eggs and sugar in a bowl until double in volume.
- Add the coconut oil and milk then stir in the almond flour and salt.
- Fold in the cranberries then spoon the batter in a 9-inch round cake pan.
- Bake in the preheated oven at 350F for 40-45 minutes or until they pass the toothpick test.
- Allow the cake to cool down before slicing and serving.

Nutritional information per serving

Calories: 182
Fat: 13.8g

Protein: 3.3g
Carbohydrates: 13.2g

C OCONUT CHIA PUDDING

Time: 1 hour

Servings: 4

Ingredients:

2 cups coconut milk
¼ cup chia seeds
¼ cup water

¼ cup maple syrup
½ cup coconut flakes

Directions:

- Mix all the ingredients in a bowl.
- Cover with plastic wrap and place in the fridge for at least 30 minutes.
- Serve the pudding fresh.

Nutritional information per serving

Calories: 373

Fat: 32.6g

Protein: 3.5g

Carbohydrates: 22.0g

INGERBREAD BAKED OATMEAL

Time: 40 minutes

Servings: 4

Ingredients:

2 cups rolled oats

½ teaspoon cinnamon powder

½ teaspoon ground ginger

¼ teaspoon ground cloves

1 tablespoon molasses

¼ cup applesauce

1 cup coconut milk

¼ cup raisins

Directions:

• Mix all the ingredients in a small deep dish baking pan.

• Cover with aluminum foil and cook in the preheated oven at 350F for 15 minutes.

• Serve the oatmeal warm or chilled.

Nutritional information per serving

Calories: 342

Fat: 17.1g

Protein: 7.1g

Carbohydrates: 43.9g

P UMPKIN SPICE LATTE

Time: 15 minutes

Servings: 2

Ingredients:

½ cup pumpkin puree

1 cup brewed coffee

½ cup coconut milk

¼ teaspoon cinnamon powder

1 pinch nutmeg

1 pinch ground ginger

Directions:

• Mix all the ingredients in a blender.

• Pulse until smooth and creamy.

• Pour the latte into serving glasses and serve it fresh.

Nutritional information per serving

Calories: 161

Fat: 14.6g

Protein: 2.2g

Carbohydrates: 8.4g

P EANUT BUTTER ENERGY BALLS

Time: 30 minutes

Servings: 10

Ingredients:

1 cup rolled oats

¼ cup smooth peanut butter

½ cup ground almonds

2 tablespoons chia seeds

2 tablespoons maple syrup

Directions:

• Place the oats in a food processor and pulse until ground.

• Add the rest of the ingredients and mix well.

• Form small balls of mixture and serve them fresh.

Nutritional information per serving

Calories: 138

Fat: 8.1g

Protein: 5.0g

Carbohydrates: 12.6g

𝓑 ANANA OATMEAL COOKIES

Time: 45 minutes

Servings: 20

Ingredients:

4 bananas, mashed

1 egg

2 ½ cups rolled oats

Directions:
- Mix all the ingredients in a bowl.
- Drop spoonfuls of mixture on a baking tray lined with baking paper.
- Bake in the preheated oven at 350F for 10-15 minutes or until golden brown on the edges.
- Allow to cool in the pan before serving.

Nutritional information per serving

Calories: 63

Fat: 1.0g

Protein: 1.9g

Carbohydrates: 12.3g

𝓗 ARVEST PANCAKES

Time: 40 minutes

Servings: 4

Ingredients:

1 cup almond flour

1 teaspoon baking soda

1 pinch salt

4 eggs

1 banana, mashed

¼ cup applesauce

¼ cup pumpkin puree

Directions:
- Mix all the ingredients in a bowl until creamy.
- Heat a non-stick pan over medium flame then drop spoonfuls of batter on the hot pan.
- Cook on each side until golden brown.
- Serve the pancakes warm and fresh.

Nutritional information per serving

Calories: 141

Fat: 8.0g

Protein: 7.6g

Carbohydrates: 11.5g

𝓥 EGAN HOT CHOCOLATE

Time: 10 minutes

Servings: 2

Ingredients:

1 cup coconut milk

½ cup water

¼ cup cocoa powder

¼ cup honey

1 teaspoon vanilla extract

Directions:
- Mix the coconut milk, water and cocoa powder and cook over low heat until thickened.
- Remove from heat and stir in the honey and vanilla.
- Pour the chocolate in serving mugs and serve it warm and fresh.

Nutritional information per serving

Calories: 435

Fat: 30.0g

Protein: 4.8g

Carbohydrates: 47.7g

*H*EALTHY BANANA BREAD

Time: 1 hour   Servings: 10

Ingredients:

½ cup coconut oil, melted   ¼ teaspoon salt
½ cup maple syrup   ½ teaspoon cinnamon powder
2 eggs   ½ teaspoon ground ginger
2 bananas, mashed   1 teaspoon baking powder
½ cup coconut milk   ½ teaspoon baking soda
1 ¾ cups whole wheat flour

Directions:

- Mix the coconut oil, maple syrup, eggs, bananas and coconut milk in a bowl.
- Add the rest of the ingredients and mix well.
- Pour the batter in a loaf cake pan lined with parchment paper.
- Bake in the preheated oven at 350 for 35-40 minutes or until golden brown and well risen.
- Allow to cool in the pan before slicing and serving.

Nutritional information per serving

Calories: 277   Protein: 3.9g
Fat: 15.0g   Carbohydrates: 33.7g

*H*EALTHY CHOCOLATE BARK

Time: 25 minutes   Servings: 4

Ingredients:

8 oz. dark chocolate chips, melted   ¼ cup dried cranberries
¼ cup sunflower seeds   ¼ cup raisins
¼ cup pumpkin seeds   2 tablespoons chia seeds

Directions:

- Spread the chocolate on a piece of baking paper.
- Top the chocolate with the rest of the ingredients then place in the fridge to set for a few minutes.
- When set, break into smaller pieces and serve.

Nutritional information per serving

Calories: 437   Protein: 9.9g
Fat: 25.4g   Carbohydrates: 53.0g

*C*HOCOLATE COVERED STRAWBERRIES

Time: 20 minutes   Servings: 20

Ingredients:

1 pound strawberries   1 tablespoon coconut oil
4 oz. dark chocolate

Directions:

- Combine the chocolate and coconut oil in a heatproof bowl and place over a hot water bath.
- Melt them until smooth.
- Dip each strawberry in melted chocolate and place on a baking tray lined with baking paper.
- Place in the fridge to set.

Nutritional information per serving

Calories: 43   Protein: 0.6g
Fat: 2.4g   Carbohydrates: 5.1g

CRANBERRY ORANGE SMOOTHIE

Time: 10 minutes

Servings: 2

Ingredients:

½ cup fresh cranberries
1 cup fresh orange juice
1 cup coconut milk

1 tablespoon honey
1 tablespoon chia seeds

Directions:
- Mix all the ingredients in a blender.
- Pulse until smooth and creamy.
- Pour the mixture into 2 serving glasses and serve it fresh.

Nutritional information per serving

Calories: 457
Fat: 33.7g
Protein: 6.8g
Carbohydrates: 36.0g

TAHINI NUTTY BONBONS

Time: 1 hour

Servings: 20

Ingredients:

1 cup macadamia nuts, ground
½ cup coconut oil, melted
2 tablespoons chia seeds

¼ cup tahini paste
2 tablespoons maple syrup
Sesame seeds to roll the bonbons into

Directions:
- Mix all the ingredients in a food processor.
- Pulse until well mixed.
- Form small balls and roll them through sesame seeds.
- Serve the bonbons fresh or store them in an airtight container.

Nutritional information per serving

Calories: 134
Fat: 13.1g

Protein: 1.7g
Carbohydrates: 4.0g

OLIVE OIL CHOCOLATE CAKE

Time: 1 hour

Servings: 8

Ingredients:

1 cup whole wheat flour
½ cup cocoa powder
1 ½ teaspoons baking powder
¼ teaspoon salt
½ cup coconut sugar

1 cup plain yogurt
2 eggs
½ cup extra virgin olive oil
½ cup dark chocolate chips

Directions:
- Mix the eggs and sugar in a bowl until double in volume.

- Add the yogurt and olive oil and mix well.
- Fold in the flour, cocoa powder, baking powder and salt.
- Stir in the chocolate chips then pour the batter in a 8-inch round cake pan lined with baking paper.
- Bake in the preheated oven at 350F for 30-35 minutes.
- Allow to cool in the pan before serving.

Nutritional information per serving

Calories: 295

Fat: 16.9g

Protein: 6.2g

Carbohydrates: 34.6g

S TRAWBERRY GRANOLA CRUMBLE

Time: 1 hour

Servings: 8

Ingredients:

2 pounds strawberries, halved

1 tablespoon cornstarch

¼ cup white sugar

1 tablespoon lemon juice

1 cup granola

½ cup whole wheat flour

¼ cup coconut oil, melted

1 pinch salt

Directions:
- Mix the strawberries, cornstarch, sugar and lemon juice in a deep dish baking pan.
- Mix the granola, flour, coconut oil and salt in a bowl. Spread the mixture over the strawberries.
- Bake in the preheated oven at 350F for 30-35 minutes.
- Allow to cool in the pan before serving.

Nutritional information per serving

Calories: 186

Fat: 14.6g

Protein: 6.1g

Carbohydrates: 38.1g

D ATE OATMEAL COOKIES

Time: 1 hour

Servings: 20

Ingredients:

1 cup oat flour

1 cup rolled oats

½ cup coconut sugar

2 teaspoons baking powder

¼ teaspoon salt

1/3 cup maple syrup

1 egg

1/3 cup coconut oil, melted

½ cup dates, pitted and chopped

½ cup walnuts, chopped

Directions:
- Mix the oat flour, rolled oats, coconut sugar, baking powder and salt in a bowl.
- Add the rest of the ingredients and mix well.
- Drop spoonfuls of batter on a baking tray lined with parchment paper.
- Bake in the preheated oven at 350F for 15-20 minutes or until golden brown.
- Allow to cool in the pan before serving.

Nutritional information per serving

Calories: 132

Fat: 6.3g

Protein: 2.3g

Carbohydrates: 18.1g

C HOCOLATE BANANA LOAF

Time: 1 hour

Servings: 10

Ingredients:

4 bananas, mashed

2 eggs

¼ cup canola oil
1 teaspoon vanilla extract
1 cup whole wheat flour
½ cup oat flour

¼ cup rolled oats
¼ cup cocoa powder
¼ teaspoon salt
1 teaspoon baking soda

Directions:
- Mix the bananas, eggs, oil and vanilla in a bowl.
- Add the rest of the ingredients and mix well.
- Spoon the batter in a loaf cake pan lined with baking paper.
- Bake in the preheated oven at 350F for 35-40 minutes or until it passes the toothpick test.
- Allow to cool in the pan before serving.

Nutritional information per serving

Calories: 180
Fat: 7.3g

Protein: 4.2g
Carbohydrates: 26.2g

P OPPY SEED ORANGE CAKE

Time: 1 ½ hours

Servings: 10

Ingredients:
2 cups whole wheat flour
½ cup oat flour
½ teaspoon baking soda
1 teaspoon baking powder
¼ teaspoon salt
¼ teaspoon cinnamon powder

¼ cup coconut oil, melted
¼ cup maple syrup
2 cups almond milk
1 orange, zested and juiced
2 tablespoons poppy seeds

Directions:
- Mix the flours, baking soda, baking powder, salt and cinnamon in a bowl.
- Combine the coconut oil, maple syrup, almond milk, orange zest and orange juice in another bowl.
- Stir in the flour mixture then fold in the poppy seeds.
- Pour the batter in a 9-inch round cake pan and bake in the preheated oven at 350F for 35-40 minutes or until golden brown.
- Allow to cool in the pan before serving.

Nutritional information per serving

Calories: 305
Fat: 18.3g

Protein: 4.8g
Carbohydrates: 33.0g

P OMEGRANATE GRANITA

Time: 4 hours

Servings: 4

Ingredients:
1 cup pomegranate juice
¾ cup water

½ cup honey
1 tablespoon lemon juice

Directions:
- Mix the water and honey in a bowl until the honey is melted.
- Add the rest of the ingredients and mix well.
- Pour the mixture in a small airtight container and freeze for at least 3 hours. To ensure a smooth granita, remove the container from the freezer from time to time and shred the frozen granita with a fork.
- Serve the granita fresh or store it in the freezer for up to 1 month.

Nutritional information per serving

Calories: 167
Fat: 0.0g
Protein: 0.2g

Carbohydrates: 44.2g

*G*RILLED CARAMELIZED PINEAPPLE

Time: 15 minutes

Servings: 4

Ingredients:
4 slices pineapple
3 tablespoons honey
1 tablespoon lemon juice

2 mint leaves, chopped
Ice cream to serve

Directions:
- Mix the honey, lemon juice and chopped mint in a bowl.
- Brush the pineapple slices with this mixture.
- Heat a grill pan over medium flame then place the pineapple on the grill.
- Cook on each side until browned.
- Serve the pineapple warm, topped with your favorite ice cream.

Nutritional information per serving
Calories: 133
Fat: 0.3g

Protein: 1.2g
Carbohydrates: 35.2g

P UMPKIN PIE PUDDING

Time: 40 minutes

Servings: 2

Ingredients:
1 ½ cups low fat milk
½ cup pumpkin puree
2 egg yolks
½ teaspoon vanilla extract
¼ cup sweetened condensed milk

¼ teaspoon cinnamon powder
¼ teaspoon ground ginger
¼ teaspoon ground cardamom
1 pinch salt

Directions:
- Mix all the ingredients in a bowl.
- Pour the mixture into 2 ramekins and arrange the ramekins in a deep dish baking pan.
- Pour hot water in the pan, around the ramekins, enough to cover them ¾ with water.
- Bake in the preheated oven at 300F for 30 minutes.
- Allow to set then serve.

Nutritional information per serving
Calories: 279
Fat: 9.8g

Protein: 12.6g
Carbohydrates: 36.0g

B LACKBERRY SWEET WINE GRANITA

Time: 4 hours

Servings: 4

Ingredients:
1 cup fresh blackberries
1 cup sweet red wine
¼ cup coconut sugar

½ cup water
½ teaspoon vanilla extract

Directions:
- Mix the sugar and water in a saucepan and bring to a boil. Allow to cool then pour into a blender.
- Add the rest of the ingredients and pulse until smooth.
- Pour the mixture in an airtight container and freeze for at least 3 hours. Remove the container from the freezer from time to time and mix with a fork.
- Serve the granita chilled.

Nutritional information per serving

Calories: 111
Fat: 0.2g

Protein: 0.5g
Carbohydrates: 17.1g

*M*int Julep Sorbet

Time: 3 hours

Servings: 4

Ingredients:

1 cup water
½ cup honey
8 mint leaves, chopped

1 cup bourbon
2 limes, zested and juiced

Directions:

- Mix the water and honey in a saucepan and place over low heat. Heat up until the honey is melted. Remove from heat and add the mint. Allow to infuse until cooled down then drain well.
- Stir in the rest of the ingredients then pour the mixture in an airtight container.
- Freeze for a few hours. Remove from the freezer from time to time and stir it with a fork to ensure a smoother, finer texture.
- Serve the sorbet fresh or store it in the freezer for up to 1 month.

Nutritional information per serving

Calories: 277
Fat: 0.2g

Protein: 1.1g
Carbohydrates: 40.3g

*O*atmeal Baked Apples

Time: 50 minutes

Servings: 8

Ingredients:

8 Granny Smith apples, halved and cored
1 cup rolled oats
¼ cup coconut oil, melted
¼ cup light brown sugar

¼ teaspoon cinnamon powder
¼ teaspoon ground ginger
1 pinch salt

Directions:

- Place the apple halves in a baking tray lined with baking paper.
- Mix the oats, sugar, coconut oil, cinnamon, ginger and salt in a bowl.
- Top the apple halves with the oat mixture and bake in the preheated oven at 350F for 30 minutes.
- Serve the baked apples chilled.

Nutritional information per serving

Calories: 210
Fat: 7.8g

Protein: 1.9g
Carbohydrates: 36.5g

*B*lueberry Cheesecake Ice Cream

Time: 1 ¼ hours

Servings: 6

Ingredients:

2 cups blueberries, halved
1 cup cream cheese

1 lemon, zested and juiced
¼ cup honey

Directions:

- Combine all the ingredients in a blender and pulse until well mixed and smooth.
- Pour the mixture in an ice cream machine and churn according to the machine's instructions.
- Serve the ice cream fresh or store it in an airtight container in the freezer for up to 1 month.

Nutritional information per serving

Calories: 208

Fat: 13.7g

Protein: 3.4g

Carbohydrates: 20.6g

S TRAWBERRY FROZEN YOGURT

Time: 1 ¼ hours

Servings: 4

Ingredients:

1 ½ cups strawberries

1 ½ cups plain yogurt

¼ cup honey

1 teaspoon lemon juice

1 teaspoon lemon zest

Directions:

- Combine all the ingredients in blender. Pulse until smooth and creamy.
- Pour the mixture in your ice cream machine and churn according to your machine's instructions.
- Serve the frozen yogurt fresh or store it in an airtight container for up to 1 month in the freezer.

Nutritional information per serving

Calories: 148

Fat: 1.3g

Protein: 5.7g

Carbohydrates: 28.2g

C OLORFUL FRUIT SKEWERS

Time: 30 minutes

Servings: 6

Ingredients:

1 cup fresh strawberries

Half cantaloupe, peeled and cubed

Half watermelon, peeled and cubed

½ pineapple, peeled and cubed

1 lemon to prevent the fruits from browning

Directions:

- Arrange the fruits on wooden skewers.
- Drizzle them with lemon juice and serve them fresh.

Nutritional information per serving

Calories: 245

Fat: 1.1g

Protein: 4.9g

Carbohydrates: 61.3g

J UICY APPLE AND PEAR CRISP

Time: 1 ¼ hours

Servings: 8

Ingredients:

1 pound apples, peeled and sliced

1 pound pears, peeled, cored and sliced

¼ cup raisins

¼ cup dried cranberries

1 tablespoon lemon juice

½ teaspoon cinnamon powder

¼ cup light brown sugar

1 cup whole wheat flour

½ cup rolled oats

1/3 cup coconut oil, chilled and cubed

Directions:

- Mix the apples, pears, raisins, cranberries, lemon juice, cinnamon and sugar in a deep dish baking pan.
- For the topping, combine the flour, oats and coconut oil in a food processor. Pulse until grainy.
- Spread this mixture over the apples and bake in the preheated oven at 350F for 35-40 minutes.
- Serve the crisp chilled.

Nutritional information per serving

Calories: 250

Fat: 9.8g

Protein: 2.8g

Carbohydrates: 40.2g

ASPBERRY YOGURT PARFAITS

Time: 20 minutes

Servings: 4

Ingredients:

1 cup graham crackers, crushed

2 cups plain yogurt

1 ½ cups fresh raspberries

4 tablespoons honey

Directions:

- Layer the crushed graham crackers, yogurt and raspberries into 4 serving glasses.
- Drizzle the parfaits with honey and serve them fresh.

Nutritional information per serving

Calories: 264

Fat: 3.9g

Protein: 9.0g

Carbohydrates: 47.6g

PICED CHERRY COMPOTE

Time: 45 minutes

Servings: 6

Ingredients:

1 ½ pounds cherries, pitted

1 cinnamon stick

1 star anise

2 cardamom pods, crushed

2 whole cloves

1 cup red wine

2 cups water

½ cup coconut sugar

Directions:

- Combine all the ingredients in a saucepan.
- Place the saucepan over low heat and cook for 10-15 minutes just until fragrant and softened.
- Allow to cool in the pan before serving.

Nutritional information per serving

Calories: 229

Fat: 0.3g

Protein: 0.6g

Carbohydrates: 50.1g

OGURT BLUEBERRY PANNA COTTA

Time: 1 ¼ hours

Servings: 4

Ingredients:

2 cups plain yogurt

1 cup heavy cream

1 tablespoon lemon zest

1 teaspoon vanilla extract

½ cup white sugar

1 ½ teaspoons gelatin powder

¼ cup cold water

1 cup fresh blueberries

Directions:

- Bloom the gelatin in cold water for 10 minutes.
- Mix the yogurt, cream, lemon zest and vanilla, as well as sugar in a bowl.
- Melt the gelatin over a hot water bath and stir it in the yogurt mixture.
- Pour the mixture in 4 ramekins and place in the fridge to set for 1 hour.
- Top with fresh blueberries just before serving.

Nutritional information per serving

Calories: 310

Fat: 12.7g

Protein: 7.9g

Carbohydrates: 40.4g

VOCADO CHOCOLATE MOUSSE

Time: 10 minutes

Servings: 2

Ingredients:

1 avocado, peeled
2 tablespoons coconut cream
2 tablespoons cocoa powder

2 tablespoons maple syrup
½ teaspoon vanilla extract
1 pinch salt

Directions:

- Combine all the ingredients in a blender and pulse until smooth.
- Spoon the mousse into serving bowls and serve it fresh.

Nutritional information per serving

Calories: 307
Fat: 23.9g

Protein: 3.2g
Carbohydrates: 26.0g

CITRUS PUDDING

Time: 1 hour

Servings: 8

Ingredients:

1 cup milk
1 cup heavy cream
1 teaspoon lemon zest
1 teaspoon orange zest
1 teaspoon lime zest

4 eggs, separated
½ cup coconut sugar
¾ cup all-purpose flour
1 pinch salt

Directions:

- Mix the milk, cream, citrus zest, egg yolks, flour and salt in a bowl.
- Whip the egg whites in a bowl until stiff. Add the sugar and mix until glossy and firm.
- Fold the meringue into the pudding.
- Pour the batter in a deep dish baking pan.
- Bake in the preheated oven at 350F for 30 minutes.
- Allow to cool in the pan before serving.

Nutritional information per serving

Calories: 187
Fat: 8.5g
Protein: 5.3g
Carbohydrates: 23.2g

Quick Breads

VANILLA APPLE BREAD

Time: 1 ¼ hours

Servings: 10

Ingredients:

1 cup white sugar
2 eggs
½ cup milk
½ cup applesauce
1 tablespoon vanilla extract

¼ cup butter, melted
2 cups all-purpose flour
¼ teaspoon salt
2 teaspoons baking powder
2 apples, peeled, cored and diced

Directions:

• Mix the sugar and eggs in a bowl until creamy.
• Add the milk, applesauce, vanilla and butter and mix well.
• Stir in the flour, salt and baking powder then fold in the apples
• Pour the batter in a loaf pan lined with baking paper and bake in the preheated oven at 350F for 40 minutes or until it passes the toothpick test.
• Allow to cool in the pan before serving.

Nutritional information per serving

Calories: 254
Fat: 6.1g

Protein: 4.3g
Carbohydrates: 46.8g

CARROT PUMPKIN BREAD

Time: 1 hour

Servings: 12

Ingredients:

2 cups whole wheat flour
½ cup oat flour
2 teaspoons baking powder
¼ teaspoon salt
½ teaspoon cinnamon powder
½ teaspoon ground cardamom
½ teaspoon ground ginger

1 cup pumpkin puree
½ cup applesauce
½ cup white sugar
½ cup olive oil
2 large carrots, grated
½ cup crushed pineapple

Directions:

• Mix the flours, baking powder, salt and spices in a bowl.
• Add the rest of the ingredients and give it a quick mix.
• Pour the batter in a loaf pan lined with baking paper.
• Bake in the preheated oven at 350F for 40-45 minutes or until golden brown and fragrant.
• Allow to cool in the pan before serving.

Nutritional information per serving

Calories: 215
Fat: 8.9g

Protein: 3.0g
Carbohydrates: 32.2g

APPLESAUCE WALNUT BREAD

Time: 1 ¼ hours
Servings: 10

Ingredients:

2 ½ cups all-purpose flour
½ teaspoon salt
½ teaspoon baking soda
1 ½ teaspoons baking powder
½ teaspoon ground ginger
1 teaspoon cinnamon powder

1 egg
1 cup applesauce
¾ cup buttermilk
½ cup light brown sugar
1 cup walnuts, chopped

Directions:

- Mix the flour, salt, baking soda, baking powder, ginger and cinnamon in a bowl.
- Add the rest of the ingredients and give it a quick mix.
- Pour the batter in a loaf pan lined with parchment paper.
- Bake in the preheated oven at 350F for 45-50 minutes or until it passes the toothpick test.
- Allow to cool in the pan before serving.

Nutritional information per serving

Calories: 244
Fat: 8.3g

Protein: 7.5g
Carbohydrates: 36.3g

$\mathcal{E}$ GGLESS PUMPKIN BREAD

Time: 1 hour

Servings: 10

Ingredients:

1 ½ cups all-purpose flour
1 teaspoon baking soda
¼ teaspoon salt
1 teaspoon pumpkin pie spices
1 cup light brown sugar

¼ cup butter, melted
1 ½ cups pumpkin puree
½ cup buttermilk
1 teaspoon vanilla extract
¼ cup pumpkin seeds

Directions:

- Mix the dry ingredients in a bowl.
- Add the rest of the ingredients and give it a quick mix.
- Pour the batter in a loaf pan lined with parchment paper.
- Bake in the preheated oven at 350F for 40 minutes or until it passes the toothpick test.
- Allow to cool in the pan before serving.

Nutritional information per serving

Calories: 202
Fat: 6.6g

Protein: 3.7g
Carbohydrates: 32.9g

$\mathcal{D}$ RIED CRANBERRY EGGNOG BREAD

Time: 1 ¼ hours

Servings: 10

Ingredients:

½ cup dried cranberries
¼ cup eggnog
1 ½ cups all-purpose flour
¼ teaspoon salt
¼ cup oat flour

1 ½ teaspoons baking powder
2 eggs
1 cup milk
1 teaspoon vanilla extract
½ cup white sugar

Directions:

- Mix the cranberries and eggnog in a bowl and allow to infuse for 10 minutes at least.
- Combine the remaining ingredients in a bowl and give them a quick mix.
- Fold in the cranberries then spoon the batter in a loaf pan lined with parchment paper.
- Bake in the preheated oven at 350F for 40 minutes or until well risen and golden brown.
- Allow to cool down before serving.

UTTERNUT SQUASH BREAD

Time: 1 ¼ hours

Servings: 10

Ingredients:

1 cup butternut squash puree
2 eggs
½ cup canola oil
½ cup buttermilk
½ cup light brown sugar
2 tablespoons maple syrup

1 ¾ cups all-purpose flour
1 teaspoon baking soda
¼ teaspoon salt
½ teaspoon cinnamon powder
½ teaspoon ground ginger
¼ teaspoon ground nutmeg

Directions:

- Mix the butternut squash puree, eggs, oil, buttermilk, sugar and maple syrup in a bowl until creamy.
- Add the rest of the ingredients and give it a quick mix.
- Pour the batter in a loaf pan lined with parchment paper on the bottom and sides.
- Bake the bread in the preheated oven at 350F for 35-40 minutes.
- Allow to cool in the pan before slicing and serving.

Nutritional information per serving

Calories: 237
Fat: 12.2g

Protein: 3.9g
Carbohydrates: 28.3g

DOUBLE CHOCOLATE BREAD

Time: 1 ¼ hours

Servings: 10

Ingredients:

½ cup coconut oil
1 cup coconut milk
2 eggs
1 teaspoon vanilla extract
1 ¼ cups all-purpose flour

½ cup cocoa powder
¼ teaspoon salt
1 ½ teaspoons baking powder
1 cup shredded coconut
1 cup dark chocolate chips

Directions:

- Mix the coconut oil, milk, eggs and vanilla in a bowl.
- Add the flour, cocoa powder, salt, baking powder and coconut and mix quickly with a whisk.
- Fold in the chocolate chips then pour the batter in a loaf pan lined with parchment paper.
- Bake in the preheated oven at 350F for 40 minutes or until it passes the toothpick test.
- Allow to cool in the pan before serving.

Nutritional information per serving

Calories: 314
Fat: 24.1g

Protein: 5.1g
Carbohydrates: 25.3g

ONE BOWL BANANA BREAD

Time: 1 hour

Servings: 10

Ingredients:

3 bananas, mashed
½ cup coconut oil, melted
¼ cup maple syrup

1 egg
½ cup applesauce
1 ½ cups all-purpose flour

1 teaspoon baking soda
½ teaspoon salt

½ cup coconut flakes
½ cup walnuts, chopped

Directions:
- Combine all the ingredients in a bowl.
- Give it a quick mix with a whisk then pour the batter in a loaf pan lined with parchment paper.
- Bake in the preheated oven at 350F for 35-40 minutes or until well risen and golden brown.
- Allow to cool in the pan before slicing and serving.

Nutritional information per serving
Calories: 279
Fat: 16.7g

Protein: 4.5g
Carbohydrates: 30.3g

*V*EGAN GLUTEN FREE BANANA BREAD

Time: 1 hour

Servings: 10

Ingredients:
½ cup brown rice flour
½ cup tapioca flour
¼ cup coconut flour
½ cup ground walnuts
2 bananas, mashed

¼ cup maple syrup
¼ cup almond butter
1 cup coconut milk
1 pinch salt
1 ½ teaspoons baking powder

Directions:
- Combine all the ingredients in a bowl.
- Give it a quick mix until well combined.
- Pour the batter in a loaf cake pan lined with baking paper.
- Bake in the preheated oven at 350F for 35-40 minutes or until well risen and golden brown.
- Allow to cool in the pan before slicing and serving.

Nutritional information per serving
Calories: 249
Fat: 13.7g

Protein: 4.6g
Carbohydrates: 30.1g

*S*PICED CORNBREAD

Time: 1 hour

Servings: 10

Ingredients:
1 cup all-purpose flour
1 cup yellow cornmeal
2 teaspoons baking powder
¼ teaspoon salt
1 teaspoon pumpkin pie spices
½ cup pumpkin puree

2 eggs
½ cup canola oil
½ cup plain yogurt
¼ cup honey
1 teaspoon vanilla extract

Directions:
- Combine all the ingredients in a bowl and give it a quick mix.
- Pour the batter in a loaf pan lined with parchment paper.
- Bake in the preheated oven at 350F for 40-45 minutes or until well risen and golden brown.
- Allow to cool down before slicing and serving.

Nutritional information per serving
Calories: 240
Fat: 12.5g
Protein: 4.3g
Carbohydrates: 28.5g

YOGURT **V**ANILLA **B**READ

Time: 1 hour

Servings: 8

Ingredients:

2 cups all-purpose flour
2 teaspoons baking powder
½ teaspoon salt
2 eggs

1 ½ cups plain yogurt
1 cup almond milk
1 teaspoon vanilla extract
¼ cup canola oil

Directions:

- Mix the flour, baking powder and salt in a bowl.
- Add the rest of the ingredients and give it a quick mix.
- Pour the batter in a loaf pan lined with baking paper.
- Bake in the preheated oven at 350F for 40 minutes or until it passes the toothpick test.
- Allow to cool in the pan before slicing and serving.

Nutritional information per serving

Calories: 294
Fat: 15.9g

Protein: 7.9g
Carbohydrates: 29.5g

PEANUT **B**UTTER **B**ANANA **B**READ

Time: 1 ¼ hours

Servings: 10

Ingredients:

1 cup whole wheat flour
½ cup all-purpose flour
¼ cup ground flaxseeds
1 teaspoon baking soda
1 teaspoon baking powder
¼ teaspoon salt
½ teaspoon cinnamon powder

4 bananas, mashed
½ cup plain yogurt
½ cup smooth peanut butter
2 tablespoons canola oil
2 eggs
¼ cup honey

Directions:

- Mix the flours, flaxseeds, baking soda, baking powder, salt and cinnamon in a bowl.
- In a different bowl, mix the bananas, yogurt, peanut butter, oil, eggs and honey.
- Add the flour mixture and mix with a spatula.
- Spoon the batter in a loaf pan lined with parchment paper.
- Bake in the preheated oven at 350F for 40 minutes or until well risen and golden brown.
- Allow to cool in the pan before slicing and serving.

Nutritional information per serving

Calories: 273
Fat: 11.5g

Protein: 8.0g
Carbohydrates: 36.6g

ZUCCHINI **B**ANANA **B**READ

Time: 1 hour

Servings: 10

Ingredients:

1 ½ cups all-purpose flour
1 teaspoon baking powder
½ teaspoon baking soda
¼ teaspoon salt
½ teaspoon cinnamon powder
½ cup light brown sugar

2 eggs
¼ cup coconut oil, melted
2 bananas, mashed
1 cup grated zucchinis
1 teaspoon lemon juice

Directions:
- Mix the eggs, coconut oil, bananas, zucchini and lemon juice in a bowl.
- Add the flour, baking powder, baking soda, salt, cinnamon and brown sugar and give it a quick mix.
- Pour the batter in a loaf pan lined with parchment paper.
- Bake in the preheated oven at 350F for 35-40 minutes or until well risen and golden brown.
- Allow to cool in the pan before slicing and serving.

Nutritional information per serving

Calories: 179

Fat: 6.6g

Protein: 3.5g

Carbohydrates: 27.5g

um Banana Bread

Time: 1 hour

Servings: 10

Ingredients:

Bread:

½ cup butter, softened

1 cup white sugar

2 eggs

2 bananas, mashed

½ cup sour cream

¼ cup dark rum

½ cup shredded coconut

2 cups all-purpose flour

2 teaspoons baking powder

½ teaspoon salt

Glaze:

2 tablespoons dark rum

1 ½ cups powdered sugar

Directions:
- For the bread, mix the butter and sugar in a bowl until creamy.
- Add the eggs, one by one, then stir in the bananas, sour cream and rum.
- Add the rest of the ingredients and mix with a spatula.
- Spoon the batter in a loaf pan lined with baking paper.
- Bake in the preheated oven at 350F for 40-45 minutes or until the bread looks golden brown and well risen.
- Allow to cool in the pan then transfer on a platter.
- For the glaze, mix the ingredients in a bowl.
- Drizzle the glaze over the bread and serve it fresh.

Nutritional information per serving

Calories: 410

Fat: 14.2g

Protein: 4.6g

Carbohydrates: 64.0g

ecan Bread

Time: 1 hour

Servings: 12

Ingredients:

1 cup all-purpose flour

1 cup whole wheat flour

1 cup pecans, chopped

¼ cup dark brown sugar

2 teaspoons baking powder

2 tablespoons ground flaxseeds

¼ teaspoon ground nutmeg

½ cup butter, melted

2 bananas, mashed

¼ cup canola oil

½ cup almond milk

Directions:
- Mix the butter, bananas, canola oil and almond milk in a bowl.
- Stir in the flours, pecans, sugar, baking powder, flaxseeds and nutmeg and give it a quick mix.
- Pour the batter in a loaf pan lined with parchment paper and bake in the preheated oven at 350F for 40 minutes or until well risen and golden brown.
- Allow to cool in the pan before serving.

Nutritional information per serving

Calories: 251

Fat: 16.1g

Protein: 3.0g

Carbohydrates: 24.8g

C INNAMON MAPLE BREAD

Time: 1 hour

Servings: 10

Ingredients:

2 cups all-purpose flour

¼ teaspoon salt

2 teaspoons baking powder

¼ cup light brown sugar

¼ cup dark brown sugar

1 teaspoon cinnamon powder

¼ cup maple syrup

½ cup butter, melted

2 eggs

½ cup low fat milk

Directions:

- Mix the maple syrup, butter, eggs and milk in a bowl.
- Add the dry ingredients and give it a quick mix with a whisk.
- Pour the batter in a loaf cake pan lined with parchment paper and bake in the preheated oven at 350F for 35 40 minutes or until it passes the toothpick test.
- Allow to cool in the pan before slicing and serving.

Nutritional information per serving

Calories: 239

Fat: 10.5g

Protein: 4.2g

Carbohydrates: 32.6g

R HUBARB BREAD

Time: 1 hour

Servings: 10

Ingredients:

1 ½ cups all-purpose flour

½ cup rolled oats

1 ½ teaspoons baking powder

¼ teaspoon salt

½ cup white sugar

¼ cup canola oil

2 eggs

½ cup sour cream

¼ cup milk

1 teaspoon vanilla extract

2 rhubarb stalks, sliced

Directions:

- Mix the sugar, oil, eggs, sour cream, milk and vanilla in a bowl.
- Stir in the flour, oats, baking powder and salt and mix quickly then fold in the rhubarb.
- Spoon the batter in a loaf pan lined with parchment paper.
- Bake in the preheated oven at 350F for 40 minutes or until the bread passes the toothpick test.
- Allow it to cool in the pan before slicing and serving.

Nutritional information per serving

Calories: 214

Fat: 9.3g

Protein: 4.2g

Carbohydrates: 28.8g

B UTTERMILK STRAWBERRY BREAD

Time: 1 hour

Servings: 10

Ingredients:

2 cups all-purpose flour

1 teaspoon baking powder

1 teaspoon baking soda

½ cup white sugar

¼ teaspoon salt

½ cup butter, melted

1 cup buttermilk

1 egg

1 teaspoon vanilla extract

2 cups strawberries, halved

Directions:
- Mix the flours, baking powder, baking soda, sugar and salt in a bowl.
- Add the butter, buttermilk, egg and vanilla and give it a quick mix.
- Fold in the strawberries then spoon the batter in a loaf cake pan lined with parchment paper on the bottom and sides.
- Bake the bread in the preheated oven at 350F for 40 minutes or until well risen and golden brown.
- Allow to cool in the pan before slicing and serving.

Nutritional information per serving

Calories: 237

Fat: 10.2g

Protein: 4.2g

Carbohydrates: 32.8g

*C*HOCOLATE BEER BREAD

Time: 1 hour

Servings: 12

Ingredients:

2 cups whole wheat flour

1 teaspoon baking soda

1 teaspoon baking powder

½ teaspoon salt

½ cup cocoa powder

1 cup dark beer stout

¼ cup canola oil

½ cup buttermilk

1 egg

1 teaspoon vanilla extract

Directions:
- Combine the flour, baking soda, baking powder, salt and cocoa powder in a bowl.
- Add the rest of the ingredients and give it a quick mix with a whisk.
- Pour the batter in a loaf pan lined with baking paper.
- Bake in the preheated oven at 350F for 40 minutes or until well risen and fragrant.
- Allow to cool in the pan before slicing and serving.

Nutritional information per serving

Calories: 12

Fat: 5.7g

Protein: 3.7g

Carbohydrates: 19.3g

ERMAN CHOCOLATE BREAD

Time: 1 ¼ hours

Servings: 10

Ingredients:

Bread:

1 cup brewed coffee

½ cup canola oil

½ cup buttermilk

2 eggs

1 ½ cups all-purpose flour

½ cup cocoa powder

1 teaspoon baking powder

1 teaspoon baking soda

½ teaspoon salt

Topping:

1 cup sweetened condensed milk

1 cup shredded coconut

½ cup dark chocolate chips

Directions:
- For the bread, mix the coffee, oil, buttermilk and eggs in a bowl.
- Add the rest of the ingredients and give it a quick mix.
- Pour the batter in a loaf pan lined with baking paper and bake in the preheated oven at 350F for 40 minutes.
- Allow to cool in the pan then transfer on a platter.
- For the topping, mix all the ingredients in a bowl.
- Spoon the topping over the bread and serve right away.

Nutritional information per serving

Calories: 347

Fat: 19.6g

Protein: 7.4g   Carbohydrates: 39.4g

I RISH SODA BREAD

Time: 1 hour   Servings: 8

Ingredients:

1 ½ cups milk   ½ teaspoon salt
1 teaspoon apple cider vinegar   1 teaspoon cumin seeds
2 tablespoons canola oil   1 teaspoon baking soda
2 cups all-purpose flour

Directions:

- Mix the milk, vinegar and oil in a bowl.
- Add the flour, salt, cumin seeds and baking soda and mix well.
- Transfer the dough in a loaf pan lined with baking paper and bake in the preheated oven at 350F for 35 minutes.
- Allow to cool in the pan before slicing and serving.

Nutritional information per serving

Calories: 169   Protein: 4.8g
Fat: 4.8g   Carbohydrates: 26.2g

M OIST BANANA BREAD WITH SALTED CARAMEL SAUCE

Time: 1 ¼ hours   Servings: 10

Ingredients:

Banana bread: ½ cup light brown sugar
1 ½ cups all-purpose flour   ¼ cup sour cream
½ cup oat flour   ¼ cup canola oil
1 ½ teaspoons baking powder   1 teaspoon vanilla extract
½ teaspoon baking soda   Salted caramel sauce:
¼ teaspoon cinnamon powder   1 cup white sugar
¼ teaspoon salt   ½ cup heavy cream
2 eggs   ½ teaspoon salt
2 bananas, mashed

Directions:

- For the bread, mix the flours, baking powder, baking soda, cinnamon and salt in a bowl.
- Add the rest of the ingredients and give it a quick mix.
- Spoon the batter in a loaf cake pan lined with baking paper and bake in the preheated oven at 350F for 35-40 minutes or until golden brown and well risen.
- Allow to cool down before slicing and serving.
- For the caramel sauce, melt the sugar in a saucepan until golden.
- Add the cream and keep on heat until melted and smooth.
- Allow to cool down before serving.
- Top the banana bread with caramel sauce right when serving it.

Nutritional information per serving

Calories: 306   Protein: 4.2g
Fat: 10.3g   Carbohydrates: 50.9g

C OCONUT RAISIN BREAD

Time: 1 hour
Servings: 8

Ingredients:

½ cup brown rice flour
½ cup tapioca flour
¼ cup coconut flour
½ cup coconut flakes
¼ teaspoon salt
1 ½ teaspoons baking powder

½ cup raisins
½ cup coconut oil, melted
1 ½ cups coconut milk
2 eggs
½ cup golden raisins

Directions:

- Mix the flours, coconut flakes, salt and baking powder in a bowl.
- Stir in the rest of the ingredients and give it a quick mix.
- Fold in the golden raisins.
- Spoon the batter in a small loaf pan lined with baking paper.
- Bake in the preheated oven at 350F for 30 minutes.
- Allow to cool in the pan then slice and serve.

Nutritional information per serving

Calories: 400
Fat: 28.0g

Protein: 4.4g
Carbohydrates: 38.1g

$\mathcal{T}$ROPICAL BANANA BREAD

Time: 1 ¼ hours

Servings: 10

Ingredients:

Bread:
2 bananas, mashed
½ cup coconut sugar
1 cup crushed pineapple
¼ cup coconut oil, melted
2 eggs
2 tablespoons orange marmalade
2 cups all-purpose flour

¼ teaspoon salt
1 teaspoon baking powder
1 teaspoon baking soda
¼ cup coconut flakes
Glaze:
1 lime, zested and juiced
1 cup powdered sugar

Directions:

- For the bread, start by mixing the bananas, coconut sugar, oil, crushed pineapple, orange marmalade and eggs in a bowl.
- Add the rest of the ingredients and mix with a spatula just until combined.
- Pour the batter in a loaf pan lined with baking paper.
- Bake the bread in the preheated oven at 350F for 35-40 minutes or until it passes the toothpick test.
- Allow to cool in the pan then transfer on a platter.
- For the glaze, mix the lime zest and juice with sugar until creamy.
- Drizzle the glaze over the bread and serve it fresh.

Nutritional information per serving

Calories: 280
Fat: 7.3g

Protein: 4.1g
Carbohydrates: 51.4g

$\mathcal{C}$INNAMON STREUSEL PEAR BREAD

Time: 1 ¼ hours

Servings: 10

Ingredients:

Bread:
1 cup buttermilk
¼ cup canola oil
1 teaspoon vanilla extract
2 eggs

1 ½ cups all-purpose flour
½ cup oat flour
¼ teaspoon salt
2 teaspoons baking powder
2 pears, peeled, cored and diced

Streusel:
1 cup pecans, chopped
½ cup all-purpose flour

1 pinch salt
1 teaspoon cinnamon powder
¼ cup butter, chilled

Directions:
- For the bread, mix the buttermilk, oil, vanilla and eggs in a bowl.
- Stir in the flours, salt and baking powder and mix well.
- Fold in the pears then spoon the batter in a loaf pan lined with baking paper.
- For the streusel, mix all the ingredients in a bowl until grainy.
- Top the bread with the streusel.
- Bake in the preheated oven at 350F for 35-40 minutes or until well risen and golden brown.
- Allow to cool in the pan before serving.

Nutritional information per serving
Calories: 256
Fat: 12.8g

Protein: 5.5g
Carbohydrates: 30.6g

EAR CARROT BREAD

Time: 1 ¼ hours

Servings: 10

Ingredients:
1 cup whole wheat flour
3/4 cup all-purpose flour
¼ teaspoon salt
2 teaspoons baking powder
½ teaspoon cinnamon powder
½ teaspoon ground ginger
½ teaspoon ground cardamom

½ cup light brown sugar
1 egg
1 cup plain yogurt
¼ cup canola oil
2 carrots, grated
2 pears, peeled, cored and diced

Directions:
- Mix the flours, salt, baking powder, spices and sugar in a bowl.
- Add the egg, yogurt and oil and mix well with a whisk.
- Fold in the carrot and pears then spoon the batter in a loaf pan lined with baking paper.
- Bake in the preheated oven at 350F for 40 minutes or until the bread passes the toothpick test.
- Allow to cool in the pan then slice and serve.

Nutritional information per serving
Calories: 210
Fat: 6.5g

Protein: 4.5g
Carbohydrates: 33.7g

B LUEBERRY WHOLE WHEAT BREAD

Time: 1 hour

Servings: 10

Ingredients:
½ cup butter, melted
½ cup white sugar
1 egg
1 teaspoon vanilla extract
¾ cup buttermilk

1 ¾ cups whole wheat flour
¼ teaspoon salt
2 teaspoons baking powder
1 ½ cups fresh blueberries

Directions:
- Mix the butter, sugar, egg and vanilla in a bowl until creamy.
- Add the buttermilk and mix well.
- Fold in the flour, salt and baking powder then add the blueberries.
- Spoon the batter in a loaf pan lined with baking paper.
- Bake in the preheated oven at 350F for 40 minutes or until well risen and the bread passes the toothpick test.

- Allow to cool in the pan before slicing and serving.

Nutritional information per serving

Calories: 227

Fat: 10.1g

Protein: 3.7g

Carbohydrates: 31.3g

UTTY RAISINS BREAD

Time: 1 hour

Servings: 12

Ingredients:

½ cup butter, softened

¼ cup orange marmalade

2 eggs

½ cup plain yogurt

½ cup milk

1 teaspoon vanilla extract

2 cups whole wheat flour

2 teaspoons baking powder

¼ teaspoon salt

½ cup white sugar

½ cup walnuts, chopped

½ cup pecans, chopped

½ cup almonds, chopped

Directions:

- Mix the butter, marmalade, eggs, yogurt and milk in a bowl. Add the vanilla and mix well.
- Stir in the flour, baking powder, salt and sugar and mix well.
- Fold in the nuts then spoon the batter in a loaf pan lined with baking paper.
- Bake in the preheated oven at 350F for 40 minutes or until well risen and golden brown.
- Allow to cool down before slicing and serving.

Nutritional information per serving

Calories: 279

Fat: 14.8g

Protein: 6.3g

Carbohydrates: 31.9g

ATMEAL CRANBERRY BREAD

Time: 1 hour

Servings: 10

Ingredients:

1 cup oat flour

½ cup all-purpose flour

½ cup rolled oats

¼ teaspoon salt

1 ½ teaspoons baking powder

½ cup white sugar

½ cup butter, melted

2 eggs

1 cup milk

1 teaspoon vanilla extract

1 cup dried cranberries

Directions:

- Mix the oat flour, all-purpose flour, oats, salt and baking powder in a bowl, adding the sugar as well.
- Stir in the butter, eggs, milk and vanilla and give it a quick mix.
- Fold in the cranberries then spoon the batter in a loaf pan lined with parchment paper.
- Bake in the preheated oven at 350F for 40 minutes or until well risen and golden brown.
- Allow to cool down before slicing and serving.

Nutritional information per serving

Calories: 226

Fat: 11.5g

Protein: 4.4g

Carbohydrates: 26.5g

ARVEST CHOCOLATE CHIP BREAD

Time: 1 hour

Servings: 10

Ingredients:

½ cup pumpkin puree
2 bananas, mashed
½ cup applesauce
¼ cup light brown sugar
1 egg
¼ cup canola oil
1 teaspoon vanilla extract

1 cup whole wheat flour
1 cup all-purpose flour
½ teaspoon cinnamon powder
½ teaspoon ground ginger
2 teaspoons baking powder
½ cup walnuts, chopped

Directions:

- Mix the pumpkin puree, bananas, applesauce, sugar, egg, oil and vanilla in a bowl.
- Add the flours, cinnamon and spices, as well as baking powder and mix quickly.
- Fold in the walnuts then spoon the batter in a loaf pan lined with baking paper.
- Bake in the preheated oven at 350F for 40 minutes or until well risen and golden brown.
- Allow to cool down before slicing and serving.

Nutritional information per serving

Calories: 231
Fat: 9.9g

Protein: 5.0g
Carbohydrates: 31.6g

𝒯HYME LEMON BREAD

Time: 1 hour

Servings: 10

Ingredients:

1 ¾ cups all-purpose flour
¼ teaspoon salt
1 ½ teaspoons baking powder
1 cup buttermilk
¼ cup sour cream

¼ cup canola oil
1 lemon, zested and juiced
1 egg
1 teaspoon fresh thyme

Directions:

- Mix the flour, salt and baking powder in a bowl.
- Add the rest of the ingredients and give it a quick mix with a whisk, just until combined.
- Spoon the batter in a loaf pan lined with baking paper.
- Bake in the preheated oven at 350F for 35-40 minutes or until golden brown and fragrant.
- Allow to cool in the pan before serving.

Nutritional information per serving

Calories: 159
Fat: 7.6g

Protein: 3.9g
Carbohydrates: 19.1g

𝒫EANUT BUTTER BREAD

Time: 1 hour

Servings: 10

Ingredients:

½ cup coconut sugar
½ cup butter, melted
2 eggs
4 bananas, mashed
½ cup buttermilk

1 teaspoon vanilla extract
2 cups whole wheat flour
¼ teaspoon salt
2 teaspoons baking powder
½ cup smooth peanut butter

Directions:

- Mix the sugar, butter, eggs, bananas, buttermilk and vanilla in a bowl.
- Add the flour, salt and baking powder and give it a quick mix.
- Spoon the batter in a loaf pan lined with baking paper.
- Drop spoonfuls of batter on top of the bread and bake in the preheated oven at 350F for 40 minutes or until well risen

and golden.
- Allow to cool in the pan before slicing and serving.

Nutritional information per serving

Calories: 346

Protein: 8.0g

Fat: 17.1g

Carbohydrates: 43.2g

C LEMENTINE BREAD

Time: 1 ¼ hours

Servings: 10

Ingredients:

4 small clementines

1 teaspoon vanilla extract

½ cup heavy cream

2 cups all-purpose flour

1 egg

¼ teaspoon salt

¼ cup canola oil

2 teaspoons baking powder

Directions:
- Place the clementines in a saucepan and cover with water. Cook until softened then drain and place in a blender.
- Add the cream, egg and oil, as well as vanilla into the blender and pulse until well mixed.
- Stir in the flour, salt and baking powder then pour the batter in a loaf pan lined with baking paper.
- Bake in the preheated oven at 350F for 40 minutes or until golden brown and well risen.
- Allow to cool in the pan before slicing and serving.

Nutritional information per serving

Calories: 205

Protein: 3.9g

Fat: 8.4g

Carbohydrates: 29.3g

P ERSIMMON BREAD

Time: 1 hour

Servings: 10

Ingredients:

2 persimmons, pureed

¼ teaspoon salt

4 eggs

1 cup all-purpose flour

¼ cup canola oil

½ cup oat flour

¼ cup bourbon

½ cup ground walnuts

2/3 cup white sugar

1 ½ teaspoons baking powder

¼ teaspoon ground nutmeg

Directions:
- Mix the persimmon puree, eggs, canola oil, bourbon and sugar in a bowl.
- Stir in the rest of the ingredients and mix well.
- Pour the batter in a loaf cake pan lined with baking paper.
- Bake in the preheated oven at 350F for 40 minutes or until it passes the toothpick test.
- Allow to cool in the pan before slicing and serving.

Nutritional information per serving

Calories: 246

Protein: 5.6g

Fat: 11.3g

Carbohydrates: 28.8g

B LACKBERRY CORNBREAD

Time: 1 hour

Servings: 10

Ingredients:

1 cup yellow cornmeal

¼ teaspoon salt

1 cup all-purpose flour

2 teaspoons baking powder

1 cup plain yogurt
2 eggs
¼ cup canola oil

¼ cup milk
1 ½ cups blackberries

Directions:
- Mix the cornmeal, flour, salt and baking powder in a bowl.
- Add the eggs, yogurt, oil and milk and give it a quick mix.
- Fold in the blackberries then spoon the batter in a loaf pan lined with baking paper.
- Bake in the preheated oven at 350F for 40 minutes or until well risen and golden brown.
- Allow to cool down before slicing and serving.

Nutritional information per serving
Calories: 181
Fat: 7.4g

Protein: 5.3g
Carbohydrates: 23.6g

WALNUT HONEY BREAD

Time: 1 ¼ hours

Servings: 10

Ingredients:
1 cup ground walnuts
1 cup all-purpose flour
¼ teaspoon salt
½ cup oat flour
¼ teaspoon cinnamon powder
¼ teaspoon ground ginger

2 teaspoons baking powder
3 eggs
¼ cup canola oil
½ cup honey
½ cup warm milk

Directions:
- Mix the eggs, oil, honey and vanilla in a bowl.
- Stir in the walnuts, flour, salt, oat flour, spices and baking powder and mix quickly with a spatula.
- Spoon the batter in a loaf pan lined with baking paper.
- Bake the loaf in the preheated oven at 350F for 40 minutes.
- Allow to cool in the pan before slicing and serving.

Nutritional information per serving
Calories: 267
Fat: 14.8g

Protein: 7.0g
Carbohydrates: 29.1g

CHOCOLATE BANANA BROWNIE BREAD

Time: 1 hour

Servings: 10

Ingredients:
½ cup coconut sugar
½ cup butter, softened
2 eggs
4 bananas, mashed
½ cup buttermilk

1 teaspoon vanilla extract
2 cups whole wheat flour
¼ cup cocoa powder
½ teaspoon baking soda
¼ teaspoon salt

Directions:
- Mix the coconut sugar and butter in a bowl until creamy.
- Add the eggs and bananas and mix well then stir in the vanilla and buttermilk and give it a quick mix.
- Fold in the flour, cocoa powder, baking soda and salt.
- Spoon the batter in a loaf pan lined with baking paper.
- Bake in the preheated oven at 350F for 40 minutes or until well risen and golden.
- Allow to cool down before serving.

Nutritional information per serving
Calories: 274

Fat: 10.9g

Protein: 5.1g   Carbohydrates: 41.4g

RANGE PUMPKIN BREAD

Time: 1 hour   Servings: 10

Ingredients:

1 cup pumpkin puree   ¼ teaspoon salt
1 orange, zested and juiced   1 ½ teaspoons baking powder
2 eggs   ½ teaspoon cinnamon powder
1 teaspoon vanilla extract   ½ teaspoon ground ginger
1 ¾ cups all-purpose flour   ¼ teaspoon ground nutmeg

Directions:
- Mix the pumpkin puree, orange zest, orange juice, eggs and vanilla in a bowl.
- Add the flour, salt, baking powder and spices and mix well with a spatula.
- Spoon the batter in a loaf pan lined with baking paper.
- Bake in the preheated oven at 350F for 40 minutes or until fragrant and well risen.
- Allow to cool in the pan before serving.

Nutritional information per serving

Calories: 112   Protein: 3.8g
Fat: 1.2g   Carbohydrates: 21.4g

THE ULTIMATE BANANA BREAD

Time: 1 hour   Servings: 10

Ingredients:

½ cup light brown sugar   1 cup all-purpose flour
½ cup butter, softened   1 cup whole wheat flour
2 eggs   2 teaspoons baking powder
4 bananas, mashed   ¼ teaspoon salt
½ cup buttermilk   ¼ teaspoon cinnamon powder
1 teaspoon vanilla extract

Directions:
- Mix the butter and sugar in a bowl until creamy.
- Add the eggs and mix well then stir in the bananas and buttermilk.
- Add the flours, baking powder, salt and cinnamon and mix with a spatula.
- Spoon the batter in a loaf pan lined with baking paper.
- Bake in the preheated oven at 350F for 40 minutes or until it passes the toothpick test.
- Allow to cool in the pan before serving.

Nutritional information per serving

Calories: 262
Fat: 10.6g
Protein: 4.7g
Carbohydrates: 38.2g

LEMON ZUCCHINI BREAD

Time: 1 hour
Servings: 12

Ingredients:

2 cups grated zucchinis
1 lemon, zested and juiced
4 eggs
1 cup white sugar
½ cup canola oil

1 teaspoon vanilla extract
2 ½ cups whole wheat flour
2 teaspoons baking powder
¼ teaspoon salt

Directions:

- Mix the zucchinis, lemon zest, lemon juice, eggs and sugar in a bowl. Add the oil and vanilla and mix well.
- Fold in the flour, baking powder and salt then spoon the batter in a loaf pan lined with baking paper.
- Bake the bread in the preheated oven at 350F for 40 minutes or until the bread passes the toothpick test.
- Allow to cool in the pan before slicing and serving.

Nutritional information per serving

Calories: 265
Fat: 10.8g

Protein: 4.8g
Carbohydrates: 38.2g

R ED WINE CHOCOLATE BREAD

Time: 1 hour

Servings: 10

Ingredients:

2 cups all-purpose flour
¼ cup cocoa powder
½ teaspoon salt
1 ½ teaspoons baking powder
½ teaspoon baking soda
1 cup red wine

½ cup canola oil
1 egg
¼ cup buttermilk
1 teaspoon vanilla extract
1 cup cherries, pitted

Directions:

- Mix the flour, cocoa powder, salt, baking powder and baking soda in a bowl.
- Add the rest of the ingredients and give it a quick mix.
- Fold in the cherries then pour the batter in a loaf pan lined with baking paper.
- Bake in the preheated oven at 350F for 45 minutes or until it passes the toothpick test.
- Allow to cool in the pan before slicing and serving.

Nutritional information per serving

Calories: 231
Fat: 11.9g

Protein: 3.8g
Carbohydrates: 23.7g

C OCONUT ZUCCHINI BREAD

Time: 1 ¼ hours

Servings: 10

Ingredients:

1 cup rolled oats
1 cup all-purpose flour
1 teaspoon baking powder
1 teaspoon baking soda
¼ teaspoon cinnamon powder
¼ teaspoon ground ginger

½ cup light brown sugar
½ cup canola oil
¼ cup buttermilk
2 zucchinis, grated
1 cup shredded coconut

Directions:

- Mix the sugar, oil, buttermilk, zucchinis and coconut in a bowl.
- Add the oats, flour, baking powder, baking soda, cinnamon and ginger and mix with a spatula.
- Pour the batter in a loaf pan lined with parchment paper.
- Bake in the preheated oven at 350F for 40 minutes or until well risen and it passes the toothpick test.
- Allow to cool in the pan before serving.

Nutritional information per serving

Calories: 238
Fat: 14.3g

Protein: 3.3g
Carbohydrates: 25.3g

$\mathcal{P}$EANUT BUTTER JELLY BREAD

Time: 1 ¼ hours

Servings: 12

Ingredients:

2 cups all-purpose flour
¼ teaspoon salt
2 teaspoons baking powder
½ teaspoon cinnamon powder
½ cup smooth peanut butter
1 cup light brown sugar

¼ cup canola oil
2 bananas, mashed
1 egg
½ cup peanuts, chopped
½ cup raspberry jelly

Directions:

- Mix the peanut butter, sugar and oil in a bowl.
- Add the bananas and egg and mix well.
- Stir in the flour, salt, baking powder and cinnamon then fold in the peanuts.
- Spoon the batter in a loaf pan lined with baking paper.
- Top the batter with dollops of jelly and bake in the preheated oven at 350F for 40-45 minutes.
- Allow to cool in the pan before slicing and serving.

Nutritional information per serving

Calories: 320
Fat: 13.6g

Protein: 7.1g
Carbohydrates: 44.9g

$\mathcal{D}$ATE LOAF CAKE

Time: 1 ¼ hours

Servings: 10

Ingredients:

1 cup dates, pitted
1 cup hot water
2 eggs
¼ cup canola oil
2 tablespoons molasses
1 teaspoon vanilla extract

1 2/3 cups whole wheat flour
½ teaspoon baking soda
1 teaspoon baking powder
¼ teaspoon salt
¼ teaspoon cinnamon powder
½ teaspoon ground ginger

Directions:

- Combine the dates and water in a blender and pulse until smooth.
- Add the eggs, oil, molasses and vanilla and mix well.
- Fold in the rest of the ingredients then spoon the batter in a loaf pan lined with parchment paper.
- Bake the bread in the preheated oven at 350F for 40-45 minutes or until well risen and golden brown.
- Allow to cool in the pan before slicing and serving.

Nutritional information per serving

Calories: 200
Fat: 6.6g

Protein: 3.7g
Carbohydrates: 32.7g

$\mathcal{C}$INNAMON RAISIN BREAD

Time: 1 hour

Servings: 10

Ingredients:

1 cup hot water

¼ cup canola oil

¼ cup light brown sugar
2 tablespoons milk powder
2 eggs
2 cups all-purpose flour

¼ teaspoon salt
2 teaspoons baking powder
1 teaspoon cinnamon powder
1 cup raisins

Directions:

- Mix the water, oil, sugar and milk powder in a bowl. Add the eggs and mix well.
- Stir in the flour, salt, baking powder and cinnamon and give it a quick mix.
- Fold in the raisins then spoon the batter in a loaf pan lined with parchment paper.
- Bake in the preheated oven at 350F for 40 minutes or until well risen and golden brown.
- Allow to cool in the pan then slice and serve.

Nutritional information per serving

Calories: 216
Fat: 6.6g

Protein: 4.7g
Carbohydrates: 35.5g

*L*EMON YOGURT POUND CAKE

Time: 1 ¼ hours

Servings: 10

Ingredients:

2 cups all-purpose flour
2 teaspoons baking powder
¼ teaspoon salt
½ cup butter, melted
4 eggs

2/3 cup white sugar
¼ cup fresh lemon juice
1 teaspoon vanilla extract
1 cup plain yogurt

Directions:

- Mix the flour, baking powder and salt in a bowl.
- In a different bowl, mix the butter, eggs, sugar, lemon juice, vanilla and lemon zest. Stir in the yogurt and mix well.
- Fold in the flour mixture then spoon the batter in a loaf pan lined with parchment paper.
- Bake in the preheated oven at 350F for 40 minutes or until well risen and golden brown.
- Allow to cool in the pan before serving.

Nutritional information per serving

Calories: 269
Fat: 11.6g

Protein: 6.3g
Carbohydrates: 34.9g

*L*EMON GLAZED BLUEBERRY BREAD

Time: 1 ¼ hours

Servings: 10

Ingredients:

Bread:
1 ¾ cups all-purpose flour
¼ teaspoon salt
1 ½ teaspoons baking powder
1 cup heavy cream
1 lemon, zested and juiced
¼ cup canola oil

1 egg
1 cup blueberries
Glaze:
1 tablespoon lemon juice
1 teaspoon lemon zest
1 cup powdered sugar

Directions:

- For the bread, mix the cream, lemon zest, lemon juice and egg in a bowl.
- Add the flour, salt and baking powder and give it a quick mix.
- Fold in the blueberries then spoon the batter in a loaf pan.
- Bake in the preheated oven at 350F for 35-40 minutes or until golden brown and well risen.
- Allow to cool in the pan then transfer on a platter.
- For the glaze, mix the lemon juice, zest and sugar in a bowl.

- Drizzle the glaze over the bread and serve it fresh.

Nutritional information per serving

Calories: 233
Fat: 10.6g

Protein: 3.2g
Carbohydrates: 32.1g

*M*ARZIPAN BANANA BREAD

Time: 1 ¼ hours

Servings: 10

Ingredients:

2/3 cup light brown sugar
½ cup butter
2 oz. marzipan, softened
2 bananas, mashed
1 egg

1 teaspoon vanilla extract
1 ½ cups all-purpose flour
¼ teaspoon salt
1 ½ teaspoons baking powder
¼ teaspoon cinnamon powder

Directions:

- Mix the sugar and butter in a bowl. Add the marzipan and mix well then stir in the bananas, egg and vanilla.
- Add the rest of the ingredients and mix with a spatula.
- Spoon the batter in a loaf pan lined with parchment paper.
- Bake the bread in the preheated oven at 350F for 35-40 minutes or until well risen and golden brown.
- Allow to cool in the pan before serving.

Nutritional information per serving

Calories: 239
Fat: 10.7g

Protein: 3.1g
Carbohydrates: 33.4g

*D*OUBLE ALMOND BREAD

Time: 1 hour

Servings: 10

Ingredients:

1 cup all-purpose flour
1 cup almond flour
½ teaspoon baking soda
1 teaspoon baking powder
¼ teaspoon salt
½ cup sliced almonds

½ cup butter, melted
½ cup white sugar
2 eggs
1 banana, mashed
1 teaspoon vanilla extract

Directions:

- Mix the butter, sugar, eggs and banana in a bowl.
- Add the rest of the ingredients and mix with a spatula.
- Spoon the batter in a loaf pan lined with parchment paper.
- Bake in the preheated oven at 350F for 40 minutes or until well risen and golden brown.
- Allow to cool in the pan before serving.

Nutritional information per serving

Calories: 233
Fat: 14.0g

Protein: 4.2g
Carbohydrates: 24.2g

*S*PICED NUTTY BREAD

Time: 1 ¼ hours

Servings: 10

Ingredients:

1 ½ cups all-purpose flour
½ cup ground walnuts

½ cup ground almonds
¼ teaspoon salt

1 teaspoon baking powder
½ teaspoon baking soda
½ teaspoon cinnamon powder
½ teaspoon ground ginger
½ teaspoon ground cardamom
¼ cup butter, softened

2/3 cup white sugar
2 tablespoons molasses
2 eggs
1 banana, mashed
½ cup buttermilk

Directions:
- Mix the dry ingredients in a bowl.
- In a different bowl, combine the butter, molasses, eggs, banana and buttermilk and mix well.
- Add the dry ingredients and mix well with a spatula.
- Spoon the batter in a loaf pan lined with baking paper.
- Bake in the preheated oven at 350F for 40-45 minutes or until well risen and golden brown, as well as fragrant.
- Allow to cool in the pan before serving.

Nutritional information per serving
Calories: 266
Fat: 11.9g

Protein: 6.2g
Carbohydrates: 36.0g

NE BOWL GINGER BREAD

Time: 1 hour

Servings: 10

Ingredients:
1 ½ cups whole wheat flour
1 cup all-purpose flour
½ teaspoon salt
1 teaspoon ground ginger
¼ teaspoon cinnamon powder
1 teaspoon baking powder

1 teaspoon baking soda
1 cup milk
2 eggs
1 cup buttermilk
¼ cup canola oil
1 teaspoon vanilla extract

Directions:
- Mix all the ingredients in a bowl.
- Give it a quick mix with a whisk then spoon the batter in a loaf pan lined with baking paper.
- Bake the bread in the preheated oven at 350F for 40-45 minutes or until well risen and golden brown.
- Allow to cool in the pan before slicing and serving.

Nutritional information per serving
Calories: 199
Fat: 7.4g

Protein: 6.0gg
Carbohydrates: 26.7g

B ANANA SOUR CREAM LOAF

Time: 1 ¼ hours

Servings: 10

Ingredients:
2 cups all-purpose flour
1 teaspoon instant coffee
1 teaspoon baking soda
1 teaspoon baking powder
¼ teaspoon salt
2/3 cup white sugar

¼ cup butter, melted
1 cup sour cream
2 eggs
2 bananas, mashed
¼ cup milk
1 teaspoon vanilla extract

Directions:
- Mix the butter, sour cream, eggs, bananas, milk and vanilla in a bowl.
- Add the dry ingredients and give it a quick mix with a whisk.
- Spoon the batter in a loaf pan lined with parchment paper.
- Bake in the preheated oven at 350F for 40 minutes or until well risen and golden brown.

- Allow to cool in the pan before slicing and serving.

Nutritional information per serving

Calories: 269

Fat: 10.7g

Protein: 4.9g

Carbohydrates: 39.4g

M OIST SUNBUTTER BREAD

Time: 1 hour

Servings: 10

Ingredients:

½ cup sunflower butter

¼ cup maple syrup

3 eggs

¼ cup canola oil

1 teaspoon vanilla extract

1 teaspoon lemon juice

¼ cup coconut flour

1 cup whole wheat flour

¼ teaspoon salt

1 teaspoon baking powder

½ teaspoon baking soda

¼ cup sunflower seeds

Directions:
- Mix the sunflower butter, maple syrup, eggs, oil, vanilla and lemon juice in a bowl until creamy.
- Add the coconut flour, wheat flour, salt, baking powder and baking soda and mix well.
- Fold in the sunflower seeds then spoon the batter in a loaf pan lined with baking paper.
- Bake in the preheated oven at 350F for 40 minutes or until golden brown and well risen.
- Allow to cool down before slicing and serving.

Nutritional information per serving

Calories: 167

Fat: 8.6g

Protein: 4.0g

Carbohydrates: 18.6g

F RENCH SPICE CAKE

Time: 1 ¼ hours

Servings: 10

Ingredients:

½ cup honey

¼ cup light brown sugar

½ cup water

½ cup orange marmalade

2 eggs

¼ cup canola oil

1 ½ cups all-purpose flour

1 teaspoon baking soda

½ teaspoon baking powder

¼ teaspoon salt

½ teaspoon ground ginger

½ teaspoon cinnamon powder

¼ teaspoon ground nutmeg

Directions:
- Mix the honey, sugar, water, marmalade, eggs and canola oil in a bowl until creamy.
- Add the rest of the ingredients and mix well.
- Spoon the batter in a loaf pan lined with baking paper.
- Bake in the preheated oven at 350F for 40 minutes or until fragrant and well risen.
- Allow to cool down in the pan before serving.

Nutritional information per serving

Calories: 235

Fat: 6.5g

Protein: 3.2g

Carbohydrates: 42.7g

O RANGE NUTMEG BREAD

Time: 1 ¼ hours

Servings: 10

Ingredients:

1 ½ cups milk
¼ cup white sugar
¼ cup canola oil
1 orange, zested and juiced
1 teaspoon vanilla extract
2 cups all-purpose flour

2 teaspoons baking powder
¼ teaspoon salt
½ teaspoon ground nutmeg
¼ cup butter, melted
½ cup cream cheese

Directions:

- Mix the milk, sugar and oil in a bowl. Add the orange zest, orange juice, vanilla, cream cheese and butter and mix well.
- Fold in the flour, baking powder, salt and nutmeg then spoon the batter in a loaf pan lined with baking paper.
- Bake in the preheated oven at 350F for 40-45 minutes or until well risen and golden brown.
- Allow to cool down before serving.

Nutritional information per serving

Calories: 269
Fat: 15.2g

Protein: 4.9g
Carbohydrates: 28.9g

ℰSPRESSO CHOCOLATE BREAD

Time: 1 hour

Servings: 10

Ingredients:

2 bananas, mashed
¼ cup light brown sugar
¼ cup dark brown sugar
¼ cup canola oil
1 teaspoon vanilla extract
½ cup espresso
½ cup buttermilk

1 egg
1 ½ cups all-purpose flour
¼ cup cocoa powder
¼ teaspoon salt
1 teaspoon baking soda
1 teaspoon baking powder

Directions:

- Mix the bananas, sugars, oil, vanilla, espresso, buttermilk and egg and mix well.
- Add the flour, salt, baking soda, baking powder and cocoa powder.
- Pour the batter in a loaf pan lined with parchment paper.
- Bake in the preheated oven at 350F for 40 minutes or until well risen and golden brown.
- Allow to cool in the pan before slicing and serving.

Nutritional information per serving

Calories: 183
Fat: 6.5g

Protein: 3.6g
Carbohydrates: 28.9g

ℱRESH ORANGE CRANBERRY BREAD

Time: 1 ¼ hours

Servings: 10

Ingredients:

2 cups all-purpose flour
¼ teaspoon salt
2 teaspoons baking powder
½ cup white sugar
1/4 cup butter, melted

1 egg
1 cup fresh orange juice
2 tablespoons orange zest
1 teaspoon vanilla extract
1 cup dried cranberries

Directions:

- Mix the butter, egg, orange juice, orange zest and vanilla in a bowl.
- Add the flour, salt, baking powder and sugar and mix well.
- Fold in the cranberries then spoon the batter in a loaf pan lined with baking paper.
- Bake in the preheated oven at 350F for 35-40 minutes or until well risen and golden.

- Allow to cool in the pan before serving.

Nutritional information per serving

Calories: 196

Fat: 5.4g

Protein: 3.4g

Carbohydrates: 33.5g

*G*LUTEN FREE PUMPKIN COCONUT BREAD

Time: 1 hour

Servings: 10

Ingredients:

1 cup coconut flour

½ cup shredded coconut

¼ teaspoon salt

1 ½ teaspoons baking powder

1 teaspoon cinnamon powder

½ teaspoon ground ginger

½ cup canola oil

5 eggs

1 ½ cups pumpkin puree

1 teaspoon vanilla extract

Directions:

- Mix the oil, eggs, pumpkin puree and vanilla in a bowl.
- Stir in the coconut flour, shredded coconut, salt, baking powder, cinnamon and ginger and give it a quick mix.
- Spoon the batter in a loaf pan lined with baking paper.
- Bake in the preheated oven at 350F for 40 minutes or until golden brown and well risen.
- Allow to cool in the pan before serving.

Nutritional information per serving

Calories: 205

Fat: 16.1g

Protein: 4.9g

Carbohydrates: 10.6g

*C*HOCOLATE CHIP ORANGE BREAD

Time: 1 ¼ hours

Servings: 10

Ingredients:

½ cup butter, softened

1 cup white sugar

2 eggs

1 teaspoon vanilla extract

1 orange, zested and juiced

½ cup buttermilk

1 ¾ cups all-purpose flour

¼ teaspoon salt

1 ½ teaspoons baking powder

½ cup dark chocolate chips

Directions:

- Mix the butter and sugar in a bowl until creamy.
- Add the eggs and vanilla and mix well.
- Stir in the orange zest, orange juice and buttermilk and mix well.
- Fold in the flour, salt, baking powder and chocolate chips then spoon the batter in a loaf pan lined with baking paper.
- Bake in the preheated oven at 350F for 40 minutes or until well risen and golden brown.
- Allow to cool in the pan before slicing and serving.

Nutritional information per serving

Calories: 292

Fat: 12.0g

Protein: 4.5g

Carbohydrates: 43.9g

*M*APLE APPLE BREAD

Time: 1 ¼ hours

Servings: 10

Ingredients:

1 ¾ cups all-purpose flour

¼ teaspoon salt

1 ½ teaspoons baking powder

½ teaspoon cinnamon powder

½ teaspoon ground ginger
2/3 cup maple syrup
2 eggs
¼ cup canola oil

1 teaspoon vanilla extract
¼ cup buttermilk
2 red apples, peeled and diced

Directions:
- Mix the flour, salt, baking powder, cinnamon and ginger in a bowl.
- Add the maple syrup, eggs, oil and vanilla and mix well. Stir in the buttermilk as well.
- Pour the batter in a loaf pan lined with baking paper.
- Top with apples.
- Bake in the preheated oven at 350F for 40 minutes or until well risen and golden brown.
- Allow to cool in the pan before serving.

Nutritional information per serving
Calories: 219
Fat: 6.7g

Protein: 3.7g
Carbohydrates: 36.6g

*H*EALTHY ZUCCHINI BREAD

Time: 1 hour

Servings: 10

Ingredients:
1 cup grated zucchinis
2 eggs
½ cup buttermilk
¼ cup canola oil
1 teaspoon vanilla extract

½ cup light brown sugar
1 ½ cups whole wheat flour
¼ cup ground flaxseeds
¼ teaspoon salt
1 ½ teaspoons baking powder

Directions:
- Mix the zucchinis, eggs, buttermilk, oil and vanilla in a bowl.
- Stir in the sugar, flour, flaxseeds, salt and baking powder and mix quickly with a spatula.
- Pour the batter in a loaf pan lined with baking paper.
- Bake in the preheated oven at 350F for 40 minutes or until well risen and golden brown.
- Allow to cool in the pan before serving.

Nutritional information per serving
Calories: 180
Fat: 7.5g

Protein: 4.1g
Carbohydrates: 23.7g

*C*HOCOLATE MARBLED BANANA BREAD

Time: 1 ¼ hours

Servings: 10

Ingredients:
1 ¾ cups all-purpose flour
½ cup whole wheat flour
¼ teaspoon salt
2 teaspoons baking powder
½ teaspoon cinnamon powder
2 eggs

3 bananas, mashed
½ cup plain yogurt
1 teaspoon vanilla extract
¼ cup canola oil
2 tablespoons cocoa powder

Directions:
- Mix the eggs, bananas, yogurt, vanilla and oil in a bowl.
- Stir in the rest of the ingredients and give it a quick mix.
- Split the batter in half. Pour half of the batter in a loaf pan.
- Mix the remaining batter with cocoa powder then pour it over the white batter. Swirl it with a fork or toothpick.
- Bake in the preheated oven at 350F for 40 minutes or until it passes the toothpick test.
- Allow to cool in the pan before slicing and serving.

Nutritional information per serving

Calories: 208

Fat: 7.0g

Protein: 5.3g

Carbohydrates: 31.6g

UTTERMILK CINNAMON BREAD

Time: 1 hour

Servings: 10

Ingredients:

1 ¼ cups buttermilk

¼ cup canola oil

¼ cup water

1 teaspoon vanilla extract

1 cup all-purpose flour

1 cup whole wheat flour

1 teaspoon cinnamon powder

½ teaspoon ground ginger

¼ teaspoon salt

1 teaspoon baking soda

1 teaspoon baking powder

Directions:

- Mix the buttermilk, oil, water and vanilla in a bowl.
- Stir in the rest of the ingredients and give it a quick mix.
- Pour the batter in a loaf pan lined with baking paper.
- Bake in the preheated oven at 350F for 40 minutes or until well risen and golden brown.
- Allow to cool down before slicing and serving.

Nutritional information per serving

Calories: 153

Fat: 6.0g

Protein: 3.6g

Carbohydrates: 20.9g

CREAM CHEESE PUMPKIN BREAD

Time: 1 ½ hours

Servings: 12

Ingredients:

Bread:

¼ cup canola oil

½ cup plain yogurt

¼ cup honey

2 eggs

1 cup pumpkin puree

2 bananas, mashed

¼ cup fresh orange juice

½ cup light brown sugar

1 ½ cups whole wheat flour

¼ cup ground flaxseeds

¼ teaspoon salt

1 ½ teaspoons baking powder

Frosting:

1 cup cream cheese

¼ cup butter, softened

1 cup powdered sugar

Directions:

- For the bread, mix the oil, yogurt, honey, eggs, pumpkin puree, bananas, orange juice and sugar in a bowl.
- Add the rest of the ingredients and mix well.
- Spoon the batter in a loaf pan lined with baking paper.
- Bake in the preheated oven at 350F for 40 minutes or until well risen and golden brown.
- Allow to cool in the pan then transfer on a platter.
- For the frosting, mix the cream cheese and butter in a bowl until creamy. Add the sugar and mix well.
- Top the bread with the cream cheese frosting and serve it fresh.

Nutritional information per serving

Calories: 339

Fat: 17.0g

Protein: 5.5g

Carbohydrates: 42.6g

BUTTERMILK CORNBREAD

Time: 1 hour

Servings: 10

Ingredients:

1 cup yellow cornmeal
1 cup hot water
2 eggs
1 cup buttermilk
¼ cup canola oil
1 teaspoon vanilla extract

1 cup all-purpose flour
¼ teaspoon salt
1 teaspoon baking powder
¼ teaspoon baking soda
1 cup strawberries, halved

Directions:

- Mix the cornmeal and hot water in a bowl.
- Add the eggs, buttermilk, oil and vanilla and mix well.
- Stir in the flour, salt, baking powder and baking soda.
- Spoon the batter in a loaf pan lined with baking paper.
- Top with strawberries then bake in the preheated oven at 350F for 35-40 minutes.
- Allow to cool down before serving.

Nutritional information per serving

Calories: 167
Fat: 7.1g

Protein: 4.3g
Carbohydrates: 21.6g

CHOCOLATE CHIP YOGURT BREAD

Time: 1 hour

Servings: 10

Ingredients:

1 cup plain yogurt
¼ cup canola oil
1 cup white sugar
2 eggs
½ cup buttermilk

1 teaspoon vanilla extract
2 cups all-purpose flour
¼ teaspoon salt
2 teaspoons baking powder
1 cup dark chocolate chips

Directions:

- Mix the yogurt, oil, sugar, eggs, buttermilk and vanilla in a bowl.
- Add the flour, salt and baking powder and give it a quick mix.
- Fold in the chocolate chips then spoon the batter in a loaf pan lined with parchment paper.
- Bake in the preheated oven at 350F for 35-40 minutes. To test the bread, insert a toothpick in the center. If it comes out clean, the bread is done, if not, keep baking a few more minutes then test again.
- Allow to cool in the pan before serving.

Nutritional information per serving

Calories: 307
Fat: 10.2g

Protein: 6.3g
Carbohydrates: 50.0g

FRESH CRANBERRY BREAD

Time: 1 hour

Servings: 10

Ingredients:

½ cup butter, softened
½ cup white sugar
2 eggs
1 teaspoon orange zest
1 teaspoon lemon zest

½ cup fresh orange juice
1 ¾ cups all-purpose flour
¼ teaspoon salt
1 ½ teaspoons baking powder
1 cup fresh cranberries

Directions:
- Mix the butter, sugar, eggs, orange zest, lemon zest and orange juice in a bowl.
- Add the flour, salt and baking powder and mix with a spatula.
- Fold in the cranberries then spoon the batter in a loaf pan lined with baking paper.
- Bake the bread in the preheated oven at 350F for 35-40 minutes or until the bread passes the toothpick test.
- Allow to cool in the pan then slice and serve.

Nutritional information per serving

Calories: 224

Fat: 10.3g

Protein: 3.5g

Carbohydrates: 29.5g

PRICOT SWEET POTATO BREAD

Time: 1 ¼ hours

Servings: 10

Ingredients:

1 ½ cups all-purpose flour

½ cup whole wheat flour

¼ teaspoon salt

2 teaspoons baking powder

½ cup butter, melted

¼ cup honey

¼ cup light brown sugar

2 eggs

1 teaspoon vanilla extract

1 cup sweet potato puree

4 apricots, pitted and diced

Directions:
- In a large bowl, mix the butter, honey, sugar, eggs, vanilla and sweet potato puree.
- Stir in the flours, salt and baking powder then fold in the apricots.
- Spoon the batter in a loaf pan lined with parchment paper.
- Bake in the preheated oven at 350F for 35-40 minutes or until well risen and golden brown.
- Allow to cool in the pan before serving and slicing.

Nutritional information per serving

Calories: 959

Fat: 10.5g

Protein: 4.5g

Carbohydrates: 37.7g

COCONUT BANANA RUM BREAD

Time: 1 ¼ hours

Servings: 12

Ingredients:

2 cups all-purpose flour

½ teaspoon salt

1 teaspoon baking powder

1 teaspoon baking soda

¼ teaspoon ground ginger

½ cup light brown sugar

1 cup shredded coconut

½ cup butter, melted

2 bananas, mashed

¼ cup dark rum

2 eggs

1 teaspoon vanilla extract

½ cup milk

Directions:
- Mix the butter, bananas, rum, eggs, vanilla and milk in a bowl.
- Add the flour, salt, baking powder, baking soda, ginger, sugar and coconut and give it a quick mix.
- Pour the batter in a loaf pan lined with baking paper and bake in the preheated oven at 350F for 40-45 minutes or until well risen and golden brown.
- Allow to cool in the pan before slicing and serving.

Nutritional information per serving

Calories: 236

Fat: 11.1g

Protein: 3.9g

Carbohydrates: 28.2g

BROWN **B**UTTER **W**HOLE **W**HEAT **B**ANANA **B**READ

Time: 1 ¼ hours

Servings: 10

Ingredients:

½ cup butter
3 bananas, mashed
½ cup light brown sugar
3 eggs
1 teaspoon vanilla extract

1 ½ cups whole wheat flour
½ cup oat flour
¼ teaspoon salt
1 ½ teaspoons baking powder

Directions:

- Place the butter in a saucepan and melt on medium heat until it begins to look golden brown. Remove from heat and allow to cool down then transfer in a bowl.
- Add the bananas, sugar, eggs and vanilla and mix well.
- Stir in the flours, salt and baking powder and mix with a spatula.
- Spoon the batter in a loaf pan lined with baking paper.
- Bake in the preheated oven at 350F for 40-45 minutes or until it passes the toothpick test.
- Allow to cool in the pan before slicing and serving.

Nutritional information per serving

Calories: 248
Fat: 11.1g
Protein: 4.7g
Carbohydrates: 33.2g

Yeasted Dough

ORANGE SWEET BREAD

Time: 1 ½ hours

Servings: 8

Ingredients:
Starter:
½ cup warm milk
¼ cup all-purpose flour
1 teaspoon instant yeast
Dough:
The starter from above
2 eggs

¼ cup butter, melted
1 tablespoon orange zest
½ cup warm milk
½ cup white sugar
2 ½ cups all-purpose flour
¼ teaspoon salt

Directions:
- Make the starter by combing then three ingredients in a bowl. Place aside, covered with plastic wrap, until it doubles in volume.
- For the dough, mix the eggs, butter, orange zest, milk and sugar in a bowl.
- Add the starter and mix well then stir in the flour and salt.
- Knead the dough for a few minutes until elastic and well mixed.
- Cover the bowl and allow to rise for 40 minutes.
- When risen, transfer the dough on a floured working surface and shape it into a loaf.
- Place the bread in a loaf pan lined with baking paper.
- Bake in the preheated oven at 350F for 40 minutes.
- Allow to cool down before serving.

Nutritional information per serving
Calories: 287
Fat: 7.9g

Protein: 7.1g
Carbohydrates: 47.2g

GARLIC THYME DINNER ROLLS

Time: 1 ½ hours

Servings: 8

Ingredients:
3 cups all-purpose flour
¼ teaspoon salt
1 ¼ teaspoons instant yeast
1 teaspoon dried thyme

1 teaspoon garlic powder
1 egg
1 ¼ cups warm milk
¼ cup olive oil

Directions:
- Mix the flour, salt, yeast, thyme and garlic powder in a bowl
- Add the egg, milk and oil and mix well.
- Knead the dough for 5-10 minutes until elastic.
- Cover the bowl and allow the dough to rise for 30 minutes.
- Transfer the dough on a floured working surface and cut it into small pieces. Roll each piece into a ball and place in a deep dish baking tray.
- Allow to rise for another 20 minutes then bake in the preheated oven at 350F for 25-30 minutes.
- Allow to cool in the pan before serving.

Nutritional information per serving
Calories: 255
Fat: 8.1g
Protein: 7.1g
Carbohydrates: 38.3g

$\mathcal{V}$EGAN DINNER BREAD

Time: 1 ½ hours

Servings: 8

Ingredients:

3 cups all-purpose flour
¼ teaspoon salt
1 teaspoon instant yeast
1 tablespoon white sugar

1 cup almond milk
¼ cup water
¼ cup canola oil

Directions:

- Mix the flour, salt, sugar and yeast in a bowl.
- Add the milk, water and oil and mix well. Knead the dough for a few minutes until elastic.
- Allow the dough to rise for 30 minutes then transfer the dough in a baking tray lined with parchment paper.
- Bake in the preheated oven at 350F for 30 minutes.
- Allow to cool in the pan before serving.

Nutritional information per serving

Calories: 307
Fat: 14.4g

Protein: 5.7g
Carbohydrates: 39.1g

$\mathcal{S}$OFT DINNER ROLLS

Time: 1 ½ hours

Servings: 10

Ingredients:

4 cups all-purpose flour
2 teaspoons instant yeast
2 tablespoons white sugar
½ teaspoon salt

2 cups warm milk
1 egg
¼ cup olive oil
1 egg for egg wash

Directions:

- Mix the flour, yeast, sugar and salt in a bowl.
- Add the milk, egg and oil and mix well then knead the dough until elastic.
- Cover the bowl and allow to rise for 30 minutes or until double in volume.
- Transfer the dough on a floured working surface and cut it into small pieces.
- Shape the dough into small balls and place in a deep dish baking tray.
- Allow to rise for 20 additional minutes then brush the rolls with egg.
- Bake in the preheated oven at 350F for 25 minutes.
- Allow to cool down before serving.

Nutritional information per serving

Calories: 274
Fat: 7.5g

Protein: 8.2g
Carbohydrates: 43.3g

$\mathcal{N}$O KNEAD PARMESAN BREAD

Time: 2 hours

Servings: 12

Ingredients:

2 cups warm water
2 teaspoons instant yeast
1 teaspoon honey

3 ½ cups all-purpose flour
½ cup grated Parmesan
¼ teaspoon salt

Directions:

- Mix the water, yeast and honey in a bowl. Allow to rest and rise for 10 minutes then add the rest of the ingredients and mix well.
- Cover the bowl with plastic wrap and allow to rise for 1 hour.

- Transfer the dough on a floured working and shape it into a baking pan lined with parchment paper.
- Bake the bread in the preheated oven at 350F for 35-40 minutes or until well risen and golden brown.
- Allow to cool in the pan before serving.

Nutritional information per serving

Calories: 144

Fat: 0.9g

Protein: 4.8g

Carbohydrates: 28.6g

H ONEY FIG BREAD

Time: 1 ½ hours

Servings: 8

Ingredients:

1 ½ cups warm milk

¼ cup canola oil

3 tablespoons honey

2 eggs

2 ½ cups all-purpose flour

¼ teaspoon salt

1 teaspoon instant yeast

1 cup dried figs, chopped

Directions:

- Mix the milk, oil, honey and eggs in a bowl.
- Add the flour, salt and yeast and knead the dough for 10 minutes until elastic, adding the figs as well.
- Allow the dough to rise for 30 minutes then transfer it on a floured working surface.
- Cut the dough in half and shape each half into a log. Braid the dough logs and place on a baking tray lined with baking paper.
- Bake the bread in the preheated oven at 350F for 25-30 minutes.
- Allow the bread to cool down before serving.

Nutritional information per serving

Calories: 328

Fat: 9.5g

Protein: 7.9g

Carbohydrates: 54.7g

C INNAMON RAISIN BREAD

Time: 1 ½ hours

Servings: 10

Ingredients:

3 cups all-purpose flour

¼ teaspoon salt

1 teaspoon cinnamon powder

1 ½ teaspoons instant yeast

½ cup white sugar

2 eggs

1 ¼ cups warm milk

¼ cup butter, melted

½ cup raisins

Directions:

- Mix the eggs, sugar, milk and butter in a bowl.
- Add the flour, salt, cinnamon and yeast and mix well. Add the raisins as well.
- Knead the dough for 10 minutes until elastic and easy to work with.
- Cover the bowl and allow to rise for 30 minutes.
- Transfer the dough on a floured working surface and shape it into a loaf.
- Place the bread in a baking tray lined with parchment paper.
- Bake in the preheated oven at 350F for 40 minutes.
- Allow to cool down before serving.

Nutritional information per serving

Calories: 266

Fat: 6.5g

Protein: 6.5g

Carbohydrates: 46.2g

UMPKIN CRANBERRY BREAD

Time: 1 ½ hours

Servings: 10

Ingredients:

1 cup pumpkin puree
1 cup warm milk
¼ cup light brown sugar
1 teaspoon instant yeast
¼ cup butter, melted

1 cup whole wheat flour
1 cup all-purpose flour
¼ teaspoon salt
½ cup dried cranberries

Directions:

- Mix the pumpkin puree, warm milk, sugar, yeast and butter in a bowl. Allow to rest for 5 minutes.
- Add the rest of the ingredients and mix well.
- Knead the dough until elastic, at least 10 minutes then cover with a clean kitchen towel and allow to rise for 30 minutes.
- Transfer the dough on a floured working surface and shape it into a bowl.
- Allow to rise 20 additional minutes then bake the bread in the preheated oven at 350F for 35-40 minutes.
- Allow to cool in the pan before slicing and serving

Nutritional information per serving

Calories: 170
Fat: 5.4g

Protein: 3.9g
Carbohydrates: 26.5g

I RISH DRIED FRUIT BREAD

Time: 3 hours

Servings: 14

Ingredients:

½ cup raisins
½ cup sultanas
½ cup dried cranberries
2 cups brewed black tea
2 tablespoons Irish whiskey
¼ cup light brown sugar
2 eggs

½ cup butter, melted
4 cups all-purpose flour
½ teaspoon salt
1 teaspoon cinnamon powder
½ teaspoon ground ginger
½ teaspoon ground star anise
2 teaspoons instant yeast

Directions:

- Mix the raisins, sultanas, cranberries, black tea, whiskey, sugar, eggs and butter in a bowl.
- Add the rest of the ingredients and mix well. Knead the dough for 10 minutes or until it gets easy to work with.
- Allow the dough to rise for 1 ½ hours then transfer it on a floured working surface and cut it in half. Roll each half into a loaf and place them in baking trays lined with parchment paper.
- Bake the breads in the preheated oven at 350F for 35-40 minutes or until well risen and golden brown.
- Allow to cool in the pan then serve.

Nutritional information per serving

Calories: 236
Fat: 7.6g

Protein: 5.0g
Carbohydrates: 35.7g

D RIED CHERRY PUMPKIN BREAD

Time: 2 hours

Servings: 10

Ingredients:

4 cups all-purpose flour
2 teaspoons instant yeast
1 teaspoon cinnamon powder

½ teaspoon salt
½ cup light brown sugar
½ cup pumpkin puree

1 cup warm milk
2 eggs
1 teaspoon vanilla extract

¼ cup canola oil
1 cup dried cherries

Directions:
- Mix the flour, yeast, cinnamon and salt in a bowl.
- In a different bowl, combine the pumpkin puree, sugar, milk, eggs, vanilla and oil.
- Pour the mixture over the dry ingredients and mix well. Knead the dough for 10 minutes or until elastic and easy to work with.
- Cover the bowl and allow to rise for 30 minutes.
- Transfer the dough on a floured working surface and shape it into a log. Place the dough in a baking tray lined with parchment paper.
- Bake in the preheated oven at 350F for 40 minutes or until well risen and golden brown.
- Allow to cool in the pan before serving.

Nutritional information per serving
Calories: 299
Fat: 7.4g

Protein: 7.6g
Carbohydrates: 50.0g

PPLESAUCE RAISIN BREAD

Time: 2 hours

Servings: 10

Ingredients:
1 cup applesauce
3 eggs
¼ cup honey
1 teaspoon vanilla extract
½ cup canola oil

3 cups all-purpose flour
¼ teaspoon salt
1 ½ teaspoons instant yeast
½ cup raisins

Directions:
- Mix the applesauce, eggs, honey, vanilla and oil in a bowl.
- Add the flour, salt and yeast and mix well. Add the raisins and knead the dough until elastic and easy to work with.
- Cover the dough and allow it to rise for 30 minutes in a warm place.
- Transfer the dough on a floured working surface and shape it into a loaf. Place the dough in a baking tray lined with parchment paper.
- Bake in the preheated oven at 350F for 35 minutes or until it's well risen, golden brown and crusty.
- Allow the bread to cool down in the pan before serving.

Nutritional information per serving
Calories: 313
Fat: 12.6g

Protein: 6.0g
Carbohydrates: 44.5g

MULTIGRAIN BREAD

Time: 2 hours

Servings: 8

Ingredients:
1 cup all-purpose flour
1 cup whole wheat flour
1 cup multigrain flour
1 teaspoon instant yeast

¼ teaspoon salt
1 ½ cups warm water
¼ cup canola oil

Directions:
- Mix the flours, yeast and salt in a bowl.
- Add the water and oil and mix well. Knead the dough for 10 minutes or until elastic and easy to work with.
- Transfer the dough on a floured working surface and shape it into a loaf.
- Place the dough in a baking tray lined with parchment paper and bake in the preheated oven at 350F for 30-35 minutes or until well risen and golden brown.

- Allow to cool in the pan before serving.

Nutritional information per serving

Calories: 185

Fat: 7.5g

Protein: 4.2g

Carbohydrates: 25.9g

W HOLE WHEAT BREAD

Time: 2 hours

Servings: 10

Ingredients:

2 cups whole wheat flour

2 cups all-purpose flour

½ teaspoon salt

1 ½ teaspoons instant yeast

2 cups warm milk

¼ cup canola oil

Directions:

- Mix the flours, salt and yeast in a bowl.
- Add the milk and oil and mix well. Knead the dough until elastic and easy to work with.
- Cover the bowl and allow the bread to rise for 30 minutes.
- Transfer the dough on a floured working surface and shape it into a loaf.
- Place the dough in a large loaf pan lined with baking paper.
- Allow to rise for 30 additional minutes then bake the bread in the preheated oven at 350F for 35-40 minutes or until well risen and golden brown.
- Allow to cool in the pan before serving.

Nutritional information per serving

Calories: 256

Fat: 7.0g

Protein: 7.0g

Carbohydrates: 40.8g

C ARAMELIZED ONION FOCCACIA

Time: 1 ½ hours

Servings: 8

Ingredients:

1 cup warm water

½ teaspoon instant yeast

¼ cup canola oil

2 cups all-purpose flour

¼ teaspoon salt

2 red onions, sliced

2 tablespoons olive oil

½ teaspoon dried thyme

Directions:

- Heat the oil in a saucepan. Add the onions and cook for 10 minutes or until caramelized, golden brown.
- Add the thyme and remove from heat.
- Mix the water, yeast and oil in a bowl. Allow to rest for 5 minutes then stir in the rest of the ingredients.
- Mix well then knead the dough for 10 minutes or until elastic and easy to work with.
- Allow the dough to rest for 10 minutes then roll it into a thin sheet.
- Place the dough on a baking tray and top it with the caramelized onions.
- Bake in the preheated oven at 350F for 20 minutes.
- Allow to cool down before serving.

Nutritional information per serving

Calories: 216

Fat: 10.7g

Protein: 3.6g

Carbohydrates: 26.6g

P LUM CINNAMON BREAD

Time: 2 hours

Servings: 10

Ingredients:

3 cups all-purpose flour
1 teaspoon instant yeast
¼ teaspoon salt
2 eggs
¼ cup white sugar
1 ¼ cups warm milk

1 teaspoon vanilla extract
¼ cup butter, melted
1 pound plus, pitted and sliced
1 teaspoon cinnamon powder
½ cup light brown sugar

Directions:

- Mix the flour, yeast and salt in a bowl.
- Mix the eggs, sugar, milk, vanilla and butter in another bowl. Pour this mixture over the flour and mix well. Knead the dough for 10 minutes or until elastic and easy to work with.
- Allow the dough to rise for 30 minutes.
- Transfer the dough on a floured working surface and roll it into a thin sheet.
- Sprinkle the dough with cinnamon and sugar and top with plums.
- Roll the dough tightly then place the bread in a loaf pan lined with parchment paper.
- Bake the bread in the preheated oven at 350F for 40-45 minutes or until well risen and golden brown.
- Allow to cool in the pan before serving.

Nutritional information per serving

Calories: 276
Fat: 6.5g
Protein: 6.3g
Carbohydrates: 47.9g

Puddings

Lemon Pudding

Time: 1 hour

Servings. 6

Ingredients:

½ cup butter, melted
2 tablespoons lemon zest
1/3 cup lemon juice
1 ¼ cups white sugar
1 cup all-purpose flour

1 teaspoon baking powder
4 eggs, separated
1 ½ cups whole milk
1 pinch salt

Directions:

- Mix the butter, lemon zest, lemon juice, sugar, flour, baking powder and salt in a bowl.
- Stir in the milk and mix well, then add the egg yolks and mix quickly.
- Whip the egg whites with an electric mixer until stiff.
- Fold the whipped egg whites into the batter.
- Pour the mixture into 6 ramekins.
- Bake in the preheated oven at 350F for 30 minutes.
- Allow to cool in the ramekins before serving.

Nutritional information per serving

Calories: 452
Fat: 20.6g

Protein: 8.1g
Carbohydrates: 61.6g

Chocolate Self Saucing Puddings

Time: 1 hour

Servings: 4

Ingredients:

Pudding:
1 cup all-purpose flour
1 teaspoon baking powder
¼ cup cocoa powder
¼ cup light brown sugar
½ cup milk
2 eggs

1/3 cup butter, melted
Sauce:
1 cup hot water
2 tablespoons cocoa powder
2 tablespoons light brown sugar
1 pinch salt

Directions:

- For the pudding, mix all the ingredients in a bowl just until combined.
- Spoon the batter in 4 ramekins and place them in a baking tray. Place aside.
- For the sauce, combine the ingredients in a bowl and mix well.
- Evenly pour the sauce over the 4 puddings.
- Bake in the preheated oven at 350F for 20 minutes.
- Allow to cool in the ramekins before serving, although it can be served warm as well.

Nutritional information per serving

Calories: 367
Fat: 29.5g

Protein: 8.6g
Carbohydrates: 43.8g

Chunky Banana Bread Pudding

Time: 1 hour
Servings: 8

Ingredients:

8 slices white sandwich bread, cubed
2 bananas, sliced
½ cup chocolate chips
4 eggs, beaten
1 ½ cups milk

½ cup white sugar
1 teaspoon vanilla extract
2 tablespoons butter, melted
½ cup walnuts, chopped

Directions:

- Combine the bread, bananas, chocolate chips and walnuts in a deep dish baking pan.
- Combine the eggs, milk, sugar, vanilla and butter in a bowl.
- Pour this mixture over the bread and allow it to soak up for 10 minutes.
- Bake in the preheated oven at 350F for 40 minutes.
- Allow to cool in the pan before serving.

Nutritional information per serving

Calories: 329
Fat: 14.8g

Protein: 9.3g
Carbohydrates: 42.7g

RANGE CHOCOLATE BREAD PUDDING

Time: 1 hour

Servings: 8

Ingredients:

8 slices bread pudding, cubed
4 eggs
1 ½ cups milk
2 tablespoons cocoa powder

½ cup orange marmalade
4 tablespoons dark brown sugar
1 pinch salt
1 cup dark chocolate chips

Directions:

- Mix the bread cubes and chocolate chips in a deep dish baking pan.
- Combine the eggs, milk, cocoa powder, marmalade, sugar and salt in a bowl. Pour this mixture over the bread.
- Bake the pudding in the preheated oven at 350F for 40 minutes or until set.
- Allow to cool in the pan before serving.

Nutritional information per serving

Calories: 384
Fat: 15.3g

Protein: 8.6g
Carbohydrates: 57.8g

UTELLA BREAD PUDDING

Time: 1 hour

Servings: 8

Ingredients:

8 slices white sandwich bread, cubed
1 cup milk
1 cup heavy cream
1 cup Nutella
3 eggs

1 teaspoon vanilla extract
¼ cup white sugar
1 pinch salt
1 pinch cinnamon powder

Directions:

- Place the bread in a deep dish baking pan.
- Mix the milk, cream, Nutella, eggs, vanilla, sugar, salt and cinnamon in a bowl.
- Pour this mixture over the bread then bake in the preheated oven at 350F for 35-40 minutes.
- Allow to cool in the pan before serving.

Nutritional information per serving

Calories: 211
Fat: 10.2g
Protein: 5.6g

Carbohydrates: 25.2g

EAR CARAMEL BREAD PUDDING

Time: 1 ¼ hours

Servings: 8

Ingredients:

Bread pudding:
8 slices whole wheat bread, cubed
4 eggs
1 ½ cups milk
½ teaspoon cinnamon powder
1 pinch salt

½ cup light brown sugar
2 pears, peeled, cored and diced
Caramel sauce:
1 cup white sugar
½ cup heavy cream
¼ teaspoon salt

Directions:

- For the bread pudding, mix the bread cubes and pears in a deep dish baking pan.
- For the sauce, combine the eggs, milk, cinnamon, salt and sugar in a bowl. Pour this mixture over the bread and allow it to soak up for 5 minutes.
- Bake in the preheated oven at 350F for 35-40 minutes.
- For the sauce, melt the sugar in a saucepan until it has an amber color.
- Add the cream and keep on heat until melted and smooth. Allow to cool down then drizzle the caramel over the pudding.

Nutritional information per serving

Calories: 308
Fat: 6.9g

Protein: 8.2g
Carbohydrates: 56.0g

RESH FRUIT BREAD PUDDING

Time: 1 ¼ hours

Servings: 10

Ingredients:

10 slices white bread, cubed
2 plums, pitted and sliced
2 apricots, pitted and sliced
1 apple, cored and diced
1 pear, cored and diced

1 orange, zested and juiced
1 ½ cups milk
3 eggs
1 teaspoon vanilla extract
½ cup golden raisins

Directions:

- Mix the bread, plums, apricots, apple, pear and raisins in a deep dish baking pan.
- Combine the milk, orange juice, orange zest, eggs and vanilla in a bowl.
- Pour the mixture over the bread and allow to soak up for 10 minutes.
- Bake in the preheated oven at 350F for 40 minutes.
- The pudding is best served chilled.

Nutritional information per serving

Calories: 117
Fat: 2.5g

Protein: 4.2g
Carbohydrates: 20.8g

HUBARB BRIOCHE PUDDING

Time: 1 hour

Servings: 8

Ingredients:

8 slices brioche bread, cubed
2 rhubarb stalks, sliced
1 cup strawberries, halved
1 ½ cups milk
2 eggs

1 teaspoon vanilla extract
½ cup white sugar
1 teaspoon lemon zest
1 pinch salt

Directions:

- Mix the brioche bread, rhubarb and strawberries in a deep dish baking pan.
- Combine the milk, eggs, vanilla, sugar, lemon zest and salt in a bowl. Pour over the bread and press it slightly to soak up the liquid.
- Bake in the preheated oven at 350F for 35-40 minutes.
- Allow to cool in the pan before serving.

Nutritional information per serving

Calories: 218

Fat: 5.3g

Protein: 5.9g

Carbohydrates: 37.2g

*E*GGNOG FLAVORED BREAD PUDDING

Time: 1 hour

Servings: 10

Ingredients:

10 slices white bread, cubed

½ cup dried cranberries

½ cup golden raisins

½ cup eggnog

1 ½ cups milk

4 eggs

¼ cup white sugar

1 teaspoon vanilla extract

Directions:

- Mix the bread, cranberries and raisins in a deep dish baking pan.
- Combine the eggnog, milk, eggs and sugar, as well as vanilla in a bowl.
- Pour this mixture over the bread and bake in the preheated oven at 350F for 35-40 minutes or until golden brown.
- Serve the pudding slightly warm or chilled.

Nutritional information per serving

Calories: 129

Fat: 3.8g

Protein: 4.8g

Carbohydrates: 19.5g

*D*ARK CHOCOLATE FUDGY PUDDING

Time: 40 minutes

Servings: 6

Ingredients:

1 ½ cups dark chocolate chips

½ cup butter

3 eggs

½ cup white sugar

2 tablespoons flour

¼ teaspoon salt

Directions:

- Combine the chocolate chips and butter in a heatproof bowl. Place over a hot water bath and melt them together until smooth.
- Remove from heat then add the eggs, sugar, flour and salt.
- Spoon the batter in 4 ramekins and bake in the preheated oven at 350F for 15 minutes.
- Serve the pudding slightly warm or chilled.

Nutritional information per serving

Calories: 379

Fat: 25.6g

Protein: 5.2g

Carbohydrates: 38.8g

*G*OLDEN SYRUP PUDDING

Time: 1 hour

Servings: 6

Ingredients:

1 cup dates, pitted

½ cup hot water

1 cup golden syrup

¼ cup butter, melted

½ cup light brown sugar
2 eggs
1 cup all-purpose flour

1 teaspoon baking powder
¼ teaspoon salt

Directions:
- Combine the dates and water in a blender and pulse until smooth.
- Add the rest of the ingredients and mix well.
- Pour the batter in 6 ramekins and bake in the preheated oven at 350F for 20 minutes.
- Allow to cool in the ramekins before serving.

Nutritional information per serving
Calories: 451
Fat: 9.4g
Protein: 4.8g
Carbohydrates: 92.9g

Basics

*F*RENCH MERINGUE BUTTERCREAM

Time: 25 minutes

Servings: 6

Ingredients:

4 egg whites

¼ teaspoon salt

1 cup white sugar

1 cup butter, softened

Directions:

- Mix the egg whites and salt in a bowl until fluffy, glossy and firm. It will take at least 5 minutes.
- Add the butter, all at once, and mix well. At first it will curdle up, but keep mixing for 2-3 minutes on low speed until it comes together.
- Use the buttercream right away or store it in the fridge or freezer until needed.

Nutritional information per serving

Calories: 408

Fat: 30.7g

Protein: 2.7g

Carbohydrates: 33.5g

*I*TALIAN MERINGUE BUTTERCREAM

Time: 30 minutes

Servings: 6

Ingredients:

1 cup white sugar

50ml water

4 egg whites

¼ teaspoon salt

1 cup butter

Directions:

- Combine the sugar and water in a saucepan and place it over low heat.
- Mix the egg whites and salt in a bowl until fluffy. When the sugar syrup is hot, pour it gradually over the egg whites and continue mixing until stiff and glossy and the bowl is cold.
- Add the butter, all at once, and mix for 2-3 minutes until fluffy and smooth. At first it will curdle up, then it will come together and become smooth and creamy.
- Use the buttercream right away or store it in the fridge until needed.

Nutritional information per serving

Calories: 408

Fat: 30.7g

Protein: 2.7g

Carbohydrates: 33.5g

*S*WISS MERINGUE BUTTERCREAM

Time: 30 minutes

Servings: 4

Ingredients:

4 egg whites

1 cup white sugar

¼ teaspoon salt

1 cup butter

Directions:

- Mix the egg whites, salt and sugar in a heatproof bowl.
- Place over a hot water bath and keep on heat until the sugar is melted.
- Remove from heat and whip until glossy and stiff, at least 5 minutes. The bowls should be cold by this time as well.
- Add the butter, all the once, and mix well for 2-3 minutes on low settings. At first it will curdle up , but then it will come back together.
- Use the buttercream right away or store it in the fridge until needed.

Nutritional information per serving

Calories: 408

Fat: 30.7g

Protein: 2.7g

Carbohydrates: 33.5g

ENOISE SPONGE CAKE

Time: 1 hour

Servings: 6

Ingredients:

6 eggs

2/3 cup white sugar

1 teaspoon vanilla extract

1 cup all-purpose flour

¼ teaspoon salt

½ teaspoon baking powder

Directions:

- Mix the eggs and sugar in a bowl at least 5 minutes or until triple in volume.
- Add the vanilla and mix well.
- Fold in the flour, salt and baking powder then pour the batter in a 9-inch round cake pan lined with baking paper.
- Bake in the preheated oven at 350F for 25-30 minutes or until golden brown and well risen.
- Allow to cool in the pan before using.

Nutritional information per serving

Calories: 225

Fat: 4.6g

Protein: 7.7g

Carbohydrates: 38.8g

ADEIRA SPONGE CAKE

Time: 1 hour

Servings: 8

Ingredients:

1 cup butter, softened

1 cup white sugar

4 eggs

1 teaspoon vanilla extract

1 cup all-purpose flour

¼ teaspoon salt

1 teaspoon baking powder

Directions:

- Mix the butter and sugar in a bowl until creamy.
- Add the vanilla, then stir in the eggs, one by one, and mix well.
- Fold in the flour, salt and baking powder and mix with a spatula.
- Spoon the batter in a 8-inch round cake pan lined with baking paper.
- Bake in the preheated oven at 350F for 35 minutes or until well risen and golden brown.
- Allow to cool down before serving or using.

Nutritional information per serving

Calories: 388

Fat: 25.4g

Protein: 4.6g

Carbohydrates: 37.5g

HOCOLATE SWISS MERINGUE BUTTERCREAM

Time: 35 minutes

Servings: 8

Ingredients:

4 egg whites

¼ teaspoon salt

1 cup white sugar

1 cup butter, softened

1 ½ cups dark chocolate

Directions:

- Start by melting the chocolate in a heatproof bowl. Allow it to cool down before using.
- Mix the egg whites, sugar and salt in a heatproof bowl and place over a hot water bath.

- Keep on heat until the sugar is melted then remove from heat and start mixing until stiff and glossy and the bowl is chilled.
- Add the butter, all at once, and mix for 2-3 minutes or until it comes back together.
- Stir in the melted chocolate and mix just until incorporated.
- Serve or use the buttercream right away or store it in the fridge until needed.

Nutritional information per serving

Calories: 474

Fat: 32.4g

Protein: 4.5g

Carbohydrates: 43.9g

*C*HOCOLATE MOUSSE

Time: 30 minutes

Servings: 6

Ingredients:

2 egg yolks

¼ cup white sugar

2 tablespoons cold water

1 pinch salt

1 cup dark chocolate chips, melted

½ teaspoon gelatin powder

2 tablespoons cold water

1 cup heavy cream, whipped

Directions:
- Bloom the gelatin in cold water for 10 minutes.
- Combine the sugar and 2 tablespoons of cold water in a saucepan and place over low heat.
- Mix the egg yolks until pale. Gradually stir in the sugar syrup and mix until light and thickened.
- Melt the gelatin and mix it with the egg mixture.
- Add the melted chocolate then allow to cool down to room temperature.
- Fold in the cream and pour the mousse into serving bowls or use it to fill a cake.
- Serve the mousse chilled, after it has set.

Nutritional information per serving

Calories: 212

Fat: 14.2g

Protein: 2.6g

Carbohydrates: 22.6g

*W*HITE CHOCOLATE MASCARPONE MOUSSE

Time: 30 minutes

Servings: 6

Ingredients:

1 cup white chocolate chips, melted

¾ cup mascarpone cheese

½ teaspoon gelatin

2 tablespoons cold water

1 ½ cups heavy cream, whipped

Directions:
- Bloom the gelatin in cold water for 10 minutes.
- Mix the chocolate and mascarpone cheese in a bowl. Add the melted gelatin then allow to cool down if needed.
- Fold in the whipped cream then pour the mousse in serving bowls.
- Serve the mousse chilled.

Nutritional information per serving

Calories: 311

Fat: 24.2g

Protein: 5.8g

Carbohydrates: 18.7g

*S*ALTED CARAMEL SAUCE

Time: 20 minutes

Servings: 4

Ingredients:

1 cup white sugar

2 tablespoons cold water

½ cup heavy cream
1 tablespoon butter

½ teaspoon sea salt

Directions:
- Combine the sugar and water in a saucepan and place it over medium heat. Cook until it begins to look golden brown and caramelized.
- Add the butter and mix well then stir in the cream. Keep on heat just until melted and smooth.
- Add the salt and remove from heat.
- Allow to cool down before serving.

Nutritional information per serving
Calories: 265
Fat: 8.4g

Protein: 0.3g
Carbohydrates: 50.4g

$\mathcal{T}$HICK CHOCOLATE SAUCE

Time: 30 minutes

Servings: 4

Ingredients:
1 cup milk
¼ cup heavy cream
2 tablespoons cocoa powder

1 pinch salt
½ cup dark chocolate chips
1 teaspoon vanilla extract

Directions:
- Mix the milk, cream, cocoa powder and salt in a saucepan. Place over low heat and cook just until thickened.
- Remove from heat and stir in the chocolate and vanilla.
- Allow to cool down before serving.

Nutritional information per serving
Calories: 135
Fat: 8.4g

Protein: 3.6g
Carbohydrates: 14.8g

$\mathcal{C}$HOCOLATE MIRROR GLAZE

Time: 30 minutes

Servings: 10

Ingredients:
1 ½ cups white sugar
1 cup heavy cream
1 cup water
1 cup cocoa powder

½ teaspoon salt
2 ½ teaspoons gelatin powder
4 tablespoons cold water

Directions:
- Combine the sugar, cream, water, cocoa powder and salt in a saucepan and place over low heat.
- Cook until thickened then remove from heat.
- Bloom the gelatin in cold water for 10 minutes then melt it for a few seconds in the microwave.
- Mix the gelatin with the glaze then strain it through a fine sieve to remove any possible lumps.
- Allow to cool to room temperature before serving.
- This glaze can also be frozen.

Nutritional information per serving
Calories: 173
Fat: 5.6g

Protein: 1.8g
Carbohydrates: 35.1g

$\mathcal{P}$HYLLO DOUGH

Time: 1 hour
Servings: 4

Ingredients:

2 cups all-purpose flour
¼ teaspoon salt
1 teaspoon apple cider vinegar

1 cup warm milk
1 tablespoon canola oil

Directions:

- Mix all the ingredients in a bowl. Knead the dough for at least 10 minutes then allow it to rest for 20 minutes.
- Cut the dough into 4 equal pieces then take one piece and place it on a working surface that has been slightly greased with canola oil.
- Roll the dough into a thin sheet then, using your fingertips, start pulling the edges of the dough until it becomes very thin, so thin that you can see through it.
- Use the dough for strudels or other desserts.

Nutritional information per serving

Calories: 289
Fat: 5.4g

Protein: 8.5g
Carbohydrates: 50.7g

*Q*UICK PUFF PASTRY DOUGH

Time: 25 minutes

Servings: 6

Ingredients:

1 cup sour cream
¼ teaspoon salt

2 cups all-purpose flour

Directions:

- Combine all the ingredients in a bowl and mix well just until the dough comes together.
- Use right away or store in the fridge for a few days.
- The dough is simple to make, but it acts just like the famous puff pastry dough.

Nutritional information per serving

Calories: 234
Fat: 8.4g

Protein: 5.5g
Carbohydrates: 33.4g

*C*HOCOLATE WHIPPED CREAM

Time: 20 minutes

Servings: 4

Ingredients:

2 cups heavy cream

1 cup dark chocolate chips

Directions:

- Melt the chocolate in a heatproof bowl over a hot water bath. Allow it to cool down for 15 minutes.
- In the meantime, whip the cream until it forms stiff peaks.
- Fold the whipped cream into the melted chocolate.
- Use the cream right away or store in an airtight container for up to 2 days.

Nutritional information per serving

Calories: 347
Fat: 30.2g

Protein: 3.2g
Carbohydrates: 21.7g

*C*RÈME CHANTILLY

Time: 10 minutes

Servings: 4

Ingredients:

2 cups heavy cream
2 tablespoons powdered sugar

1 teaspoon vanilla extract

Directions:
- Combine the cream with sugar in a bowl and whip until the cream form stiff peaks.
- Add the vanilla extract and mix gently.
- Use the crème Chantilly fresh.

Nutritional information per serving

Calories: 226
Fat: 22.2g

Protein: 1.2g
Carbohydrates: 5.8g

C RÈME ANGLAISE

Time: 20 minutes

Servings: 4

Ingredients:

1 cup milk
¼ cup white sugar

3 egg yolks
1 teaspoon vanilla extract

Directions:
- Pour the milk in a saucepan and bring it to the boiling point.
- Mix the egg yolks and sugar in a small bowl until fluffy and pale. Pour the hot milk over the egg yolks then transfer the mixture back into the saucepan.
- Cook over low heat until it thickens and leaves a trail on the back of the spoon.
- Remove from heat and allow to cool down then stir in the vanilla.
- Serve the crème anglaise with puddings, strudels or meringues.

Nutritional information per serving

Calories: 121
Fat: 4.6g

Protein: 4.0g
Carbohydrates: 16.1g

V ANILLA PASTRY CREAM

Time: 25 minutes

Servings: 4

Ingredients:

2 cups milk
4 egg yolks
1/3 cup white sugar

¼ cup cornstarch
1 pinch salt
1 teaspoon vanilla extract

Directions:
- Pour the milk in a saucepan and place over low heat to bring it to the boiling point.
- Mix the egg yolks and sugar in a bowl until creamy and pale. Add the cornstarch and mix well then pour the hot milk over the mixture.
- Transfer back into the saucepan and cook on low heat until thickened.
- Remove from heat and stir in the vanilla.
- Cover with plastic wrap on the surface and allow the cream to cool down before serving.

Nutritional information per serving

Calories: 211
Fat: 7.0g

Protein: 6.7g
Carbohydrates: 30.7g

D ARK CHOCOLATE GANACHE

Time: 10 minutes

Servings: 4

Ingredients:

1 cup heavy cream
8 oz. dark chocolate chips
1 pinch salt

Directions:
- Bring the cream to the boiling point in a saucepan. Don't allow it to boil as it spoils the texture of the final cream.6
- Remove from heat and stir in the chocolate and salt. Allow to sit for 5 minutes then mix with a whisk until smooth and thick.
- Allow to cool down before serving.
- Use the ganache to fill cakes, frost them or for chocolate truffles.
- For dark chocolate, the ratio is 1 to 1.

Nutritional information per serving

Calories: 368

Fat: 26.2g

Protein: 4.4g

Carbohydrates: 38.6g

W HITE CHOCOLATE GANACHE

Time: 15 minutes

Servings: 6

Ingredients:

1 cup heavy cream

12 oz. white chocolate chips

1 pinch salt

1 tablespoon butter

Directions:
- Bring the cream to the boiling point in a saucepan. Don't allow it to boil.
- Remove from heat and stir in the chocolate and salt. Allow to rest for 5 minutes then mix until melted and smooth.
- Add the butter and mix well then allow to cool down before serving or using.
- The ratio for white chocolate ganache is 1 part cream, 2 parts white chocolate.

Nutritional information per serving

Calories: 392

Fat: 27.5g

Protein: 3.8g

Carbohydrates: 34.2g

F UDGY CHOCOLATE SAUCE

Time: 15 minutes

Servings: 4

Ingredients:

1 cup white sugar

½ cup corn syrup

½ cup water

3 oz. dark chocolate chips

1 pinch salt

1 tablespoon butter

Directions:
- Mix the sugar, corn syrup and water in a saucepan. Place over low heat and cook just until melted.
- Remove from heat and allow to cool down for 5 minutes then add the chocolate, salt and butter and mix well until smooth.
- Allow the sauce to cool down before serving.

Nutritional information per serving

Calories: 421

Fat: 8.6g

Protein: 1.4g

Carbohydrates: 93.6

D ULCE DE LECHE

Time: 1 hour

Servings: 6

Ingredients:

1 can sweetened condensed milk (14 oz.)

Directions:
- Open the can and pour the condensed milk in a small heatproof baking pan.
- Cover the pan with aluminum foil and place in the preheated oven at 350F.

- Cook for 20 minutes, then remove from the oven and mix into the condensed milk. Place back in the oven and cook 10 additional minutes then remove again and mix.
- Continue cooking and mixing once every 5 minutes until the milk has turned into a thick caramel.
- Allow to cool down then serve.

Nutritional information per serving

Calories: 22

Fat: 0.5g

Protein: 0.5g

Carbohydrates: 3.9g

C LASSIC PIE DOUGH

Time: 30 minutes

Yields: 1 9-inch pie crust 8 servings

Ingredients:

2 cups all-purpose flour

¼ teaspoon salt

½ cup butter, chilled and cubed

1 tablespoon white sugar

¼ cup shortening, chilled and cubed

2-4 tablespoons cold water

Directions:

- Combine the flour and salt in a food processor.
- Add the butter and shortening and pulse until grainy.
- Add 2 tablespoons of water at first and pulse. If needed add the remaining water as well and pulse until it comes together.
- Place the dough on a floured working surface. Form a disc of dough and wrap it in plastic wrap.
- Place in the fridge for 30 minutes then roll and place in a pie pan.
- Press the dough on the bottom and sides of the pan and trim the edges as needed.
- Use right away, baking it, or freeze for up to 1 month.

Nutritional information per serving

Calories: 278

Fat: 18.2g

Protein: 3.4g

Carbohydrates: 25.4g

P ATE A CHOUX FOR ÉCLAIRS

Time: 40 minutes

Servings: 20

Ingredients:

1 cup water

½ cup butter

1 pinch salt

1 cup all-purpose flour

4 eggs

Directions:

- Combine the water, butter and salt in a saucepan.
- Bring to a boil. The moment it boils, add the flour, all at once and mix well with a spatula.
- Keep on heat until the dough comes together into a ball.
- Remove from heat and allow to cool down for 10 minutes.
- Add the eggs, one by one, and mix well.
- Spoon the dough in a pastry bag and pipe it into small logs on a baking tray lined with parchment paper.
- Bake in the preheated oven at 350F for 20 minutes or until golden brown and crisp.
- You can use this dough for small choux or profiteroles.

Nutritional information per serving

Calories: 76

Fat: 5.5g

Protein: 1.8g

Carbohydrates: 4.8g

C RUNCHY MERINGUES

Time: 2 ¼ hours

Servings: 30

Ingredients:

4 egg whites

1 cup white sugar

1 pinch salt

½ teaspoon lemon juice

Directions:

- Combine all the ingredients in a heatproof bowl. Place over a hot water bath and heat up until the sugar has melted.
- Remove from heat and whip with an electric mixer for 5-7 minutes or until stiff and glossy.
- Spoon the meringue into a pastry bag and pipe small dollops on a baking tray lined with baking paper.
- Bake in the preheated oven at 200F for 1 ½ hours.
- Allow them to cool in the pan before serving.

Nutritional information per serving

Calories: 27

Fat: 0.0g

Protein: 0.5g

Carbohydrates: 6.7g

COCONUT DACQUOISE

Time: 45 minutes

Servings: 6

Ingredients:

1 cup ground almonds

½ cup powdered sugar

¼ cup all-purpose flour, softened

¼ cup shredded coconut

5 egg whites

1 pinch salt

½ cup white sugar

Directions:

- In a bowl, mix the almonds, powdered sugar, flour and coconut.
- In a different bowl, whip the egg whites and salt until stiff. Add the sugar, gradually, and continue mixing until stiff and glossy.
- Add the almond mixture, gradually, mixing gently with a spatula.
- Spoon the batter in a square baking tray lined with parchment paper.
- Bake in the preheated oven at 350F for 15-20 minutes or until golden brown.
- Allow to cool in the pan before using.

Nutritional information per serving

Calories: 238

Fat: 9.1g

Protein: 7.0g

Carbohydrates: 34.7g

CONCLUSION

Baking is the joy of many people's life, whether they are home bakers or professionals. It is the one activity that takes simple things, like flour, sugar and eggs, and turns them into showstopper cakes, moist muffins, outstanding cupcakes, rich quick breads, silky cheesecakes, delicious pies or tarts or juicy puddings. Baking is a part science, a part motivation, dedication, passion and maybe just a touch of talent. But beyond these big words, the truth is that everyone can bake something with the right recipe. And from the 1001 recipes found in this book, you'll surely find something to fit your taste and impress your family or friends. Just keep in mind that it's not as hard as it may sound and focus on the final result. You're a baker! You're an amazing baker! Don't ever let anyone tell you otherwise!

Made in the USA
Middletown, DE
02 November 2018